P9-CSV-954

Project WET

Curriculum & Activity

Guide

The Watercourse
201 Culbertson Hall
Montana State University
Bozeman, Montana 59717-0570

Council for Environmental Education

Council for Environmental Education
5555 Morningside, Suite 212
Houston, Texas 77005-3216

PROJECT WET
Water Education for Teachers

Project WET

201 Culbertson Hall

Montana State University

Bozeman, Montana 59717-0570

Phone: (406) 994-5392

Fax: (406) 994-1919

e-mail: projectwet@montana.edu

WET Web Site: www.montana.edu/wwwwet

 Printed on recycled paper.

Original Production Team, Contributors, and Reviewers

Project WET Staff, 2000

Dennis Nelson, Executive Director

Sandra Chisholm DeYonge, Director

Gary Cook, Project WET Coordinator

Sally Unser, Administrative Assistant

Stephanie Ouren, Accountant

Production Team for Project WET Curriculum and Activity Guide

Production Managers/Writers: Dennis Nelson, Sandra Robinson, and Jennie Lane

Writers: Susan Higgins, Alan Kesselheim, and George Robinson

Production Business Manager: Linda Hveem

Publication Assistant: Nancy Carrasco

Researchers: Corbin Lang, Kate McLean, and Chris McRae

Editor: Mike Durney

Support Services: Mary Byron and Jennifer Zahrobsky

Conceptual Framework Development: Michael Brody (former Associate Director)

Design/Production Firm and Staff: Thibeault Advertising and Design: Mark and Diane Thibeault, Scott Morrison. SkyHouse Publishers and their associates: Rick Newby, Director; Jeff Wincapaw, Art Director; Julie Schroeder, Assistant Director for Natural History; Susan Ferber, Chief Designer and Cover Artist; Laurie "gigette" Gould, Illustrator; Marita Martiniak, Production Artist; and Will Harmon, Lee Esbenshade, and Noelle Sullivan, Copyeditors/Proofreaders.

Photography: Victoria Enger, unless indicated otherwise.

Project WET Advisory Council Members

Chuck Evans, U.S. Environmental Protection Agency

Rosanne Fortner, Ohio State University

Robert Halliday, Environment Canada, National Hydrology Research Centre

Don Hollums, Colorado Department of Education

Gina Morrison, State Project WET Coordinator's Representative

David Sprynczynatyk, North Dakota State Water Commission

Vivienne Torgeson, Oregon Water Resources Department

Patrick Weasel Head, Northwest Regional Education Laboratories

Keith Wheeler, Global Rivers Environmental Education Network

Josetta Hawthorne, Western Regional Environmental Education Council

Kurt Cunningham (former Advisory Council Member), Montana Fish, Wildlife, and Parks

Financial Sponsors

The developmental phase (1991-1994) of Project WET was funded by the United States Department of the Interior, Bureau of Reclamation.

Special thanks to the National Fish and Wildlife Foundation, Phillips Petroleum Company, Church & Dwight Co., Inc. for supporting the implementation of Project WET's state sponsor WETnet network.

Western Regional Environmental Education Council

Mark Hilliard, President; Josetta Hawthorne, Executive Director; Executive Committee Members: Dave Sanger, John Gahl, and Gini Mitchell; and Members: Peggy Cowan, Alaska Department of Education, Colleen Matt, Alaska Department of Fish and Game, and Robert Warren, University of Alaska S.E.; California: Bill Andrews, California State Department of Education, Elena Tarailo, California Department of Fish and Game, and Darleen Stoner, Ph.D., California State University; Colorado: Don Hollums, Colorado Department of Education, Dale Lashnits, Colorado Division of Wildlife, and Cece Forget, U.S. EPA; Hawaii: Kathy Kawaguchi, Hawaii Department of Education, and Randy Honebrink, Hawaii Division of Aquatic Resources; Idaho: Dr. Richard Kay, Idaho Department of Education, John Gahl, Idaho Fish and Game Department, and Mark Hilliard, U.S. Bureau of Land Management; Montana: Russ Hartford, Montana Office of Public Instruction, Kurt Cunningham, Montana Department of Fish, Wildlife, and Parks, and Mary Ellen Wolfe, Montana Watercourse; Nevada: Bob Lawson, Rose Bullis Center for Curriculum and Instruction, Dave Sanger, Nevada Department of Wildlife, and Gini Mitchell, Nevada Cooperative Extension; New Mexico: Sam Ornelas, New Mexico Department of Education, Don MacCarter, New Mexico Game and Fish Department, and Terry Zubchenok, New Mexico State Forestry; Oregon: Vivienne Torgeson, Oregon Water Resources Department, and Steve Andrews, Beaverton School District; Utah: Brett Moulding, Utah State Office of Education, Bob Ellis, Utah Division of Wildlife Resources, and Terry

Messmer, Utah State University; Washington: Beverly Isenson, Washington Department of Wildlife, and Rhonda Hunter, Washington Department of Ecology; and Wyoming: Dr. William Futrell, Wyoming Department of Education, Joe Vogler, Wyoming Game and Fish Department, and Donn Kesselheim, Wyoming Riparian Association.

State Project WET Program Coordinators, June 2000

ALABAMA: Jerry deBin, Dept. of Conservation & Natural Resources, (334) 242-3623

AMERICAN SAMOA: Michael Kirschman, EPA (684) 633-2304

ARIZONA: Kerry Schwartz, Water Resources Research Center/University of Arizona, (520) 792-9591, Ext.22

ARKANSAS: Rob Beadel/Philip Osborne, AR Dept. of Pollution Control & Ecology, (501) 682-0024

CALIFORNIA: Judy Wheatley, Water Education Foundation, (916) 444-6240 Ext.12

COLORADO: Don Hollums, Colorado Department of Education, (303) 866-6787

CONNECTICUT: Roger Lawson, Kellog Env. Ctr., (203) 734-2513

DELAWARE: Nancy Rolli, Dept. of Natural Resources and Environmental Control, (302) 739-4506

DISTRICT OF COLUMBIA: Hyder Houston, Greater Washington Urban League, (202) 265-8200 Ext. 248

FLORIDA: Eileen Tramontana, St. Johns River Water Management District, (904) 329-4572

GEORGIA: Petey Giroux/Monica Kilpatrick, DNR/Environmental Protection Division, (404) 675-1638

IDAHO: Julie A. Scanlin, Univ. of Idaho, (208) 422-0737

ILLINOIS: Randy Wiseman, Illinois Department of Natural Resources, (217) 785-1256

INDIANA: Susan M. Schultz, Natural Resources Education Center, (317) 562-0788

IOWA: Marcy Seavey, The Iowa Academy of Science, (319) 273-7486

KANSAS: Diane Maddox/John Strickler, KACEE, (913) 894-2069

KENTUCKY: Jennifer Lynn, North Central 4-H Center, (606) 289-5308

LOUISIANA: Joey Breaux, Office of Soil & Water Conservation, (225) 922-1269

MAINE: Mary Ann McGarry, Water Research Institute (WRI), (207) 581-3107

MARSHALL ISLANDS: Hackney Takju, MWSC (692) 625-3838

MARYLAND: Cindy Grove, Department of Natural Resources, Conservation Education, (410) 260-8716

MASSACHUSETTS: Jim Lafley, MDC- (508) 792-7423 Ext 231

MICHIGAN: Janet Vail, Grand Valley State University, (231) 895-3048

MINNESOTA: April Rust, Department of Natural Resources, (651) 297-4951

MISSISSIPPI: Martha Cooper/Betsy Sullivan, MS Museum of Natural Science/MDWFP, (601) 354-7303

MISSOURI: Joe Pitts, Missouri Department of Natural Resources, Technical Assistance Program, (573) 751-3131

MONTANA: Rab Cummings, Montana Watercourse/Montana State University, (406) 994-6425

NEBRASKA: Brooke Levey, University of Nebraska-Kearney, School of Natural Resource Sciences, (308) 865-8809

NEVADA: Bob Lawson, Division of Water Planning, (775)-358-0862

NEW HAMPSHIRE: Nicole Clegg, NH Department of Environmental Services, (603) 271-4071

NEW JERSEY: Colleen Gould, Wetlands Institute, (732) 776-5308

NEW MEXICO: Bryan Swain, WERC, New Mexico State University (505) 646-1378

NEW YORK: Alan Mapes, Bureau of Environmental Education, Dept of Environ. Conservation, (518) 457-3720

NORTH CAROLINA: David Wojnowski, Division of Water Resources, DENR, (919) 715-5433

NORTH DAKOTA: Bill Sharff, ND State Water Commission, (701) 328-4833

NORTHERN MARIANA ISLANDS: Pamela Mathis, Commonwealth Utilities Corporation, (670) 235-6973

OHIO: Leonard Black, Ohio Department of Natural Resources, (614) 265-6758

OKLAHOMA: Karla Beatty, Oklahoma Conservation Commission, (405) 521-6788

OREGON: Sue McWilliams, The High Desert Museum, (541) 382-4754

PALAU: Helen Sugiyama, MWSC (680) 488-1310

PENNSYLVANIA: Patricia Vathis, Office of Environment and Ecology/Dept. of Education, (717) 783-6994

RHODE ISLAND: Christine Dudley, Dept. of Environmental Management, Div. of Fish and Wildlife, (401) 789-0281

SOUTH CAROLINA: Janice Conner, Dept of Natural Resources, Land, Water & Conservation Div., (803) 737-0808, Ext. 134

SOUTH DAKOTA: Terry Lewis, SD Discovery Center & Aquarium, (605) 224-8295

TENNESSEE: Laurina Lyle, Biology Dept./, Austin Peay State University, (931) 552-9432

TEXAS: Sara Kneipp, Caddo Lake Institute, (903) 938-3545

UTAH: Ann Evans, Div of Water Resources, (801) 538-7299

VERMONT: Amy Picotte, Dept of Environ. Conservation, Water Quality Division, (802) 241-3777

VIRGINIA: Jim Speckhart, Department of Environmental Quality, (804) 698-4049

WASHINGTON: Rhonda Hunter, State Dept. of Ecology, (360) 407-6147

WEST VIRGINIA: Rosanna Long, Division of Environmental Protection, (304) 558-3614

WISCONSIN: Dorothy Snyder, UWEX-CNR, University of Wisconsin—Stevens Point, (715) 346-4978

WYOMING: Sue Perin, Teton Science School, (307) 733-4765

CANADA: Pauline Nystrom, Project WET Canada, (306) 780-8312

Dear Educator:

In his timeless *Seven Laws of Teaching*, noted educator John Milton Gregory said, "the lesson to be mastered must be explicable in terms of truth already known by the learner. . . the unknown must be explained by means of the known." He spoke of educational relevance, suggesting that learning occurs best when the subject taught is within the personal experience of the learner. Water is within the experience of all of us. It touches the past, present, and the future. It covers 70 percent of Earth's surface, comprises nearly three-fourths of the human body, and connects and sustains Earth systems. Water is a "truth already known."

In developing the *Project WET Curriculum and Activity Guide*, Project WET accepted these challenges:

- to create a guide that represented the thoughts, needs, and concerns of a vast cross section of grassroots educators and resource managers and was **relevant and meaningful** to young people,

- to accommodate diverse learning styles with activities that were not only practical but also thought-provoking and engaging;

- to address water from the widest possible angle with Project WET modules and existing regional water education programs bringing local issues into sharper focus;

- to provide educators with a large selection of creative teaching strategies;

- to promote the tenet of "water for all water users";

- to generate enthusiasm for further, more in-depth study of topics introduced through the activities.

To meet these challenges, in 1991 Project WET enlisted the support of thousands of dedicated and creative educators and resource people to help generate activities. These people provided insight into critical water issues and, referring to their own school and state curricula standards, they indicated what was most important to be included in a national water education program. These individuals contributed hundreds of ideas and completed activities.

Because the *Project WET Curriculum and Activity Guide* is "by educators and for educators" it serves not only veteran instructors seeking new ideas to infuse into their curricula but also new arrivals to the field of water education. For individuals seeking more in-depth training and instruction, Project WET and leading water resource organizations from across the country and around the world will collaborate in the development of an array of materials designed to supplement the *Guide.*

Project WET's commitment to you does not end when you receive the *Guide;* instead, it marks the beginning of a service relationship. Your state Project WET sponsor, coordinator, his or her local facilitator network, and the individuals and organizations that support your state program all share your commitment to young people.

Project WET believes that the efforts of educators, resource managers, and state Project WET coordinators and their facilitators will stimulate young people to become involved in a myriad of projects in their homes, schools, and communities and that this commitment will stay with them throughout their lives. With all of us working together, the waters of the future will reflect our care and stewardship today. Thank you.

Dennis Nelson
Executive Director, Project WET

A Cruise Through the Guide

Introductory Material

Teaching Strategies

Water education involves a variety of **teaching strategies**.

Teachers can use many approaches to educate students about water. A variety of strategies for assessment, student action, and cooperative learning provide educators with the means to monitor and facilitate student learning.

Project WET Activities

Water has unique **physical and chemical characteristics**.

The nature of the water molecule determines the physical properties of water and its behavior. The physical and chemical properties of water are unique and complex.

Water is **essential for all life** to exist.

Life processes, from the level of the cell to that of the ecosystem, depend on water. Both the quantity and quality of water contribute to the sustainability of life on Earth.

Water connects all **Earth systems**.

Water is an integral part of Earth's structure and plays a unique role in Earth's processes. It is found in the atmosphere, on the surface, and underground. The water cycle is central to life on Earth and connects Earth systems.

Water is a **natural resource**.

All living things use water. The available freshwater supply on Earth is limited and must sustain multiple users. Multiple uses of water can lead to water resource issues.

Water resources are **managed**.

Multiple use of water resources leads to diverse and sometimes conflicting demands, which require water resource management practices. Management decisions involve distribution of water resources and protection of acceptable water quality and quantity.

Water resources exist within **social constructs**.

Over time, societies develop water management systems and practices to meet the needs of diverse water users. People's values, attitudes, and beliefs shape political and economic systems that are dynamic.

Water resources exist within **cultural constructs**.

Cultures express connections to their unique water environments through art, music, language, and customs. Cultures around the world hold similar and contrasting views toward water.

Appendices

Project WET

Water in the 21st Century

Water takes away, but also leaves behind; it depletes, but also restores. Water changes form, and yet its molecular structure remains the same. Partnered with gravity, water can exert tremendous force. In driving rainstorms, single droplets loosen tons of soil and carry it from mountaintops to the sea. Water freezing in crevices fractures rocks. In concert with the moon, the rise and fall of tides continually rearrange shorelines. Flowing in swollen rivers, water carves canyons and sculpts rocky monuments.

Clear, colorless, tasteless, and odorless, a compound made up of two atoms of hydrogen and one of oxygen, water is deceptively simple in structure and form. Despite this simplicity, however, the behavior of water and its interrelationships on the blue planet are wondrously complex.

Every organism is composed mainly of water. The human body is about 70 percent water, a cactus nearly 90 percent. A universal solvent, water carries nourishment to plant and animal cells and removes wastes.

Since ancient times, civilizations have prospered or faltered in response to water availability. Early people knew that rain supported life and drought brought death. They carved messages in stone (spirals symbolizing hidden sources of water) or created instruments, like rainsticks, that imitated the sound of the rain to celebrate its arrival.

Roughly the same amount of water exists on Earth today as when it first formed on the planet. However, our demand for water has increased. According to some water resource specialists, world water usage has tripled since 1950. With the increase in demand for a finite resource, all countries face diverse water issues. How can we satisfy human needs while protecting the ecological integrity of natural systems? How can populations balance their need to use water with their responsibility for its quality and availability?

Water-related issues will continue to evolve and will grow more critical as we move into the 21st century. The resolution of these issues depends on a populace sensitive to and knowledgeable of water and water resources. Education provides one of the best approaches to ensuring responsible behavior toward water. Project WET (Water Education for Teachers), through its education services and programs, will help prepare learners for citizenship in the next century.

History of Project WET

Project WET is a nonprofit water education program for educators and young people, grades K-12, located on the Montana State University campus in Bozeman, Montana. The original WET program was established in 1984 by the North Dakota State Water Commission. In 1989, the director of Project WET was invited by Montana State University—with funding from the U.S. Department of the Interior, Bureau of Reclamation—to duplicate the original North Dakota program in Montana, Idaho, and later, Arizona. The success of this pilot multi-state initiative led to a decision to develop a national Project WET program. In 1990, the Council for Environmental Education, (formerly the Western Regional Environmental Education Council) became an official cosponsor, in partnership with The Watercourse, of Project WET. The Council for Environmental Education (CEE) is a national leader in the field of environmental education, and its cosponsored programs—Project WILD and Project Learning Tree—are among the most long-lived and successful national efforts in environmental education.

The Goal of Project WET

The goal of Project WET is to facilitate and promote awareness, appreciation, knowledge, and stewardship of water resources through the development and dissemination of classroom-ready teaching aids and through the establishment of state and internationally sponsored Project WET programs.

Project WET believes:
• water moves through living and nonliving systems and binds them together in a complex web of life.
• water of sufficient quality and quantity is important for all water users (energy producers, farmers and ranchers, fish and wildlife, manufacturers, recreationists, rural and urban dwellers).
• sustainable water management is crucial for providing tomorrow's children with social and economic stability in a healthy environment.
• awareness of and respect for water resources can encourage a personal, lifelong commitment of responsibility and positive community participation.

In support of the stated goal, Project WET is guided by the following objectives:
• Research: To stay abreast of emerging state and national water education trends and standards, and to stay in touch with the educational needs of citizens.
• Publications: To produce and publish creative and informative materials to meet the needs identified through research.
• Instruction and Training: To provide leadership training and

instruction to ensure that materials and services are fully utilized, and to foster grass-roots participants in their capacities to educate others.
- Networking and Partnerships (WETnet): To form partnerships with organizations to enhance awareness, distribution, and use of materials and services.
- Evaluation: To improve the program through an aggressive, ongoing, and multifaceted evaluation program.
- Recognition: To seek ways to acknowledge and recognize people and organizations for their contributions to water education.

The Watercourse

The Watercourse was created with funding from the U.S. Department of the Interior, Bureau of Reclamation. The original mission of The Watercourse was to establish state Project WET programs in Montana, Idaho, and Arizona. These were modeled after North Dakota's highly successful WET program. The Watercourse was also commissioned to develop an adult water education program targeting major water issues in western states.

Since its inception in 1989, The Watercourse has expanded to accommodate the varied interests of water users nationwide. Watercourse programs provide opportunities for young people and adults to learn about water through materials that are educationally sound, interdisciplinary, interactive, and creative and can be used immediately in the field, classroom, or home.

The goal of The Watercourse is to promote and facilitate public understanding of atmospheric, surface, and ground water resources and related management issues through publications, instruction, and networking.
The Watercourse's scope is nation-wide, its delivery is unbiased, and its mission is to build informed leadership in resource decision making. The Watercourse responds to the information needs of many diverse interest groups. Above all, The Watercourse relies on cooperation with other resource managers, policy makers, water educators, and citizens.

Currently, The Watercourse sponsors two programs: The Watercourse Public Education Program and Project WET. The Watercourse Public Education Program focuses on contemporary management issues through the use of creative materials and teaching aids. The program assists citizens in expanding their knowledge of topics important to all water users.

Council for Environmental Education (CEE)

The Council for Environmental Education (formerly Western Regional Environmental Education Council) is a nonprofit educational organization founded in 1970 in a unique effort to create a partnership and network between education and natural resource professionals. The specific and primary purpose of the Council is to support environmental education through the management and development of environmental education programs, to publish and disseminate environmental education materials, and to facilitate the development and maintenance of partnerships for environmental education. As a cosponsor of two of the most widely used programs in environmental education, Project Learning Tree and Project WILD, CEE has established itself as a national leader in the field of environmental education. The national and international reputation of CEE cosponsored programs has paved the way for the successful incorporation of Project WET into education programs nationwide.

Project Learning Tree (PLT) is the first program CEE cosponsored and was one of the first environmental education programs designed for classroom use. PLT uses the forest as a "window on the world" to increase students' understanding of our complex environment; to stimulate critical and creative thinking; to develop the ability to make informed decisions on environmental issues; and to instill the confidence and commitment to take responsible action on behalf of the environment. PLT's new and revised curriculum for grades preK-8 and their upcoming secondary modules offer teachers and students state-of-the-art products with hands-on, interdisciplinary activities that **work** in the classroom. PLT is administered nationally by the American Forest Foundation. For more information on this program contact: Project Learning Tree, 1111 19th Street NW, Suite 780, Washington, DC 20036.

Project WILD is an interdisciplinary environmental education program emphasizing wildlife. Project WILD has been the recipient of several awards, including the President's Environmental and Conservation Challenge Award. The Project WILD Aquatic Education Activity Guide is part of the Project WILD program and emphasizes aquatic wildlife and aquatic ecosystems. This resource is an excellent companion to Project WET. Cosponsored by CEE and the Western Association of Fish and Wildlife Agencies, Project WILD is dedicated to developing an informed public that is better prepared to make decisions about wildlife and the environment. Contact Project WILD, 5430 Grosvenor Lane, Bethesda, MD 20814.

Introduction

The *Project WET Curriculum and Activity Guide*, for kindergarten through twelfth grades, is a collection of innovative, water-related activities that are hands-on, easy to use, and fun! Project WET activities incorporate a variety of formats, such as large and small group learning, whole-body activities, laboratory investigations, discussion of local and global topics, and involvement in community service projects. Developed, field-tested, and reviewed by hundreds of educators and resource managers around the country, the *Project WET Curriculum and Activity Guide* addresses the goals of Project WET and The Watercourse.

People's relationships to water are a major theme of the *Project WET Curriculum and Activity Guide.* Providing a thorough water education program, the guide also addresses water's chemical and physical properties, quantity and quality issues, aquatic wildlife, ecosystems, and management strategies. Project WET activities promote critical thinking and problem-solving skills and help provide young people with the knowledge and experience they will need to make prudent decisions regarding water resource use.

The *Project WET Curriculum and Activity Guide* is available to all formal and nonformal educators through workshops provided by state Project WET coordinators or trained facilitators. Classroom teachers, park naturalists, museum educators, environmental education specialists, and others can adapt and integrate these activities to satisfy the needs of their curriculum, setting, time frame, and/or audience. The activities cut across many disciplines in the study of water and water resources—chemistry and physics, life science, earth systems, natural resources management, history, and culture.

Using tools provided within the guide, educators may easily organize activities into units of study or pick and choose their individual favorites. Many Project WET activities require little preparation and can be conducted within one class period. However, other activities cause students to experience a variety of approaches to learning water-related concepts, thus involving more preparation and class time. These thorough, extensive activities help students construct multiple connections among knowledge, experiences, feelings, and actions, thereby promoting the retention of relevant water concepts.

Because of the number and diversity of activities and the space restraints of the guide, background information is necessarily brief. Educators desiring further information can refer to the list of selected resources provided for each activity. For a more in-depth investigation of specific topics—such as wetlands, water conservation, ground water, watersheds, and water history—Project WET modules (publications that focus on a single topic and include an extensive reference section and 25 to 50 activities) are available. For more information about Project WET modules, see page 505.

Project WET acknowledges and appreciates the support of WREEC and the efforts of hundreds of educators and resource specialists in conceptualizing, developing, writing, reviewing, and testing the *Project WET Curriculum and Activity Guide.* By utilizing these activities, educators and young people nationwide will travel through the water cycle, conduct a water festival, solve the mystery of a waterborne disease, and debate contemporary water management issues. Through these experiences, today's learners and tomorrow's citizens will view water not only as a shared resource, but also as a shared responsibility.

A note about word usage, grammar, and writing style. The writing style within the guide follows *The Chicago Manual of Style*, 14th edition; spelling is based on *The Random House Unabridged Dictionary*, 2nd edition. The term ground water is presented as two words within the guide based on the recommendation of the United States Geological Survey (USGS), the primary water management data agency for the country. Ground water (two words) correlates with surface water (two words). When referring to Earth, the planet, a capital *E* is used and the article *the* is omitted. The word earth, with a lowercase *e*, is used to designate soil and rock materials.

Project WET Guide and Modules

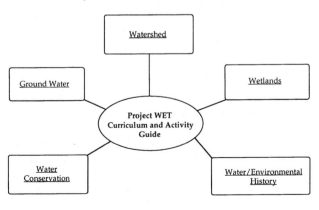

Activities Listed Alphabetically

Dive In!

Implementation of Project WET Activities

What might health, chemistry, and history classes have in common? One thing is water. Because water is a ubiquitous substance, water-related concepts can be found in almost any discipline. By recognizing these aquatic connections, you will discover many opportunities to implement Project WET activities in your curriculum.

Project WET activities are designed to satisfy the goals of educational programs by complementing existing curricula rather than displacing or adding more concepts. Project WET activities provide many opportunities to address curricular objectives and educational standards.

Within the curriculum or standards for your school or district, you will likely find objectives that relate to water (climate, historic water travel, use of water colors, etc.). Additionally, topics that seem unrelated to water can be addressed by using skills and teaching approaches associated with Project WET activities. For example, if an objective relates to debating skills, it might be accomplished through activities such as "Hot Water," "Perspectives," and "Water Court," which use these skills.

Several tools are available within the guide to help you locate activities to meet your teaching needs. These include the following:

• **Activity Icons** identify the water-related concept addressed within the activity. Each activity includes an icon label. For more information about the icons, see **A Cruise Through the Guide**.

• **Summary, Objectives,** and **Assessment** of each activity provide insight into the process of the activity and the learning that is to be accomplished. For more information about activity components, see the **Activity Format** on page xii.

• The **Charting the Course** section of each activity describes related Project WET activities. Again, see the **Activity Format** on page xii.

• **Cross-Reference and Planning Charts** located in the back of the guide classify the activities by topic, subject area, time requirement, grade level, setting, teaching methods, skills, assessment strategies, and environmental education standards.

• **Water Units** chart provided on page xiii includes suggestions on how to organize activities by topic.

• **Glossary**.

The following scenarios describe how educators might select activities to meet the needs of their curricula.

Health Teacher

A health educator plans to teach about health issues related to water. He turns to the **Cross-Reference and Planning Charts** titled **Subject Areas** and **Topics**. Scanning down the column, he finds several activities related to health and water. After locating the activities in the guide, he reads each **Summary** and the **Objectives** to determine which meet his needs. He refers to **Charting the Course** for suggestions on how to arrange the activities.

Science Teacher

A science teacher focuses her unit on watersheds. She flips to the **Water Units** chart and finds a sample unit

consisting of a set of activities on watersheds (e.g., "Rainy-Day Hike," "Color Me a Watershed," "Branching Out!"). For alternate or related activities, she can supplement the list by looking at the **Cross-Reference and Planning Chart**, titled **Topics**. "Supplementary Resources" (in the back of the book) describes additional materials (e.g., the education module *Discover a Watershed: The Everglades*) that could be used to enrich the watershed unit.

Elementary Teacher

An elementary teacher instructs a very active, inquisitive group of first graders. Every day before lunch, they allow the water to run while all students wash their hands. Although the teacher has asked them to turn off the water so that it is not wasted, the students have not been convinced of the importance of this action. The teacher turns to the *Project WET Curriculum and Activity Guide,* and first scans the titles in the **Grade Levels** chart. She notices that "A Drop in the Bucket" has a K-2 Option. She flips to the front of the guide and reads the summary for this activity. Satisfied that she is on the right track, the teacher turns to the page number indicated and reads the entire activity. After students have become aware of the amount of potable water available to them, the teacher monitors hand washing to assess if the lesson has had an impact on their behavior. She may decide to reinforce the concept by conducting other activities that emphasize water as a shared, finite resource, such as "Common Water" (K-2 Option) and "Water Meter" (an activity that can be adapted for lower elementary).

Art Teacher

An art teacher who wants to know what activities in the *Project WET Curriculum and Activity Guide* relate to her discipline turns to the **Cross-Reference and Planning Chart** titled **Subject Areas**. Under the column titled **Fine Arts**, she finds several activities that involve application of artistic methods. She reads through the **Summary** and **Objectives** of each activity to select one that best fits her teaching needs. She notes that the activity includes a section called **Charting the Course** that provides suggestions on other Project WET activities that could precede, complement, or follow this activity.

Nonformal Educator

A ranger-naturalist in Everglades National Park is scheduled to lead a two-hour hike for park visitors. She scans the **Water Units** chart and locates "Watersheds." She quickly reviews activity titles and selects "Stream Sense." She prepares a "Touch and Feel Bag" with items that visitors may encounter on the hike (e.g., an apple snail shell, a limestone rock, a blade of sawgrass). She follows the activity procedure, explaining to participants how to use all of their senses to collect information about the slough that they will visit on the hike. A ranger in Yellowstone National Park consults the **Glossary** of the *Project WET Curriculum and Activity Guide* and locates "geysers." He turns to the appropriate page number and discovers the activity "Geyser Guts." It includes a simple demonstration that he can use to illustrate for park visitors the conditions necessary for a geyser to erupt. Naturalists, guides, docents, and others who may have a single opportunity to impress upon an audience the value of water resources can adapt several Project WET activities to their needs.

Resource Specialist

A resource specialist is invited to a fourth-grade class and given four hours to present a unit about water. The teacher would like the students to conduct hands-on activities in the classroom. This is the resource manager's first visit to the class, and she wants to make this experience meaningful and relevant. She turns to the **Teaching Strategies** section of the guide and reads "Idea Pools"; she makes plans to assess what students already know about water. Turning to the **Cross-Reference and Planning Charts** in the back of the guide, she locates activities that are appropriate for the grade level and topic area.

She narrows her search by referring to the **Time Requirement**, **Setting**, and **Teaching Methods** charts. She confirms her selections by reading the **Summary** of each activity. Based on her study, she develops a concise unit about water consisting of four activities. She is also able to provide the teacher with a list of resources and related activities he can use to reinforce the experience through further study.

These are a few suggestions for selecting and organizing Project WET activities. As you become more familiar with the guide, you will discover many ways in which activities can be arranged to provide students with thorough and fascinating investigations into our world of water.

KEN DE YONGE

Activity Format

Icon indicates the activity's placement within the conceptual framework.

■ **Grade Level:**
Suggests appropriate learning levels; Lower Elementary (K-2), Upper Elementary (3-5), Middle School (6-8), and High School (9-12).

■ **Subject Areas:**
Disciplines to which the activity applies.

■ **Duration:**
Preparation time: The approximate time needed to prepare for the activity. NOTE: Estimates are based on first-time use. Preparation times for subsequent uses should be less.
Activity time: The approximate time needed to complete the activity.

■ **Setting:**
Suggested site.

■ **Skills:**
Skills applied in the activity.

■ **Charting the Course**
Concepts and related Project WET activities that could be performed prior to, in conjunction with, and after the activity.

■ **Vocabulary**
Significant terms defined in the glossary.

A snappy, thought-provoking teaser introduces the activity. This can be presented as an ice breaker.

▼ Summary
A brief description of the concepts, skills, and affective dimensions of the activity.

Objectives
The qualities or skills students should possess after participating in the activity. NOTE: Learning objectives, rather than behavioral objectives, were established for Project WET activities. To measure student achievement, see **Assessment**.

Materials
• *Supplies needed to conduct the activity.* (Describes how to prepare materials prior to engaging in the activity.)

Making Connections
Describes the relevance of the activity to students and presents the rationale for the activity.

Background
Relevant information about activity concepts or teaching strategies.

Procedure
▼ *Warm Up*
Prepares everyone for the activity and introduces concepts to be addressed. Provides the instructor with preassessment strategies.

▼ *The Activity*
Provides step-by-step directions to address concepts. The primary component of each step is presented in bold-faced type.
NOTE: Some activities are organized into "parts." This divides extensive activities into logical segments. All or some of the parts may be used, depending on the

objectives of instruction. In addition, a few activities provide Options. These consist of alternative methods for conducting the activity.

▼ *Wrap Up*
Brings closure to the lesson and includes questions and activities to assess student learning.
NOTE: Many Project WET activities include an "action" component *Wrap Up and Action*. Action moves learners beyond the classroom and involves friends, family, community, state, national, and/or international audiences.

Assessment
Presents diverse assessment strategies that relate to the objectives of the activity, noting the part of the activity during which each assessment occurs. Ideas for assessment opportunities that follow the activity are often suggested.

Extensions
Provides additional activities for continued investigation into concepts addressed in the activity. Extensions can also be used for further assessment.

☺ K-2 Option
Describes more concrete approaches to illustrate specific concepts for kindergarten through second-grade levels. This option is included in selected activities.

Resources
Lists references providing additional background information. Resources for direct use by students are marked with an 🍎.

NOTE: This is a limited list. Several titles are suggested, but many other resources on similar topics will serve equally well.

Water Units

Unit of study	Charting the Course			
	K-2	3-5	6-8	9-12
1.Life Systems	Aqua Bodies, (63) Aqua Notes, (66)	Water Address, (122)	Let's Even Things Out, (72) Thirsty Plants, (116)	
2.Atmospheric Water/ Precipitation	Water Match, (50) A House of Seasons, (155)	The Thunderstorm, (196)	Poetic Precipitation, (182), Wet Vacation, (206)	Piece It Together ,(174)
3.General Surface Water/ Distribution	A Drop in the Bucket (238), (K-2 Option)	Branching Out! (129)	Old Water, (171) Wet Vacation, (206)	Piece It Together, (174) Dust Bowls and ... (303)
4.Movement of Water Over Earth's Surface		The Incredible Journey, (161)	Water Models, (201)	Great Water Journeys, (246)
5.Ground Water			Get the Ground Water Picture, (136)	The Pucker Effect, (331) A Grave Mistake, (311)
6.Natural Disasters		The Thunderstorm, (196)	AfterMath, (289)	Nature Rules!, (262) Hot Water, (388)
7.Waterborne Disease		No Bellyachers, (85)	Poison Pump, (93)	Super Sleuths, (107)
8.Public Process	Choices & Preferences... (367) (K-2 Option)	Dilemma Derby, (377)	Water Bill of Rights, (403)	Whose Problem Is It?, (429) Hot Water, (388) Water Court, (413)
9.Wastewater Management	Rainy-Day Hike, (186) (K-2 Option)	A-maze-ing Water, (219)	Macroinvertebrate Mayhem, (322) Reaching Your Limits, (344)	Sparkling Water, (348) The Price Is Right, (333) Perspectives, (397)
10.Water Rights		A Drop in the Bucket (238)	Wet Vacation, (206) Pass the Jug, (392)	Hot Water, (388) Water Court, (413)
11.Water History		Water Messages in Stone, (454) The Rainstick, (442) Water Concentration, (407)	Old Water, (171) Water Crossings, (421) The Long Haul, (260) Wish Book, (460)	Easy Street, (382)
12.Water Science	Water Match, (50)	Molecules in Motion, (47) H₂Olympics, (30)	Hangin' Together, (35) Adventures in Density, (25) What's the Solution?, (54) Is There Water on Zork? (43)	
13.Water Users	Water Meter, (271)	Choices and Preferences, Water Index, (367) Every Drop Counts, (307)	Common Water, (232) Energetic Water, (242)	Water Works, (274)
14.Watersheds		Capture, Store, and Release (133)	Rainy-Day Hike, (186) Branching Out! (129)	Color Me a Watershed (223)
15.Wetlands		Salt Marsh Players (99)	Life in the Fast Lane (79)	Wetland Soils in Living Color (212)

Water education involves a variety of teaching strategies.

▼

Teachers can use many approaches to educate students about water. A variety of strategies

for assessment, student action, and cooperative learning provide educators with

the means to monitor and facilitate student learning.

Check It Out!

- **Grade Level:** K-12

- **Subject Areas:** All

- **Duration:**
Preparation time:
Depends on activity
Activity time:
Depends on activity

- **Setting:**
Depends on activity

- **Skills:**
Depends on activity

- **Charting the Course**
Assessment strategies described in this activity can be conducted prior to, during, and after many of the activities in this guide.

- **Vocabulary**
assessment, criteria, survey

"Wa-ter" we trying to learn here?

▼ Summary
Through teacher observations and student feedback, student learning via Project WET activities can be assessed.

Objectives
Students will:
- present what they know about water and water resources.
- express how they feel toward water and water resources.
- exhibit skills related to water resource investigations.

Materials
- *Depends on Project WET activity being assessed*

Making Connections
We learn about the world through our senses and by integrating new observations, experiences, and perceptions with existing thoughts and feelings. Assessment strategies are incorporated throughout each Project WET activity to support meaningful and purposeful learning.

Background
Each activity in this guide includes an assessment component. It is designed to provide strategies to assess students' knowledge, thoughts, feelings, and behaviors related to water.

While many aspects of assessment can be addressed in pencil and paper tests, sometimes students can be evaluated more comprehensively while they are involved in an activity. Such assessments are based on teacher observations of student behaviors. This approach to assessment involves establishing a set of criteria, often presented as a checklist. In many schools, teachers work together to prepare these checklists and then share them with students to help them understand what is expected.

The checklist of criteria may include a list of skills (e.g., measuring, comparing), desired behaviors (e.g., following directions, working cooperatively) or competencies (e.g., accurately defining a concept, defending a point of view). Because students' actions may provide evidence of additional, unintended—but valuable—learning, flexibility should be built into the checklist.

Some of the objectives of the activities in this guide are not directly observable (e.g., attitudes, actions outside of class). Through self-reporting assessments, interviews, and open discussions, teachers can gain insight into students' attitudes, values, and behaviors toward water.

The students themselves are the best source of information about student learning. They should be encouraged to share their understandings derived from an activity. In the activity "Water Logs," students keep a journal or log to record their thoughts and feelings related to water.

The information gained from teacher observations and student feedback is important for curriculum planning processes. In addition, the results of the assessment may show that supplemental lessons or activities are needed.

Procedure
▼ Warm Up
After selecting one or more Project WET activities, refer to the **Objectives**, **Procedure**, and **Assessment** components to identify the skills, behaviors, or attitudes you will observe to assess student learning. In some cases, students can help

develop a list of criteria to use for evaluation (e.g., "wAteR in moTion," "Wet Vacation").

▼ *The Activity*

Following are several suggested strategies to assess student learning and brief descriptions of how they can be used in Project WET activities.

Part I
Snowflakes

Younger students can be encouraged to set criteria for their own learning processes through the use of a snowflake. After an activity is explained to students, have them establish six different criteria to gauge their progress. Each criterion is placed on a point of the snowflake. (Students can make their own snowflakes or a basic pattern can be used each time.) When a student has met a particular criterion, he or she can decorate that section of the snowflake. Teachers check the snowflakes and students' work to confirm outcomes.

For example, in the activity "A House of Seasons," students create a collage of weather scenes arranged by season. The collage is covered by a piece of construction paper with openings like windows to view the scenes. Before beginning the activity, students could suggest criteria for monitoring their work. These suggestions could be arranged around a snowflake. After students complete the activity, they can evaluate their product and the process by the criteria.

Part II
Process Skills Checklist

Acquisition and accomplishment of process skills are important components of many Project WET activities. To help determine whether students have achieved the skills and to promote student un-

POSSIBLE SNOWFLAKE FOR "A HOUSE OF SEASONS"

COLLAGE INCLUDES ALL SEASONS

STUDENT SHARES COLLAGE WITH A FRIEND

COLLAGE IS COLORFUL

STUDENT CLEANS UP AFTERWARD

COLLAGE SHOWS WATER

STUDENT FOLLOWS DIRECTIONS

derstanding of what is expected of them, a process skills list can be created for each activity. Following are three examples.

In "Adventures in Density," students perform simple density experiments and relate learned information to segments from literature. A suggested assessment strategy is to have students conduct activities and identify the relationship of water temperature and salinity to density.

One approach provides students with two samples of fresh water of the same temperature, one dyed blue and the other red. Directions ask students to float the red water on the blue water (teacher provides a variety of materials such as a Bunsen burner, ice, and salt). The following checklist could be used to evaluate the students' performance.

Procedure	Points Possible	Points Awarded
Student heats red water	2	
Student cools blue water	2	
Student adds salt to blue water	2	
Student slowly pours blue water into red water	1	
Student uses other strategy to float red water Describe:	up to 2 pts.	
Results successful	3	
Reasons provided why did/did not work	4	
Total		

In "Branching Out!" students build a watershed out of papier-mâché and rocks. One suggested assessment strategy has students predict where water will flow and collect in their watershed model. After determining the criteria needed to make a valid prediction, the following checklist could be used.

PREDICTION STRATEGY	POINTS POSSIBLE	POINTS AWARDED
Students refer to points of elevation	2	
Students identify low points as collection sites	2	
Students describe water flowing from points of higher elevation to collection sites	4	
Students base predictions on other factors Describe:	up to 3 pts.	
Total		

In "Hangin' Together," students demonstrate the role of hydrogen bonding in evaporative cooling. Students role-play water molecules being heated and eventually breaking away, leaving cooler molecules behind.

DEMONSTRATION	POINTS POSSIBLE	POINTS AWARDED
Students work cooperatively	up to 3 pts.	
Students correctly use suggested demonstration	2	
Accuracy of demonstration: simulates how heat energy increases kinetic energy	2	
simulates how heated water molecules break away from liquid water	2	
simulates how remaining water is cooler	3	
Creativity of demonstration Describe:	up to 3 pts.	
Total		

Part III
Opinion and Behavior Surveys

Several Project WET activities help students evaluate their own and others' feelings, attitudes, and behaviors toward water resources (e.g., "Perspectives," "Idea Pools," "Common Water"). On the following page are examples of statements that could be used in the form of a survey. For more in-depth analysis of student responses to the survey, students could be asked to provide reasons for their choices. Because students are reporting their own feelings, perceptions, and behaviors, the information should not be used as a grading criterion. In many cases students do not need to write their names on surveys, as class averages rather than individual responses are needed to evaluate the activity. NOTE: In any situation where students are asked to express opinions, assure them the results will remain confidential.

Younger students may respond to the statements in an interview or in written form with simpler options (e.g., Never, Sometimes, Almost Always). Children may also react to illustrations of actions and indicate their opinions with thumbs up or down, or by circling a picture of a happy, sad, or neutral face.

▼ Wrap Up
Use the checklists to compare the **Objectives** of the activities with the results. What did students learn? What areas need improvement? Were there any unexpected accomplishments?

Discuss with students the results of the assessment strategies. What was the overall effectiveness of the activity? What worked? What activities could precede or follow (see suggestions under **Charting the Course**). What changes would you make to the activity? Other teachers and the

Circle the response that best indicates the extent to which you agree or disagree with each statement.
Strongly Agree (SA)   Agree (A)   Unsure (U)   Disagree (D)   Strongly Disagree (SD)

a.	It is important to consider the needs of other people who use water.	SA A U D SD
b.	There is plenty of fresh water available for us to use.	SA A U D SD
c.	Pesticides and fertilizers put on the land can affect nearby streams and water underground.	SA A U D SD
d.	I can help keep water clean.	SA A U D SD
e.	Some water issues are too big for me to help.	SA A U D SD
f.	My efforts to conserve water will make a difference.	SA A U D SD

How often do you take part in the following activities:
Almost Always (A)   Frequently (F)   Seldom (S)   Never (N)

a.	I wash my hands before I eat to avoid the spread of germs.	A F S N
b.	I write my representative to express my views about water resource issues.	A F S N
c.	I leave the water running when I brush my teeth.	A F S N
d.	I encourage my parents to vote.	A F S N
e.	I share water facts I have learned with my friends and family.	A F S N
f.	I throw trash in the toilet.	A F S N

staff at Project WET will be interested in what you discover.

Assessment
(Strategies will vary based on the activity used; following are a few generic examples.)

Have students:
- set criteria for their own learning process.
- demonstrate their water-related knowledge and skills.
- express their feelings, attitudes, and values about water.

Extensions
Have students work cooperatively to develop a checklist assessment strategy for evaluating students' "Water Logs."

Involve parents or room monitors in completing a survey (at the beginning and end of the school year or of a unit on water) indicating how each child's water habits have changed. For example: Does the child wash his or her hands before eating? Does the child leave the water running while brushing his or her teeth?

Resources
Doran, R., et al. 1993. "Authentic Assessment." *Science Teacher* 60 (6): 36-41.

Hart, Diane. 1994. *Authentic Assessment: A Handbook for Educators.* Menlo Park, Calif.: Addison-Wesley Publishing Company.

LeBuffe, J. 1993. "Performance Assessment." *Science Teacher*, 60 (6): 46-48.

Marcinkowski, T. 1993. "Assessment Strategies in Environmental Education." In *Environmental Education: Teacher Resource Handbook*, ed. R. Wilke. Millwood, N.Y.: Kraus International Publications.

Moran, J., and W. Boulter. 1992. "Step by Step Scoring." *Science Scope*, 15 (6): 46-47.

Shavelson, R., and G. Baxter. 1992. "What We've Learned About Assessing Hands-on Science." *Educational Leadership*, (May).

Idea Pools

- **Grade Level:** K-12

- **Subject Areas:** All

- **Duration:**
Preparation time:
Depends on activity
Activity time:
Depends on activity

- **Setting:**
Depends on activity

- **Skills:**
Depends on activity

- **Charting the Course**
This activity provides a good strategy to introduce a unit on water. "Idea Pools" can also be conducted following activities on water, to explore changes in thoughts and feelings. For a more in-depth look at perceptions, feelings, and thoughts related to water, students can participate in "Choices and Preferences, Water Index" and "Dilemma Derby."

- **Vocabulary**
pre-assessment

Students pool their ideas, interests, feelings, experiences...

▼ Summary
This teaching strategy involves using a network of ideas to pool (categorize) students' interests, thoughts, feelings, and experiences related to water and water concepts.

Objectives
Students will:
- express their interests, thoughts, experiences, and feelings concerning water-related concepts.

Materials
- *Index cards (3 per student)*
- *Markers*
- *Masking tape*

Making Connections
When a new concept is introduced to students, they may already possess a variety of beliefs. Being aware of students' prior knowledge, interests, and feelings regarding a water-related topic helps educators better prepare students for new learning. "Idea Pools" is a strategy that can be used to monitor students' own learning processes and progress.

Background
Learning is an interconnected, interdependent, and ordered process. Assessing students' prior knowledge or preconceptions is a vital component of effective teaching. Students' preconceptions may be accurate and facilitate learning, or they may be misconceptions that can impede learning. Students' prior knowledge related to water can be used to plan activities and to make concepts more relevant to the learner.

Teachers introducing new concepts or nonformal educators who are contacting students for the first time need to assess the class's level of understanding of the topic to be presented. Project WET activities include a variety of pre-assessment strategies, allowing teachers to determine what students know and think about water before introducing a new concept.

Procedure
▼ Warm Up
The *Warm Up* section of each Project WET activity usually includes suggested methods for assessing what students currently think and feel about the forthcoming water-related concepts. These approaches include the following: asking students thought-provoking questions; having students create a diagram to illustrate their perceptions; providing students with a demonstration and soliciting explanations.

These strategies can help educators determine if students already have a strong understanding of the topic. If they do, further study may not be necessary, or the activity could be conducted for reinforcement. On the other hand, students may have limited information and require additional instruction prior to the activity. If students have naive conceptions, these should be adjusted to eliminate any obstacles to constructive learning.

Following is a strategy that can reveal student cognitions regarding water-related concepts.

▼ The Activity
1. **Present students with the topic to be studied (e.g., the states of water, the water cycle, the uses of water in the body). Give each student three index cards and ask him or her to write or draw one relevant idea related to that topic on each card.** They should limit

Ideas pooled by workshop participant. PROJECT WET

their writing to a few words or a single sentence.

2. **Ask a student to describe or read aloud one of his or her cards. Ask the class if anyone has a similar description. Collect related cards and tape them in a group on the wall.** Repeat the procedure and continue forming groups until all the cards are posted. The number of groups generated will depend on the size of the class.

3. **Draw or tape a circle around each group and ask students to suggest a title that describes the common element among the cards in the group. Write this on a card and attach it to the surrounding circle. Explain that each group is a separate "idea pool" (a collection of related ideas, topics or concepts).** Students may note overlaps among pools.

4. **Have students describe the links among pools.** Discuss the network of idea pools.

5. **Challenge groups of students to create a story or write a paragraph using all of the idea pools.** Encourage them to present their story using a variety of techniques, such as role-playing, storytelling, or pantomime.

6. **Ask students to evaluate their stories or presentations.** What information did they feel confident in using? What connections seemed weak? Have them identify what they think is factual information about water and note areas they would like to learn more about.

▼ Wrap Up

The *Wrap Up* of Project WET activities is used to bring closure to activities; however, it can also confirm acquisition of knowledge. One approach is to compare students' responses to identical questions found in the *Warm Up* and *Wrap Up*. If the "Idea Pools" strategy is used, students can be asked to create a network of pools prior to and following an activity. Their thoughts, descriptions, and groupings can be compared to determine if progress was made.

Assessment

Have students:
- present what they currently know about a water-related concept (*Warm Up* and step 1).

Upon completing the activity, for further assessment have students:

- generate a list of questions they have about water topics and issues and research ways to answer their questions.

Extensions

Students can supplement their stories with references to current events. A summary of their findings can be written and submitted to the school or city newspaper, to let others know what the class thinks and feels about water.

Idea pools can also be used to facilitate the formation of small working groups of individuals who share common interests or concerns. Give each person three index cards and request that he or she write on each card one water topic that is of particular importance. Have participants organize the topics into idea pools. One technique is to collect cards and briefly discuss them one at a time and allow the group to determine the set to which each card belongs. Cards can be grouped and taped or tacked to a wall. Participants can then locate their cards on the wall and decide in which group they would like to place themselves.

Resources

Biehler, Robert F., and Jack Snowman. 1986. *Psychology Applied to Teaching*, 5th ed. Boston, Mass.: Houghton Mifflin Company.

Gagné, Ellen D. 1985. *The Cognitive Psychology of School Learning*. Boston, Mass.: Little, Brown & Company.

Novak, J. D., and D. Bob Gowin. 1986. *Learning How to Learn*. New York, N.Y.: Cambridge University Press.

Saunders, Walter L. 1992. "The Constructivist Perspective: Implications and Teaching Strategies for Science." *School Science and Mathematics* 92(3): 136-141.

Let's Work Together

If two heads are better than one . . . how about four or five?

■ **Grade Level:** K-12

■ **Subject Areas:**
Depends on activity

■ **Duration:**
Preparation time:
Depends on activity
Activity time:
Depends on activity

■ **Setting:**
Depends on activity

■ **Skills:**
Depends on activity

■ **Charting the Course**
This activity can be used whenever group work is required.

■ **Vocabulary**
cooperative learning

▼ Summary
While conducting Project WET activities, students working in small groups use cooperative learning strategies to build teamwork skills.

Objectives
Students will:
• work cooperatively in a group during Project WET activities.
• assess personal and group strengths and weaknesses and use talents appropriately to conduct the activity.

Materials
• *Depends on activity*

Making Connections
Students are often assigned group projects and have voluntarily worked in groups to complete an activity. Students will recognize that a group of people working together can accomplish more than one person working alone. They will also have experienced groups not functioning smoothly, and disputes reducing group productivity. Working cooperatively in groups helps students benefit from the knowledge and experience of others and enhances the effectiveness of Project WET activities. It will also prepare them for myriad future opportunities requiring participation in real life groups.

Background
The idea of people working together in groups to accomplish a shared task is an age-old concept. The skills needed to work effectively in groups can be taught and developed through cooperative learning strategies.

The goal of cooperative learning is to help young people gain the knowledge and skills necessary to work effectively with others as productive team members. Involving students in cooperative learning engenders the following: increased motivation, improved academic performance, active learning, respect for individual differences, and refined language skills. Helping everyone become a productive group member results in group unity, which will extend beyond the classroom to the playground and other social situations.

Experience and practice are essential to cooperative learning. Structuring a cooperative learning environment begins by converging students of diverse abilities, cultures, backgrounds, and interests. The five components of cooperative learning are: (1) face-to-face interaction, (2) individual accountability, (3) group cohesion (building a consensus), (4) social skill development, (5) monitoring and evaluating the process. These five components need to be practiced for the cooperative learning experience to occur.

Cooperative group interaction starts by setting clear goals and establishing realistic tasks matched to student interests and abilities. (The student determines his or her own strengths.) In these groups, each member is responsible for a particular task and is accountable to other group members to complete work in a timely and precise fashion.

Procedure
▼ Warm Up
Many Project WET activities involve group work. Review the Project WET activity you plan to conduct to determine the various tasks group members perform. Students can help identify roles and responsibilities. For example, all Leaders could meet and determine their

Students work together to find pictures for their house of seasons.

responsibilities; all Recorders could similarly meet, etc.

▼ The Activity

1. **Divide the class into groups of diverse student aptitudes and backgrounds. (Group size will depend on the needs of the activity.)**

2. **Present students with the different roles or responsibilities. Assign, or have each choose, a role. The roles can be given water-related terms, such as Headwater for the Leader.** Following are examples of roles students in cooperative learning groups can assume.

- **Leader:** This student presents the group with the purpose of their assignment, leads group discussions, gives directions, etc. (For younger students the teacher may be the leader.)

- **Recorder:** This student acts as the checker/recorder. He or she takes notes, records observations, keeps track of what other group members are doing, and reports to the Leader.

- **Researcher:** This person is the materials coordinator. He or she collects necessary materials, gathers sources for research, and makes sure materials are returned.

- **Reader:** This is the presenter of the group. He or she reports the outcomes and conclusions of the group's actions.

- **Caregiver:** This student maintains group cooperation and support.

The following roles may be more appropriate for younger students in cooperative learning groups: Materials-Gatherer, Housekeeper, Messenger.

3. **Examples of how cooperative learning groups could operate in three Project WET activities are provided below:**

- In the activity "Rainy-Day Hike," students work in groups to explore how water flows through their school yard. The Researcher would get the *Legend* and give it to the Leader. The Leader would read the sheet and tell group members what they should look for. The rest of the group would present their findings to the

Recorder, who would record them on the map. The Reader would be responsible for reporting the findings to the class.

- In "wAterR in moTion," students create a sculpture that involves moving water. The Leader conducts a group discussion on how they should design their artwork. The Recorder writes down the ideas. Once a design is selected, the Researcher gathers the materials. The Caregiver makes sure students work together and support each other's ideas. The Reader presents the artwork to the rest of the class.

- In "A House of Seasons," the roles can be Leader (the teacher), Researcher, Materials-Gatherer, and Housekeeper. The Leader assigns Researchers to locate or draw pictures of water through the seasons. The Leader also coordinates the production of the collage. The Materials-Gatherer is responsible for getting and

Notes ▼

returning materials, and the Housekeeper cleans up.

▼ *Wrap Up*

During evaluation, look for student participation, responsibility, and cooperation. Students can express, in a class discussion or during student/teacher conferences, what they did and did not like about working together. Students can also do self- and peer-evaluations of their cooperative learning roles. The role groups (Leaders, Recorders, etc.) could meet again and assess their accomplishments and make recommendations for future group tasks.

Assessment

Have students:
- cooperate as members of a group to complete an activity (steps 2 and 3).
- identify ways the group could have functioned more efficiently and effectively (*Wrap Up*).
- evaluate student contributions to group work (*Wrap Up*).

Extensions

Through a cooperative learning group, students may investigate procedures for resolving local water issues. They may want to keep a journal, collect data, and prepare case studies. This information may be stored in class computer databases and later used for comparative studies.

Resources

Coley, Elaine P. 1989. *Learn the Value of Cooperation*. Vero Beach, Fla.: Rourke.

Culp, Linda, and V. Malone. 1992. "Peer Scores for Group Work." *Science Scope*, 15 (6): 35-36.

Johnson, R., and D. Johnson. 1986. "Action Research: Cooperative Learning in the Science Classroom." *Science and Children*, 24 (2): 31-32.

Slavin, R. 1983. *Cooperative Learning*. New York, N.Y.: Longman.

Water Actions

■ **Grade Level:**
Middle School, High School

■ **Subject Areas:**
Depends on activity

■ **Duration:**
Preparation time:
Depends on activity
Activity time:
Depends on activity

■ **Setting:**
Classroom and community

■ **Skills**
Applying (developing and implementing investigations and action plans); Evaluating; Presenting

■ **Charting the Course**
In "Choices and Preferences, Water Index" students learn that people have varying views about water resources. The activities "Perspectives," "Whose Problem Is It?" and "What's Happening?" (use of surveys) help students learn about the complexity of water-related issues. Many activities in this guide have an action component. "Water Actions" can be used in conjunction with these activities to help guide student participation in various action projects.

■ **Vocabulary**
water-related issue, values

Acid rain, ground water contamination, water shortages—how can we resolve these seemingly overwhelming issues?

▼ **Summary**
Investigating, analyzing, and participating in projects that address water resource issues give students a sense of accomplishment and provide motivation to help manage and protect water.

Objectives
Students will:
• explain the importance of considering the feelings and values of others involved in water-related issues.
• analyze the appropriateness of proposed action strategies.
• plan and evaluate the steps needed to investigate and conduct an action project.
• conduct water action projects.

Materials
• *Depends on the project selected*

Making Connections
Ground water contamination, water shortages, acid rain, nonpoint source pollution—these are just a few of the water-related issues people hear about every day in the news. Several Project WET activities provide students opportunities to gain a better understanding of water-related issues. Students can acquire first-hand experience in water issue resolution by educating and involving others in learning about these issues as well.

Background
After students become aware of a water resource issue, they may be interested in learning how they can help resolve the problem. Many Project WET activities

have an action component that encourages students to share their knowledge about water or water issues with their families and community and to explore options for resolving these issues.

Active participation in local, state, and national decision-making processes is important. However, people should consider all sides of an issue during the process. **This is especially critical when formal and nonformal educators and young people consider issues.**

To learn about all aspects of an issue, people should conduct an investigation and analysis. This consists of researching the problem and learning how others perceive it. Research includes finding out who is (or was) involved in creating the issue and who will be needed to help remedy it. Who are the key players? Who has been affected by the issue, and are they involved in the solution?

People can become involved in protecting water resources in a variety of ways. One of the most powerful methods is education. Helping other people better understand the background and implications of an issue promotes appreciation of and concern for it. Through class-sponsored water festivals, letter writing to the editors of newspapers, public debates, presentations to community groups, and informational posters about water-related issues, people become more familiar with issues.

Some problems can be corrected by people taking direct action, such as community service projects (trail work, litter patrol, and designating and protecting sensitive areas). Implementing water conservation practices helps with water quantity problems. Cleaning up a river or refraining from pouring toxic chemicals down storm drains reduces the burden placed on wastewater treatment plants.

People can use economic strategies to bring about change. For example, fund-raising activities can help provide monetary support for a group or organization. If people believe laws and regulations are needed to correct a situation, they can contact their representatives to voice their opinions. Voting for a person who supports your views helps ensure that your voice will be heard. While most students in grades K-12 are too young to vote, they can encourage adults to exercise this right.

When contemplating a project, establish a goal and determine objectives. The goal is the purpose or intent of the project. Objectives are specific and achievable tasks related to accomplishing the goal. The specific steps to accomplishing the objectives are the methods.

An example of a goal is: "To improve stream habitat." One objective is to inventory the macroinvertebrates to assess the quality of the stream. This method involves collecting and analyzing macroinvertebrate populations. Setting time lines and laying out a budget are intrinsic components of a project.

The saying "Look before you leap" relates directly to student-led service projects and is critical to their success. **Only projects that comply with policies of the school system or of nonformal organizations should be considered.** Planning is important. Select realistic projects that have clear goals, obtainable objectives, and appropriate tasks. Safety must always be a primary concern.

After thoroughly researching the issue and deciding upon an action

strategy you will still need to consider several factors before beginning a project. An action analysis criterion developed by Hungerford et al. (1992) can be organized into a checklist to determine if action is warranted and appropriate.

- Is there sufficient evidence to warrant this action?
- Is the chosen action the most effective one available?
- Are there legal (social, economic, ecological) consequences of this action? If so, what are they?
- Do my personal values support this action?
- Do I understand the beliefs and values of others who are involved in this issue?
- Do I understand the procedures necessary to take this action?
- Do I have the skills, time, courage,

Storm drain stenciling project. COURTESY: KING COUNTY SURFACE WATER MANAGEMENT, WASHINGTON

and resources to complete this action? (Hungerford et al. 1992, 145-47).

Educators should be aware of considerations and needs unique to their school and community, and include these in the checklist. Relevant to the needs of the school setting, Lane and Rossow (1993) have added an additional set of considerations for the teacher. These include the following:

- Is the project relevant to the objectives of the class?
- How does the project fit into the curriculum?
- What are the interdisciplinary connections?
- Will student motivation and ownership be generated?
- Will the project include a diversity of learning techniques? (Lane and Rossow 1993, 241).

When action projects are conducted in a school setting, purposeful learning must occur. The decision to become involved should come from the students. They may need guidance to determine if the project is within their capabilities.

Student measures salinity with a refractometer.
DAVID MAKEPEACE

Procedure
▼ *Warm Up*
Share with students one or both of the case studies at the end of this activity. Have students identify specific projects described within the case studies and discuss what they think was involved in completing them.

▼ *The Activity*
1. **Have students identify a water-related issue that interests them.** Students can obtain information by reading newspapers or magazines, and watching news programs and documentaries; guest speakers, field trips, and videos can also provide students with ideas. If possible, involve students in Project WET activities that will help them learn about this issue (e.g., "Whose Problem Is It?"). (If students decide to work in groups, the activity "Idea Pools" suggests a technique for organizing individuals according to common interests and issues.)

2. **If students decide they want to become active in helping resolve this issue, have them generate research questions.** These research questions should include: What caused the problem? What are the environmental implications of the problem? How do other people perceive the problem? How are their values related to their viewpoints? What efforts have been taken to resolve it? These questions are answered by reading textbooks and news articles, interviewing experts, and conducting surveys. Once the information has been collected, it should be organized in a report or chart for easy reference. This information can be used to determine if action should be taken regarding this issue.

Regardless of the goal and objectives of the action, students should anticipate and assess potential responses/reactions that their action could elicit from classmates, school officials, and community members. The action should be weighed against the response.

3. **Involve students in a discussion of what can be done to correct this problem.** Students can participate in the activity "Perspectives" to consider the pros and cons of various solutions. Can the action be initiated by individual students (e.g., water conservation) or will they need to involve other people? Ask students to create a list of potential action strategies.

4. **After students have developed a list of potential action strategies, help them evaluate the strengths and weaknesses of the strategies.** Lead them through an analysis criteria checklist similar to the one in the **Background**. Make sure local considerations and concerns are added to the list.

5. **Provide students with the student activity sheet, *Project Action Planning Form for Teachers and Students*. Discuss the information on this form.** Review the research procedures required for students to complete this form. Conduct group meetings and discussions to help students execute the forms, initiate action, and complete their projects. For long-term projects, arrange for students to submit progress reports on a regular basis.

Students use storm drain stencils to inform residents in their watershed. COURTESY: CITY OF BELLEVUE, WASHINGTON

▼ *Wrap Up and Action*

When students have completed their projects or taken some kind of action, have them discuss their feelings and experiences. Do they think they were effective? What evidence supports their opinion? What problems did they encounter? What were the rewards? What would they change if they were to repeat the project? Are they interested in becoming involved in a similar project in the future? What advice would they give to other students who would like to conduct a similar project?

Discuss ways that students can inform others about what they have accomplished. They may want to write a feature article for a local newspaper. Would the local television news program be interested? Perhaps they could present a summary of their efforts to another class or at a town or school meeting.

Assessment

Have students:
* investigate and research a water-related issue (steps 1 and 2).

* recognize the feelings and values of individuals representing diverse viewpoints regarding the issue (step 2).
* identify potential strategies to resolve the issue (step 3).
* assess the strengths and weaknesses of the proposed action strategies (step 4).
* plan and conduct a project designed to address a water-related issue (step 5).
* evaluate the outcomes of the project (*Wrap Up*).
* publicize and publish the results of the project (*Wrap Up*).

Extensions

Have students form a water-action club.

Resources

Hammond, Bill. 1993. "The Monday Group." *Project WILD*. Bethesda, Md.: Western Regional Environmental Education Council.

Hungerford, Harold, et al. 1992. *Investigating and Evaluating Environmental Issues and Action Skill Development Modules*. Champaign, Ill.: Stipes Publishing Company.

Lane, Jennie, and Catherine Rossow. 1993. "Sources and Ideas for Special Projects." In *Environmental Education: Teacher Resource Handbook*, ed. R. Wilke. Millwood, N.Y.: Kraus International Publications.

🍎 Lewis, Barbara. 1991. *The Kid's Guide to Social Action*. Minneapolis, Minn.: Free Spirit Publishing.

Pennock, M., and L. Bardwell. 1994. *EE Tool Box—Workshop Resource Manual: Approaching Environmental Issues in the Classroom*. Ann Arbor, Mich.: NCEET.

Project WILD. 1992. Activity "Living Research: Aquatic Heroes and Heroines." *Aquatic Project WILD*. Bethesda, Md.: Project WILD.

Project WILD. 1995. *TAKING ACTION! An Educator's Guide to Involving Students in Environmental Action Projects*. Houston, Tex.: Western Regional Environmental Education Council.

🍎 Wallace, Aubrey. 1993. *Eco-Heroes: Twelve Tales of Environmental Victory*. San Francisco, Calif.: Mercury House.

For Information

On storm drain monitoring and stenciling programs, contact:

Step Coordinator, Oregon Department of Fish and Wildlife, P.O. Box 59
2501 S.W. First Avenue
Portland OR 97207

Earthwater Stencils
4425 140th S W , Dept. WT
Rochester WA 98579

Center for Marine Conservation
306A Buckroe Avenue
Hampton VA 23664

REAL in the Florida Keys

Case study submitted by David Makepeace and the students of Coral Shores High School in Tavernier, Florida. CSHS is located in the Florida Keys and is part of the Okeechobee-Kissimmee-Everglades-Florida Bay watershed.

Conducting a literature review of an environmental problem . . . attending public meetings . . . managing a school recycling program . . . teaching middle school students about the problems of the Everglades and Florida Bay . . . organizing a "Concert for the Bay" . . . taking part in a water quality monitoring program . . . These are a few of the projects that students organized and engaged in as participants in REAL (Responsible Environmental Action and Leadership). Instructor David Makepeace developed this "service learning" program with the support of a Serve-America grant. To gain credit in the class, students contract to participate in four different areas: Awareness, Leadership, Advocacy, and Community Service.

Developing awareness, students research the literature, view videos, attend public meetings, and take part in field trips to enhance their knowledge of South Florida problems or issues. Specialists from diverse government agencies, citizen organizations, and universities are frequent guest speakers in the classroom and train students in the field.

Related to an identified problem or issue, students are required to assume a leadership role. REAL students manage the recycling program at their high school. As a result of student efforts, the county has identified Coral Shores High School as a pilot site for school recycling programs. Also, REAL students prepare two-week lesson plans and use slides, videos, and lab demonstrations to teach seventh and eighth graders about the problems of Florida Bay and the Everglades.

As part of their advocacy commitment, students are required to support a position on an environmental issue, as well as plan and perform an action related to their issue. The only stipulation is that their plan must be "for"—not "against"—something. Several students have elected to become involved in a Florida Bay water quality monitoring program. Partnering with an existing water quality monitoring organization (Baywatch), REAL students are trained by specialists in data collecting protocol. Students generally participate in two data-collecting trips per month during the school year

and continue the program over the summer vacation.

To receive a semester credit, students must provide a minimum of 75 hours of community service and must work with a community partner or partners. Guided by their individual interests, students have chosen to work with: a bird rehabilitation center; local, state, and national parks; a historical preservation society and others.

Are REAL students effective? "YES!" say their instructor, their parents, their school and community, several federal and state government agencies, and local organizations. "Yes," says a state senator who heard their call. Students decided that admission to "Concert for the Bay" should be a well-written, informed letter sent to one of several public officials to draw attention to the problems of Florida Bay. Three hundred letters were forwarded as a result of the concert. Receiving over 30 student letters, one state senator contacted a Florida Water Management District official and said he wished to be updated on the issue—he's been a Florida Bay supporter ever since!

Dump No Waste—Drains to Stream

Case study submitted by Rhonda Hunter, Environmental Education Coordinator, Washington State Department of Ecology, and Sheila Yule, teacher and coordinator of the Environmental Club at St. Francis of Assisi, Louisville, Kentucky.

Beargrass Creek was visibly deteriorating due to the used oil, antifreeze, litter, and pollutants that had washed down storm drains. The Louisville Nature Center selected an environmental youth group (Friends of the Future) of St. Francis of Assisi school to work toward a solution for this Kentucky stream.

After researching the history of the creek, students discovered their storm water runoff was part of a combined sewer overflow system that drained directly into Beargrass Creek. They wrote a mini-grant to acquire test kits and did their own water quality stream monitoring with tests for pH, nitrogen, phosphorus, chlorine, fecal coliform, dissolved oxygen, sediment, and more.

Their tests showed high fecal coliform counts from *E. coli* that indicated raw sewage was entering from the combined sewer overflow system. High levels of phosphorus came from lawn fertilizers. Used oil was apparent, probably from

driveways and automotive oil changes. High levels of turbidity and sediment were also found.

The students worked with two engineers from the Metropolitan Sewer District who explained the combined sewer overflow systems, and even discussed environmental career opportunities. Now, with a full understanding of the problem, the students decided to help educate the rest of the community.

They chose a storm drain stenciling project. They mapped the area around their school and carefully stenciled their message, "Dump No Waste . . . Drains to Stream," next to the storm drains. Students created a brochure that explained the effect of storm drain runoff on Beargrass Creek and that offered environmental protection tips, such as using less fertilizer, recycling used oil instead of dumping it, and disposing of household hazardous waste on collection days.

The students distributed the brochure door-to-door and discussed it with neighbors who were surprised to learn that their storm drains led directly to the creek. Many residents agreed to manage their wastes differently in the future. One eighth grader said she liked the door-to-door visits, because "People were glad we made an effort to help the community." She added, "I like knowing that we made a difference."

The storm drain stenciling program was started in the Northwest where Washington's city and county local governments provide stencils and technical support to involve teachers and students in grades 4–12, Scouts and Campfire, youth at risk programs, retired seniors programs, and others.

For more information, contact: Earthwater Stencils, Dept. WT, 4425 140th Avenue Southwest, Rochester, WA 98579-9703.

Project Action Planning Form for Teachers and Students

Title of Project: _____ Teacher: _____

Name(s): _____ Date: _____

Briefly describe your special project and why it is important:

1. Project Goals and Objectives

Describe the expected results of your project. What goals do you hope to accomplish by doing this special project?

What do you hope to learn by completing your project?

2. Research and Background Information

Identify any obstacles you may encounter when conducting your special project and describe possible solutions.

Has your project been done before? If so, how was it done and what worked best?

Make a list of information and/or data you need to gather in order to complete your special project. Identify possible sources of information relevant to your project and where you might find them.

Identify any community, state, or national organizations that might provide you with information, materials, or services.

Identify other people such as teachers, administrators, parents, or community members who might help you with your special project. Describe how they can help.

3. Planning

On a separate sheet of paper, create a workable project outline.

a. Begin by listing all of the tasks you will need to accomplish in order to finish your project.

b. For each task, assign responsibility to someone.

c. Assign a date by which that task will need to be completed. This will help you finish your project on time.

Make a list of all the materials and resources you will need to complete your project. Use the project outline to identify materials and resources you will need to complete each task.

Determine the costs (if any) of doing your special project. Make a list of ways you can minimize your costs.

4. Other Considerations

What special equipment or arrangements will you need in order to complete your project (transportation, use of computers or telephone, special field equipment, etc.)? How will you obtain them?

When will you work on your special project?

If your project will be submitted for a grade, have you met all of the established criteria?

5. Project Completion

How and where will you present the results of your project to others? Will your presentation require space (for example, for a display or booth) or equipment?

How will you decide if your project has been successful?

Will your special project require long-term follow-up? If so, who will continue your project after you are finished? What long-term maintenance costs are associated with your project?

SOURCE: LANE, JENNIE F., AND CATHERINE E. ROSSOW. "SOURCES AND IDEAS FOR SPECIAL PROJECTS," IN *ENVIRONMENTAL EDUCATION TEACHER RESOURCE HANDBOOK*, PP. 243-45. MILLWOOD, N.Y.: KRAUS INTL. PUBLICATIONS, 1993. REPRODUCED WITH PERMISSION.

Water Log

Grade Level: K-12

Subject Areas: All

Duration:
Preparation time: 15 minutes
Activity time: Variable

Setting: Anywhere

Skills:
Depends on activity

Charting the Course
Prior to this activity, students should be familiar with methods of recording information (e.g., drawing, outlining, concept mapping, diagramming). Water logs can be used throughout the year with lessons and activities related to water.

Vocabulary
journal, portfolio

▼ Summary

Students use a water log (journal or portfolio) to write or illustrate their observations, feelings, and actions related to water. The log serves as an assessment tool to monitor changes over time related to knowledge of and attitudes toward water. Maintaining journals can keep students "afloat" while participating in Project WET activities.

Objectives
Students will:
• keep a journal to express what they think and feel about water and to reference experiences.
• use a journal to monitor their learning, by identifying water concepts and skills they need to improve.

Materials
• *Journals, notebooks, or folders*
• *Pencils and pens*
• *Crayons, markers, and other art materials*

Making Connections
Some students keep diaries. They may know that famous researchers and explorers have used journals or logs to record their thoughts and feelings. In some classes, students may be responsible for maintaining a portfolio, or file, of their work. By keeping a journal about their water education and experiences (field trips, water festivals, activities, etc.), students are encouraged to record and monitor their learning.

Background
After teaching one or more activities in this guide, how do you know what students have learned? Assessment strategies provided with the activities will help you determine if student learning objectives have been achieved. But do you know what was important to your students? Have they internalized the concepts? Will they use acquired skills to protect and maintain water quality or to conserve water? A journal or log provides teachers with unique insights into students' thoughts and feelings.

People have been documenting events in their lives for thousands of years. Similarly, water-related skills, feelings, and knowledge can be chronicled in a water log. The approach and format of water logs vary with the discipline and the needs of students and teachers. Logs may be structured, open ended, or both.

The log can be a journal or diary: Students write, draw, or diagram to reflect upon what they have learned. Many older students have read Anne Frank's diary. Her entries tell of her life in hiding. For two years (1942-1944) she and seven others lived in an attic to escape capture by the Nazis. Anne Frank's diary expresses the hopes and concerns common to young girls facing adulthood, and the fears and uncertainties unique to her time.

The log can serve as a source book: Students keep track of important concepts by including vocabulary lists, diagrams, or descriptions in their logs. Scientists use journals to postulate ideas or to interpret observations. Much current knowledge of primates is based on the findings of Jane Goodall. Goodall began studying chimpanzees in Tanzania in 1960. She recorded her observations in a journal, including the birth dates and names of the chimpanzees and descriptions of their personalities. This gave her a record to study as she continued learning about these chimpanzee families.

The log can inventory student work: Descriptions, drawings, or photos of student activities and projects may be included in the log. Historians and naturalists often refer to records of the Lewis and Clark expedition. While Meriwether Lewis was traveling in the early 1800s across the wilderness west of the Mississippi, he filled his journal with sketches of Native Americans, birds, plants, and fish, and maps of waterways. He also wrote about his discoveries during this exploration of land in the Louisiana Purchase.

The log functions as an evaluation tool: Whether the log is used as a diary, source book, or inventory guide, it allows teachers access to how students' understandings, feelings, and attitudes change over time. Teachers and students can designate those components of the log to be used for assessment. Teachers may look for students' perceptions of a specific concept. In other cases, students may present to the teacher their best achievements. Water logs may be submitted to the teacher throughout the year, or they can be discussed during student/teacher conferences.

Procedure
▼ Warm Up
Read to older students the excerpt from the journals of Lewis and Clark reproduced below. For younger students, copy and distribute the picture journal ("When I think of water, I think of . . .").

Have students list things that could be learned from this entry (e.g., the challenges and rewards the explorers faced) or from the picture journal. Ask students if they have ever kept a journal. Have them describe the purpose of journals and daily logs. Ask students to indicate how a journal helps people organize their thoughts and feelings.

▼ The Activity
1. **Tell students that they will be keeping a journal or water log in which to write or draw their feelings, thoughts, or experiences related to water or water resources.**

2. **Following are two approaches for keeping a water log.** Both forms can be used to assess student progress. (For younger children, teachers may need to provide boxes or cubbyholes for students to store water logs.)

Open-ended:
Request that students use their water logs to record experiences, knowledge, thoughts, and feelings about water. They may write or draw in them daily or whenever they wish. For example, they may want to record something just learned in a lesson about water, or they may compose a poem during a snow storm. Younger children can decorate the outside of their journals with water scenes. One approach for primary students is to have them draw pictures about something related to water they saw, heard, or felt. They can use their writing skills by developing simple sentences to describe these pictures. Or, the students can dictate their ideas to the teacher, who writes them down. At various times during the year, students share sections of the logs with the teacher and/or class. Selection should be up to the students; however, the teacher can request students to choose within a

---

July 2, 1806.

    The Indians who accompanied us intended leaving us in order to seek their friends, the Ootlashoots; but we prevailed on them to accompany Captain Lewis on part of his route, so as to show him the shortest road to the Missouri, and in the meantime amused them with conversation and running races, on foot and with horses, in both of which they proved themselves hardy, athletic, and active. To the chief Captain Lewis gave a small medal and a gun, as a reward for having guided us across the mountains; in return the customary civility of exchanging names passed between them, by which the former acquired the title of Yomekollick, or White Bearskin Unfolded. The Chopunnish, who had overtaken us on the 26th, made us a present of an excellent horse for the good advice we gave him, and as a proof of his attachment to the whites, as well as of his desire to be at peace with the Pahkees.

July 3, 1806.

    All our preparations being completed, we saddled our horses, and the two parties, who had been so long companions, now separated with an anxious hope of soon meeting, after each had accomplished the destined purpose.

                              — *Lewis and Clark*

QUOTED FROM: *HISTORY OF THE EXPEDITION UNDER THE COMMAND OF LEWIS AND CLARK, VOLUME III*, EDITED BY ELLIOTT COUES.

specific topic or criteria (e.g., something that shows positive feelings toward water, something that shows what they learned or gained from an activity, a sample of their best work).

Structured:
Instruct students to follow a set format or to comply with certain criteria. Individual expression and creativity should be a component of this approach as well. Require students to use their water logs in one or more of the following ways:

- Record their experiences, knowledge, thoughts, and feelings about water.
- Summarize what they have learned in an activity.
- Maintain a reference file of important water concepts and water study skills.
- Inventory projects and activities to demonstrate their knowledge, attitudes, and skills related to water.

3. **All or parts of the water log are reviewed or assessed.** Students may wish to record their personal reflections in code, in a special section of the log, or in a separate journal.

4. **If the water log is graded, one or more of the following criteria can be used: accuracy of content, creativity, originality, evidence of increased knowledge about water, thorough expression of attitudes toward water, completeness, etc.** Each of these criteria can be graded on a scale of 1-5 or 1-10. An explanation for the rating should be supplied as well. In some cases, students can grade themselves, explaining reasons for grades. Students' work should be reviewed to determine the validity of their self-evaluations.

5. **One of the main objectives of the water log is to allow students to record and monitor their own learning. Students should be encouraged to identify areas of** water education in which they feel competent or need to improve through additional study or experiences.

▼ *Wrap Up*
Discuss with students their opinions about keeping a water log. Ask about other ways they could use the water log. Throughout the year or grading period, ask students how they can use the water log to monitor their work.

Assessment
Have students:
- maintain water logs (steps 1 and 2).
- present their water-related knowledge, attitudes, and skills in a water log (steps 1 and 2).
- evaluate their water logs (step 4).

Upon completing the activity, for further assessment have students:
- identify areas of strengths and weaknesses regarding understanding of water concepts and acquisition of skills (for upper level students).

Extensions
If students have identified water-related concepts and skills that they do not understand, have them develop strategies to improve their understanding or performance. Younger students may wish to display their best water log entries.

Students can use their logs as field journals, sketching pictures of aquatic plants and animals.

Resources
Barrow, Lloyd. 1993. "A Portfolio of Learning." *Science and Children*, 31 (3): 38-39.

Belanoff, Pat, and Marcia Dickson, eds. 1991. *Portfolios: Process and Product*. Portsmouth, N.H.: Boynton/ Cook Publishers, Inc.

Benjamin, Carol Lea. 1985. *Writing for Kids*. New York, N.Y.: T.Y. Crowell.

Caduto, Michael. 1985. *Pond and Brook: A Guide to Nature Study in Freshwater Environments*. Englewood Cliffs, N.J.: Prentice Hall.

Cornell, Joseph. 1987. *Listen to Nature*. Nevada City, Calif.: Dawn Publications.

Coues, Elliott, ed. 1965. *History of the Expedition Under the Command of Lewis and Clark, Volume III*. New York, N.Y.: Dover Publications, Inc.

Evans, Christine S. 1993. "When Teachers Look at Student Work." *Educational Leadership*, 50 (5): 71-72.

🍎 Leslie, Claire. 1987. *The Naturalist's Sketchbook: Pages from the Seasons of a Year*. New York, N.Y.: Dodd-Mead.

🍎 Twain, Mark. 1989. *Following the Equator: A Journey Around the World*. New York, N.Y.: Dover.

Name _____ Date: _____

When Gigette* thinks of water, she thinks of ...

When I think of water, I think of ...

*Gigette is the illustrator for the *Project WET Curriculum and Activity Guide!*
She lives in Helena, Montana, and loves to take a long walk on a snowy day!

Water has unique physical and chemical characteristics.

▼

The nature of the water molecule determines the physical properties of

water and its behavior. The physical and chemical properties

of water are unique and complex.

Adventures in Density

Floating on a raft on the Mississippi . . . shipwrecked on an iceberg . . . being towed to sea by a great fish . . . How are these accounts (penned by authors Mark Twain, Arthur Roth, and Ernest Hemingway) adventures in density?

▼ Summary
Students conduct investigations to discover how the density of water is affected by heat and salinity, and relate their "discoveries" to literary adventures.

■ **Grade Level:**
Middle School

■ **Subject Areas:**
Physical Science, Language Arts

■ **Duration:**
Preparation time:
Part I: 50 minutes
Part II: 10 minutes

Activity time:
Part I: 50 minutes
Part II: 50 minutes

■ **Setting:** Classroom

■ **Skills:**
Organizing (matching); Analyzing (comparing, contrasting, inferring); Interpreting (relating)

■ **Charting the Course**
While aspects of density are introduced in this activity, a basic understanding of density supports this activity. Participating in "Molecules in Motion" helps students relate closeness of particles to amount of heat energy. Activities illustrating hydrogen bonding, such as "Hangin' Together" or "H$_2$Olympics," supplement this activity.

■ **Vocabulary**
density

Objectives
Students will:
- demonstrate how heat and salinity affect the density of water.
- relate the compactness of water molecules to the density of water in different states.
- recognize that concepts of density can be found in literature and daily life.

Materials
- *2 soft-sided plastic bottles of the same size* (Fill each with equal amounts of water, cap, and place one in the freezer until frozen.)
- *Copy or overhead transparency of* **Density Diagram**
- *Copies of* **Adventures in Density Activity Sheet** *and* **Heavy and Light Reading**

Each group of students will need the following:
- *Very hot water*
- *Very cold water*
- *Food coloring (e.g., red and blue)*
- *Beakers or clear plastic cups*
- *Oven mitts or heat protective gloves*
- *Straws or eyedroppers*
- *Ice cubes containing blue food coloring*
- *Hard-boiled egg*
- *Salt (at least ½ cup [0.12 l])*
- *Spoon*
- *Heat source*

Making Connections
Through reading or personal experiences, most students have enjoyed adventures about icebergs, fishing, rafting, etc. All these adventures involve density. Investigating how heat and salinity affect the density of water helps increase students' understanding of the basic properties of water.

Background
Water is one of the few substances on Earth that can be naturally found in all three states: solid, liquid, and gas. One difference between each of these states is density: how close water molecules are to each other. The amount of particles (mass) within a certain space (volume) determines the density of a substance. Water vapor is the least dense of water states because the molecules are furthest apart from each other. The molecules of warm water are less dense (less compact) than cold water. However, ice is less dense than liquid water. The density of water can be influenced by a variety of factors, and many aspects of water density play important roles for life on Earth.

Heating and cooling water affect the density of water. Heating water speeds up the movement of water molecules. When their movement is increased, water molecules are less able to stay near each other. As they move faster, the molecules bounce off each other more frequently and move farther apart, decreasing the density of water molecules. Therefore, warm water is less dense than cold water.

As water cools, water molecules lose heat energy and move more slowly. This allows water molecules to move closer together, becoming more dense. Therefore, cold water will sink and warm water will rise. Since the molecules of cold water are closer together, they can support the less dense warm water above it. Warm water will sit on top of cooler water; where these two layers meet is called a thermocline.

But what happens when water gets very cold and turns to ice? Since ice is extremely cold water, one might expect the molecules to move very little and be very close together (very dense). However, one only needs to put ice cubes in a soft drink or go ice-skating to know that ice does not sink; therefore, it cannot be denser than liquid water. The molecules in ice do move very slowly; however, they are farther apart from each other in ice than when in liquid form. This is because when water freezes, the molecules spread out and are arranged in a lattice-like pattern. This formation increases the distance between water molecules, making ice less dense than liquid water. (See "Hangin' Together.")

Adding certain materials to water, such as salt, increases its density. If salt is added to fresh water, the amount of material within the space water occupies increases. Whereas only water molecules previously consumed space, now salt molecules are crowded into the same space. This makes salt water more dense than fresh water.

Pressure also increases the density of water. Deep water has greater pressure than surface water because the weight of the water molecules above pushes down on the deeper molecules, forcing them closer together and making them more dense. Temperature also decreases with depth, and cooler water has greater density than warmer water. As the depth of water increases, the density of water increases. A large body of water contains many density levels. Each level provides a different habitat in which certain plants and

animals may live. Many factors determine where organisms live—sunlight, water temperature, pressure, food supply, etc. People who harvest food from lakes and oceans know this and will drop their nets or fishing lines to the depth (density level) at which they will most likely find the food they are seeking.

Lakes in temperate climates benefit from the formation and melting of ice. As water cools in the fall, water molecules slow down and move closer together (becoming more dense). The density of water continues to increase until the temperature reaches 39 degrees F (4°C); this is when the density of water is at its greatest. When the temperature of water falls to 39 degrees F, the water begins to sink. As the temperature of water drops below 39 degrees F, it begins to freeze and molecules become arranged in the lattice-like pattern. As it freezes, ice rises and

A density difference causes icebergs to float; these provide refuge for many animals. ARCHIE SATTERFIELD

floats above the denser liquid water. Ice also acts as an insulator, preventing the water beneath from freezing. In the spring, when ice melts and the water temperature rises to 39 degrees F, the water begins to sink. This rise and fall of water, or turnover, circulates nutrients and oxygen throughout the lake.

Procedure
▼ Warm Up

Discuss this riddle: Which weighs more, a pound of feathers or a pound of lead? They both weigh the same, but since lead is more dense, it will take a much greater volume of feathers to make a pound than it will lead.

Ask students to define density. Show students the *Density Diagram* and have them discuss which graphic represents the denser material? Have them note the differences between the two pictures. Which is most like lead? If necessary, students can refine their definition of density; help students relate density to compactness of particles or molecules.

Show students two bottles of water, one frozen. Explain that they each contain equal amounts of water. Ask students to describe what happened to the frozen bottle. (The sides of the bottle should be forced outward by the ice.) Which diagram in the *Density Diagram* best represents ice?

▼ The Activity

Part I

Have students work in small groups. Provide each group with a copy of the *Adventures in Density Activity Sheet*. Present them with the necessary materials and have them complete the activities and readings. They may need help in providing reasons why the density of ice is less than water (see **Background**).

DENSITY DIAGRAM

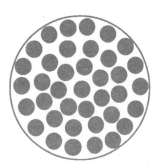 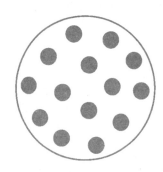

Part II

Distribute *Heavy and Light Reading*. Have students determine the role of density in each selection. In the first selection, wildlife finds refuge on floating ice. (Ice is less dense than liquid water.) In the second story, the density of water increases as the depth of water increases. In the last selection, the raft would more easily float on the denser salt water.

▼ Wrap Up

Have students summarize the results of their activities. Have students cite situations in their lives that have involved different densities of water (e.g., ice-skating, feeling cool water at the bottom of a pool or lake). Ask students to identify density concepts in daily events and further readings.

Assessment

Have students:
- demonstrate the relationship of water temperature and salinity to density (*Part I*).
- cite examples of different densities of water in excerpts from literature (*Part II*).
- interpret a diagram representing closeness of water molecules to the density of ice and to liquid water (*Warm Up* and *Wrap Up*).

Upon completing the activity, for further assessment have students:

- identify which of each of the following pairs represents a denser material: cool water or warm water; fresh water or salt water; ice or liquid water.
- set up a demonstration to show why fish don't freeze in winter.

Extensions

Have students construct miniature rafts that can float and write imaginative stories about their adventures on them. Students may also create science-fiction stories about life on a planet where air is denser than water or ice is denser than liquid water.

Resources

Cuevas, Mapi M., and William G. Lamb. 1994. *Physical Science*. Austin, Tex.: Holt, Rinehart, & Winston.

🍎 Hemingway, Ernest. 1952. *The Old Man and the Sea*. New York, N.Y.: Macmillan Publishing Company.

🍎 Roth, Arthur. 1974. *The Iceberg Hermit*. New York, N.Y.: Four Winds Press.

Scheckel, Larry. 1993. "How to Make Density Float." *Science and Children* (31) 3: 30-33.

Sinclair, Patti K. 1992. *e for Environment*. New Providence, N.J.: R. R. Bowker.

🍎 Twain, Mark. 1953. *The Adventures of Huckleberry Finn*. New York, N.Y.: Dodd, Mead & Co., Inc.

Adventures in Density

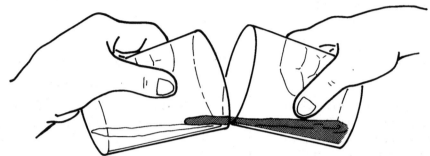

Temperature

a.   Get a beaker (or cup) of cold water and a beaker of hot water (wear protective gloves). Put a drop of red food coloring in one and a drop of blue in the other (it doesn't matter which). *Gently* **tilt both beakers so that the liquids almost touch and allow hot water to flow over cold.**

Look at the containers from the side; draw a picture of what you see.

Which is more dense, cool water or warm water? Answering the next two questions should support your response.

How does heat energy affect the movement of water molecules? (Hint: Compare boiling water to cool water.)

When do you think it is easier for molecules to stay close together: when they move slowly or when they move quickly?

b.   Add food coloring to cold water. Put a straw in the cold water; position your finger over the opening. When you lift the straw above the surface, water should stay in the straw. Put the straw on the inside edge of the cup of hot water and slowly release the cold water. Where does it go?

c.   Float a blue-colored ice cube in a glass of warm water. Look from the side: what happens to the blue coloring as the ice melts?

Even though ice is colder than liquid water, ice floats. Considering this, how would the density of molecules in ice compare to molecules in liquid water?

Salinity

a.   Fill two glasses with water. While stirring, add salt to one of the glasses until no more salt dissolves. Place a hard-boiled egg in each glass. The egg should float in the salt water; if not, try adding more salt.

How does salt affect the density of water? (Hint: Which has more particles within the same amount of space, fresh water or water with salt added to it?)

b.   Try to float fresh water (dyed with food coloring) on top of salt water. Be careful when pouring; try to flow the fresh water gently over the salt water.

Temperature and Salinity

a.   See how you can alter the above experiments by adding salt and heating or cooling water.

For example, when floating fresh water on salt water, how would heating the fresh water affect the result? Is warm salt water less dense than cold salt water?

Describe how you altered the experiment and record your observations.

Heavy and Light Reading

Read the following selections. Relate density concepts learned in the above activities to information in the excerpts (especially to those terms and questions in bold type).

The Iceberg Hermit by Arthur Roth

Summary: Allan Gordon was shipwrecked on an iceberg where he lived for two years. He finally made contact with the native people and lived with them for an additional five years, until he was rescued by a Dutch whaling ship. Allan Gordon observed the following about the Arctic wilderness that surrounded him.

Excerpt:

*Then too there was plenty of wildlife. He often saw seals sleeping on pans of **ice**. Small herds of walrus sometimes **used the iceberg as a resting platform**, between dives to the sea floor after clams and other shellfish. Birds of all descriptions flew over and often **landed briefly on his ice island**. On several occasions Allan spotted the high feather of mist that came from a sounding whale, and once he even saw the long twisting horn of a narwhal.*

Explain how the wildlife observed by Allan Gordon depended on density.

The Adventures of Huckleberry Finn by Mark Twain

Summary: This famous story recounts the adventures of a young boy and a runaway slave on a raft floating down the Mississippi River.

Excerpt:

*. . . It's lovely to live on a **raft**. . . . Once or twice a night we would see a steamboat slipping along in the dark . . . and by and by her waves would get to us, a long time after she was gone, and **joggle the raft** a bit . . .*

Would it be easier to float a raft on salt water or fresh water? Did the egg float more easily in salt or fresh water?

The Old Man and the Sea by Ernest Hemingway

Summary: An old Cuban fisherman struggles to land a giant marlin and is pulled far out into the Gulf Stream.

Excerpt:

*They sat on the Terrace and many of the fishermen made fun of the old man and he was not angry. Others, of the older fishermen, looked at him and were sad. But they did not show it and they spoke politely about the **current and the depths they had drifted their lines at** and the steady good weather and of what they had seen . . .*

*This far out, he [the marlin] must be huge in this month, he thought. Eat them [sardines], fish. Eat them. Please eat them. How fresh they are and you **down there six hundred feet in that cold water in the dark.** Make another turn in the dark and come back and eat them.*

How would the density of water near the surface of the ocean compare to water at greater depths? (Hint: Which would be warmer?)

Plants and animals live in many places or habitats within the layers of the ocean. (The layers are created by differences in density, pressure, light, etc.) People who fish often take advantage of this knowledge by weighting their baits to fall within the range of a particular fish. Anglers also take advantage of currents within the ocean. Density currents occur because of differences in salinity, temperature, and the amount of material dissolved in water. (However, currents vary; the Gulf Stream current is driven more by wind.)

H₂Olympics

■ **Grade Level:**
Upper Elementary, Middle School

■ **Subject Areas:**
Physical Science, Mathematics

■ **Duration:**
Preparation time: 40 minutes
Activity time: 50 minutes

■ **Setting:** Classroom

■ **Skills:**
Analyzing (formulating questions, identifying components and relationships)

■ **Charting the Course**
Preceding this lesson, introduce the structure and behavior of the water molecule ("Molecules in Motion"). This activity can be done in conjunction with "Hangin' Together" to help students understand the forces that contribute to water's properties. This activity supports concepts presented in "Thirsty Plants," "Get the Ground Water Picture," "Let's Even Things Out," and "Aqua Notes."

■ **Vocabulary**
adhesion, cohesion, capillary action, surface tension

Can you make water defy gravity?

▼ Summary
Students compete in a Water Olympics to investigate two properties of water, adhesion and cohesion.

Objectives
Students will:
- demonstrate adhesive and cohesive properties of water.
- relate adhesion and cohesion to daily activities.

Materials
- *Beaker or measuring cup with narrow spout*
- *Yarn (soaking wet)*
- *Container to hold water*
- *Colored water*
- *Music taped from the Olympics or other sports programs (optional)*
- *Copies of H₂Olympics Score Sheet*
- *Water*
- *Paper and drawing materials*

To simplify setting up the activity, materials for each event are listed separately. (Each event requires water.)

Event 1
- *Clear plastic cups*
- *Two dollars in pennies*

Event 2
- *Eyedropper*
- *Penny*

Event 3
- *Boat pattern*
- *Stiff cardboard*
- *Scissors*
- *Soap chips (shaved from a bar of soap)*
- *Large aluminum trays*
- *Stopwatch*

Event 4
- *Paper clips*
- *Fork*
- *Magnifying glass*
- *Clear plastic cups*

Event 5
- *Several brands of paper towels*
- *Tall glasses*
- *Tape*
- *Ruler*
- *Scissors*

Making Connections
Students see signs of water's adhesive properties daily (e.g., water beading on the surface of a glass); however, they may not appreciate how unique this quality is. Learning how a water strider skates over the surface of water or how water travels upward through soil gives students opportunities to explore further the structure and behavior of the water molecule.

Background
The nature of the water molecule causes it to be attracted to other water molecules as well as to molecules of other substances. Without these qualities, plants could not get water, and blood would have difficulty traveling through the body. The attraction between water molecules is called cohesion. The attraction of the water molecule to other materials, like glass or soil, is called adhesion.

Evidence of water's attraction to itself can be seen by simply looking at its surface. If a glass is filled to the brim and more water is added gently, the level of the water will exceed the top of the glass. The cohesive force between water molecules causes the water surface to behave as though it is covered by a thinly stretched membrane that is always trying to contract. This phenomenon is

Water striders can skate on water because they do not break the surface tension. JENNIE LANE

called surface tension. In many ways, surface tension is like water's skin.

Water's surface is so strong it can even support paper clips and needles. Surface tension is important to the survival of many aquatic organisms, including insects. The water strider lives on the surface of fresh water. Compared to a piece of wood floating in the water, paper clips and water striders are not actually floating. Instead, they are held up by bonds between water molecules (see "Hangin' Together"). Floating objects do break the surface tension of water. They stay afloat because water molecules deeper in the water can support the weight of the objects.

Soap also breaks surface tension. For example, when a small piece of cardboard cut into the shape of a boat is placed on water, it will stay in one place. This is because water is equally attracted to all sides of the cardboard. When soap is placed at the back end of the cardboard boat, water molecules are still pulling at the front end of the boat, but not the

back end. (The soap reduces the pull of water molecules on the back end of the boat.) This causes the boat to move forward. (An analogy would be a tug of war. The rope is the boat and the people pulling on each side are the water molecules. If several people on one end let go [representing the addition of soap], the rope [boat] would be pulled toward the opposite end.)

The same forces that cause water to be attracted to itself cause it to adhere to other substances. If this didn't happen, water would slide off everything like water off a duck's back.

Water appears to defy gravity as it moves up a paper towel, through spaces among soil particles, or along a piece of yarn at an angle to the

ground. This is called capillary action and results from water molecules being attracted to molecules of the towel (or soil or yarn) and to each other. However, the molecules can only travel so far before the force of gravity overcomes the attraction of water to itself and to other molecules.

Procedure
▼ *Warm Up*

Show students a beaker partially filled with colored water, an empty container, and the yarn. Tell them that you are going to make water defy gravity as it "walks a tightrope" from the beaker to the container. Hold beaker and yarn as indicated in the illustration, *Water Walks a Tightrope*. Slowly pour the water down the yarn. (You might want to practice first!) Can students explain how water moves along the yarn? Tell them they will conduct a series of events that will help them understand this demonstration and other feats of water.

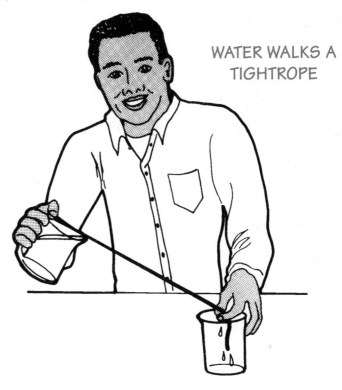

WATER WALKS A TIGHTROPE

H₂Olympics Scoreboard

	EVENT 1 Pole Vaulting (number of pennies)	EVENT 2 Balance Beam (number of drops)	EVENT 3 Sculling (number of seconds)	EVENT 4 Backstroke (number of paper clips)	EVENT 5 Slalom (height)	
					1st Towel	2nd Towel
Team:						
Team:						
Etc.						

▼ The Activity

1. **Divide the classroom into sections; an Olympic event will take place in each area.** Banners can be designed to identify each event.

2. **Divide the class into small teams.** Each team should represent a body of water (e.g., the Atlantic Ocean team, the Columbia River team, the Lake Travis team, etc.). Begin the games with each team presenting its members to the class.

3. **Play the Olympics theme song. Tell students they will be participating in a Water Olympics to demonstrate some amazing feats of water.**

4. **Students complete the events in any order.** Directions for the events are on the H₂Olympics Score Sheet. Results should be recorded on their score sheets and on a scoreboard posted in the front of the room.

▼ Wrap Up

Have students compare the results of the different events. Ask them to explain the role of cohesion (water's attraction to itself) and adhesion (water's attraction to other materials) in each activity.

Remind students of the water walking the tightrope during the **Warm Up.** Can they explain how water's attraction to the yarn and to itself keeps water from falling

toward the ground? If water is poured too quickly, gravity will overpower water's cohesive and adhesive forces.

Have students develop a system to hand out medals to the winners of each event. Students should be encouraged to make sure each team gets some type of medal (include criteria such as teamwork, creativity, cooperation, etc.).

Assessment

Have students:
- demonstrate water's cohesive and adhesive properties (step 4).
- draw a picture of water moving along yarn or of a water drop and identify where adhesion and cohesion occur (**Wrap Up**).

Extensions

Students can investigate how soil absorbs water to explore adhesion and cohesion further. Challenge students to concoct a soil that will absorb the most water. Have students collect soil samples and remove excess water by leaving the samples spread out in the sun for about six hours. Instruct them to describe their soil recipe and why they think it will absorb water well. After the samples are dried, provide students with the following instructions:

- Use a cup with tiny holes punched in the bottom. Record the weight of the cup: ____. Fill the cup with your soil; pack it tightly. Record the weight of the cup and the soil, and subtract the weight of the cup. How much does the dry soil weigh? ____ Place the cup in a pan filled with a shallow layer of water. After thirty minutes, remove the cup from the water and carefully wipe excess water from the sides and bottom. Weigh the cup and soil and subtract the weight of the cup and dry soil. How much water did your soil absorb? ____

Compare the surface tension of other liquids. Using a magnifying glass, investigate drops of water, hydrogen peroxide, and alcohol. How do they differ? Can a paper clip be supported on the surface of each of these liquids?

Resources

Hurd, Dean, et al. 1988. *Prentice Hall Physical Science.* Englewood Cliffs, N.J.: Prentice Hall, Inc.

Lamb, William G., et al. 1989. *HBJ Physical Science.* Orlando, Fla.: Harcourt Brace Jovanovich, Inc.

Watson, Philip. 1982. *Liquid Magic.* New York, N.Y.: Lothrop, Lee & Shepard Books.

H₂Olympics Score Sheet

TEAM NAME: _____   Date: _____

Team member(s): _____

Event 1. Pole Vaulting: Over the Top!

Read the directions through before you begin this event. How many pennies do you think you'll be able to add before the water spills over? _____

Directions: Fill a clear plastic cup with water until it is even with the rim. Add pennies, one at a time. Keep track of the number of pennies added. Continue until the water spills over the side. Repeat for the other team member.

Describe or draw the surface of the water:

Number of pennies added,
team member 1: _____ team member 2: _____

Event 2. The Balance Beam: A Penny for Your Thoughts!

Read the directions before you begin this event. How many drops of water do you think you'll be able to put on the penny? _____

Directions: Using an eyedropper, place as many drops of water on the penny as possible without spilling over the edge. Keep track of the number of drops. Continue until water spills over or the water drop collapses. Repeat for the other team member. Record the scores.

Describe or draw how the water appeared on the penny before the drop collapsed:

Number of drops,
team member 1: _____ team member 2: _____

Event 3. Sculling: Bubble Power!

Directions: Cut out two boat shapes from a piece of cardboard (see pattern). In the rear of each boat, cut out a small notch. Place a soap chip in the notch of one boat. Place the boats in a tray of water and describe what happens.

What caused the boat to move? (Hint: Place a drop of water on the table. What happens to it when you put a soap chip in it?)

Design a better shape for the boat so that it will move faster and in a straight line. Experiment with different shapes of boats, placement of the soap chip, and size of the soap chip.

Choose the best design and place the boat at one end of the tray at the start line. Time it until it crosses the finish line.

How long did it take to cross the finish line?

_____

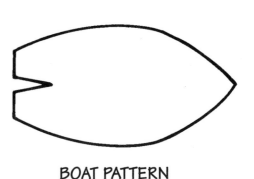

BOAT PATTERN

Event 4. Backstroke: Clipping Along!

Read the directions before you begin this event. How many paper clips do you think your team can suspend on the surface of water?

_____

Directions: Try placing a paper clip on the surface of water. (Hint: Lay the paper clip on the prongs of a fork and lower it into the water.) Use a magnifying glass to observe the surface of the water where it comes in contact with the paper clip. Draw a picture or describe what this looks like.

_____

_____

_____

_____

_____

See how many paper clips you can suspend on the water's surface. Repeat for your other team member.

Number of paper clips suspended on the surface of water,

team member 1: _____

team member 2: _____

Event 5. Slalom: Weaving In and Out!

Directions: Cut out strips of two brands of paper towels—one you think will absorb the most water and one you think will absorb the least. Explain your reasoning.

_____

_____

_____

_____

_____

_____

_____

_____

_____

_____

_____

_____

_____

_____

Tape one end of each towel to the middle of a pencil. Lay the pencil on top of a tall glass. Figure out how much water will need to be added to the container to immerse the ends of the paper towels ½ inch (1.5 cm) into the water. Remove the towels, fill the container to that level, and put the towels back in. Let the paper towels absorb water until the water stops rising. Use a ruler to measure the height absorbed above the water for each towel.

Height for first towel: _____

Height for second towel: _____

Hangin' Together

What has a tough skin, can make a mountain of sugar disappear, can keep elephants cool, and can crack giant boulders?

▼ Summary

Students mimic the water molecule's special ability to hold onto other water molecules; they also present four properties of water that are critical to life on Earth.

Objectives

Students will:
- illustrate the structure and intermolecular forces of the water molecule in relation to hydrogen bonding.
- explain the role of hydrogen bonding and its relationship with some of the unique characteristics of water.
- deduce how these unique molecular properties of water are critical to life on Earth.

Materials

- *Dark-colored bottle*
- *Wool material* (optional)
- *Balloon* (optional)
- *Comb*
- *Running water* (if a water source is not available, have a student pour a slow, steady stream of water from a gallon jug)
- *3-foot-long (1 m) pieces of string or strips of cloth, one per student*
- *Copies of **Student Activity Cards***
- *Magnets*
- *Paper clips*
- *Forks*
- *Cups*
- *Sugar*
- *Oil*
- *Paintbrushes*
- *Copies of **Hydrocharade Cards***
- *Broom or meter stick*
- *Water*
- *Scrap paper*
- *Several pieces of string 13 inches (about 0.33 m long), 2 per student*
- *Tape*
- *Marking pens*
- *Chalk*

Making Connections

Children are familiar with rain, salt water, perspiration, and ice, but do they realize that the same unique feature of water makes all these forms of water possible? The water molecule's ability to bond with other water molecules allows it to bead up, to dissolve substances, to evaporate, to condense, and to be less dense as a solid. If water did not possess these qualities, life on Earth could not exist.

Background

Understanding the intermolecular forces of water requires a basic understanding of atomic and electromagnetic theories. These theories explain why the water molecule's shape causes it to be attracted to other water molecules.

The water molecule consists of two elements, hydrogen and oxygen, in the ratio of two hydrogen for every one oxygen. The formula for water is H_2O. Water molecules are said to be polar; that means they are like magnets. One end has a negative charge and the other has a positive charge.

The positive end of one molecule is attracted to the negative end of another molecule. When the molecules stay in contact with each other, a bond—called a hydrogen bond—forms between the two molecules. The structure and nature of the water molecule give it various interesting properties that are critical to life on Earth.

■ **Grade Level:**
Middle School

■ **Subject Areas:**
Physical Science

■ **Duration:**
Preparation time:
Part I: 20 minutes
Part II: 30 minutes
Part III: 30 minutes

Activity time:
Part I: 10 minutes
Part II: 50 minutes
Part III: 30 minutes

■ **Setting:** Classroom

■ **Skills:**
Gathering information (observing); Interpreting (inferring, translating); Presenting

■ **Charting the Course**
"Molecules in Motion" and activities on the structure of the water molecule can precede this activity. Follow with activities focusing on the physical characteristics and behavior of water (e.g., "H₂Olympics," "What's the Solution?"), evaporation/condensation ("Water Models"), ice ("Cold Cash in the Icebox"), and density ("Adventures in Density").

■ **Vocabulary**
heat sink, hydrogen bond, electromagnetic forces, polar, surface tension, solution

---

• **Water bonds to itself and other substances.**

The surface of water acts like a skin that keeps some things out. The skin is actually a layer of water molecules held tightly together by hydrogen bonds. This is why water forms drops, and why some insects can skate on the surface of water. To demonstrate water's "skin," place a paper clip on the prongs of a fork and gently lower the fork into water; surface tension supports the paper clip.

Molecules of water are also attracted to other materials that have negative and positive charges. Its ability to stick to other surfaces allows water to move into small spaces in soil or be absorbed by paper towels.

• **Water dissolves a variety of substances.**

More things dissolve in water than in any other substance. Compounds like sugar, which are magnetically charged (polar), dissolve easily in water. Water molecules dissolve sugar by forming hydrogen bonds with each sugar molecule. Sugar appears to disappear as it mixes thoroughly with water. If water could not dissolve sugar, sugar molecules could not travel through blood to our cells. Some substances, like oil and fats, are not charged (nonpolar). These do not dissolve or mix in water because hydrogen bonds are not formed. Cells within our body are made of fatty substances. If fat and oil dissolved in water, we would all end up like mush!

• **Water cools as it evaporates.**
Water is constantly evaporating from the surface of our skin, as well as from the skin of other animals such as elephants. Without this, the body, which con-

stantly produces energy, would overheat. Water in the body is heated by the metabolism of digested nutrients. Sweat glands excrete the heated water to the skin's surface. Because the water molecules contain heat energy, they move quickly (see the activity "Molecules in Motion"), making it difficult for hydrogen bonds to form. Individual water molecules are able to break away or evaporate, becoming gas molecules. The power-packed gas molecule takes heat energy with it, leaving slower moving molecules behind, which makes the body feel cooler. Evaporation also helps to cool water in oceans, lakes, or a cup of coffee.

- **Water expands when it freezes.** Ice floats on the surface of ponds. One might expect the slower moving molecules of frozen water to be closer together than liquid water molecules; however, in ice, water molecules are actually farther apart from each other (less dense) than they are in liquid form. Hydrogen bonds easily form when water molecules have little heat energy and are moving slowly (see "Molecules in Motion"). The strong hydrogen bonds force water molecules into a pattern, holding them apart from each other. How can water crack rock? Water that seeps into the fissures of rocks may freeze and melt as often as 70 times a year in some regions. Freezing water expands and exerts a force of about 30,000 pounds per square inch on the surrounding rock.

Procedure
▼ *Warm Up*
Show students a dark-colored bottle and say that it contains a wonderful liquid. This liquid keeps elephants cool, can support some six-legged

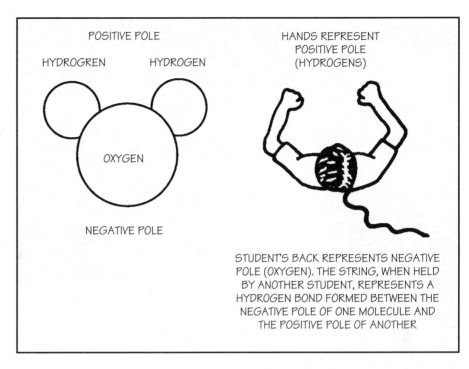

POSITIVE POLE

HYDROGREN   HYDROGEN

OXYGEN

NEGATIVE POLE

HANDS REPRESENT POSITIVE POLE (HYDROGENS)

STUDENT'S BACK REPRESENTS NEGATIVE POLE (OXYGEN). THE STRING, WHEN HELD BY ANOTHER STUDENT, REPRESENTS A HYDROGEN BOND FORMED BETWEEN THE NEGATIVE POLE OF ONE MOLECULE AND THE POSITIVE POLE OF ANOTHER

creatures on its surface, can make mountains of sugar or salt appear to vanish, and can crack giant boulders! Tell students that the most amazing thing about this liquid is that it is available by simply turning on a faucet.

List the accomplishments of water mentioned above (dissolving sugar, supporting insects, cooling elephants, cracking rock). Assess students' prior knowledge by having them offer possible explanations for how water accomplishes these feats.

Tell students you will give them a hint. Ask students if they have experienced static electricity. If necessary, demonstrate it by rubbing a balloon against some wool and sticking it to wool clothing or holding it near a head of hair. Explain that electrical charges in the balloon attract opposite charges in wool and hair.

Transfer electrical charges to a comb by running it through a student's hair. Ask the class if they think water

has electrical charges. Have the student bring the comb close to, but not touching, a slow, continuous stream of water. The stream should bend, moving closer to the comb.

What do students think gives water electrical charges? Tell them they are each going to become the smallest possible particle of water, and they will investigate how and why water behaves as it does.

▼ *The Activity*

Part I
1. **Tell students they are water molecules. Explain that a water molecule is like a magnet. It has a negative charge (or pole) and a positive charge. Tell them to stand and hold their arms straight out from their bodies, parallel to the ground.** Their arms should form a "V" in front of them.

2. **Have students tie strings around their waists, leaving a tail hanging behind each student.** Identify their hands as the positive

poles (hydrogen atoms) and their bodies, specifically their backs, as the negative poles.

3. **Explain that water molecules attract each other like magnets. Show how two magnets attract each other. Tell students they can demonstrate how water molecules act like magnets: one student holds another student's string. Explain that when the negative part of one molecule attaches or bonds to the positive part of another molecule, this forms a hydrogen bond. The string represents the hydrogen bond.**

4. **Have students summarize how hydrogen bonding occurs in water molecules.**

Part II

1. **Divide the class into groups and provide each group with a set of four *Student Activity Cards*.** Each card provides information and a simple hands-on or mental lab relating to a certain behavior of water that involves hydrogen bonding.

2. **Discuss the results of the investigations and the role hydrogen bonding plays in each.**

Part III

1. **Divide the class into four groups. Each group will act out one of the behaviors of water related to hydrogen bonding. Explain that this will be like a game of charades in which the audience tries to guess the property of water being presented.** The presentations relate to each of the investigations just completed.

2. **Provide each group with a *Hydrocharade Card*.** The card provides a suggestion for acting out a particular behavior of water (creating surface tension, dissolving, evaporating, freezing). Students

should read the card and assign each group member a role to play. The skit can be altered to add more drama or humor; make sure the basic principles are still clear. Allow time for groups to practice their skits.

3. **Each group presents its skit to the class. Audience members (the three groups not currently presenting) write down which property they think is being portrayed and why they think so.**

▼ *Wrap Up*

After each presentation or at the end of all the demonstrations, have students reveal their guesses for which skit demonstrated which behavior of water. Challenge students to apply the demonstrations to real-life situations, such as those discussed in the *Warm Up*. How does water make sugar seem to

disappear? (Dissolving.) How does it help keep elephants cool? (Evaporation.) How can insects walk on water? (Surface tension.) How can it crack giant boulders? (Freezing water expands.)

Assessment

Have students:

- describe how hydrogen bonding occurs in water molecules (*Part I*, step 4).
- demonstrate, through role-playing, hydrogen bonding in solutions, surface tension, evaporative cooling, and formation of ice (*Part III*, step 3).
- interpret a skit to identify whether surface tension, solutions, evaporation, or ice formation is being demonstrated (*Wrap Up*).

Upon completing the activity, for further assessment have students:

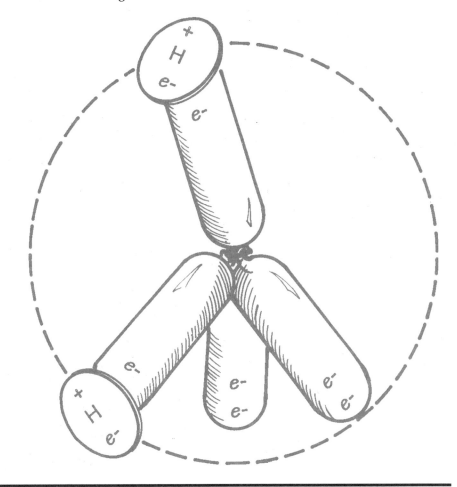

- compose a paper, draw a picture, or perform a play representing what life would be like without hydrogen bonding (ice would sink, water might too easily evaporate, water drops couldn't form, etc.).
- design a simulation to demonstrate how ice (less dense than water) floats on water.

Extensions

Students wishing to further explore the structure of the water molecule and its polarity can do the following activity. Inflate four elongated balloons and tie the ends of the balloons tightly together. (The balloons should spread out from each other in different directions: three should stand like a tripod with the fourth sticking straight up.) These four balloons represent an atom of oxygen. Where the balloons are tied together represents the nucleus (eight protons and eight neutrons), and each balloon represents the location of electrons (the orbitals). Oxygen has eight electrons; the first two are located near the nucleus. The remaining six electrons are located in the four orbitals. Each orbital would "like" to have two electrons; however, because there are only six electrons, two orbitals will have only one electron each. Do the following to show the distribution of electrons.

Use a marking pen to write an "e-" (representing an electron) on the outer end of the four balloons. Then mark another "e-" on the end of two balloons (preferably two that are near each other). You should end up with two orbitals with two electrons each and two orbitals with only one each. The two orbitals lacking an electron would like to get another electron. In the water molecule, oxygen fills its orbitals by sharing electrons with hydrogen. (This is called a covalent bond.)

Hydrogen has one proton and one electron, and room for another electron. By sharing electrons with each other, oxygen and hydrogen can fill their orbitals. The electrons of two hydrogens are needed to fill each orbital of oxygen.

Make two models of hydrogen by cutting out a circle of paper; write "H" in the middle, "e-" on one end, and "+" (representing a proton) on the other end. Tape the hydrogens onto the oxygen orbitals that only have one electron (the "e-" should face oxygen's nucleus). Now all oxygen's orbitals have two electrons; one electron in two of the orbitals is shared with the hydrogens. This represents a molecule of water: two hydrogens and one oxygen.

The eight protons (positive charges) of oxygen's nucleus pull the hydrogens' electrons toward the center of the water molecule. This leaves the protons of the hydrogens toward the outside of the water molecule. The protons of hydrogen create the positive pole of the water molecule. The oxygen orbitals containing two pairs of electrons form the negative pole of the water molecule.

Resources

Ardley, Neil. 1991. *Science Book of Water*. Orlando, Fla.: Harcourt, Brace, Jovanovich, Inc.

Dorin, Henry, Peter D. Demmin, and Dorothy L. Gabel. 1992. *Chemistry: The Study of Matter*, 4th ed. Needham, Mass.: Prentice Hall, Inc.

Leopold, Luna B., and Kenneth S. Davis. 1980. *Water*. Alexandria, Va.: Time-Life Books.

🍎 Watson, Philip. 1982. *Liquid Magic*. New York, N.Y.: Lothrop, Lee & Shepard Books.

Notes ▼

Student Activity Cards

Activity: *CALL ME BOND, HYDROGEN BOND*

Information: The surface of water acts like a skin that keeps some things out. The skin is actually a layer of water molecules held tightly together by hydrogen bonds. This is why water forms drops, and why some insects can skate on water's surface.

Challenge: Can you make water demonstrate the properties described in the paragraph above? Describe or draw a picture of how you did it. If you need help, send one group member to ask the teacher for suggestions.

Materials you will need: cup of water, paper clip, fork

Activity: *HOW CAN YOU TELL A POLAR MOLECULE FROM A POLAR BEAR?*

Information: More things dissolve in water than in any other substance. Some materials are magnetically charged (polar) and dissolve easily in water. Water molecules dissolve these materials by forming hydrogen bonds with each molecule in the material. Other substances are nonpolar. These do not dissolve or mix in water because hydrogen bonds are not formed.

Challenge: Which of these two materials is polar, oil or sugar? How can you tell? Send one group member to check with the teacher to see if your response is correct.

Materials you will need: cup of water, oil, sugar

Activity: *IT'S NO SWEAT . . . OR IS IT?*

Information: It is a very hot day. You and some friends decide to race around the block to the playing field. Suddenly, one of your friends stops and complains about feeling overheated. You happen to be carrying a bottle of suntanning oil and a bottle of water. One friend says oil will help cool down the overheated friend; the other claims water will work better.

Challenge: Which of your friends is right? Try spreading a thin layer of each liquid on your hand. Which one feels cooler? Suggest reasons for the outcome. Send one group member to check with the teacher to see if your response is correct.

Materials you will need: oil, water, paintbrush for each person

---

Activity: *FREEZING WATER IS A SWELL IDEA*

Information: You plan to go on a hike tomorrow. You want to bring along some water. You have water in both glass and plastic bottles. A friend suggests freezing the filled bottles overnight, so the water will still be cool when you need a drink.

Challenge: Which container of water should you put in the freezer? Draw a picture of and provide an explanation for what you think each might look like when you check the freezer in the morning. (Don't try this one at home!) Send one group member to check with the teacher to see if your response is correct.

No materials needed; this is a mental lab!

Hydrocharade Cards

Hydrocharade Card

HOW THE SURFACE OF WATER SUPPORTS A PAPER CLIP

All members of your group except one represent water molecules at the surface of a cup of water. Tie strings around your waists, leaving a tail hanging in back. Your backs represent the negative pole or end of the molecule. Indicate the positive end by holding your arms outstretched in front of you like a "V." Now hold tightly onto each other's strings; this symbolizes hydrogen bonding among water molecules.

To show a paper clip or a pin being supported by water's surface, one group member gently lays a broom handle or meter stick across several of the bonds (strings). You can also illustrate your failed attempts at floating the paper clip by placing the broom handle at an angle between the bonds.

Materials you will need: strings, broom or meter stick

Hydrocharade Card

HOW WATER DISSOLVES SUGAR

Get several sheets of scrap paper and write a large "+" at one end and a "-" at the other end of each piece. The "+" represents the positive pole of a sugar molecule, and the "-" represents the negative end. Put the papers in a pile. (This represents a cube of sugar that has just been placed into a cup of water.)

All members of your group except one represent water molecules swirling around the sugar cube. Each water molecule holds a string in each hand and has another string tied around his or her waist, leaving a tail hanging in back. Your backs represent the negative pole or end of the molecule. Indicate the positive end by holding your arms outstretched in front of you like a "V."

One group member, representing a spoon, "stirs up" the sugar and the water. This student tapes the positive end of the sugar molecules (pieces of paper) to the negative charge (the tail) of the water molecules. This student may also tape the negative end of the sugar molecule to the strings held in the water molecules' hands. The strings represent hydrogen bonds. The sugar molecules are kept in solution because they have formed hydrogen bonds with (are taped to) water molecules.

Materials you will need: strings, scraps of paper, tape, marking pen

Hydrocharade Cards

Hydrocharade Card

HOW EVAPORATING WATER MOLECULES REMOVE ENERGY

All members of your group except one represent water molecules in a liquid state. Tie strings around your waists, leaving a tail hanging in back. Your backs represent the negative pole or end of the molecule. Indicate the positive end by holding your arms outstretched in front of you like a "V."

In liquid form, the water molecules remain close together, weaving in and about each other. Because molecules are in motion during the liquid state, hydrogen bonds are constantly formed, broken, and reformed as molecules pass by each other. Represent this by weaving around each other, grasping onto and releasing the strings of other molecules as they pass by. The strings represent hydrogen bonds.

To show some molecules being heated up, have one group member, representing a heat source, tag a few water molecules. Tagged molecules become energized. They move about more rapidly, making it more difficult for other molecules to hold onto them (to form bonds). Eventually, they break away, becoming gas molecules (evaporating). The molecules that are left behind have less heat energy, making the water feel cooler.

Materials you will need: string, a sign labeled "heat source"

Hydrocharade Card

HOW WATER EXPANDS WHEN IT FREEZES

All members of your group except one represent water molecules in a liquid state. Tie strings around your waists, leaving a tail hanging in back. Your backs represent the negative pole or end of the molecule. Indicate the positive end by holding your arms outstretched in front of you like a "V."

Mark a boundary with chalk on the floor around all group members to represent the sides of a container. As a liquid, the molecules must stay within the boundary, standing close to each other. Another group member (a cool student), representing a heat sink (something that "absorbs" heat energy, such as the cool air in a freezer), tags molecules (taps them on the shoulder). When you are tagged, begin to move more slowly. (Your heat energy has been transferred to the heat sink.)

When water molecules move more slowly, hydrogen bonds form more easily. To represent this, group members who are slowed down should grasp each other's strings. Move apart from each other until the string is straight. Eventually, there will not be room within the boundary, and some group members will need to step outside the chalk marks.

Materials you will need: string, a sign labeled "heat sink", chalk

Is There Water on Zork?

You're stranded on the planet Zork and you're thirsty. The Zorkians present you with a clear liquid. Is it water? Will you drink it? How in the Zork would you know?

▼ Summary
Students describe the unique characteristics of water and design investigations to distinguish water from other clear liquids.

Objectives
Students will:
- describe qualities that distinguish water from other clear liquids.
- design an investigation to test characteristics of water.
- analyze the efficiency and effectiveness of the investigation.

Materials
Liquids to be tested. (Place liquids in separate beakers, numbered 1-7; label the water with a different number for each group. Depending upon time and grade level, use seven or fewer liquids.)
- *Water*
- *White vinegar*
- *Hydrogen peroxide*
- *Corn syrup*
- *Alcohol*
- *Glycerin or mineral oil*
- *Clear soda*

Testing materials. Possible tests are provided in parentheses for students needing more guidance. Items may be deleted or added to the list to fit the needs of the investigations.
- *Salt (solubility)*
- *Pepper (surface tension)*
- *Sugar (solubility)*
- *Baking soda (solubility, chemical reactions)*
- *Corn starch (solubility)*
- *Wax paper (surface tension)*
- *Aluminum foil (chemical reactions)*
- *Hot and cold water baths (evaporation, condensation, specific heat)*
- *Ice (density)*
- *A scale (mass)*
- *Objects of different density: metal to wood (density)*
- *Paper clips (surface tension)*
- *Toothpicks (density, surface tension)*
- *Food coloring (density)*
- *Graduated cylinders (volume)*
- *Thermometers (temperature, phase change)*
- *pH strips (acidity)*
- *Liquid soap (surface tension)*

Testing equipment.
- *Goggles*
- *Extra beakers or cups for conducting tests*
- *Eyedroppers*
- *Glass rods*

Making Connections
Students have seen and used a variety of clear liquids in their lives, but have they stopped to think why a particular liquid is or is not water? Focusing on students' inquisitiveness, this activity encourages students to use scientific processes to investigate how water is unlike other clear liquids.

Background
We all use scientific methods to answer questions about our lives and the world. Farmers study their fields, confer with agronomists, and conduct tests to learn why a certain crop is producing low yields. Teachers, when selecting an approach to best convey a concept, gather resources, attend workshops, and try out activities with their students. Consumers selecting among brands of shampoo read labels, talk with friends, listen to commercials, and test samples.

■ Grade Level:
Middle School

■ Subject Areas:
Physical Science

■ Duration:
Preparation time:
Part I: 60 minutes
Part II: Completed for Part I

Activity time:
Part I: 50 minutes
Part II: 50 minutes

■ Setting:
Classroom or laboratory

■ Skills:
Applying (experimenting, designing, hypothesizing); Evaluating (testing, assessing); Presenting

■ Charting the Course
This activity can be used at the beginning or end (or both) of a unit on water chemistry and physics. Students can discover what they do and do not know about water and apply concepts they have learned.

■ Vocabulary
investigation

All these actions are guided by questions: Why are my crops failing? What's the best way to teach this? Which shampoo should I buy?

Scientists use questions to guide their research as well. How scientists answer questions depends on current understandings, available resources, and the nature of the questions themselves. There is no one scientific method. Nonetheless, investigations are often guided by a series of questions:

• What is the question we are trying to answer?
• What do we know that is related to this question? (This can involve forming a hypothesis.)
• What are the procedures to answer the question?
• What are the results of the investigation?
• What conclusions can we draw?
• What is the value of these conclusions? (Can these conclusions be used to answer the question?)

This process facilitates thorough, organized investigations. The questions need not be followed in sequential order. Sometimes researchers first recall what they know about the problem, or they come up with a conclusion first, and then test it.

Even when these questions are used to guide an investigation, the problem may not be solved, or more questions may arise. Results may be erroneous. The farmer may not learn why crop yields are low. The teaching strategy may reveal gaps in student knowledge requiring the teacher to develop supplementary lessons. The consumer may find that his or her choice of shampoo causes frizzy hair.

Investigations into problems are ongoing. As they learn, people continue to ask questions.

Procedure
▼ Warm Up
Present the following situation to the class. Some students are visiting planet Zork. They are running low on water. Through remote sensing techniques, they know that water exists on Zork, but they're not sure where it is. Fortunately, they encounter some friendly Zorkians who speak English; unfortunately, their words for water, clear, and liquid are different from ours. The visiting students need to explain to the Zorkians that they are looking for water.

Have several students play the visiting students and others play the Zorkians. The class can help the Zorkians think of questions they can ask about this commodity (e.g., What does it feel like? What is it used for? Why do you need it?). Mindful that the Zorkians do not understand the words clear and liquid, the visiting students must try to describe the characteristics of water.

After a few minutes, have students summarize their responses. How much do students think they know

about water? Did they think it was difficult to describe water?

Ask students to list the words and phrases they use to describe water. Encourage them to use all five senses. Make a master list and post it in the classroom. This list of words and descriptions provides students with a synopsis of what they know about water. It also provides information they can use to solve the problem presented in this activity.

▼ The Activity
Part I
1. **Tell students the Zorkians brought forth seven different clear liquids, based on the stranded travelers' descriptions.**

2. **Divide the class into small groups. Provide each group with samples of the clear liquids. Present students with the problem: Which of these liquids is water?**

3. **Based on what they know about water, have students write out several questions they have about the liquids.** Ask them to brainstorm different ways to answer the questions. Display the materials they can use in the front of the room.

4. **Have students develop a set of procedures to determine which**

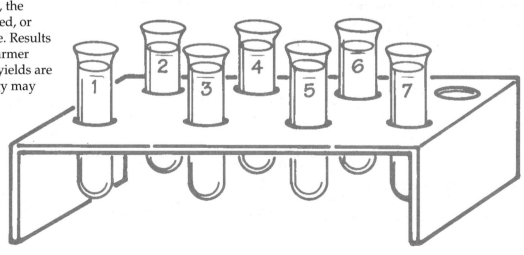

liquid is water. Check the designs for safety and feasibility. **TASTE TESTS ARE NOT ALLOWED! IF STUDENTS HEAT THE LIQUIDS, THEY SHOULD USE A HOT WATER BATH, LIMIT THE HEATING TIME TO THREE MINUTES, AND BE IN A WELL-VENTILATED AREA. ANY TIME A SUBSTANCE IS HEATED, GOGGLES MUST BE WORN.**

5. **Have students write out the questions and procedures in a table or diagram.** A suggested format is provided in this activity, but students may design their own to match the needs of their investigation. (See *Problem: Which of these liquids is water?*)

Part II

1. **Students can now conduct the tests to answer the questions. Make sure they record their results or answers.** These can be included in the table as well.

2. **At the end of their investigations, students should draw conclusions based on their findings.** If they were unable to determine which liquid was water, they should still summarize the results by indicating liquids they know are **not** water. Explain that the investigative process is more important than determining which liquid is water. If the investigation stimulated other questions, these should be listed in the conclusion as well.

▼ *Wrap Up and Action*

Discuss the investigative process and results with students. What was the value of the conclusions? Did the investigation solve the problem? To confirm their results, students can run identical tests on a sample of tap water. If students were to repeat the activity, would they revise their procedure or alter their conclusions?

If time allows, have students conduct the investigations a second time.

What do they know about water that they didn't know before? Match these discoveries to the list of words and phrases used to describe water in the *Warm up*. Ask students if they think the list is accurate or if descriptions should be changed or added.

Have students design a poster presenting water as both a common and unique substance. Display student work in a public place such as a grocery store, library, or water treatment center.

Assessment

Have students:

- design an investigation that distinguishes water from other clear liquids (*Part I*, steps 3 and 4).
- draw conclusions to investigations based on their findings (*Part II*, step 2).
- describe the properties of water

that distinguish it from other clear liquids (*Wrap Up*).

- assess how effectively the investigation addressed the needs of the problem (*Wrap Up*).

Extensions

Have students collect water samples from sources throughout the community. To compare and contrast the samples, have them design tests for: smell, temperature, clarity, pH, and precipitates.

Resources

Dorin, Henry, Peter D. Demmin, and Dorothy L. Gabel. 1992. *Chemistry: The Study of Matter*, 4th ed. Needham, Mass.: Prentice Hall, Inc..

Haber-Schaim, Uri, John H. Dodge, and James A. Walter. 1986. *PSSC Physics*. Lexington, Mass.: D. C. Heath & Co.

Novak, J. D., and D. Bob Gowin. 1986. *Learning How to Learn*. New York, N.Y.: Cambridge University Press.

Problem: Which of these liquids is water?

Name: _____ Date: _____

Question asked	What do we know?	Procedure	Results							Conclusions
			Liquid 1	Liquid 2	Liquid 3	Liquid 4	Liquid 5	Liquid 6	Liquid 7	
Which materials dissolve in the liquid (check salt, sugar, baking soda, etc.—note reactions)										
Which materials float on the liquid (check ice, tooth-pick, paper clip, colored oil, etc.)										
What does a drop of the liquid look like on wax paper?										
How much does the temperature change when placed in a hot water bath for three minutes? Cold water bath?										
How long does it take for ½ teaspoon (2.5 ml) of the liquid to evaporate?										
What is the pH of the liquid?										
Student designed tests:										

Molecules in Motion

Ever had a close encounter with a water molecule?

▼ Summary

This activity brings water molecules up to size (student-size!) by physically involving students in simulating molecular movement in each of water's physical states (solid, liquid, gas).

Objectives
Students will:
- model the effects of heat energy on the state of water.

Materials
- *Samples of water in each state* (ice, a glass of water, and boiling water or water evaporating on a sunny window ledge) (optional)
- *2 flashlights* (one covered with a red filter or transparency and one with a blue filter or transparency)

Making Connections
Students have had close encounters with all three states of water: they drink water; inhale and exhale water vapor; and crunch ice cubes. Understanding the behavior of water molecules helps students acquire a fundamental knowledge of the physical properties of water.

Background
Water is made of molecules; each water molecule contains two hydrogen atoms and one atom of oxygen. Molecules constantly move. Heat energy contributes to the motion of molecules (kinetic energy). When water feels warm, molecules are moving very rapidly. Water molecules with little heat energy, such as those in an ice cube, move more slowly.

The motion of molecules determines the state of water. In the gaseous state (water vapor), water molecules have a large amount of heat energy and move rapidly. This rapid movement causes molecules to bounce off each other, resulting in greater distances between the molecules. (Compare the amount of space needed by a person who is moving around rapidly to someone who is standing still.) The molecules in liquid water move more slowly. The molecules require less space and are closer to each other. In ice, the molecules contain the least amount of heat energy, so their movement is very slow. (Water molecules in ice form a lattice pattern, see "Hangin' Together.")

Water changes from one state to another when heat energy is added or lost. Heat travels from areas of high temperature (rapidly moving molecules) to low temperature (slower-moving molecules).

Ice melts in your hand because the heat from your body transfers to the colder material. Sometimes, when molecules near the surface of liquid water move very rapidly, they break away or evaporate, becoming water vapor. Eventually water vapor will lose energy and return to liquid form. This can be seen when steam condenses on a cool bathroom mirror. Water will also change from a liquid to a solid as heat energy continues to be lost. However, even as ice, water molecules contain some heat energy. Therefore, although the movement is limited, the molecules are still in motion.

Procedure
▼ *Warm Up*
Have students write down or draw pictures of what happens to an ice cube on a window ledge as the weather turns warmer. Discuss their views and collect their papers.

■ **Grade Level:**
Upper Elementary

■ **Subject Areas:**
Physical Science

■ **Duration:**
Preparation time: 40 minutes
Activity time: 50 minutes

■ **Setting:**
Classroom or open area

■ **Skills:**
Analyzing (identifying patterns); Interpreting (summarizing); Presenting (drawing, writing)

■ **Charting the Course**
This activity serves as a good introduction to the properties of water and the water cycle ("The Incredible Journey," and "Imagine!"). How heat energy affects water is further addressed in "Water Models," "Water Match," and "Cold Cash in the Icebox." Investigations into the role of hydrogen bonding are provided in "Hangin' Together."

■ **Vocabulary**
kinetic energy, heat energy, evaporation, condensation, solid, liquid, gaseous (gas), water molecule

Discuss and compare the three states of water. (A sample of each can be available for reference.) Have students identify the conditions needed for each to exist.

What happens when water evaporates? Where does the water go? Students may know or guess the answer. Help them to understand that water has been broken down to its tiniest form—a water molecule.

Tell students that water is made up of millions of tiny molecules. A cookie appears to be one solid piece, but when crumbled it is made up of many tiny pieces. This analogy can be used to help young learners understand the particulate nature of matter.

▼ The Activity

1. **Tell the class they are going to become water molecules. They will begin as water in its solid form, ice.** As ice, students stand in place and move very little.

2. **Inform students that for this activity a flashlight with the red filter will be used to represent the addition of heat energy.** Shining the light on a student represents heat energy traveling from an outside source to that water molecule (student), resulting in increased temperature and molecular motion (kinetic energy).

3. **Beam the flashlight on a few students.** They should begin to move slowly in place, gently bumping into each other. Through a chain reaction, all students begin moving.

4. **Tell students they are now liquid.** As a liquid, students should stay close together.

5. **Add more heat; the liquid turns into a gas.** In its gaseous state, water molecules move freely. Students step away from each other and roam randomly around the room. Music may enhance the flow of "molecules" around the room.

6. **Explain that eventually heat energy will be lost.** The loss of heat energy is represented by the flashlight with the blue filter. (Heat travels from the molecule to the colder object.)

7. **Shine the blue flashlight on a group of students.** Droplets of water form around the room as molecules lose energy and move together. After all the students are liquid, continue to shine blue light (representing a continued loss of energy) on students until they become ice.

▼ Wrap Up

Have students write in their own words or draw a picture or diagram to represent how water behaves in each state and what happens during the transition from one state to another. Provide students with a scenario, such as a glass of ice set on a sunny porch, and have them describe in molecular terms what is happening to the ice. Have students keep their descriptions of molecules in motion in a handy place (such as a Water Log), to be used as a reference when learning other water concepts.

Solid

Liquid

Gas

COURTESY: YELLOWSTONE NATIONAL PARK

This activity should be repeated a number of times throughout the year. A story or different scenario may be used to illustrate the activity.

Assessment

Have students:

- demonstrate and compare the movement of water molecules in solid, liquid, and gaseous form (steps 1-7).
- write about or draw a picture of what happens to water as it changes from one state to another (*Wrap Up*).

Extensions

Have students create a musical interpretation of "Molecules in Motion." Students can select music that represents the various energy levels of molecules and the resulting states of water. Loud music with a rapid tempo may create the impression of water vapor. Intense, concentrated, slow music may symbolize the solid state of ice. Harmonies incorporating the sounds of flowing water or patterns of rainfall may accompany the liquid state. Students may produce a musical journey by drawing pictures or collecting photographs or slides that illustrate the various states of water. They may

create a slide show coordinating images with their musical selections. Student drawings or pictures from magazines may also be organized on a flip chart. Students turn the pages in time with the music.

Resources

Cooper, et al. 1985. *HBJ Science.* Orlando, Fla.: Harcourt, Brace, Jovanovich, Inc.

Dorin, Henry, Peter Demmin, and Dorothy L. Gabel. 1992. *Chemistry: The Study of Matter*, 4th ed. Needham, Mass.: Prentice Hall, Inc.

Mallison, George et al. 1987. *Silver Burdett Science.* Morristown, N.J.: Silver Burdett Co.

Water Match

There's no ace in the hole in this game; just water under the bridge, and in the lake, and in the sky . . .

▼ Summary
Students match up pairs of water picture cards and in the process learn to distinguish the three states of water—solid, liquid, and gas.

Objectives
Students will:
- identify the three states of water: solid, liquid, and gas.
- recognize that water can become polluted and that some water can be cleaned.

Materials
- *Ice cube*
- *Glass of water*
- *Cold spoon*
- *A set of water match cards* (Photocopy the page of cards 2 times for each group of players. Each deck should have 22 cards including 1 Washer Wild Card and 1 Polluter Joker.)

Making Connections
Young students have observed water in two states in their environment such as ice cubes (solid) or rain showers (liquid). They may not have recognized water in its gaseous state-water vapor in air or their breath. Young children are usually aware of the types of water pollution that they can see. Provided with a basic understanding of the three states of water, students have the information to learn other water-related concepts.

Background
Water is found throughout our planet in one of three states: solid, liquid, and gas. It is the only substance on Earth that is able to exist naturally in all of these forms.

Water that is in a solid form is either in an ice or crystal formation. Ice forms include ice cubes, hailstones, and frozen surface water. Crystallized water is better known as snowflakes. To form ice or crystals, water requires freezing temperatures (32 degrees F [0°C] or lower).

Water in its liquid form is found in rivers, lakes, streams, and underground. It requires temperatures above the freezing point, but below the boiling point (212 degrees F [100°C]) to remain in a liquid state.

Water, when in a gaseous state, is fine particles of matter (molecules) suspended in the air and invisible to the eye most of the time. We usually identify the vapor as steam. By applying sufficient heat, we can change water from a liquid to a gaseous state. Water evaporates and enters the atmosphere as vapor. Fog and clouds are actually in liquid form; they are composed of tiny water droplets.

Water can be polluted in any form. Pollution can result from an act of nature or from human carelessness. Some types of water pollution can be cleaned up. Certain pollutants are removed from water through the water cycle. When water evaporates, it usually leaves waste materials behind. Contaminants are filtered out as water moves through soil. As water flows through a lake or stream, some pollutants will settle out. Humans have developed ways to speed up the cleaning process through wastewater treatment plants and other forms of technology. However, waste removal may not be a permanent solution. Even though a contaminant is removed, it doesn't disappear. Therefore, it may recontaminate water when it re-enters the water cycle.

■ Grade Level:
Lower Elementary

■ Subject Areas:
Earth Science

■ Duration:
Preparation time:
Part I: 30 minutes
Part II: Completed for Part I

Activity time:
Part I: 50 minutes
Part II: 30 minutes

■ Setting: Classroom

■ Skills:
Organizing (matching)

■ Charting the Course
Students can explore their feelings about water in "Idea Pools." Students can learn how water changes states in "Molecules in Motion." The three states of water play an important role in the water cycle ("The Incredible Journey").

■ Vocabulary
solid, liquid, gas, pollution, sublimation

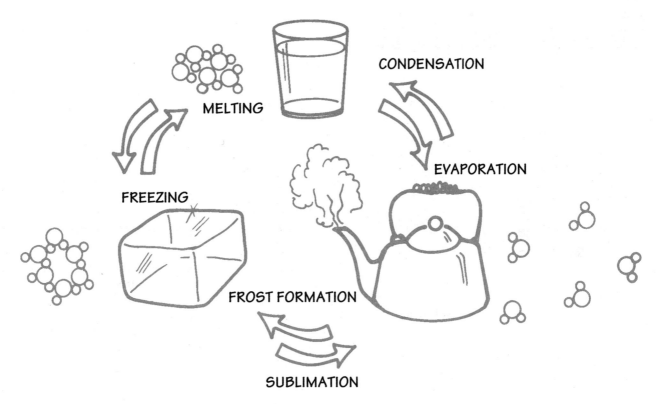

CONDENSATION

MELTING

EVAPORATION

FREEZING

FROST FORMATION

SUBLIMATION

Procedure
▼ Warm Up
Show students the ice cube, glass of water, and indicate their breath while identifying the state of each (solid, liquid, gas). Discuss the characteristics of water in each of these states (e.g., snowflakes and ice are in the solid state, while water vapor in breath is a gas). To demonstrate water vapor in breath, blow on a cold spoon and have students observe the condensed water droplets.

▼ The Activity
Part I
1. **Tell students they are going to match cards that have pictures of water as solid, liquid, or gas (e.g., solid with solid, etc.). Hold up the** *Water Match Cards* **(excluding the** *Polluter Joker* **and** *Washer Wild* **cards) one at a time. Ask students to identify the picture and the state they think the water is in** (e.g., a picture of a lake is water in its liquid

state, a picture of hail or a glacier is water in its solid state).

2. **Divide the class into groups of four. Give each group a set of cards to be evenly distributed among players. Tell them to look at their cards without letting other players see them.**

3. **Discuss the rules of the game:**
    *   If any player is holding matching cards, he or she lays them down, face up. (An example of a match is the rain and the wave because both pictures show water as a liquid.)
    *   Decide who will go first, second, third, and fourth.
    *   The first player draws a single card from one other player.
    *   If the card matches, he or she lays the pair down and takes another turn.
    *   If there is no match, the second player takes a turn and draws from any other player.
    *   Continue taking turns until all cards are paired.

*   The player with the most matches wins!

Part II
1. **Ask students to describe water pollution.** Discuss ways water can be polluted. How do they feel about pollution?

2. **Tell students they are going to play the game again, but a new card will be added. Show them the** *Polluter Joker* **card, and explain that this is a card they do not want.**

3. **Add a** *Polluter Joker* **card to each group's set of cards. When the cards are dealt, tell students that the one with the** *Polluter Joker* **card should not tell anyone she or he has it. The object is to get someone else to draw it. Continue playing until everyone has an empty hand except the one holding the** *Polluter Joker.*

4. **How did the players feel who ended up with the** *Polluter Joker* **card? Discuss ways pollution can naturally be removed from water and how humans have developed**

Students playing Water Match.

wastewater treatment plants to remove pollutants as well.

5. **Show students the *Washer Wild* card and add one to each set of cards. The *Washer Wild* card is a match for the *Polluter Joker*. Have students play the game again. The winner is the player with the most matches.**

▼ *Wrap Up and Action*

Ask students to identify the three states of water and where they might find water in each state. How did they feel about the *Polluter Joker* and the *Washer Wild* cards? If students are on a field trip to a lake and have just finished eating a candy bar, what should they do with the wrapper? Why?

Assessment

Have students:

- describe the three states of water and where they may be found (*Wrap Up*).

- express their views about pollution (*Part II*, step 4 and *Wrap Up*).

Extensions

In a variation of the game, students match cards of different states of water if they can explain how water moves between the two forms. For example, if the card shows rain and the player draws a lake, he or she must explain that rain falls into the lake.

Have students illustrate different water cards to add to the deck.

Divide a poster board into three sections with a broad-tipped marking pen and label each section as solid, liquid, or gas. From old magazines, have students cut out pictures of water in each of these states and glue them to the poster board. Ask students to look for pictures of polluted water. Ask them if they want to add them to the collage. Why or why not? Do they

think water can be polluted in all of the three states?

Resources

🍎 Gunston, Bill. 1982. *Water*. Morristown, N.J.: Silver, Burdett & Ginn, Inc.

🍎 Leutscher, Alfred. 1983. *Water*. New York, N.Y.: Dial Books for Young Readers.

🍎 Watson, Philip. 1983. *Liquid Magic*. New York, N.Y.: Lothrop, Lee, & Shepard Books.

🍎 Webb, Angela. 1987. *Water*. New York, N.Y.: Watts, Franklin, Inc.

Water Match Cards

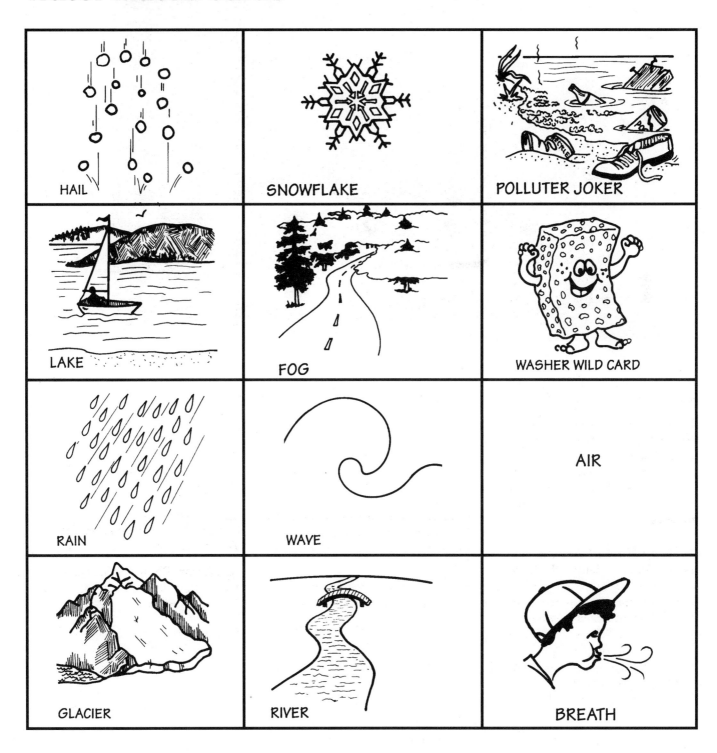

HAIL

SNOWFLAKE

POLLUTER JOKER

LAKE

FOG

WASHER WILD CARD

RAIN

WAVE

AIR

GLACIER

RIVER

BREATH

What's the Solution?

Mr. Charles Mum II has been robbed! Can you use your water wisdom to solve this mystery?

▼ Summary

While investigating the dissolving power of water, students solve a crime.

Objectives

Students will:
- discriminate solutions from other mixtures.
- demonstrate water's ability to dissolve solids, liquids, and gases.

Materials

- Copies of *The Case of the Missing Coin Collection, Part I* and *Part II*
- Copies of *Solution Investigation Sheet*

Each group of students will need the following:
- *Container, lid labeled "A", sugar and water*
- *Container, lid labeled "B", sand and water*
- *2 100-ml graduated cylinders*
- *Water*
- *Rubbing alcohol*
- *Vegetable oil*
- *3 sealed bottles of clear, carbonated soda: one available for observation; one left in a hot water bath; the third left in a cold water bath (each for about 15 minutes)*
- *2 balloons*
- *Chilled water*

Making Connections

Students come in contact with solutions every day. Many students have heard of antifreeze, and most have sipped sweetened, carbonated soda. These are both examples of solutions. Understanding the nature of solutions helps students further their knowledge of the properties of water and can even aid in solving mysteries!

Background

A solution is a homogeneous mixture of two materials. In a solution the following conditions exist: the two materials are evenly dispersed among each other; the solution is transparent; it is not possible to distinguish one material from the other; and one material will not settle out when left standing. Water is found in many solutions because the structure of the water molecule enables it to dissolve many materials.

The structure of the water molecule causes it to have a positive end (or pole) and a negative end. Because it has opposite charges at either end, the water molecule is said to be polar.

WATER MOLECULE

positive pole

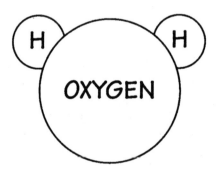

negative pole

Polar molecules act like magnets: opposites attract. The positive end of one molecule is attracted to the negative end of another molecule. This quality enables water to dissolve other substances.

Water is often called the universal solvent—it can dissolve many materials. The individual molecules of the sub-

- **Grade Level:**
Upper Elementary, Middle School

- **Subject Areas:**
Physical Science

- **Duration:**
Preparation time: 50 minutes
Activity time: 50 minutes

- **Setting:** Classroom

- **Skills:**
Gathering information (observing, measuring); Interpreting (generalizing, drawing conclusions); Applying (problem solving)

- **Charting the Course**
Activities on water's molecular structure and its reaction to heat energy ("Molecules in Motion") should precede this activity. To further explore the role of electromagnetic properties of the water molecule, students could participate in "Hangin' Together." This activity supports concepts presented in "Aqua Notes," "Let's Even Things Out," "Where Are the Frogs?" and "The Pucker Effect."

- **Vocabulary**
solution, solvent, solute

stance being dissolved (the solute) are dispersed evenly throughout the solvent (the material dissolving the solute). During the dissolving process, the positive end of the water molecule (hydrogen) seeks out the negative charge of the solute. Similarly, a water molecule's negative end (oxygen) will be attracted to the positive charge of the solute's molecule. The magnetic attractions between the water molecules and the molecules of the solute keep the mixture in solution.

Solids, liquids, and gases can dissolve in water. Examples of solids that dissolve in water include sugar and salt. Sugar, like water, is a polar molecule. The negative end of the sugar molecule is attracted to the positive end of the water molecule, and vice versa. Salt (sodium chloride or NaCl) is not a polar molecule; it is an ionic molecule. Salt dissolves in water because it is pulled apart by the water molecule—separating the salt molecule into positive and negative parts or ions. The negative ion of the salt molecule (Cl^-) is attracted to the positively charged hydrogen, and the positive ion of the salt (Na^+) is pulled toward the negatively charged oxygen of water.

Sometimes when two materials, such as sand and water, are mixed, they appear to be a homogeneous mixture. However, water does not dissolve sand, and sand, being denser than water, will eventually settle to the bottom. If one substance eventually settles out, the mixture is called a suspension.

Alcohol is a liquid that dissolves in water. When alcohol is poured into water, the alcohol molecules mix evenly among the water molecules. This is why mixing equal amounts of alcohol and water will result in slightly less than the volume of both liquids combined (i.e., a mixture of 50 ml water and 50 ml

WATER MOLECULE — MAGNETIC ATTRACTION — SUGAR MOLECULE

OXYGEN
H
H
POSITIVE POLE OF WATER MOLECULE

NEGATIVE POLE OF SUGAR MOLECULE

alcohol will be around 98 or 99 ml rather than 100 ml).

Carbonated beverages contain dissolved gas. When water has a smell, it is often because it contains a dissolved gas, such as sulfur or chlorine. (Water vapor mixed in with other air molecules [oxygen and nitrogen] is an example of a gaseous solution.)

The ability of water to dissolve gases is affected by pressure (forcing molecules closer together) and temperature. Pressure *increases* the ability of water to dissolve a gas. Soft drink bottlers use increased pressure to pump carbon dioxide gas into sodas. When a carbonated soda is opened, carbon dioxide gas escapes because the pressure is reduced (there is more space for molecules to move about).

Higher temperatures *decrease* the ability of water to dissolve a gas. Increased temperatures cause gas molecules to move faster and spread farther apart, including out of the water. If an opened soda is left at

room temperature, it becomes warm and the movement of the liquid molecules increases; this promotes the escape of carbon dioxide gas molecules as well.

Higher temperatures *increase* the ability of water to dissolve solids and liquids. The increased temperatures cause the water molecules to move faster, promoting quicker distribution of the solute (e.g., sugar).

Procedure
▼ Warm Up
Ask students about mysteries they have read or seen on television. Have them list elements common to many mystery stories. Have students describe what clues are and how to look for them. Tell them they will be reading a short mystery story and conducting experiments to help solve the mystery.

▼ The Activity
1. **Have students read the short mystery story, *The Case of the Missing Coin Collection—Part I.***

2. **After they have read *Part I*, ask students to summarize what happened. Can they identify clues that might help them solve the mystery?**

3. **Hand out copies of the *Solution Investigation Sheet*. Students work in small groups to conduct experiments similar to Clarissa's and to learn about solutions.** The investigations are divided into three sections. Each investigation has several questions for students to read and answer. Answers to the *Solution Investigation Sheet* are found in the **Background**.

▼ *Wrap Up and Action*

Ask students to summarize the results of their findings, and to include a definition of solutions. Based on their investigations, have students solve The Case of the Missing Coin Collection. Hand out copies of *The Case of the Missing Coin*

Collection—Part II. Were students correct in their guesses? Have them write their own stories based on "solutions." They can share their stories with classmates and family; can readers solve the mystery?

Assessment

Have students:
- discriminate between solutions and suspensions (step 3).
- compare water and alcohol with water and oil mixtures, and identify which is the solution and why (step 3).
- summarize what keeps gas in solution (step 3).

Extensions

Create a supersaturated solution of sugar and water by dissolving as much sugar as possible in hot water. Tie a string around a pencil and suspend the end of the string in the

solution. Place the mixture on the windowsill. Watch as crystals form on the string. A supersaturated solution means there are actually more sugar molecules in the solution than the water molecules can bond with. The string acts like a seed or base, onto which excess sugar molecules cling.

Resources

Dorin, Henry, Peter Demmin, and Dorothy L. Gabel. 1992. *Chemistry: The Study of Matter*, 4th ed. Needham, Mass.: Prentice Hall, Inc.

🍎 Watson, Philip. 1982. *Liquid Magic*. New York, N.Y.: Lothrop, Lee & Shepard Books.

WonderScience 7 (6). Contact: Wonder Science, American Chemical Society, 1155 16th Street N.W., Washington DC 20036. 1-800-333-9511.

Notes ▼

The Case of the Missing Coin Collection—Part I

Aquaville was a small town where few crimes occurred, but whenever an incident transpired the police always called the Professor. It was generally known that the Professor had traveled all over the world, had studied at numerous universities, and had even been friends with Albert Einstein. But what the community did not know was that the Professor's success at solving cases was largely the result of his niece, Clarissa.

Clarissa was twelve years old and had been helping her uncle solve cases since she was six. In exchange for her help she had full use of her uncle's library and lab, and could

have anything she chose to eat on Friday nights. (To her uncle's dismay she always selected pizza and pop.)

Because solving cases meant that someone usually ended up angry at being "found out," Clarissa and her uncle agreed that, for her protection, she would be a silent partner. When Clarissa found something significant at the crime scene she and her uncle communicated in code.

One day last week Clarissa and her uncle found themselves ringing the doorbell of the richest estate in Aquaville. Apparently Mr. Charles Mum II had been robbed. According to Mr. Mum, he was working on his priceless coin collection in his study. With his magnifying glass he was examining a 1787 Brasher's Doubloon when a voice from behind told him to continue looking straight ahead. The voice was muffled as if the speaker was wearing a mask.

Mr. Mum recounted that he was blindfolded and tied to his chair. And that is exactly how he was found when the butler returned early that evening.

With Clarissa at his side, the Professor interviewed the butler. The man said he had served Mr. Mum his lunch at noon; in fact, the glass of soda pop,

ham sandwich, and chips were still on the tray placed upon Mr. Mum's desk. When the butler returned six hours later, he found Mr. Mum bound and blindfolded—and the coin collection gone!

As the police and the Professor questioned Mr. Mum and the butler, Clarissa wandered about the library. She searched the worn carpet for anything the robber might have dropped. She examined the tattered curtains covering the glass doors that opened onto the patio from Mr. Mum's study. She noted a basket full of unopened correspondence—power, phone, and credit card bills.

She overheard Mr. Mum tell the police with a sigh, "Well, I had better contact the insurance company. Although I will never recover my wonderful coins, I can at least collect their value. With a seven-hour lead and no clues to speak of, I'm sure the robber and my coins will never be found."

As the police and the Professor moved out of the study into the hall and commiserated with Mr. Mum, Clarissa looked more closely at the items on Mr. Mum's desk—a magnifying glass, a letter opener, a copy of *The Numismatist*, and the tarnished silver lunch tray.

She abruptly turned and walked into the hallway. "Uncle, I'm thirsty."

Mr. Mum looked annoyed.

The Professor started to frown and then hurriedly said, "Of course. Excuse me, gentlemen. Point me in the direction of the kitchen and I shall get my niece a drink of water."

In the kitchen the Professor turned on the faucet. "Well?"

"Uncle, Mr. Mum and the butler are lying; no crime except fraud occurred here today. Mr. Mum appears to have fallen on hard times and only wanted to make it look like the coins had been stolen so he could collect the money from the insurance company."

"But Clarissa, how do you know?"

"You're wasting water, Uncle. Turn off the faucet and I'll tell you."

- How did Clarissa solve the mystery???

- List things that were in the room and what Clarissa noted. Which of these could be clues for solving the mystery?

- Clarissa found something that indicated Mr. Mum had been lying. She based this on investigations with liquid solutions she had been conducting in her mom's kitchen. After you complete the following investigations, you should be able to figure out how Clarissa came to her conclusion.

Solution Investigation Sheet

One of Clarissa's teachers told her that water could dissolve many solids, liquids, and gases. She decided to experiment with each of these.

DISSOLVING SOLIDS IN WATER:
Look at the two mixtures, A and B, presented by the teacher. Shake each 10 times. Observe what happens to the two containers over the next five minutes. List differences between mixtures A and B. Container A is a sugar and water mixture and is a solution. Container B contains sand and water and is a suspension. Why do you think the sand settles out but the sugar does not?

From your observations, write your own definition of a solution.

DISSOLVING LIQUIDS IN WATER:
Next Clarissa tried to dissolve a liquid in a liquid. This meant that the molecules of one liquid would spread evenly throughout the molecules of the second. Fill two graduated cylinders with 50 ml of water each. Add 50 ml of oil to one and 50 ml of rubbing alcohol to the other. Carefully observe the water levels in both cylinders. Are they the same? (Look closely, the solution should be slightly less than 100 ml.)

Based on your observations and your definition, which one is the solution?

DISSOLVING GASES IN WATER:
Clarissa wondered about gases being dissolved in liquids. She asked her mother, who showed Clarissa a bottle of clear soda. Clarissa knew that sugar and carbon dioxide gas were mixed in the soda.

Observe a sealed bottle of clear soda. Does the carbon dioxide gas and water mixture fit your description of a solution? Why or why not?

When Clarissa opened the bottle, she noticed a sound like air escaping. Her mother explained that carbon dioxide gas was escaping from the soda. To make carbonated soda, manufacturers pump carbon dioxide gas into the soda, forcing the gas molecules closer together and increasing the pressure. This increased pressure restricts the movement of gas molecules and causes them to stay in solution.

Clarissa looked at the glass of soda she was drinking and saw that it had bubbles rising. She knew the bubbles were carbon dioxide gas escaping. She wondered how long it would take for all of the gas to come out of solution. She had to wait six hours before it went flat! She noticed that a bottle left open in the refrigerator took longer to stop bubbling.

To see how temperature affects the rate of gas leaving a solution, try the following. Get two bottles of clear soda, one from the hot water bath and one from the cold. Open each and put balloons over the openings. Which balloon blows up faster? Consequently, what two things help keep gases in solution?

NOTE: You might want to check this out at home to see if you get the same results. Leave a bottle of soda open and check to see how long it takes for it to stop bubbling. Does it take longer if it is left in the refrigerator?

The Case of the Missing Coin Collection—Part II

Now you know the experiments Clarissa had performed to help her recognize that Mr. Mum and his butler were lying. Which of these findings do you think Clarissa used? Why? Have you solved The Case of the Missing Coin Collection? Read on to see if your guesses are correct.

Clarissa's discovery related to a knowledge of solutions and time. The butler and Mr. Mum reported that the lunch tray was served at noon. The butler left Mr. Mum alone in the house until he returned that evening at six o'clock. Supposedly, as soon as Mr. Mum

was freed—a little after six o'clock—he called the police, who arrived with the Professor at about half past six. Therefore, about six and one-half hours had passed since the coin collection was allegedly taken.

Clarissa, however, took a closer look at the untouched lunch tray. The soda in the glass was still giving off bubbles. Clarissa knew that soft drinks are made from flavored syrup and carbonated water. Carbon dioxide gas is mixed with water. However, once soft drinks are opened, the carbon dioxide slowly escapes from the solution into the air. This makes the liquid bubble and fizz.

If the soda pop had been sitting for six and one-half hours, as the butler and Mr. Mum maintained, then it should have been "flat." All the gas would have gone out of the solution. Therefore, the lunch tray was intended as a prop to create the illusion of lapsed time.

Water is essential for all life to exist.

▼

Life processes, from the level of the cell to that of the ecosystem, depend

on water. Both the quantity and quality of water contribute to the

sustainability of life on Earth.

Aqua Bodies

What is the difference between a raisin and a grape? Water!

▼ Summary
Students trace their bodies and color portions to represent the amount of water their bodies contain. How does their water content compare to that of a cactus, lettuce, or a whale?

Objectives
Students will:
• conclude that water is the main ingredient of living organisms.

Materials
• *Dried fruit*
• *Ripe fruit*
• *Balance (optional)*
• *Butcher paper (about 120 feet [36 m] for a class of 30) or 2–3 sheets of newspaper taped together for each student*
• *Chalk (optional)*
• *Crayons*
• *Scissors*
• *Bathroom scale*
• *Containers to hold water (e.g., gallon jug, buckets, zip-lock bags, balloons)*
• *4" x 6"(10 x 15 cm) index cards*
• *Tape*

Making Connections
People drink water every day, but they rarely think about the proportion of their bodies that is composed of water. Learning how much of their bodies are composed of water encourages students to appreciate life's dependence on water.

Background
Active living organisms are composed of at least 50 percent water. This is true whether they live in a desert (certain cacti have 90 percent water content) or in the oceans (body water content of many whales is 75 percent). Regardless of the environment, organisms are able to acquire and maintain a healthy water balance.

The human body is about 65 to 70 percent water. If humans lose more than 8 percent of their body water, they will die. Where is this water located within the human body? About 67 percent of the water in the body is located within cells; about 25 percent is located between cells; and the rest, about 8 percent, is located in the blood.

Procedure
▼ *Warm Up*
Present students with the following situation: two people are stranded in a desert. One person has a basket of food including canned meats, bread, cake, etc.—enough to last a month. The other has only a one-month's supply of water. Which of the two will survive longer? Compare how long we can go without food (about a month) to how long we can go without water (approximately three days).

Explain that the bodies of most living organisms are at least 50 percent water. Display samples of ripe and dried or wilted fruits and vegetables and compare water content (see table) or weight (e.g., raisin versus grape or plum versus prune). Demonstrate the percentage of the fruit or vegetable that is water by cutting off a representative piece. (For example, carrots are 88 percent water, so cut off about 88 percent of the carrot.) Emphasize that the 88 percent water in the carrot is actually within tissues and cells and therefore did not spill out when the carrot was cut. (This may counter a misconception that water is loosely sloshing throughout the body.) Do students think humans have water in their bodies? Ask students to guess what

---

■ **Grade Level:**
Lower Elementary, Upper Elementary

■ **Subject Areas:**
Life Science, Health, Mathematics

■ **Duration:**
Preparation time:
Part I: 15 minutes
Part II: 15 minutes
Part III: 10 minutes

Activity time:
Part I: 30 minutes
Part II: 30 minutes
Part III: 30 minutes

■ **Setting:**
Large, open room

■ **Skills:**
Organizing information (estimating, calculating, categorizing); Analyzing (comparing, identifying patterns)

■ **Charting the Course**
This activity is a good introduction to other activities regarding life systems and water. "Aqua Notes" provides further information about how the body uses water. Water-related adaptations are addressed in "Water Address."

■ **Vocabulary**
body water content

percentage of their bodies is made up of water.

WATER CONTENT IN SELECTED FOODS	
Food	Percent Water
Potato Chips	2
Pizza	49
Ice Cream	61
Beef Liver	70
Bananas	74
Grapes	81
Oranges	87
Carrots	88
Tomatoes	94
Lettuce	96

(Source: Calculated by van der Leeden, Frits, Fred Troise, and David Todd. 1990. *The Water Encyclopedia*, 2nd ed. Chelsea, Mich.: Lewis Publishers, Inc., using weight and water content values provided by Bowes and Church's *Food Values of Portions Commonly Used*, 14th ed. Harper and Row.)

▼ *The Activity*

Part I

NOTE: K–2 teachers may wish to focus on *Part I* only.

1.   **Have students work with partners to trace their body shapes onto butcher paper.** An alternative is to have students stand against a wall or lie on the blacktop and trace each other with chalk.

2.   **Explain to students that the percentage of water in their bodies is approximately 65-70 percent.** (For this activity, 70 percent [about $^3/_4$] will be used; the actual amount varies with age and gender. For younger students, demonstrate $^3/_4$ by showing them a circle, or a block divided into four equal parts, and remove three of the four equal pieces.)

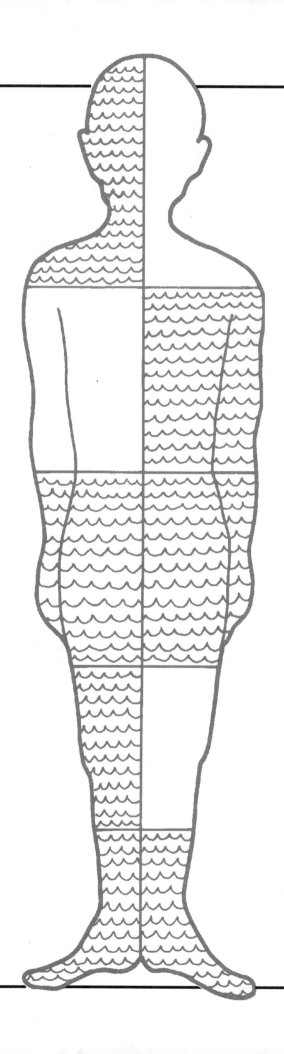

3. **Have students color 70 percent of the figures they have traced onto the paper.** It may help to show 70 percent of various objects. Or students might fold their drawing into ten equal parts and color seven of the ten sections. Have students color (using a contrasting shade) the rest of their bodies, then cut them out for display.

Part II

Assign students a random body weight and have them calculate the approximate amount of water, using the following formula: multiply body weight by 0.70. For example, 100 pounds x 0.70 = 70 pounds of water. Students can then calculate the amount of water in their own bodies. Containers can be filled with 70 pounds of water, to represent the water weight of a 100-pound person. (Because one gallon of water weighs about 8.3 pounds, 70 pounds of water is around 8.3 gallons [70 lbs. x 1 gallon/8.3 lbs. = 8.4 gallons]). Students can do the same for their own weights. (This activity may be coordinated with the school nurse's weigh-in health program.)

Part III

1. **Either assign or have students select a plant or animal.**

2. **On 4" x 6"(10 x 15 cm) index cards, have each student draw the outline of the organism. Direct students to estimate the organism's percentage of water content and color the corresponding portion of the outline.** Despite dry or wet conditions, all living organisms have at least 50 percent water content. If necessary, students can correct their drawings to represent more accurate proportions of water in the organisms. Exact proportions of body water content are not necessary, but actual amounts may be available in reference books. Following are the body water contents of several organisms:

ORGANISM	PERCENT WATER
Cat	62
Dog	63
Deer	64
Corn Plant	71

3. **Tape cards to the wall in groups, based on habitat.** Put all desert plant and animals in one group, while another has rain forest organisms.

▼ Wrap Up

Have students compare the water content of plants and animals in their drawings to that of humans. Students' outlines of themselves may be given to parents as gifts ("growth charts") or displayed in school halls. Students could calculate the number of gallons (liters) of water contained in the bodies of their parents or friends.

Assessment

Have students:
- indicate what proportion of their bodies is water (**Part I**, step 3).
- calculate how much of a body's weight is water (**Part II**).
- represent water content values of different organisms (**Part III**, step 2).

Upon completing the activity, for further assessment have students:
- produce a comic strip that illustrates how organisms would look without water.

Extensions

Obtain a food drier or build a solar food drier; have students dehydrate several food items (such as grapes—they can make their own raisins). Have students predict what the foods will look like when dried.

Compare the taste of dried foods to the hydrated forms. Use the dehydrated food to prepare a meal for the class.

Older students may illustrate body organs on their cutout figure and research the water content of each organ (e.g., the brain is 74.8 percent water). Challenge students to identify places in their bodies without water. (Water in the wrong places—such as the lungs—can be deadly).

Resources

Amos, William H. 1981. *Life in Ponds and Streams*. Washington, D.C.: National Geographic Society.

Berger, Gilda. 1989. *The Human Body*. New York, N.Y.: Doubleday.

Burnie, David. 1989. *Plant*. New York, N.Y.: Alfred A. Knopf.

Cole, Joanna. 1989. *The Magic School Bus: Inside the Human Body*. New York, N.Y.: Scholastic.

Gamlin. Linda. 1988. *The Human Body*. New York, N.Y.: Gloucester Press.

Parker, Steve. 1988. *Pond and River*. New York, N.Y.: Alfred A. Knopf.

Peavy, Linda, and Ursula Smith. 1982. *Food, Nutrition, and You*. New York, N.Y.: Charles Scribner & Sons.

Aqua Notes

■ **Grade Level:**
Lower Elementary, Upper Elementary

■ **Subject Areas:**
Fine Arts, Health, Life Science

■ **Duration:**
Preparation time: 30 minutes
Activity time: 30 minutes

■ **Setting:** Classroom

■ **Skills:**
Gathering information (listening); Interpreting (summarizing); Applying (designing, composing)

■ **Charting the Course**
Prior to this activity, have students learn what percentage of their bodies are water in "Aqua Bodies." Older students can learn how water passes between and through cells via osmosis in "Let's Even Things Out." Following this activity, students can learn how to keep their bodies healthy by participating in "No Bellyachers."

■ **Vocabulary**
osmosis, respiration, metabolism, excretion, temperature regulation

What helps to transport nutrients throughout your body, keep your temperature stable, protect your brain, and leave your body clean?

▼ Summary
While singing simple songs about water in the body, students gain an appreciation for the many ways they need water.

Objectives
Students will:
• note the different ways the body uses water.
• determine that they need water.

Materials
• *Copies or overheads of* **Aqua Tunes** (optional)
• *Copies of* **Color Me Blue Body Chart**

Making Connections
People drink water and visit the rest room everyday. Students may have learned that their bodies are made mainly of water. Learning the many ways the body uses water increases students' appreciation of their dependency on water.

Background
The human body is 65 to 70 percent water. A person without water for three to four days will not survive. Why is all this water needed? It is needed for nearly all physical and metabolic reactions in the body. Following are some of the ways the body uses water.

TRANSPORT:
Water carries essential nutrients throughout the body and moves waste out. Blood, which is mainly water, carries nutrients, hormones, enzymes, oxygen, and other life-sustaining materials to our cells.

Water travels from the heart through blood vessels called arteries. The arteries get tinier and tinier until their walls are only one cell-layer thick. These vessels are called capillaries. At the capillaries, oxygen and nutrients leave the blood and enter cells. Water also passes back and forth between cells and capillaries through the process of osmosis. Waste (such as carbon dioxide and uric acid—the by-products of breaking down or burning proteins for energy and building materials) passes from the cells into the blood stream. On the way back to the heart, blood travels through veins, and waste materials are deposited and processed in the kidneys and lungs for eventual removal from the body.

TEMPERATURE CONTROL:
Water has a high heat capacity, that is, it will take in or give off large amounts of heat energy before changing from a solid to a liquid or a liquid to a gas. In this way, water helps our bodies to maintain a constant body heat. Water also helps control body temperature through sweating. Heat energy is dissipated when water evaporates off the skin. The adult body has over 2.5 million sweat glands.

LUBRICATION:
The mucous linings of various organs and the fluids between internal organs contain water. These materials ease movement and reduce friction between internal organs. In joints, such materials help bones slide more smoothly.

DIGESTION:
Water plays important roles in breaking down ingested food. It dissolves some food to help reduce it to simpler substances. Water helps synthesize enzymes and transport

66

them to the stomach and intestines. Enzymes are used in many digestive processes.

SYNTHETIC REACTIONS:

Water helps build hormones and enzymes that are used to control reactions in the body. Hormones are chemical messengers produced in special organs (e.g., adrenal gland, pituitary gland, pancreas). They affect the growth and behavior of various cells. Enzymes are special proteins that increase the speed and reduce the energy needed for chemical reactions to take place.

EXCRETION:

Water aids in cleansing the body. Respiration, digestion, and various metabolic reactions produce waste materials that need to be removed from the body. The kidneys and the large intestines use water to help remove waste materials. Water helps transport

wastes out of the skin through sweating. When we exhale, we lose carbon dioxide and water— both by-products of respiration.

Procedure
▼ Warm Up
Ask students why they should drink plenty of water. Have them list ways they think the body uses water.

▼ The Activity
1. **Have the class sing *Aqua Tunes* to learn how water functions in the body.** Some songs can be simplified or omitted for younger students. Teach students songs line by line. If necessary, supplement lines with background information about the particular body functions. Actions to accompany the songs are written in bold.

2. **Once students are familiar with the songs, distribute the *Color Me Blue Body Chart* and have them color body parts to which the songs**

refer. (NOTE: To facilitate student coloring, location and size of organs are altered.)

▼ Wrap Up
Have students summarize ways the body uses water. Students may wish to choreograph their own movements to the songs. Performances may be recorded or video-taped. They can perform songs in a school play or for their families. Students may want to create their own song about how the body uses water. Older students may write a science fiction story based on the use of water in the human body, or design a maze or board game.

Assessment
Have students:
- cite ways the body uses water (*Wrap Up*).
- write their own song or science-fiction story, or design a maze or board game, illustrating how water is used in the human body (*Wrap Up*).

Upon completing the activity, for further assessment have students:
- provide reasons why water is important.

Extensions
Students may be interested in watching the movie *Fantastic Voyage*, where humans are shrunk to molecular size and travel through the human body. Students could identify scenes in the movie that involve water.

Resources
🍎 Berger, Gilda. 1989. *The Human Body*. New York, N.Y.: Doubleday.

🍎 Cole, Joanna. 1989. *The Magic School Bus: Inside the Human Body*. New York, N.Y.: Scholastic.

🍎 Gamlin. Linda. 1988. *The Human Body*. New York, N.Y.: Glouchester.

Color Me Blue
Body Chart

Date: _____

Name: _____

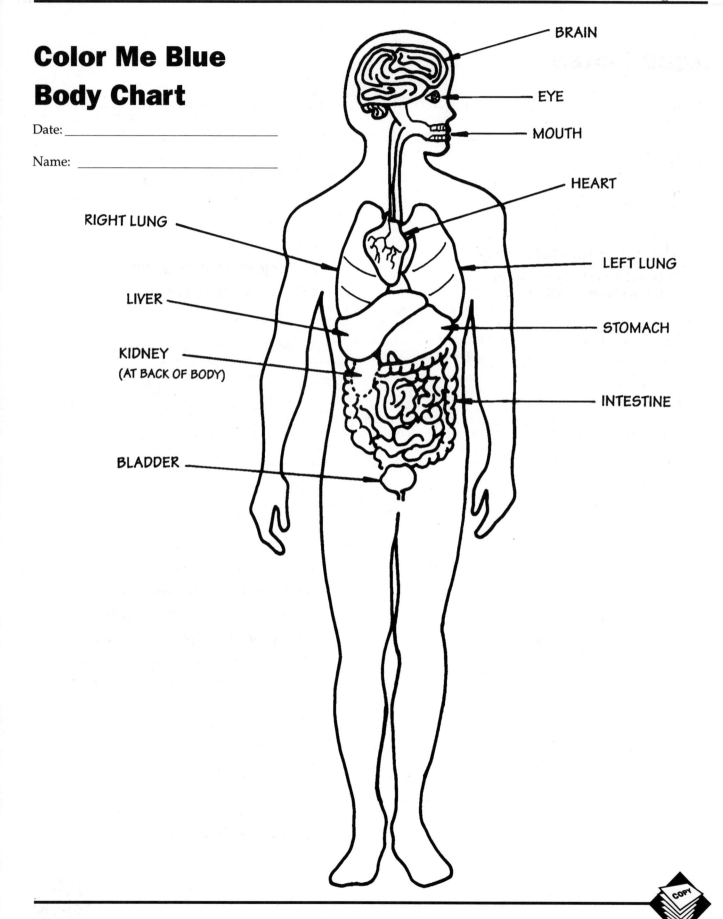

BRAIN

EYE

MOUTH

HEART

RIGHT LUNG

LEFT LUNG

LIVER

STOMACH

KIDNEY
(AT BACK OF BODY)

INTESTINE

BLADDER

Aqua Tunes

This song explains generally where water is found in the human body.

(Just a four count beat . . . **students can march in place to keep a beat)**

> Water, water, I have water
> everywhere in my body!
> Water, water, where is water
> Where is water in your body?
>
> **(Point to the body part when
> it is mentioned in the song)**
>
> Is there water in your arms? YES!
> Is there water in your eyes? YES!
> How about your bones? YES!
> There's even water in your toes!
> Is there water in your liver? YES!
> Is there water in your brain? YES!
> How about your mouth? YES!
> There's even water in your nose!
> Water, water, I drink water
> I drink water everyday!
> Water, water, I use water,
> I use water many ways!

Use the following song to help students understand how water helps lubricate the body and facilitates movement.

(To the tune of "Are You Sleeping" . . . **make body motions to follow the lyrics)**

> Bend your elbow, move your shoulder
> Up and down
> Up and down.
> If your joints lacked water
> this would not be easy.
> Bend your knee!
> Flex your foot!
> Suck your tummy in, swing your middle
> Twist and shout
> Twist and shout.
> Imagine what this'd feel like
> without water padding.
> Shake your head!
> Take a breath!

The following song introduces the topic of how water helps maintain body heat.

(To the tune of "Do Your Ears Hang Low")

> Do you shiver when it's cold **(shiver)**
> Do you sweat when it's hot **(wipe brow)**
> Does your temperature stay even
>   when you're smiling or you're not?
>   **(smile/don't smile)**
> Water helps to keep you cool
>   **(act cool)**
> Water helps to keep you warm
>   **(act warm)**
> You need water in your body
> So your temp can conform.

Aqua Tunes

This song sums up how water leaves the body and helps remove waste.

(To the tune of "Mary Had a Little Lamb")

> Water leaves me nice and clean, nice and clean, nice and clean
>
> Water leaves me nice and clean
>
> Taking waste away.
>
> Everyday I breathe and sweat, breathe and sweat, breathe and sweat
>
> Water leaves when I breathe and sweat
>
> Taking waste away.
>
> Water leaves me another way, 'nother way, 'nother way
>
> Water leaves me another way
>
> But I'm too polite to say!
>
> **(spoken)** Don't forget to flush!

The following song, provided by Vivian Werner's first grade elementary class 1993-94 (Jefferson Elementary, Pullman, Washington), will help students understand their need for water.

(To the tune of "Old McDonald")

> We need water to survive,
>
> it keeps us alive!
>
> And if you drink it everyday
>
> You can run and play.
>
> ....It's in our food,
>
> It's in the air,
>
> You'll find water everywhere,
>
> We need water to survive,
>
> it keeps us alive!

The following two songs contain technical terms and are better for older students. Involve students in defining new words.

This song presents basic information of how water is used in digestion and the chemical processes that produce molecules such as hormones and enzymes.

(To the tune of "My Bonnie Lies over the Ocean" or a contemporary tune selected by students)

> With water my cells can create things
>
> Cells also need water to break things
>
> You might wonder what must be broken
>
> It's food that's too big for my cells.
>
> Oh, break down, break down
>
> Break down the food into tiny pieces
>
> Break down, break down
>
> Break down the food for my cells!
>
> The food in my cells are the makin's
>
> Of hormones and enzymes I need
>
> To help me to grow and to function
>
> But without water these won't be made.
>
> Oh, make up, make up
>
> Water helps cells make these chemicals
>
> Make up, make up
>
> Make up these things that we need.

Aqua Tunes

(Have students adapt this as a rap tune)

I have water in my blood

Lub, dub, lub, dub, lub

To pump my blood I need my heart **(point to heart)**

Lub, dub, lub, dub, lub

Blood goes to my cells **(spread hands all over body to represent blood's movement)**

Through my arteries

Capillary here, osmosis over there

My heart pumps my blood around

Lub, dub, lub, dub, lub

I have water in my blood

Lub, dub, lub, dub, lub

And in my blood there're nutrients **(point to belly)**

Lub, dub, lub, dub, lub

With a sugar over here **(spread hands all over body to represent movement of nutrients)**

And a protein over there

Here's a fat, there's some starch

Everywhere in arteries

My blood carries nutrients

Lub, dub, lub, dub, lub

I have water in my blood

Lub, dub, lub, dub, lub

And in my blood there's oxygen **(point to lungs or chest)**

Lub, dub, lub, dub, lub

A hemoglobin here **(spread hands all over body to represent movement of oxygen)**

Goes from lungs to cells

Here's a breath, there's some air

Everywhere in arteries

My blood carries oxygen

Lub, dub, lub, dub, lub

Oxygen helps burn the food

Lub, dub, lub, dub, lub

Burning food makes energy **(jump up and down or run in place)**

Lub, dub, lub, dub, lub

With respiration here

Makes energy right there

So I can jump

And I can run

Every time that I play

I burn food for energy

Lub, dub, lub, dub, lub

All this action does make waste **(wipe brow)**

Lub, dub, lub, dub, lub

That's okay 'cause I have blood

Lub, dub, lub, dub, lub

With a carbon dioxide here

And a uric acid there

To my lungs **(point to chest)**

To my kidneys **(point to back)**

Water helps remove this waste

Lub, dub, lub, dub, lub

Let's Even Things Out

■ **Grade Level:**
Upper Elementary, Middle School

■ **Subject Areas:**
Life Science

■ **Duration:**
Preparation time: 30 minutes
Activity time: 50 minutes

■ **Setting:** Classroom

■ **Skills:**
Gathering information; Interpreting (summarizing)

■ **Charting the Course**
In conjunction with this activity, students could participate in "What's the Solution?" to learn how water dissolves substances. Understanding concepts in this activity supports other activities that address how living things use water ("Aqua Notes" and "Thirsty Plants").

■ **Vocabulary**
osmosis, diffusion, concentration, solution, solvent, solute

Have you ever tried to learn something through osmosis?

▼ Summary
Students simulate the role water plays in balancing concentrations of solutes through osmosis and diffusion.

Objectives
Students will:
• describe and demonstrate the processes of osmosis and diffusion.

Materials
• *Air freshener*
• *Food dye*
• *Dropper*
• *Water in a glass jar or beaker*
• *Copies of **Professor Osmo and the Recalcitrant Student** (optional)*

Making Connections
Students experience diffusion when they smell perfume wafting across the room. Students may not realize osmosis and diffusion are also occurring constantly inside their bodies. Learning the role water plays in dispersing solutes helps students understand how nutrients are diffused and how cells maintain water balance.

Background
In nature, things tend to move from an organized to a less structured state (entropy). Hence, buildings crumble, rooms become messy, and substances break apart and disperse. When a large number of molecules are crowded together within a limited space, they are said to be concentrated; their arrangement is usually quite organized. Organization requires an input of energy; as things become disorganized or more random, energy is released. When molecules naturally spread from areas of high concentration to areas of low concentration, this is called diffusion.

Diffusion occurs in the human body when nutrients spread throughout the blood. Sugar flows through plant systems by this same process of diffusion.

Sometimes molecules are restricted from dispersing evenly. For example, they may be enclosed by a cell membrane. In some cases, water molecules are able to pass through the membrane (that is, the membrane is permeable to water). If the concentration of solute (e.g., salt) is greater outside the membrane than inside, and the concentration of water molecules is greater inside the membrane than outside, water will pass out of the cell to where it is less concentrated. In the process, the solute outside the membrane is diluted by water. When water moves through a membrane, this is called osmosis. Osmosis is the diffusion of water through a selectively permeable membrane. Osmosis occurs throughout the cells of living organisms. For example, water travels through plants as it diffuses from one cell into another.

Ideally, water will continue to diffuse in or out of the membrane until concentrations of water on both sides of the membrane are equalized. For example, water balance in our blood cells is maintained because the concentration of salt inside the cell and outside the cell is equal. Sometimes equal distribution is neither possible nor desired. For example, in lab situations if too much water enters a cell to dilute the contents, the cell will burst. Conversely, it will collapse if too much water leaves the cell. When the body requires an unequal

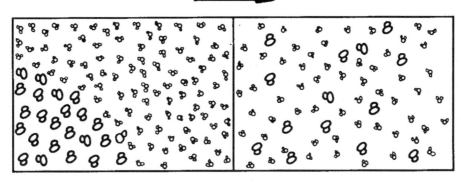

DIFFUSION

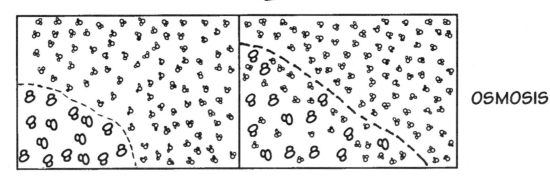

OSMOSIS

∞ = SUCROSE MOLECULES   ჿ = WATER MOLECULES

concentration of materials inside and outside a cell, the cell must use energy to maintain this uneven distribution.

Procedure
▼ Warm Up
Spray air freshener from the front of the room. Ask students in the middle and back of the room if they smell anything. Put a drop of dye in water and have students observe what happens. Have them describe how they think the odor made its way to distant parts of the room and how the dye spread throughout the water.

▼ The Activity
1. **Read or have students read** *Professor Osmo and the Recalcitrant Student* **and tell them they will be acting it out to represent osmosis and diffusion.**

2. **Explain that the process of molecules spreading from an area of high concentration to one of low concentration is called diffusion.** Compare an area of high concentration to an organized, compact state. Ask students which is easier to maintain, a clean room or a sloppy room (that is, which state requires less energy). In the first scenario from *Professor Osmo and the Recalcitrant Student,* keeping the sugar in an organized, concentrated lump requires an input of energy. Allowed to move about randomly, the sugar molecules release the energy.

3. **To demonstrate the story's first scenario (diffusion), designate an area of the floor to represent the glass. Have half the students represent sugar molecules and half water molecules. Tell the students who are sugar to congregate in one** corner of the glass and the water molecules to move about freely within the glass. Correlating with the story, have water molecules gently bump sugar molecules and disperse them throughout the glass. Encourage students to have fun and be dramatic when acting their roles.

4. **Explain that diffusion of water through a membrane is called osmosis.** Water moves from where its concentration is high (and the concentration of solutes is low) to where the concentration of water is low (and the concentration of solutes is high). In the process, the solute becomes diluted and more spread out.

5. **For the second scenario (osmosis) from** *Professor Osmo and the Recalcitrant Student,* **have two or three groups, consisting of three students each, stand close together;**

explain that they are sugar molecules (concentrated).

6. **Ask another group of students to stand shoulder-to-shoulder in a circle around the sugar molecules and take one half-step backwards.** The circle represents the membrane, and the spaces between students are the pores.

7. **The rest of the students represent water molecules outside the membrane. Correlating with the story, water molecules step into the membrane.** Each time a water molecule enters the membrane, students representing the membrane take one small step backwards. Continue doing this until students representing the membrane are stretched to their limit (arm's length apart).

8. **Students should note that the number of water molecules outside the membrane is less; there are more water molecules mixed with the sugar molecules within the membrane. Therefore, the sugar concentration has been diluted.**

▼ *Wrap Up*

Have students summarize the processes of osmosis and diffusion. Challenge them to present their summary with a diagram. Explain that air, like water, can help disperse materials. Ask students to apply diffusion to the situations in the *Warm Up*.

Tell students that diffusion is important for maintaining water balance in our cells. Explain that the concentration of salt in our plasma equals the amount inside red blood cells. Ask students to describe what could happen to red blood cells if there was too much salt in them (the cells could burst as water moved into them). Have students describe a situation in which a cell might shrink (the concentration of salt outside the cell

is greater than that inside). Remind students that blood cells bursting or shrinking would only happen in a laboratory experiment and never in the body. The human body has regulatory mechanisms that prevent this from occurring.

Ask students this question: if the salt concentration in their blood serum was high, how might this make them feel? Higher concentrations of salt in the blood cause water to move from the kidneys to the blood. This triggers mechanisms in the body to make you feel thirsty.

Assessment

Have students:
- simulate the processes of osmosis and diffusion (steps 3-8).
- summarize and diagram the processes of osmosis and diffusion (*Wrap Up*).

Upon completing the activity, for further assessment have students:
- research and cite examples of osmosis and diffusion within their bodies and within the environment.

Extensions

Osmosis can also be demonstrated by putting a sealed plastic bag of starch solution in a beaker full of water colored with a few milliliters of iodine. Starch molecules are too large to pass through the pores of the bag, but water molecules are not. To achieve a balance, iodine-colored water will pass into the bag. This can be seen when the iodine turns the starch dark blue. The iodine outside the bag will retain its original color.

Another way to see osmosis is to remove flecks of shell from the top and bottom of a raw egg without puncturing the membrane. Insert a straw into the top of the egg through the membrane. Place the egg in water. The top of the straw should be

above the level of the water. Water will flow through the membrane into the egg (the inside of the egg is more concentrated), forcing the contents of the egg out of the straw.

Students can see cells collapsing by observing through a microscope a wet-mount slide of an elodea leaf (an aquatic plant found in most pet stores) using a solution of salt water.

Resources

Biological Science Curriculum Study. 1987. *Biological Science: An Ecological Approach.* Dubuque, Iowa: Kendall/Hunt Publishing Company.

Watkins, Patricia A., Glen K. Leto, and Tommy E. Wynn. *Life Science.* Orlando, Fla.: Harcourt Brace Jovanovich, Inc.

Notes ▼

Professor Osmo and the Recalcitrant Student

It's the future. You attend a school that is experimenting with virtual reality as a teaching technique.

You failed to turn in your semester project on diffusion. Professor Osmo informs you that if you wish to pass the course, you must "volunteer" for one of her experiments. Professor Osmo assures you that you will be perfectly safe, and before you have time to say your farewells you're reduced to molecular size. You find yourself riding a sugar molecule—part of a lump of sugar in a glass of water. You can feel the tension, the energy put forth by the sugar molecules. You vibrate in concert with the millions of sugar molecules condensed around you. There are surges of increased energy as water molecules bombard the sugar particles. Suddenly, the sugar molecule you're riding takes a direct hit. You spin off like a billiard ball. Hanging on for dear life, you speed toward other water molecules—hitting some, missing others. As you slow down, you find yourself out of the sugar matrix and surrounded by both water and sugar molecules. You shout at the top of your lungs, "Professor Osmo, I get it! Diffusion is the movement of molecules from places of high concentration [the sugar cube] to areas of low concentration [the water]."

You are immediately transformed to normal size, dripping wet. You lick your lips and the water tastes sweet. The Professor thoughtfully observes you and says, "So, now you comprehend diffusion, but what about osmosis?"

You start to sweat as you stammer a response. With a gleam in her eye, the Professor says, "How about extra credit, hmmmm?"

Before you can run for the door, you're once again reduced to the molecular level, but this time you're riding a water molecule. It's a rough ride, as you're bouncing against and off of other water molecules. Ahead of you is a barrier—a translucent wall. As you watch, water molecules

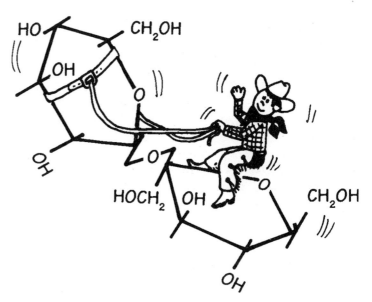

pass through pores in the wall. On the other side, you can make out a mixture of sugar molecules (too large to pass through the tiny holes) and a few water molecules. Suddenly, you feel the water molecule you're riding being drawn toward this mixture. Clinging to the particle, you squeeze your eyes shut as you pass through one of the pores. Finally, you take a breath and open your eyes. You're surrounded by sugar and water molecules. As more water molecules enter, you notice that the ratio of sugar to water molecules is beginning to even out. In passing through the wall, you moved from a place of many water molecules (high concentration) to a place of few (low concentration). Eureka! You understand osmosis. Again, you shout, "Professor Osmo, I get it! Osmosis is the diffusion of water from a place of high concentration through a membrane to an area of low concentration."

Instantly, you are transformed to normal size. As you back toward the door, you thank Professor Osmo for the close encounters with osmosis and diffusion. Professor Osmo calls out, "But how about plasmolysis?"

"Maybe next week, Professor Osmo," you reply. "I've got another project due, and I don't want to be late . . . it's on the bubonic plague!"

The Life Box

■ Grade Level:
Lower Elementary, Upper Elementary

■ Subject Areas:
Life Science

■ Duration:
Preparation time: 30 minutes
Activity time: 50 minutes

■ Setting: Classroom

■ Skills:
Analyzing (identifying relationships and components); Interpreting (deducing)

■ Charting the Course
This is a foundation activity and can be used to introduce other activities on water and how water is needed for life. For example, in "Aqua Bodies" students learn that a large percentage of the human body is water. They are introduced to how the body uses water in "Aqua Notes."

■ Vocabulary
soil, water, photosynthesis

Plants and animals have four things in common; can you guess what they are?

▼ Summary
Through a thought-provoking activity, students discover four essential factors needed to sustain life.

Objectives
Students will:
- identify four essential factors necessary for life.
- explain how living things use these four factors.

Materials
- *Potted plant*
- *Rock*
- *Cups of soil*
- *Bottles of water*
- *Life Boxes (Assemble several boxes, each with 1 cup [240 ml] of soil and a bottle of water inside. Label each box "The Life Box." Place lids securely on boxes.)*
- *1 half-pint (240 ml) milk carton for each student (Wash cartons and pull apart the top flaps so the cartons completely open up.) (optional)*
- *Soil (optional)*
- *Water (optional)*
- *Glue (optional)*
- *Scissors (optional)*
- *Drawing materials (optional)*

Making Connections
Most students know that they require water and air to survive. Some may have learned that plants also require water, air, minerals found in soil, and sunlight. Through deduction, students learn that animals and plants depend upon four crucial factors, an awareness that heightens students' appreciation of these resources.

Background
Why all this fuss about water? Why worry? The answer is really quite simple: the availability of water is a matter of life and death. Throughout history people have engineered ways to secure quantities of water to meet their needs and to protect themselves from water-related natural events like floods and droughts. You cannot simply snap your fingers and get water. You cannot wish water out of the sky or locate it below the ground where it does not exist. Plants, wildlife, and human communities have formed around water.

Four factors are necessary for life to exist:

SOIL
Soil is the result of rock that has been broken down by physical and/or chemical processes called weathering. Soil contains organic matter from decomposed plants and animals. Soil provides plants with minerals and nutrients, and it helps transport water to plants' roots.

SUNLIGHT
Radiant energy from the sun illuminates and warms Earth's surface. Plants use the sun's energy to make sugar from carbon dioxide and water—a process called photosynthesis.

Sunlight and soil are used directly by plants and indirectly by animals. Plants get minerals from the soil. Animals get their nutrients and energy from plants (or from animals that eat plants).

AIR
Air is a mixture of numerous gases that make up Earth's atmosphere, including nitrogen, oxygen, hydrogen, carbon dioxide, argon, neon, helium, and others. During plant photosynthe-

sis, carbon dioxide is used to build sugar. Oxygen helps many plants and animals metabolize sugar in their cells. This burning of sugar, or respiration, supplies energy to living things.

WATER

Water is the combination of two colorless and odorless gases—hydrogen and oxygen. It is needed to dissolve and carry nutrients in solution for transport of food and waste within organisms. The process of photosynthesis also requires water.

Soil erosion and air or water pollution compromise the life-supporting properties of these resources. Through awareness of our dependence on clean water, soil, and air, and perhaps through more direct use of sunlight for energy resources, we can learn to sustain the quality of our resources for future generations.

Procedure
▼ Warm Up

Show students a live potted plant, a rock, and a child selected from the class. Ask them to identify the two things that are "living." Tell students that they will discover what is needed for life.

▼ The Activity

1. Circulate the *Life Boxes* among your students. Ask each student to open a box and note what is inside. (Older students can list items on a sheet of paper.) After each student has examined the contents, he or she should place the cover back on the box and give it to the next student.

2. Ask students what they found in each box. They will likely answer soil and a bottle of water. Their interest should grow when you tell them that each box contains two more items.

3. Circulate the boxes again and repeat the question: "What is in the box?" If, after a short brainstorming session, your students still have not identified air and light, provide the answer.

4. Tell students that each box contains the four things necessary for most life. Actually, three things are in the box—water, soil, and air. *The fourth, light, entered when the box was opened!*

5. Explain how each of these factors is used by living things.

NOTE: An alternative is to have each student make his or her own *Life Box*. Students can put soil and water into a milk carton and try to guess which four things needed for life are in the box. After identifying these factors, they can decorate the outside of the box. For example, the carton can be covered with construction paper and each of the factors illustrated. Or

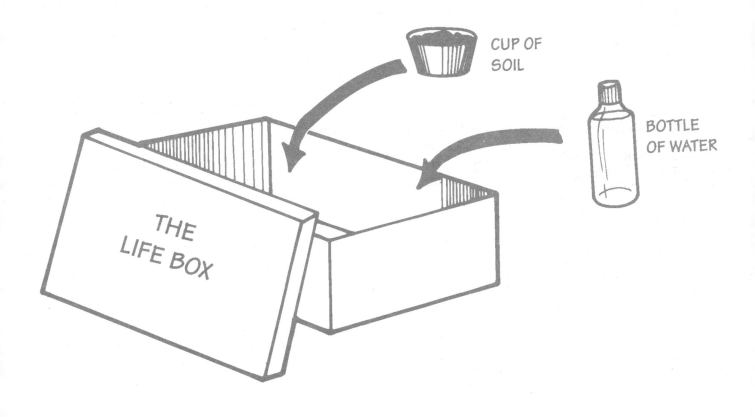

CUP OF SOIL

BOTTLE OF WATER

THE LIFE BOX

they could cover each side of the box with drawings or photographs of their favorite people or things (e.g., parents, siblings, pets, food). Challenge them to explain how each pictured person or thing needs (or once needed) the four life factors.

▼ Wrap Up and Action
Bring the selected student back to the front of the room; also display the potted plant. Ask the class how each of these organisms uses the four life factors.

Encourage students to take a *Life Box* home and test their family members about the four factors needed for life.

Assessment
Have students:
- identify four essential factors of life (step 3).
- describe how living things use the four factors of life (**Wrap Up**).

Upon completing the activity, for further assessment have students:
- create an experiment to prove or disprove that water, sunlight, air, and soil are essential for life.

Extensions
In addition to the four essential life factors, discuss with students the important concept that living things require a healthy environment: food, shelter, water, and adequate space. Then have the students plant two or three seeds or beans in each *Life Box* and water them lightly each day, thus verifying that the four factors necessary for life will cause dormant seeds to germinate and grow. Remind students that they must keep open the top of the carton to allow sunlight to enter.

Resources
Caduto, Michael, and Joseph Bruchac. 1989. *Keepers of the Earth.* Golden, Colo.: Fulcrum, Inc.

 Leutscher, Alfred. 1983. *Water.* New York, N.Y.: Dial.

 Williams, Jay. 1980. *The Water of Life.* New York, N.Y.: Four Winds Press.

Life in the Fast Lane

■ **Grade Level:**
Upper Elementary, Middle School

■ **Subject Areas:**
Ecology, Life Science

■ **Duration:**
Preparation time:
Part I: 50 minutes
Part II: 50 minutes

Activity time:
Part I: One week to a month (for long-term investigation)
Part II: 50 minutes

■ **Setting:**
Large space and outdoors

■ **Skills:**
Gathering information (observing, collecting); Analyzing (identifying components and relationships, comparing, discussing)

■ **Charting the Course**
Prior to this activity, students could learn how puddles are affected by the water cycle (e.g., "The Incredible Journey"). How water collects in wetlands is explored in "Capture, Store, and Release." Students can study wetland soils in "Wetland Soils in Living Color." Other wetland environments are studied in "Salt Marsh Players."

■ **Vocabulary**
temporary wetland

Instant wetlands—just add water!

▼ Summary
Through a scavenger hunt and investigations of temporary wetlands in their neighborhood, students learn the benefits of and challenges to organisms living in temporary wetlands.

Objectives
Students will:
- describe physical and biological components of temporary wetlands.
- recognize the importance of temporary wetlands to larger ecosystems.
- explain how organisms in temporary wetlands race against time to obtain water, shelter, food, and a mate.

Materials
The following are needed for the investigation of temporary wetlands:
- *Temporary wetlands or large spring puddles within walking distance of school*
- *Copies of Temporary Wetland Data*
- *Field study equipment (1 kit per group), consisting of a plastic bag filled with the following: thermometer, aquarium fishnet, magnifying glass, ruler, string*
- *Field guides (optional)*
- *Water test kits, pH strips, dissolved oxygen tests, etc. (optional)*
- *Classroom aquariums or large jars (optional)*
- *Microscope (optional)*

The following items (about one per student for each item) should be distributed around the school or in a playing field:
- *Snack food (e.g., hard sugar candies, peanuts, or crackers)*
- *Toothpicks*
- *Soil*

Other items for scavenger hunt include:
- *Plastic cups or bags (3 per student)*
- *Pins or tape*
- *Paper*
- *Copies of Scavenger Hunt (Prey) and Scavenger Hunt (Predator)*
- *Prizes for successful scavengers (optional)*

Making Connections
April showers bring May flowers, but they also create puddles. A source of wet fun for a youngster, a puddle may become a temporary home for a plant or animal. Temporary wetlands provide excellent field sites for student investigations. Learning about these special kinds of wetlands helps students appreciate their role in the ecological balance of larger ecosystems.

Background
With the addition of water, a once dry, dormant low area erupts with plant and animal life. These temporary wetlands usually appear during the wet season, then dry up later in the year. In some parts of the country, such wetlands appear in the spring and are called vernal pools. Where do all the grasses, mosquitoes, and frogs come from? Buried in the soil, many wait for the essential ingredient that allows them to become active—water! Water collects in large puddles or wetlands when flatland soils become saturated with rain or snowmelt. Depending on topography and amount of precipitation, these wetlands may only be a few yards in diameter or they may cover an acre.

Water that collects in these wetlands either evaporates, percolates into the ground, or flows downstream. Consequently, these temporary wetlands rarely last through the dry season. A temporary wetland may exist for one day or up to four or five months. A whole world of life appears in such a wetland, with a

fast-paced lifestyle designed to win the race against time—the time when the wetland dries up. During this limited time, organisms such as mosquitoes, salamanders, frogs, toads, fairy shrimp, and microorganisms must secure shelter, find food, locate a mate, and reproduce.

One benefit of living in a temporary wetland is the concentration of food sources (algae and other plant species). This rich supply of food makes these wetlands an attractive home and a productive nursery for many animals. Some species (e.g., fairy shrimp) are found primarily in temporary wetlands, and their existence depends on these pools. If they lay their eggs or deposit their seeds before the wetland dries up, their offspring will be born when the water returns next season. Other organisms bury themselves and become dormant when the water dries up (in some cases, for as long

as 20 years!). Other animals are transient residents (e.g., visiting during migration) and relocate when the wetland disappears. In this way, temporary wetlands contribute to larger, permanent ecosystems, such as deserts or forests.

Procedure
▼ Warm Up
Have students write a paragraph describing an area of their neighborhood that retains water on a temporary basis. Explain that this collection of water might be classified as a temporary wetland. Have students share what they know and think about wetlands and list how temporary wetlands could be important to the environment.

▼ The Activity
Part I
1.   **Ask students to note when puddles begin to form around the**

school. (This may be assigned as an out-of-school project.) Have them construct a neighborhood map and mark the location of significant pools (or wetlands). Give each wetland a name and assign students to monitor each throughout its existence.

2.   **Have students use the *Temporary Wetland Data Sheet* to record observations of their wetland every other day during the wetland's existence. The variables to monitor include, but are not limited to:**

WATER TEMPERATURE
Changes in temperature affect animal activity and the amount of oxygen in water. (Cooler water can hold more oxygen.)

DIAMETER AND AVERAGE DEPTH
Large, deep wetlands have more room for diverse organisms. Wide, shallow wetlands will evaporate more quickly.

80

ANIMAL AND PLANT TYPES AND NUMBERS

Organisms can be collected with an aquarium fish net or studied at the site. Animals and plants may be brought temporarily to the classroom and returned to the wetland within a few hours. Be sure students keep animals in wetland water and do not touch them. Students can look for indirect evidence of animals (tracks, egg cases, molted shells, etc.). If a field guide is available, students can identify organisms. Students may conduct additional research on organisms living in temporary wetlands.

3.   **Explain to students how organisms function within the time span of a puddle forming and drying up;** describe life processes (obtaining food, seeking shelter, reproducing) that must occur during the existence of the wetland.

Part II

1.   **Tell students they are going to participate in a scavenger hunt to simulate this race against time. Explain that they are organisms living in a newly formed temporary wetland.**

2.   **Have students count off by fives. Tell all number ones to write the word** *predator* **on a piece of paper and pin it to their shirts. Predators, which eat insects and other organisms, include frogs, salamanders, and turtles. The rest of the students are prey organisms, such as insects, crustaceans, etc.**

3.   **Tell students the temporary wetland will dry up in a specified amount of time. Players must search their school or playing field to acquire what they need to survive.** The amount of time will depend on the size of the school or playing field and the distribution of items. Start with a ten-minute time limit.

4.   **Distribute** *Scavenger Hunt (Prey)* **and** *Scavenger Hunt (Predator)* **and plastic cups to students. The four main categories are water, shelter, food, and a partner. Students must obtain all items in one category before they can begin to fill the next.** That is, all items in one category must be brought to the classroom and initialed on the scavenger sheet. The first three categories can be completed in any

Prairie potholes provide temporary homes for many migratory species. JIM STUTZMAN

order, but all three must be completed before students can identify a partner.

5. **Warn students that they must avoid predators while scavenging. If they are tagged by a predator, they become the food of the predator. The prey must stop searching and travel with the predator.**

6. **After students acquire partners, they return to the classroom and have their scavenger sheets finalized. All students must return once the allotted time has elapsed.**

7. **Set the timer and release students.** Departures of predators and prey should be staggered to give the prey time to scatter. Prizes can be awarded to students who return within the time limit.

▼ Wrap Up and Action

Discuss the outcome of the scavenger hunt. What might be the fate of organisms that do not obtain what they need before the wetlands dry up? Have students summarize the challenges of living in temporary wetlands. Explain that, despite such limited time, one advantage over permanent water bodies is that food and shelter are generally more accessible, with predators less common.

Have students discuss the results of their local temporary wetlands study. What organisms did they find? Did any wetlands dry up during the study period? How might their results relate to the scavenger hunt? Have students discuss how wetlands could benefit their community. Why might people want to eliminate temporary wetlands? Compare students' comments in class discussion, to identify differing points of view. Local governments or state resource agencies may be interested in students' findings.

Assessment

Have students:
- record observations of physical and biological elements of a temporary wetland over time (*Part I*, step 2).
- describe the benefits and challenges of life in a temporary wetland (*Wrap Up*).
- research and write a paper identifying how temporary wetlands benefit their community (*Wrap Up*).

Extensions

Compare the longevity of several wetlands during the same season. Explain differences.

Students may be interested in researching how human actions can protect or endanger temporary wetlands.

Read *Neighborhood Puddle* to students and have them write a story about their temporary wetlands.

Resources

Braus, Judy, ed. 1987. *NatureScope: Let's Hear It for Herps!* Washington, D.C.: National Wildlife Federation.

Caduto, Michael. 1990. *Pond and Brook: A Guide to Nature in Freshwater Environments.* Hanover and London, England: University Press of New England.

Downer, Anne. 1992. *Spring Pool: A Guide to the Ecology of Temporary Ponds.* New York, N.Y.: Watts.

Mitsch, W. J., and J. G. Gosselink. 1993. *Wetlands*, 2nd ed. New York, N.Y.: Van Norstrand Reinhold.

Project WILD. 1992. "Micro Odyssey" and "Puddle Wonders." *Aquatic Project WILD.* Bethesda, Md.: Western Regional Environmental Education Council.

🍎 Waters, John F. 1971. *Neighborhood Puddle.* New York, N.Y.: Frederick Warne and Co., Inc.

Temporary Wetland Data Sheet

Name: _____ Date: _____

Wetland Name: _____

Location: _____

Date/time	H$_2$O temp.	Diameter	Depth	Animals	Plants

Scavenger Hunt (Prey) Name: _____

WATER Teacher initials	Three cups of water
SHELTER Teacher initials	A toothpick and some soil
FOOD Teacher initials	Four pieces of food (such as one hard candy, one piece of chocolate, peanut, cracker)
PARTNER Teacher initials	A partner (the first student you see who has found water, shelter, and food)

Scavenger Hunt (Predator) Name: _____

WATER Teacher initials	Three cups of water
SHELTER Teacher initials	A toothpick and some soil
FOOD Teacher initials	Eight pieces of food. The actual food items (hard candy, chocolates, peanuts, crackers) count as one piece each. Students (prey organisms) represent two pieces of food each. You can scavenge eight pieces of food or four prey students, or any combination of food pieces and students to equal eight pieces. (For example, three prey students and two pieces of food equal eight pieces.)
PARTNER Teacher initials	A partner (the first student you see who has found water, shelter, and food)

No Bellyachers

Grade Level:
Upper Elementary, Middle School

Subject Areas:
Health, Life Science

Duration:
Preparation time:
Part I: 10 minutes
Part II: 20 minutes

Activity time:
Part I: 20 minutes
Part II: 30 minutes

Setting:
Classroom, gym, and/or playground

Skills:
Gathering information (calculating); Interpreting (relating)

Charting the Course
Students may be interested in learning more about pathogens ("Super Sleuths"). In "Poison Pump," students investigate how water is the culprit in the spread of cholera. In "Water Concentration," students analyze how water use practices have evolved to prevent the spread of waterborne diseases.

Vocabulary
pathogens, bacteria, virus

Have you ever shared a soda with someone who came down with the flu the next day? Did you ever think you got a cold from someone who sneezed on you?

▼ Summary
Students will participate in a series of demonstrations and a game of tag to show how illness-causing bacteria and viruses are spread by water.

Objectives
Students will:
- recognize factors that contribute to avoiding a cold or influenza.
- describe how some infectious diseases are spread by water or water droplets.
- identify ways to reduce the chances of becoming infected with a disease.

Materials
- *Ladle, water dipper, or cup (optional)*
- *Clean spray bottle*
- *Water*
- *Food coloring*
- *Clear container filled with water*
- *Paper*
- *Tokens (peanuts, macaroni, cotton balls, etc.)*
- *Small bags*
- *Timer or watch with second hand*

Making Connections
Everyone has had a cold, influenza, or a stomach virus. Each year these common infectious diseases spread across the country and around the world affecting millions of people. Students know that many diseases are contagious. Learning how pathogens are spread may promote healthy habits.

Background
The human body is home to all kinds of bacteria. Most bacteria are beneficial. In fact, if it were not for bacteria, people could not exist. Microorganisms digest food and produce substances such as vitamin K that help blood to clot. They form the body's first line of defense because they out-compete pathogens (harmful viruses or bacteria) on the skin or in the mouth. Sometimes people get infected with an overwhelming number of pathogens that settle in their nasal passages, throat, lungs, stomach, and other parts of the body. The infected person in turn expels water droplets from his or her lungs through saliva or mucus, and expels water in urine or feces. The spread of germs from one person to another is the basis of infection by communicable diseases.

Population density is also an important factor in the spread of colds and influenza. The chance of pathogens spreading is greatly enhanced when people are in close contact with each other. A classroom full of students is an ideal setting for spreading cold and flu microorganisms.

Fortunately, our bodies have many ways to combat infection. Nasal passages and the trachea are lined with tiny hairs that trap microorganisms. Once the body has been invaded by pathogens, it can mount various attacks. Certain white blood cells can seek out pathogens and consume them. Other white blood cells produce antibodies that fit the structure of pathogens much like puzzle pieces. When an antibody finds a pathogen, it attaches to it and destroys it. This requires some time, which is usually why it takes about a week to recover from a cold, flu, or stomach virus.

To help our bodies stay clear of some diseases (such as colds or influenza), parents, teachers, and the medical community stress the importance of preventive measures to avoid the spread of pathogens. These precautions include the following:

- covering the mouth when sneezing or coughing.
- washing hands after going to the rest room and before each meal.
- avoiding shared eating utensils, food, or beverages.

Precautions also include ways to keep the body healthy so that it can mount an attack when threatened by a pathogen:
- drinking eight glasses of water each day.
- getting eight hours or more of sleep each night.
- eating three balanced meals a day, including grains, fruits, and vegetables.
- exercising regularly.
- wearing weather-appropriate clothing.

Procedure
▼ Warm Up
Open the discussion by asking students to name some contagious diseases. How many of them presently have a cold or have had a cold or the flu in the last month? What were some of the symptoms? Ask students how they think they got the cold.

Tell students how they might have gotten the cold or flu through contact with water. Read the following stories: "The Sneeze," "Reach Out and Touch Someone," and "The Common Cup."

Reinforce the stories with the following demonstrations:

- Simulate a sneeze by spraying water into the air. Have students observe how the water dissipates throughout the room.
- Show how bacteria and viruses are passed through touch. Ask a student to cover his or her mouth and fake a sneeze. Wet his or her hand thoroughly with water. Tell that student to shake hands with another student; the second student shakes hands with a third, etc. They should not dry their hands between shakes. How many students shook a wet hand? What if pathogens were in the "sneezed" fluids? How do microorganisms on the hand get to the mouth?

THE SNEEZE
Think of the person who has a cold and sneezes in a crowded room without covering his or her mouth. Picture thousands of water droplets laden with mucus flying through the air. As the droplets disappear, laughter erupts because of the loudness of the sneeze. Where do the droplets go? Some are still in the air and some land on food, on you, and on your friends. How could you get a cold from these water droplets?

REACH OUT AND TOUCH SOMEONE
Would you believe most intestinal, stomach, and cold viruses are spread by our hands? Through touch, microorganisms are transferred from the fluids in the nose and mouth of one person to something (e.g., a pencil, food, a phone) or to someone else. When other people bring their hands or the object near their

mouths, the bacteria or viruses may find a new home.

NOTE: Intestinal and stomach viruses are spread by improper hand washing after using the toilet.

THE COMMON CUP
About 150 years ago, in a one-room school, students dipped the long-handled ladle into the water bucket for a drink. Schools and most homes did not have running water, so the bucket was filled and everyone drank from the same dipper. As people learned that a shared cup meant shared pathogens, states outlawed the common dipper. What role did the water play in the spread of pathogens?

NOTE: Remind students that improper hand washing after using the toilet also promotes the spread of disease through contact.

• Demonstrate how microorganisms can permeate water in a jug. Place several drops of food coloring in a clear container of water. What happens to the water? How is this similar to the spread of pathogens? How does the dispersion of color throughout the water show how water helps spread bacteria and viruses?

▼ The Activity

Part I

1. **Have students list preventive measures that help their bodies resist disease. Have students discuss why each is important. Once the list is complete, rewrite each item in the form of a question.** (Example: Did you get eight hours of sleep last night?) The questions will form the basis for a class survey.

2. **Conduct the class survey as follows. Have students answer each question with a "+" for yes and "-" for no. After all questions have been answered, have each student add up the +'s and the -'s. Have them find the difference between the two sums.** For example, a student with 6 yeses (+6) and 4 noes (-4) has a score of +2. A student with 4 yeses (+4) and 6 noes (-6) has a score of -2. Assign a negative, neutral, or positive score to each student. (The student with +2 has a positive score; the one with -2 has a negative score.)

3. **Discuss the results of the survey.** Why can it be difficult to maintain healthy habits?

Part II

1. **Have students participate in a game of "No Bellyachers Tag" to**

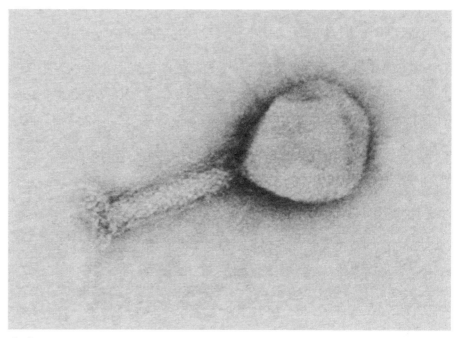

A virus. COURTESY: CAROLINA BIOLOGICAL SUPPLY COMPANY

simulate how diseases spread throughout a population. This game will reinforce the importance of healthy living and demonstrate the rapid transmission of microorganisms.

2. **Use a mock run to teach the game procedure.** Tag one student. Both you and the student each tag one student for a total of four people tagged. The four tagged players each tag another student for a total of eight. Eventually the entire class should be tagged.

3. **Assign restrictions and bonus tokens as follows:** Students who had (-) scores must hop on one leg. Students with neutral (0) scores will have no restrictions and can be tagged once. Students with (+) scores will be given a single token.

4. **Start the game by designating one student to have a virus or a bacterial infection.** This player must place a hand over his or her mouth to indicate a sneeze or place hands over

stomach to represent a bellyache. The goal is to tag as many people as possible.

5. **Players who are tagged must also hold hands over their mouths or stomachs and proceed to chase other players who have not been tagged.** Players with tokens who are tagged do not become it. Instead, a tagged player relinquishes his or her token to the person who is it. If tagged a second time, he or she becomes infected (i.e., becomes it). (Students who are it can carry small bags for collecting tokens.)

6. **Stop the game after two minutes and record the number of tagged and untagged students.**

7. **Adapt the game to demonstrate how population density affects the spread of disease. Expand the tag-playing area. Population density (number of people per foot of space) can influence the transmission of disease. With students dispersed over a larger playing area,**

a widespread population is simulated. How did the greater space between players influence the outcome of the game? Ask students why people tend to get colds more often in winter than in summer. In what season are people more likely to be indoors and in proximity to others? Is it easier for microorganisms to travel among people when they are close together or far apart? Students can simulate indoor living conditions and the transfer of disease by reducing the size of the area. How does this influence the outcome?

▼ Wrap Up and Action

Discuss what happened during each game of "No Bellyachers Tag." Determine how restrictions and

bonus tokens affected results. How many students remained healthy after two minutes?

Based on the results of the game, discuss how healthy habits may protect against disease. Have the class prepare and conduct a presentation about healthy habits for other students. Students may wish to play the game with friends and family.

Assessment

Have students:
- explain how water and water droplets spread microorganisms (*Warm Up*).
- demonstrate how microorganisms spread within a population by playing a tag game (*Part II*, steps 4-7).

- relate how healthy habits help to protect against disease (*Part I*, step 1 and *Warm Up*).

Extensions

Invite a public health nurse to speak to the class about communicable diseases.

Why do we stay healthy as much as we do? How do our bodies resist disease? Have students research how the body resists disease. With this new information, have students alter the game.

Have students compare the growth of bacteria from washed and unwashed hands. Order petri dishes from a biological supply company. Have one group of students wash their hands and press their thumbs into the agar of separate petri dishes; have a second group do the same, but without washing their hands. Cover the petri dishes and incubate at 90 degrees F (32°C) for 48 hours. Compare results. Dispose of petri dishes properly.

Resources

Brock and Madigan. 1991. *Biology of Microorganisms*, 6th ed. Englewood Cliffs, N.J.: Prentice Hall.

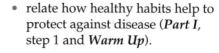 Dashefsky, H. Steven. 1994. *Microbiology: 49 Science Fair Projects*. New York, N.Y.: McGraw-Hill.

Pelagos, Chan, and Kreig. 1993. *Microbiology, Concepts and Applications*. New York, N.Y.: McGraw-Hill.

Ward, Brian R. 1988. *Health and Hygiene*. New York, N.Y.: Watts.

People of the Bog

Feeling bogged down? You're in good company—except they're 3,000 years old!

▼ Summary

Students construct a classroom bog and a mini-composter to observe the rate of decomposition in anaerobic (little or no oxygen present) and aerobic (oxygen available) environments.

Objectives

Students will:
- describe characteristics of bog environments.
- explain the conditions of bogs that allow for the preservation of artifacts from the past.
- compare the rates of decomposition of articles in aerobic and anaerobic environments.

Materials

(Encourage students to contribute materials.)

For one bog:
- *20-gallon (76 liter) glass tank (aquarium/ terrarium)* (An alternative is for students to make individual bogs in plastic soda bottles.)
- *Small water container* (cut-off cottage cheese container or fruit juice bottle)
- *Watering can*
- *Clear plastic soda bottle* (mini-composter)
- *5 pounds (2 kg) gravel*
- *1 pound (0.5 kg) perlite* (purchase at garden center)
- *3.5 pounds (1.6 kg) activated charcoal*
- *10 pounds (4.5 kg) dry peat moss* (purchase at garden center)
- *3 pounds (1.5 kg) sphagnum moss*
- *Several plants* (a carnivorous plant or two, like a Venus fly trap, and several water-tolerant plants, like ferns or violets)
- *Potting soil*
- *Several snails* (optional)
- *Items to represent artifacts:*
  3 3-inch (7.5 cm) long nails
  3 thin pieces of wood (popsicle sticks will work)
  6-8 pieces of fruit (pear, banana, apple)
  other things students want to test
- *Distilled/dechlorinated water* (An inexpensive way to dechlorinate water is to keep a 5-gallon (19 liter) bucket of water in a closet. Within one day the chlorine should evaporate out of solution. Chemicals from pet stores can also be obtained to remove chlorine from the water.)

Making Connections

A student's experience with bogs may be limited to images from horror movies. By constructing an artificial bog in a classroom, students become acquainted with the complicated balance of environmental circumstances that must combine to create and maintain this unique environment.

Background

Bogs (sometimes called peatlands) are wetland environments created over thousands of years. Vast sections of northern Europe and northern North America qualify as peatlands, along with many alpine and tropical settings where environmental conditions favor the accumulation of organic material (dead plant and animal litter).

Bog formation requires a location with standing or slow-moving water (where the water inflow exceeds outflow or where the ground water table is at the surface). Certain plants, such as sphagnum moss, grow well in these still or stagnant waters. As these plants live and

---

■ **Grade Level:**
Middle School, High School

■ **Subject Areas:**
Earth Science, History, Life Sciences

■ **Duration:**
Preparation time: 50 minutes
Activity time: a semester or school year for artifact observation

■ **Setting:**
Classroom (keep bog and mini-composter in a well-ventilated location)

■ **Skills:**
Gathering information (observing, researching, recording); Analyzing (comparing and contrasting); Interpreting (summarizing)

■ **Charting the Course**
Students can learn more about wetlands in the following activities: "Capture, Store, and Release," "Wetland Soils in Living Color," and "Salt Marsh Players." Ground water concepts are further explored in "Get the Ground Water Picture."

■ **Vocabulary**
bog, decomposition, aerobic, anaerobic

Northern peatland of the tundra. ALAN KESSELHEIM

die, their by-products increase the acidity of the soil and water. Other plants, such as cranberries, Labrador tea, pitcher plants, and Venus fly traps are adapted to live in these acidic conditions. For example, the pitcher plant and Venus fly trap are carnivores; they compensate for living in these nutrient-poor soils by trapping and digesting insects.

In bogs, the supply of dead organic material exceeds the rate of decomposition, so that layers accumulate through time. Waterlogged conditions inhibit the level and distribution of oxygen (resulting in anaerobic conditions), which, in turn, inhibits bacterial action and other processes of decay. Cool environments (in alpine or northern latitudes) further reduce bacterial activity. As organic material (mostly dead plants) builds up, it is compressed into peat by its own weight.

Variation in bog types depends on the level of acid in the water, available nutrients, and the extent of saturation. A bog in Florida is quite different from a bog in northern Ireland because the plant types and climates are so different.

In northern Europe peatlands have, for centuries, been mined for fuel. Strips of peat are cut away, allowed to dry, and then burned to heat houses and to fire factory furnaces. Peat miners have made many startling discoveries as they dig through the organic layers. The same lack of oxygen that retards the decay of plant material also slows the decomposition of archaeological artifacts and even human bodies, so that it sometimes takes thousands of years.

Imagine the peat farmer suddenly face-to-face with a human who perished 3,000 years ago, a body that looks fresh enough to have died only weeks earlier! Wetland bog sites have preserved remarkable archaeological evidence. Clothing, pieces of rope, undigested food in the stomachs of ancient people, and building materials have all been found preserved in a state of freshness.

Hundreds of bodies scattered throughout northern Europe have added substantially to our under-standing of our ancestors. Sites such as Little Springs, Florida, and Monte Verde, in the Andes Mountains of South America, have brought into focus new parts of the picture of human existence: parts that could never have been reconstructed without the ability of bogs to preserve material.

Procedure
▼ Warm Up
Ask students what they know about building and maintaining a compost pile. Why is it necessary to "stir" a compost pile weekly? Help them to understand that stirring helps introduce the oxygen needed by microorganisms for decomposition. What would happen to a compost pile if it were not stirred? This would promote anaerobic conditions, inhibiting the growth of decomposers. If any students have ever been to a bog, ask them to describe it.

Readings about archaeological finds (see resource books) might heighten students' curiosity. (Make sure students understand that not all bogs have people or things buried in them.)

▼ The Activity
1. **Discuss the process of and conditions for bog formation as outlined in the Background.**

2. **Tell students that artifacts are remarkably well preserved in bogs because of anaerobic conditions, and that such evidence has contributed significantly to the study of our ancient ancestors.**

3. **Provide students with the *Bog-Making Activity Sheet*. Have them work in groups or as a class to prepare the bog and to bury the artifacts. For comparison, set up a mini-composter bottle.** This consists of a plastic soda bottle with the top cut off and holes cut in the bottom

90

for drainage. Fill the bottle with soil and add similar artifacts. Water periodically to keep the soil damp, but not soggy, and stir the mini-composter once every week or two—being careful to position artifacts so they can always be clearly seen through the plastic. (Place in a well-ventilated area; it may be odorous.)

4. **Have students predict what will happen to the artifacts. Discuss the conditions of each container. Which is anaerobic? Note that the soil in the bog is saturated. (All spaces between sand particles are filled with water.) Ask students what they think usually fills these spaces.** If necessary, to demonstrate the presence of air (oxygen), fill a clear container half full with dry sand. Add water until the water line is even with the top of the container. As water displaces the air between sand particles, air bubbles will rise to the surface.

5. **At regular intervals throughout a semester or school year, have students rotate responsibility for observing and documenting the decomposition of the different artifacts in each container. For each artifact at each level in the bog, they should describe any changes or note that no obvious change has occurred.** (Do not remove artifacts from the bog; observe them through the glass.)

6. **Have students conduct research to study bog ecology.** What lives in bogs? Of what value are bogs? Why are bogs unique ecosystems? What kinds of adaptations do plants living in a bog have to make? Why do they need these adaptations? How are bogs different from other types of wetlands? Students should relate findings to what is occurring in their bog model.

▼ Wrap Up and Action

Instruct students to write a report summarizing their observations and conclusions about their bog and mini-composter. Can students confirm that "Artifacts are remarkably well preserved in bogs"? Ask them to describe the characteristics of a bog (relate to their own model bog) and include reasons why bogs are important ecosystems that should be managed and preserved. Encourage students to determine if bogs exist in their state or region. What is the condition of a local bog? If possible, arrange a field trip to a bog. Students can write articles for their local paper to inform others in their community about the importance of bogs.

Assessment

Have students:
- compare conditions in the bog and the mini-composter (step 4).
- record and interpret their observations of the bog and mini-composter (step 5).
- provide reasons why bogs are unique environments and should be managed and protected (step 6, *Wrap Up*).
- relate items in the model of a bog to characteristics of a real bog (*Wrap Up*).

Extensions

Students can research several archaeological sites found in wetland bogs. Encourage discussion of these sites and the mysteries presented by the artifacts found there. Students can write "site reports" focusing on a particular area, and then make presentations to the rest of the class.

Try other artifact burials in the classroom bog and observe the rates of decomposition.

If a local bog is near the school, organize a field trip to compare the real thing with the classroom variety.

Resources

Coles, B. and J. Coles. 1989. *People of the Wetlands.* New York, N.Y.: Thames and Hudson.

Glob, P. V. 1965. *The Bog People.* Ithaca, N.Y.: Cornell University Press.

Hanif, Muhammad. 1990. "The Vanishing Bog." *Science and Children* 27 (7): 25–26.

Williams, M., ed. 1990. *Wetlands: A Threatened Landscape.* Cambridge, Mass.: Basil Blackwell.

Notes ▼

Bog-Making Activity Sheet

1. To create the permeable lower layer of an artificial bog, first spread the perlite to an even depth on the bottom. Add 1-2 inches (2-3 cm) of gravel above that, followed by an even layer of the activated charcoal. These materials facilitate the processes of drainage and evaporation that occur in a natural bog.

2. Before adding the next layer, place several artifacts against the glass on top of the charcoal. A piece of wood, a nail, several pieces of fruit, and one cube of meat should be adequate.

3. Place 1-3 inches (2-4 cm) of peat moss above the charcoal. Compress this layer of peat with a block of wood or pack with your hands.

4. Arrange more artifacts on top of the compressed peat, so they can be seen through the tank glass.

5. Loosely pack sphagnum moss and the remaining peat moss, creating some topography, with a gentle slope toward a marked depression. Place a final layer of artifacts on the surface of the loose peat moss.

6. In the depressed section of your "landscape" bury the small water container, so that it is slightly below the surface of the bog. This simulates a small bog pond and helps add humidity to the tank.

7. Plant the carnivorous plants in the peat at the low end of the tank (with the dirt intact) and the water-tolerant varieties at the high end (gently remove dirt and separate the roots). Pack soil around the plant bases. Aquarium may be covered with plastic wrap or sheet of glass.

8. Water the bog evenly with distilled or dechlorinated water (chlorine may harm the plants). Water the bog often enough to maintain a high level of humidity. Condensation droplets should appear on the tank glass. Place the tank near an outside window or alternate daily periods of light and darkness, so that photosynthesis occurs.

9. Every two weeks, feed insects to the carnivorous plants. (Don't overfeed.)

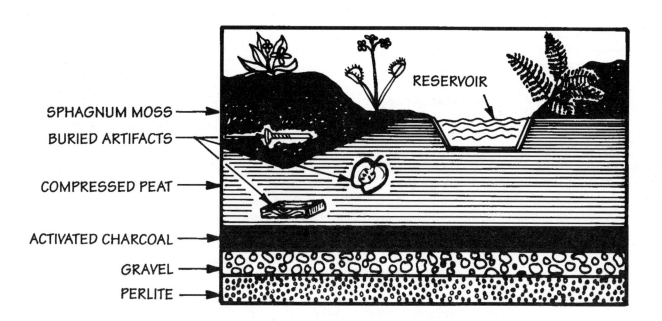

BOG CONSTRUCTION ADAPTED FROM "THE VANISHING BOG," BY MUHAMMAD HANIF, NSTA PUBLICATIONS, COPYRIGHT 1990 FROM *SCIENCE AND CHILDREN* 27 (7):25-26, NATIONAL SCIENCE TEACHERS ASSOCIATION, 1840 WILSON BOULEVARD, ARLINGTON, VA 22201-3000.

Poison Pump

A killer has swept through the streets of London; hundreds are dead! Would you believe that an accomplice to this terrible crime is something you use everyday?

■ **Grade Level:**
Middle School

■ **Subject Areas:**
History, Life Science, Health

■ **Duration:**
Preparation time: 30 minutes
Activity time: 50 minutes

■ **Setting:** Classroom

■ **Skills:**
Analyzing (identifying patterns); Interpreting (identifying cause and effect)

■ **Charting the Course**
Students should understand that water is a shared resource ("Common Water"). Students may wish to continue to learn about other waterborne diseases ("Super Sleuths"). Students are introduced to ways humans can prevent the spread of disease in "No Bellyachers."

■ **Vocabulary**
epidemic, waterborne, bacteria, pathogen

▼ Summary

Through a series of clues, students solve a mystery to discover that water can also produce negative effects for people.

Objectives
Students will:
• apply investigative methods used by epidemiologists to trace the source of contagious diseases.

Materials
Each group of students will need the following:
• *Student activity sheet,* **Broad Street Area Map** (The map is a fictionalized representation of London streets in 1854.)
• *Copies of* **Victim Cards**
• *Colored marking pens*
• *Copies of* **Clue Cards**

Making Connections
Of the world's leading diseases, over half depend on water for their transmission. These diseases often occur in catastrophic proportions. Epidemics of the past and present intrigue many students. Through following the clues used by scientists in the past, students use investigative and analytic skills to locate the source of a killer disease.

Background
Cholera is a disease caused by the *Vibrio cholerae* bacterium. The bacterium travels through untreated water contaminated by human or animal feces. Cholera is spread by sharing contaminated water or by eating contaminated food. Since the body does not produce lasting immunity against the bacterium, the disease can be contracted more than once.

Cholera is characterized by rapid dehydration resulting from simultaneous vomiting, diarrhea, and profuse perspiration. As victims dehydrate, their skin darkens, shrivels, and loses its elasticity. Depending on general health, body mass, age, and amount of ingested bacteria, cholera victims may suffer only mild symptoms or can die in less than an hour.

In 1854, hundreds of people living in London died during a cholera epidemic. The disease spread from India to London on ships that carried contaminated drinking water. If a ship was known to carry disease, the London port authorities refused to grant docking privileges. Rather than lose money on their cargo, some ship captains deceived the authorities by dumping contaminated water overboard into the Thames River, London's water source.

London was served by competing water companies in 1854. At least one, in an effort to cut costs, failed to filter adequately the river water being pumped into the city. While upper- and most middle-class citizens had indoor plumbing, the poor of London relied on public pumps for their water needs.

Dr. John Snow, considered the father of epidemiology, is credited with tracking and identifying the source and transmission agent of the 1854 cholera epidemic. The agent for spread of the disease was found to be the Broad Street public pump.

Today, most people understand that unclean water carries organisms that cause disease. In the mid-nineteenth century, the idea of waterborne disease was an unpopular and frightening theory. Many people believed that the poor suffered as a result of their shiftlessness and sinful living and deserved retribution in the form of catastrophic disease.

Even though many people doubted and disapproved of Snow's contaminated water theory, Dr. Snow persuaded the authorities to remove the Broad Street pump handle. This simple act saved the lives of many people and marked the beginning of the end of a tragic situation.

We now know that people can avoid cholera infection by making sure their water supplies are clean. Unfortunately, in developing countries where only 35 percent of the population has access to clean water, cholera epidemics continue.

Modern medicine has produced a vaccine against cholera, but it must be repeated every six to twelve months because the antibodies are short lived. Too often, though, citizens of impoverished nations do not have the funds to procure the vaccine. Used for centuries in India, the most effective treatment is to provide the victim with copious amounts of liquids and rehydration salts. This method replaces lost body fluids and electrolytes and flushes out the bacteria. After the pathogen has been purged from the body, antibiotics can promote the victim's recovery.

Cholera has been absent from the Western Hemisphere for most of this century. Nonetheless, health officials warn that the United States could experience outbreaks of cholera and other waterborne diseases. As population increases, more waste

products are generated, a situation that can strain the abilities of municipalities to maintain plentiful and clean water supplies.

Procedure
▼ *Warm Up*
Ask students to share mysteries they have read or seen on television. Discuss how detectives solve crimes in general: they identify the crime,

Dr. John Snow is considered to be the father of epidemiology.

determine the method or weapon used, seek and question eyewitnesses, search for clues, etc.

Narrow the discussion to serial crimes, such as a series of burglaries. How do investigators track the culprit? Have students list what they would look for. Students may have seen television shows in which detectives post a map of an area and mark the location of each crime, looking for a pattern. The detectives then try to determine if the crimes occurred within similar time frames

and if the victims shared common characteristics.

Explain that scientists, particularly epidemiologists, identify, trace, and arrest diseases in the same manner that detectives solve crimes.

▼ *The Activity*
1.   **Tell students that in 1854 a cholera epidemic broke out in the slums of London. *Without mentioning water* describe the symptoms of cholera.** Tell the class that throughout history this disease has killed millions of people, and that hundreds died in the 1854 epidemic. One man, Dr. John Snow, discovered the source and stopped the epidemic.

2.   **Inform the class that they will be given the same information that Dr. Snow possessed and will try to solve the mysterious epidemic.**

3.   **Divide students into groups and give each group a *Broad Street Area Map*, a set of *Victim Cards*, and a marking pen.** (If after five minutes, any group has not begun to mark the location of victims on the map, suggest this as a logical strategy.)

4.   **Allow the class 20 minutes to fill out the map, study the *Victim Cards*, and write down all common characteristics.**

5.   **Ask if any group has located the source of the epidemic.** Without telling the groups whether they are right or wrong, ask how they arrived at their conclusions.

6.   **One at a time, have different students read the *Clue Cards* aloud.** The cards reveal additional information uncovered by Dr. Snow. As more information is given, students will either confirm or revise their conclusions.

▼ Wrap Up and Action

Have students discuss how water from the pump became contaminated. Tell them that the disease broke out in India prior to the London epidemic. Point out that since ships travel to many countries, they often transport diseases.

Discuss with students why most North Americans need not worry about becoming infected with cholera. Some students who have traveled abroad may have received a cholera vaccination. Why was this necessary?

Have students research how pathogens are prevented from entering their water supplies. Students can make a poster of water diseases that have occurred in their community and how people can avoid contracting them.

Assessment
Have students:
- use investigative skills to trace the source of a waterborne disease (steps 4, 5, and 6).

Notes ▼

Extensions
Students can research recent outbreaks of waterborne epidemics in the United States (e.g., Alabama–1991; Milwaukee–1993).

Have students study their community's water resources. Obtain a map of the water system. Visit a water treatment plant. Talk with community water managers and determine the methods and frequency of water testing. How would water suppliers and health department officials manage outbreaks of disease?

By visiting local museums and reading old diaries and newspapers, students may research the history of waterborne diseases and epidemics in their community, region, and/or state. A host of other diseases depend on water-breeding insects to survive. These include malaria, yellow fever, dengue fever, and encephalitis. Malaria alone infects 800 million people annually and over 1 million die each year.

Have students research diseases that directly result from water scarcity—trachoma, leprosy, conjunctivitis, and scabies. Cholera, typhus, infectious hepatitis, diarrhea, and dysentery occur because of poor water quality. Diarrhea and dysentery kill tens of thousands of children around the world each year.

Resources
Balows, Albert, and William J. Hausler, et al. 1991. *Manual of Clinical Microbiology*, 5th ed. Washington, D.C.: American Society for Microbiology.

Baron, Finegold, and Peterson. 1994. *Diagnostic Microbiology*, 9th ed. St. Louis, Mo.: Mosby Publishing Co.

Howard, Barbara J., ed. 1994. *Clinical and Pathogenic Microbiology*, 2nd ed. St. Louis, Mo.: Mosby Publishing Co.

Snow, John, M.D. 1965. *Snow on Cholera*, New York, N.Y.: Hafner Publishing Co.

Broad Street Area Map

Name: _____ Date: _____

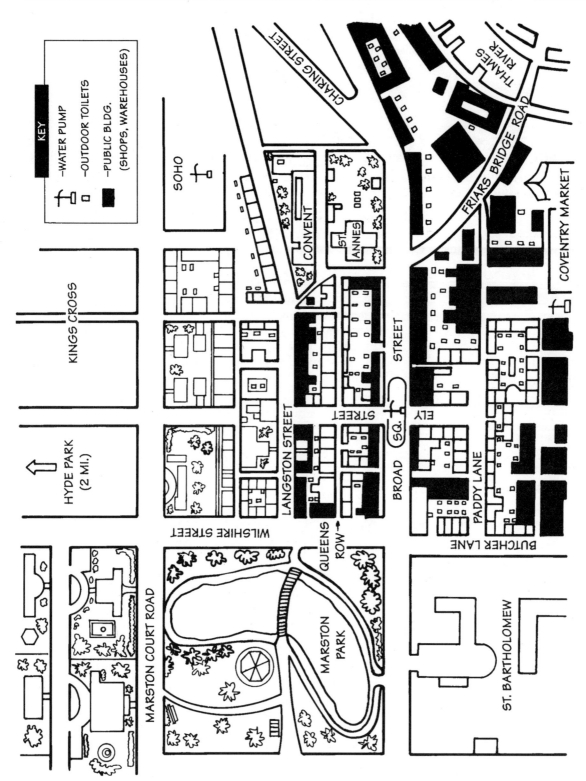

Victim Cards

THOMAS SUTTERFIELD, ESQUIRE, lawyer:
- Lives in Hyde Park with wife and two children.
- Only member of his immediate family to contract cholera.
- Won most recent case, defending a Broad Street butcher accused of selling spoiled meat.
- Recovering.

MATILDA WRIGHT, wealthy 90-year-old spinster:
- Lived alone (with her three servants) in the family mansion in Marston Court.
- Great-aunt of Thomas Sutterfield.
- Only member of the household to contract cholera.
- Died in a matter of hours.

TOLLY MARTIN, 10 years old, professional pick-pocket:
- Homeless orphan who slept in doorways around Soho Square.
- Occasionally roamed quite far from Soho, looking for wealthier citizens to rob.
- Died of cholera two days after a fist fight with another boy at Broad Street Square.

OWEN AND OBEDIENCE TURNER and their three children:
- Lived on Paddy Lane behind butcher shop on Broad Street.
- Owen Turner, who was lame, earned small change cleaning up the day's slops at the butcher shop.
- Entire family died of cholera.

Nine families on Butcher Lane:
37 individuals dead; 8 recovering

Twelve families on Ely Street:
60 individuals dead; 10 recovering

SLYE CHILDREN, ages 7, 8, and 10:
- Three of the eight children of Gideon and Lucy Slye.
- Gideon Slye is a Broad Street butcher accused of selling spoiled meat.
- Slye family recently moved to Kings Cross from Broad Street and now have indoor plumbing.
- When not in school, three of the Slye children often accompanied their father to work and played on Broad Street Square.
- These three are the only family members to contract cholera.
- Two died; one recovering.

MUCKY JOHNSON, 18, delivery boy from Coventry Circle:
- Delivered fresh seafood from Coventry Market to wealthy homes in Marston Court.
- Often stopped to eat lunch and talk to people on Broad Street Square; said the water from the Broad Street pump was the best in the city.
- Died of cholera.

JOHN AND MARY CANTY, tinkers from Soho:
- Pulled their cart through wealthy neighborhoods, mending pots and pans for the well-to-do.
- Often stopped to visit John's ailing mother who lived on Butcher Lane.
- Both died of cholera.

Twenty-five families on Queens Row:
89 individuals dead; 31 recovering

Eighteen families on Paddy Lane:
83 individuals dead; 7 recovering

Clue Cards

1. The people living around Broad Street are poor. Large families are crowded into one- and two-room apartments. None has indoor plumbing; residents use outdoor toilets and haul their water from the nearest public pump.

4. Matilda Wright refused to drink water from the faucets in her home. She would only drink the sweet-tasting water that her gardener hauled from the Broad Street pump.

2. Thomas Sutterfield fell ill two hours after stopping off to visit his great-aunt "Tilda." He had tea, biscuits, and sausages with his great-aunt. It was a hot day and he took a drink of cool water before leaving.

5. Ausley and Marthy Brown and their two children are the only people on Ely Street who haven't gotten cholera. Marthy's family lives in Soho. The Browns haul their water from the Soho pump, which allows them to visit their relatives.

3. Following his fight with another boy, Tolly Martin washed the blood off his mouth at the Broad Street pump and ran off with a sausage stolen from the butcher shop.

Salt Marsh Players

How would you react if, a part of each day, your home was covered with water?

▼ Summary

Students role-play how organisms adapt to life in a salt marsh—a coastal, marine habitat that is alternately flooded and drained by tides.

■ **Grade Level:**
Upper Elementary

■ **Subject Areas:**
Ecology, Fine Arts, Language Arts

■ **Duration:**
Preparation time: 50 minutes
Activity time: 50 minutes

■ **Setting:** Large classroom

■ **Skills:**
Analyzing (identifying components and relationships); Interpreting (identifying cause and effect); Applying (designing); Presenting

■ **Charting the Course**
How plants and animals adapt to wet and dry environments is presented in "Water Address." Other wetland ecosystems are explored in "Life in the Fast Lane," and "People of the Bog."

■ **Vocabulary**
adaptation, salt marsh, habitat

Objectives

Students will:
• demonstrate how various salt marsh plants and animals adapt to environmental conditions.
• recognize various plants and animals that live in salt marshes

Materials

• *Photos, slides or a video of salt marshes and organisms that live in the salt marsh (optional)*
• *Copies of **The Salt Marsh Players Character Cards** (make duplicates for larger classes)*
• *4"x 6" (10 x 15 cm) index cards*
• *Glue*
• *Scissors*
• *String*
• *2 cardboard tubes (paper towel)*
• *Blue cloth, or a piece of blue ribbon approximately 12 feet (4 m) long and 1 foot (30 cm) wide (use the paper towel tubes to roll the cloth like a scroll)*
• *Soap bubble bottle and bubble maker*

Making Connections

People see, hear of, and read about salt marshes and other wetlands in the media. Some students may have visited coastlines where salt marshes exist. Students may also have learned how certain species adapt to various conditions. By physically enacting behavioral strategies of salt marsh organisms encountering high and low tides, students are introduced to the complex and interrelated world of animal and plant adaptations.

Background

Salt marshes are grassy wetland habitats that occur within temperate estuarine environments. In the United States, marshes exist on the Atlantic and Pacific coasts and the shores of the Gulf of Mexico. They are part of the intertidal zone (the area between high and low tide) and are flooded once or twice a day by incoming tides.

The dominant plants of a salt marsh include grasses and algae. These plants seasonally die and regenerate, adding tremendous amounts of detritus (decaying organic matter) to the food chain. Scavengers and bacteria break down the detritus into nutrients and minerals. These provide the nutritional foundation for a complex food web, including fish, crabs, shellfish, and larger animals.

The pulsing action of tides delivers and distributes nutrients that plants and animals can consume. The comings and goings of tides also pose great challenges to salt marsh life. Regularly, a salt marsh is flooded with salt water during high tide. When the tide recedes, the land becomes exposed, and fresh water runoff often flows through the marsh. Not only are organisms exposed to varying degrees of moisture but also changes in salinity and temperature.

This produces an obvious distribution of plants and animals that are adapted to specific conditions within the marsh. This situation is called zonation and is often described as:

High Marsh—covered briefly each day by the tides, and

Salt marsh on the coast of Maine. SUSAN HIGGINS

Low Marsh—beneath the level of the tide for many hours each day.

The area which is never exposed to the air is called the subtidal zone. Both the high marsh and low marsh comprise the intertidal zone.

This altering environment requires residents to adapt, both physiologically and behaviorally. Changes in physiology, like marsh plants' ability to excrete salt, have evolved over long periods of time. Behavioral responses, like crabs burrowing into the mud at low tide, allow animals to adapt quickly to changes in the environment.

Some salt marsh species, like marsh snails, move away from incoming water. Others retreat into underwater burrows and remain inactive during high tides. Still others adjust their activities to suit the varying degrees of salinity or temperature. Salt marsh residents may have to adapt to both aquatic and terrestrial conditions within the same day!

Procedure
▼ *Warm Up*
Ask students to list human behavioral responses to environmental change. What do we do in response to heat or cold? How do we prepare for a flood, cope with lack of food, or respond to physical pain?

Have the class brainstorm some obvious behavioral adaptations of common animals to the environment (pet dogs begging for scraps from the table, cattle seeking shade, birds migrating away from winter conditions).

Describe, display pictures of, or show a video of salt marshes and the organisms that reside there. Have students list some basic characteristics of the salt marsh and some plants and animals they think may live there. Explain that the marsh is flooded by the tide each day. Have students list ways they think plants and animals adapt to life in the salt marsh.

▼ *The Activity*
1.   **Hand each student a *Salt Marsh Player Character Card* and *Salt Marsh Player Picture*, string, and a large index card. Provide tape, glue, and scissors. Ask students to read the cards. Have them glue the pictures to one side the index cards and the descriptions to the other, punch two holes, and thread the**

string so that the cards can be worn around the neck.

2. Designate a section of the classroom, at least 12 feet (4 m) x 15 feet (5 m). One end of the area will be a body of water (subtidal zone); and the other end is upland. The marsh is located between the two. Low marsh lies near the subtidal zone and high marsh near the upland.

3. Ask the water characters to unroll the scroll of water and take their places at low tide (see diagram). Tell them to read their cards aloud and to make gentle wave motions with the fabric.

4. Ask, "What makes waves?" Have student holding the wind card read about making waves, then make blowing sounds, dancing around while the waves move.

5. Taking turns, all the plants should read their *Salt Marsh Players Character Cards* and move into the appropriate area of the marsh. Each animal character does the same. Fish and blue crab live in the water, moving forward and back with the tides. The rest of the animals should take their low tide positions.

6. When all are in place, tell the wind to blow again. Ask, "What makes the tides move in and out?"

Sun and moon should read their *Salt Marsh Players Character Cards,* then stand on chairs making circles above their heads with their arms, indicating a full moon and bright sun.

7. Have the oxygen character enter the water and read his or her *Salt Marsh Player Character Card* aloud. Tell students that wind churning the water helps mix oxygen into the water. Have the oxygen character blow soap bubbles while the wind howls.

8. Tell the characters to get ready to perform together. Remind students to notice what the other

THE SALT MARSH "STAGE"

Shown at low tide; arrows show movement as tide rises

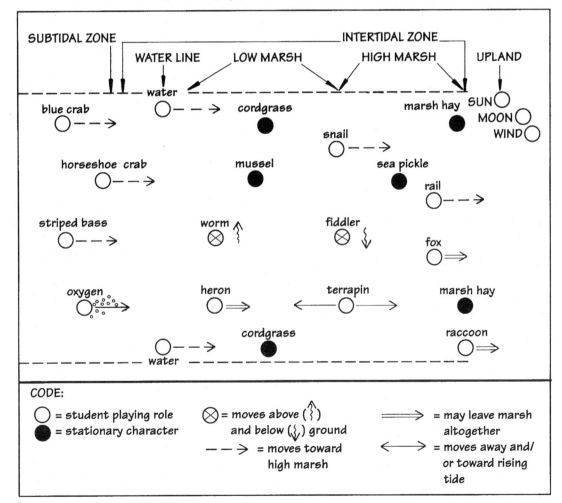

characters are doing. Announce that the sun and moon are high in the sky, the wind begins to blow, the waves start moving gently, and plants sway.

9. After several minutes, say, "The tide is rising!" The water characters should walk very slowly toward the high marsh, with fish, crab, and oxygen following behind. Remind plants that since they are rooted in the ground, they must stand in place but should bend and sway in response to wind and water movement; plants should duck below the scroll of water as it passes. Animals should adopt high tide behavior (as described on their *Salt Marsh Players Character Cards*).

10. As the water reaches its high mark (just past the high marsh), announce that "It is high tide!" Ask the characters to explain their behavior briefly. Now reverse the sequence and have the water retreat back to low tide while players adjust their behaviors. The performance may be videotaped.

▼ Wrap Up and Action

Have students write character sketches and locate materials from home to create costumes to dramatize the hardships and rewards of their existence. They may wish to do additional research. They should include ways that plants and animals adapt to the changing tides. They may be interested in learning how people adjust who live in tidal or storm-prone areas (houses on stilts, boats instead of cars, etc.).

Students may wish to choreograph a modern dance interpretation with their salt marsh players. This may be performed for school and community members.

Assessment

Have students:
- identify various plants and animals that live in salt marshes (*Warm Up*)
- enact the behavioral responses of salt marsh characters to tides (steps 3–10).
- describe how various salt marsh plants and animals adapt to environmental conditions (step 10 and *Wrap Up*).
- write a sketch of a salt marsh player (*Wrap Up*).
- design a costume to characterize a salt marsh player (*Wrap Up*).

Extensions

Take a field trip to or show a video of a salt marsh and have students look for plants and animals from the play.

Classes might study other environments (rain forest, desert, tundra, etc.) and pinpoint the adaptations of plants and animals who live there. A class can develop a similar game for the residents of another environment, using seasonal change as the environmental factor, for example.

Resources

Environmental Concern Inc., The Watercourse, and Project WET. 1995. *WOW!: The Wonders Of Wetlands.* Published through a partnership between Environmental Concern Inc., St. Michaels, Md. and The Watercourse, Bozeman, Mont.

Mitchell, John G. 1992. "Our Disappearing Wetlands." *National Geographic*, 182 (4).

Mitsch, William J., and James G. Gosselink. 1993. *Wetlands,* 2nd ed. New York, N.Y.: Van Nostrand Reinhold.

Niering, William A. 1985. *Wetlands.* The Audubon Society Nature Guides. New York, N.Y.: Alfred A. Knopf.

Notes ▼

ADAPTED WITH PERMISSION FROM "THE SALTMARSH PLAYERS," PAGES 65-67. *WOW!: THE WONDERS OF WETLANDS,* © 1991 BY ENVIRONMENTAL CONCERN INC., P.O. BOX P, ST. MICHAELS, MD

The Salt Marsh Players Character Cards

NOTE: These characters represent the mid-Atlantic coast of the United States—species are different for other areas.

RED FOX — (*Vulpes vulpes*)

I am a mammal who does not live in the salt marsh, but I do come here to hunt for rabbits, rodents, small marsh birds and eggs, and invertebrates. As the tide rises, I leave the marsh. I usually hunt in drier areas in winter.

CORDGRASS* — (*Spartina alterniflora*)

I grow in the low marsh where the ground gets flooded by water for long periods of time each day. During the highest tides (spring tides), I might be completely underwater! Since I am a rooted plant, I can't move about except to sway with the breeze. I must tolerate sea water.

RACCOON — (*Procyon lotor*)

Though I do not live in the salt marsh, I do come here to hunt for dragonflies, crabs, oysters, clams, fish, and other good bits of food. I am not fond of swimming, so when the tide rises, I leave the marsh for higher ground.

"SEA PICKLE" (saltwort)* — (*Salicornia virginica*)

I am a rather stiff, plump little plant that "crouches" down in the lower end of the high marsh, where I am alternately covered with water and exposed. I absorb a lot of salt water, which gives me my fleshy appearance. Considered a delicacy, sea pickles make a crunchy, salty addition to salads!

MOON

I am the moon and I am the major force driving the tide! I create a gravitational pull as I rotate around the earth. This causes the water to "pile up," making a high tide, or to pull away from shore, causing a low tide. I am about 70 percent responsible for the changing tide. (You will stand on a chair and make a big circle above your head with your arms and "shine" over the marsh.)

SALT MEADOW (salt marsh) **HAY** * — (*Spartina patens*)

I am a grass, often called "marsh hay" because at one time I was harvested and fed to cattle. I grow in the high marsh where I get flooded for a few hours each day. When the wind blows, my neighbors and I sway softly, looking as though we were painted in watercolors. At low tide, we lie in swirly cowlicks, with roots still in the mud.

SUN

I am the sun and I help to drive the tide! The sun's gravitational pull occurs as the Earth rotates daily on its axis. This causes the water to "pile up," making a high tide, and then later to pull away from shore, causing a low tide. I am about 30 percent responsible for the changing tide. (You will stand on a chair and make a big circle above your head with your arms and "shine" over the marsh.)

WATER — (H_2O, salty)

I am water and I am the tide! When it is time for the tide to rise, I move slowly into the low marsh, then up into the high marsh. At the high tide point, I stop and rest a minute, then turn in place and move slowly "out to sea." (You will need a partner to help you make and move the strip of "water.")

GREAT BLUE HERON — (*Ardea herodias*)

I am a large, beautiful bird that wades gracefully in the shallow water, hunting for food. With my long neck and long, pointed bill I snatch fish, crabs, water insects, and even small mammals out of the water. As the tide comes in, I move to higher parts of the marsh to stay in shallow water. Sometimes I just fly away.

OXYGEN — (O_2, what a gas!)

Water must contain oxygen to support all the living things that live in it! As the tide moves in and out, I move along just behind the water line, showering all things I encounter with bubbles! Bubbles are made by carbon dioxide gas (which contains O_2) that animals exhale, or by the oxygen given off by underwater plants.

*(Make two copies of each plant)

STRIPED BASS ("rockfish") — (*Morone saxatilis*)

Like many kinds of fish, I use the marsh as a nursery area, a protected place to raise my young (called "fry" or "fingerlings" at different stages). My tiny offspring dart in and out of the marsh plants as they move with the tides. (Remember, fish filter oxygen from water with gills!) These hungry youngsters find lots of food here.

(make two copies of water card)

WIND

I help the sun and moon to drive the tide in and out. If I blow very hard, I can force the water to come in or go out farther than usual. I also add oxygen to the water, which helps to make the water healthy and keeps plants and animals alive. Sometimes I can be very noisy as I sweep across the marsh!

DIAMONDBACK TERRAPIN — (*Malaclemys terrapin terrapin*)

I am the only turtle that lives year-round in salty wetlands. I must breathe air, but I am really not affected much by tide, since I can swim to the surface and poke my head or nose out for a breath. I like to eat snails, crabs, worms, insects, and fish, so I go where the food is!

FIDDLER CRAB — (*Uca pugnax*)

I run about the marsh at low tide, searching for bits of dead plants and animals to eat, which I shove into my mouth with my one large and one small claw (females have two small claws). I am an air breather, so when the tide comes in, I plop down into my mud burrow and shut the "door" (a mud ball) so I don't drown!

SEA WORM (clam worm) — (*Nereis succinea*)

I am a colorful worm who burrows in the mud in the subtidal zone or in the low marsh, where I build a tube out of sand. When the tide is high and my tube is underwater, I look for food, such as the soft insides of clams, dead fish, or other small water animals. When the tide is low, I stay deep inside my tube.

HORSESHOE CRAB — (*Limulus polyphemus*)

I'm really not a true crab at all! Some think I am an odd, primitive creature. I stay at sea until a full moon in May, when it is time to lay eggs. Female crabs, with the smaller males in tow, swim ashore with the incoming tide, crawl onto the sand above the tide line, burrow, lay thousands of tiny eggs, then catch an outgoing tide a few days later.

CLAPPER RAIL — (*Rallus longirostris*)

I am an elusive, hen-like bird, often called the "marsh hen" because I live and nest in salt marshes. At low tide, I forage and probe my long bill into the mud, looking for fiddler crabs, worms and other small creatures, and seeds. High tide limits my territory to the high marsh, but here I can still eat snails that climb up grasses to escape the water.

BLUE CRAB — (*Callinectes sapidus*)

I am the tasty blue crab who comes into the marsh with the tide. Here, I find lots of oysters, fish, and many other creatures to eat. Since I breathe with gills, I must swim out of the marsh with the retreating tide. When I am "soft" (I shed my shell to grow), the marsh is a great place to hide from predators!

RIBBED MUSSEL — (*Geukensia demissa*)

I am a bivalve, a two-shelled animal, like a clam. I live in mud in the low marsh, but half of me sticks above the mud. I can't move about. At high tide I open my shell a bit, take in water, and strain out oxygen and tiny plants and animals to eat. At low tide I close up tightly to hold moisture in my gills for breathing until next high tide.

SALT MARSH SNAIL — (*Melampus bidentatus*)

I prefer to live in the high marsh, since I am an air breather and don't like to be too wet. During low tide, I glide around the mud flats looking for algae and bits of dead plants to eat. As the tide comes in, I crawl up the stems and leaves of grasses to keep from drowning!

Super Sleuths

■ Grade Level:
Middle School, High School

■ Subject Areas:
Health, Life Science, Geography

■ Duration:
Preparation time: 50 minutes
Activity time: 50 minutes

■ Setting: Classroom

■ Skills:
Organizing (matching, recording); Analyzing (inferring, determining cause and effect); Interpreting (drawing conclusions)

■ Charting the Course
A similar sleuthing activity is presented in "The Poison Pump," in which students identify the source of a cholera epidemic. "No Bellyachers" addresses how waterborne diseases spread and can be prevented. This activity can serve as an ice breaker. When two people who have the same disease meet, the facilitator provides them with the disease and its description.

■ Vocabulary
waterborne disease, epidemiologist, pathogen, bacterium, protozoan, virus, water treatment

If you like mystery and intrigue, this activity is for you.

▼ Summary
Students learn about the diversity of waterborne illnesses and the role of epidemiology in disease control by searching for others who have been "infected" with the same water-borne illness as they have.

Objectives
Students will:
- identify the role of water in transmitting diseases.
- compare symptoms of several waterborne diseases.
- analyze the characteristics of environments that promote the transmission of these diseases around the world.

Materials
- *Symptoms of diseases* (Make at least 2 copies of the **Symptom Cards** pages; cut and put them into separate envelopes, one disease per envelope. Make sure the order of **Symptom Cards** is different for envelopes containing the same disease. If more than 24 students in class, make extra sets. See illustration, page 110.)
- *Copies of **Disease Descriptions***
- *Pencils and note pads* (optional)
- *World map*
- *Newspapers/magazines*

Making Connections
Students may remember news stories about contaminated water causing disease or recall camping when they purified lake or stream water by boiling it. Some students may know that waterborne diseases are the number one killer of children worldwide. Learning about all the diseases that could be contracted through contaminated water helps students gain an appreciation for clean drinking water.

Background
Waterborne diseases are those acquired through the ingestion of contaminated water. About 80 percent of all diseases are water-related. In many of these illnesses, water infiltrated with sewage spreads the disease. An infected person or animal may pass pathogenic bacteria, viruses, or protozoa through waste into the water supply.

The microorganisms that cause illness cannot be seen, smelled, or tasted; contaminated water often appears fresh and clear. This causes particular concern with municipal water supplies. Contamination may not be detected until a noticeable number of people have become ill.

Most ailments caused by ingestion of water infiltrated with sewage are intestinal, causing gas, cramping, and diarrhea. Some pathogens (harmful microorganisms) attach to intestinal linings and produce toxic materials which the body then tries to purge. Others invade intestinal epithelial cells and cause inflammation but do not produce toxins. Fluids containing disease-fighting white blood cells are secreted into the intestine to aid in attacking or flushing the harmful organisms from the body. Unfortunately, this loss of fluids also causes dehydration, the major concern in patients with these types of diseases.

If the patient is very young, elderly, or malnourished, dehydration can be life-threatening. Children with diarrhea must be closely monitored. They have not developed the immunities of adults, and their systems can be quickly overwhelmed by the sheer number of pathogens. As many as one-third of pediatric deaths in developing countries are attributed to diarrhea and the resulting dehydration. Africa, Asia, and Latin America experience an estimated 3-5 billion cases of diarrhea, with 5-10 million deaths, each year. *Vibrio cholerae, Salmonella* sp., and *Shigella* species of bacteria are among the leading causes of bacterial diarrhea.

Bacteria are everywhere, including in our water. However, water supplies are monitored to prevent contamination by fecal pathogens in concentrations that will produce infections in humans. Water treatment facilities routinely test for these pathogens by checking levels of indicator bacteria, such as *Escherichia coli* (a common organism in our intestines). If these organisms rise above a set level, fecal contamination has occurred and more intensive water testing should begin. This does not mean other pathogens are present, but serves as an "indicator" that they may be. It may be necessary to accelerate water treatment procedures. Also, the source of contamination must be located and protective measures taken to avoid further contamination.

Until recently, Americans have regularly suffered through epidemics of waterborne illness such as cholera and typhoid fever. Improvements in wastewater disposal practices and the development, protection, and treatment of water supplies have significantly reduced the incidence of these diseases. The treatment and chlorinating of municipal water have made infection by microorganisms rare in developed countries; however, in many developing countries treatment of wastewater is minimal or nonexistent. In some cases, sewage and other wastes are dumped directly into rivers that are used by people downstream for drinking and washing.

Epidemiologists study the incidence, transmission, distribution, and control of disease. When outbreaks of a particular disease occur, epidemiologists research symptoms, incidence, and distribution of the cases; they try to determine the cause of the disease, its means of spreading, and possible methods for controlling or preventing the illness. With waterborne diseases, determining how the water supply was contaminated is critical to solving the problem. The case histories of affected patients and any associations among patients help epidemiologists solve the mysteries of disease.

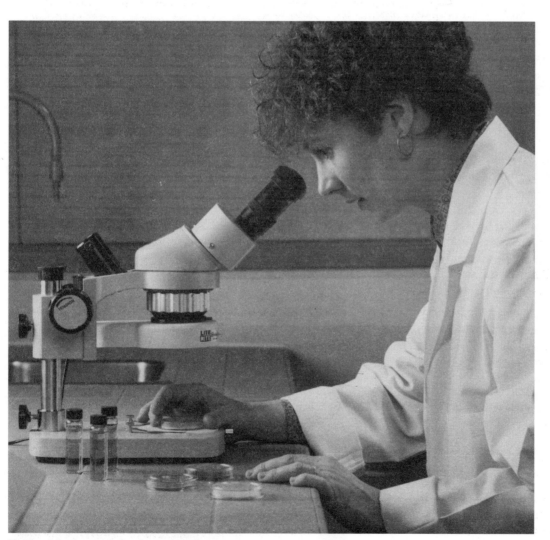

Epidemiologist studying bacteria cultures. COURTESY: HACH COMPANY

Procedure

▼ Warm Up

Ask students if they can identify the world's number one killer. Explain that thousands of children die each year from diarrhea. Tell students that diarrhea is caused by microorganisms such as bacteria, viruses, and protozoa. What do students think is the source of these organisms?

Show students two glasses of water: one murky due to sediment, the other clear—but possibly containing pathogens. Ask them, "Which glass of water would you prefer to drink?" Make the point that disease-causing organisms can be found in clear, "clean-looking" water.

▼ The Activity

1.   **Tell students that, like epidemiologists, they are going to compare symptoms and mode of transmission of diseases that they and a few others in the class have "acquired."**

2.   **Hand out the symptom envelopes and** *Disease Descriptions,* **one to each student.** Students will consider symptoms, who was infected, and the site of infection, attempting to find others in the class who have the same illness. Many students in the class will have similar symptoms, but only a few will have the same disease.

3.   **Direct students to select one card or clue randomly from the envelope. Have them circulate throughout the room and ask others about their symptoms. Their goal is to locate other students who have similar symptoms.** Students may take notes or this may be a memory exercise. Students can have fun acting out certain symptoms.

4.   **After one or two minutes, tell students to remove a second symptom card from their envelopes. They** **should continue to search for others with the same illness.** Continue this process until all clues have been removed from the envelopes and everyone has found at least one other person sharing the same waterborne disease.

▼ Wrap Up and Action

Reading their list of symptoms to the class and reviewing *Disease Descriptions,* students should identify their illnesses. Have them infer how they contracted the disease, how the disease was transmitted, and how it can be prevented. Discuss the control cards; these cards describe conditions that are not related to waterborne diseases. (For example, the person was tired in the late afternoon because he or she worked long days, and the pain and rattling in the chest were likely caused by smoking.)

Students may conduct research to confirm their answers and to investigate where these diseases occur throughout the United States and the rest of the world. They can plot their diseases on a world map and discuss conditions that might allow for the spread of these diseases (e.g., inadequate water treatment systems, concentrated population, political upheaval that forces large migrations of people suffering from lack of food and water, the presence of disease-spreading organisms such as beavers or snails).

Discuss the role of water in the transmission of disease. Emphasize that most waterborne diseases result from inadequate water treatment and poor sanitation practices. However, contamination occasionally occurs despite sound water treatment practices. An outbreak of illness in Milwaukee was caused by contamination of the city's drinking water with *Cryptosporidium* sp. This outbreak was particularly disturbing because modern filtration systems were not effective; that is, the organism was so small it passed through the filters. Discuss cases of hikers and travelers becoming ill after consuming water they thought safe. Stories or films may be available on these subjects. Discuss how the cause and transmission of disease are studied by epidemiologists.

Assessment

Have students:

*   describe the symptoms of several waterborne diseases (step 3 and *Wrap Up*).
*   relate how some waterborne diseases are transmitted (*Wrap Up*).
*   analyze conditions that promote the spread of waterborne diseases (*Wrap Up*).
*   research the occurrence of diseases and plot their locations on a world map (*Wrap Up*).

Extensions

Some chemical contaminants that cause illness can also be transmitted by water. Read the following case study to students.

Pete Smith is a 40-year-old carpenter. Pete does not smoke. For three months he has been complaining of numbness and tingling in his toes and fingertips. Within the last two weeks the tingling has become a burning pain, and he is experiencing weakness in his hands when attempting to grip tools. He is generally in good health, but about four months ago he experienced three to four days of fever, cough, diarrhea, and muscular pain.

When he was examined, a doctor discovered that Pete had dark-colored skin lesions and that his skin had thickened in areas. The palms of his hands and soles of his feet had cornlike elevations. He was also found to be anemic (depleted of red blood cells, causing paleness, weakness, and breathlessness).

For ten years Pete has lived in the same house in an agricultural area, and his water comes from a well. He has been married for one year. His wife does not share his symptoms.

Ask students to speculate if Pete's illness is a waterborne disease. Have them cite reasons for their answers.

After a physician conducted numerous tests and studied Pete's family health history, Pete was found to be suffering from chronic arsenic poisoning. When Pete's well water was tested, it was found to contain high levels of arsenic. Arsenic can enter water from natural sources (such as arsenic-containing bedrock) or from arsenical pesticide runoff. (Pete's wife did not get ill because she had only lived in the area for one year, and frequently drank juice and other liquids instead of well water.)

Students may wish to research other illnesses associated with chemical contaminants and create clue cards. Another example is infantile methemoglobinemia, a.k.a. blue baby disease, which is caused by high levels of nitrates in water.

Resources

Craun, Gunther. 1986. *Waterborne Diseases in the United States.* Boca Raton, Fla.: CRC Press.

Craun, Gunther. 1990. *Waterborne Disease Outbreaks: Selected Reprints of Articles on Epidemiology, Surveillance, Investigation, and Laboratory Analysis.* Cincinnati, Ohio: Health Effects Research Laboratory, Office of Research and Development, U.S. Environmental Protection Agency.

Kroehler, Carolyn. 1990. *What Do the Standards Mean: A Citizens' Guide to Drinking Water Contaminants.* Blacksburg, Va.: Virginia Water Resources Research Center.

Rouech, Berton. 1953. *Eleven Blue Men and Other Narratives of Medical Detection.* Boston, Mass.: Little Brown.

U.S. Department of Health and Human Services. Agency for Toxic Substances and Disease Registry. 1990. *Arsenic Toxicity* (June).

Zinsser, Hans, Wolfgang Joklik et al., eds. 1992. *Microbiology.* Norwalk, Conn.: Appleton & Lange.

For information about occurrences of specific diseases within the United States and around the world, students can contact the Center for Disease Control, 1600 Clifton Road NE, Atlanta, GA 30333. (404) 639-3311.

INSTRUCTIONS FOR PREPARING SYMPTOM CARDS

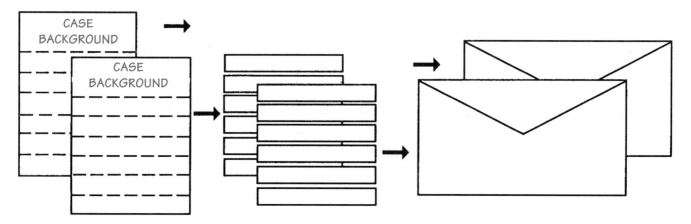

Make two photocopies of each case background card (more for larger classes).

Cut each set of cards into strips along the dotted lines.

Put each set of case background strips into separate envelopes (exclude name of the disease) and hand out to students. (Be sure the case background strips are mixed up within the envelope.)

Common Waterborne Diseases and Symptom Cards

Typhoid fever, caused by *Salmonella typhi* bacteria.

Case background:

> Symptoms occurred ten days after attending a family camp

> Discovered that camp's sewage system was faulty and chlorinator was not functioning

> Family reunion used same camp the previous week; two people attended who had recently recovered from typhoid fever.

> Began feeling lethargic with general aches and pains

> Malaise — general weakness and discomfort, and anorexia — loss of appetite

> Developed high fever, became delirious

> Tender abdomen with rose-colored spots on skin

Legionnaire's disease, caused by *Legionella pnuemophilia* bacteria.

Case background:

> Chain smoker living in warm climate

> Lives in a home that is constantly air conditioned during summer months

> Sudden onset of fever that progressed to a high fever with shaking chills

> Developed a cough and excessively rapid breathing

> Pain in chest; lungs have rattling sound when breathing

> General, diffuse muscular pain and tenderness

> Intense headache and mental confusion

Cholera, caused by *Vibrio cholerae* bacteria.

Case background:

> Recently returned from Bangladesh

> Symptoms occurred two days after eating fruit thoroughly washed at outdoor pump

> Family members have begun coming down with the same symptoms

> Severe dehydration

> Painless diarrhea, vomiting

> Severe muscular cramps in arms, legs, hands, and feet

> Eyes and cheeks appear sunken; hands have dish-washing appearance

Amebiasis, caused by *Entamoeba histolytica*, a protozoan.

Case background:

- Returned from Thailand two weeks ago
- Drank unbottled water
- Feverish
- General abdominal discomfort and tenderness, especially on lower right side
- Dysentery
- Tires easily, mental dullness
- Moderate weight loss

Enterotoxigenic *E. coli* gastroenteritis, caused by *E. coli bacteria*.

Case background:

- Just returned from visiting friends in Mexico
- Symptoms began 12 hours after drinking several swallows of water from a bucket pulled from a well
- Experiencing dehydration caused by diarrhea
- General, diffuse muscular pain and tenderness
- Low-grade fever
- Nausea, vomiting
- Abdominal cramps

Giardiasis, caused by the *Giardia lamblia* protozoan.

Case background:

- Symptoms occurred two weeks after backpacking trip
- Filled water bottle with clear, fresh-tasting water from a stream below a beaver dam
- Abdominal cramps
- Intermittent dysentery (which is greasy and odorous)
- Excessive intestinal gas
- Malaise — general weakness and discomfort
- Weight loss

Salmonellosis, caused by species of *Salmonella* bacteria.

Case background:

Lives on a ranch that raises cattle and chickens

Symptoms occurred 10 hours after drinking from pump outside of barn (ground water may have been contaminated by surface water in the pasture after heavy rain)

Malaise — general weakness and discomfort

Fever

Dysentery

Abdominal cramps

Nausea and vomiting

Shigellosis, caused by species of *Shigella* bacteria.

Case background:

Four years old

Symptoms began 15 hours after bobbing for apples in pre-school class

Severe abdominal cramps

Frequent, painful dysentery

Blood and mucus in stool

High fever, chills

Dehydration

Hepatitis A. caused by *Hepatitis A* virus.

Case background:

Visited favorite beach and swam with friends

Malaise — general weakness and discomfort

Anorexia — loss of appetite

Fever

Nausea, mild diarrhea

Jaundice — yellowing of skin and whites of eyes

Sick for a week

Control Card. (Individual has no waterborne illness.)

Case background:

> Lives in an apartment in the city

> Chain smoker living in a warm climate

> Drinks tap water

> Pain in chest; lungs have rattling sound when breathing

> Visited favorite beach and swam with friends

> Recently visited an alligator farm

> Eats lots of fresh seafood

Cryptosporidiosis, caused by *Cryptosporidium*.

Case background:

> Four years old

> Attends a daycare center five days a week

> Diarrhea

> Nausea and vomiting

> Fever

> Sucks thumb

> Recently swam in a local pond

Control Card. (Individual has no waterborne illness.)

Case background:

> Lives on a ranch that raises cattle and chickens

> Just returned from visiting friends in Mexico

> Lives in a home that is constantly air conditioned during summer months

> Is tired in the late afternoon

> Often conducts pack trips in the mountains

> Works 14 hours a day, usually seven days a week

> Drinks eight glasses of water per day

Disease Descriptions

Typhoid fever, caused by *Salmonella typhi* bacteria.

(Now uncommon in the U.S., this is usually acquired during foreign travel. During the first half of this century it was the most commonly reported cause of waterborne disease in the U.S. It can be acquired by contact with contaminated water, swimming, etc. In 1907, Mary Mallon, nicknamed "Typhoid Mary," was identified as a carrier of the disease. She transmitted the disease while working as a cook in restaurants and private homes in New York City. She escaped authorities for eight years, but was finally apprehended in 1915. She infected some 50 people, with three cases resulting in death. In 1973 a major outbreak of typhoid fever affected 225 people in a migrant labor camp in Dade County, Florida. The well that supplied water to the camp was contaminated by surface water.)

Legionnaire's disease, caused by *Legionella pnuemophilia* bacteria.

(Found naturally in water environments; bacteria often colonize artificial water systems such as air conditioners and hot water heaters, and can be inhaled with aerosols produced by such systems. Smoking and lung disease increase susceptibility to disease.)

Cholera, caused by *Vibrio cholerae* bacteria.

(This disease is extremely contagious; if untreated, dehydration can lead to death. Cholera originated in Europe and was spread to the United States by transatlantic liners through New Orleans. It reached California through the forty-niners in their quest for gold. Recent outbreaks of cholera have occurred throughout the United States. Along the Gulf Coast, water and seafood were identified as contributing to the outbreaks. In Louisiana, undercooked crab was the culprit, and in Texas in 1981, people were infected by eating cooked rice that had been washed with contaminated water.)

Amebiasis, caused by *Entamoeba histolytica*, a protozoan.

(This disease usually occurs in tropical areas where crowding and poor sanitation exist. Waterborne outbreaks are now rare in the United States.)

Enterotoxigenic *E. coli* gastroenteritis, caused by *E. coli bacteria*.

(Leading cause of infant morbidity worldwide. Visitors to Latin American countries who partake of the food and water occasionally come down with "traveler's diarrhea," also known as "turista" or "Montezuma's Revenge." A large outbreak of this disease occurred in 1975 in Crater Lake National Park, Oregon. About 2,000 park visitors and about 200 park employees became ill after consuming water that had been contaminated by sewage.)

Giardiasis, caused by the *Giardia lamblia* protozoan.

(Sickness results with only a low dose of the protozoan; it is the most commonly reported causative pathogen of waterborne outbreaks. The giardia protozoan is killed by boiling water for at least five minutes or is removed by passing water through a filter whose pore size is at least 0.2 microns.)

Salmonellosis, caused by species of *Salmonella* bacteria.

(This is carried by humans and many animals; wastes from both can transmit the organism to water or food. The largest waterborne salmonella outbreak reported in the United States was in Riverside, California, in 1965 and affected over 16,000 people.)

Shigellosis, caused by species of *Shigella* bacteria.

(Most infection is seen in children 1-10 years old; a very low dose can cause illness. Waterborne transmission is responsible for a majority of the outbreaks.)

Hepatitis A. caused by *Hepatitis A* virus.

(Third most common cause of waterborne disease in U.S. The term hepatitis relates to inflammation of the liver.)

Cryptosporidiosis, caused by *Cryptosporidium*.

(This was first identified as a cause of diarrhea in people in 1976. It can be transmitted through contact with animals [particularly cattle and sheep], other humans [especially in daycare centers], and contaminated water supplies.)

Thirsty Plants

■ Grade Level:
Middle School

■ Subject Areas:
Life Science, Mathematics

■ Duration:
Preparation time:
Part I: 15 minutes
Part II: 30 minutes

Activity time:
Part I: 20 minutes
Part II: 50 minutes

■ Setting:
Classroom and schoolyard

■ Skills:
Gathering information (collecting, researching); Organizing (estimating, calculating); Analyzing (comparing); Applying (designing)

■ Charting the Course
An understanding of osmosis and diffusion ("Let's Even Things Out"), evaporation ("Water Models"), and adhesion and cohesion ("H₂Olympics") supports this activity. This activity relates to concepts in "Irrigation Interpretation."

■ Vocabulary
capillary action, xylem, stomata, transpiration, evapotranspiration, xeriscaping

What do the plants in your backyard have to do with the water cycle?

▼ Summary

Through demonstration and field studies, students learn about transpiration and the significant role plants play in the water cycle.

Objectives

Students will:
- explain how plants transport water through transpiration.
- describe the importance of plants in the water cycle.
- recognize that certain plants are appropriate for xeriscaping.

Materials

- *Copies of the student activity sheet,* **Water Cycle Diagram**
- *Celery stalks or white carnations*
- *Clear container with water colored with red or blue food coloring* (Place celery or carnation in water for several hours, until leaves or petals are colored with the dye.)
- *Paper towel tube*
- *Paper that is cut into a series of connecting circles* (See diagram; the circles are inserted through the paper towel tube. If possible, the width of the circles should equal the diameter of the tube so that the tube holds the paper in place. An alternative is to thread Popbeads—the kind that lock into each other, used in children's necklaces—through a straw)
- *Clear plastic bag and twist tie for each group*
- *Balance or scale* (optional)
- *Forceps or tweezers*

Making Connections

Most people are familiar with house plants and gardens and basically understand the need for watering plants to ensure successful growth. Students may have observed that plants wilt because of lack of water. How plants take in and transport water throughout their structure may be less understood. Learning how water moves through plants helps students appreciate the role of vegetation in the water cycle.

Background

Plants require water to live. Plants need water to transport nutrients and minerals necessary for plant metabolism and use water in photosynthesis. Since most photosynthesis takes place in the leaves, and the leaves of a plant can be many meters above ground level, how does water from the soil get to these leaves?

Transpiration (evaporation of water from pores, or stomata, on trunk, stem, and leaf surfaces) aids plants to transport water upward through their tissues. Root pressure, the cohesive and adhesive qualities of water (capillary action), and evaporation all contribute to water's circulation through a plant.

Many plants have a vascular system: narrow tubes or vessels that run the length of the plant's body. Like veins and arteries in humans, these tubes in plants carry nutrients and liquids. The vascular tissue through which water travels up a plant is called xylem. Xylem begins in the roots and ends as stomata in the leaves.

Through the process of osmosis (filtering of water into plant cells), water enters the roots and exerts an upward pressure (root pressure), that prevents it from flowing backward down the xylem. The cohesive and adhesive characteristics of water help support its placement in the tubing. Cohesion is water's attraction to itself—i.e., the formation of hydrogen bonds between water molecules. Adhesion is water's attraction to other materials, such as the inside of the tubing. This process, called capillary action, essentially creates a column of water in the xylem. Since the molecules are attached (or bonded) to each other, a tension is created among the molecules in the column.

However, root pressure and capillary action alone are unable to push water many meters above ground level. Evaporation is likely the main process whereby water is pulled up the tubing.

When water molecules reach the stomata, they are exposed to air and the sun's energy. The exposed molecules receive heat energy from the sun and begin to move faster. This motion makes it easier for the molecules to break away and become water vapor. However, because of capillary action, a tension still exists among water molecules in the xylem. Therefore, as one molecule is drawn away, it pulls on water molecules still bonded to it, bringing those molecules closer to the surface.

Plants can absorb large quantities of water; however, they lose most of this water through transpiration. Transpiration coupled with evaporation of surface water is called evapotranspiration. It plays a crucial role in the water cycle. Evapotranspiration returns water to its gaseous state, in which it can be carried by winds through the atmosphere until it condenses and returns to Earth as precipitation. This process helps purify water and move it around the planet.

The rate of transpiration from plants depends on humidity and the nature

COURTESY: EVERGLADES NATIONAL PARK

of the plants. Water evaporates readily in dry, warm air because room is available for more water. Some plants, such as Rocky Mountain juniper, Russian sage, and golden currant, require little water to survive. Frugal water users such as these have smaller leaves, deeper root systems, thick waxy surfaces, and other qualities that limit water

loss. (A method of landscaping, called xeriscaping, entails garden layouts incorporating plants that require little water.) In addition to plant selection, xeriscaping also involves specialized placement of plants, watering techniques, mulching, and monitoring garden drainage patterns. Many communities promote xeriscaping, especially those that experience water shortages.

Procedure
▼ Warm Up
Distribute copies of the *Water Cycle Diagram* student activity sheet. Ask students to share what they know of the water cycle and then draw arrows indicating how water moves through the environment represented in the diagram. Note whether or not they included plants.

Show students the celery that has been soaking in blue- or red-dyed water. Ask them to make a list of possible explanations for how the water traveled through the cutting.

▼ *The Activity*
Part I
1.   **Ask students to consider a 20-foot-tall tree; how do its leaves get water?** Students may think that plants suck water up to the leaves. Do they think they could draw water up a straw that length?

2.   **Show students the paper towel tube with the cut-out circles inserted. See diagram below. Explain that the tube represents part of the tissue inside a plant (xylem), similar to veins inside our bodies. The paper circles represent water molecules.** Explain that in plants,

water molecules remain inside the tube because they are attracted to each other and to the sides of the tube.

3.   **Point out the water molecule near the top of the tube. Explain that this represents a molecule at a stoma or pore in a leaf. During the day, increased heat energy will cause water to evaporate.** Evaporation occurs when the energy of movement (caused by heat energy) is stronger than the forces holding the molecule to other water molecules.

4.   **To show evaporation, pull on the top circle to draw the next circle**

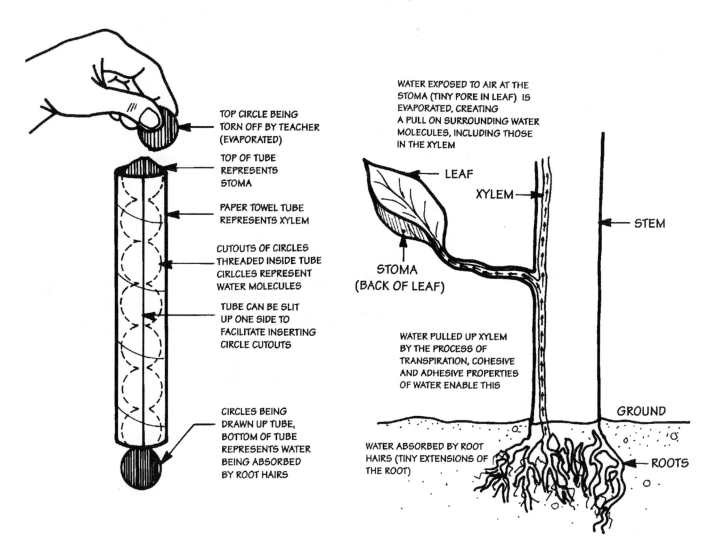

TOP CIRCLE BEING TORN OFF BY TEACHER (EVAPORATED)

TOP OF TUBE REPRESENTS STOMA

PAPER TOWEL TUBE REPRESENTS XYLEM

CUTOUTS OF CIRCLES THREADED INSIDE TUBE CIRLCLES REPRESENT WATER MOLECULES

TUBE CAN BE SLIT UP ONE SIDE TO FACILITATE INSERTING CIRCLE CUTOUTS

CIRCLES BEING DRAWN UP TUBE, BOTTOM OF TUBE REPRESENTS WATER BEING ABSORBED BY ROOT HAIRS

WATER EXPOSED TO AIR AT THE STOMA (TINY PORE IN LEAF) IS EVAPORATED, CREATING A PULL ON SURROUNDING WATER MOLECULES, INCLUDING THOSE IN THE XYLEM

LEAF

XYLEM

STEM

STOMA (BACK OF LEAF)

WATER PULLED UP XYLEM BY THE PROCESS OF TRANSPIRATION, COHESIVE AND ADHESIVE PROPERTIES OF WATER ENABLE THIS

GROUND

WATER ABSORBED BY ROOT HAIRS (TINY EXTENSIONS OF THE ROOT)

ROOTS

118

near the top, then tear off the top circle. **Explain that this represents a water molecule being evaporated from the leaf (transpiration).** When the top molecule leaves the plant, it must break away from surrounding water molecules. This creates a pull on those water molecules, drawing them further up the xylem.

5. **Have students write descriptions of transpiration based on the demonstration, identifying areas where clarification is needed.**

Part II
NOTE: This activity will work best on a sunny day after a rain storm or after an area has been watered.

1. **Divide the class into small groups; give each group an empty plastic bag and have them record its weight.** If the scale is not sensitive enough to weigh one bag, the class can weigh all their bags together, or they can simply describe the appearance of the bag.

2. **Identify trees, shrubs, or small plants located on the school grounds. Assign each group to a plant. (More than one group to a plant also works.)**

3. **Have each group carefully place its bag over part of a limb of its tree or shrub. (Facing the sun works best.) Tie the bag with a twist tie or string. Each group should count and record the number of leaves in its bag.**

4. **Challenge the students to develop a method to estimate the number of leaves on the tree.** After the groups have recorded their estimates, ask each group to carefully examine its bag for changes.

5. **After 30 minutes (it can be longer, but all bags should be removed at the same time), carefully remove the bag from the limb; take it to the class and weigh it.** If leaves or debris are in the bag, remove them with forceps or tweezers before weighing it, trying not to remove any of the moisture. Again, if a scale is not available, students can observe the bags, looking for condensation.

6. **Have each group measure the amount of moisture accumulated in its bag by using the following formula: weight gain = total weight – starting weight.**

7. **Pool the class data and have each group answer the following questions based on the data collected by the class:**

a. Which plant transpired the most water?

b. Which plant transpired the least water?

c. Estimate the mass of water each plant would transpire during seven hours of sunlight. Assume a constant rate of transpiration.

PLANT NAME OR DESCRIPTION	TRANSPIRATION RATE (OUNCES [OR GRAMS] PER 30 MIN.)	TRANSPIRATION PER SEVEN-HOUR DAY
Plant 1 _____		
Plant 2 _____		
Plant 3		

Water Cycle

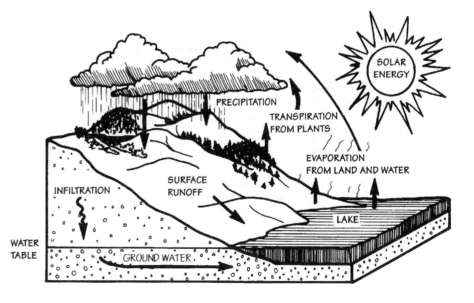

▼ *Wrap Up and Action*

Have students summarize the process of transpiration. How did the water get into the plastic bags? Discuss the amount of water transpired by plants in the schoolyard and where water goes after it leaves the plant. Have students relate their answers to the role these plants play in the water cycle.

Return students' attention to the arrows they drew on the *Water Cycle Diagram* student activity sheet in the *Warm Up*. Do they think the placement of their arrows is correct? Are revisions needed? Show students copies of the *Water Cycle* that includes arrows and labels and have students compare the two.

Students may have found that some plants transpired more water than others. Discuss the use of xeriscaping techniques to conserve water. Invite an extension agent or someone from the state natural resources department to provide additional information. Students can also conduct their own research. Have students survey their community for examples of residences or businesses that practice xeriscaping. What plants do they use? Why are these particular plants selected? Have students design a xeriscaped yard or garden.

Assessment

Have students:
- describe the process of transpiration (*Part I*, step 5 and *Wrap Up*).
- estimate and/or calculate the mass of water transpired from plants in the schoolyard (*Part II*, step 7).
- indicate the role of plants in the water cycle (*Wrap Up*).
- design a garden using xeriscape techniques (*Wrap Up*).

Upon completing the activity, for further assessment have students:
- write a paragraph envisioning what the water cycle would look like without plants; they might want to consider Earth's poles and the pre-Cambrian period.

Extensions

Have the students use microscopes to look carefully at the leaves and stalk of the celery. They should be able to see that the dyed water has traveled though major tubes to individual cells. Explain that the dye in the water is similar to essential nutrients for plant growth, in that the nutrients, like the dye, are dissolved in water and are transported to each individual cell. The difference is that, whereas nutrients are essential for successful plant metabolism, the dye is not. Wet-mount slides of leaf epidermis can be made to enable students to study stomata.

Resources

Biological Science Curriculum Study. 1987. *Biological Science: An Ecological Approach.* Dubuque, Iowa: Kendall/ Hunt Publishing Company.

Knox, Kim, ed. 1989. *Landscaping for Water Conservation—Xeriscape!* Denver, Colo.: City of Aurora and Denver Water Company.

Taylor's Guide to Water-Saving Gardening. 1990. Boston, Mass.: Houghton-Mifflin Company.

🍎 Walker, Sally M. 1992. *Water Up, Water Down: The Hydrologic Cycle.* Minneapolis, Minn.: Carolrhoda Books.

Notes ▼

Water Cycle Diagram

Name: _____ Date: _____

Use arrows to show all the places you think water moves throughout this land area.

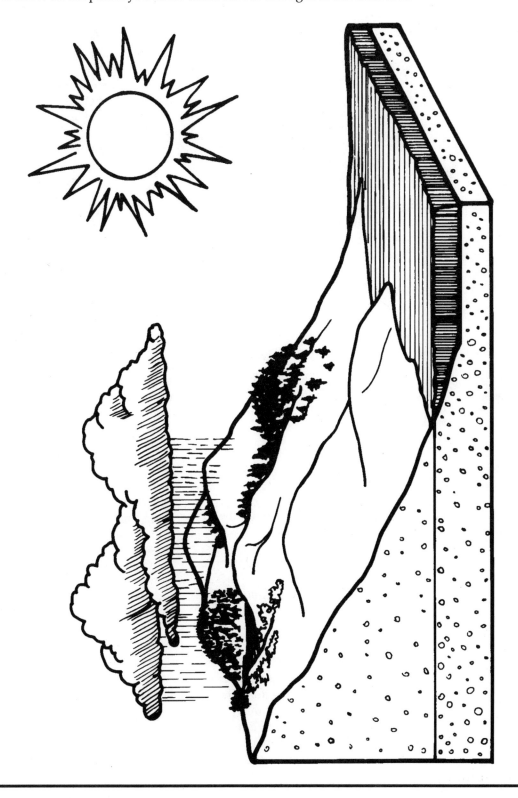

Water Address

When I was born, I moved about; but now that I'm older, I'm a real homebody in the limestone house I built. What's my water address?

■ **Grade Level:**
Upper Elementary, Middle School

■ **Subject Areas:**
Life Science, Ecology, Geography, Language Arts

■ **Duration:**
Preparation time: 30 minutes
Activity time: 50 minutes

■ **Setting:** Classroom

■ **Skills:**
Organizing (matching); Analyzing (identifying components); Interpreting (summarizing); Applying

■ **Charting the Course**
Before doing the activity, students should understand the importance of water to living organisms (e.g., "Aqua Bodies" and "Aqua Notes"). More information about global climates and ecosystems is found in "Piece It Together," "Wet Vacation," and "Water Models." Wetland ecosystems are presented in "Salt Marsh Players."

■ **Vocabulary**
adaptation

▼ Summary
Students identify plants and animals and their habitats by analyzing clues that describe water-related adaptations of aquatic and terrestrial organisms.

Objectives
Students will:
• recognize water-related adaptations of some plants and animals.

Materials
• *A set of **Water Address Cards** for each group of students* (These cards can be mounted on cardboard for durability.)
• *Pencils and paper for scorekeeping*
• *Pictures or photographs of organisms listed on **Water Address Cards*** (optional)
• *Map of the world* (optional)
• *Encyclopedia* (optional)
• *3" x 5" index cards*

Making Connections
Children have seen pictures of camels and cacti, beavers and pine trees. One common element among all these organisms is that they have adaptations related to water. Learning about these specific adaptations helps students appreciate the importance of water for survival.

Background
Living organisms can be found all over Earth's surface. Since three-quarters of Earth is covered with water, many plants and animals live in water environments such as oceans, lakes, and rivers. Other organisms are able to live on land, including deserts, wetlands, mountains, grasslands, etc. To survive in these varying environments, plants, animals, and other living things have special features, or adaptations. Developed over time, these adaptations help organisms acquire available nutrients and energy, protect themselves against enemies, and cope with diverse conditions (e.g., arid, aquatic, tropical). Because water covers most of the planet and is essential for life, many adaptations relate to water.

Animals and plants have become suited to live in aquatic environments in many ways. For example, fish have stream-lined bodies and fins to help them maneuver through water. Ducks have webbed feet for swimming and glands that produce a waxy oil for waterproofing feathers. Other organisms have developed the means to filter oxygen from water; for example, fish have gills. To live in fast-flowing water, such as a mountain stream, some organisms have modified mouth parts or fins that resemble suction cups, to keep them from being swept downstream. Water lilies anchor themselves on the bottoms of ponds and lakes, but their large leaves float on the surface, gathering light.

Some land animals have adaptations that help them obtain and conserve water. The kangaroo rat, a desert dweller, feeds only on dry seeds. The animal metabolizes proteins and fats in a way that provides all the fresh water it needs. A camel can survive for days or even months without water. This animal gets moisture from its food and retains most of the water that is in its body. Camels do not sweat much and can tolerate an increase in body temperature of 11 degrees F (6°C). A camel stores water in fat cells throughout its body.

Plant adaptations for dry conditions include large root systems for collecting water, decreased leaf size, and a thick,

DUSTY PERIN, N E STOCK PHOTO

protective outer covering that resists water loss. The ribs of the saguaro or giant cactus expand or contract like an accordion for water storage.

Plants and animals also possess adaptations related to cold water. Seals, penguins, and whales have insulation called blubber (a thick layer of oily fat beneath their skin) that keeps their body heat from escaping. Plants in cold environments must adapt to water scarcity, since the water in the soil around their roots is often frozen. The pine needle, a specialized leaf, has a thick, waxy coat and a small surface area to reduce the amount of water loss.

The behavior pattern of an animal can be a response to the lack or abundance of water. Elk, moose, and deer migrate, sometimes great distances, to avoid heavy snows

during winter. Migration patterns of birds correlate with winter and summer seasons. To prevent water loss during the heat of the day, some desert animals seek shade. When water dries up in a pond, certain species of frogs bury themselves in the mud and can hibernate for many years, waiting for the rains to return.

Procedure
▼ Warm Up
Discuss the importance of water to life. What is the longest time students can remember going without water? Inform them that humans cannot survive more than three or four days without water. While some organisms can live without oxygen, and some without light, all living things need water.

Have students list different ecosystems and compare water availability in these areas. Ask students to list plants and animals that they think might be found in these areas and describe how these organisms either live in or use water.

Review the concept of adaptation. Ask students if they have pets or plants that have special water adaptations. Fish have many physical adaptations for living in water. Some students may have a cactus or an air plant (epiphyte) growing in their homes.

▼ The Activity
1. **Tell students they are going to play a riddle game in which they must guess an organism's identity and "water address." Ask them to form groups of three or four.**

2. **Hand out a set of the *Water Address Cards* to each group. Instruct students not to look at the cards before the game starts.**

3. **Explain that each card lists four adaptations to water of a certain plant or animal. Based on the clues, students will try to guess the name of the plant or animal and the habitat in which it is usually found.**

4. **Each group should initially pick one student as "reader." This student will read clues, one at a time and in any order, until someone else in the group can guess the plant or animal. Answers are listed at the bottom of each card.** If photos of organisms are available, have students place the image on a map to indicate where it lives.

5. **The student who correctly guesses both the name of the organism and its water address receives points based on the number of clues that were read before he or she was able to guess.** Assign one student in each group to be scorekeeper and keep track of the score as follows:

   One clue read = four points

   Two clues read = three points

   Three clues read = two points

   All four clues read = one point

6. **The student who correctly guessed the previous water address riddle becomes the new reader and begins reading the clues on the next card. Continue the game until all cards have been read.**

▼ Wrap Up and Action
Discuss how adaptations enable organisms to live in their environment. Have students summarize water-related adaptations included in the game. Relate adaptations to living in water (e.g., swimming, filtering oxygen from water, keeping

out excess water) and to living with little water (e.g., preventing water loss, storing water, efficient methods of gathering water).

Remind students that each of the thousands of plants and animals not included in this activity has many adaptations. Have students visit the library and view videos to research additional organisms' adaptations to water, and then make additional clue cards for their own game. The game can then be played with these new cards, and groups can swap sets for longer games. Encourage students to play this game with friends and family.

Assessment

Have students:
- identify an organism and its environment based on a set of clues describing adaptations to water (steps 4 and 5).
- explain how adaptations enable plants and animals to live in diverse environments (*Wrap Up*).

- create clue cards for different organisms, listing water-related adaptations (*Wrap Up*).

Extensions

Students can create a new organism in an environment of the future, or in a fictional water environment on a different planet, such as "Zork." Have them imagine special features or behaviors the organism would need to live in this environment; encourage them to be creative. Students should write a detailed description or draw a picture of the habitat, depicting how the organism blends into the environment and how it obtains and conserves water. Have students evaluate each other's designs and provide suggestions for improvement. The portraits and descriptions can be posted in a "Water Address" gallery. The display should include descriptions of the organisms and their water-related adaptations. The "Water Address" game could be adapted to include these new organisms.

 **K-2 Option**

Show children drawings or magazine pictures of plants and animals that have various water-related adaptations, such as the ones described in the "Water Address" game. Discuss ways the plants and animals live in water or use it. Cut each picture into strips and place each cut-up picture in a separate envelope. Divide the class into small groups and give each group an envelope. A student in each group pulls out one strip of paper at a time and the group members try to guess what the plant or animal is. If they cannot guess, another strip is selected, and so on, until they figure out the organism. The group then summarizes the special features or adaptations that help the organism live in its environment. The groups can trade envelopes.

Resources

Attenborough, David. 1984. *The Living Planet*. Boston, Mass.: Little, Brown & Co.

Parker, Steve. 1988. *Pond and River*. New York, N.Y.: Knopf.

Parker, Steve, and Jane Parker. 1990. *Migration*. New York, N.Y.: Gloucester Press.

Simon, Seymour. 1990. *Oceans*. New York, N.Y.: Morrow.

Taylor, Barbara. 1992. *Desert Life: A Close-up Look at the Natural World of a Desert*. New York, N.Y.: Dorling Kinderley.

Videos:

Desert Animals and Plants. 1988. Eastman Kodak Company.

Strange and Unusual Animals: Adaptations to Environment. 1992. Diamond Entertainment Corporation.

ARCHIE SATTERFIELD

Water Address Cards

° I have dense, oily fur, webbed hind feet, and ears and nostrils that close when underwater.
° I sink green branches into my pond to retrieve during winter for food.
° I use my wide tail as a paddle.
° I build a home in water with sticks, and it has an underwater entrance.

Answer: Beaver—lives in streams or rivers

° My accordion-like stems expand to hold great volumes of water.
° My root system is widespread and shallow for absorbing water.
° My thick skin limits evaporation, reducing water loss.
° I have a spiny skin to prevent other organisms from trying to get to my stored water.

Answer: Cactus—lives in the desert

° I am able to drink great volumes of water and store it in the fat cells throughout my body.
° I sweat and urinate rarely, and don't pant or breathe rapidly (to reduce evaporation).
° I can travel without drinking water 10 times longer than a human can.
° Fat stored in my hump is broken down for energy, and in the process, water, which I can use, is released.

Answer: Camel—lives in the desert

° Where I live, I must swim constantly to stay in one place.
° I lay my eggs in stream channels and cover them with gravel.
° I am smooth and slippery, with fins and a large tail.
° I breathe using gills, which take oxygen from water.

Answer: Trout—lives in fast-flowing water

- I live in water, but can survive out of water for many hours because my limestone doors can close, keeping me from drying.
- When submerged, I reach out and wave my legs to pull nutrient-filled water into my mouth.
- When first born I move about in the water; when older I stay in one place—I use a special adhesive to glue myself to a rock, a boat, or a whale.
- I create my own limestone house from materials that I filter from the water.

Answer: Barnacles—live at the edge of the ocean

- My leaves have a waxlike coating that limits water loss through evaporation.
- I have tiny, needlelike leaves that contain very little moisture to freeze in winter.
- Pointy, thin leaves and sturdy, flexible branches keep snow from weighing me down.
- My buds contain a chemical and are covered with a protective layer to keep them from freezing.

Answer: Pine tree—found in northern forests, cold and/or dry areas

- My feet are webbed and used for steering.
- I wear a matted feather coat that keeps out wind and water.
- Blubber helps keep my body heat inside.
- I have wings that I use for flippers.

Answer: Penguin—lives in the Antarctic

- I can be found on still water.
- I have six wax-coated feet.
- I stand with legs splayed to distribute my weight, so I won't break through the water's surface.
- I appear to glide across the water's surface.

Answer: Pond skater or water strider—lives in ponds and quiet streams

Water connects all Earth systems.

▼

Water is an integral part of Earth's structure and plays a unique role in Earth's processes.

It is found in the atmosphere, on the surface, and underground. The water

cycle is central to life on Earth and connects Earth systems.

Branching Out!

Grade Level:
Middle School

Subject Areas:
Earth Science, Geography

Duration:
Preparation time: 50 minutes
Activity time: two 50-minute periods

Setting: Classroom

Skills:
Organizing (mapping); Analyzing (contrasting and comparing); Applying (predicting); Evaluating (testing, critiquing)

Charting the Course
Prior to or in conjunction with this activity, students can investigate the role their schoolyard plays in a watershed in "Rainy-Day Hike." The concept of watersheds is explored further in "Just Passing Through" and "Color Me a Watershed." Students can investigate how drainage patterns influence human settlements and ecosystems in "Water Crossings."

Vocabulary
drainage basin, watershed, divide, tributary, runoff

Is it possible to cross the Mississippi River in one step?

▼ Summary
Students build a model landscape to investigate how water flows through and connects watersheds.

Objectives
Students will:
- predict where water will flow in watersheds.
- describe drainage patterns in watersheds.

Materials
- *Overhead transparency or copies of* **Branching Patterns**
- *Blue-colored water*
- *Spray bottles or sprinkling cans*
- *Drawing paper and pencil*
- *Blue pencils*
- *Tracing paper or blank transparency sheets*
- *Copies of a local map showing rivers*

NOTE: In this activity students build a model of a watershed. This is presented as a class activity, but smaller groups of students can construct their own models. Students can build a temporary, simple model or a more durable version that can be used in subsequent activities. The materials for both are listed below.

Temporary model*
- *White scrap paper, newsprint, or butcher paper*

Permanent model
- *Papier-mâché materials (strips of newspaper dipped in a thick mixture of flour and water)*
- *Water-resistant sealer and white paint (or white waterproof paint)*

Both models will require:
- *5 to 10 rocks, ranging from 2 to 6 inches (5 to 15 cm) in height (If groups of students are making their own models, each group will need its own rocks.)*
- *Square or rectangular aluminum tray, large enough to hold rocks*
- *Plastic wrap (Thick plastic wrap from a grocery or butcher shop works well.)*

Making Connections
Children have watched water flowing down a street during a heavy rainstorm and may have asked: Where does all the water go? Viewing turbulent waters in a stream, students may have wondered: Where does all the water come from?

The pattern water makes as it flows through a watershed is familiar to students who have drawn pictures of trees or studied the nervous system. By investigating drainage patterns, students consider how watersheds distinguish different land areas.

Background
When the ground is saturated or impermeable to water during heavy rains or snowmelt, excess water flows over the surface of land as runoff. Eventually, this water collects in channels such as streams. The land area that drains water into the channels is called the watershed or drainage basin.

Watersheds are separated from each other by areas of higher elevation called ridge lines or divides. Near the divide of a watershed, water channels are narrow and can contain fast-moving water. At lower elevations, the slope of the land decreases, causing water to flow more slowly. As smaller streams merge together, the width of the channel

TEMPORARY MODEL ADAPTED WITH PERMISSION FROM "FLOWING TO THE RESERVOIR: WHAT IS A WATERSHED?" WATER WISDOM. BOSTON, MASS.: MASSACHUSETTS WATER RESOURCES AUTHORITY.

increases. Eventually, water collects in a wide river that empties into a body of water, such as a lake or ocean.

From an aerial view, drainage patterns in watersheds resemble a network similar to the branching pattern of a tree. Tributaries, similar to twigs and small branches, flow into streams, the main branches of the tree. Streams eventually empty into a large river, comparable to the trunk. Like other branching patterns (e.g., road maps, veins in a leaf, the human nervous system), the drainage pattern consists of smaller channels merging into larger ones.

Watersheds are either closed or open systems. In closed systems, such as Crater Lake in southwest Oregon or the Great Salt Lake in Utah, water collects at a low point that lacks an outlet. The only way water naturally leaves the system is through evaporating or seeping into the ground. Most watersheds are open: water that collects in smaller drainage basins overflows into outlet rivers and eventually empties into the sea.

Procedure

▼ *Warm Up*

Show students copies or an overhead of *Branching Patterns* (the outlines of a watershed's drainage pattern, a tree in winter, the human nervous system, and a road map). Ask them what all the pictures have in common.

▼ *The Activity*

1.   **Depending on whether a temporary or more permanent model is being built, have students do the following:**

Temporary model:

Instruct students to wrap rocks with white scrap paper and lay them in a square or rectangular aluminum tray. Place larger rocks near one end of the tray. Cover the rocks snugly with plastic wrap.

Permanent model:

Have students lay rocks in a square or rectangular aluminum tray, with larger rocks near one end. Snugly cover the rocks and exposed areas of the tray with plastic wrap. Apply strips of papier-mâché to cover the rocks. For a sturdier model, apply several layers of papier-mâché. When the mâché has dried, coat the model with waterproof sealant and white paint or waterproof white paint.

2.   **Have students sketch a bird's-eye view of the model.** (See model sketch.) They should mark points of higher elevation with "H"s and low spots with "L"s. To identify possible ridgelines, connect the "H"s.

3.   **Tell students that the model will soon experience a rainstorm. Where do they think water will flow and collect in the model? Have them sketch predictions on their drawings.** Show them crevices in the model and possible locations of watersheds.

4.   **Spray blue-colored water over the model and note where it flows.** (See photo.) Water may need to be sprayed for several minutes to cause a continual flow. Assist students in identifying branching patterns as water from smaller channels merges into larger streams.

5.   **Have students use blue pencil to mark on their drawings the actual branching patterns of water.** Some imagination and logic may be required. Ask them to confirm the locations of watersheds by noting where water has collected in the model.

6.   **Have students determine if smaller watersheds overflow into larger ones.** Does all the water in the model eventually drain into one collection site (open watershed system)? Does the model contain several closed watershed systems (collection sites that lack an outlet)?

130

▼ Wrap Up

Have students place tracing paper or an overhead transparency over their drawings and draw the drainage pattern. Compare the traced lines to the branching patterns presented during the **Warm Up** and contrast with drawings of other students. Discuss how all the networks involve smaller channels merging together and becoming larger.

Provide each student with a copy of a local map. Have students locate streams and rivers and note where smaller rivers flow together or merge into larger ones. Ask them to encircle land areas they think drain into the rivers.

Have them pick one river on the map and follow its path in two directions. If all of the river is pictured, one direction should lead to the headwaters or source (where the line tapers off). In the opposite direction, the river will merge with another river or empty into a body of water.

Have students write a story or draw a picture about a local river. Have them describe how water moves to the river from surrounding land areas or tributaries and then flows to a larger body of water.

Assessment

Have students:

- predict where water will flow and collect in their watershed model (step 3).
- test their predictions and use the results to confirm or modify their projected drainage patterns (steps 4 and 5).
- compare the drainage pattern of watersheds to other branching networks, such as a road map, tree, or the human nervous system (**Warm Up** and **Wrap Up**).
- write a story about or draw a map of drainage patterns in their watershed (**Wrap Up**).

Extensions

Have children compare their drawings or stories to *Where the River Begins*, a story by Thomas Locker. In the book, two boys and their grandfather follow a river to its source.

If the model were a real land area, do students think the drainage patterns would be the same thousands of years from now? Have students consider the effects of natural and human-introduced elements (e.g., landslides, floods, erosion, evaporation, water consumption by plants and animals, runoff from agricultural fields or residential areas, dams).

Students may want to finish their models by painting landscapes and constructing scale models of trees, wetlands, and riparian areas. They may introduce human influences such as towns and roads. Natural and human-made environmental problems, such as landslides and erosion, could be incorporated into the design.

As in the game "Pin the Tail on the Donkey," blindfold students and have them randomly touch a point on a map of the North American continent, the U.S., or their state. Have students explain likely routes water would flow to that area.

Advanced students may want to make a topographic map of their model. Totally waterproof the model. Submerge it, 1/2 inch (1-2 cm) at a time, in water. At each increment, while viewing from above, trace the water level onto a sheet of glass or plastic covering the model.

☺ K-2 Option

Have children focus on how smaller streams merge into larger ones. Gather pruned branches and let students investigate how the main branches "branch out" into smaller ones. If branches are not available, students can make a branching system out of pipe cleaners.

Help students imagine a drop of water flowing down the twig to the larger branches and finally to the main branch. Students can paint or decorate the branch and name the rivers. Into what body of water might the large river (the main branch) flow?

Relate the branch to a river flowing near or through the community. What smaller channels might feed into this river? Where do students think the water in the river goes? Help them to imagine the water flowing into a larger river and finally to a lake or to the sea.

Lead them in the following hand motions to represent small rivers flowing into larger rivers. A simple song about rivers can accompany the motions.

A babbling brook (hold arm in front of body and wiggle fingers) flows into a small river (place both arms together and wave them in a serpentine motion). The water from smaller rivers goes into a large river (have students merge together in a column) and travels to the sea or lake (students move to a place in the room designated as the sea or a lake and dance in the area like waves splashing about).

Resources

Coble, Charles, et al. 1988. *Prentice Hall Earth Science*. Englewood Cliffs, N.J.: Prentice Hall, Inc.

🍎 Holling, Clancy. 1941. *Paddle to the Sea*. Boston, Mass.: Houghton Mifflin Company.

🍎 Locker, Thomas. 1984. *Where the River Begins*. New York, N.Y.: Dial Books.

🍎 Tresselt, Alvin. 1990. *Rain Drop Splash*. New York, N.,Y.: Morrow.

Branching Patterns

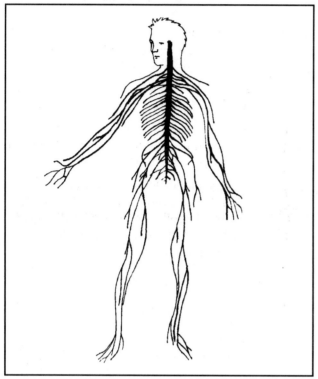

Human nervous system

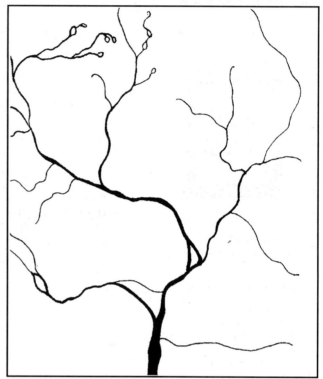

Watershed drainage pattern

Road system

Tree in winter

©The Watercourse and Council for Environmental Education (CEE).

Capture, Store, and Release

How much water will a watershed shed if a watershed sheds its wetlands?

▼ Summary
Students use a household sponge to simulate how wetlands capture, store, and release water.

Objectives
Students will:
- recognize that ground water, surface water, and precipitation can contribute water to wetlands.
- describe how wetlands capture, store, and release water.

Materials
- *Pictures or slides of wetlands*
- *Colored water*
- *Aluminum trays (one per group)*
- *Large, light-colored sponges—1 sponge per group (Fold sponges and cut along the fold removing a lengthwise strip; the strip should extend from one end of the sponge to the other. Do not cut all the way through the sponge.)*
- *Strips of cardboard cut to fit in strip cut from sponge*
- *Pencils or rulers*
- *Pieces of absorbent cloth*
- *Measuring cups*
- *Shovel or trowel*

Making Connections
Most children have dug holes in sand or soil, poured in water, and watched it seep into the ground. This experience helps students understand how soils in some wetlands absorb water. Understanding the source of water in wetlands and how wetlands can capture, store, and release water helps students appreciate the importance of wetlands in watersheds.

Background
Wetlands form in a variety of places under myriad conditions—along edges of rivers, streams, lakes, and ponds; in low-lying woods; in highway ditches built to collect rainwater draining from the road; in low areas of fields; even on mountains and hillsides where snowmelt and rainwater constantly run.

Although the definition of wetlands is still debated, most agree they are areas where the soil is saturated for all or parts of the year. Wetlands have qualities of both aquatic and terrestrial habitats. Many variables contribute to the formation of wetlands, including soil type, elevation, and water source. The main determinant, however, is always *water*.

Surface water, ground water, and precipitation can each contribute water to wetlands. When it rains, much of the water that hits the ground runs over the surface of the land, until it eventually collects in low spots (e.g., ponds, rivers, or lakes). If it saturates the surrounding land, wetlands may form.

Wetlands are also formed and fed by ground water seepage from uplands and from waterways. Some wetlands are located where the ground water level is above the surface. When the ground water level drops, the wetland seems to disappear (unless it is fed by surface water). In this circumstance, any water that enters the now dry wetland will be absorbed by the ground below.

The ability of wetlands to hold water is one reason they are valuable for watershed management. Many wetlands store water and slowly release it over time. Although all wetlands capture, store, and release water, significant differences exist among wetlands.

One of the primary variables is soil type. If a wetland forms on clay or other semi-

Grade Level:
Upper Elementary

Subject Areas:
Earth Science, Geography

Duration:
Preparation time:
Part I: 50 minutes (teacher preparing sponges)
Part II: 15 minutes

Activity time:
Part I: 50 minutes
Part II: 50 minutes

Setting:
Classroom and outdoors

Skills:
Gathering information (observing); Organizing (measuring); Analyzing (comparing and contrasting)

Charting the Course
Students should participate in "The Incredible Journey" to learn how water is released after it is captured and stored. "Get the Ground Water Picture" supports this activity. "Wetland Soils in Living Color" provides a good follow-up. Wetland habitats are investigated in "Life in the Fast Lane."

Vocabulary
wetland, ground water, surface water, water table, watershed

impervious soil, a small amount of water infiltrates the ground; standing water will be present. Most of the water in such a wetland will be released into the atmosphere through evaporation. At the other extreme is a wetland located on sandy ground. Water moves into the soil at a rapid pace, and unless the ground water level is above the surface, most of the water will filter underground.

Procedure
▼ Warm Up
Show students pictures or slides of wetlands. Discuss what the pictures have in common. Ask students to describe why these areas are called wetlands. Have them list possible sources of water for the wetland.

▼ The Activity

Part I
1.   **Divide the class into small groups. To demonstrate how the ground stores water, have students pour a shallow layer of water into the bottom of an aluminum tray. Place a sponge in the tray; it absorbs water much like soil. Have a student press his or her finger into the sponge to create a depression that collects water from the stored ground water.**

2.   **Have students simulate how surface water helps form wetlands. Dampen and distribute sponges. Explain that the cutaway portion represents a stream. Tell them to cover the bottom of the cutaway portion with a strip of cardboard, which represents the bed of the stream.**

3.   **Have students place two pencils or rulers across the top of the aluminum tray. Instruct them to lay the sponge on top of the pencils. (Elevate one end of the tray.) Slowly pour colored water into the stream. Eventually, the banks of the stream**

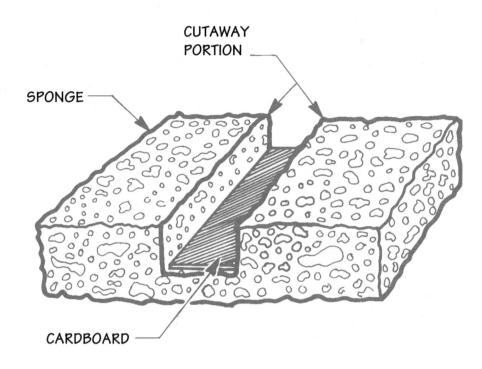

CUTAWAY PORTION

SPONGE

CARDBOARD

absorb the water and it seeps to the surrounding land area. If the borders of streams remain moist, wetlands may form on the banks. Sprinkling water on the sponge shows that precipitation also feeds wetlands.

Part II
1.   **Ask students to imagine water flowing over a land area containing a wetland. What happens to the water when it reaches the wetland? Students should understand that wetlands collect and store water.** Explain that, eventually, water is released when it evaporates, seeps into the ground water system, or flows out of the wetland and travels further downhill or downstream.

2.   **Tell students that through a demonstration, they are going to compare watersheds that do and do not have wetlands.**

3.   **Provide students with the following instructions (or do as a demonstration). Poke a hole in one**

end of an aluminum tray and prop up the other end of the tray to form a slope. Put in as many sponges as will fit into the tray (making sure the sponges have been wrung dry). The set-up represents a watershed with wetlands (sponges) in it, and the hole simulates where water is discharged.

4.   **Instruct students to pour two cups (473 ml) of water on the top portion of the tray. This represents water entering the watershed. Water flowing through the watershed should be collected as it comes out of the hole. How much water is collected compared to the amount poured in? Keep track of the time it takes for the water to drain.**

5.   **Ask students how they think the watershed would be affected if the wetlands were removed? Have them remove the sponges, dry the tray, and again pour two cups (473 ml) of water on the top portion of the tray. Compare the quantity of water drained and the time required**

134

for draining to when sponges (wetlands) were present. Explain that if a wetland is covered by concrete or pavement, the above scenario is representative. However, in the case of a wetland removed from a field, some infiltration into the soil and ground water will occur. This can be shown by placing a few layers of cloth on the bottom of the tray when conducting the activity.

▼ Wrap Up and Action

Have students summarize sources of water that feed wetlands and how wetlands can help regulate surface water runoff. Discuss problems that can result if the volume and rate of runoff in a watershed are increased.

Take the group on a walk around the school or community to find a body of water (puddle, pond, or stream) or a muddy location. Have students carefully dig holes at varying distances from the site and investigate the moisture content of the soil. If the soil is damp, ask students where the water originated. Make sure students fill the holes afterward. Students can talk to community planners to learn how city planners manage wetlands.

Assessment
Have students:
* identify sources of water in wetlands (*Wrap Up*).

After completing the activity, for further assessment have students:
* write a paragraph that includes the terms *capture, store*, and *release*, comparing the flow of water through watersheds that have and that lack wetlands.

Extensions

If students collect soil samples, have them determine the amount of water in the soil. This is done by comparing the weights of samples before and after drying. (Remove water from soil by setting it in the sun until the soil is dry or in an oven at 300 degrees F [150°C] for 30 minutes.)

Students can enhance the simple sponge activity, making a more detailed model of a wetland. They can design the area to show how wetlands differ in their ability to capture, store, and release water. They can add vegetation and wildlife that live in wetland habitats.

Students can make crossword puzzles for each other incorporating words and definitions to support understanding of wetlands. They may choose from the following list or select their own words: wetland, marsh, sawgrass, cattail, absorption, filtration, swamp, saturated, muskrat, everglades.

Resources
Environmental Concern Inc., The Watercourse, and Project WET. 1995. *WOW!: The Wonders Of Wetlands.* Published through a partnership between Environmental Concern Inc., St. Michaels, Md. and The Watercourse, Bozeman, Mont.

Lynn, Brian. 1988. *Discover Wetlands: A Curriculum Guide.* Olympia, Wash.: Washington State Department of Ecology Publications Office.

Mitsch, William J., and James G. Gosselink. 1993. *Wetlands*, 2nd ed. New York, N.Y.: Van Norstrand Reinhold.

Project WILD. 1992. Activity "Wetland Metaphors." From *Aquatic Project WILD.* Bethesda, Md.: Western Regional Environmental Education Council.

Get the Ground Water Picture

Have you ever wished you had a window into the earth so you could see what's beneath your feet?

▼ Summary

Students will "get the ground water picture" and learn about basic ground water principles as they create their own geologic cross section or earth window.

Objectives

Students will:
- identify the parts of a ground water system.
- compare movement of water through diverse substrates.
- relate different types of land uses to potential ground water contamination.

Materials

- *Clear, 12-ounce plastic soda bottles or the same number of plastic cups* (with top cut off and holes punched in bottom)
- *Gravel*
- *Sand*
- *Clay* (If unable to obtain clay locally, place unscented, nonclumping kitty litter in a blender and grind until fine. Mix with enough water to make moist.)
- *Hand-held magnifying lens*
- *25 1" x 12" strips of white paper* (Number the back of the strips 1 through 25.)
- *Blue crayon or colored pencil*
- *Copies of **Well Log Data Chart***
- *Copies of **Ground Water Student Page***

Making Connections

Out of sight is out of mind. Because ground water is hidden below Earth's surface, students do not have a visible reference point as they do when they look at water in lakes or rivers. However, because ground water is so widely used as a source of drinking water, students likely drink ground water every day. (Students may have seen a windmill or pump that draws water from the ground.) Windmills can serve as surface indicators of ground water. They also generate electricity. Creating a geologic cross section helps students become aware of this hidden source of water.

Background

Ground water is one of Earth's most valuable natural resources. The water stored in the pores, cracks, and openings of subsurface rock material is ground water. Wells dug by hand or machine have been used throughout history to retrieve water from the ground. Scientists use the word *aquifer* to describe an underground formation that is capable of storing and transmitting water.

Aquifers come in all shapes and sizes. (See pages 140-141 for identification and definition of the parts of a ground water system.) Some aquifers may cover hundreds of square miles and be hundreds of feet thick, while others may only cover a few square miles and be a few feet thick. Water quality and quantity vary from aquifer to aquifer and sometimes vary within the same system. Some aquifers can yield millions of gallons of water per day and maintain water levels, while others may only be able to produce small amounts of water each day. In some areas wells might have to be drilled thousands of feet to reach usable water, while in other areas water can be located only a few feet down. One site might contain several aquifers located at different depths, and another site might yield little or no ground water.

The age of ground water varies from aquifer to aquifer. For example, an unconfined surface aquifer might hold

---

Grade Level:
Middle School, High School

Subject Areas:
Environmental Science, Mathematics, Government

Duration:
Preparation time:
Part I: 30 minutes
Part II: none needed
Part III: 15 minutes

Activity time:
Part I: 30 minutes
Part II: 30 minutes
Part III: 50 minutes

Setting: Indoors

Skills:
Organizing (matching, charting); Analyzing (identifying patterns); Interpreting (inferring, translating)

Charting the Course
To help students appreciate the amount of time water can spend underground and how ground water relates to the water cycle, they can participate in "The Incredible Journey" and "Imagine!" Issues concerning ground water contamination are addressed in "The Pucker Effect" and "A Grave Mistake." Students investigate soil profiles in "Wetland Soils in Living Color."

Vocabulary
ground water system

water that is only a few days, weeks, or months old. On the other hand, a deep aquifer that is covered by one or more impervious layers may contain water that is hundreds or even thousands of years old.

The rate of movement of ground water varies based on the rock material in the formation through which the water is moving. After water percolates down to the water table, it becomes ground water and starts to move slowly down gradient. Water movement responds to differences in energy levels. The energies that cause ground water to flow are expressed as gravitational energy and pressure energy. (These are both forms of mechanical energy.) Gravitational energy comes from the difference in elevation between the recharge area (where water enters the ground water system) and discharge area (where water leaves the system). Pressure

energy (hydraulic head) comes from the weight of overlying water and earth materials. Ground water moves toward areas of least resistance. (Ground water encountering semi-impervious material, such as clay, will slow down significantly; when it moves toward an open area, such as a lake, water's rate of movement will increase.)

Hydrogeologists, scientists who study ground water, know that the above variables exist and that to really "get the ground water picture" they must drill wells. Wells provide the best method of learning the physical, hydrologic, and chemical characteristics of an aquifer. As a well is drilled deeper and deeper into the ground, the drill passes through different rock formations. The driller records the exact location of the well, records the depth of each formation, and collects samples of the rock material penetrated (sandstone,

sand, clay, etc.). This data becomes part of the well's record or *well log*. The driller's record provides valuable information for determining ground water availability, movement, quantity, and quality. The well driller then caps and seals the well to protect it from contamination.

If hazardous waste, chemicals, heavy metals, oil, etc. collect on the surface of the ground, rain or runoff percolating into the soil can carry these substances into ground water. When hydrogeologists or water quality specialists analyze the quality of ground water, they consider land-use practices in the watershed and in the vicinity of the well.

Procedure
▼ *Warm Up*
Tell students they are about to learn how they can "get the ground water picture." Explain that hydrogeologists study wells to learn the types

JENNIE LANE

of rock material located below ground. Ask students to draw pictures representing what they think it looks like underground (texture and color of rock formations) or to write brief descriptions of what happens to water after it seeps into the ground.

▼ *The Activity*

Part I

Ground Water Demonstration.

Have students conduct the following activity to learn how water moves through rock materials such as gravel, sand, and clay.

Place gravel, sand, and clay in separate clear containers. Have students look closely at each container. (A hand-held magnifying glass works well.) To demonstrate that ground water moves through underground rock formations, pour water into each container; observe and discuss the results. Which container emptied the fastest? The slowest? How would the different materials influence water movement in natural systems?

Part II

(May be appropriate for younger students.)

Ground Water Movement Activity.

Conduct the following activity to show how different sizes and kinds of rock material affect water movement. Select three or four students to become molecules of water. The rest of the students will be rock material.

a. Water Movement Through Gravel: Students become gravel by raising arms outstretched. Students should be able to rotate and not touch other students. The goal of the students representing water molecules is to move (flow) through

A
WATER MOVEMENT THROUGH GRAVEL

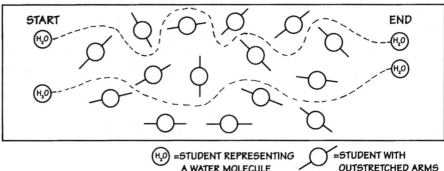

(H₂O) =STUDENT REPRESENTING A WATER MOLECULE   ⊘ =STUDENT WITH OUTSTRETCHED ARMS REPRESENTING GRAVEL

B
WATER MOVEMENT THROUGH SAND

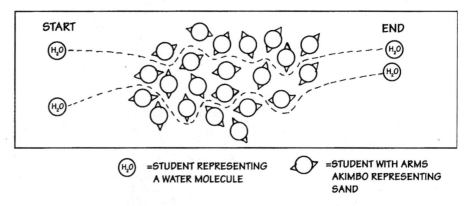

(H₂O) =STUDENT REPRESENTING A WATER MOLECULE   ⊘ =STUDENT WITH ARMS AKIMBO REPRESENTING SAND

C
WATER MOVEMENT THROUGH CLAY

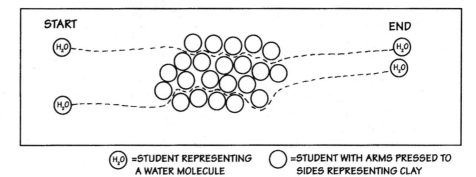

(H₂O) =STUDENT REPRESENTING A WATER MOLECULE   ○ =STUDENT WITH ARMS PRESSED TO SIDES REPRESENTING CLAY

138

students representing gravel to the other side of room. (See illustration *A*.)

b. Water Movement Through Sand: Students become sand by extending arms, bending them at the elbows, and touching waists with fingertips. Students should stand so their elbows are almost touching. The water molecules will experience some difficulty this time, but should still reach the other side. (See illustration *B*.)

c. Water Movement Through Clay: Students become clay particles by keeping arms at their sides and huddling together. They should be very close together, making it a formidable task for water molecules to move through the clay. Without being rough, the water molecules should slowly push their way through the clay. The water molecules may be unable to move through the clay at all. (See illustration *C*.)

Part III

1. **Hand out strips numbered 2-24 to students (students can work individually or in pairs) and copies of the *Well Log Data Chart*. The paper represents the length of a well that has been dug. They will receive data about the location and types of rock materials in their wells, and transfer this information to their strips of paper to make well logs.**

2. **Demonstrate how to record the types of rock materials. Divide the strip labeled 1 into 12 inches. Show students**

the data from Well #1. Mark the level of the water table by drawing a double line at the appropriate point (2" from the top) of the paper strip; this corresponds with the level found in the first column of the chart. In the second column find the level of fine sand (0–1). Measuring from the top of the column, the first inch should be speckled with dots. From 1" to 2 1/2", the formation is composed of medium sand.**

SAMPLE STRIP

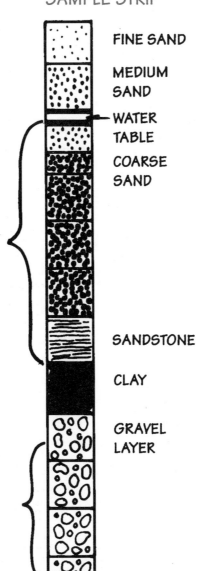

FINE SAND

MEDIUM SAND

WATER TABLE

COARSE SAND

BLUE COLORED

SANDSTONE

CLAY

GRAVEL LAYER

BLUE COLORED

Course sand exists from 2 1/2" to 6", and so forth, until the gravel layer, which exists from 8" to 12". Complete the drawing by coloring (light blue) the area between the water table and the top of the clay layer. Also color the gravel layer.

3. **Have students fill in their log based on the number on their strip of paper (if a strip is labeled 6, the student uses data from Well # 6) and the information in the *Well Log Data Chart*. Make sure students note the land use existing above their well sites.**

4. **When they have completed their well logs, ask students to answer questions based on their well logs.**

a. The horizontal scale of the cross section is 1 inch = 1 mile. The vertical scale is 1 inch = 50 feet. How many miles are horizontally represented in the cross section? How many feet are vertically represented in the cross section?

b. How many feet below the surface is the water table?

c. Ask each student to imagine a drop of water falling on the surface above his or her well. What pollutants might this drop of water pick up as it filters into the ground? (Students can refer to the land use practice above their well, but may conclude they need additional information.)

d. Have students describe the drop's movement down the column. Through which layers would it move the fastest? The slowest?

e. At which layer might the drop's movement be restricted? Explain to students that only a slight amount of water would pass through the clay. Have them speculate on the source of the water beneath the clay level (in the gravel layer).

5. **Have students assemble their well logs in order, and tape to a wall. Distribute to each student the** *Ground Water Student Page.* **Compare students' well log cross section to the chart.**

a. Provide the definitions listed in the box at right and have students locate these parts of a ground water system on the *Well Log Ground Water Chart (Cross Section).*

b. Ask students what direction the ground water is moving in the unconfined aquifer. (Predominantly moves from left to right.)

c. What are water sources for the unconfined aquifer? (rainfall, wetlands, the river)

d. How long would it take the water in the sandstone formation to move from Well #1 to Well #15? (Assume the water moves at a constant rate and flows at 100 feet per day [1 mile = 5280 feet].)

e. Now that students know about the land use above other well sites, and the direction water flows, how would they answer question 4c?

f. Have students refer to the *Cone of Depression* diagram. Explain that the cone of depression results from water being drawn up the well. Ask them to locate the cone of depression on the *Well Log Ground Water Chart (Cross Section).*

g. Instruct students to refer to the *Ground Water System (Simplified).* What are possible sources of water in the confined aquifer portion of their well? (Compare answers to 4e.)

▼ *Wrap Up*

If they had to drill a well, which sites would students consider most favorable on the *Well Log Ground Water Chart (Cross Section)?*

- **WATER TABLE:**
The top of an unconfined aquifer; indicates the level below which soil and rock are saturated with water.

- **CONFINED AQUIFER:**
An aquifer that is bounded above and below by nonpermeable layers that transmit water significantly more slowly than the aquifer. The water level in a well that taps a confined aquifer will rise above the top of the aquifer because the confined aquifer is under pressure. Also called artesian aquifer.

- **UNCONFINED AQUIFER:**
An aquifer in which the upper boundary is the top of the water table.

- **PERMEABLE LAYER:**
Portion of aquifer that contains porous rock materials that allow water to penetrate freely.

- **IMPERMEABLE LAYER:**
Portion of aquifer that contains rock material that does not allow water to penetrate; often forms the base of unconfined aquifers and the boundaries for confined aquifers.

- **ZONE OF SATURATION:**
The part of a water-bearing formation in which all spaces (between soil particles and in rock structures) are filled with water.

- **ZONE OF AERATION:**
Portion of unconfined aquifer above the water table where the pore spaces among soil particles and rock formations are filled with air.

Students may be interested in learning about the rock formations beneath their community. The city water department might have a geologic cross section for the city or region. Students could attempt to interpret the maps.

Assessment
Have students:
- compare the movement of water through diverse substrates (*Part I*).
- construct a well log (*Part III*, steps 2 and 3).
- analyze possible effects on ground water based on interpretations of the well logs (*Part III*, steps 4 and 5).

- identify the parts of a ground water system (*Part III*, step 5).
- determine when additional data are needed to draw valid conclusions (*Part III*, steps 4 and 5).

Extensions
Does your school have its own well? If so, consider visiting the well site and performing a survey of possible pollution sources in the well's vicinity. What are they and where are they located? Should something be done to remove them? What are the options? The water quality of your school's well is public information and would make an interesting study. Has your school experienced water quality problems?

140

To demonstrate surface water filtration of sediment and materials carried by water, ask four students to represent water molecules and to lightly attach balloons to themselves with tape. These balloons represent materials picked up by water molecules as they move across the surface of the ground. Have several students representing soil particles stand elbow to elbow to form Earth's surface. As the "water molecules" pass through the "soil," the balloons will be "brushed off" (because of the proximity of the students). This represents how soil can filter out sediment and debris carried by water.

Have each of the water molecules rub a little flour on the sides of their arms. The flour represents the small but visible materials that can still be carried by water as it moves downward from the surface as it becomes part of ground water. The students who were soil particles are now rock particles and stand side by side to represent different types of rock material (gravel, sand, and clay). As the water molecules move through the rock material, some of the flour rubs off on the rock material. Although some material is removed by rock filtration, some is still retained by the water molecules.

Water that looks or tastes pure and is odorless is not necessarily potable. Water quality specialists know that odorless, colorless, and tasteless contaminants are found in water. These substances are detected through testing; a sample of water is collected and analyzed for specific contaminants (bacteria, nitrates, arsenic, and so forth).

Assign half of the students in class to be water molecules and the rest rock particles. Cut small pieces of paper and on each write one of the following: bacteria, nitrate, arsenic, lead, etc. Secretly distribute these pieces of paper to about half of the water molecules and tell students to hide them in their pockets. Have the water molecules move through the students, standing side by side, who represent rock particles.

After they have all passed through, ask students (except for the "contaminated" water molecules), "Do you believe that the water that just filtered through the rock particles is clean; that is, would you be willing to drink it?" Students will likely answer yes. Have the contaminated water molecules remove the contaminants from their pockets. Remind students that even though water may "appear" clean, it may still carry contaminants that are only detected through testing.

Resources

Ground Water Flow Model: A Plexiglas sand tank model, video, and user's guide that demonstrates basic ground water principles and management concerns. Contact: The Watercourse, 201 Culbertson Hall, Montana State University, Bozeman, MT 59717. (406) 994-5392. Fax: (406) 994-1919.

🍎 Hoff, Mary, and Mary M. Rogers. 1991. *Our Endangered Planet: Ground water.* Minneapolis, Minn.: Lerner.

🍎 Taylor, Carla, ed. 1985. *Groundwater: A Vital Resource.* Knoxville, Tenn.: Tennessee Valley Authority.

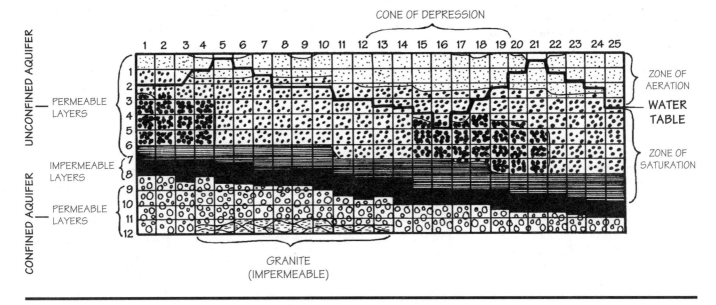

WELL LOG GROUND WATER CHART (CROSS SECTION)

Well Log Data Chart

						KEY			
				Note: numbers in vertical columns are in inches					
Well No.	Land Use Type	Water Table	Fine Sand	Medium Sand	Coarse Sand	Sand-stone	Clay Layer	Gravel Layer	Granite
1	farmland	2	0 - 1	1 - 2½	2½ - 6	6 - 7	7 - 8	8 - 12	—
2	farmland	2	0 - 1	1 - 3	3 - 6	6 - 7	7 - 8	8 - 12	—
3	farmland	2	0 - 1½	1½ - 3	3 - 6	6 - 7	7 - 8½	8½ - 12	—
4	wetland	1	¼ - 1½	1½ - 3	3 - 6	6 - 7	7 - 8¼	8¼ - 11½	11½ - 12
5	wetland	¼	½ - 1½	1½ - 6	—	6 - 7¼	7¼ - 8¼	8¼ - 11½	11½ - 12
6	wetland	1	¼ - 1¾	1¾ - 6	—	6 - 7¼	7¼ - 8½	8½ - 11	11 - 12
7	farmland	1¾	0 - 1¾	1¾ - 6	—	6 - 7¾	7¾ - 8¾	8¾ - 11	11 - 12
8	farmland	2½	0 - 1¾	1¾ - 6	—	6 - 7¾	7¾ - 8¾	8¾ - 11	11 - 12
9	landfill	2½	¾ - 1¾	1¾ - 6	—	6 - 7¾	7¾ - 8¾	8¾ - 11	11 - 12
10	industry	2½	0 - 1¾	1¾ - 6	—	6 - 7¾	7¾ - 9	9 - 11	11 - 12
11	industry	3	0 - 2	2 - 7	—	7 - 8	8 - 9¼	9¼ - 11½	11½ - 12
12	urban area	3	0 - 2¼	2¼ - 7	—	7 - 8¼	8¼ - 9½	9½ - 11½	11½ - 12
13	urban area	3½	0 - 2¼	2¼ - 7	—	7 - 8¼	8¼ - 9½	9½ - 11½	11½ - 12
14	urban area	3¾	0 - 2¼	2¼ - 7	—	7 - 8½	8½ - 9¾	9¾ - 11½	11½ - 12
15	urban area	4	0 - 2¾	2¾ - 4½	4½ - 7	7 - 9	9 - 9¾	9¾ - 12	—
16	urban area	5	0 - 2¾	2¾ - 4½	4½ - 7	7 - 9	9 - 9¾	9¾ - 12	—
17	farmland	4	0 - 2¾	2¾ - 4½	4½ - 7½	7½ - 9	9 - 10	10 - 12	—
18	wastewater treatment plant	3	¼ - 2½	2½ - 4	4 - 7½	7½ - 9	9 - 10	10 - 12	—
19	farmland	2½	0 - 2¼	2¼ - 4½	4½ - 8	8 - 9	9 - 10¼	10¼ - 12	—
20	river	1½	¼ - 2½	2½ - 4½	4½ - 8	8 - 9¼	9¼ - 10½	10½ - 12	—
21	river	½	1 - 2½	2½ - 5	5 - 8	8 - 9¼	9¼ - 10½	10½ - 12	—
22	river	1½	¼ - 3	3 - 8	—	8 - 9¼	9¼ - 10½	10½ - 12	—
23	national park	2	0 - 3	3 - 8	—	8 - 9½	9½ - 10¾	10¾ - 12	—
24	national park	3¼	0 - 2¾	2¾ - 8	—	8 - 9¾	9¾ - 11	11 - 12	—
25	national park	3¾	0 - 3	3 - 8	—	8 - 10	10 - 11¼	11¼ - 12	—

Ground Water Student Page

Name: _____ Date: _____

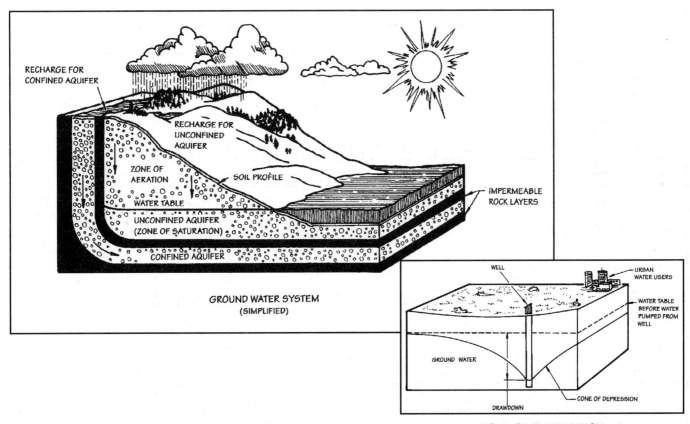

WELL LOG GROUND WATER CHART (CROSS SECTION)

RECHARGE FOR
CONFINED AQUIFER

RECHARGE FOR
UNCONFINED
AQUIFER

ZONE OF
AERATION

SOIL PROFILE

WATER TABLE

UNCONFINED AQUIFER
(ZONE OF SATURATION)

CONFINED AQUIFER

IMPERMEABLE
ROCK LAYERS

GROUND WATER SYSTEM
(SIMPLIFIED)

WELL

URBAN
WATER USERS

WATER TABLE
BEFORE WATER
PUMPED FROM
WELL

GROUND WATER

DRAWDOWN

CONE OF DEPRESSION

CONE OF DEPRESSION

Geyser Guts

Daisy, Pork Chop, Old Faithful . . . names of a favorite pet? First born child? No. They're geysers in Yellowstone National Park.

▼ Summary
Students observe a mini-erupting geyser and interpret and diagram how a geyser works.

Objectives
Students will:
- list the conditions necessary for a geyser.
- compare and contrast a geyser, hot spring, fumarole, and mud pot.

Materials
- *Copies or overheads of photographs of* **Geothermal Features**
- *Copies of* **Geyser Guts Maze**

For **Option 1**:
- *Percolator coffee pot, with lid, basket, and stem (These are available in camp stores and may be found at rummage sales.)*
- *Rocks*
- *Water*
- *Heat source (e.g., Bunsen burner, hot plate, stove top)*
- *Pliers*
- *Duct Tape (to seal the spout of the pot)*

For **Option 2**:
- *Heat source*
- *Glass beaker*
- *1-hole rubber stopper (snugly fits into glass beaker)*
- *Glass tube (about 8 inches [20 cm] high)*
- *Funnel*

Making Connections
Students may have had little previous experience with geysers and other geothermal features. Some may have visited or heard of Yellowstone National Park, where more than half of Earth's geysers are found. Helping students become aware of this natural phenomenon may promote student involvement in protecting these rare and beautiful features.

Background
Yellowstone National Park has between 200 and 250 active geysers, and is the largest geyser field in the world. Geysers are also found in Iceland (site of Geysir and Strokkur), New Zealand, Chile, and Russia. Why are geysers not found in our backyards? Geysers have very specific requirements: a generous water supply, a heat source, a plumbing system, and porous rock.

Rain and snow fulfill the water requirement. With each eruption, some geysers spew tens of thousands of gallons of water. Therefore, geysers will only occur in areas of abundant water.

Geysers require hot water. Precipitation is cold, so how is water heated? Geyser basins exist in areas that have a strong heat source of molten rock (magma) beneath the ground water. Cold water from the surface trickles through underground rocks and comes in contact with rocks that are heated by magma. The water is heated and rises, because hot water is less dense. The temperature of this water can reach 500 degrees F (260°C), but still does not turn into vapor, because the rocks encasing the liquid increase the pressure on the water, preventing it from turning into gas. This is superheated water because it is heated above the normal boiling point of 212 degrees F (100°C) at sea level. At the surface of Yellowstone National Park, water's boiling point is 199 degrees F (93°C), because of its high elevation (six to eleven thousand feet, averaging about eight).

Sidebar

■ **Grade Level:**
Upper Elementary, Middle School

■ **Subject Areas:**
Earth Science, Geography

■ **Duration:**
Preparation time:
Part I, Option 1: 50 minutes
Option 2: 10 minutes
Part II: 30 minutes

Activity time:
Part I, Option 1: 30 minutes
Option 2: 30 minutes
Part II: 30 minutes

■ **Setting:** Outdoors

■ **Skills:**
Gathering information (observing); Interpreting (relating); Applying (designing)

■ **Charting the Course**
Prior to this activity, students should understand the effect heat energy has on molecules (e.g., "Molecules in Motion"). Other aspects of ground water systems are explored in "Get the Ground Water Picture."

■ **Vocabulary**
geyser, vapor

Iceland

Kamchatka

Yellowstone

New Zealand

El Tatio

Locations of geysers around the world.

USED WITH PERMISSION FROM *GEYSERS: WHAT THEY ARE AND HOW THEY WORK*, T. SCOTT BRYAN. 1990. NIWOT, CO: ROBERTS RINEHART PUBLISHERS.

A geyser must have a *plumbing system*. In most of the world's geyser locations, water is moving through rhyolite, a volcanic rock. Water dissolves a mineral in rhyolite called silicon dioxide, or silica, creating tunnels and pathways (the geyser's gut) throughout the rock. An opening in the Earth's surface (a vent) allows heated water to escape via these cracks when enough pressure is produced. Dissolved materials are carried by water and deposited along the plumbing system, constricting the pathways and openings. This narrowing of the geyser's network is important, because it allows pressure to build up within the system. The underground network of fractures and channels is unique to each geyser and actually helps to determine its appearance and behavior.

What causes a geyser to erupt? Water in a geyser system is superheated and kept in a liquid state by the pressure above and all around it. However, at some place in the

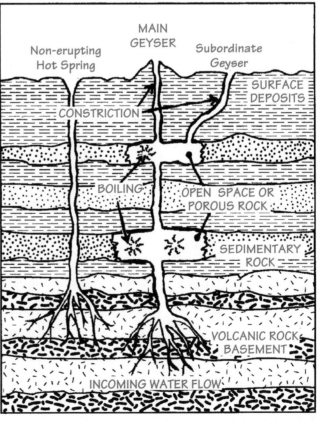

MAIN GEYSER

Non-erupting Hot Spring

Subordinate Geyser

SURFACE DEPOSITS

CONSTRICTION

BOILING

OPEN SPACE OR POROUS ROCK

SEDIMENTARY ROCK

VOLCANIC ROCK BASEMENT

INCOMING WATER FLOW

ADAPTED WITH PERMISSION FROM *GEYSERS: WHAT THEY ARE AND HOW THEY WORK*, T. SCOTT BRYAN. 1990. NIWOT, CO: ROBERTS RINEHART PUBLISHERS.

plumbing system the heat of the water will rise so high that it will overcome the pressure suppressing it. It will then boil, creating steam bubbles. Steam bubbles manage to force some water out of the vent. (To the viewer this looks like a mini-eruption and is called "preplay.") The escaped water creates a sudden drop in pressure within the plumbing system, and superheated water within the system flashes to steam. The geyser continues to erupt until equilibrium between the pressure created by superheated water and the atmospheric pressure above is achieved.

Natural and human events alter geysers. Earthquakes or a buildup of silica within a geyser's gut can stop eruptions. In some areas hot water has been tapped for powering turbines to create electricity or other energy uses—a practice that has destroyed some nearby geysers. This deprives geysers of either sufficient heat or water or both.

In addition to geysers, three other types of thermal features exist: hot springs, fumaroles, and mud pots. While geysers erupt, hot springs do not, because of inadequate heating or cooling of their large surfaces. However, most large hot pools in Yellowstone were once geysers. Fumaroles occur when there is ample heat but insufficient water for a geyser—all of the water turns to steam. When hot clay accumulates, resulting from acid attacking rock and soil and breaking it down, a popping and bubbling mud pot occurs.

Procedure
▼ Warm Up
Show students pictures of geysers. Ask where they would go to find geysers. Have they ever traveled to areas where geysers exist (Yellowstone National Park; Mam-

moth Lakes, California)? Why aren't geysers found in their backyards? Have students draw a picture or diagram showing how they think a geyser works.

To show what happens to a liquid that has gas dissolved in it when pressure is suddenly released, shake a bottle of soda pop and open the cap quickly and carefully. Stand back. Be sure to stage this outdoors. This demonstration involves two of the factors required for a geyser to function: liquid and pressure. Heat and a plumbing system will be illustrated later with a more complex demonstration.

▼ The Activity
THIS ACTIVITY INVOLVES BOILING WATER. EXERCISE EXTREME CAUTION DURING DEMONSTRATION. KEEP STUDENTS AT A SAFE DISTANCE TO AVOID BURNS. TO TEST THE SAFETY OF YOUR EQUIPMENT, COMPLETE A PRACTICE DEMONSTRATION PRIOR TO THE CLASS PRESENTATION.

Part I
Following are two options for simulating a geyser. The first option is more dramatic but the materials may be more difficult to locate.

Option 1
1. **Present the following demonstration to show how a geyser works. Place the stem and coffee basket of a percolator into the coffee pot.**

2. **Put rocks inside the coffee basket to keep the stem resting on the bottom of the pot. Fill the coffee-pot halfway with water. Seal the spout with duct tape.**

3. **Using pliers, slightly pinch the tube of the stem near the top. (Do not close off the stem completely.) Make sure the lid is securely on the pot. The basket lid does not need to be in place. Position the pot over a heat source. It may be necessary to heat the water for 5 to 10 minutes.**

4. **Explain to students that the water that first spits out of the stem is called "preplay." This overflow**

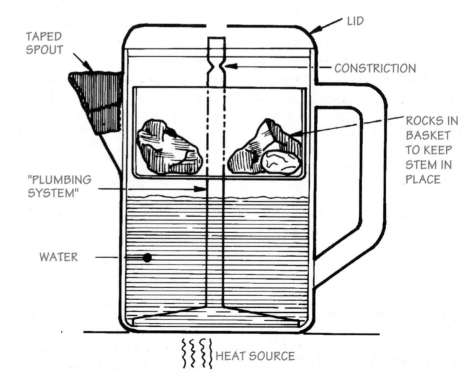

TAPED SPOUT

LID

CONSTRICTION

"PLUMBING SYSTEM"

ROCKS IN BASKET TO KEEP STEM IN PLACE

WATER

HEAT SOURCE

and splashing will occur prior to the eruption. **CAUTION: STAND BACK—HOT WATER WILL BE ERUPTING FROM THE STEM.** You can expect the height of the eruption to be from 1 ¹/₂ to 3 feet (0.5 m to 1 m).

5. **Have students identify the components of the demonstration that caused the water to erupt. They should list a plumbing system, a constriction in the plumbing system, and a heat source. Describe how these conditions exist in the natural world.**

Option 2

1. **Assemble the materials as illustrated below. The funnel is used to finish pouring water into the glass tube until it is about three-fourths full. Remove funnel after filling.**

2. **Apply the heat source. Be sure that students are observing from a safe distance. A spout of hot water will erupt from the glass rod to an approximate height of 1 to 3 feet (0.3 m to 1 m).**

Part II

1. **Provide students with descriptions of other thermal features (hot springs, fumaroles, and mud pots).**

2. **Have students brainstorm ideas for demonstrating these features.** Students may diagram their ideas. After careful evaluation of students' ideas, the teacher may wish to perform the actual demonstrations. Because of the danger of boiling water and steam, students should not conduct the demonstrations.

▼ Wrap Up

Ask students to draw a diagram of the geyser demonstration and explain its relationship to the eruption of a natural geyser. Compare their drawings to the ones they made in the *Warm Up*. Discuss how

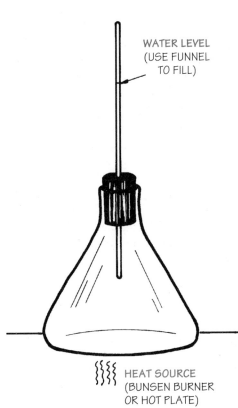

WATER LEVEL
(USE FUNNEL TO FILL)

HEAT SOURCE
(BUNSEN BURNER OR HOT PLATE)

altering parts of the set-up might affect the eruption. For example, what might result from placing only one cup of water in the beaker (reducing the water supply) or pinching the stem in more than one place (changing the shape of the plumbing system)?

Have younger students guide the water drop through the *Geyser Guts Maze*. Older learners may want to create their own maze that illustrates how a geyser works. Have students present mazes to friends and families to complete.

Ask students to compare and contrast the four geothermal features.

Assessment

Have students:
*   draw a diagram of the geyser demonstration and relate it to a natural eruption (*Warm Up* and *Wrap Up*).
*   design demonstrations for mud pots, fumaroles, and hot springs

(*Part II*, Step 2).
*   trace the water drop's path through the maze or design their own maze (*Wrap Up*).

Extensions

Have students research geothermal energy production and its effect on geysers around the world. In some areas geysers are located on protected lands such as national parks. However, individuals and companies may own lands adjacent to geyser fields and wish to tap the hot water. Scientists, managers, and others often contest this action because geyser systems are sometimes interconnected, and draining the water has potential to destroy the geysers. Have students discuss the rights of an adjacent landowner versus the rights of the public regarding these features.

Resources

Bryan, T. Scott. 1990. *Geysers: What They Are and How They Work*. Niwot, Colo.: Roberts Rinehart, Inc. Publishers.

"Geothermal Energy and Our Environment." Available from the United States Department of Energy, For Energy Information write: Energy, P.O. Box 62, Oak Ridge, TN 37830.

Robinson, Sandra C., and George, Robinson. 1991. *In Pictures, Yellowstone, The Continuing Story*. Las Vegas, Nevada: K.C. Publications.

Selleck, Jeff. "Build Your Own Model Geyser." In The Idea File, available from the interpretive staff of Yellowstone National Park.

White, Donald E. 1984. *Geysers*. Washington, D.C.: Government Printing Office. Available free from the U.S. Geological Survey (#1984-421-618/10002)

Geothermal Features

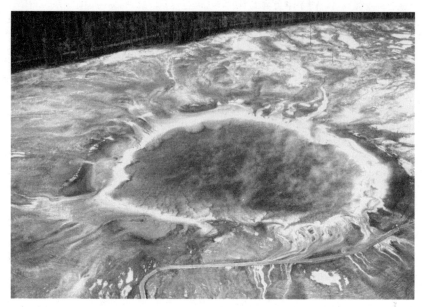

Hot Spring. COURTESY: YELLOWSTONE NATIONAL PARK

Geyser. COURTESY: YELLOWSTONE NATIONAL PARK

Mud Pot. COURTESY: YELLOWSTONE NATIONAL PARK

Fumarole. COURTESY: YELLOWSTONE NATIONAL PARK

©The Watercourse and Council for Environmental Education (CEE).

PROJECT WET
Water Education for Teachers

Geyser Guts Maze

Name: _____

Date: _____

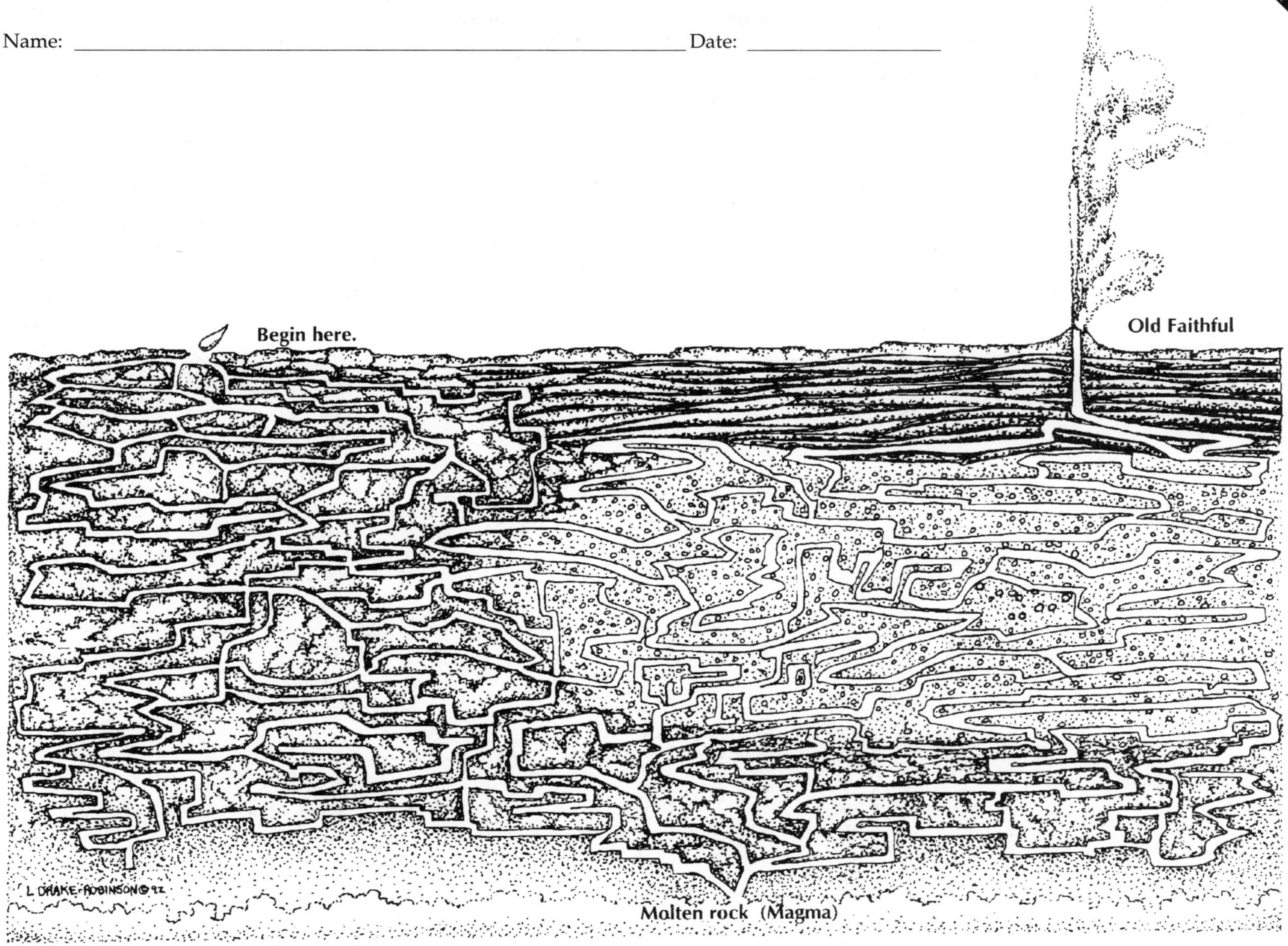

Begin here.

Molten rock (Magma)

Old Faithful

L. DRAKE-ROBINSON © '91.

The Great Stony Book

You are walking along a path one mile above sea level, when suddenly you step on a sea shell . . . how did it get there?

▼ Summary
Students create layers of buried fossils to learn how ancient, elevated ocean floors create a history book of stone.

Objectives
Students will:
- demonstrate water's involvement in the processes of sedimentation and erosion.
- recognize that layers of sedimentary rock can contain a record of earlier life (fossils) and environments.

Materials
- *3 different colors of soft modeling clay or modeling dough* (The different colors represent types of sedimentary rock in which fossils are most commonly found—limestone, sandstone, and shale. See the activity "A-maze-ing Water" for recipe for dough. One recipe will make enough dough for about one layer.)
- *A small, empty, rectangular aquarium* (must be at least 12 inches [30 cm] tall)
- *A rolling pin*
- *Student-provided fossils or artifacts*
- *A putty knife* (or other implement to cut into layered modeling dough)
- *Pencils*
- *Marking pens*
- *Large piece of poster board*
- *Water* (to sprinkle on clay)
- *Glass sheet or plastic wrap* (to cover aquarium)

Making Connections
Some students know that ancient oceans covered much of Earth's surface at different times during the geologic past. Many will be aware of major landforms like the Grand Canyon, where dozens of once buried rock layers are exposed. Investigating how history is preserved in stone helps students learn about Earth's past.

Background
In 1869, Major John Wesley Powell led an expedition down the Colorado River. He and his companions were the first people known to record their travels through the Grand Canyon. As the explorers ventured deeper into the great incision cut into Earth by the river, Powell observed that the Colorado had opened a "Great Stony Book," the pages of which contained a record of millions of years of Earth's history.

Powell, head of the United States Geological Survey, knew that some of the layers of exposed rock in the canyon walls had formed in ancient seas and contained evidence of earlier environments and life forms. These layers, dating back millions of years, also held clues to Earth's water history.

The Great Stony Book tells an interesting story. Traces of the plants and animals that lived during various time periods are now preserved as fossils in the Earth's rock record. Nature continually adds pages to the book, which in some places is open to reveal chapters in the history of Earth and its inhabitants.

Change is an enduring quality of the process that we call nature; but in the short span of a human life, alterations to the landscape are often nearly imperceptible. People observe changes that occur as a result of sudden, spectacular events—a flash flood gouging a new stream channel or washing away topsoil, a sandstorm reshaping a desert landscape, or an earthquake creating a lake. But the slow, endless process of water

---

■ Grade Level:
Middle School

■ Subject Areas:
Earth Science

■ Duration:
Preparation time: 50 minutes

Activity time: 2 weeks (1 hour on first and last day, 30 minutes on other days)

■ Setting: Classroom

■ Skills:
Gathering information (observing); Organizing (manipulating materials, categorizing); Interpreting (relating)

■ Charting the Course
A related activity is "Branching Out!" in which students build a model of a watershed to explore how water flows over the landscape. In "Wetland Soils in Living Color," students explore a soil profile, which involves sedimentation on a smaller scale. Other aspects of rock formation are covered in "Get the Ground Water Picture." The history of water on Earth is further explored in "Old Water." "What's the Solution?" presents some concepts relevant to this activity.

■ Vocabulary
sediment, erosion, deposition

TOP VIEW OF CLAY LAYERS

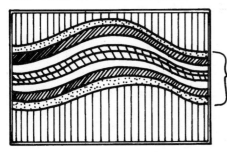

PATH OF RIVER

MOCK GEOLOGIC CHART   SAMPLE CUTS INTO ROCK LAYERS

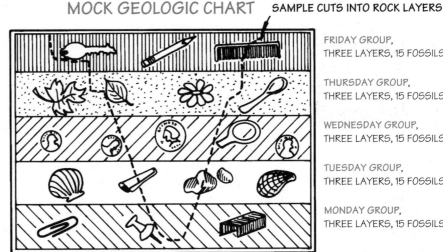

FRIDAY GROUP,
THREE LAYERS, 15 FOSSILS

THURSDAY GROUP,
THREE LAYERS, 15 FOSSILS

WEDNESDAY GROUP,
THREE LAYERS, 15 FOSSILS

TUESDAY GROUP,
THREE LAYERS, 15 FOSSILS

MONDAY GROUP,
THREE LAYERS, 15 FOSSILS

and wind picking up soil, weathered rock particles, and other debris; transporting them; and depositing them in other places (only to become rock again) is measured in *mountain time*—millions of years. As rivers, moving relentlessly toward the sea, cut into layers of rock, they open the pages of the stony book and reveal evidence of the earlier work of wind, water, and other natural agents of change.

Some of the rock layers of the Grand Canyon were formed from sediments that settled to the floor of shallow seas that once covered this land-scape, when it was lower and flatter. Other layers are the remnants of vast deserts that covered this area at other times in the past.

The process of sedimentation is slow and continuous. Over time, layer upon layer of sediments may stack up to great thicknesses. The weight of one layer upon another creates pressure. This pressure compacts the sedimentary particles tightly to-gether. Given enough time and the addition of a cementing agent, usually calcium carbonate ($CaCO_3$) or silica (SiO_2), this process results in the formation of a sedimentary rock. Three examples of sedimentary rock are sandstone, shale, and limestone. Sandstone is formed from deposits of sand. Shale is created from silt and clay; thus shale is finer grained than sandstone. Limestone is of either organic or inorganic origin. It may

consist of decomposed shells and skeletons of marine organisms that settled to the seafloor and combined with calcium carbonate; or it may be composed of only calcium carbonate that chemically precipitates from the water.

When a plant or animal dies, its remains are often buried by sedi-ments. Most of the organisms buried in the sediments decompose and leave no trace of their existence. In some cases, organisms leave an imprint of their shape in the sedi-ments before they solidify. Some-times parts of the organisms—such as shells and bones—are replaced by minerals, but retain their shape and internal structure and are preserved in the rock. These records of early life are called fossils. In addition to fossils, the surface of a sedimentary layer often has *ripple marks*; these are made by water flowing over an exposed surface (a beach or tidal mud flat) or by wind (as on the surface of a sand dune).

Over millions of years, immense geologic processes associated with mountain building raise these layers of sedimentary rock above the surface of the sea. Most sedimentary rocks, including those that are now far from the sea or other large bodies of water, were formed in marine or freshwater environments. According to a geologic principle, the principle of original horizontality, the sedi-ments were originally deposited in horizontal layers. Another geologic principle, the principle of superposi-tion, tells us that the bottom layer or formation is the oldest; the newest or youngest layer is on top. Thus, we must read the Great Stony Book backward in time, from the top down.

We can take the metaphor of the Great Stony Book further: It is a book with many parts and characters. The rock pages and chapters are exposed as water (and wind) erode Earth's surface. Earth is the author, illustra-tor, and designer. Each geologic formation is a new chapter and the story line for each chapter is provided by the environmental conditions that existed during the time the sediments were deposited. The pages contained in each chapter reflect minor variations in the environment over time, and support the main theme. The main characters are the sedimentary layers and the fossilized plants and animals they contain. The publisher is time. The author of the Great Stony Book, Earth, is also its editor. Earth is a restless editor, continually making changes. In some editing sessions, large parts of chapters have been altered. Some have even been deleted.

We, too, are characters in the most recent chapter. What will be our contribution to the Great Stony Book?

Procedure
▼ Warm Up
Tell the class about a careless student who, after undressing at night, throws her clothes on the floor. She does not pick them up the next day. Instead, she throws another layer of clothes on top of the pile. Tell students that this pile represents a record or storybook of the clothes this student has worn. Where would students find the clothes she had worn the first day?

Inform students that geologists use this same principle when studying layers of rock. They view the layers as a Great Stony Book.

Present students with information about the sedimentation process. Discuss how ancient ocean bottoms can now be found far above sea level. Refer them to the Grand Canyon and how water erodes the layers of rock, slowly revealing history—from the present to the distant past.

Have students list things they think geologists might find when studying

these layers. Make students aware that many sedimentary layers do not contain fossils. Have students keep a journal throughout the activity, recording observations, sketches, and interpretations.

▼ The Activity
1. **Explain that during the next two weeks, students will be creating a stony book that will record each day's events. Each day will represent several hundreds of thousands, or millions, of years.**

2. **Each day for a week, a different group of students will deposit layers of rock (clay) and randomly place "fossils" or artifacts in the layers. The days of the week will represent periods of geologic time.**

3. **Discuss with students what types of fossils they should use. Each group should think of approximately 15 small fossils they would like to bury. The groups should not see each other's fossils.** They will discover many of them next week. The fossils should be unique or have some special significance, but should not be valuable or sentimental. All items should somehow relate to the day during which they are placed in the layers (i.e., the fossils of Monday's group should be objects they brought to school or found in the classroom on Monday).

4. **Divide students into five small groups. Give the first group three mounds of modeling dough or clay, each a different color. Instruct students to roll out the mounds into layers about 3/4 inch (1.9 cm) thick. The length and width should match the inside dimensions of the aquarium.**

5. **Have students place one layer of modeling dough on the bottom of the aquarium. Explain to students that this represents the process of deposition of ocean sediments,**

which normally occurs over a great period of time.

6. **Tell students that, along with sediments, sometimes shells and bones of animals settle to the bottom of the ocean floor. To represent this, each student in the group should then randomly press a fossil or artifact into the surface of the layer. Repeat the process for the next two layers.** The last layer can contain ripple marks to serve as an additional clue to the marine origin of the sediments. Ripple marks can be made by lightly and repeatedly pressing the rounded surface of the rolling pin into the surface of the modeling dough.

7. **The next day, another group will repeat this same procedure. They should vary the arrangement of layers, so that layers of the same color are not adjacent.** For example, students on the first day layered red, then white, then blue. The second group could put a red or white layer next, but not a blue layer.

8. **Repeat the above steps with a different group each day, until each group has deposited three layers of sedimentary rock (modeling dough) and has randomly embedded their fossils in the layers.** By the end of the first week, the aquarium should contain a total of 15 layers and 75 different fossils or artifacts. To keep the clay moist, sprinkle it with water and cover the tank with a glass sheet or plastic wrap.

9. **Inform students that geologic processes have lifted the sea bottom thousands of feet above sea level. Mark a serpentine outline of a river on the surface of the top layer (the last and youngest), using a pencil. Refer to the illustration on page 151.**

10. **Using poster board, draw a cross section chart depicting the 15 layers of the model. Refer to the**

COURTESY: NATIONAL PARK SERVICE

illustration on page 151. **Assign dates along one side of the diagram, with each arrangement of three layers representing one period of time.** It is not necessary to use actual geologic dates and terms, but each group of layers should represent a large span of time (e.g., thousands or millions of years). Students may wish to create names for their group's time periods.

11. **On the first day of the second week, have a group from the previous week begin forming the canyon by** *carefully* **cutting about 1/5 of the way into the layered model, tracing the outline of the river. Be certain to vary the order so that no group discovers its own fossils. This represents water eroding through layers of rock. As they encounter fossils or artifacts in the layers, students should record, in the group's journal, a description of the items as well as the layer in which they were found. The fossils or artifacts should then be placed on the appropriate spot on the cross-sectional chart.** Students may wish to include a sketch of the fossil or artifact in the journal.

12. **Repeat the above process with each group throughout the week until the bottom (oldest) layer is reached. Each successive group will need to increase the width of the canyon as they cut deeper.**

▼ Wrap Up

Have students explain the Great Stony Book metaphor, and discuss how layers of rock and the fossils they contain are windows into the past. What is the role of water in this process? Ask students to look at each group's records and compare observations, sketches, and interpretations. Moderate a class discussion on the role of water as an agent of geologic change. (Water deposits the layers of sediments and wears them away.) Display the model and the "Mock Geologic Chart" derived from it in other classrooms or a school hallway.

Assessment

Have students:
- use a mock fossil record to interpret geologic events or classroom daily events (step 11).
- record and/or sketch fossils or artifacts in their journals (step 11).
- relate how water and its role in erosion and sedimentation help create a book of stone that contains a record of Earth's history (*Wrap Up*).

Extensions

If a stream-cut canyon or valley exists nearby, take a field trip to it. Otherwise, go to a nearby quarry or roadside where students can observe the layering of sediments. Sometimes fossils can be seen in these locations.

Visit a local natural history museum or the geology/paleontology department of a local college or university.

Write to Grand Canyon National Park and request titles of books, films, videos, and other educational materials. Grand Canyon Natural History Association, P.O. Box 399, Grand Canyon, AZ 86023. (602) 638-2481.

Depending on time and student interest, a more elaborate model (using real sediments [sand, gravel, mud], real bones and shells, and flowing water) might be made for display at a school science fair or in the classroom throughout the year. To construct a model, enlist the aid of an industrial arts teacher.

Resources

Bates, L. Robert, and Julia A. Jackson, eds. 1984. *Dictionary of Geological Terms*. New York, N.Y.: Doubleday.

Braus, Judy, ed. 1988. *Nature Scope: Geology, The Active Earth*. Washington, D.C.: National Wildlife Federation.

Coble, Charles et al. 1988. *Prentice Hall Earth Science*. Englewood Cliffs, N.J.: Prentice Hall, Inc.

Geological Society of America, 3300 Penrose Place, Boulder, CO 80301.

Judson, Sheldon, and Marvin E. Kauffman. 1990. *Physical Geology*. Englewood Cliffs, N.J.: Prentice Hall, Inc.

McPhee, John. 1980. *Basin and Range*. Toronto, Canada: Collins Publishers.

———. 1982. *In Suspect Terrain*. Toronto, Canada: McGraw-Hill Ryerson Ltd.

———. 1986. *Rising from the Plains*. Toronto, Canada: Collins Publishers.

Schlenker, Richard M., and Sarah J. Yoshida. 1991. "Learning about Fossil Formation by Classroom Simulation." *Science Activities*, 28 (3).

NOTE: MacTimeliner (Tom Snyder Productions) is a computer program that can be used to generate geologic time lines.

A House of Seasons

"April showers bring May flowers," "Sunshine and showers make up summer hours," "Frost on the pumpkin," and "A winter wonderland" . . . What do all these descriptions have in common?

■ **Grade Level:**
Lower Elementary

■ **Subject Areas:**
Earth Science, Fine Arts, Geography

■ **Duration:**
Preparation time: 30 minutes
Activity time: 50 minutes

■ **Setting:** Classroom

■ **Skills:**
Gathering information (collecting); Organizing (sorting); Analyzing (comparing); Presenting (drawing)

■ **Charting the Course**
Conducting "Water Match" prior to this activity helps students identify the three states of water. Aspects of water in the seasons can be further researched in "The Thunderstorm."

■ **Vocabulary**
seasons

▼ Summary
By constructing a "House of Seasons" collage, students observe the role of water in each of the seasons.

Objectives
Students will:
• recognize the presence of water within each season.

Materials
• *Old children's or nature magazines* (Check libraries and recycling centers.)
• *Scissors*
• *Glue*
• *Construction paper*
• *Tape*

Making Connections
People have different attitudes about each of the seasons. Often these relate to the presence of water and its various forms. Students' observation skills can be enhanced when they look for signs of water in photographs of different seasons.

Background
As the seasons change, so can the quantity and forms of precipitation. In the summer, long, hot, humid days can produce spectacular thunderstorms. In late fall, water can be seen when dew forms frost on the grass and windowpanes. Water in winter is used in snowball fights and in snow fort building. In spring, melting snow and plentiful showers create puddles, which are often a nuisance but can also be great fun!

Not all parts of the country experience four distinct seasons. Some places, such as the South, have a dry season, a wet season, and a cool season. No matter where in the country we live, variations in weather occur throughout the year. These wet, wonderful changes influence how we plant our crops, plan vacations, and perhaps even view the world.

Procedure
▼ *Warm Up*
Ask students to describe the different seasons. Write down or note their responses. Circle or have students identify how many of their descriptions involve water in some form (snow, rain, puddles, etc.) Which season do they like best? Why?

▼ *The Activity*
1. **Organize students into small groups. Have students look through children's or nature magazines. Ask them to locate and cut or tear out pictures that show the different seasons. Encourage students to look especially for pictures that contain water images.** Students may also draw pictures of the seasons.

2. **Tell students to arrange the pictures in four piles, one pile for each season.** For organizational purposes, have students sort by placing each picture on a different colored piece of construction paper, representing each season (i.e., white for winter; green for spring; yellow for summer; red for fall). (For regions of the country with just two or three seasons, classify pictures accordingly.)

3. **Have each student fold a piece of paper into quarters, dividing it into**

four equal sections. Instruct students to make collages of the photographs. Keep each season within its quarter section. (An option is to have students contribute their pictures to a large class collage, constructed by the teacher.)

4. **Discuss the presence of water in each season. Have students compare how water looks in spring, summer, fall, and winter.** Do they think there is a different quantity of water in each season? Does water have anything to do with why they do or do not like a season? How do people manage water during different seasons (e.g., sprinkle lawns during hot and dry times, shovel snow)?

5. **Give each student a sheet of construction paper. Have them cut four shuttered windows in the paper. The location of the cuts should correspond to the placement of the seasons in the collage.** Teachers may wish to pre-cut the windows. (An alternative activity is to create a "Book of Seasons." Collages of different seasons can be stapled together and students can design an attractive cover.)

6. **Have students lay the construction paper over their collage and tape the edges to the collage. When they open the windows, they should see winter, summer, fall, and spring scenery.** Students may want to draw a house around their windows. Have them tell or write a story, poem, or song about the House of Seasons, that is, a house in which each window offers a view of a different season.

▼ *Wrap Up and Action*

Have students share their collage with a friend. See if the friend can identify the season and describe what water looks like in that season.

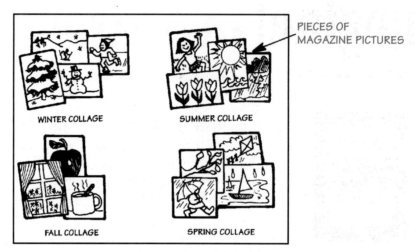

WINTER COLLAGE   SUMMER COLLAGE

PIECES OF MAGAZINE PICTURES

FALL COLLAGE   SPRING COLLAGE

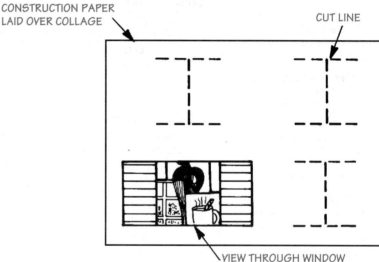

CONSTRUCTION PAPER LAID OVER COLLAGE

CUT LINE

VIEW THROUGH WINDOW WHEN "SHUTTERS" ARE OPEN

Assessment
Have students:
*   identify or draw pictures of the seasons (step 1).
*   sort pictures into seasons (step 2).
*   design a House of Seasons collage (steps 5 and 6).
*   compare the appearances of water in each season (step 4).

Extensions
Older students could add to their collage newspaper headlines about water in the seasons. They can also investigate how the angle of the Earth's axis, and Earth's rotation around the Sun causes seasons.

Have students use their own photographs of the seasons to create a collage.

Resources
Borden, Louise. 1989. *Caps, Hats, Socks, and Mittens: A Book about the Four Seasons.* New York, N.Y.: Scholastic.

Gilmore, Julie, et al. 1993. *Pathways: Increasing Environmental Literacy Through the Arts.* Kelly, Wyo.: Teton Science School.

Hughes, Shirley. 1988. *Out and About.* New York, N.Y.: Lothrop.

Kahl, Jonathan. 1992. *Wet Weather: Rain Showers and Snowfall.* Minneapolis, Minn.: Lerner.

Imagine!

■ **Grade Level:**
Upper Elementary, Middle School

■ **Subject Areas:**
Earth Sciences, Life Sciences, Language Arts, Fine Arts

■ **Duration:**
Preparation time: 10 minutes
Activity time: 20 minutes

■ **Setting:** Anywhere

■ **Skills:**
Gathering information (listening); Interpreting (relating)

■ **Charting the Course**
Prior to this activity, students should learn about physical and chemical processes of water, specifically "Water Models," which covers evaporation and condensation. To support student understanding of the water cycle they can participate in the activity "The Incredible Journey."

■ **Vocabulary**
evaporation, condensation, precipitation

What would it be like to take a journey as a water molecule?

▼ Summary
Students take an imaginary journey with water in its solid, liquid, and gaseous forms as it travels around the world.

Objectives
Students will:
• identify changes in states of water that enable water to move through the water cycle.
• describe the water cycle.

Materials
• *Audio recordings of water sounds* (water lapping on the shore of a pond, a storm, ocean waves, streams, a waterfall) (optional)
• *Copy of Water Cycle Journey* (script)

Making Connections
Students usually learn about the processes in the water cycle through indirect approaches such as diagrams and experiments. Using their imaginations, students discover what happens to water as it moves above, over, and under Earth's surface.

Background
Water can be found almost everywhere at any given time. As it changes forms, it travels throughout the world in the water cycle.

If you were able to travel with a water molecule, you would explore ocean depths, float through the atmosphere, splash down on a prairie, and weave among soil particles deep underground. How does water travel to all these places?

The processes that drive the water cycle are evaporation, condensation, transpiration, and precipitation. They are powered by solar energy and gravity. Causing water vapor to rise into the atmosphere, solar energy evaporates water from soil, plants, oceans, lakes, and streams. When it condenses in the atmosphere as rain, snow, hail, or sleet, gravity pulls it down again.

Because of the nature of water movement, a water molecule may be used over and over again throughout the centuries. The water you drink today could have dribbled down the back of a dinosaur, been locked in a glacier during the last ice age, spent 30,000 years in the ocean depths, or floated in a cloud over ancient Egypt!

Procedure
▼ *Warm Up*
Ask students to diagram or write a description of the water cycle and describe the processes that occur as water moves from one location to another.

▼ *The Activity*
1. **Ask students what it would be like to travel with water as it moves through the water cycle.**

2. **Tell students that you are going to take them on a journey through the water cycle with their imaginations. They should sit quietly and may wish to close their eyes.** You will be relating ideas and events and they should create pictures in their minds.

3. **Begin the tape of water sounds and start reading the script, *Water Cycle Journey*. Keep your voice even, level, and clear. Pause 2–3 seconds when you encounter the symbol "..............." to let students imagine what you are describing.**

COURTESY: EVERGLADES NATIONAL PARK

or, when river water is used for industrial or municipal purposes?

Students can create drawings, poems, or other artwork to reflect their perceptions of the water cycle.

Resources

Alexander, Gretchen. 1989. *Water Cycle Teacher's Guide*. Hudson, N.H.: Delta Education, Inc.

Ewing, Margaret S., and Terence J. Mills. 1994. "Water Literacy in College Freshmen: Could a Cognitive Imagery Strategy Improve Understanding?" *Journal of Environmental Education* (25) 4: 36-40.

🍎 Mayes, Susan. 1989. *What Makes It Rain?* London, England: Usborne Publications.

🍎 Schmid, Eleonore. 1990. *The Water's Journey*. New York, N.Y.: North-South Books.

Audio recordings of water sounds:

Alpine Stream. 1994. North Sound, North Word Press Inc.

Ocean Encounter. 1994. North Sound, North Word Press Inc.

Solitude Series. Contact: The Moss Music Group Inc., 48 West 38th Street, New York, NY 10018.

▼ *Wrap Up*

After the reading, ask students for their impressions. Have students list the major parts of the journey. Where did they go and how did they get there? Have each student diagram or write a description of the water cycle and relate events in the exercise to the diagram/description.

Instruct students to look for and record water movements that occur in the water cycle in their everyday lives (rain, evaporating puddles, a cloud, an animal drinking water). Have students keep track of relative humidity reports to remind them that even when they can't see water, it is moving in the air around them. Keep a class record of these events and reports. Have students create their own water journeys. An alter-

native is for students to create a comic strip of a water molecule traveling through the water cycle.

Assessment

Have students:
*   identify the states of water as it moves through the water cycle (*Warm Up* and *Wrap Up*).
*   describe the places water goes as it moves through the water cycle (*Wrap Up*).
*   describe the processes that enable water to move (*Wrap Up*).

Extensions

Have students write a script for other parts of the water cycle. What happens when ground water is absorbed by a plant, when water from a stream is drunk by an animal,

Water Cycle Journey

THE POOL

It is a beautiful summer day.........the sky is blue.........white puffy clouds float overhead ....the sun is shining.........the ground is warm......a songbird sings in a nearby tree ....Imagine a still pool of water.........it is surrounded by soft green grass and tall trees .... you are a water molecule in the pond ....moving gently back and forth......... you can feel other water molecules around you .... you are all gently moving against each other ....touching.........close.........a gentle wind ripples the surface.........tiny waves move along ....you are bounced into each other......... you are all rocking back and forth ....the sun warms the surface of the water ....you are close to the surface.........now you are right at the surface.........you begin to move more rapidly ....the warmth and energy of the sun continue to strike you.........you become more energized and move more quickly.........suddenly you burst from the surface.........you are released into the air.........you have moved away from the others and you gently float alone.........invisible to the human eye.........apart from any other water molecules.

THE ATMOSPHERE

You float in the air and rise slowly.........there is great space around you.........you can see the pond below.........it grows more distant......... you continue to rise.........around you, you can see other water molecules.........but they are on their own.........you cannot reach out and touch them.........they, like you, continue to float and rise into the atmosphere......... as you rise, it is getting cooler.........your movement becomes slower.........a tiny particle floats by you .... you grab on to it.........another water molecule

grabs on to the same particle......... then another and another......... you all begin to bond to each other making the particle larger and larger......... you see other particles with water molecules attached......... everything around you begins to form patterns......... the patterns are like giant diamonds.........light passes through these ice crystals and creates prisms and tiny rainbows ....more and more water molecules come together.........you feel them surround you .... you are becoming heavier......... heavier .... heavier......... you begin to fall.........

THE SNOW

You are falling faster.........faster......... wind blows you up and around......... you swirl about......... trees appear.........then a white blanket below.........gravity takes you to the blanket......... you land on the surface......... above you and around you other particles fall .... you become part of the white blanket ....everything becomes quiet and cold......... all around you stillness settles in.........

THE BIG MELT

Gently, ever so slowly......... a soft light begins to appear around you......... a gradual brightness .... the light brings warmth with it......... you begin to move ever so slowly......... as the light brightens the warmth increases .... you move back and forth......... around you water molecules begin to slip away......... they seem to move downward, sliding along......... you and surrounding water molecules are suddenly released and begin to slide.........

DOWN THE MOUNTAIN

As you tumble downward, you feel other water molecules push together around you........ suddenly you burst to the surface........ the sun is bright........the air is fresh and dry........it invigorates you........ all around you there are water molecules .... traveling quickly........ all moving down a hill........ more groups of molecules join you........ more........ and more........ all traveling down quickly........ as you travel you see trees, grasses........ you come upon a large tree........you bump against the roots and slow down........

INTO THE GROUND

Gravity begins to pull at you........you seep into the ground, weaving among sand and soil particles........flowing underground is like moving, slow motion, through a dark obstacle course........you are now deep underground, surrounded by soil particles........suddenly, your movement seems to be more horizontal, the pressure of other molecules behind you pushes you along........it appears lighter up ahead........you and surrounding molecules spring out of the ground........ tumbling over ground, you continue your gradual descent to the foot of the mountain........

BIG RIVER

Gradually you slow down........ you sense a gradual decrease in the slope of the land........ you now move gracefully in a large mass of water........ other streams contribute to your journey........ more and more water molecules collect together ....this is the big river........ along you travel........ other particles swirl around you........ you and other molecules work together to carry the particles........you move more slowly now........the slope is slight........ the slower you go the less energy you have to carry the particles .... the particles slip from your grasp and sink but you move on........

THE GIANT POOL

Ever so slowly the water moves toward the open........ grassy banks give way to cement canals........ all around you civilization makes itself known........ cars........ people .... even an airport........ the sounds are loud and constant........ eventually you feel a change ....all around you are new materials .... molecules of other substances........they are strongly attracted to you........ these are the salts........they fill in the gaps between you and other water molecules........ you and other particles continue to move about........

WHAT NEXT?

There are many options open to you........ where will you go?........ the sun's energy may invigorate you, you could break away and float into the sky again ....other water molecules may hold on to you, you could swirl around the surface........ gravity may pull at you, you could explore the darkness of the deep........ a fish swims by, now there's a possibility........ imagine where you will go next........ picture it in your mind........ when you know where you are or will go, when you are ready, open your eyes........

The Incredible Journey

■ Grade Level:
Upper Elementary, Middle School

■ Subject Areas:
Earth Science

■ Duration:
Preparation time: 50 minutes
Activity time: two 50-minute periods

■ Setting:
A large room or playing field

■ Skills:
Organizing (mapping); Analyzing (identifying components and relationships); Interpreting (describing)

■ Charting the Course
Other water cycle activities include "Water Models" and "Imagine!" In-depth investigations of how water moves can supplement this activity: condensing and evaporating ("Water Models"), filtering through soil ("Get the Ground Water Picture"), traveling over Earth's surface ("Branching Out!"), and moving through the atmosphere ("Piece It Together").

■ Vocabulary
condensation, evaporation, electromagnetic forces

Where will the water you drink this morning be tomorrow?

▼ Summary
With a roll of the die, students simulate the movement of water within the water cycle.

Objectives
Students will:
- describe the movement of water within the water cycle.
- identify the states of water as it moves through the water cycle.

Materials
- *9 large pieces of paper*
- *Copies of* **Water Cycle Table** *(optional)*
- *Marking pens*
- *9 boxes, about 6 inches (15 cm) on a side* (Boxes are used to make dice for the game. Gift boxes used for coffee mugs are a good size or inquire at your local mailing outlet. There will be one die [or box] per station of the water cycle. [To increase the pace of the game, use more boxes at each station, especially at the clouds and ocean stations.] The labels for the sides of the die are located in the *Water Cycle Table*. These labels represent the options for pathways that water can follow. Explanations for the labels are provided. For younger students, use pictures. Another option is to use a spinner—see the activity "A Drop in the Bucket" for spinner design. It is necessary to design a spinner for each station.)
- *A bell, whistle, buzzer, or some sound maker*

Making Connections
When children think of the water cycle, they often imagine a circle of water, flowing from a stream to an ocean, evaporating to the clouds, raining down on a mountaintop, and flowing back into a stream. Role-playing a water molecule helps students to conceptualize the water cycle as more than a predictable two-dimensional path.

Background
While water does circulate from one point or state to another in the water cycle, the paths it can take are variable.

Heat energy directly influences the rate of motion of water molecules (refer to the activity "Molecules in Motion"). When the motion of the molecule increases because of an increase in heat energy, water will change from solid to liquid to gas. With each change in state, physical movement from one location to another usually follows. Glaciers melt to pools which overflow to streams, where water may evaporate into the atmosphere.

Gravity further influences the ability of water to travel over, under, and above Earth's surface. Water as a solid, liquid, or gas has mass and is subject to gravitational force. Snow on mountaintops melts and descends through watersheds to the oceans of the world.

One of the most visible states in which water moves is the liquid form. Water is seen flowing in streams and rivers and tumbling in ocean waves. Water travels slowly underground, seeping and filtering through particles of soil and pores within rocks.

Although unseen, water's most dramatic movements take place during its gaseous phase. Water is constantly evaporating, changing from a liquid to a gas. As a vapor, it can travel through the atmosphere over Earth's surface. In fact, water vapor surrounds us all the time. Where it condenses and returns to Earth depends upon loss of heat energy, gravity, and the structure of Earth's surface.

Using station illustrations, create a one page graphic on which students record their movements during the Incredible Journey.

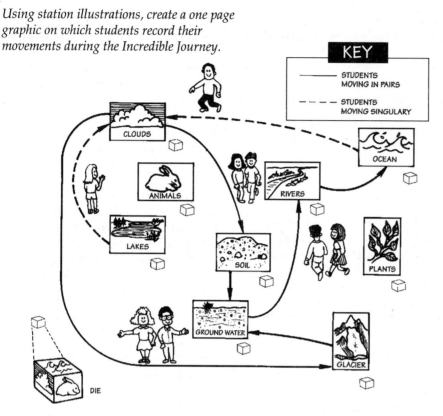

KEY

—————— STUDENTS MOVING IN PAIRS

- - - - - - STUDENTS MOVING SINGULARY

CLOUDS

ANIMALS

LAKES

RIVERS

OCEAN

SOIL

PLANTS

GROUND WATER

GLACIER

DIE

Water condensation can be seen as dew on plants or water droplets on the outside of a glass of cold water. In clouds, water molecules collect on tiny dust particles. Eventually, the water droplets become too heavy and gravity pulls the water to Earth.

Living organisms also help move water. Humans and other animals carry water within their bodies, transporting it from one location to another. Water is either directly consumed by animals or is removed from foods during digestion. Water is excreted as a liquid or leaves as a gas, usually through respiration. When water is present on the skin of an animal (for example, as perspiration), evaporation may occur.

The greatest movers of water among living organisms are plants. The roots of plants absorb water. Some of this water is used within the body of the plant, but most of it travels up through the plant to the leaf surface.

When water reaches the leaves, it is exposed to the air and the sun's energy and is easily evaporated. This process is called transpiration.

All these processes work together to move water around, through, and over Earth.

Procedure
▼ *Warm Up*
Ask students to identify the different places water can go as it moves through and around Earth. Write their responses on the board.

▼ *The Activity*
1. **Tell students that they are going to become water molecules moving through the water cycle.**

2. **Categorize the places water can move through into nine stations: Clouds, Plants, Animals, Rivers, Oceans, Lakes, Ground Water, Soil, and Glaciers. Write these names on large pieces of paper and put them** in locations around the room or yard. (Students may illustrate station labels.)

3. **Assign an even number of students to each station. (The cloud station can have an uneven number.) Have students identify the different places water can go from their station in the water cycle. Discuss the conditions that cause the water to move.** Explain that water movement depends on energy from the sun, electromagnetic energy, and gravity. Sometimes water will not go anywhere. After students have come up with lists, have each group share their work. The die for each station can be handed to that group and they can check to see if they covered all the places water can go. The *Water Cycle Table* provides an explanation of water movements from each station.

4. **Students should discuss the form in which water moves from one location to another.** Most of the movement from one station to another will take place when water is in its liquid form. However, any time water moves to the clouds, it is in the form of water vapor, with molecules moving rapidly and apart from each other.

5. **Tell students they will be demonstrating water's movement from one location to another.** When they move as liquid water, they will move in pairs, representing many water molecules together in a water drop. When they move to the clouds (evaporate), they will separate from their partners and move alone as individual water molecules. When water rains from the clouds (condenses), the students will grab a partner and move to the next location.

6. **In this game, a roll of the die determines where water will go.** Students line up behind the die at

162

their station. (At the cloud station they will line up in single file; at the rest of the stations they should line up in pairs.) Students roll the die and go to the location indicated by the label facing up. If they roll **stay**, they move to the back of the line.

When students arrive at the next station, they get in line. When they reach the front of the line, they roll the die and move to the next station (or proceed to the back of the line if they roll *stay*).

In the clouds, students roll the die individually, but if they leave the clouds they grab a partner (the person immediately behind them) and move to the next station; the partner does not roll the die.

7. **Students should keep track of their movements.** This can be done by having them keep a journal or notepad to record each move they make, including *stays*. Students may record their journeys by leaving behind personalized stickers at each station. Another approach has half the class play the game while the other half watches. Onlookers can be assigned to track the movements of their classmates. In the next round the onlookers will play the game, and the other half of the class can record their movements.

8. **Tell students the game will begin and end with the sound of a bell (or buzzer or whistle). Begin the game!**

▼ *Wrap Up and Action*

Have students use their travel records to write stories about the places water has been. They should include a description of what conditions were necessary for water to move to each location and the state water was in as it moved. Discuss any *cycling* that took place (that is, if any students returned to the same station).

Provide students with a location (e.g., parking lot, stream, glacier, or one from the human body—bladder) and have them identify ways water can move to and from that site. Have them identify the states of the water.

Have older students teach "The Incredible Journey" to younger students.

Assessment

Have students:
- role-play water as it moves through the water cycle (step 8).
- identify the states water is in while moving through the water cycle (step 4 and *Wrap Up*).
- write a story describing the movement of water (*Wrap Up*).

Extensions

Have students compare the movement of water during different seasons and at different locations around the globe. They can adapt the game (change the faces of the die, add alternative stations, etc.) to represent these different conditions or locations.

Have students investigate how water becomes polluted and is cleaned as it moves through the water cycle. For instance, it might pick up contaminants as it travels through the soil, which are then left behind as water evaporates at the surface. Challenge students to adapt "The Incredible Journey" to include these processes. For example, rolled-up pieces of masking tape can represent pollutants and be stuck to students as they travel to the soil station. Some materials will be filtered out as the water moves to the lake. Show this by having students rub their arms to slough off some tape. If they roll *clouds*, they remove all the tape; when water evaporates it leaves pollutants behind.

Resources

Alexander, Gretchen. 1989. *Water Cycle Teacher's Guide.* Hudson, N.H.: Delta Education, Inc.

🍎 Mayes, Susan. 1989. *What Makes It Rain?* London, England: Usborne Publications.

🍎 Schmid, Eleonore. 1990. *The Water's Journey.* New York, N.Y.: North-South Books.

Where will this student go next on water's incredible journey?

Water Cycle Table

STATION	DIE SIDE LABELS	EXPLANATION
Soil	one side *plant*	Water is absorbed by plant roots.
	one side *river*	The soil is saturated, so water runs off into a river.
	one side *ground water*	Water is pulled by gravity; it filters into the soil.
	two sides *clouds*	Heat energy is added to the water, so the water evaporates and goes to the clouds.
	one side *stay*	Water remains on the surface (perhaps in a puddle, or adhering to a soil particle).
Plant	four sides *clouds*	Water leaves the plant through the process of transpiration.
	two sides *stay*	Water is used by the plant and stays in the cells.
River	one side *lake*	Water flows into a lake.
	one side *ground water*	Water is pulled by gravity; it filters into the soil.
	one side *ocean*	Water flows into the ocean.
	one side *animal*	An animal drinks water.
	one side *clouds*	Heat energy is added to the water, so the water evaporates and goes to the clouds.
	one side *stay*	Water remains in the current of the river.
Clouds	one side *soil*	Water condenses and falls on soil.
	one side *glacier*	Water condenses and falls as snow onto a glacier.
	one side *lake*	Water condenses and falls into a lake.
	two sides *ocean*	Water condenses and falls into the ocean.
	one side *stay*	Water remains as a water droplet clinging to a dust particle.

Water Cycle Table, continued

STATION	DIE SIDE LABELS	EXPLANATION
Ocean	two sides *clouds*	Heat energy is added to the water, so the water evaporates and goes to the clouds.
	four sides *stay*	Water remains in the ocean.
Lake	one side *ground water*	Water is pulled by gravity; it filters into the soil.
	one side *animal*	An animal drinks water.
	one side *river*	Water flows into a river.
	one side *clouds*	Heat energy is added to the water, so the water evaporates and goes to the clouds.
	two sides *stay*	Water remains within the lake or estuary.
Animal	two sides *soil*	Water is excreted through feces and urine.
	three sides *clouds*	Water is respired or evaporated from the body.
	one side *stay*	Water is incorporated into the body.
Ground Water	one side *river*	Water filters into a river.
	two sides *lake*	Water filters into a lake.
	three sides *stay*	Water stays underground.
Glacier	one side *ground water*	Ice melts and water filters into the ground.
	one side *clouds*	Ice evaporates and water goes to the clouds (sublimation).
	one side *river*	Ice melts and water flows into a river.
	three sides *stay*	Ice stays frozen in the glacier.

Just Passing Through

■ **Grade Level:**
Upper Elementary, Middle School

■ **Subject Areas:**
Earth Science, Environmental Science, Ecology

■ **Duration:**
Preparation time:
Part I: 30 minutes
Part II: completed in Part I
Part III: 20 minutes

Activity time:
Part I: 20 minutes
Part II: 20 minutes
Part III: 30 minutes

■ **Setting:** Large space

■ **Skills:**
Analyzing (comparing and contrasting); Interpreting (relating, summarizing); Applying (designing)

■ **Charting the Course**
In "Get the Ground Water Picture," students are introduced to how water moves through soil. Students explore the role of their schoolyard in a watershed in "Rainy-Day Hike." In "Color Me a Watershed" and "Capture, Store, and Release," students learn how changes to a watershed affect stream discharge.

■ **Vocabulary**
erosion, sediment, Best Management Practices

Who am I? Plants and soil slow me down, but I pass on through. I may be stored in a lake, but I will be released; I'm just passing through! Who am I?

▼ **Summary**

In a whole-body activity, students investigate how vegetation affects the movement of water over land surfaces.

Objectives
Students will:
- compare the rates at which water flows down slopes with and without plant cover.
- identify Best Management Practices that can be used to reduce erosion.

Materials
- *Copies or overhead transparencies of photographs of hillsides with and without plant cover*
- *Yarn or rope* (the length of the playing field)
- *Tray of soil*
- *Container of water* (to be poured on tray of soil)
- *Planting pot containing only soil*
- *Container of water including shredded paper*
- *Biodegradable items* (such as peanuts) (optional)

Making Connections
Children have observed how water flows downhill and how it often transports litter or sediment. When watering plants, students have seen how soil and plant matter absorb and hold water. Understanding how vegetation affects water's movement through a site promotes student appreciation of the relationship between water quality and landscape.

Background
As it flows over and through soil, water filters through spaces among particles and around plant roots and vegetative matter. This process slows the movement of water. Sediment (soil and other natural materials carried by water) may be removed from the water as it is captured and stored by vegetation, lakes, ponds, and wetlands. Vegetation also helps to hold soil in place. When vegetation is removed (by human or natural causes), soil particles are more likely to be dislodged and carried away by water. This is called erosion.

Soil being carried by water is a natural, ongoing process. Erosion has occurred since water appeared on the planet. (Consider the formation of the Grand Canyon or the gradual leveling of the Appalachian Mountains.) When soil and organic matter are carried by water from one location to another, the destination site may be enriched and its surface area increased (e.g., the floodplain of a river or delta). However, the effects of erosion are not always desirable. Erosion of topsoil decreases the fertility of soil, and sediment build-up in streams and lakes can harm aquatic life.

Ensuring that the condition of a land area does not promote deleterious erosion and other water resource problems involves the use of Best Management Practices (BMPs). Watershed managers rely on BMPs that reduce erosion and nonpoint source pollution problems. BMPs that prevent erosion include: landscaping areas to promote plant cover; replanting areas cleared by logging; monitoring water that enters and leaves cut areas; building terraces, catch basins, and natural filters to mitigate sediment deposition in lakes, streams, etc.; and leaving a green or planted zone in riparian areas.

Slope With Plant Cover

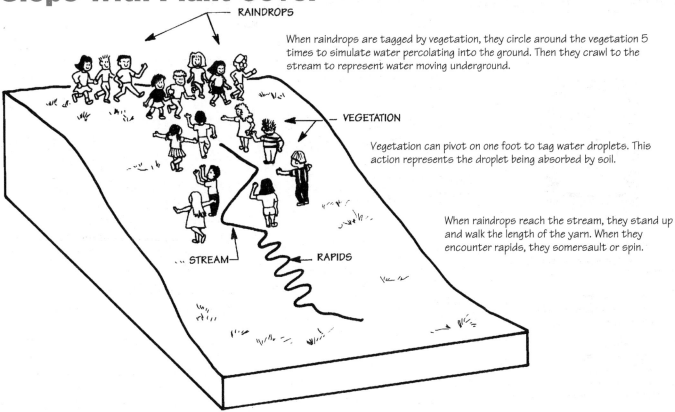

RAINDROPS

When raindrops are tagged by vegetation, they circle around the vegetation 5 times to simulate water percolating into the ground. Then they crawl to the stream to represent water moving underground.

VEGETATION

Vegetation can pivot on one foot to tag water droplets. This action represents the droplet being absorbed by soil.

STREAM — RAPIDS

When raindrops reach the stream, they stand up and walk the length of the yarn. When they encounter rapids, they somersault or spin.

Procedure

▼ Warm Up

Show students pictures of hillsides that are covered with vegetation. Ask them to imagine a gentle rain falling on these slopes. What do they think would happen to the water? Now show photographs of hillsides with barren slopes. How would rainfall affect these areas, compared to the previous sites?

▼ The Activity

Part I

1. **Inform students they are going to act out the role of water as it flows through a site (down a slope and into a stream). Arrange the playing field according to the diagram Slope With Plant Cover.** Lay yarn or a piece of rope down the middle portion of the field to indicate the stream. (A section of the yarn can be crumpled up to represent rapids.) Have half of the class assemble at one end of the playing field. These students represent "raindrops." The remaining students represent "vegetation" and should position themselves somewhere between the raindrops and the stream.

2. **To begin, have students participate in Part I of the activity "The Thunderstorm." At the height of the storm, raindrops move into the site and take the most direct route to the stream (walking swiftly).** This represents water falling on and flowing over the land's surface.

3. **Vegetation on the slope slows the flow of water. To show this, students representing vegetation try to tag the raindrops. Vegetation** **must keep one foot in place, but can pivot and stretch their arms (representing roots trapping water).**

4. **If a raindrop is tagged, the student simulates filtering into the ground by circling five times around the vegetation. To represent water moving underground toward the stream and passing through spaces among soil particles, raindrops should crawl toward the yarn.** (In reality, this process can take many days, weeks, or months, depending on rock material and gradient.) Raindrops cannot be tagged a second time.

5. **Once raindrops reach the stream, they stand up and walk the length of the yarn.** If they encounter rapids, they can spin about or do forward rolls to represent water spilling over rocks. At the end of the

stream, they should wait for the rest of the raindrops.

6. **Record the time it takes all the raindrops to pass through the site.** If they want, students can exchange roles and repeat the simulation.

7. **Discuss the results of the activity. Ask students to describe water's movement.** Help students to understand how vegetation slows the rate of flow, which allows time for water to percolate into the soil.

Part II

1. **Ask students how the results of the activity will differ when vegetation is removed. Have students perform the second version of the activity. (See diagram *Barren Slope*.)** Half of the class simulates raindrops and the other half represents "small rocks." Students representing small rocks should sit or lie down, curling themselves into tight balls.

When raindrops move near a rock, they can walk around or jump over it, continuing to flow down the slope.

2. **Compare the time required for raindrops to flow through sites with and without plant cover. Discuss the implications of water racing down a barren slope.**

Part III

1. **Prior to the third simulation, demonstrate what happens when raindrops dislodge and transport soil and other materials.** Sprinkle water on a tray of soil to demonstrate how falling and flowing water can loosen soil and other materials (e.g., pieces of wood, decaying matter, and litter). Water can transport the loosened soil great distances. Help students to recognize how soil acts like a filter. Pour water containing shredded paper (representing sediment) into a pot of soil and note

the water that drains out the bottom. Students should see that most of the sediment has been removed.

2. **Set up the playing field as in *Part I*. As raindrops flow through the site, they pick up sediment (pebbles, twigs, dead leaves, or biodegradable items, such as peanuts, scattered by the instructor). If tagged, raindrops percolate or filter into the ground. They drop all the tokens they have collected (symbolizing soil filtering raindrops and removing sediment).** Once raindrops are tagged, they circle five times around vegetation and crawl to the stream. (They do not pick up any more sediment.) Remind students about gravity; raindrops must keep moving as they bend down to collect materials.

3. **After raindrops make it through the site, have them count the**

Barren Slope

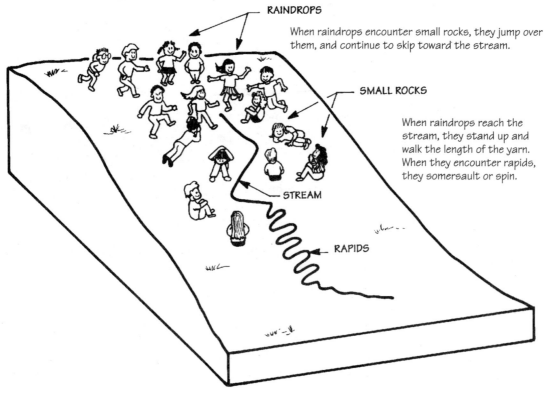

RAINDROPS

When raindrops encounter small rocks, they jump over them, and continue to skip toward the stream.

SMALL ROCKS

When raindrops reach the stream, they stand up and walk the length of the yarn. When they encounter rapids, they somersault or spin.

STREAM

RAPIDS

number of items that they are still holding.

4. **Arrange the playing as in *Part II* and have raindrops flow through the site picking up sediment.** At the conclusion, students should find that a larger amount of sediment has been collected by the raindrops than in the previous simulation.

5. **Discuss problems associated with erosion and unchecked transport of sediment. Introduce Best Management Practices that can be used to control erosion.** Remind students that erosion is a natural process (necessary for adding minerals to streams and creating landscapes). However, because a large amount of sediment is being removed within a short period of time, this simulation (*Part III*, step 4) represents erosion that could be harmful.

▼ Wrap Up and Action

Have students inventory their school grounds or community, looking for land areas that compare to those demonstrated in the activity. During a rainfall, students can observe the area's runoff and the amount of sediment carried by the water. Students can plant trees or landscape a garden to improve an area that has erosion problems.

Assessment

Have students:
• demonstrate how water flows down a slope and into a stream (*Part I*).
• compare water's movement through sites that have and that lack plant cover (*Part II*, step 2 and *Part III*, steps 4 and 5).
• inventory their school grounds or community to assess areas likely to have erosion problems (*Wrap Up*).

• design a landscape using BMPs to control erosion (*Wrap Up*).

Extensions

How does a lake affect the movement of water through a site? Make the playing field similar to that in *Part I*, but add a lake (a large circle of yarn or rope at the end of the stream). Have raindrops move through the playing field. When a student enters the lake, he or she cannot leave until four more raindrops enter the area. (They can stand in line and make a "wave," moving their arms up and down in a waving motion.) How did the lake affect the rate of water movement? Students may respond that after moving quickly through the stream, they were slowed by the lake.

To introduce how lakes can be affected by surrounding areas with and without plant cover, try the following. Show students a clear glass of water and pour in some sand or soil. Note how materials begin to settle out. Explain that this happens when water is standing in a lake as well. Arrange the playing field as in *Part II* and have raindrops pick up sediment as they move toward the stream. When a student enters the lake, he or she waits for the fifth student to enter. Raindrops discard their sediment before leaving the lake. Discuss how a lake could be affected by an accumulation of sediment. (If stream sediment continues to be deposited in the lake, over time the lake could become shallow or even fill. High levels of sediment can adversely affect aquatic plants and animals.) What could be done to decrease the quantity of sediment flowing into the lake? Students may want to repeat this simulation, but with a playing field similar to that in *Part I* (site with plant cover) and compare sediment levels.

Resources

Huff, Barbara A. 1990. *Greening the City Streets: The Story of Community Gardens*. St. Louis, Mo.: Clarion Publishing Co.

Miller, G. Tyler, Jr. 1990. *Resource Conservation and Management*. Belmont, Calif.: Wadsworth Publishing Company.

National Arbor Day Foundation. Contact: 100 Arbor Avenue, Nebraska City, NE 68410. (402) 474-5655.

Society of Municipal Arborists. Contact: 7000 Olive Boulevard., University City, MO 63130. (314) 862-1711.

Notes ▼

Hillside without plant cover. JENNIE LANE

Hillside with plant cover. JENNIE LANE

Old Water

Is it possible you brushed your teeth this morning with water that was once slurped by a Tyrannosaurus rex?

▼ Summary

Students construct a time line to illustrate and interpret water's history.

Objectives
Students will:
- appreciate the age of water.
- compare the proportion of time that water and life processes have existed on Earth.

Materials
- *Glass of water*
- *33-foot (10 m) length of rope*
- *Clothespins*
- *Tape*
- *Index cards*
- *Piece of yarn*
- *Geologic time line (optional)*
- *Butcher paper or newsprint*
- *A variety of drawing and painting materials*

Making Connections
Compared to water's existence on Earth, humans have been around a significantly shorter amount of time. This can be difficult to conceptualize. Through proportional reasoning skills, students apply the abstract concept of time to a concrete example.

Background
According to geologists, Earth was formed about 4.5 billion years ago. At that time, Earth was composed mainly of molten rock and was barren of water. The heat generated from Earth's core caused massive eruptions from volcanoes, releasing various gases and creating a primitive atmosphere; water vapor was one of these gases. About 3.8 billion years ago, when Earth cooled to below 212 degrees F (100°C), the vapor condensed and it rained and rained and rained. This water poured over the planet's surface and collected in depressions, giving rise to seas and oceans. Today, Earth has essentially the same amount of water as when water first formed long ago.

This water supported life on Earth, even before the presence of atmospheric oxygen. This water continues to support life now, and will do so into the future.

NOTE: This activity is based on a geologic time scale. The rope is 10 meters (33 ft) long, representing 5 billion years—every 2 meters (6.6 ft) equals 1 billion years, every 2 centimeters (³/₄ in) equals 10 million years. Throughout the activity, varying cultural beliefs of students should be considered. Specific time periods need not be mentioned. The time line can be divided into sections to represent any length of time. For simplicity (i.e., even increments of measurement), metric units are listed first in this activity. Most Earth Science texts contain a geologic time scale that can be used as a resource by teachers.

Procedure
▼ Warm Up
Fill a glass with water. After looking at the water for a few seconds, ask students to speculate how old it is. The water in the glass has been around since the time water formed on Earth.

Have each student draw a line down the middle of a piece of notebook paper. Turn the paper lengthwise, so the line runs horizontally across the page. On one end of the line write the words "Earth formed" and on the other end write "Now." Tell students that this line

---

■ **Grade Level:**
Upper Elementary, Middle School

■ **Subject Areas:**
Earth Science, Mathematics, Fine Arts, History

■ **Duration:**
Preparation time: 20 minutes

Activity time: two 50-minute periods

■ **Setting:** Classroom

■ **Skills:**
Organizing (plotting data); Analyzing (comparing and contrasting); Presenting (drawing)

■ **Charting the Course**
"Old Water" can set the stage for other activities concerning water resource use, such as "Common Water," "Water Concentration," and "Water Works." Following this activity, students should learn about the water cycle ("The Incredible Journey," "Imagine!") to investigate how this same water has been used over and over again and by billions of people. Students can learn how much of this water is available for our use in "A Drop in the Bucket."

■ **Vocabulary**
precipitation

represents a time line measuring from Earth's beginning to the present. Have students indicate a point on the line when they believe water was formed; label the point with a "W." Then have them label when they believe life began with an "L". Finally, have students mark with an "H" when they believe humans appeared. Students should write one or two sentences explaining why they chose these proportions. Collect the students' time lines.

▼ The Activity

1. **Read or have a student read the following paragraph.**

A long time ago, when Earth was first formed, it was composed of hot, barren rock. This rock released gases that produced steam. Later, Earth's atmosphere cooled and the steam condensed, becoming rain. It rained for many years. This rain cascaded down hillsides and mountains and collected in land depressions, creating oceans and lakes. So much rain fell that Earth became a water planet: almost three-quarters of its land surface was and still is covered with water.

Show students the glass of water again and tell them that some of the water that fell on Earth long ago is before them now. What could have happened to this water from the time it first fell on Earth to its current presence in this glass?

2. **Hang the piece of rope across the room, from corner to corner. Label one end "Earth formed" and label the other end "Now."**

3. **Label an index card "Water on Earth," and attach it with a clothespin 7.5 meters (24.75 ft) from the end labeled "Now."** This is to indicate when liquid water formed.

4. **Explain to the class that this rope represents a time line. It will be used to measure events that have occurred since Earth's formation.** So far, three events are recorded on the time line: Earth's formation, the formation of liquid water, and the present.

5. **Distribute index cards to students. Have each student write something that happened a long time ago that could have involved water.**

6. **Have students attach their cards where they think the events occurred on the time line.** Assist students in placing their cards in the desired locations. Since most life forms appeared recently in Earth's history, most or all of the students' index cards will likely be concentrated near the *Now* end.

According to the geologic time scale, human existence on Earth would consume the final 2 millimeters ($^3/_{32}$ in) of this 10-meter-long time line. Hang a piece of yarn on the *Now* end of the rope. Students who have described human events can clip their cards onto the yarn.

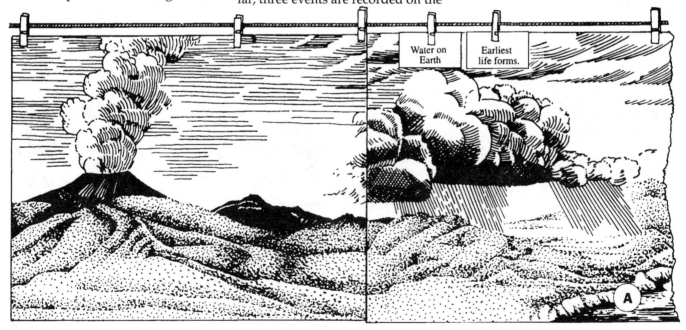

Water on Earth

Earliest life forms.

Divisions of the time line are based on the geologic time scale, which may or may not be stressed.

To adapt the mural to this book, two meters of the time line (between points A and B, on the following page) have been deleted. Illustrations on these sections would be similar to those in panel A.

NOTE: The earliest life forms appeared on Earth approximately 3.5 billion years ago, or about 7 meters (23 ft) from the *Now* end of the rope. Dinosaurs were the dominant land animals during the period from 230 million to 65 million years ago, or about 40 centimeters (16 in) from the *Now* end of the rope.

7. **Have students compare the amount of time water, life, and humans have been on Earth.** Students should note that humans have existed on Earth a relatively short period of time.

8. **Hang butcher paper on the rope. Assign students to sections of butcher paper along the time line. They should illustrate events that occurred during Earth's history specific to that section of the time line.** Students can refer to the index cards, geologic time scales, and Earth Science texts for ideas.

NOTE: Students assigned to illustrate human activities will only have paper 2 millimeters wide! Because this space is so small, students can be allowed to expand their drawings to a larger piece of butcher paper. A footnote should be added to the mural explaining that all the drawings with human events apply to a 2-millimeter-wide section of the mural.

▼ Wrap Up

Have students reattach their drawings in the correct locations on the rope. Compare the drawings of earlier periods (probably filled with rock and water) to those of more recent times (full of life forms). Discuss the role of water in each period. Post the mural in the hallway. Based on the mural, how would students alter the time lines they sketched in the **Warm Up**?

Assessment

Have students:
- indicate on a time line drawn on a piece of paper the appearance of water, life, and humans on Earth (**Warm Up** and **Wrap Up**).
- compare the proportions of time that humans, other life forms, and water have occupied Earth (step 7).

Extensions

Make a time line that focuses on human history. Record how human use of water has changed or remained the same through time.

Have students create a mural of future human events related to water.

Take a *Water Trek* into the future. Students can record their impressions in a short story.

Resources

Benton, Michael. 1986. *The Story of Life on Earth: Tracing Its Origins and Development Through Time.* New York, N.Y.: Watts, Franklin, Inc.

Branley, Franklyn M. 1972. *The Beginning of the Earth.* New York, N.Y.: Harper Collins Publishers, Inc.

Burton, Virginia L. 1989. *Life Story.* Boston, Mass.: Houghton Mifflin Co.

Gallant, Roy A. 1986. *Our Restless Earth.* New York, N.Y.: Watts, Franklin, Inc.

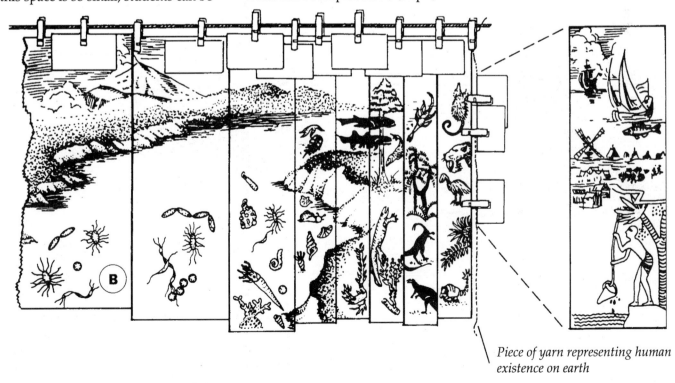

Piece of yarn representing human existence on earth

Piece It Together

■ **Grade Level:**
Upper Elementary, Middle School

■ **Subject Areas:**
Earth Science, Language Arts, Anthropology, Geography

■ **Duration:**
Preparation time:
Part I: 15 minutes
Part II: 15 minutes
Part III: 15 minutes

Activity time:
Part I: 30 minutes
Part II: 30 minutes
Part III: 30 minutes

■ **Setting:** Classroom

■ **Skills:**
Organizing; Analyzing (comparing and contrasting); Interpreting

■ **Charting the Course**
Students should understand how water evaporates and condenses ("Water Models," "Molecules in Motion," and "Poetic Precipitation"). In "Wet Vacation," students focus on water distribution in the United States. Relationships between culture and water are also addressed in "The Rainstick," and "Raining Cats and Dogs".

■ **Vocabulary**
climate, weather, ecosystem

Welcome to the lifestyles of the cold and polar . . . or would you prefer the hot and arid?

▼ Summary

Students analyze and plot global temperature and precipitation distributions to determine climate patterns and how they influence human lifestyles.

Objectives
Students will:
- locate global climates based on their interpretation of data (annual temperature and precipitation).
- provide reasons for the locations of climates.
- identify how humans adjust to a diversity of climates.

Materials
- *Planet Pieces*, *cut into 6 sections (1 section per group)*
- *Average Yearly Temperatures & Precipitation for Climatic Regions*, *cut into 6 sections (1 section per group)*
- *Globe*
- *Flashlight*
- *Photographs of tropical environments (optional)*
- *World map*
- *Population Densities for Climatic Regions*, *cut into 6 sections (1 section per group)*
- *Copies of Regional Stories*

Making Connections
Students have seen images of different climates in magazines, on television, and in movies. While they may be able to describe the weather in these places, they may be unaware of how Earth's shape determines the location of temperate, tropical, and polar climates. Studying how people adapt to different climates

promotes a global appreciation of the distribution of water.

Background
Earth's climates are divided into polar, tropical, and temperate. Climates (average temperatures and long-term precipitation patterns) are primarily influenced by the uneven heating of Earth's surface. Earth's shape causes its surface to heat unevenly. Sunlight shines directly on the equator, while at the poles it strikes the surface at an angle, and is less intense.

The region of the equator heats quickly, and this heat transfers to the surrounding air. This warm air rises and flows north and south toward the poles. The poles of Earth receive little warmth from the sun and experience colder temperatures. The colder, denser air of the poles tends to flow over Earth's surface toward the equator. Temperate or mid-latitude climates receive a mixture of polar and tropical air.

Global winds further affect tropical, temperate, and polar climates. When moisture-laden air passes overland from the ocean, it carries water vapor, creating wet or marine ecosystems. As air continues moving inland, it eventually loses its moisture via precipitation. This dry air creates arid conditions, such as desert ecosystems, usually around 30° latitude north and south (within the temperate climate region).

Human populations inhabit all climates and ecosystems. Over the years, people have learned to adjust their lifestyles to their environment. Some Native Americans living in polar regions make homes out of ice, while in certain places of Southeast Asia, people build homes on stilts to avoid floods and to allow air to circulate. In tropical climates, people dress to allow body heat and moisture to flow from their bodies. In North American deserts, some people build adobe or mud houses to provide insulation from the heat. Some desert dwellers are herders who travel from place to place to find grass and water for their animals. Throughout the world, proximity to and availability of water significantly influence human lifestyles.

Procedure
▼ Warm Up
Show students a globe and ask them to describe the temperature and humidity at the poles and the equator. Ask them to explain why the poles are so cold and the equator so warm.

Provide students with the data about cities X, Y, and Z provided in the box at right. Ask them to describe where they think each would be located on a globe.

▼ The Activity
Part I
1. **Write the words "polar," "temperate," and "tropical" on the board. Ask students to locate each area on a globe.** Have students list differences and similarities among them. Underline the descriptions that relate to temperature and precipitation.

2. **Divide the class into six groups. Assign each group one section from** *Planet Pieces* **and provide them with data about cities located within their section** (*Average Yearly Temperatures & Precipitation for Climatic Regions*).

3. **Based on the average annual precipitation and monthly temperatures of those cities, have students summarize the weather pattern for their section. Have each group locate another group that has a similar weather pattern. The groups**

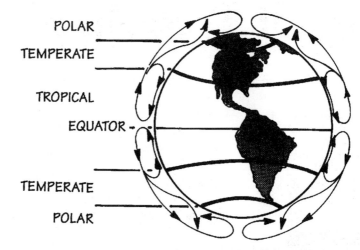

CITY	TEMP. IN JULY	TEMP. IN JAN.	ANNUAL PRECIPITATION
X	40°F (4°C)	-26°F (-32°C)	4 inches (10 cm)
Y	75°F (24°C)	25°F (-4°C)	25 inches (62.5 cm)
Z	75°F (24°C)	75°F (24°C)	100 inches (250 cm)

should piece their sections together to form a circle.

Part II
1. **Demonstrate how Earth's shape causes its surface to heat unevenly.** Tell students that the beam of a flashlight represents a ray of light from the sun. Shine the light at the equator of a globe. The beam will form a circle of light. When the light is directed at the poles, the beam spreads out and appears oblong.

2. **Discuss each of the following questions:**

- **Which part of Earth receives the most intense sunlight?** (Explain that the atmosphere is heated by Earth's surface, which is heated by the sun.)
- **Why does warm air hold more moisture than cold air?** Ask a group of students to stand close together. They represent cold, dense air. Have a second group simulate warm air. These students stand further apart from each other. Which has more room for water vapor?

- **What are the characteristics of tropical weather?** Show students pictures of or describe tropical environments and emphasize the warm, humid weather of these areas.
- **How do polar climates compare to tropical climates and desert regions?** Students may be surprised to learn how little precipitation polar and desert areas receive. The poles are among the driest places in the world. Remind them that cool air is less able to hold moisture.
- **In which climate is the United States located?** Tell students that the United States is located in a temperate or mid-latitude climate. Have them compare and contrast mid-latitude climates to the poles and the tropics.
- **Many deserts are located at 30° latitude north and south. Why?** Explain that parts of the world experience wet conditions near the coasts and dry weather further inland. Global winds at 30° latitude are descending (compared to the rising air at the equator).

Generally, descending air contains little moisture. Discuss the characteristics of deserts. Compare air carrying water over land to a person carrying a bucket of water with holes in the bottom. The further inland air moves, the more moisture is lost. Have students locate major deserts on a map of the world.

Part III

1. **Discuss reasons why people might prefer to live in one climate over another.** The class may want to list pros and cons for living in each climate. Ask them to predict which sections of the globe are most heavily populated. Provide students with *Population Densities for Climatic Regions*. Discuss ways people manage to live in arid as well as humid climates. Compare and contrast regional water problems.

2. **Refer to *Regional Stories*. Students can read the stories about children as they begin their day in different regions of the world. Ask students to match each story with a climate or ecosystem.** Discuss the following aspects of each story: weather patterns (temperature and precipitation), amount of water

available for use, and lifestyle adaptations. Students may want to research further how people around the world live in different climates. They may extend what happens in the regional stories or role-play people from these regions. They may be interested in writing and illustrating their own stories.

▼ Wrap Up and Action

Refer students to the *Warm Up* and their locations for cities X, Y, and Z. Ask students if they wish to change the locations of cities. Discuss what they think the population of each city might be. How would people adapt to each location?

Create a display showing how various world cultures dress and behave in response to climate, particularly precipitation. Produce a fashion show displaying how people dress for different climates.

Assessment

Have students:
- interpret temperature and precipitation data to identify three primary global climates (*Part I*, step 3).

- compare the angle of the sun's rays striking the equator to the angle at the poles (*Part II*, step 1).
- match characters in a story to the climates in which they live (*Part III*, step 2).
- describe and demonstrate how people adapt to different climates (*Part III*, step 1 and *Wrap Up*).

Extensions

Help students start writing to a pen pal in a different part of the world. Embassies, sister-cities programs, or the Peace Corps may have ideas about locating students from other countries. Ask students to discuss climate, precipitation, and water-related lifestyles with their new friends.

Interested students can research some hypothetical climatic changes. Following are some examples: receiving 25 percent less (or more) precipitation per year, increasing or decreasing average temperature by 41 degrees F (5°C), changing the direction of prevailing winds.

Resources

Braus, Judy, ed. 1989. *Nature Scope: Rain Forests, Tropical Treasures*. Washington, D.C.: National Wildlife Federation.

deBlij. H. J., and Peter O. Muller. 1993. *Physical Geography of the Global Environment*. New York, N.Y.: John Wiley & Sons, Inc.

Lands & Peoples. 6 vols. 1993. Danbury, Conn.: Grolier, Inc.

🍎 Robinson, Sandra, and The Watercourse. 1994. *The Rainstick, A Fable*. Published through a partnership between Falcon Press Publishing Co., Inc., Helena, Mont., and The Watercourse, Bozeman, Mont.

🍎 Wood, Jenny. 1993. *The Children's Atlas of People and Places*. Brookfield, Conn.: Millbrook Press.

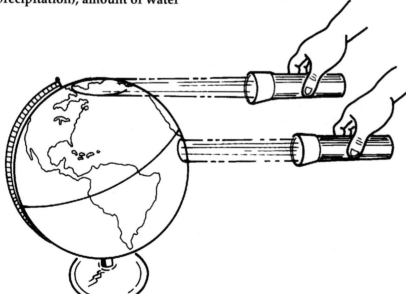

Planet Pieces

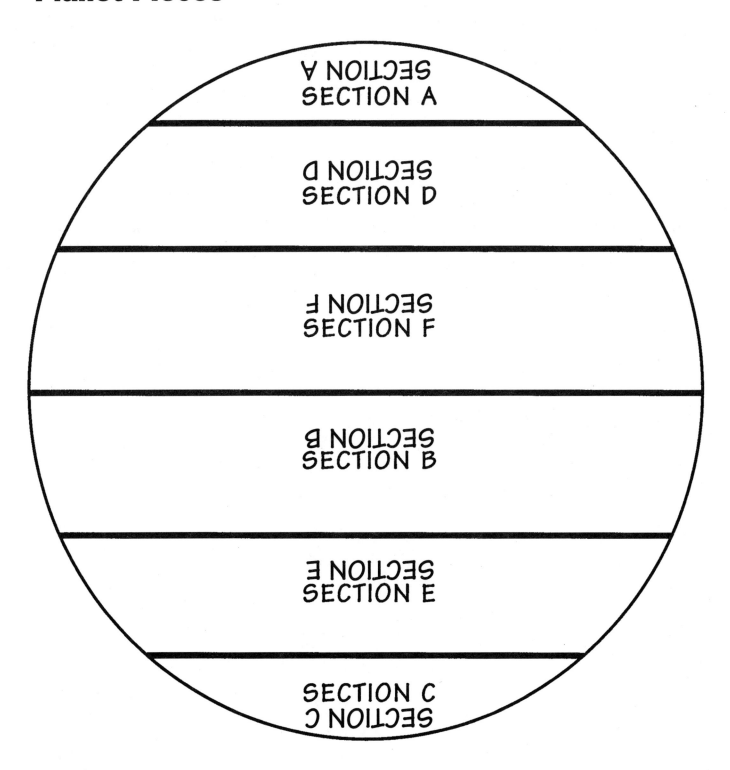

Average Yearly Temperature & Precipitation for Climatic Regions

Section A

Barrow, Alaska, United States
Temperature: Jan. 4°F (-16°C) — July 50°F (10°C)
Precipitation: 4.3 in. (10.75 cm)

Resolute, Northwest Territory, Canada
Temperature: Jan. -26°F (-32°C) — July 40°F (4°C)
Precipitation: 5.5 in. (13.75 cm)

Verkhoyansk, Russian Federation
Temperature: Jan. -54°F (-48°C) — July 61°F (16°C)
Precipitation: 6 in. (15 cm)

Section B

Belem, Brazil
Temperature: Jan. 80°F (27°C) — July 65°F (18°C)
Precipitation: 92 in. (230 cm)

Nairobi, Kenya
Temperature: Jan. 66°F (19°C) — July 60°F (16°C)
Precipitation: 38 in. (95 cm)

Cairns, Queensland, Australia
Temperature: Jan. 81°F (27°C) — July 70°F (21°C)
Precipitation: 86 in. (215 cm)

Section C

South Pole
Temperature: Jan. -20°F (-29°C) — July -74°F (-59°C)
Precipitation: 0.1 in. (0.25 cm)

Wilkes Land (Region), Antarctica
Temperature Jan. 31°F (-1°C) — July 3°F (-16°C)
Precipitation 12.2 in. (30.5 cm)

Section D

London, England
Temperature: Jan. 39°F (4°C) — July 63°F (17°C)
Precipitation: 22.9 in. (57.3 cm)

Moscow, Russian Federation
Temperature: Jan. 10°F (-12°C) — July 64°F (18°C)
Precipitation: 22 in. (24.5 cm)

Edmonton, Alberta, Canada
Temperature: Jan. 5°F (-15°C) — July 61°F (16°C)
Precipitation: 17 in. (42.5 cm)

Las Vegas, Nevada, United States
Temperature: Jan. 43°F (6° C) — July 90°F (32°C)
Precipitation: 3.8 in. (9.5 cm)

Section E

Perth, Western Australia
Temperature: Jan. 74°F (23°C) — July 55°F (13°C)
Precipitation: 36 in. (90 cm)

Casablanca, Morocco
Temperature: Jan. 54°F (12°C) — July 70°F (21°C)
Precipitation: 17 in. (42.5 cm)

Buenos Aires, Argentina
Temperature: Jan. 75°F (24°C) — July 48°F (9°C)
Precipitation: 39 in. (97.5 cm)

Riyadh, Saudi Arabia
Temperature: Jan. 58°F (14°C) — July 95°F (35°C)
Precipitation: 3.2 in. (8 cm)

Section F

San Jose, Costa Rica
Temperature: Jan. 74°F (23°C) — July 74°F (23°C)
Precipitation: 105 in. (262.5 cm)

Madras, India
Temperature: Jan. 77°F (25°C) — July 84°F (29°C)
Precipitation: 50 in. (125 cm)

Abidjan, Ivory Coast
Temperature: Jan. 86°F (30°C) — July 78°F (26°C)
Precipitation: 77 in. (192.5 cm)

Population Densities for Climatic Regions

Section A

Barrow, Alaska, United States
Pop. 3,469
Density—under 3/sq. mile (2/km²)

Resolute, Northwest Territory, Canada
Pop. 168
Density—under 3/sq. mile (2/km²)

Verkhoyansk, Russian Federation
Pop. 2,000
Density—3-25/sq. mile (2-10/km²)

Section B

Belem, Brazil
Pop. 1,000,349
Density—130-260/sq. mile (50-100/km²)

Nairobi, Kenya
Pop. 509,286
Density—over 260/sq. mile (100/km²)

Cairns, Queensland, Australia
Pop. 48,557
Density—under 3/sq. mile (2/km²)

Section C

South Pole
Uninhabited

Wilkes Land (Region), Antarctica
Pop. small population of researchers
Density—under 3 sq. mile (2/km²)

Section D

London, England
Pop. 7,566,620
Density—over 260/sq. mile (100/km²)

Moscow, Russian Federation
Pop. 8,769,000
Density—over 260/sq. mile (100/km²)

Edmonton, Alberta, Canada
Pop. 657,057
Density—130-260/sq. mile (50-100/km²)

Las Vegas, Nevada, United States
Pop. 461,816
Density—130-260/sq. mile (50-100/km²)

Section E

Perth, Western Australia
Pop. 809,305
Density—25-130/sq. mile (10-50/km²)

Casablanca, Morocco
Pop. 1,506,373
Density—over 260/sq. mile (100/km²)

Buenos Aires, Argentina
Pop. 2,908,000
Density—over 260/sq. mile (100/km²)

Riyadh, Saudi Arabia
Pop. 666,840
Density—130-260/sq. mile (50-100/km²)

Section F

San Jose, Costa Rica
Pop. 391,107
Density—25-130/sq. mile (10-50/km²)

Madras, India
Pop. 3,169,930
Density—over 260/sq. mile (100/km²)

Regional Stories (Read each story and try to identify where each child lives.)

Region 1

When Shada wakes up, the cool of the night is still in the air, but she knows that by afternoon the temperatures will be over 104 degrees F (40°C). She dresses in a light shift and goes outside to check the water. There is still some water left in the large urn. Before leaving for school, she will walk to the town's well to fill the urn. Fortunately, her family only uses two urns of water per day. She is now quite good at balancing a jug of water on her head, but her younger sister is just learning and still finds it challenging.

Her sister is already at the table eating her millet porridge and listening to her uncle, who is sharing stories of his travels through the desert. He recalls one time when he nearly died of thirst. Fortunately, he recognized a plant with a large root that stored water. He was able to break open the tuber and get enough liquid to help him survive.

After the morning meal and chores, Shada and her sister prepare for the walk to school. The sun is already well over the horizon. The sisters wrap themselves in lightweight cloaks and cover their heads with cloths. The coverings are needed to protect their skin from the sun and to keep them cool.

Region 2

Teshka is awakened by sounds in the kitchen; her father is back from ice fishing. Teshka turns on the small lamp near her bed. She looks forward to the few hours of sunlight they will get today and hopes it will not be cloudy. Reluctantly leaving her warm bed, Teshka quickly puts on her slippers and robe. She knows the temperature today will stay well below 32 degrees F (0°C).

The smell of frying fish wafts to her bedroom and draws her toward the kitchen. A wave of cold air washes over her as her brother opens, then closes, the door. He is carrying a pail which contains snow that he will melt on the stove. Some places in town have running water, but problems with freezing pipes and limited water supplies make it impossible for Teshka's home to have indoor plumbing.

After breakfast, Teshka and her brother prepare for school. They dress in many warm layers of animal fur and wool. Teshka goes out and disconnects the snowmobile from the generator, while her brother prepares their lunches of dried fish and caribou meat. When her brother finishes, Teshka starts the snowmobile, turns on the headlight, and they begin their 12-mile (20 km) drive to school.

Region 3

Prem awakes to the sound of roosters crowing and people talking in the road. His brother is still asleep. Lifting the mosquito netting, he gets out of bed and wraps a long cloth around his waist. He waits for his mother to finish her bath, then goes outside to bathe himself. The water is always cold in the morning and sometimes he considers skipping the morning washing. He knows it won't be long before the humidity and the day's heat will make him feel uncomfortable. At the end of the school day he never hesitates to bathe, but by then he usually feels hot and sticky.

Seeing that the urns are nearly empty, Prem turns on the electric water pump. Not long ago, his family had to carry water from the river, as some people in the village still do. Dressing in light cotton clothes, Prem prepares for school.

For breakfast, his mother serves rice and stir-fried pork with basil. Before leaving, Prem and his brother feed the pigs. Already, a film of sweat has formed on the boys' skin. Walking to school, Prem notices that the rice farmers are opening the levees to flood the paddies. As the heat of the day increases, Prem looks forward to the cooling afternoon rain.

Region 4

The sound of thunder wakes Paul; he looks out the window to see pouring rain. He knows his father will not need to irrigate the crops today. Paul dresses quickly in his work clothes and goes out to do his morning chores. As he enters the barn, the cows and horses are restless, anticipating their morning feeding.

He returns to the house to clean and dress for school. Turning on the shower's faucet, he receives a welcome spray of warm water. Dressing for school, he puts a light sweater over his cotton shirt. He knows that, depending on the rain, the weather could stay cool or become warm.

When he arrives in the kitchen, his mother has bacon and eggs frying on the stove. His sister already sits at the table. She says that unless the rain continues, they will harvest potatoes after school. After breakfast, their mother warns them to hurry so they won't miss the school bus. Leaving the house, he and his sister grab their raincoats. On the 15-minute bus ride to school, the rain eases and Paul notices that the leaves are beginning to change color.

Poetic Precipitation

Grade Level:
Upper Elementary, Middle School

Subject Areas:
Earth Science, Language Arts

Duration:
Preparation time:
Part I: 30 minutes
Part II: 10 minutes

Activity time:
Part I: 50 minutes
Part II: 50 minutes

Setting: Classroom

Skills:
Analyzing; Interpreting (inferring); Presenting (writing)

Charting the Course
This activity involves density, evaporation, and condensation concepts that are addressed in "Water Models" and "Molecules in Motion." Students participating in "Wet Vacation" gain a broader understanding of weather patterns. "The Thunderstorm" adds drama to weather investigations as students mimic the sounds of a rainstorm.

Vocabulary
humidity, precipitation, condensation, evaporation, vapor

Shel Silverstein and Robert Louis Stevenson found rhymes in rain. Can you?

▼ Summary
While learning about the conditions that produce condensation, students create poems that express thoughts and feelings about rain, snow, and other forms of precipitation.

Objectives
Students will:
- describe how clouds are formed.
- recognize that thoughts and feelings are influenced by weather conditions.

Materials
- *Balloons* (about half as many as there are students in the class)
- *Garbage bags* (1 for every 5 students in the class)
- *Samples of poems and songs about precipitation* (optional)

Making Connections
Rain, snow, fog, drizzle, and hail—these are all forms of precipitation that have been used in songs and poems. Children have heard these words in nursery rhymes and the lyrics of popular music. Students' interest in music and poetry provides an excellent avenue for students to interpret what they know and feel about precipitation.

Background
Precipitation affects our lives in a variety of ways. Plans for daily outings are adjusted or canceled as weather changes. People's moods may fluctuate in response to changes in cloud shapes or colors. Variations in the amount of rainfall cause crop yields and grocery store prices to increase and decrease.

Culture reflects how weather affects human lives. Language, artwork, and poetry often contain weather terms. For example, one might be said to have a stormy personality. Words may describe the physical environment or be used symbolically to relay emotions or perceptions. For example, an author might set the mood for her story by stating that it was a dark, stormy night; a beautiful snow-covered land might be described as a "winter wonderland."

An indication of the importance of precipitation to lifestyles is the popularity of weather reports on daily news broadcasts. Watching cloud shapes and measuring temperature and the amount of moisture in the air helps people predict when and what type of precipitation is likely to occur.

Clouds form when water vapor in the atmosphere condenses into tiny ice crystals or water droplets. When droplets or crystals merge, they become larger and heavier, and gravity pulls them to the ground. They fall as rain or snow, depending on the temperature of the air. Because the upper atmosphere is so cold, precipitation usually starts out as snow and melts to rain as it falls nearer Earth's warm surface.

Cloud formation depends on the amount of moisture in the air, temperature, and presence of condensation nuclei (dust particles onto which water vapor condenses). Water vapor condenses when the temperature decreases. (Refer to illustration on page 183.)

Temperature decreases when molecules lose heat energy or when pressure is reduced. When molecules lose heat energy, they slow down. At higher elevations, there is less pressure, allowing air and water molecules to spread out. When air and water molecules are further apart, they bump into each other

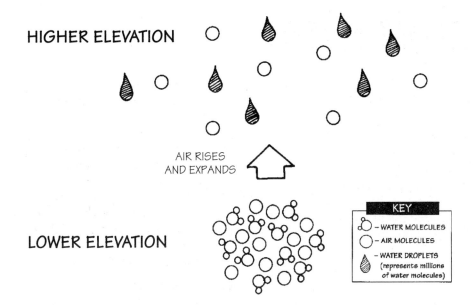

HIGHER ELEVATION

LOWER ELEVATION

AIR RISES
AND EXPANDS

KEY
– WATER MOLECULES
– AIR MOLECULES
– WATER DROPLETS
(represents millions
of water molecules)

less often and lose energy. (The motion of molecules—kinetic energy—is maintained when molecules collide with each other.) Slower moving water molecules do not have enough energy to remain a vapor and will settle on condensation nuclei floating in air. The temperature at which water molecules condense is called the dew point.

Procedure
▼ Warm Up
Ask students to describe current weather conditions. What kinds of weather do they like and dislike? Discuss why people are interested in reading or listening to weather reports. How do different weather conditions influence moods or feelings? Share a poem (see list of *Weather Poems*), song, or saying that includes weather terms and ask students to interpret its meaning or message.

Ask students how they know when it will rain. Some students may listen to weather reports; others may look for environmental clues. Ask students to describe how rain is formed.

If necessary, review the processes of evaporation and condensation. Show

water condensed on the outside of a glass of ice. Describe how water vapor in the air is a source of that water.

▼ The Activity

Part I

1. **Have students identify times when they have seen condensation. Ask students what they think water condensed in the upper atmosphere would look like.** If there are clouds outside, point them out as collections of floating water droplets. What does a cloud feel like? Ask students if they have walked through fog. Explain that fog is a cloud formed at ground level.

2. **Tell students they are going to demonstrate how water droplets form in the upper atmosphere. Explain that the molecules in air (oxygen, nitrogen, water vapor, and other gases) move about freely, bumping into each other, maintaining their speed of motion. When they do not collide into**

each other or gain heat energy, the molecules slow down.

3. **Have the students count off by fives. Give the "ones" large plastic bags and tell them they are "condensation nuclei." The rest of the students are "air molecules."**

4. **Tell the air molecules to stand at arm's length from each other. They must keep one foot in place at all times, but can pivot about that foot.** Explain that in reality, air molecules move about freely, bumping into each other. However, for this exercise their movements will be limited.

5. **Tell the students that when you clap your hands, they increase the space between themselves by taking two steps away from each other.** Explain that the clapping represents air rising further into the atmosphere. At higher altitudes there is less pressure, and molecules move further apart. Therefore, the molecules are not pressed together, making it harder for them to transfer heat energy to each other. NOTE: If space is limited, have certain students leave the playing area when you clap your hands.

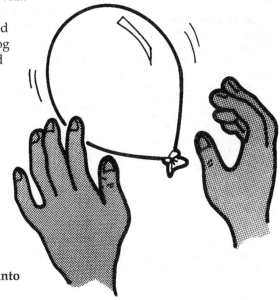

6. **Tell students that the balloons represent water molecules. Explain that when the demonstration begins, you will toss balloons in the air; air molecules should volley the balloons to keep them aloft. Every time a student taps a balloon, he or she should call out "energy!"** This represents energy of motion (kinetic energy) being transferred between air and water molecules, keeping heat levels constant.

7. **Explain that when a balloon falls to the ground, it means that heat energy has been lost from the water molecule. The condensation nuclei should gather the fallen balloons in their plastic bags. When two or more balloons have been collected, the condensation nuclei becomes a "water droplet."**

8. **Begin the activity. Clap your hands about every minute. As the distance increases between students, more balloons should fall to the ground. When most of the balloons are collected, stop the**

ARNOLD JOHN KAPLAN, N E STOCK PHOTO

activity. Ask students what all these water droplets represent. (A collection of water droplets makes a cloud.)

9. **Explain that the water droplets are too heavy to float in air. Designate one side of the room as Earth's surface; have water droplets represent precipitation falling to the ground by moving to that wall.** Air molecules can flash the classroom lights and make the sound of thunder by stomping their feet.

10. **Based on this demonstration, have the students diagram the formation of a cloud (water droplets).** They may wish to use other science books to enhance their diagram.

Part II

1. **Have students list different types of precipitation they know or have experienced. Ask them to describe what each looks and feels like. What moods, feelings, or thoughts are associated with each precipitation type?**

2. **Tell students to create a poem about a type of precipitation.** They can use their descriptions, thoughts, and feelings for topic material. Share poetry from Robert Frost, Walt Whitman, Emily Dickinson, e. e. cummings, Shel Silverstein, or your personal favorites.

▼ *Wrap Up and Action*

Have students share and analyze each others'

poems. They should determine if the poems were written to educate about weather types, set a mood, and/or express emotion. What is unique or interesting about the work?

Students can produce a book of their weather poems. The poems should be grouped according to seasons or particular weather patterns. Copies of the book could be given to friends and family. Local weather stations may be interested in presenting the poems on their programs.

Assessment
Have students:
- diagram how a cloud forms (*Part I*, step 10).
- write poems that include weather terms and thoughts and feelings about weather (*Part II*, step 2).
- analyze poems about weather (*Wrap Up*).

Extensions
Students may be interested in setting up a simple weather monitoring station. Some simple instruments include a rain gauge (a jar with a plastic ruler taped inside), a thermometer, and a wind vane (a piece of ribbon stapled to a stick). They could conduct a weekly cloud watch and learn the names of different cloud types. They may want to contact another school in a different town or state to compare weather reports. The National Geographic Society has a **Weather in Action Kit** with which students set up a weather monitoring station and share findings with other student observation stations around the country through telecommunication software systems. Write to: National Geographic Society, Educational Services, 1145 17th Street N W, Washington, DC 20036-4688 or call 1-800-368-2728 for information.

Before meteorologists were able to use advanced technology to track

184

and interpret weather, people used to look at other environmental clues to predict the weather. Following is a list of some old sayings. Students may want to test them out to see if they make accurate forecasting tools.

- If a dog eats grass, it is a sign it will rain.
- Robins in the bush are a sign of an oncoming storm.
- Fall is coming when the blackbirds start to bunch up in big flocks.
- When people have aching joints, they say the weather is changing for the worse.
- When dew is on the grass, rain will never come to pass.
- Cold is the night when the stars shine bright.
- If the ants build up their hills, rain from the clouds will be spilled.
- A ring around the moon means cold weather.
- Red sky at night—sailors' delight. Red sky in morning—sailors take warning.
- An early, heavy coat on farm animals (or city park squirrels) means a long, cold winter is ahead.
- When leaves stay on the trees in the fall, it is a sign of a cold winter.
- Rain will occur on the 3rd, 30th, and 60th day after a fog.
- It won't snow very long if large snowflakes are falling.
- It's a sign of rain when cattle bunch together.
- If it rains when the sun is shining, it is going to rain tomorrow.
- Students acting up in school indicate that a change in the weather is coming.
- When corn husks are thick, it is going to be a long, hard winter.

Have students generate a hypothetical weather report using some of these old sayings. Have them pretend they are weather personalities and present their weather report to classmates.

K-2 Option

Rhyming poems or other favorites about water could be used in a shared reading lesson (e.g., *The Snow* by F. Ann Elliott, *Little Raindrops* by Ann Hawkins, *Rain in Summer* by Henry Wadsworth Longfellow). Read the poems with children, discussing the words and ideas. Have students illustrate the poems; vocabulary words or stanzas can be written under the pictures. Children can use the rhyming words to identify patterns among words. Have students create a short skit for the poems, focusing on vocabulary words. Have children add hand motions to the poems.

Resources

Weather:

Abbott, Marti, and Betty Jane Polk. 1991. *Clouds, Rain, Wind and Snow*. New York, N.Y.: Fearon Teacher Aids, Simon & Schuster Supplementary Education Group.

Branley, Franklyn M. 1987. *It's Raining Cats and Dogs: All Kinds of Weather and Why We Have It*. Boston, Mass.: Houghton Mifflin Co.

Braus, Judy, ed. 1985. *Nature Scope: Wild About Weather*. Washington, D.C.: National Wildlife Federation.

de Paola, Tomie. 1975. *The Cloud Book*. New York, N.Y.: A Holiday House Book.

Poetry:

Blisher, Edward, comp. *Oxford Book of Poetry for Children*. 1991. Oxford, England: Oxford University Press.

Denman, Gregory A. 1988. *When You've Made it Your Own . . . Teaching*

Poetry to Young People. Portsmouth, N. H.: Heinmann Educational Books, Inc.

Dunn, Sara, and Alan Scholefield, eds. 1991. *Poetry for the Earth*. New York, N.Y.: Fawcett Columbine.

Kennedy, X. J., and Dorothy M. Kennedy, eds. *Talking Like the Rain: A First Book of Poems*. 1992. Boston, Mass.: Little, Brown & Company.

WEATHER POEMS

"Address to a Child During a Boisterous Winter Evening" by Dorothy Wordsworth

"The Cloud" by Percy Bysshe Shelley

"Clouds" by Aileen Fisher

"Cynthia in the Snow" by Gwendolyn Brooks

"The First Snowfall" by James Russell Lowell

"Fog" by Carl Sandburg

"In the Fog" by Lilian Moore

"The Muddy Puddle" by Dennis Lee

"Rain" by Shel Silverstein

"Rain" by Robert Louis Stevenson

"Rain Clouds" by Elizabeth-Ellen Long

"The Rain Has Silver Sandals" by May Justus

"Spring Rain" by Marchette Chute

"Summer Shower" by David McCord

"The Tide In the River" by Eleanor Farjeon

"When All the World is Full of Snow" by N. M. Bodecker

"When I Went Out" by Karla Kuskin

"The Wind Has Such a Rainy Sound" by Christina Rossetti

"Winter Morning" by Ogden Nash

Rainy-Day Hike

What do a puddle on your playground and a nearby lake or stream have in common?

▼ Summary
Students are introduced to the concept of watersheds by collecting data about water flowing over school grounds.

Objectives
Students will:
- identify the watershed in which their school is located.
- explain the role the schoolyard plays in the watershed.

Materials
- *Maps of the local community, showing streams, lakes, and topography*
- *Drawing paper*
- *2 sets of copies of the **Legend***
- *Waterproof outerwear*
- *Clipboards or sturdy cardboard with rubber band to secure paper (Tape 2 pieces of cardboard to form a book; students can close map inside cardboard to keep it dry.)*
- *Plastic wrap*
- *Pencils*

Making Connections
Students may be familiar with the idea of a watershed, but unaware that they live and attend school within one. Observing water flowing through and collecting on their school grounds provides students with direct experience in their watershed.

Background
Puddles, streams, and lakes all have something in common. They collect water that has drained from watersheds. Watersheds are like funnels; they are drainage basins where surface water runs off and drains into a common collection site. Watersheds are separated from each other by land forms (ridge lines or mountain divides). Water falling on each side of the divide drains into different watersheds and collection sites.

Surface runoff flows over a school's grounds on its way to the collection site (e.g., a river); therefore, schoolyards are part of a watershed. (Puddles are the collection sites of mini-watersheds: land surrounding puddles are the mini-drainage basins that empty into the puddle.) When the puddles overflow or the soil becomes saturated, water is released.

Often, materials carried by water to the school grounds (e.g., litter, twigs, leaves, oil) are left behind. Surface water leaving the school grounds may carry materials to the collection site of the watershed. These materials include soil, leaves, and twigs; litter; oil and gasoline from parking lots; and fertilizer from lawns.

As water flows from the school grounds, it combines with runoff from other land areas within the drainage basin. Materials from these other places are added to the water. While some substances decompose, settle out, or are filtered by soil, other matter continues to travel long distances downstream. Organic materials carried by the water nourish aquatic life. Some substances are toxic, however, and can endanger organisms consuming or living in the water.

Contaminants whose entry point into the watershed is difficult to locate are classified as nonpoint source pollutants. Along with residential areas, agricultural fields, and paved parking lots, school grounds can contribute nonpoint source pollutants. The schoolyard contributes point source pollution when the source of the pollutant can be traced back to a specific location on the school grounds (e.g., sewer, ditch, pipe).

■ **Grade Level:**
Upper Elementary, Middle School

■ **Subject Areas:**
Earth Science, Environmental Science, Geography

■ **Duration:**
Preparation time:
Part I: 30 minutes
Part II: 30 minutes

Activity time:
Part I: 50 minutes
Part II: 50 minutes

■ **Setting:**
Classroom, schoolyard

■ **Skills:**
Gathering information (collecting, observing); Organizing (mapping); Analyzing; Interpreting

■ **Charting the Course**
This activity provides a good introduction to watersheds. Students make a model of a watershed in "Branching Out!" Students can investigate the possible effects of the run-off from their schoolyard in "A-maze-ing Water." Following this activity, students can explore aspects of nonpoint source pollution in "Sum of the Parts."

■ **Vocabulary**
watershed, nonpoint source pollution

Procedure

▼ Warm Up

Show students a map of the community and identify local rivers or lakes. Ask the class if they think a connection exists between their schoolyard and these bodies of water. Tell the class they will take a fair-weather and a rainy-day hike, to study what happens to the water that falls on and flows over their school property.

Although plans for a rainy-day hike will generate student excitement, the wait for a wet day may prove discouraging. The lack of rain offers the opportunity to discuss with students the idea that people do not control the rain or other aspects of the weather. Remind students that even if people cannot "control" the weather, they can often predict it.

Have students listen to, watch, or read weather reports. When is rain predicted? Students can mark the calendar with the date and continue "preparations" for the hike.

▼ The Activity

Part I

1.   **In planning for the rainy day, have students create a map of the school grounds. Divide the grounds into sections and assign groups to** map each area. Orient students to which direction is north so all maps face the same direction.

2.   **Remind groups to include the following: school buildings, parking lots, designated playgrounds, natural areas (trees, grass, flower gardens), with emphasis on water features like streams, temporary and permanent ponds, and constructed water features like bird baths and fountains.**

3.   **After students have completed their initial mapping, if there is a school building in their area, have them consider the following questions.** Can they determine where the water that falls on the roofs goes? Does it flow off the roof into gutters that lead to waterspouts or does it fall directly onto the ground? Have students place an "X" on the buildings to indicate the location of waterspouts.

4.   **Make two copies of student maps, one for the fair-weather hike where students make predictions of water flow and one for the rainy-day hike when students check their predictions.**

5.   **For the fair-weather hike, give each group a copy of their mapped section and the** *Legend.* **Have each** group predict the direction water will flow through their section. Where do students think water will be stored? Are there ponds or low spots?

6.   **Have students survey the ground area of their section for possible sources of point and nonpoint contamination (oil stains on parking lots, trash, tainted soil near the school dumpster). What materials could be on the roof of the school building that could be washed off during a rain (bird and rodent droppings, insects, dirt, roofing materials, leaves, twigs, etc.)?**

7.   **Assemble the map sections from the groups and post in the classroom. Have them summarize their predictions.** How do the predictions of individual groups relate to each other? Where do students think water flows onto the school grounds? Where will it flow off the school grounds?

Part II

1.   **On a rainy day, have students dress properly; take them outside and begin a simple tour of the school grounds. Have students identify patterns of water flow.** Discuss what influences the direction water moves. Have students:

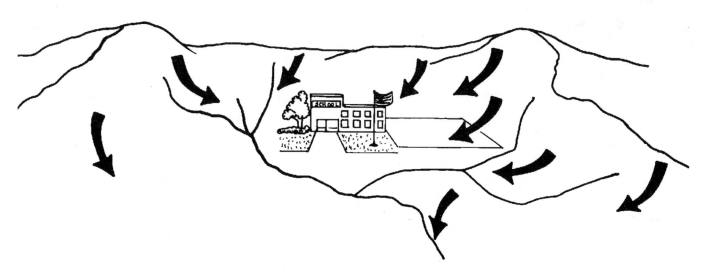

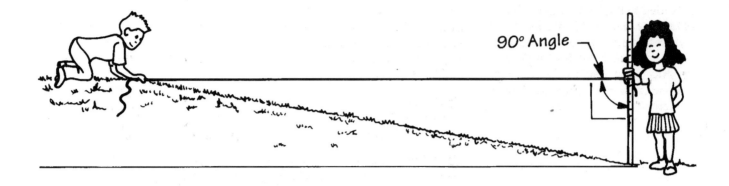

90° Angle

- note slopes, depressions, cracks in the sidewalk, erosion trails, rocks, buildings, gardens, trees, etc.
- compare how fast or slow water flows in different places.
- identify ways water affects the surface of the school grounds (e.g., watering plants, eroding soil, piling up litter, washing away litter).
- note water flowing from the roofs of buildings and waterspouts.

2. **Divide the class into their original groups and give each group a copy of their unmarked map section and the *Legend*.** Have students indicate the following on their maps: direction and patterns of flowing water; natural and unnatural materials being carried onto and off their study area; and areas of standing water. Remind students to use pencils—ink runs. They can cover their note pads with plastic wrap or cardboard when they are not writing.

3. **When students have completed their investigations, assemble the map sections and post.** Arrows of adjacent map sections should line up. If they don't, discuss reasons for discrepancies.

▼ *Wrap Up and Action*

Have students summarize the general pattern of surface water as it flows across the school property. They should identify areas where the flow of water is slowed by landforms and vegetation, collects in depressions, and flows off school property. Have them compare the completed map on the rainy-day hike to the map indicating their predictions. How accurate were their predictions?

Referring to a community map, discuss the school's location within a watershed. Trace the likely course of runoff from the school grounds into a local lake or river.

City engineers or planners have information on storm drainage systems, or can identify destinations of storm water runoff from streets and parking lots.

Have the class list uses of water in local lakes or rivers (e.g., drinking water, animal habitat, irrigation, swimming, fishing, etc.). Do any activities occurring on your school grounds affect, positively or negatively, the water moving across it?

Some school property plans incorporate surface water treatment systems, such as detention ponds, to reduce materials carried by runoff. Ask the principal for a copy of the school site plan. Does the plan show the surface water management system for the school?

If students believe their school grounds contribute to erosion or to point or nonpoint source pollution, they may want to develop a plan to improve the area. They can plant trees or a garden, encourage parking lot patrons to keep their cars in tune, promote wise use of fertilizers and pesticides, etc.

Assessment

Have students:
- predict the movement of water and possible contaminants across their school grounds (*Part I*, steps 5 through 7).
- identify the school's location within a watershed or in relation to a body of water (*Wrap Up*).
- list ways the school grounds positively affect water passing through the watershed (*Wrap Up*).
- locate sources of point and nonpoint source pollution on the school grounds (*Wrap Up*).

Extensions

To increase the detail of their study area maps, students may include measurements of slope. Slopes can be classified as level, gentle, moderate, or steep. How does steepness of slope affect rates of water flow, erosion, and sediment load? To measure slope, one student stands at the top of the study area (top of the slope) and another student, holding a meter stick, stands at the bottom. The run or distance between the two students is measured. The student at the top holds one end of a string at his ground level and the other end is extended to the student at the bottom of the slope. A level is needed to ensure the string is held straight. The point at which the string intersects the meter stick held by the second student is the rise. Slope gradient is calculated by dividing the rise by the run.

$$\frac{rise}{run} = \text{slope gradient}$$
(expressed as a percentage)

On a community map, have students use pins to locate the school and their homes. Do students share the same watershed address as the school? They can observe surface runoff to see where the water goes. Topographic maps may help locate ridge lines within the community.

☀ K-2 Option

Have students work in small groups to investigate sites of flowing water on the school grounds. They should observe what is in the water. Caution them not to touch the water, especially if the water is running off a parking lot. Children can search the area for natural materials with which to construct tiny boats. Have boat races to see how far and where the boats travel. Students can draw pictures describing what the tiny boat might encounter if it flowed off the school grounds. Discuss reasons why the school grounds must be kept clean.

Resources:

Doppelt, Bob. 1993. *Entering the Watershed: A New Approach to Save America's River Ecosystems.* Washington, D.C.: Island Press.

🍎 Dorros, Arthur. 1991. *Follow the Water From Brook to Ocean.* New York, N.Y.: Harper Collins.

🍎 Holling, Clancy. 1941. *Paddle to the Sea.* Boston, Mass.: Houghton Mifflin Company.

🍎 Locker, Thomas. *Where the River Begins.* New York, N.Y.: Dial Books.

Miller, G. Tyler, Jr. 1990. *Resource Conservation and Management.* Belmont, Calif.: Wadsworth Publishing Company.

Project WILD. 1992. Activities "Puddle Wonders," "Where Does Water Run Off After School?" and "Watershed." *Aquatic Project WILD.* Bethesda, Md.: Western Regional Environmental Education Council.

Notes ▼

Legend

arrows indicate direction of water flowing onto and away from study area

a leaf indicates natural materials, such as leaves, soil, and twigs, that might have been carried onto study area from another location

a puddle shows where water collects in the study area

a crumpled ball of paper indicates unnatural materials, such as litter, oil, and chemicals, that might have been carried onto the study area from another location

a flower shows things that help slow the flow of water

a shaded leaf indicates natural materials that are being or could be carried away from the study area

a shaded, crumpled ball of paper indicates unnatural materials that are being or could be carried away from the study area

Stream Sense

■ Grade Level:
Lower Elementary, Upper Elementary

■ Subject Areas:
Earth Science, Fine Arts, Language Arts

■ Duration:
Preparation time: 50 minutes
Activity time: two 50-minute periods

■ Setting: A local stream

■ Skills:
Gathering information (observing, recording)

■ Charting the Course
Have students explore what they think and feel about streams with an adapted version of "Idea Pools." In "Rainy-Day Hike," students study how their schoolyard may affect the health of neighboring streams. Activities on watersheds (e.g., "Branching Out!") could follow this activity. Journaling (see "Water Log") could be introduced through this activity.

■ Vocabulary
observation

What does your nose know and your ear hear about a stream?

▼ Summary
Students use their senses to observe a stream, learning there is more to flowing water than meets the eye.

Objectives
Students will:
- recognize how their senses provide them with details about stream ecosystems.

Materials
- *Touch-and-feel bags* (a dark-colored bag with sample materials that could be found near a stream: a cattail, a pebble, a shell, a twig, etc.)
- *Copies of the **Sensory Observation Sheet***
- *Pencils and crayons*
- *Journals (optional)*
- *Camera (optional)*
- *Tape recorder (optional)*
- *Binoculars (optional)*
- *Magnifying lenses (optional)*
- *Sample foods (edible plants and seeds) that could be found near a stream (optional)*
- *Spray bottle (optional)*
- *Collecting apparatus, such as buckets, tweezers, nets, etc. (optional)*

Making Connections
Many people enjoy the sights and sounds of a babbling brook. People find comfort through the sense of touch and recall distant memories through certain smells. Often people depend on only their vision to gather details about their environment. By making careful observations, students experience how their other senses (besides sight) provide them

with additional information about the environment.

Background
Sense organs—eyes, ears, nose, tongue, and skin—are needed to detect the surrounding environment. With information it receives through the senses, the brain interprets what we see, hear, smell, taste, and feel. In addition to translating the information it receives, the brain also relates these details to memories and thought processes. In this way, recognition and learning take place.

In most humans, sight is the predominant sense organ. When an individual uses *all* of his or her senses to investigate the environment, the brain receives a broader range of information. This information provides the opportunity for more thorough learning.

A stream provides an ideal opportunity for people to use all their senses. People hear water rushing over rocks and lapping at the banks. They feel a breeze against their skin, and hear insects buzzing and chirping among the willows. The air around the stream feels moist and carries a variety of particles from flowers, damp earth, and chemicals in the water to their noses. Along the banks and in shallow portions of the stream, a variety of materials of different shapes and textures can be touched.

It is important to protect the senses. Safety rules should be followed when students explore a stream.

Procedure
▼ Warm Up
Review the five senses (sight, sound, touch, smell, and taste). Discuss how they are used in daily life. Ask students about previous trips or visits to natural areas. How were their senses involved in these visits?

Ask students to describe how they observe things. Do they think it is possible to observe using all their senses?

▼ The Activity

1. **Distribute touch-and-feel bags to groups of students. Ask them to identify the objects inside by touch alone. Ask where they might find all these items.**

2. **Tell students they will be visiting a stream and will be recording how they use their senses to observe the stream. Discuss the** *Stream Walk Safety Rules.*

3. **Hand out copies of the** *Sensory Observation Sheet.* **Explain that when they record their observations, students should write things down or draw things as they perceive them.** For example, when they look at things they should describe shapes and colors. When they hear things they can write down imitations of the sound (e.g., peep, peep, gurgle, gurgle, swish, swish, shoooosh!).

4. **Throughout the trip, remind students about using their senses. Ask students to find a quiet spot near the stream and have them sit very still to look, smell, listen, and feel.** Older children may want to sit for 15 minutes or more, while for younger students 2 or 3 minutes is probably enough. During this time, students can complete their observation sheets. If they bring their journals, they may be inspired to write poems or draw pictures. Students may want to take photographs or tape record sounds.

5. **Other sensory activities that students could do at the stream include the following:**

- Have them block one or more of their senses (e.g., close their eyes, cover their ears, plug their noses). How does this affect their other

senses? Did students hear better when they could not see?

- Have a student guide a blind-folded partner to his or her quiet site. Have the partner recall sounds, smells, and feelings he or she experienced along the way.

- Supply students with ways to improve the ability of their senses (e.g., use binoculars, spray water on their noses [moisture traps scent particles], cup their hands behind their ears).

6. **Following are questions that could be asked of students before, during, or after the stream visit:**

Sight: What plants and animals do they see? Does the appearance of the stream vary with location? Is the stream fast or slow moving? How can they

determine its speed?

Sound: What sounds does the stream make? Can they hear animals? What does the wind sound like?

Smell: How do smells near the stream compare to those on a road or in a home? Does the water smell the same as tap water?

Touch: What does the stream water feel like? How does soil near the stream feel compared to soil in the woods or schoolyard? Are the rocks in the stream smooth or rough?

▼ Wrap Up and Action

Have students share their *Sensory Observation Sheets* with the class. Ask them to create a mobile that includes things they observed with each of

---

Stream Walk Safety Rules

Notes for the Teacher:

1. Visit the stream first to determine if it is safe for students to visit. Check stream depth, velocity, and temperature. Also look for walking conditions, potentially dangerous wildlife, poisonous plants, etc.

2. Bring along a first-aid kit.

3. Define stream walk boundaries; make sure students understand that staying within the boundaries protects wildlife and students.

4. Locate a place where students can wash hands after the visit.

Rules for the Students:

1. Students should stay with their assigned buddies.

2. Students should wear old athletic shoes or boots because they will likely get wet and muddy.

3. Students should not enter the stream without supervision.

4. Students should not touch wildlife or taste anything (plants or water) unless permitted by teacher.

VIVIAN LINDEN

their senses at the stream. Have students create a display board titled *Sensory Observations of a Stream*.

Assign students to create sensory guide sheets for other people who visit the stream. The brochure or sheet could identify specific locations where people could make observations or it could be more general, listing sights, sounds, smells, and touchable objects near the stream.

Assessment

Have students:
- record observations (sights, sounds, smells, or textures) of a stream environment (steps 3 and 4).
- create a mobile that includes things perceived through their senses at the stream site (*Wrap Up*).
- create a sensory guide sheet to educate others about what they

might see, hear, touch, and smell at a stream (*Wrap Up*).

Extensions

Many state departments of natural resources, government agencies, water conservation agencies, education departments, and extension agencies have developed programs for studying and monitoring streams. Check the **Resources** section for a selected list of agencies and programs. Following is a brief description of some stream-related activities.

Resources

Water quality monitoring programs:

The Adopt-a-Stream Foundation, P.O. Box 5558, Everett, WA 98206.

Adopt-a-Watershed, Education Coordinator, California Association of Resource Conservation Districts, 1970 McKain Rd., Calabasas, CA 91302.

Global Rivers Environmental Education Network, 721 East Huron Ave., Ann Arbor, MI 48104. (313) 761-8142.

Sensory awareness resources:

Carson, R. 1956. *A Sense of Wonder.* New York, N.Y.: Harper & Row.

Cornell, J. 1979. *Sharing Nature with Children.* Nevada City, Calif.: Dawn Publications.

Herman, M., J. Passineau, A. Schimf, and P. Treur. 1985. *Teaching Kids to Love the Earth: Sharing a Sense of Wonder . . . 186 Outdoor Activities for Parents and Other Teachers.* Duluth, Minn.: Pfeifer-Hamilton Publishers.

Milord, S. 1989. *The Kids' Nature Book: 365 Indoor/Outdoor Activities and Experiences.* Charlotte, Vt.: Williamson Publishing Co.

Following is a partial list of agencies, organizations, and authors who offer stream-related resources:

Cromwell, Mare, et al. 1992. *Investigating Streams and Rivers.* Global Rivers Environmental Education Network, 721 East Huron Ave., Ann Arbor, MI 48104. (313) 761-8142.

Delta Labs. 1987. *Adopt-A-Stream Teacher's Handbook.* Rochester, N.Y.: Delta Laboratories, Inc.

McCollim, Lori. 1994. *Water We Here For?* Bozeman, Mont.: Project WET Montana.

Save our Streams Program. Izaak Walton League of America, 1401 Wilson Blvd., Level B, Arlington, VA 22209.

The Stream Scene: Watersheds, Wildlife and People. 1990. Portland, Oreg.: Oregon Department of Fish & Wildlife.

Other Things to Do at a Stream

Observations

What color is the water?

Is it always this color? Does it change throughout the day? What about during different seasons? Find an object that has a similar color to the water. Learn how water gets its color . . . Hint: it has something to do with light!

Can you see the bottom?

Is the water clear or murky? Collect a jarful of water and time how long it takes material to settle. Try this at different times of the year. Is it the same each time?

What is on the bottom?

Look at the bottom. Obtain a sample and describe what it feels like. Is it sandy or rocky? Is it mushy or coarse? Record the size of the rocks or pebbles. Are they rough and angular or round and smooth? Can you tell where they came from?

What lives in the stream?

Look for big things and little things, plants and animals, fast movers and slow movers. Filter the water, look under logs and rocks, stir up the bottom and see what flows into a net. Keep a record of what you find. NOTE: Try not to disturb or harm living things. Return them after observation.

What's along the banks?

Look at the different plants and animals that live near the stream. Keep an inventory of trees, flowers, birds, mammals, and insects that you see. Remember to look and not touch. If samples are collected for classroom study, try to return them safely.

Describe the soil on the banks. Are the banks easy to walk on or are they slippery? Do you see signs of erosion or parts of the banks sliding into the river?

Take measurements!

Is the water cold or warm?

Measure its temperature with a thermometer. Check different locations along and within the river—are they all the same temperature? What about at different times of the day or year?

How fast is the water moving?

See how long it takes for an object to float a certain distance (e.g., 20 yards). Divide the time into the distance to determine how fast the water is moving (e.g., yards per second).

Water quality

(See list of water quality monitoring programs in **Resources** section.)

Many state agencies and biological supply companies have information and kits you can use to test water quality. Check out why and/or how to test for each of the following: dissolved oxygen, pH, nitrates, phosphates, chlorine, hardness.

Taking action

Do you see any signs of pollution or litter? Talk with teachers or parents about organizing a stream cleanup. Collect and dispose of litter. (Be sure to wear heavy gloves.)

Design posters or make announcements on the radio about caring for the stream. (Ask local radio stations about making a public service announcement.)

Water Log

Record monthly observations in water journals to monitor changes over time.

Sensory Observation Sheet

Sights	Smells

Touch	Sounds

The Thunderstorm

■ **Grade Level:**
Lower Elementary, Upper Elementary

■ **Subject Areas:**
Earth Science, Language Arts

■ **Duration:**
Preparation time:
Part I: none needed
Part II: 30 minutes

Activity time:
Part I: 30 minutes
Part II: 50 minutes

■ **Setting:** Classroom

■ **Skills:**
Gathering information (calculating); Organizing (plotting data, mapping); Analyzing

■ **Charting the Course**
Activities on condensation and precipitation should precede this activity (see "Water Models"). To learn about the effects of precipitation on a watershed, students could participate in "Branching Out!" and "AfterMath." For further understanding of precipitation processes, have students participate in "Poetic Precipitation."

■ **Vocabulary**
precipitation, isohyetal line

What rumbles but is never hungry and crashes but never gets hurt?

▼ Summary

Students simulate the sounds of a thunderstorm through an aerobics activity and generate precipitation maps through a mock monitoring network.

Objectives
Students will:
• work cooperatively to mimic the sounds of a thunderstorm.
• become more aware of the various sounds of a thunderstorm.
• monitor and record "precipitation."

Materials
• *Hundreds of small pieces of paper* (¹/₂-inch [1 cm] squares)
• *Paper and pencil*
• *Containers with lids* (Ask students to collect containers of the same size, one per student.)
• *Plastic rulers*
• *Local map*

Making Connections
A discussion of thunderstorms will evoke diverse reactions from students. Most will have experienced the sights and sounds of a storm. Some will be aware of thunderstorms' effects through reading newspapers or watching television. Students should learn how thunderstorms can affect their lives and how meteorologists study thunderstorms.

Background
Thunderstorms are one of nature's most spectacular phenomena. They are common throughout the country. It would be difficult to listen to a national weather report in the spring or summer and not hear that thunderstorms were moving through different regions.

What distinguishes a thunderstorm from other types of storms? Thunder and lightning. Electrical charges build up and move about within certain kinds of clouds (for example, a cumulonimbus cloud that contains large amounts of moisture). When these charges jump from one area of the cloud to another, to another cloud, or to the ground, lightning occurs. The electric current in the lightning stroke heats the air it passes through. This heat causes an expansion of the air along its path and creates a shock wave of sound—thunder.

If you count five seconds from the time you see the lightning until you hear the thunder, the storm is about one mile away. Why? The lightning one sees is traveling at the speed of light (186,282 miles [299,792 km] per second); whereas the thunder one hears is traveling much slower at the speed of sound (1,100 feet [335 m] per second).

The sights and sounds that accompany a thunderstorm are impressive—lightning flashes illuminate the sky, thunder rumbles and shakes houses, rain falls on roofs, the wind sways tree branches, and an occasional hailstone rattles windows. In watching a thunderhead grow in the distance on a warm summer evening, we witness a spectacle of great beauty. However, when we are in a thunderstorm, safety becomes a priority.

Rain is one of the primary benefits of thunderstorms. Although thunderstorms can cause destruction through high winds, hail, heavy rains, and even tornadoes, most storms only pass through, bringing moisture.

It is important to monitor the amount of precipitation released by a thunderstorm. For example, 10 inches (25 cm) of rainfall in a 24-hour period in a limited area may cause extensive flooding. If, on

COURTESY EVERGLADES NATIONAL PARK

the other hand, a large area receives this amount of precipitation over several months, a flood may not be imminent. In the Midwest floods of 1993, continuous storms pounded the entire basin over a period of months.

A record of rainfall measurements helps watershed managers predict possible water shortages. If there is a chance the water table may be depleted, managers will need to implement water conservation strategies.

Precipitation is monitored through a network of recording stations. Each station collects data that is transmitted to scientists. The quality of the data generated by a network is related to the size of the area being monitored, the number of data collection stations, and the duration of the monitoring.

Scientists use graphs to illustrate their measurements. Graphs and maps make the data easier to visualize and understand.

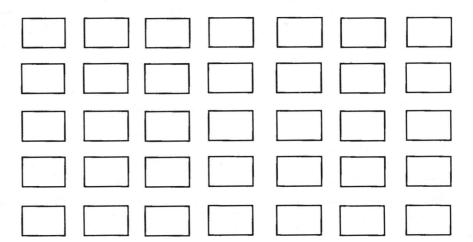

Procedure
▼ *Warm Up*

Have students describe how they would feel if they heard this report on their car radios:

A large thunderstorm with lightning, heavy rain, small hail, and gusty winds is moving toward (your town's name) at 25 miles (40 km) per hour. People in the path of the storm are advised to take precautions, according to the National Weather Service.

Have students outline the precautions they should take.

Ask students to create a mental picture of the approaching thunderstorm. Have them list some of the sights and sounds of the storm. What do they think causes the sound of thunder? Provide them with a brief explanation. Explain that they are going to create the sounds of a thunderstorm and also calculate how much "rain" was released as the storm passed through the classroom.

198

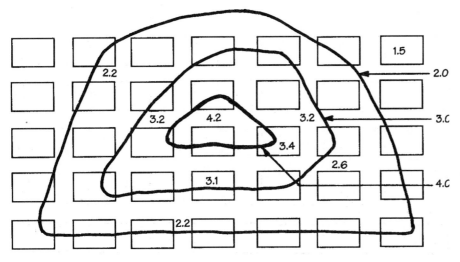

▼ The Activity

Part I

1. **Ask students to stand in a semicircle in front of you. Explain that when you make eye contact with or point to a student, he or she should imitate your motion. The student should continue making the motion until you make eye contact again and show a new motion. Start with a student on one end and begin the first motion. Continue the motion as you make eye contact with each student down the line. Return to the first student and start the second motion. This will create a crescendo as the sounds produced move from one end to the other. Using this strategy, lead students through the following series of motions:**
- rub your hands together
- snap your fingers
- clap your hands together in an irregular cadence
- slap your hands on your legs (Optional: At this time, a student flicks a light switch on and off to represent lightning, while another beats a drum to symbolize thunder.)
- stomp your feet
- slap your hands on your legs and stomp your feet (represents height of the storm)
- stomp your feet
- slap your hands on your legs
- clap your hands together in an irregular cadence
- snap your fingers
- rub your hands together
- open palms (quiet)

2. **When all students are standing with open palms, have them remain silent for a minute to think about the exercise and to catch their breath. Ask students to be seated.**

Discuss each motion and the effect it mimics.

3. **Have students write stories or draw pictures about thunderstorms they have experienced.** Create a collection, "Tales of Thunderstorms," and place it in the school library for everyone to read.

Part II

1. **Have students arrange their chairs or desks in rows to form a grid and stand behind them.**

2. **Give a container filled with pieces of paper to one student. Tell the student that when you say "Now!" he or she should toss the paper into the air.**

3. **Repeat the thunderstorm activity. At the height of the storm, when students are stomping feet and slapping hands on legs, say "Now!"**

4. **After the last sounds fade, ask students to be seated. Tell students that the pieces of paper represent the amount of rainfall.**

5. **Discuss the importance of monitoring rainfall. Tell students they each represent one point in the monitoring network. Have students gather as many pieces of paper as they can without leaving their seats.**

6. **Calculate the amount of precipitation by counting each piece collected as a tenth of an inch of rain.** (10 pieces equal 1 inch [2.5 cm] of rain, 5 pieces equal 0.5 inch [1.25 cm], 23 pieces equal 2.3 inches [5.75 cm] and so on.) For younger students, round the measurement to the nearest inch (e.g., 3, 8, or 12 pieces of paper would be rounded to 1 inch and 15, 19, or 24 pieces of paper would be rounded to 2 inches).

7. **Draw the grid of the student monitoring stations on the board. Record the number of pieces of paper collected by each student in the corresponding square on the grid. Have students locate the area that received the most precipitation and mark it with an "X."**

8. **Divide the class into groups. Have each group copy the grid and rainfall measurements.**

9. **Have each group make a precipitation map.** The purpose of the map is to identify areas that had similar amounts of precipitation. Ask students how they would categorize or group the stations. Suggest that they refer to the number of inches of rainfall. For example, if the area with the heaviest rainfall received 4.8 inches (12 cm), have them locate all other sites that received 4 inches (10

cm) of rain or more. They should draw a line connecting all those stations. The end result will be a circle—make sure the circle does not enclose any stations that received less than 4 inches (10 cm) of rain. The same should be done with the 3-, 2- and 1-inch (7.5, 5, and 2.5 cm) rainfall measurements. The 3-inch (7.5 cm) circle will encompass or surround the 4-inch (10 cm) circle, the 2-inch (5 cm) will surround the 3-inch (7.5 cm), and so on. The lines should not cross.

10. **The circles are called isohyetal lines. Theoretically, they indicate that every point along the line is of equal value. Ask students how a hydrologist might use the data from this map (flood predictions, irrigation, soil erosion, etc.).**

▼ *Wrap Up and Action*
Check students' maps to make sure they were drawn correctly. Have students discuss the following questions:
- What change could have been made to the monitoring network to get better results?
- Would the results have been that much better if there had been more collection points?

Repeat the activity several times to generate different maps.

Post a map of the community and have each student mark the location of his or her house. Have students place containers in open areas near their homes. Instruct them to measure the amount of rain collected after the next storm and bring the

results to class. Tell students to record the measurements on the community map. Have them use the results to produce a precipitation map.

Assessment
Have students:
- mimic the sounds of a thunderstorm (*Part I*, step 1).
- relate the sounds to actual thunderstorm events (*Part I*, step 2).
- recount experiences of thunderstorms (*Part I*, step 3).
- draw and interpret a precipitation map (*Part II*, step 9 and *Wrap Up*).

Extensions
Introduce the process of estimating the distance of a thunderclap. Challenge students to incorporate this into the thunderstorm activity (i.e., ask them to simulate a storm that is five seconds away).

Have students suggest ways to vary the intensity of the thunderstorm or to mimic different types of rain. Make an audio cassette recording of each type of storm or rain sound produced. Play back the recordings and have students match the recording to the type of storm or rain intensity they tried to mimic.

Convert the precipitation amounts on the map to snow depth. For example, 1 inch (2.5 cm) of precipitation equals 10 inches (25 cm) of snow. If you collected 24 pieces of paper you would have 2.4 inches (6 cm) of rain or 24 inches (60 cm) of snow. This type of data is important

when anticipating spring runoff, recreating in avalanche country, predicting wildlife migrations to winter feeding areas, and in river basin planning. If snowpack is low and holds little moisture, how might this affect river water levels later in the year?

Use blue pieces of paper to represent rain and white to represent hail. Run the activity the same way. This time count the total for each color. This will allow you to draw isohyetal lines for rain and hail on the same map.

Create a wild weather report. To stimulate some creative thinking, have students write a weather report like the one prepared by the National Weather Service, but from the perspective of a gopher, a robin, a fox, a trout, or an oak tree. What would they say about a thunderstorm? What would they tell their wild friends to do?

Resources
🍎 Branley, Franklyn M. 1985. *Flash, Crash, Rumble and Roll.* New York, N.Y.: Harper.

Fariel, Robert E., et al. 1984. *Addison-Wesley Earth Science.* Menlo Park, Calif.: Addison-Wesley Publishing Company.

Lambert, David, and Ralph Hardy. 1984. *The World of Science: Weather and Its Work.* New York, N.Y.: Facts on File, Inc.

🍎 Whipple, A. B. C. 1982. *Storm.* Morristown, N.J.: Silver Burdett.

Water Models

■ Grade Level:
Upper Elementary, Middle School

■ Subject Areas:
Earth Science, Ecology, Geology, Physical Science

■ Duration:
Preparation time: 30 minutes
Activity time: two 50-minute periods

■ Setting: Classroom

■ Skills:
Gathering information (observing, researching); Analyzing; Applying (making models); Presenting

■ Charting the Course
"Piece It Together" and "Wet Vacation" help students understand more about climates and ecosystems. Other water cycle activities include "The Incredible Journey," and "Imagine!" Further investigations of climate and culture are found in "The Rainstick" and "Raining Cats and Dogs."

■ Vocabulary
climate, condensation, ecosystem, evaporation, precipitation, transpiration, water cycle

Does water move through the water cycle in a desert as it would in a rain forest?

▼ Summary
Students construct models of the water cycle to illustrate its major components and processes, and adapt their models to show how they think water would cycle in various ecosystems.

Objectives
Students will:
- recognize the roles of condensation and evaporation in the water cycle.
- relate the water cycle to different climates and ecosystems around the world.

Materials
- *Heat source*
- *Frying or cooking pans*
- *Ice*
- *Duct tape*
- *Large plastic or glass jars with tops* (Students can bring empty pickle or peanut butter jars from home.)
- *Water*
- *Sand*
- *Rocks*
- *Items that represent components of different climates or ecosystems* (collected by students)
- *Heat-resistant gloves* (or oven mitts)
- *Copies of* **Water Cycle in a Jar**
- *Copies of* **Observation Sheet**

Making Connections
When it rains and when water flows down a river, students see evidence of water moving through the water cycle. But some components of the water cycle are not visible to the eye and may be overlooked. Constructing water cycle models can help students better appreci-ate how evaporation and condensation help move water through the environment and around the world.

Background
Earth's water supply is finite, and this same water has been moving over, on, and under Earth's surface for thousands of years. The continual movement of water— often called the water cycle— collects, purifies, and distributes water around the world. The pull of gravity, electromagnetic forces, and the sun's energy keep water in continual motion.

Solar energy heats water on Earth's surface and in oceans, streams, lakes, soil, and vegetation and causes it to evaporate into the atmosphere. Heat from the sun also causes snow and ice to melt and then evaporate. Sometimes snow and ice can evaporate directly rather than going to the liquid state first; this process is called sublimation. Winds and air masses, also energized by the sun, flow around the globe, carrying water vapor with them. Falling temperatures cause water vapor to condense into tiny droplets that form clouds or fog. Water then leaves the atmosphere as precipitation (rain, snow, hail, etc.). Water often leaves the atmosphere many miles from where it originated. About 77 percent of the precipitation over the surface of Earth falls into the oceans. Water that falls on the ground seeps downward through soil and permeable rock formations, flows over the surface, or evaporates again.

There are three major climates (polar, temperate, and tropical). At the poles the air is cold and dry. The Arctic and the Antarctic are covered with snow throughout most of the year. Limited sunlight and cold temperatures allow very few plants to exist. Examples of plants that live in the tundra of the Arctic include mosses, lichens, and other plants that grow close to the ground. Although water at the poles stays frozen for a long time, sometimes it does evaporate. The water vapor eventually condenses and falls back to Earth as snow or it may be carried by global wind currents to other parts of the planet. At lower latitudes, the snow may melt and be absorbed by plants or flow for a while over the surface.

Tropical climates are hot and humid. The tropics, especially the rain forests, are densely populated by a great diversity of plants. Very tall trees, whose tops form a dense canopy, cover much of the land area. Some plants growing beneath this crown cover have large leaves to catch sunlight that filters through the canopy, while others (epiphytes) grow far above the ground on the branches of taller trees. The ground is moist throughout most of the year, so plants do not need to grow deep roots to find water. Rain forests create their own weather systems. Water evaporates from the ground or from plants (through transpiration) and rises to the top level of the trees, where it condenses and then falls back to the ground. The water may flow over the surface, be absorbed by plants, or filter to the ground. Some water vapor does eventually escape to the atmosphere, where global winds carry it to other places.

While weather at the poles and in the tropics is fairly consistent throughout the year, the temperate climates (Earth's mid-latitude regions) experience seasons. A variety of plants live in this climate, such as deciduous trees, flowering plants, mosses, and grasses. Their life cycles and growing patterns must comply with the changing seasons. In this climate, water flows over the surface, seeps underground, freezes, and evaporates. Water moves through the atmosphere as vapor, eventually

falling back to Earth—sometimes many miles away or in a different climate.

Geographic qualities, such as nearness to the ocean, elevation, and extent of land mass, create a variety of ecosystems within the temperate climate. For example, deserts are hot and dry. To live in these conditions, some plants, such as mesquite, have extremely deep root systems. Other plants, such as cacti, have fleshy tissue and very few pores, so they can retain large quantities of water instead of losing it through transpiration.

The processes of evaporation and condensation within all these climates help water move around Earth's surface. In this way, water is used and reused, with all parts of Earth eventually sharing the same water.

Procedure
▼ Warm Up
Set up the following teacher demonstration:
- Place a hot plate or other heat source on a table at the front of the room.
- Place a pot of water over the heat source.

- Once the water is hot, hold a pan of ice above the rising water vapor. (Wear heat resistant gloves for protection.)
- Drops of water vapor should condense on the bottom of the pan of ice.
- The drops of liquid water will fall and return to the pan of hot water.

Have the students make a list of observations and explain each. Ask students to list the processes that are occurring and how these might be exhibited in nature.

▼ The Activity
1. **Provide groups of students with a copy of** *Water Cycle in a Jar* **and have them construct their model and record observations on the** *Observation Sheet*.

2. **Have students summarize their observations, identifying and explaining the processes of evaporation and condensation. Help students understand the role of solar energy in these processes.** Runoff, filtration through sand, and other aspects of the water cycle can also be discussed.

3. **Discuss the role of plants in the water cycle. Have students research different climates (polar, temperate,**

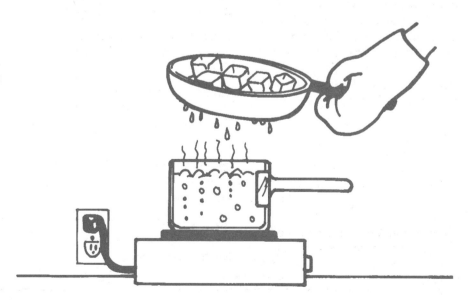

tropical) and/or ecosystems around the world (rain forest, desert, tundra, etc.). They should focus their search on learning how water moves in the area. Would water evaporate quickly? Would there be much standing water? Does water remain frozen? Students could further their investigations by finding out what plants live in the area. How do they manage to live in these different climates?

4. **Challenge students to adapt their jar model to represent the climate or ecosystem they are studying.** For example, if the model represents a desert, they could put in tiny cacti, sand, and a little water, and place it in the sunlight.

▼ Wrap Up

Have students present their models to the class and describe how water moves within the model and within the climate or ecosystem represented by the model.

After the presentations are complete, draw a large circle on the floor that represents Earth. Bisect the circle with a line to indicate the equator. Have students arrange their models comparable to where they are located on Earth. (An alternative is to lay a world map on the ground.) Students should extrapolate how evaporation and condensation and other processes of the water cycle help water travel from one part of the world to another. Have students summarize how the world shares water.

Assessment

Have students:
- construct a simple model of the water cycle and identify the processes of evaporation and condensation (steps 1 and 2).
- create a model simulating the water cycle of different climates or ecosystems throughout the world (step 4).

- use the model to explain how the world shares water (*Wrap Up*).

Extensions

Involve students in the following activities to further explore condensation and evaporation. Hand out paper towels soaked with equal amounts of water to groups of students. Charge them with finding the fastest way to dry the towels using only things they find in the room. Students should discover that motion, heat, and increasing the exposed surface help the water evaporate more quickly. Discuss where the evaporated water goes. Challenge students to retrieve water from the air. Discuss the process of condensation. Provide helpful hints by having metal or glass containers and ice water available.

Resources

Alexander, Gretchen. 1989. *Water Cycle Teacher's Guide*. Hudson, N. H.: Delta Education, Inc.

Biological Science Curriculum Study. 1987. *Biological Science: An Ecological Approach*. Dubuque, Iowa.: Kendall/Hunt Publishing Company.

🍎 Cast, Vance C. 1992. *Where Does Water Come From?* Hauppauge, N.Y.: Barron's Educational Series, Inc.

Hurd, Dean et al. 1988. *Physical Science*. Englewood Cliffs, N.J.: Prentice Hall.

Lamb, William G., Mapi M. Cuevas, and Robert L. Lehman. 1989. *Physical Science*. Orlando, Fla.: Harcourt Brace Jovanovich, Inc.

🍎 Mayes, Susan. 1989. *What Makes It Rain?* London, England: Usborne Publications.

🍎 Schmid, Elenore. 1990. *The Water's Journey*. New York, N.Y.: North-South Books.

Notes ▼

Water Cycle in a Jar

1. Take two identical jars; put a pile of sand in one and saturate with water. Place a rock in the sand. Tape together the open ends of the two jars. (See diagram.)

2. Put the jars near a sunny window.

3. Observe the jars several times during the day for a period of at least a week.

4. Record your observations on the observation sheet.

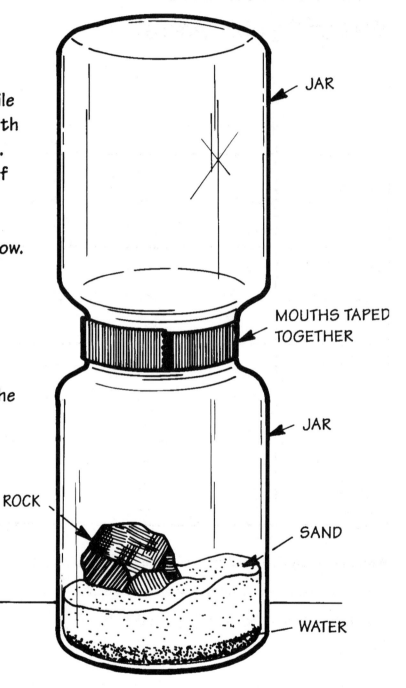

JAR

MOUTHS TAPED TOGETHER

JAR

ROCK

SAND

WATER

Observation Sheet
Water Cycle Model

Team Members: _____   Date: _____

_____

	Day 1	Day 2	Day 3	Day 4	Day 5
Solar Energy Record: Good/Fair/Poor	obs. 1: obs. 2: obs. 3:	obs. 1: obs. 2: obs. 3:	obs. 1: obs. 2: obs. 3:	obs. 1: obs. 2: obs. 3:	obs. 1: obs. 2: obs. 3:
Evaporation Record: Good/Fair/Poor	obs. 1: obs. 2: obs. 3:	obs. 1: obs. 2: obs. 3:	obs. 1: obs. 2: obs. 3:	obs. 1: obs. 2: obs. 3:	obs. 1: obs. 2: obs. 3:
Condensation Record: Good/Fair/Poor	ob. 1: obs. 2: obs. 3:	obs. 1: obs. 2: obs. 3:	obs. 1: obs. 2: obs. 3:	obs. 1: obs. 2: obs. 3:	obs. 1 obs. 2: obs. 3:
Water Level (measure in inches or centimeters)	obs. 1: obs. 2: obs. 3:	obs. 1: obs. 2: obs. 3:	obs. 1: obs. 2: obs. 3:	obs. 1: obs. 2: obs. 3:	obs. 1 obs. 2: obs. 3:

What time of day does condensation usually appear? _____

What processes are occurring to make these changes? _____

What is the role of sunlight and temperature? _____

Conclusions: _____

_____

_____

_____

_____

_____

Wet Vacation

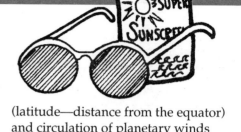

Do you take a parka when you travel to Florida? Do you pack a beach towel when you visit Nebraska in December?

▼ Summary

After plotting annual precipitation and average temperatures, and researching climatic conditions of places around the country, students design attractive travel brochures.

Objectives

Students will:
- identify factors that affect temperature and precipitation patterns.
- analyze how weather conditions influence tourism.

Materials

- *Map of the United States*
- Copies of **Temperature and Precipitation Statistics for Cities Across the United States**
- *Samples of travel brochures*
- *Atlases, reference manuals, encyclopedias, etc.*
- Copies of **Tips for Designing a Brochure for a Wet Vacation**

Making Connections

Every year thousands of people plan trips. Students are familiar with popular vacation spots, but may not know why people prefer one area over another. Often weather is the primary criterion for choosing a destination. By investigating seasons and topographic features, students learn how unique weather patterns create attractive vacation sites.

Background

A region's climate is based on long-term weather conditions. Temperature ranges and amounts of precipitation characterize climates. Location on Earth's surface (latitude—distance from the equator) and circulation of planetary winds mainly determine an area's temperature and precipitation.

The United States is located within a temperate climate region. Temperate climates have definite winter and summer seasons (compared to polar regions that experience no true summer, and tropical regions where winter never occurs).

Even though the United States is classified as having a temperate climate, arctic tundra, deserts, high mountains, rain forests, and subtropical conditions are found within the country. In addition to latitude and planetary winds, other factors influence precipitation and temperature. These include elevation, proximity to large bodies of water, and nearness to mountain ranges. These conditions can alter or even override typical temperate climate patterns and create deserts and tropical regions.

For example, the weather on one side of a mountain range often differs from that on the other side. As wind carries moist air over a mountain range and the air mass rises, it cools and loses its ability to hold water. By the time air passes to the other side, it contains little moisture. Lands near oceans and large freshwater lakes are subject to milder weather patterns. This is because water takes longer than air to gain or lose heat energy. After the sun goes down, heat slowly escaping from water will continue to warm the air.

Weather patterns often influence where people live and vacation. Some people prefer cool, dry weather, while others enjoy basking in the sun. People also consider the amount of precipitation. They want to avoid floods and droughts, but they enjoy rafting down rivers churning with whitewater. In winter,

---

Sidebar

■ **Grade Level:**
Middle School, High School

■ **Subject Areas:**
Geography, Earth Science, Fine Arts, Language Arts

■ **Duration:**
Preparation time:
Part I: 30 minutes
Part II: 30 minutes

Activity time:
Part I: 50 minutes
Part II: up to one week

■ **Setting:** Classroom

■ **Skills:**
Organizing (plotting data); Analyzing (comparing and contrasting, identifying components and relationships); Applying (designing); Presenting

■ **Charting the Course**
The activity "Idea Pools" could be used to help students brainstorm what aspects of weather and climate they find attractive. In "Piece It Together," students learn about global climate patterns. For a closer look at precipitation and weather, have students participate in "Poetic Precipitation."

■ **Vocabulary**
temperature, precipitation, climate, weather

---

deep snowfall promises an exciting ski season.

Travel agencies keep in mind the likes and dislikes of people when creating brochures. Knowing the weather patterns of a region helps them design fun, comfortable vacations for travelers.

Procedure
▼ Warm Up
Point out locations on a map of the United States and have students describe what they think the weather patterns (temperature and precipitation) of an area are. Have students list factors that they think contribute to an area's weather.

▼ The Activity
Part I
1. **Provide students with a copy of** *Temperature and Precipitation Statistics for Cities Across the United States.* **Tell students to locate the cities on a map of the United States.** When they are done, three to four cities should be plotted for each state.

2. **Have students look for similarities and differences in temperatures and precipitation within states and regions of the country.** Is the information consistent for the areas? Do some states have cities that differ greatly from each other in average temperatures and/or precipitation? Have students look for expected patterns of temperature and precipitation ranges and note where the information differs from their expectations.

Part II
1. **Divide the class into groups; have each group select a state (or portion of a state) and identify the seasons and weather patterns for the area. Have them research if and how latitude, elevation, large**
bodies of water, ocean and air currents, and mountains affect the area's temperature and precipitation.** For organization, they may want to arrange these influences into a table. Sources for research include atlases, encyclopedias, Geography and Earth Science texts, reference books about the region, etc. They may want to contact the tourist department of the state to request information.

2. **Have students plan a wet vacation to the area. Explain that a wet vacation focuses on how water determines the best times for travel or the most appealing quality of the region (e.g., dry deserts are good for allergy sufferers; spring thaws create river rapids for whitewater enthusiasts).**

3. **Tell students they are to design a travel brochure or guide for their study area. Provide them with** *Tips for Designing a Brochure for a Wet Vacation.*

4. **Involve students in establishing a grading criteria for the brochures.** This could consist of a list of the recommended components (e.g., accurate information, persuasive language, suggested activities) followed by a rating scale.

▼ Wrap Up and Action
Have students evaluate their own and/or other groups' travel brochures using the grading criteria they developed. Ask them to summarize the factors that contribute to an area's temperature and precipitation. Other classes or family members can read the brochures to learn about different parts of the country and to see if they would be interested in a wet vacation.

Assessment
Have students:
- identify factors that influence a region's temperature and precipitation (*Part II*, step 1).
- design a travel brochure that highlights the attractive water-related components of a location (*Part II*, step 2).
- evaluate travel brochures developed in class (*Part II*, step 4 and *Wrap Up*).

Extensions
Establish a travel agency in the classroom. Display all the students' brochures and a large map. Have train, plane, and cruise ship schedules available. Ask students to choose a brochure (not their own) and determine how they would travel to that destination. What would they pack? How long would the trip take? How much would it cost?

Students may want to explore water's resistance to temperature change. Have the students place two cups in a refrigerator: one filled with warm water, the other empty. Place a thermometer in the water and another thermometer in the empty cup. Compare the change in temperature of the water to that of the air over a 30-minute period. Leave the cups in the refrigerator overnight and remove them in the morning. Have students once again compare changes.

Resources
Entine, Lynn, and Ellen Fisher, eds. 1985. *Our Great Lakes Connection: A Curriculum Guide for Grades Kindergarten through Eight.* Madison, Wis.: Wisconsin University, Madison University Extension, Environmental Resources Center.

Ruffner, James A., ed. 1985. *Climates of the States,* 3rd ed. Detroit, Mich.: Gale Research Co.

Ruffner, James A., and Frank E. Blair, eds. 1985. *Weather of U.S. Cities,* 2nd ed. Detroit, Mich.: Gale Research Co.

Temperature and Precipitation Statistics for Cities Across the United States

CITY	STATE	PRECIPITATION INCHES	PRECIPITATION CENTI- METERS	TEMPERATURE DEGREES F	TEMPERATURE DEGREES C	CITY	STATE	PRECIPITATION INCHES	PRECIPITATION CENTI- METERS	TEMPERATURE DEGREES F	TEMPERATURE DEGREES C
Huntsville	ALABAMA	56.19	142.72	60.4	15.8	Tallahassee	FLORIDA	59.04	149.96	67.7	19.8
Mobile		63.76	161.95	67.5	19.7	Tampa		48.83	124.03	72.2	22.3
Montgomery		51.23	130.12	65.5	18.6	Miami		58.90	149.61	75.5	24.2
Birmingham		53.74	136.50	63.1	17.3	Jacksonville		51.49	130.78	67.9	19.9
Anchorage	ALASKA	15.06	38.25	35.1	1.7	Columbus	GEORGIA	51.51	130.84	64.8	18.2
Barrow		4.39	11.15	9.6	-12.4	Augusta		44.50	113.03	64.3	17.9
Fairbanks		11.16	28.35	26.1	-3.3	Savannah		48.78	123.90	66.8	19.3
Nome		16.80	42.67	25.9	-3.4	Atlanta		48.62	123.49	61.5	16.4
Yuma	ARIZONA	3.36	8.53	72.8	22.7	Hilo	HAWAII	127.40	323.60	73.5	23.1
Phoenix		7.49	19.02	70.6	21.4	Honolulu		22.83	57.99	76.4	24.7
Tucson		11.32	28.75	67.5	19.7	Kahului		18.76	47.65	75.4	24.1
Flagstaff		20.67	52.50	45.6	7.6	Lihue		43.92	111.56	74.1	23.4
Fort Smith	ARKANSAS	39.91	101.37	61.3	16.3	Boise	IDAHO	12.14	30.84	51.2	10.7
Little Rock		48.39	122.91	62.1	16.7	Lewistown		13.05	33.15	52.1	11.7
Texarkana		45.25	114.94	64.4	18.0	Coeur d'Alene		25.79	65.51	48.3	9.1
Blytheville		49.43	125.55	61.0	16.1	Pocatello		12.40	31.50	47.3	8.5
San Diego	CALIFORNIA	9.93	25.22	62.2	16.8	Cairo	ILLINOIS	43.58	110.69	58.7	14.8
Fresno		9.89	25.12	63.1	17.3	Chicago		33.55	85.22	49.9	9.9
Eureka		39.44	100.18	52.0	11.1	Springfield		35.47	90.09	53.2	11.8
San Francisco		21.49	54.58	56.6	13.7	Moline		35.73	90.75	49.9	9.9
Grand Junction	COLORADO	8.52	21.64	52.7	11.5	Evansville	INDIANA	42.47	107.87	56.6	13.7
Alamosa		7.09	18.01	41.4	5.2	Fort Wayne		34.36	87.27	50.0	10.0
Pueblo		11.56	29.36	52.3	11.3	Indianapolis		39.90	101.35	52.6	11.4
Denver		14.59	37.06	50.2	10.1	South Bend		36.09	91.67	49.5	9.7
Bridgeport	CONNECTICUT	43.93	111.58	51.1	10.6	Burlington	IOWA	35.20	89.41	51.4	10.8
Hartford		47.13	119.71	50.0	10.0	Des Moines		31.68	80.47	49.9	9.9
Danbury		48.17	122.35	49.6	9.8	Sioux City		25.45	64.64	48.4	9.1
						Dubuque		34.71	88.16	47.8	8.8
Wilmington	DELAWARE	41.38	105.11	54.1	12.3						
Dover		44.44	112.88	56.2	13.4	Concordia	KANSAS	26.50	67.31	53.7	12.1
Lewes		45.08	114.50	55.2	12.9	Dodge City		20.44	51.92	54.8	12.7
Bridgeville		44.36	112.67	55.5	13.06	Topeka		33.53	85.17	54.7	12.6
						Wichita		29.86	75.84	56.8	13.8

CITY	STATE	PRECIPITATION		TEMPERATURE		CITY	STATE	PRECIPITATION		TEMPERATURE	
		INCHES	CENTI-METERS	DEGREES F	DEGREES C			INCHES	CENTI-METERS	DEGREES F	DEGREES C
Louisville	KENTUCKY	43.82	111.30	56.8	13.8	Columbia	MISSOURI	37.86	96.16	54.8	12.7
Hopkinsville		49.16	124.87	56.9	13.8	Kansas City		36.67	93.14	55.3	12.9
Middleboro		52.33	132.92	55.7	13.2	St. Louis		36.83	93.55	56.1	13.4
Lexington		43.66	110.90	55.1	12.8	Springfield		40.97	104.06	56.0	13.3
Lake Charles	LOUISIANA	55.68	141.43	68.0	20.0	Kalispell	MONTANA	15.35	38.99	43.1	6.2
New Orleans		60.14	152.76	68.9	20.5	Miles City		13.94	35.41	45.5	7.5
Alexandria		53.86	136.80	64.8	18.2	Havre		12.64	32.11	42.6	5.9
Shreveport		44.60	113.28	65.8	18.8	Bozeman		19.20	48.00	37.9	3.3
Caribou	MAINE	36.95	93.85	38.8	3.8	Valentine	NEBRASKA	18.50	46.99	47.1	8.4
Portland		42.54	108.05	45.5	7.5	Scottsbluff		15.16	38.51	48.5	9.2
Eastport		43.82	111.30	43.5	6.4	Omaha		28.51	72.42	51.0	10.6
Rumford		43.84	111.35	42.7	5.9	North Platte		18.70	47.50	49.1	9.5
Baltimore	MARYLAND	41.84	106.27	55.0	12.8	Ely	NEVADA	9.17	23.29	44.3	6.8
Hagerstown		38.84	98.65	53.5	11.9	Las Vegas		4.16	10.57	66.1	18.9
Salisbury		44.83	113.87	57.2	14.0	Reno		7.69	19.53	49.9	9.9
Rockville		40.91	103.91	55.0	12.8	Winnemucca		8.51	21.62	48.8	9.3
Boston	MASSACHUSETTS	41.50	105.41	50.4	10.2	Concord	NEW HAMPSHIRE	38.09	96.75	45.9	7.7
Springfield		44.87	113.97	50.5	10.28	Durham		43.23	109.80	47.0	8.3
New Bedford		43.94	111.61	52.3	11.3	Hanover		36.67	93.14	44.9	7.2
Worcester		47.46	120.55	47.0	8.3	Keene		40.31	102.39	46.7	8.2
Alpena	MICHIGAN	29.11	73.94	42.7	5.9	Atlantic City	NEW JERSEY	41.23	104.72	53.0	11.7
Detroit		31.49	79.98	49.2	9.6	Newark		42.53	108.03	53.9	12.2
Grand Rapids		33.43	94.91	48.4	9.1	Trenton		43.85	109.63	53.9	12.2
Marquette		31.93	81.10	41.6	5.3	Newton		44.03	111.84	48.4	9.1
Duluth	MINNESOTA	28.48	72.34	38.5	3.6	Albuquerque	NEW MEXICO	8.31	21.11	55.8	13.2
International Falls		24.99	63.47	36.7	2.6	Clayton		14.83	37.67	52.9	11.6
Minneapolis		26.84	68.17	44.9	7.2	Roswell		12.43	31.57	59.5	15.3
Marshall		25.33	64.34	44.4	6.9	Lordsburg		10.40	26.42	60.8	16.0
Jackson	MISSISSIPPI	52.33	132.92	65.4	18.6	Albany	NEW YORK	36.52	92.76	48.0	8.9
Aberdeen		54.85	139.32	63.0	17.2	Buffalo		35.66	90.58	47.3	8.5
Biloxi		61.00	154.94	68.1	20.1	New York		43.72	111.05	54.1	12.3
Clarksville		51.19	130.02	63.0	17.2	Syracuse		36.83	95.55	47.7	8.7
						Ashville	NORTH CAROLINA	47.94	121.77	55.3	12.9
						Charlotte		44.89	114.02	60.4	15.8
						Greensboro		42.46	107.85	57.9	14.4
						Wilmington		50.83	129.11	63.4	17.4

| CITY | STATE | PRECIPITATION | | TEMPERATURE | | CITY | STATE | PRECIPITATION | | TEMPERATURE | |
		INCHES	CENTI-METERS	DEGREES F	DEGREES C			INCHES	CENTI-METERS	DEGREES F	DEGREES C
Bismarck	NORTH DAKOTA	16.08	40.84	41.2	5.1	Corpus Christi	TEXAS	27.76	70.51	71.2	21.8
Fargo		20.89	53.06	40.2	4.6	Dallas-Fort Worth		32.14	81.64	65.6	18.7
Williston		14.25	36.20	40.5	4.7	El Paso		8.51	21.62	63.8	17.7
Grand Forks		18.29	46.46	38.9	3.8	Lubbock		18.02	45.77	59.8	15.4
Cincinnati	OHIO	40.59	103.10	53.5	11.9	Salt Lake City	UTAH	15.75	40.01	51.8	11.0
Cleveland		34.33	87.20	49.8	9.9	Wendover		4.83	12.27	52.6	11.4
Columbus		37.12	94.28	52.2	11.2	Moab		8.00	20.32	56.6	13.7
Toledo		31.74	80.62	49.5	9.7	Beaver		11.13	28.27	47.5	8.6
Oklahoma City	OKLAHOMA	31.73	80.59	60.1	15.6	Burlington	VERMONT	32.94	83.67	44.5	6.9
Tulsa		37.97	96.44	60.6	15.9	Montpelier		33.94	86.21	42.1	5.6
Boise City		15.84	40.23	55.6	13.1	Rutland		34.91	88.67	46.3	7.9
Lawton		29.20	74.17	62.1	16.7	Newport		39.94	101.45	41.8	5.4
Astoria	OREGON	70.06	177.95	50.8	10.4	Lynchburg	VIRGINIA	40.71	102.03	56.9	13.8
Eugene		45.87	116.51	52.4	11.3	Norfolk		45.28	115.01	59.8	15.4
Pendleton		13.02	33.07	52.3	11.3	Winchester		38.27	97.21	54.4	12.4
Medford		18.90	48.01	53.7	12.1	Fredricksburg		40.99	104.11	56.2	13.4
Allentown	PENNSYLVANIA	43.89	111.48	51.1	10.6	Seattle-Tacoma	WASHINGTON	39.14	99.42	51.3	10.7
Erie		37.92	96.32	49.0	9.4	Spokane		16.23	41.22	48.1	8.9
Philadelphia		41.38	105.11	54.6	12.6	Walla Walla		16.32	41.45	53.9	12.2
Pittsburg		36.23	92.02	53.3	11.8	Yakima		7.60	19.30	50.7	10.4
Block Island	RHODE ISLAND	40.57	103.05	50.0	10.0	Charleston	WEST VIRGINIA	43.65	110.87	56.2	13.4
Providence		41.73	105.99	50.5	10.3	Parkersburg		38.88	98.76	54.4	12.4
Kingston		48.49	123.16	49.2	9.6	Elkins		45.75	116.21	50.0	10.0
Charleston	SOUTH CAROLINA	48.73	123.77	65.7	18.7	Wheeling		38.06	96.67	52.2	11.2
Columbia		45.42	115.37	63.6	17.6	Green Bay	WISCONSIN	28.38	72.09	44.2	6.8
Greenville		52.03	132.16	59.8	15.4	La Crosse		30.94	78.59	46.3	7.9
Aiken		47.69	121.13	63.8	17.7	Milwaukee		30.53	77.55	46.4	8.0
Aberdeen	SOUTH DAKOTA	18.74	47.60	43.5	6.4	Superior		28.73	72.97	39.7	4.3
Rapid City		17.55	44.58	46.8	8.2	Casper	WYOMING	11.83	30.05	45.3	7.4
Sioux City		25.13	63.83	46.1	7.8	Cheyenne		14.53	36.91	45.2	7.3
Gettysburg		18.08	45.92	44.0	6.7	Jackson		15.27	38.79	38.0	3.3
Chattanooga	TENNESSEE	52.31	132.87	60.3	15.7	Green River		7.74	19.66	42.7	5.9
Knoxville		47.83	121.49	58.8	14.9	Guam	PACIFIC ISLANDS	100.90	256.29	78.8	26.0
Memphis		49.19	124.94	61.9	16.6	San Juan	PUERTO RICO	55.30	140.46	79.8	26.6
Nashville		46.88	119.08	59.5	15.3						

Tips for Designing a Brochure for a Wet Vacation

Content of the brochure

The main portion of the brochure should describe the temperature and precipitation range of the area, listing factors that contribute to its weather patterns.

Other information to include:

- What seasons does the area experience? How wet are the spring months and how much snow does it receive in winter?
- Should weather precautions be considered, specifically, water-related disasters (e.g., floods, hailstorms, drought)?
- What water-related recreational activities are available (e.g., boating, skiing, scenic water views).
- When would be the best time of year to visit the area and why?

Design considerations

1. Pay attention to the size of your brochure. A brochure is intended to be a "quick read." It should fold in an interesting but uncomplicated way, so that the reader can easily follow the flow of the text.

2. The cover of the brochure should indicate the subject of the document. Usually the front cover contains a title, a logo, and an illustration or photograph. If possible, use color; generally, color has more impact than black-and-white.

3. Within the text of the brochure, highlight main points by using a larger, or bolder, type. Details of the main points should be in smaller type.

4. Use photographs or illustrations to complement the text. We live in a visual world.

5. Professional designers use the term FAB (features and benefits). In your brochure, tell readers the features of your particular wet vacation and how these features benefit them.

6. In a brochure, you don't have much time to capture your audience's attention, so make the design appealing. Use color and don't clutter. That is, leave plenty of white or negative space.

Wetland Soils in Living Color

Have you ever thought about identifying soils with a box of crayons?

■ **Grade Level:**
Middle School

■ **Subject Areas:**
Earth Science

■ **Duration:**
Preparation time:
Part I: 40 minutes
Part II: 50 minutes

Activity time:
Part I: 50 minutes
Part II: (field trip) 1-2 hours

■ **Setting:**
Classroom and wetland site

■ **Skills:**
Gathering information (collecting); Organizing (matching, classifying, manipulating materials); Analyzing (identifying patterns); Interpreting (confirming)

■ **Charting the Course**
The activity "Capture, Store, and Release," which relates how water settles in a wetlands, could precede this activity. Understanding the parts of a ground water system ("Get the Ground Water Picture") supports concepts in this activity. Wetland ecosystems are explored in "People of the Bog" and "Salt Marsh Players."

■ **Vocabulary**
anaerobic, aerobic, organic, wetlands

▼ Summary
Students learn about the properties of wetland soils and classify soil types using a simple color key.

Objectives
Students will:
• classify soils according to color to confirm that an area is a wetland.
• describe conditions that create the color characteristics of wetland soils.

Materials
• *A collection of pencils of varying sizes, conditions, colors, and shapes—and a pen*
• *3 soil samples, preferably of varying colors*
• *Several packs of 64 Crayola® crayons*
• *Scissors*
• *Paste*
• *Poster board or manila folders*
• *Copies of **Soil Sample Data Chart and Wetland Soils Color Chart***
• *Spade, shovel, or auger*
• *Yardstick*
• *Notebooks and pencils*
• *A wetlands area near the school (Likely locations include the edges of ponds and streams, low-lying topography that is often wet and muddy, drainage ditches that are frequently full of water, or sites with obvious wetland vegetation—cattails, willows, and reeds. Try to chose a location that has not been developed or filled with soil from another area. Selection of a site will be influenced by accessibility, sufficient room for students to work, landowner permission, etc.)*

Making Connections
People use classification skills every day to arrange clothes in a closet, identify a species of bird, or prioritize a list of things to do. Soil can be classified as well. All of us see dirt in a plowed field, layers of soil in a stream bank, or rich earth in a vegetable garden. However, we likely think of soil as having little variation in character or quality. By analyzing soil samples and using a color key, students learn that a broad spectrum of characteristics help classify soils as productive or sterile, wet or dry, mineral or organic, etc. This information plays a part in determining if a land area is a wetland.

Background
The topic of wetlands frequently receives attention from the media and consideration in courts of law or legislative sessions. One issue frequently raised is the method used to determine whether or not a land area warrants the label of wetland. Soil classification provides valuable information when designating wetlands, and color is a key characteristic in classifying soils.

Wetland soils are saturated, flooded, or covered to a shallow depth with water; they remain wet long enough during the growing season that the upper soil layers are deprived of oxygen (anaerobic). Over time, this lack of oxygen produces chemical reactions that change the soil's color, as well as other of its characteristics such as texture, organic content, etc.

Even when water is not present, the color of soil can be used to identify an area as a wetland. By reading these soils, scientists can determine a great deal about the length and frequency of wet conditions.

Wetland soils are divided into two major types: organic and mineral. Wet organic soils look like black muck or dark brown or black peat. Decomposed plants and animals contribute to the color of organic soils. In water-logged, anaerobic environments, organic materials tend to accumulate rather than decompose (as they would in aerated environments).

Soils lacking organic material are classified as mineral and are usually found deeper under the surface. Sand, silt, and clay are common mineral soil components. Mineral wetland soils can be gleyed (pro-nounced "glade") or mottled. Gleyed soils range from neutral gray to greenish or bluish gray, depending on the degree of saturation. Mottled soils are gray, with splotches of brown, orange, red, or yellow, as a result of being alternately wet and dry. When oxygen mixes with iron, water, and other components in soil, the iron rusts and creates these splotches of color. Soils that contain manganese can develop black mottling in waterlogged conditions.

Wetland scientists use a complicated set of color charts, a Munsell soil color book, to identify soils. The charts classify soils into different types, based on their color, lightness and darkness, and the degree of mixture of colors.

In addition to color, a soil's texture and degree of wetness, along with other qualities like smell and the presence or absence of living matter, provide clues to its classification. A rotten-egg smell indicates the presence of hydrogen sulfide, a product of anaerobic bacteria. Various layers of soil in the same hole may exhibit striking differences in color, texture, and smell, caused by the presence of water, the parent soil material, aerobic or anaerobic conditions, and so on.

Procedure

▼ *Warm Up*

Show students a pencil and a pen and have them list qualities that distinguish one from the other. Explain that these qualities are used to *classify* one item as a pen and the other as a pencil. Show students an assortment of pencils. Challenge them to classify the pencils into three groups. Ask students to describe the system (e.g., size, degree of sharp-ness, number of teeth marks) they used to classify the pencils.

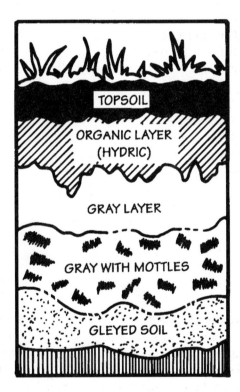

Tell students that wetlands are classified to distinguish them from other land areas. Ask students to list characteristics of wetlands.

▼ *The Activity*

Part I

1. **Provide students with the following description of a land area and ask if they would classify it as a wetland.**

The land area contains some long-leafed plants that look like grasses. Most of the year the land is dry; however, almost every spring the area is flooded.

Ask students to vote whether or not this is a wetland. Disparity may exist in their opinions, and they may conclude they need more informa-tion.

2. **Tell students that soils are often used to determine whether or not an area is a wetland. Show students three soil samples. Ask students how they would classify them or distinguish one from the other.**

3. **Explain that color provides important clues used by scientists when classifying soils.** Provide students with background about how moisture content and mineral composition influence the color of soils.

4. **Distribute copies of the *Wet-land Soils Color Chart* and review the directions at the top of the page. Explain that this is a simplified version of a chart actually used by wetland managers. Also distribute and discuss the *Soil Sample Data Chart* with students. Have them complete the *Wetland Soils Color Chart* individually or in small groups.**

Part II

1. **Take a field trip to a nearby wetland, to test the *Wetland Soils Color Chart* against actual soil samples. At the wetland, dig a hole approximately 2 feet (60 cm) deep. Refill the holes before leaving.**

2. **Remove soil samples about the size of Ping-Pong balls from several different depths; inspect and compare them against the *Wetland Soils Color Chart*. Tell students to break open the samples to check for the truest color.**

3. **Have students complete their** *Soil Sample Data Chart.* If possible, dig another hole or holes in several sites (other wetlands, upland dry areas) to compare soil variations.

▼ *Wrap Up and Action*

Have students share and combine their conclusions to create and label a diagram of the soil layers in the hole. Ask students to determine if soil samples are organic or mineral and to describe conditions that could contribute to soil color. Do results confirm this area as a wetland?

Discuss soil characteristics. Questions might include the following:
- What physical characteristics of the soil do you observe (color, texture, main ingredients, presence of earthworms and other organisms, rotten-egg smell)?
- How does the soil at the bottom of the hole differ from that at the top? What might account for the variation?
- Can you identify evidence in the surroundings to indicate where the soil material came from (decayed material, weathered rocks, river sediments)?

Consider other local wetland sites and their present status. Students could further their investigation of wetlands by participating in field trips to local wetland sites (bird-watching, canoeing, etc.) conducted by community organizations.

If wetland areas are located near the school, students can conduct interpretive walks, including explanations of soil classification, for other students.

Assessment

Have students:
- classify soil type based on color (*Part II*, step 2).
- describe the conditions that contribute to the soil color characteristics of a wetland (*Wrap Up*).
- confirm an area as a wetland, according to soil color (*Wrap Up*).

Upon completing the activity, for further assessment have students:
- identify reasons why it is important for land and water managers to use soil classification when designating wetlands.

Extensions

Have students write a short story creating a history of events leading to the development of a particular wetland soil.

Students can use computer technology to increase their understanding of geographical features, mapping, and wetlands through Geographic Information Systems (GIS). Contact Charlie Fitzpatrick, ESRI K-12 Education & Libraries, 3460 Washington Drive, Suite 101, St. Paul, MN 55122; (612) 454-0600 ext. 26 or e-mail cfitzpatrick@esri.com for information about how to order and use ArcView, a computer program that enables learners to investigate GIS files.

Resources

Environmental Concern Inc., The Watercourse and Project WET. 1995. *WOW!: The Wonders Of Wetlands.* Published through a partnership between Environmental Concern Inc., St. Michaels, Md., and The Watercourse, Bozeman, Mont.

Williams, M., ed. 1990. *Wetlands: A Threatened Landscape.* Cambridge, Mass.: Basil Blackwell, Inc.

Notes ▼

Wetland Soils Color Chart

Use crayons to color the squares on the chart below. Using the correct colors is very important! Press firmly when coloring, unless the name says "light." Cut out the whole chart and paste it to a piece of poster board or half of a folder. Carefully cut out the black circles through all thicknesses.

Use this color chart when studying soil "in the field." (This is what ecologists and other scientists call going outside to examine a site.) Wetland professionals use similar, but much more complicated, color charts to help them correctly identify

wetland soils. Hold the chart in one hand; in the other hand hold a sample of soil behind the chart, so that it is visible through one of the holes. Move the sample around until you find a color that nearly matches the **main** color of the soil.

Numbers 1, 5, 6, 9, 10, 13, 14, 15, 16, and sometimes 2 are probably wetland soils; the others are probably **not** wetland soil. Numbers 14–16 are *gleyed* wetland soils and are most likely made of clay. You can also use numbers 4, 8, and 12 to match *mottles* ("rust spots") that may be found in wetland soil.

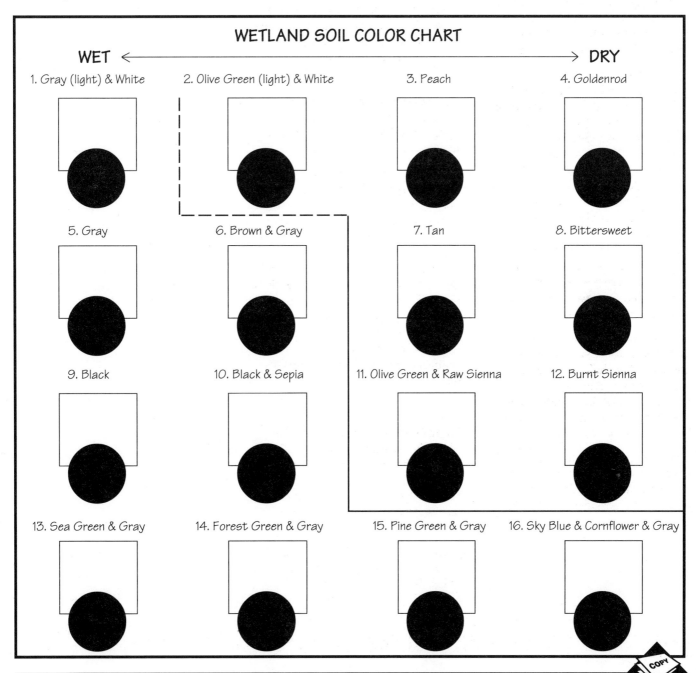

Soil Sample Data Chart

Student name(s): _____ Date: _____

Description of location: _____

_____

Description of plants present: _____

_____

Possible evidence of animals (burrows, insects, human artifacts—of value or trash): _____

_____

_____

Possible sources of water: _____

_____

_____

DEPTH OF SOIL SAMPLE	SOIL SAMPLE COLOR CLASSIFICATION	DAMPNESS OF SOIL SAMPLE (Does it stick in a ball? Can water be squeezed out?)	SOIL SAMPLE TEXTURE (Is it like coarse sand, fine silt, or clay?)

Water is a natural resource.

▼

All living things use water. The available freshwater supply on Earth

is limited and must sustain multiple users. Multiple

uses of water can lead to water resource issues.

A-maze-ing Water

■ **Grade Level:**
Lower Elementary,
Upper Elementary,
Middle School

■ **Subject Areas:**
Environmental Science,
Health

■ **Duration:**
Preparation time:
Option I: 15 minutes
Option II: 50 minutes

Activity time:
Option I: 30 minutes
Option II: three 50-minute
periods (includes drying
time for maze)

■ **Setting:** Classroom

■ **Skills:**
Organizing (manipulating
materials); Interpreting
(identifying cause and effect); Applying (designing)

■ **Charting the Course**
Prior understanding of how
water flows through a wa-
tershed supports this activity ("Branching Out!"). Students can investigate the role
their school plays in adding
to the city's runoff in "Rainy-
Day Hike." The activity
"Sum of the Parts" can be
adapted to include the
schoolyard as a nonpoint
source contributor.

■ **Vocabulary**
storm drain, nonpoint
source pollution, runoff,
contaminants

*Imagine turning on your water tap and
having everything that you dumped into the
gutter last week flow into your glass.*

▼ Summary
Students guide a drop of water
through a maze of "drainage pipes" to
learn how actions in the home and yard
affect water quality.

Objectives
Students will:
- describe urban forms of pollution.
- provide reasons why people should
  monitor what they put on their lawns
  or in streets.
- identify ways to treat urban runoff.

Materials
For **Option 1:**
- *Can or bottle labeled "chemicals" or "oil"*
- *Chalk*
- *Pieces of self-sticking paper, flour, or other
  materials to represent pollutants found in
  urban runoff*

For **Option 2:**
- *Cardboard 8 inches (21.3 cm) x 10 inches
  (25.4 cm) (1 per student or group)*
- *Wax paper*
- *Tape*
- *Wood glue*
- *Clay or modeling dough (Following is a
  simple recipe for modeling dough:
  Knead together 1 cup (22.4 g) flour, 1/2
  cup (11.2 g) salt, 3/4 cup (180 ml)
  boiling water, 1 tablespoon (15 ml)
  salad oil, and 1 tablespoon (5 g) alum
  [optional]; if too sticky, add more
  flour and salt.)*
- *Water*
- *Sugar, salt, pepper, food coloring, oil, and
  other materials to represent pollutants
  found in urban runoff*
- *Wax marking pencil*
- *Pipette or eyedropper*
- *Pencil and paper*

Making Connections
Most students have washed family cars,
seen litter on the sidewalk, or walked a
dog. In urban settings, car wash deter-
gent, litter, animal waste, paint, and oil
all wash into the street and down storm
drains. Investigating what happens to
these materials after they enter drainage
systems helps students understand how
these materials can affect water supplies
and aquatic plants and animals.

Background
Removing water quickly and efficiently
from city streets, parking lots, and
schoolyards following precipitation or
snowmelt is an important task for
municipal governments. Water flowing
through city drainage pipes is often
referred to as an urban watershed. Before
storm drainage systems were common,
cities experienced localized flooding
because of poor or nonexistent drainage
patterns and flooded sewer systems that
overflowed with storm water. Both
circumstances caused significant health
and safety concerns that warranted
solutions. Today, most city governments
require housing developers to install
city-approved storm water drainage
systems.

Traditionally, water diverted to storm
water systems received little or no
treatment before flowing into a stream or
body of water. Environmental agencies
found that water draining off lawns,
sidewalks, driveways, parking lots, and
streets carried significant amounts of
pollutants. These pollutants included
fertilizers, motor oil, litter, pesticides,
animal waste, and other contaminants.
Receiving waters were degraded, and
aquatic plants and animals were affected.
Some communities resolved the problem
by channeling storm runoff into a
wastewater treatment plant. But this is
an expensive procedure, and some plants
are unequipped to process the inorganic

materials found in urban runoff. A more cost-effective system was needed to treat storm water discharge. The scenario below describes one such water treatment system.

Imagine the parking lot of a large shopping center. Each year thousands of cars park in the lot, each depositing a small amount of engine oil- and grit (loosened road materials). A gentle rain begins to wash the lot. At the lot's lowest point, oil- and gas-tainted runoff water begins to flow into the street's gutter. A few blocks away, an urban river flows, filled with floating debris, sediment, and multi-colored water from another street, then another, and another. The flow now nearly fills a ditch constructed to channel urban runoff. From a distance the storm water in the drainage system appears dark-colored. Perhaps the road salt used to melt ice on roads and sidewalks has mixed in. How about the paint a neighbor pours into the gutter? The pet waste near the sidewalk? Whoosh, more water moves by! What next? What about the nearby stream and the people using water downstream for their drinking supply?

You follow the water to a large pond that the city constructed to catch storm water. The water in the pond is now moving slowly through cattails and other emergent wetland vegetation, and its color has started to change. Where is the debris and the sediment? And what about other waste materials? A woman from the city health department tests the water as it enters a small stream; she concludes that the water is cleaner than the river it is about to enter.

DUMP NO WASTE
DRAINS TO STREAM

Solutions to urban storm water pollution problems require participation by everyone. Homeowners can help by carefully following directions when applying pesticides and fertilizers, using biodegradable products whenever possible, cleaning up pet wastes, not disposing of household wastes in the street, and fixing oil leaks in vehicles. City sanitation departments can supply information on proper disposal procedures for paint cleaners, used oil, or leftover paint. In addition to developing wetland systems to help treat urban runoff, many city governments periodically sweep roadways to remove wastes. They plant greenways and preserve green space to help filter runoff from streets and parking lots.

Procedure
▼ Warm Up
Show students a can or bottle labeled "chemicals" or "oil." Tell students you need to dispose of the chemicals and plan to dump them in the street in front of the school. Ask students if they think this is a good idea. Have students describe what they think will happen to the waste material. Read the first paragraph of the scenario in the **Background**. Ask students what they think might happen to the runoff.

▼ The Activity
Following are two options for simulating urban runoff being collected within a storm drain system.

Option 1
1. **Discuss how water is used to clean things, such as the surface of a table after a spill. Relate how rainwater washes the outdoors.** Explain that as it flows over plants, soil, and sidewalks, it picks up and carries away soil and other materials. Inform students that cities use water to clean the waste from city streets and sidewalks. Often the water goes down storm drains, collects in pipes, and flows to a river or a treatment plant. (If a media center or water table is available, younger students can use pieces of tubing and plastic pipe to create a mini-water transport system. They can explore how pipes help water travel over distances by pouring water into one end of a tube and watching it run out in a different location.)

2. **Draw a simple but large maze on the school blacktop (see example on page 222) or arrange the chairs in the classroom to form the maze. The maze represents underground pipes that collect and transport surface water that has flowed down storm drains. Have students run the maze. Inform them they are water flowing through the drainage pipes to the river or treatment plant.**

3. **Discuss sources of water that run into the storm sewer system (streets, lawns, parking lots, etc.).** What might this water carry? (Oil from cars, fertilizers, litter.)

4. **To simulate surface water transporting pollutants into drainage pipes, have several students**

position themselves along edges of the maze. They represent storm drains and the contaminated water flowing through them. They should hold pieces of self-sticking paper or bowls of flour to symbolize the pollutants. When other students run through the maze, the students representing storm drains stick pieces of paper or sprinkle flour onto the clothing of the maze runners to represent contaminated water mixing with water (that may or may not be clean) flowing through the system. Allow students to take turns playing different roles.

5. **After several trips through the maze, discuss what happens to this dirty water.** What if it flows into the river? Can treatment plants process all the waste? Have students summarize why they should not litter.

6. **To represent a treatment system, have two students stand at the maze exit. Similar to the game London Bridge, the two treatment students "trap" each passing water student and remove as many pollutants as possible before he or she goes into the river.** What are students' attitudes about the quality of this water passing into the river?

Option 2

1. **Prepare or have students make mazes representing storm pipes carrying away street runoff.** A suggested pattern is provided on page 222. Build each maze on a piece of cardboard covered with wax paper. The walls of the maze are made from clay or modeling dough. Coat the walls and floors of the maze with wood glue and allow to dry. (Allow one day for clay to dry, and one day for glue to dry.)

2. **The maze should have one starting point and two exits.** One exit leads to a sewage treatment plant, and the other flows into a stream. Use a wax pencil to label the exits.

3. **Have students list materials people purposefully or inadvertently add to gutters and storm drains.** Have students draw a picture of a city street depicting these activities. They can switch drawings with a partner to see if their classmates can identify the polluting activities.

4. **Place drops of food coloring, salt water, and sugar water mixed with pepper on different places in the maze.** (See *Suggested Maze Pattern*.) Allow one day for the water to evaporate. Drops of oil can also be placed at certain locations. These all represent contaminants added to urban waste systems.

5. **Tell students to place a drop of water at the starting point and to tilt the maze so that the drop flows slowly toward one of the exits.** Toward which one should they aim?

6. **As the drop flows through the paths, it should pick up dye from the food coloring, particles from the salt and pepper, and possibly oil droplets.** This represents water moving through a municipal storm water system.

7. **When the drop reaches the exit, have students describe what the drop looks and feels like. If it ended in the treatment plant, the drop gets replaced with a clean drop of water. If it ended in the overflow**

("untreated water" exit), the drop is added to a cup labeled "stream."

▼ Wrap Up and Action

Discuss the problems associated with untreated urban runoff entering rivers or other bodies of water. Have students identify or research ways contaminated water affects aquatic life and drinking water supplies.

Introduce students to the many actions people can take to limit contaminants entering urban runoff. These include properly disposing of pet waste and litter, and discarding chemicals and oils according to manufacturer's directions. Inform students that many cities have developed systems to treat runoff. Refer to the scenario in the **Background** and read the second paragraph.

Have students contact their local wastewater treatment plant or public works department to determine whether their street runoff enters the treatment plant or if it flows directly into the river or filters into ground water systems.

Students may want to begin a storm drain monitoring program. This involves sending messages to the community illustrating how and why it should monitor what flows down streets into storm drains. Students can design a brochure describing ways individuals can reduce their contribution to surface and ground water pollution via urban runoff. Students can contact recycling centers, wastewater facilities, or their state department of natural resources to research ways individuals can reduce the amount of fertilizers and pesticides they use, choose alternatives to home and garden chemicals, and safely dispose of household wastes. If the city or county recycling office has a hazardous waste collection program, this could be included in the brochure as well.

In addition to the brochure, students can start a stenciling program. Students can make or purchase a stencil (see **Resources**) with a message about monitoring what flows down storm drains (e.g., "DUMP NO WASTE—DRAINS TO STREAM"). The stencils are used to spray-paint the message near neighborhood storm drains. Students can include information about the stenciling and its intent in their brochure, which they deliver to community members who live near the drains. Make sure students obtain permission from city or county public works departments before beginning the project.

Assessment
Have students:
- identify urban sources of pollution (**Warm Up**, **Option 1**, step 3, and **Option 2**, step 3).
- design mazes to simulate storm water drainage systems (**Option 2**, steps 1-4)
- explain why certain materials should not be dumped into the

street or used carelessly (**Option 1**, step 5 and **Wrap Up**).
- design a brochure describing steps individuals and communities can take to prevent surface water contamination (**Wrap Up**).

Extensions
Students can research alternatives to house and lawn chemicals and cleaning agents. Contact the local recycling center, the waste treatment facility, or a local environmental group for details. Invite a representative from the local water treatment plant to enrich the activity. Visit a local gas station and have the manager explain what happens to oil after cars are serviced.

Resources
Cole, Joanna. 1986. *The Magic School Bus at the Waterworks.* New York, N.Y.: Scholastic, Inc.

Environmental Concern Inc., The Watercourse, and Project WET. 1995. Activities "Treatment Plants" and "Water Purifiers." *WOW! The Wonders of Wetlands.* Published through a partnership between Environmental Concern, Inc., St. Michaels, Md., and The Watercourse, Bozeman, Mont.

The Water Education Foundation, 717 K Street, Suite 517, Sacramento, CA 95814. (916) 448-7699.

For information on storm drain monitoring and stenciling programs, contact:

Step Coordinator, Oregon Department of Fish and Wildlife, P.O. Box 59, 2501 S.W. First Avenue, Portland, OR 97207.

Earthwater Stencils, 4425 140th SW, Dept. WT, Rochester, WA 98579.

Center for Marine Conservation, 306A Buckroe Avenue, Hampton, VA 23664.

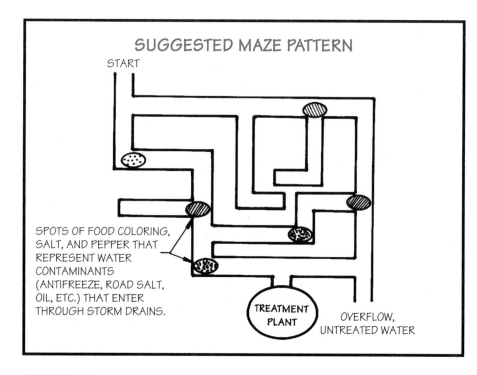

SUGGESTED MAZE PATTERN

START

SPOTS OF FOOD COLORING, SALT, AND PEPPER THAT REPRESENT WATER CONTAMINANTS (ANTIFREEZE, ROAD SALT, OIL, ETC.) THAT ENTER THROUGH STORM DRAINS.

TREATMENT PLANT

OVERFLOW, UNTREATED WATER

Color Me a Watershed

■ Grade Level: High School

■ Subject Areas:
Environmental Science, Mathematics, History

■ Duration:
Preparation time:
Option 1: 10 minutes
Option 2: 10 minutes
Option 3: 10 minutes

Activity time:
Option 1: 40 minutes
Option 2: 50 minutes
Option 3: 40 minutes

■ Setting: Classroom

■ Skills:
Gathering information (calculating); Analyzing (comparing); Interpreting (identifying cause and effect)

■ Charting the Course
Prior to this activity, students should have a general understanding of watersheds ("Rainy-Day Hike" and "Branching Out!"). Activities in which students compare runoff from different surfaces are "Capture, Store, and Release" and "Just Passing Through."

■ Vocabulary
discharge, watershed, runoff

What might make a watershed blue . . . or brown . . . or green?

▼ Summary
Through interpretation of maps, students observe how development can affect a watershed.

Objectives
Students will:
- recognize that population growth and settlement cause changes in land use.
- analyze how land use variations in a watershed can affect the runoff of water.

Materials
- *Maps and photographs of community, past and present* (optional)
- *Copies of **Maps A, B,** and **C***

For **Option 1:**
- *Colored pencils*

For **Options 2** and **3:**
- *Calculator*
- *Copies of the chart **Area of Land Coverage***
- *Copies of the chart **Volume of Rain and Volume of Runoff***

Making Connections
Learning about the past refines our current perspectives and helps us plan for the future. Historical, sequential maps provide graphic interpretations of watershed history. By comparing past and current land use practices, students can recognize trends in development; this knowledge can help them appreciate the importance of watershed management.

Background
Resource managers and policymakers use maps to monitor land use changes that could contribute to increased amounts of runoff flowing into a river. Vast amounts of public and private time, energy, and money have been invested in research projects specifically designed to collect land use data. Land uses that are monitored include, but are not limited to: urban (residential, parks, and businesses); agriculture (pastures and corn, soybean, wheat, sunflower, tomato, pineapple, and lettuce production); industry; transportation systems (roads, railroads, and trails); and public lands (refuges, parks, and monuments).

Land use changes can have significant impact on a region's water resources. Streams, lakes, and other bodies of water collect water drained from the surrounding land area, called a watershed or drainage basin. After periods of precipitation or during snowmelt, surface water is captured by the soil and vegetation, stored in ground water and in plants, and slowly released into the collection site (e.g., a stream).

Resource managers are developing and using Geographic Information Systems (GIS) to store data and generate land use maps electronically. Although the process of collecting the data is tedious work, the ease of generating usable maps and map overlays is significant. For example, a water manager could generate a map that shows a river's watershed and major tributaries, its floodplains, and the locations of urban dwellings (homes and businesses), to display areas likely to be impacted by floods. This information is valuable to local governments, planners, Realtors, bankers, homeowners, and others. This map could also be compared to similar land use maps from 10, 20, or 30 years ago.

One way watershed managers study drainage basins is by measuring streamflow. Determining how much water is discharged by a watershed involves measuring the amount of water (volume) that flows past a certain point over a period of time (velocity). Streamflow is measured in cubic feet per second (cfs) or cubic meters per second (cms).

By measuring the amount of water flowing through a stream channel over a period of years, scientists calculate average streamflow. When streamflow changes significantly from its normal quantities, watershed managers investigate reasons for this anomaly. The amount of water discharged by a watershed is influenced by soil conditions, vegetative coverings, and human settlement patterns. Wetlands, forests, and prairies capture and store more water than paved roads and parking lots. Consequently, urban areas will have more runoff than areas covered with vegetation.

Water managers carefully assess land use changes and set development policy accordingly. For example, in areas that are susceptible to erosion, the incorporation of soil conservation measures (e.g., planting cover crops on farmland and establishing grassed waterways) can significantly reduce erosion and stream sediment load. Managers may designate lands so susceptible to erosion that landowners are required to plant vegetation on them. In urban areas, local governments may set aside natural areas to serve as filters for storm water runoff, based on runoff data and stream water quality problems. In each situation, using maps to understand past and present land use helps water managers better predict future problems.

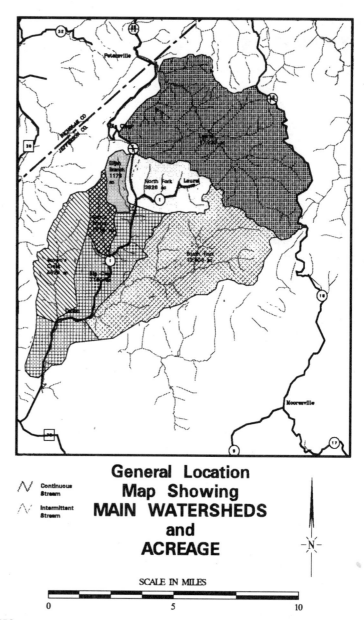

General Location Map Showing MAIN WATERSHEDS and ACREAGE

/N/ Continuous Stream

/N/ Intermittent Stream

-N-

SCALE IN MILES

0   5   10

Sample GIS map.

Procedure
▼ *Warm Up*

What did the land and water around cities like Los Angeles, Portland, Minneapolis, Houston, Chicago, New Orleans, Miami, or Washington, D.C., look like 100 or 50 years ago? How has growth changed each region? Ask students to imagine their community 100 years ago. They may want to refer to old photographs or news stories. Was the school in existence? What happened when water fell on the ground then, compared to now? If a body of water is near the school, would its appearance and condition have been altered over the years? Tell students that maps can teach us about the past and possibly answer questions such as these.

▼ The Activity

Provide students with copies of *Maps A, B,* and *C.* Explain that they represent aerial views of a watershed taken at different times. To simplify map interpretation, the borders of the watershed coincide with the edges of the grid. In addition, the outlines, of various land areas (e.g., wetlands, forests) align with grid lines.

Following are three options for interpreting changes in the watershed presented on the maps. The first option may be more appropriate for younger students, but can help all students complete **Options 2** and **3.** Students should be able to multiply and calculate percentages to complete the second and third options.

Option 1

1.   **Tell students to look at *Maps A, B,* and *C.* Explain that they represent changes in this land over a 100-year period. Have students look at the key for each map. Instruct them to designate each land area with a different color (e.g., color all forest areas green).** They should use the same color scheme for all maps.

2.   **When students finish coloring, have them compare the sizes of the different areas on each map and among maps.** Ask them to compare plant cover and land use practices in each of these periods. They may note changes in croplands, forests, grasslands, wetlands, urban land uses, etc.

3.   **Discuss one or more of the following questions:**
*   What happens to the amount of forested land as you go from *Map A* to *Map C*?
*   Which map has the most land devoted to human settlements?
*   Where are most of the human settlements located?
*   What effect might these human settlements have on the watershed?
*   Would you have handled development differently?

Option 2

1.   **Have students determine the land area of each of the maps.** Each unit in the grid represents 1 square kilometer; there are 360 square kilometers (or 360,000,000 m²) on each map.

2.   **For each map, have students determine how much area is occupied by each type of land coverage (e.g., forest, wetland, and farmland).** Responses can be guesses or exact calculations. For example, for *Map A,* 17 of the grid units are occupied by wetlands. By dividing 17 by the total number of units (360), students should calculate that 4.7% of the land area is wetlands. The amount of land allotted to wetlands, forests, etc. will change for each map, but the amount of stream coverage (111 squares or 30.8%) will remain constant. Students should record their answers in the *Area of Land Coverage* chart.

NOTE: Most watershed calculations employ standard measurements: inches and cubic feet per second (cfs). However, to facilitate students' computations, metric measurements are used here.

3.   **Tell students that the watershed has received 5 cm (0.05 m) of rain. (Although rain does not normally fall evenly over a large area, assume that the 5 cm of rain fell evenly over the entire watershed.) By converting both the rainfall and the land area to meters, students can calculate the amount of water (m³) which fell on the land.** 18,000,000 m³ of rain fell on the watershed (0.05 m x 360,000,000 m² = 18,000,000 m³). Of this 18,000,000 m³ of rain, 5,550,000 m³ landed on the stream (111,000,000 m² x 0.05 m = 5,550,000 m³). This might seem like a large quantity of water, but if 5 cm of rain did fall evenly on a watershed of this size, the stream would receive this volume of water. (NOTE: 100 cm = 1 m; 1,000,000 m² = 1 km².)

4.   **Ask students to estimate the amount of water that would be drained from the land into the stream.** Tell students that for the watershed represented by *Map A,* 2,767,500 m³ of rain was runoff (i.e., the water flowed into the stream and did not soak into the ground, did not evapo-

ANSWER KEY: AREA OF LAND COVERAG3E

Land coverage	MAP A 100 years ago		MAP B 50 years ago		MAP C Present	
	km²	%	km²	%	km²	%
Forest	189	52.5	162	45	111	30.8
Grassland	20	5.6	14	3.9	6	1.7
Wetland	17	4.7	13	3.6	5	1.4
Residential	13	3.6	33	9.2	58	16.1
Agriculture	10	2.8	27	7.5	69	19.2
Stream	111	30.8	111	30.8	111	30.8

rate, and was not used by plants or animals). (Runoff volumes are provided in the *Answer Key* below. In **Option 3**, students can calculate runoff for each land area.)

5. **Discuss changes in land coverage represented in *Maps A* through *C*. Ask students if they think the amount of runoff would increase or decrease.**

6. **Tell students that when 12,450,000 m³ of rain fell on the land represented by *Map A*, 2,767,500 m³ was runoff. For *Map B*, 3,612,500 m³ was runoff. For the *Map C*, 4,797,500 m³ was runoff. Discuss the following questions in addition to those listed in Option 1.**

- Which absorbs more water, concrete or forest (or wetlands or

grasslands)?
- Which map represents the watershed that is able to capture and store the most water?
- What problems could arise if water runs quickly over surface material, rather than moving slowly or soaking in?
- How might the water quality of the stream be affected by changes in the watershed?

Option 3
Have students determine how the figures in Option 2 were obtained. In the chart *Volume of Rain and Volume of Runoff*, each land area has been assigned a proportion of the water that is not absorbed or that runs off its surface. Using the information from this chart and from the

Area of Land Coverage chart, have students calculate the amount of water each land area does not absorb. For example, for the forested land in *Map A*, 189 km² x 1,000,000 m²/km² = 189,000,000 m² of land. Multiply this by the amount of rainfall (189,000,000 m² x 0.05 m = 9,450,000 m³). Since 20% of the rainfall was runoff, 1,890,000 m³ of water drained into the stream from the forested land (9,450,000 m³ x .20).

NOTE: The figures for percent runoff are based on hypothetical data. To determine how much water is absorbed by surface material, one needs to know soil type and texture, slope, vegetation, intensity of rainfall, etc. In addition, many farms and urban areas practice water conservation measures that help retain water

ANSWER KEY: VOLUME OF RAIN AND VOLUME OF RUNOFF

Land coverage and % runoff	MAP A 100 years ago		MAP B 50 years ago		MAP C Present	
	volume m³	runoff m³	volume m³	runoff m³	volume m³	runoff m³
Forest 20% runoff	(9.45×10^6) 9,450,000	(1.89×10^6) 1,890,000	(8.1×10^6) 8,100,000	(1.62×10^6) 1,620,000	(5.55×10^6) 5,550,000	(1.11×10^6) 1,110,000
Grassland 10% runoff	(1.0×10^6) 1,000,000	$(.1 \times 10^6)$ 100,000	$(.7 \times 10^6)$ 700,000	$(.07 \times 10^6)$ 70,000	$(.3 \times 10^6)$ 300,000	$(.03 \times 10^6)$ 30,000
Wetland 5% runoff	$(.85 \times 10^6)$ 850,000	$(.0425 \times 10^6)$ 42,500	$(.65 \times 10^6)$ 650,000	$(.0325 \times 10^6)$ 32,500	$(.25 \times 10^6)$ 250,000	$(.0125 \times 10^6)$ 12,500
Residential 90% runoff	$(.65 \times 10^6)$ 650,000	$(.585 \times 10^6)$ 585,000	(1.65×10^6) 1,650,000	(1.485×10^6) 1,485,000	(2.9×10^6) 2,900,000	(2.61×10^6) 2,610,000
Agriculture 30% runoff	$(.5 \times 10^6)$ 500,000	$(.15 \times 10^6)$ 150,000	(1.35×10^6) 1,350,000	$(.405 \times 10^6)$ 405,000	(3.45×10^6) 3,450,000	(1.035×10^6) 1,035,000
Total runoff		2,767,500		3,612,500		4,797,500
Total runoff plus stream discharge (5,550,000 m³)		(8.3175×10^6) 8,317,500		(9.1625×10^6) 9,162,500		(10.347×10^6) 10,347,500

and prevent it from streaming over the surface. The information in the chart is intended only for practice and comparisons.

▼ Wrap Up and Action
Have students summarize how changes in the land affect the quantity and quality of runoff in a watershed. Discuss land use practices in the community and how they may affect water discharge in the watershed. Take students on a walking tour around the school and community, and note areas that contribute to or reduce storm runoff. (For example, parking lots, paved roads, and sidewalks promote runoff; parks, wetlands, and trees capture water.)

Students could attend a public meeting in which changes in land use for their community are being discussed.

If students were to draw a fourth map of the same area 100 years in the future, how would it appear? Have students plan a city that contributes positively to a watershed. They should contact city planners or conduct library research to support their projections.

Assessment
Have students:
- compare land area occupied by farms, towns, and natural areas in a watershed during different time periods (**Options 1** and **2**).
- describe how surface runoff is influenced by changes in land use (**Option 2**).
- calculate quantities of runoff from different land areas in a watershed (**Option 3**).

Upon completing the activity, for further assessment have students:
- design a city plan that regulates urban runoff.

Extensions
Have students explore changes in their own community. Sources of historical and current maps include the Natural Resource Conservation Service, the Bureau of Land Management, the U.S.D.A. Forest Service, the U.S. Geological Survey, or a local public works department. Sometimes libraries contain historical, hand-drawn maps from the 1700s to the 1900s. Resource people in these agencies or the community will also have information and perspectives about past, present, and future water use.

Students may want to conduct a more accurate analysis of the degree to which different surface areas are permeable to water. Contact conservation agencies or extension agents in the community to learn how different soil types affect runoff.

Several books for young people powerfully describe and illustrate the effects of human development on land areas. Students may want to compare the changes indicated by the maps to changes portrayed in *Window*, by Jeannie Baker, or other sources.

Students can use computer technology to increase their understanding of geographical features, through Geographic Information Systems (GIS). Contact Charlie Fitzpatrick, ESRI K-12 Education and Libraries, 3460 Washington Drive, Suite 101, St. Paul, MN 55122. (612) 454-0600, ext. 26).

Or e-mail cfitzpatrick@esri.com for information about how to order and use ArcView, a computer program that enables learners to investigate GIS files.

Resources
Baker, Jeannie. 1991. *Window.* New York, N.Y.: Greenwillow Books.

Guling, Cynthia L., and Kenneth I. Helphand. 1994. *Yard Street Park.* New York, N.Y.: John Wiley & Sons.

Huff, Barbara A. 1990. *Greening the City Streets: The Story of Community Gardens.* St. Louis, Mo.: Clarion Publishing Co.

Leopold, Luna B. 1974. *Water: A Primer.* San Francisco, Calif.: W. H. Freeman & Co.

Patterson, Mark, and Ron Mahoney. 1993. *Environmental Education Software and Multimedia Source Book.* Moscow, Idaho: University of Idaho Agricultural Publications.

Smith, Daniel S., and Paul Cawood Hellmund. 1993. *Ecology of Greenways.* Minneapolis, Minn.: University of Minnesota Press.

Notes ▼

Name: _____ Date: _____

Chart for Option 2 AREA OF LAND COVERAGE

Land coverage	MAP A 100 yrs. ago		MAP B 50 yrs. ago		MAP C Present	
	km²	%	km²	%	km²	%
Forest						
Grassland						
Wetland						
Residential						
Agriculture						
Stream						

Chart for Option 3 VOLUME OF RAIN AND VOLUME OF RUNOFF

Land coverage and % runoff	MAP A 100 years ago		MAP B 50 years ago		MAP C Present	
	volume m³	runoff m³	volume m³	runoff m³	volume m³	runoff m³
Forest 20% runoff						
Grassland 10% runoff						
Wetland 5% runoff						
Residential 90% runoff						
Agriculture 30% runoff						
Total runoff						
Total runoff plus stream discharge (5,550,000 m³)						

Map A

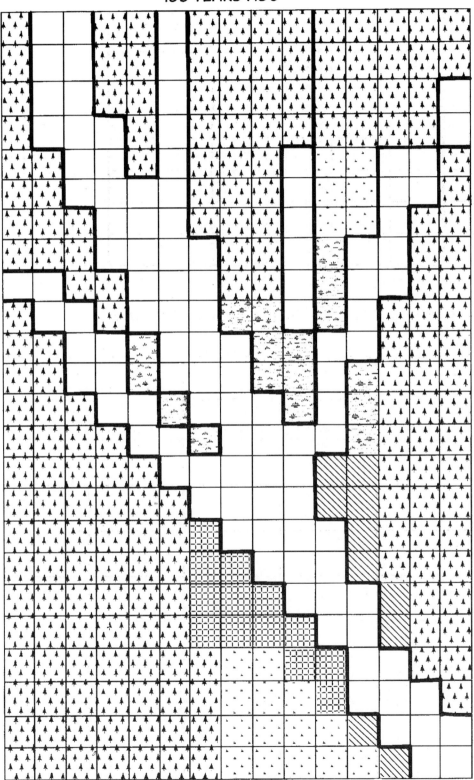

100 YEARS AGO

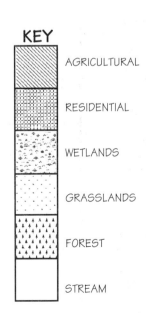

KEY

AGRICULTURAL

RESIDENTIAL

WETLANDS

GRASSLANDS

FOREST

STREAM

Map B

50 YEARS AGO

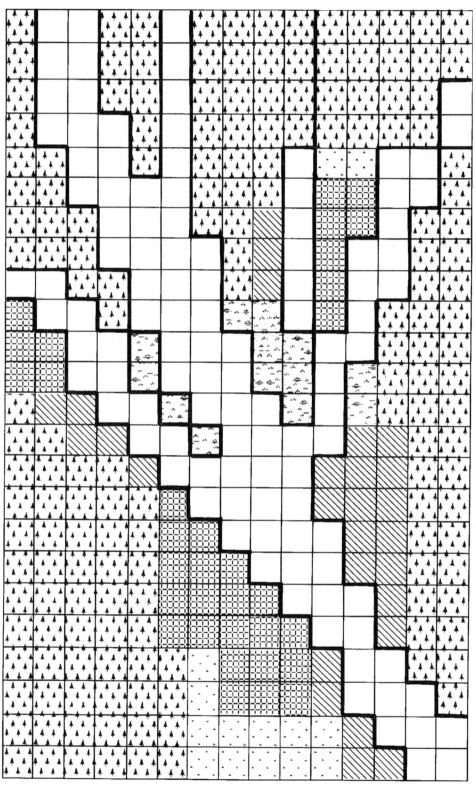

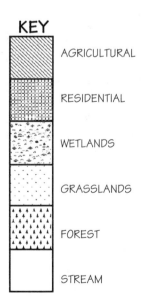

KEY

AGRICULTURAL

RESIDENTIAL

WETLANDS

GRASSLANDS

FOREST

STREAM

Map C

PRESENT

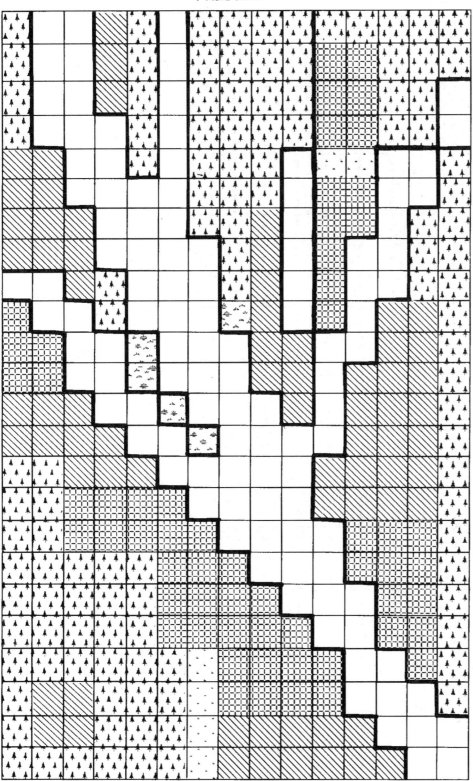

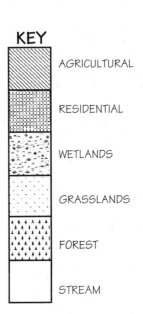

KEY

- AGRICULTURAL
- RESIDENTIAL
- WETLANDS
- GRASSLANDS
- FOREST
- STREAM

Common Water

What do you, your parents, your neighbors, a plant in your home, a squirrel in the park, and your classmates have in common?

▼ Summary
Students analyze the results of a simulation to understand that water is a shared resource and is managed.

Objectives
Students will:
- illustrate how multiple users of water resources can affect water quality and quantity.
- examine the complexities of providing water for all water users.

Materials
- *The Yellow Pages of a phone book*
- *A large bucket* (The bucket should hold several gallons of water. The amount of water in the bucket should be visibly reduced when 5 spongefuls of water are removed.)
- *Containers* (Bowls or milk cartons with the tops cut off, 1 for each student.)
- *17 large household sponges* (Cut 3 of the sponges into fourths, 5 into thirds, 5 into halves, and leave the last 4 whole. Increase or decrease the number of sponges to fit the number of students. Pieces of absorbent terry cloth can be substituted.)
- *Various colors of food coloring or washable paints* (Put several drops of food coloring of any color on all the sponges and sponge pieces.)
- *Markers*
- *Poster board*

Making Connections
Students should be aware that every living thing on Earth uses water and that water is a finite resource. They know how their family members use water,

and they may have learned how industries and farms use water. In the news, they read about problems with water quality and quantity. This activity helps students recognize that it is vital for water users to consider each other's needs and to share this finite resource.

Background
Many of us have experienced standing up in a large crowd to watch a performer or speaker on stage. Often, to get a better view, someone will sit on the shoulders of a friend. How does this make people standing behind the couple feel? Sometimes what works for the individual may not work for the group.

Water is used by all members of a community. Because water is important to all water users, as demands for this finite resource grow, the need to conserve and manage supplies also grows.

Fortunately, water is a reusable resource; given time, biological (e.g., filtering through soil and vegetation) and physical (e.g., rain, settling out of sediments) processes in healthy ecosystems replenish water quality and quantity. Wastewater treatment plants facilitate these processes as well.

Since the recent enactment of water quality control laws, many rivers and lakes are cleaner than they were in the 1960s. There is good news regarding water quantity as well. Farmers throughout the country have reduced ground water consumption through efficient water use practices (planting crops that require less water, adopting irrigation methods that use less water, capturing and reusing runoff, etc.).

Conservation and practical use of water can be employed by water users (homeowners, businesses, industry, etc.) to prevent water shortages and ensure long-term supplies. If sharers of a water

■ **Grade Level:** Middle School

■ **Subject Areas:**
Environmental Science, History

■ **Duration:**
Preparation time: 50 minutes
Activity time: 50 minutes

■ **Setting:**
Outdoors or an area with non-slippery floors such as cement (This activity may involve large quantities of spilled water.)

■ **Skills:**
Analyzing; Applying (problem solving)

■ **Charting the Course**
Students can be introduced to various water users in "Water Works," "Irrigation Interpretation," "Energetic Water," and "Water Meter." Students can discuss and debate the prioritizing of different uses of water in "Choices and Preferences, Water Index." In "Every Drop Counts" students are introduced to approaches to conserving water.

■ **Vocabulary**
conservation, consumptive use, water quality

source consider the needs of all water users, and plan for and manage those needs, then water of sufficient quality and quantity should be available. We can all make a difference!

Procedure
▼ Warm Up
Have students list major water user groups in their community and how they use water. The Yellow Pages can be a source of ideas. Ask students to arrange the water users, from those who they think use the most water to those who use the least.

▼ The Activity
NOTE: This activity may involve spilled water and should be conducted outdoors or in an area that can get wet.

1. **Fill a large bucket to the brim with water. Tell students that the bucket represents water stored in a reservoir, pond, or lake.** Some communities depend on ground water. If this is the case, the bucket represents water underground (and the sponges symbolize wells).

2. **Tell students they are going to simulate changes in a watershed over several time periods. Each 30-second round represents a time period (see Round Scenarios).** In each round, students represent different water users; they may want to make nametags to identify their roles.

3. **For each round, students should position themselves an equal distance from the water source. When the round starts, students fill their sponges with water from the reservoir (bucket). To represent water consumption, have them squeeze water out of the sponges into individual containers. Students can refill their sponges as often as they like during the round.**

4. **At the end of each round, note how much water remains in the bucket. Tell students to empty half of the water from their containers back into the bucket. This** represents used water that makes it back to the reservoir (i.e., when it percolates through soil, when it is discharged from a factory, after it runs off the surface). Students will notice that the water is colored. Inform them this represents sewage and runoff from urban and rural areas.

5. **Record students' comments about the amount of water used and the amount of waste materials generated; compare after each round. To represent the water source eventually cleaning and replenishing itself over time, fill the bucket to the brim with clean water before each round.**

Round Scenarios

Following are four suggested rounds to symbolize use of a common source of water over time. The relationship of the rounds and the allotment of sponges is shown in the chart *Suggested Distribution of Sponges for the Rounds* on page 234. Depending on time considerations or extent of investigation, rounds can be added or deleted.

Round 1.
It is 200 years ago. The watershed is inhabited by a few homesteaders operating small farms. Have three students represent the homesteaders. Give each of them one-fourth of a sponge and a container.

Round 2.
One hundred years have passed. A large farm and a small town are now located in the watershed. Distribute sponges, cut in fourths, to six students (town dwellers) and a half sponge to a student representing the farm. Provide each student with a container. Complete another round.

Round 3.
It is now just after World War II. The size of the town has increased. Many of the town residents are employed in an industry that makes typewriters. The factory is represented by half a sponge. Two farming areas supply milk and some food (meat, grains, vegetables) for the town; they get one sponge each. Give one sponge to a student who represents a power company. Several community services, such as hospitals, schools, and stores, are now part of the town; each student representing such a service agency gets half a sponge. Provide each family (about 10 students) with a third of a sponge. Provide each student with a container. Complete a round.

Round 4.
It is the present. The town has continued to grow. A new industry that makes household cleaning products has moved in (another sponge). Represent residential expansion by giving sponge pieces and a container to any remaining students. Complete a round.

▼ Wrap Up and Action

Have students discuss the quantity and quality of water in the round. Discuss proportions of sponge pieces distributed to different community members. Are water users in their own community represented by the characters in the simulation? Do students think the sponge sizes were appropriate? Were there any groups who used too much water or did not get enough? Schools were a service agency in the demonstration. Have students identify the different ways their school uses water. Do students think the school uses water wisely?

How could the activity be adjusted to ensure enough clean water for all users? Students may suggest making fewer trips to soak their sponges or reducing the size of their sponges. They may suggest adding another bucket of water to increase supply. Where would this water come from? Would another community experience water shortage as a result of these diversion projects? Methods to reduce waste discharge can also be discussed (e.g., using organic fertilizers, reducing litter, upgrading sewage treatment plants). Have students interview local water managers to identify water distribution policies and conservation programs. Students may want to run another round to test their adjustments.

Discuss the statement: "Water for all water users." Do students think this is possible? What can communities do to ensure everyone gets enough clean water? Students can create a display or mural, titled *Water for all Water Users*, depicting ways a community shares its water supply. If water quality or quantity is an issue in the community, students can research what the community is doing or should do to maintain clean water supplies. These actions should be included in the display as well.

Assessment

Have students:
- demonstrate scenarios in which water quality and quantity are threatened when water users use the resource without considering the needs of others (steps 3-5).
- propose and illustrate ways a community could supply its members with clean and ample water supplies (*Wrap Up*).

Extensions

Have students list groups of water users in the community. Explain that a water shortage exists. Working in groups, tell students they must determine who has rights to use water first and how much water each group can use. Are students able to determine which group most deserves water? Remind students that communities, like ecosystems, are interconnected and interdependent. For example, if students believe an industry uses too much water and should limit consumption, determine if production may need to be reduced. This would entail laying off workers, which will affect families. Some farms use large quantities of water, yet they supply people with large quantities of inexpensive food. Solutions to limited water supplies

SUGGESTED DISTRIBUTION OF SPONGES FOR THE ROUNDS				
	1/4 SPONGE	1/3 SPONGE	1/2 SPONGE	WHOLE SPONGE
Round 1 (200 years ago)	3 students (homesteaders)			
Round 2 (early 1900s)	6 students (residents of small town)		1 student (large farm)	
Round 3 (after WW II)		10 students (residents of town)	1 student (factory) 3 students (service agencies)	2 students (farms) 1 student (power company)
Round 4 (present)	3 students (town residents)	15 students (town residents)	1 student (factory) 4 students (service agencies)	2 students (farms) 1 student (power company) 1 student (industry)

involve individual and group cooperative efforts, with everyone conserving water and using water efficiently.

☺ K-2 Option

Use a simple story based on the rounds described in the activity. Designs for finger puppets have been provided so students can illustrate portions of the story. You will need three sponges (large, medium, small) and two large basins (one filled with water). Below is a sample story; the words in italics are spoken and the words in parentheses are directions.

Discuss how a water shortage might affect the people in the story. What changes could be made to keep more water in the lake? Help students understand the needs and interdependencies of the different water users in the story (e.g., the farmer needs large quantities of water to produce food for the people; water is used by factories to manufacture products such as cars and dishwashers). Place several basins and sponges at a learning center or a water table. Allow students time to create their own stories.

Resources

Andrews, Elaine. 1992. *Educating Young People About Water*. Madison, Wis.: University of Wisconsin-Madison, Environmental Resources Center.

🍎 Baker, Jeannie. 1991. *Window*. New York, N.Y.: Greenwillow Books.

"e." 1992. Distributed by Millennium Communications, Educational Development Specialists, 5505 East Carson Street, Suite 250, Lakewood, CA 90713. Videocassette.

🍎 Geisel, Theodore (Dr. Seuss). 1971. *The Lorax*. New York, N.Y.: Random House Publishing Company.

Hardin, Garrett. 1968. "Tragedy of the Commons." *Science* (December).

Montana Watercourse. 1993. *A Catalogue of Water Conservation Resources*. Bozeman, Mont.: Montana Watercourse.

🍎 Pringle, Laurence. 1982. *Water: The Next Great Resource Battle*. New York, N.Y.: Macmillan.

Thompson, Suzanne, and Kirsten Soutemyer. 1991. "Water Use as a Common Dilemma: The Effects of Education that Focuses on Long-Term Consequences and Individual Action." *Environment and Behavior* 23(3): 314-33.

Once there was a lake. (Show basin of water.) *Some animals lived near the lake and drank from it everyday.* (Use the small sponge and collect a few spongefuls of water, transferring the water to a different basin that is out of sight. Discuss how animal use of the lake minimally affects the level of water.) *Some years later, people began to move into the area.* (Ask students how they use water; use the medium-sized sponge and remove a spongeful of water as you name each water use in the next sentence—include student suggestions.) *Like you, these people drank water, washed, watered their plants, etc. Everyone used as much water as he or she wanted, without thinking about other people's needs. The people thought there would be plenty of water because even though they took water away from the lake, the rain would eventually bring the level of the water back up.* (Pour some water back into the basin.) *People kept moving into the area; large farms and factories were built.* (Use the largest sponge and take out water until the basin is almost empty.) *After several years, people noticed that, despite the rain, the level of the lake was going down.* (Show students the water level.)

Water User Finger Puppets

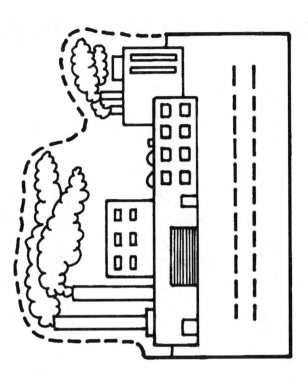

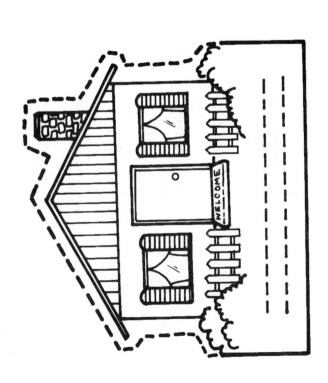

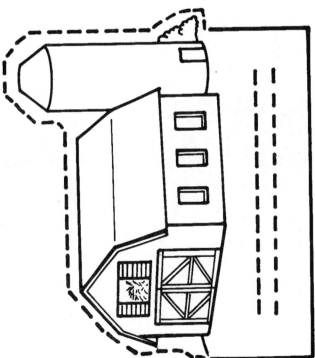

A Drop in the Bucket

Grade Level:
Middle School

Subject Areas:
Earth Science, Mathematics, Geography

Duration:
Preparation time: 30 minutes
Activity time: 30 minutes

Setting: Classroom

Skills:
Gathering information (observing, calculating); Organizing; Interpreting (drawing conclusions)

Charting the Course
Prior to this lesson, students should review percentages and should know the portion of Earth's surface covered with water. In "Old Water," students explore how long water has been on Earth. This activity supports concepts related to the water cycle ("The Incredible Journey"), watersheds ("Branching Out!"), and water distribution ("Piece It Together," "Wet Vacation," and "Dust Bowls and Failed Levees").

Vocabulary
salt water, fresh water, consumptive use

What is abundant and rare at the same time?

▼ Summary
By estimating and calculating the percent of available fresh water on Earth, students understand that this resource is limited and must be conserved.

Objectives
Students will:
- calculate the percentage of fresh water available for human use.
- explain why water is a limited resource.

Materials
- *2 colors of construction paper*
- *Sheets of white paper*
- *Markers*
- *Water*
- *Globe or world map*
- *1000-ml beaker*
- *100-ml graduated cylinders*
- *Small dish*
- *Salt*
- *Freezer or an ice bucket*
- *Eyedropper or glass stirring rod*
- *Small metal bucket*
- *Copies of* **Water Availability Table**

Making Connections
Students may know Earth is covered mainly by water, but they may not realize that only a small amount is available for human consumption. Learning that water is a limited resource helps students appreciate the need to use water resources wisely.

Background
Ironically, on a planet extensively (71 percent) covered with water, this re-source is one of the main limiting factors for life on Earth. The *Water Availability Table* summarizes the major factors affecting the amount of available water on Earth. If all the clean, fresh water were distributed equally among people, there would be about 1.82 million gallons (7 million liters) per person. This is only about .003 percent of the total water on Earth.

On a global scale, only a small percentage of water is available, but this percentage represents a large amount per individual. The paradox is that, for some, water may appear plentiful, but for others it is a scarce commodity. Why are some people in need of more water? Geography, climate, and weather affect water distribution. Agriculture, industry, and domestic use also affect availability.

Procedure
▼ *Warm Up*
Tell students they are going to estimate the proportion of potable water on Earth and compare it to the rest of the water on the planet. Have students work in small groups. Instruct them to draw a large circle with a marker on a white sheet of paper. Offer them two sheets of different-colored construction paper. One color represents available fresh water; the other represents the rest of the water on the planet.

Tell students that they will be tearing the two sheets of paper into a total of 100 small pieces. Ask them to estimate how many pieces will represent potable water and how many pieces will indicate the rest of the water on the planet. Instruct each group to tear up their paper and arrange the 100 pieces within the circle so that these pieces reflect their estimates. Have groups record the number of pieces representing "potable" and "remaining" water.

238

ANSWER KEY: Water Availability Table

Total water (100%) on Earth divided among all people (based on a world population of 6 billion people)	= 233.3 billion liters/person
Minus the 97% of each share (226.3 billion liters) that contains salt (oceans, seas, some lakes and rivers) 233.3 billion liters - 226.3 billion liters	= 7 billion liters/person
Minus the 80% of this 7 billion that is frozen at the poles (5.6 billion) 7 billion liters - 5.6 billion liters	= 1.4 billion liters/person
Minus the 99.5% of the 1.4 billion that is unavailable (too far underground, polluted, trapped in soil, etc.) (1.393 billion) 1.4 billion liters - 1.393 billion liters	= 7 million liters/person

▼ The Activity

NOTE: For simplicity, measurements have been retained in metric. To convert to standard measurements, refer to the *Metric Conversion Table* in the **Appendix**.

1. **Show the class a liter (1000 ml) of water and tell them it represents all the water on Earth.**

2. **Ask where most of the water on Earth is located. (Refer to a globe or map.) Pour 30 ml of the water into a 100-ml graduated cylinder.** This represents Earth's fresh water, about 3 percent of the total. Put salt into the remaining 970 ml to simulate water found in oceans, unsuitable for human consumption.

3. **Ask students what is at the Earth's poles.** Almost 80 percent of Earth's fresh water is frozen in ice caps and glaciers. Pour 6 ml of fresh water into a small dish or cylinder and place the rest (24 ml) in a nearby freezer or ice bucket. The water in the dish (around 0.6 percent of the total) represents non-frozen fresh water. Only about 1.5 ml of this

water is surface water; the rest is underground.

4. **Use an eyedropper or a glass stirring rod to remove a single drop of water (0.003 ml). Release this one drop into a small metal bucket.** Make sure the students are very quiet so they can hear the sound of the drop hitting the bottom of the bucket. This represents clean, fresh water that is not polluted or otherwise unavailable for use, about

.003 percent of the total! This precious drop must be managed properly.

5. **Discuss the results of the demonstration.** At this point many students will conclude that a very small amount of water is available to humans. However, this single drop is actually a large volume of water on a global scale. Have students use the *Water Availability Table* to calculate the actual amounts.

▼ Wrap Up

Referring to the **Warm Up**, remind students of their earlier guesses at how much water on Earth is available to humans and compare the actual percent of Earth's water available. Have students explain their reasoning for their initial estimates. How would they adjust their proportions? (One-half of one of the pieces of paper represents potentially available water [0.5 percent]. Only one small corner of this half [.003 percent] is actually potable water.)

Ask students again if enough water is currently available for people. If the amount of usable water on the planet is divided by the current population of approximately 6 billion, 7 million liters of water is available per person. Theoretically, this exceeds the amount of water a person would require in a lifetime.

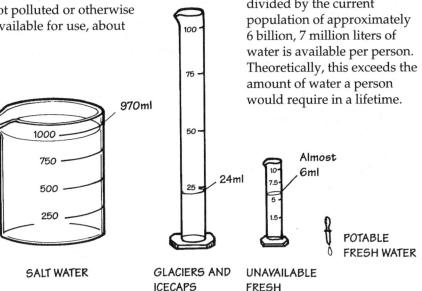

970ml

SALT WATER

GLACIERS AND ICECAPS

24ml

Almost 6ml

UNAVAILABLE FRESH WATER

POTABLE FRESH WATER

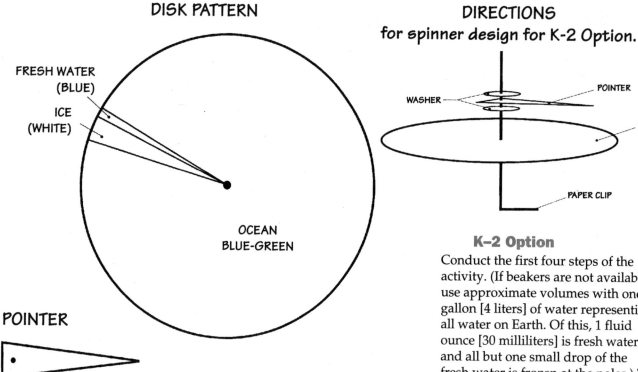

DISK PATTERN

FRESH WATER
(BLUE)

ICE
(WHITE)

OCEAN
BLUE-GREEN

DIRECTIONS
for spinner design for K-2 Option.

WASHER

POINTER

DISK

PAPER CLIP

POINTER

So, why does more than one-third of the world's population not have access to clean water? Discuss with the class the main factors affecting water distribution on Earth (e.g., land forms, vegetation, proximity to large bodies of water). Other environmental influences affect availability of water (drought, contamination, flooding). Students can also consider that other organisms use water, not just humans.

Assessment
Have students:
- determine the proportion of Earth's available fresh water (*Warm Up* and *Wrap Up*).
- calculate the volume of water available for human use (step 5).

Upon completing the activity, for further assessment have students:
- develop a television commercial outlining reasons why water is a limited resource.

Extensions
Students can calculate how much water they might use in a lifetime. Provide them with the following instructions: Keep track of how much water they use in one day. (The average person in the United States uses about 50 gallons [190 l] per day.) Multiply daily use by 365 days and then by 70 years (estimated life span). How does this compare to the 1.82 million gallons (7 million liters) available to them? (This applies to direct water use only.)

Students can identify areas of the globe where water is limited, plentiful, or in excess and discuss the geographical and climatic qualities contributing to these conditions. For example, large variations in precipitation occur within states. (Death Valley receives as little as 2 to 5 inches [5 to 12.5 cm] per year; only 100 miles [160 km] away, mountain ranges receive more than 30 inches [76 cm] per year.) These variations dramatically impact plants, people, and other animals.

K–2 Option
Conduct the first four steps of the activity. (If beakers are not available, use approximate volumes with one gallon [4 liters] of water representing all water on Earth. Of this, 1 fluid ounce [30 milliliters] is fresh water, and all but one small drop of the fresh water is frozen at the poles.) To help students appreciate these proportions, have them participate in the following activity. Construct, or have students make, spinners. (Make the disk, pointer, and washers out of sturdy cardboard.) Give each child a copy of the *Water Chart*. Children spin the pointer and color a box of the chart in the appropriate row to indicate where the pointer landed. Which row of the chart do students think will fill up first?

Resources
Miller, G. Tyler, Jr. 1990. *Resource Conservation and Management.* Belmont, Calif.: Wadsworth Publishing Company.

🍎 Goldin, Augusta. 1983. *Water: Too Much, Too Little, Too Polluted?* Orlando, Fla.: Harcourt, Brace, Jovanovich, Inc.

🍎 Hammer, Trudy J. 1985. *Water Resources.* New York, N.Y.: Watts.

🍎 Pringle, Laurence. 1982. *Water: The Next Great Resource Battle.* New York, N.Y.: Macmillan.

Water Availability Table

Name: _____ Date: _____

Quantity to be divided among people on Earth	Amount Available liters/person	% of total water
All the water on Earth	233.3 billion	100%
Only the fresh water (calculate 3% of the amount available)		3%
Only the non-frozen fresh water (calculate 20% of the remaining amount available)		0.6%
Available fresh water that is not polluted, trapped in soil, too far below ground, etc. (calculate 0.5% of the remaining amount available)		.003%

Water Chart ———————————————— K-2 Option

FRESH WATER

FROZEN WATER

OCEAN WATER

Energetic Water

What works without moving a muscle or breaking into a sweat?

▼ Summary
Students invent devices or create activities that demonstrate how moving water can accomplish work.

Objectives
Students will:
- identify the forms of energy in water.
- demonstrate how water can be used to do work.

Materials
- *Two 1-pound (450-g) coffee cans with plastic lids (Using hammer and nails, pound several equally spaced holes around the side of the bottom of one can. Do the same with the second; however, when you drive the nails into the second can, force the nail sharply to the left. Cover the holes on the bottom of both cans with masking tape. Poke a pair of holes near the top of each can through which to thread a string, making a handle.)*
- *Student Invention Kits, trays containing the following items:*
  - *blocks of wood*
  - *coarse sandpaper*
  - *glue*
  - *masking tape*
  - *paper cups of different sizes*
  - *pieces of Styrofoam*
  - *pipe cleaners*
  - *plastic spoons*
  - *plastic straws (flexible and non-flexible)*
  - *scissors*
  - *several corks of varying size*
  - *several dowels of varying length*
  - *several pieces of cardboard*
  - *string or monofilament line*
  - *tongue depressors*

■ Grade Level:
Upper Elementary, Middle School

■ Subject Areas:
Physical Science, History

■ Duration:
Preparation time: 50 minutes

Activity time: Depends on extent of student projects

■ Setting: Classroom

■ Skills:
Gathering information (observing); Applying (designing, problem solving); Evaluating

■ Charting the Course
Physical properties of water are introduced in the activities "Molecules in Motion," "Hangin' Together," and "Adventures in Density." Students can explore how the movement of water is used in three-dimensional art projects in "wAteR in moTion."

■ Vocabulary
work, energy, kinetic energy, potential energy

NOTE: Because of the experimental nature of the student activity, this listing includes suggested materials. Other items that are readily available in the classroom can be included at the teacher's discretion.

Making Connections
Many students have witnessed the energy in water when they looked at a waterfall, river, or dam. However, they may not relate the movement of water to turning lights on and off or moving heavy objects. Designing equipment or simple machines that use water to move things helps students appreciate the energy in water and how water can work for us.

Background
For thousands of years, inventive people have tapped the natural energy in water to do useful work. Water has been used to help play a musical instrument (the water organ invented by Ctesibius, a Greek engineer); grind grain into flour (water-driven grist mills); spin silk; pump bellows; operate sawmills; tell time (the clepsydra or water clock); operate flush toilets, dishwashers, water meters, and centrifugal pumps in automobile cooling systems; lift heavy ships over land separating bodies of water (through locks in the Panama Canal, C & O Canal, etc.); operate automobiles, locomotives, and ships (steam engines); generate electricity; vary the buoyancy of submarines; and do a host of other jobs.

Following this activity is a time line (*Water Through Time*) showing a sampling of the historic human adaptations of water power.

Moving water can be used to do work because its potential energy changes to kinetic energy. When water is elevated (such as on the brink of a waterfall or in

242

a reservoir behind a dam) it has gravitational potential energy. This potential energy changes to kinetic energy when the water falls or is allowed to flow. For example, when holes in the bottom of a container allow water to escape, the water's potential energy becomes kinetic energy.

The energy generated by moving water can be transferred to other objects, causing them to move and thus accomplishing work. Work involves applying force (a push or a pull) to an object to create movement. Sometimes humans use water alone to help execute work (e.g., carrying logs or moving boats downstream). Water has also been used to complement the actions of many simple machines that lift, push, turn, and pull objects. These include levers, pulleys, wheels and axles, and screws. Using the energy in water involves locating or creating places where potential energy is changed to kinetic energy (such as a waterfall or dam). Water can also be channeled and diverted to where it is used to produce work (such as over a turbine or into a lock).

Procedure
▼ Warm Up

Show students the coffee can (with the straight-punched holes) and fill it with water. Ask students if they think there is any energy in the can. Discuss what forces might be present that could produce energy. Indicate gravitational pull and explain that it causes the water to have potential energy. Have students define potential energy and relate it to the water in the can.

Hold the can by its handle above a sink or tray. (This could be messy, so it may be done outdoors.) Remove the tape from the can with the straight holes so students can observe what happens. Water will

Lock on C & O Canal, Seneca, Maryland, circa 1900. COURTESY: NATIONAL PARK SERVICE, E. B. THOMPSON

drain from the can in straight streams, but the can should remain motionless.

Ask students what happened to the potential energy of the water. Explain that it was converted to kinetic energy when water was allowed to flow. Define work (application of force to create movement) and ask if students think any work was accomplished. The force of gravity caused the water to move, but did the can do any work? Since it did not move, no work was done.

Repeat the procedure with the other can. The streams of water draining the can will be directed sideways by the bent holes, and the can will spin in the opposite direction. Explain how you can make the flowing water do work by altering or directing its flow as it drains from the can (a simple classroom example of engineering).

▼ The Activity
1. **Share the *Water Through Time* time line with students. Discuss how water has been used throughout history to do work.**

2. **Tell students they are going to create their own designs to use water to do work. Their task is to build a machine, develop a technique, or demonstrate an action that illustrates how the energy generated by water (changing from potential to kinetic) lifts, moves, pulls, twists, smashes, or in some way changes the present placement or condition of an object.**

The following are suggested challenges. Use water to:
*   lift a pencil 3 inches (7.5 cm) off a flat surface.
*   move a pencil 10 inches (25 cm) across a surface.
*   wind a piece of thread around a pencil.
*   drop a pencil from a height of 5 inches (12.5 cm) .
*   throw a soft object 2 feet (60 cm).
*   grind a cracker into small pieces.
*   break open a hollow object.
*   rotate a series of gears.

3. **Divide the class into small groups or "engineering teams." Give each team a *Student Invention Kit* containing common materials from the classroom and describe the challenges. They may use the**

materials in their trays (or others that they may find in the classroom) and the knowledge they have acquired by observing the *Warm Up* demonstration.

4. **Allow groups several hours to complete projects; more challenging endeavors may take a few weeks.** Encourage students to visit with engineers and architects to help with their design.

▼ *Wrap Up and Action*

Have "engineering teams" tell the class how they approached the challenge or task, and explain and/or demonstrate their team's solution. They should identify what form of energy was used and what work was accomplished. Encourage them to relate the action to work done in real life (in the past or the present). Other teams can evaluate the design and provide suggestions for improvement. Designs can be presented in a school display case.

Assessment

Have students:
- invent or build a simple device

Old mill at Cades Cove, Great Smoky Mountains.
COURTESY: UNITED STATES DEPARTMENT OF INTERIOR

that demonstrates the ability of water to do work (step 4).
- identify forms of energy present in water (*Wrap Up*).
- relate inventions to examples of how water has actually been used to conduct work (*Wrap Up*).
- evaluate water inventions and provide suggestions for improvement (*Wrap Up*).

Extensions

Further alterations can be made to the cans used in the *Warm Up*. Explain that energy is transferred to the suspended can, causing it to spin in the opposite direction of the force applied by the jets of water, and that the can spins at a rate equal to the force of the water leaving the can.

Discuss how the flow of water draining from the cans can be increased or decreased by changing the rate of flow (e.g., by having fewer or smaller holes, by changing the angle at which water drains from the can, or by creating a vacuum or partial vacuum by covering the open end of the can with a plastic lid). Note that as the water level drops and the weight of the column of water decreases, the pressure of water escaping from the can decreases and so does the rate of spinning. Thus, a constant flow of water into the can would be required to keep the can spinning at a constant rate.

Have students collect images (photographs, paintings, drawings) depicting the movement of water in nature (raindrops striking the ground, a river valley, a glacier or ice field, etc.) Students can use the pictures they have gathered to make a hallway exhibit or a portfolio for the classroom.

Using the time line presented at the end of this activity (supplemented with other events if desired), instruct students to make a montage of pictures showing the natural power of water intermixed with images of ways people have tapped the power of water through the ages.

Visit a local power plant and have a representative explain the role of water in the generation of electricity. Advanced students can try to build a mini-turbine able to generate an electrical current.

Resources

🍎 Ardley, Neil. 1983. *Working With Water*. New York, N.Y.: Watts.

🍎 Catherall, Ed. 1981. *Water Power*. Morristown, N.J.: Silver Burdett.

Cuevas, Mapi M., and William G. Lamb. 1994. *Physical Science*. Austin, Tex.: Holt, Rinehart & Winston.

🍎 Macaulay, David. *The Way Things Work*. 1988. Boston, Mass.: Houghton Mifflin Company.

Tennessee Valley Authority Environmental Education Program Development Group. 1992. *The Energy Sourcebook—Junior High Unit*. Norris, Tenn.: TVA.

🍎 Zubrowski, Bernie. 1982. *Messing Around With Water Pumps and Siphons*. New York, N.Y.: Little Paper.

Water Through Time

3000 B.C. – 2500 B.C.	Egyptians use water power to carry stones from distant quarries to build pyramids at Giza
A.D. 100	Greeks invent first waterwheel
A.D. 100	Greek scientist Hero invents simple steam engine called the aeolipile. Its potential is not tapped for over a thousand years
159	First water clock, or clepsydra, invented in Rome
1019	First water-driven mechanical clock built in Peking (Beijing), China
1328	Sawmill is invented. Early versions are powered by water
1510	Leonardo da Vinci designs a horizontal water wheel, the precursor of the water-driven turbine
1543	Blasco da Garay designs first steam-driven ship
1582	First waterworks founded in London. Waterwheels are installed on London Bridge
1589	First flush toilet, or water closet, designed by Sir John Harrington
1700	Mills driven by water power in common use throughout Europe
1705	Thomas Newcomen invents first practical steam engine. Water turbine invented by Pierre-Simon Girard
1764	James Watt invents condenser, first step leading to development of efficient steam engine
1769	First steam-operated "road carriage" invented by N. J. Cugnot
1775	James Watt perfects development of steam engine
1782	James Watt invents rotary steam engine
1783	Jouffroy d'Abbas sails paddlewheel steamboat on the Saône River
1785	James Watt and Mathew Bolton install steam engine in cotton spinning factory
1803	Robert Fulton invents steam-powered boat
1814	First practical steam locomotive invented by George Stephenson. *London Times* printed by steam-operated press
1815	First steam-driven warship (the *Fulton*) built
1818	First steamship (the *Savannah*) crosses the Atlantic
1830	Steam-driven cars common on the streets of London
1850	The Francis turbine, now in use in many powerplants, invented by James Francis
1859	Steamroller invented
1884	Sir Charles Parson develops first practical steam turbine engine
present	Water used as coolant in nuclear power plants

Great Water Journeys

Grade Level:
Middle School, High School

Subject Areas:
Geography, Earth Science, History

Duration:
Preparation time: 20 minutes
Activity time: 50 minutes

Setting: Classroom

Skills:
Gathering information (reading, listening, researching); Organizing (mapping); Applying (designing); Presenting

Charting the Course
How water travels over Earth's surface is addressed in "Branching Out!" In "Water Crossings," students investigate how early travelers overcame or utilized watercourses. How water moves around the world through the water cycle is introduced in "Imagine!". "Piece It Together," "Wet Vacation," and "A Drop in the Bucket" are related activities that investigate distribution of water around the world.

Vocabulary
migration

What do Lewis and Clark, gray whales, and coconuts have in common?

▼ Summary
Using a global map and a set of clue cards, students locate some significant water journeys.

Objectives
Students will:
- locate a few of the diverse pathways water travels around the globe.
- describe how water provides an important mode of transportation for plants and animals.

Materials
- Pencils
- Copies of **Water Journey Trivia Clues and Summaries**
- An encyclopedia (optional)
- Copies of **Global Map**
- A world atlas
- Wall map

Making Connections
Students are accustomed to thinking of airplanes and cars, highways and train tracks when they consider making a journey. But, unless they live in a region where water transportation is common, water travel is not likely to play a part in their lives. In "Great Water Journeys," students learn the vital role water has played in transporting plants, people, and other animals around the world.

Background
Water is a restless element, driven by solar energy, wind, gravity, and pressure (for glaciers and some ground water). It can be an obstacle to travel, as in the case of river crossings, and a dangerous medium (ocean storms or fast rivers), but it can also be the very highway that makes travel possible.

People, other animals, and plants move (and migrate) in response to a variety of environmental and social conditions. Sometimes water journeys are a matter of accident or coincidence. A tree falls into a flooding river, travels halfway across a continent, and ends up snagged in the trestles of a railroad bridge. In other cases, plants and animals have evolved to take advantage of water travel as part of their survival strategy. Some water plants have buoyant seeds that will float until they reach a favorable habitat in which to take root. Many aquatic species rely on water transportation in the course of their seasonal migrations, traveling to and from food sources, spawning grounds, and suitable climates.

Human water journeys throughout history have been motivated by various factors. Social oppression can cause whole sectors of a population to move away, sometimes by boat or across frozen expanses of water. Starvation, changing climate, and natural disasters are all capable of precipitating mass human movements. Curiosity or a desire for riches has sparked other water explorations. In island and coastal cultures, people constantly move across the water out of necessity or to benefit from their aquatic surroundings.

Gravity pulls water downhill, eventually into the sea. Winds and the rotation of Earth combine to power ocean currents, like rivers within the sea. On many of these journeys, water carries myriad passengers along with it, destined for new homes, new discoveries, and unexpected adventures.

Procedure
▼ Warm Up
Ask students to think back to the last journey they took that involved water travel (even a short trip or water cross-

ing). If they have never traveled by water, ask if they would like to take a water journey. Ask them to think about places where water provides the most efficient, or perhaps the only, transportation (oceans, swamps, cliffy coastlines, tropical forests).

Briefly discuss how plants and animals have been transported around the world by water. Have students think of three famous water journeys taken by humans. (People of local fame or from folklore and fiction, like Huck Finn, are acceptable.) See if students can think of examples of any plant, animal, or water molecule journeys.

▼ The Activity

1. **Divide the class into small groups. Tell students that they will be playing a geographic water journey trivia game.** They should pool their knowledge to identify specific water journeys.

2. **Inform the groups that they will hear three clues about each of nine water journeys, labeled "A" through "I." Based on the clues, they should try to guess who or what did the traveling. The first group to guess correctly receives a point and a summary card describing the journey.**

3. **Read the clues out loud for each card and allow time for the groups to discuss their guesses.** Make sure each group gets at least one summary card. (Some groups may receive a point but no card for a correctly guessed journey; the card is given to another group.)

4. **After all the summary cards have been distributed, tell groups to read their cards and, if possible, supplement the information with readings from science texts and history books.**

5. **Hand out copies of the *Global Map* to each group. Based on their summary cards and any other information, each group should sketch the path they think the subject of their summary card(s) traveled.** The starting and ending points are indicated on their summary cards, but remind students that the shortest distance between A and B is not always the best path. Mountain ranges or deserts, contrary winds or stormy seas may create obstacles. Students may consult a world atlas, if necessary.

6. **When students think they have the correct pathway, have them check the master map and compare their routes against the actual ones.** Discuss any major discrepancies. What explanations for the differences can they provide? (Consult the atlas or world map as necessary.) Ask students to erase and redraw any of the routes that were inaccurate on their first attempt.

▼ Wrap Up

Have each group give a class presentation about the water journey they studied. Encourage them to be accurate, but creative. On a class map, they should show the pathway of the journey and tell the other groups to copy the route onto their own maps. Have the class make one master map of great water journeys, to be posted in the school library.

Have each small group brainstorm a few other great water journeys. After selecting one, they should come up with several appropriate clues and try to draw a route on their map as accurately as possible. (Some research time may be necessary.) Groups can take turns presenting clues and trying to stump other teams with their water journey trivia.

Assessment

Have students:
- plot water pathways based on geographic clues (step 5).
- compare and evaluate projected water journeys versus actual travel routes (step 6).
- develop a presentation about a great water journey (*Wrap Up*).
- research and create their own water journey trivia clues and summary cards (*Wrap Up*).

Extensions

Students may be interested in writing short fictional adventure stories about a character (plant, animal, water molecule) as it makes a water journey, such as the one described in *Paddle to the Sea* by Clancy Holling (1941). In *Paddle to the Sea*, a young boy living within the St. Lawrence River drainage basin carves a Native American figure paddling a canoe. He places the carving on a snow bank and waits for spring, when the snow will melt and carry "Paddle to the Sea" away. The little boat encounters many people as it makes its way through the Great Lakes and beyond. The story provides insight into watersheds and the culture of the Great Lakes regions.

Orient students to watercourses by having them trace the routes of the major North American rivers (e.g., Colorado, Columbia, Mississippi, Missouri, Rio Grande), as the water moves from each river's headwaters (starting point) to its confluence (end point or where it enters another river). Have students estimate the distances water travels using the map scale.

Resources

🍎 Fritz, Jean. 1994. *Around the World in 100 Years*. New York, N.Y.: G. P. Putnam's Sons.

🍎 Holling, Clancy. 1941. *Paddle to the Sea*. Boston, Mass.: Houghton Mifflin Company.

🍎 Mason, Anthony. 1993. *Children's Atlas of Exploration*. Brookfield, Conn.: Quarto Publishing.

Zebra Mussel Watch, University of Wisconsin Sea Grant Institute, 1800 University Ave., Madison, WI 53705-4049. (608) 262-0645.

Answer Key for Global Worksheet

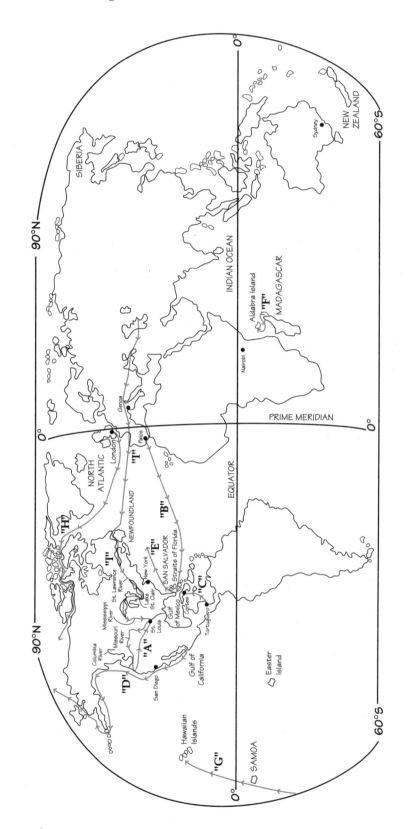

Water Journey Trivia Clues and Summaries

Journey "A"

Clues:

- The president of the United States requested this journey in the first years of the 1800s. If it hadn't been for the Louisiana Purchase, the trip might never have been taken.
- Many new species of plants and animals were discovered and named, including the grizzly bear.
- They were just a couple of ramblin' guys, but sometimes they had help from an extraordinary Native American woman, Sacajawea.

Summary:

Meriwether Lewis and William Clark, along with their company (consisting of more than 30 people), spent more than two years (1804-1806) exploring the wild frontiers of what is now the western United States. Their journey took them up the Missouri River to its headwaters, across the Continental Divide and the Rocky Mountains, and down the watershed of the Columbia River to reach the Pacific Ocean. After spending a miserable winter there, they retraced their route to St. Louis, exploring the Yellowstone River along the way.

They were sent on their mission by President Thomas Jefferson, largely to secure America's claim to the recent Louisiana Purchase. Accompanying the party were William Clark's slave, York, and the wife of an interpreter, Sacajawea, who brought her young son. Remarkably—in a journey of that duration and covering thousands of uncharted miles—only one man in the expeditionary party perished. Charles Floyd died of appendicitis on August 20, 1804.

Water Path:
Start: St. Louis, Missouri **End:** St. Louis, Missouri

Journey "B"

Clues:

- My three ships were the *Pinta*, the *Niña*, and the *Santa Maria*.
- When I touched land at the end of my voyage, I thought I had reached the Orient.
- My claim to be the first European in the New World is now in doubt.

Summary:

Christopher Columbus, born in 1451 in Genoa, Italy, went to sea at the young age of 14. After a decade or more of sailing adventures, Columbus harbored a growing ambition to achieve great glory, and great wealth, by sailing westward over the Atlantic. As years passed he became obsessed with his goal.

It wasn't until 1492 that Columbus secured the support of Ferdinand and Isabella, sovereigns of Spain, that would allow him to set out. He left from the port of Palos on August 3, 1492. His voyage to a landfall on the Caribbean island of San Salvador covered 3,066 miles (4,913 km) and took 33 days. On October 12, 1492, Columbus set foot on land he thought was part of the Orient. It was a misconception he carried to his deathbed in 1506.

His voyage has been credited with the "discovery" of America, a land long inhabited by native peoples. But more recent information indicates that the first European visitor here may well have been Saint Brendan of Ireland or Norse explorer Leif Ericson.

Water Path:
Start: Palos, Spain **End:** San Salvador

Journey "C"

Clues:

- I was tagged on a beach in Costa Rica, late one moonlit night, and was found one year and 800 miles later on the coast of Cuba.
- My children were hidden under layers of warm sand.
- Chances for my survival have improved since humans started putting escape devices on fishing nets.

Summary:

Green sea turtles are a threatened and endangered species. They live in both the Atlantic and Pacific Oceans and migrate across long stretches of open water. Browsing in beds of turtle grass, they prefer shallow water vegetation for their food. Their habit of basking in the sun out of water is unique for marine turtles. Adults can attain shell lengths of 3-6 feet (1-2 m) and weigh up to 300 pounds (150 kg).

Along with other species of marine turtles, green sea turtles lay their eggs in sand pits at specific beach locations scattered around the world. Green sea turtles are known to live as long as 20 years, and will, in that life span, travel many thousands of kilometers. (This specific journey was verified by tagging studies.)

As with many marine turtles, the green sea turtle's future is uncertain. Destruction of nesting beaches and the practice of raiding nests for eggs threaten the species' continuation.

Water path:
Start: Tortuguero, Costa Rica **End:** Cortes, Cuba

Journey "D"

Clues:

- I "talk" in songs.
- Each year I migrate between two watery homes—one in the Arctic and one off the west coast of Mexico.
- My babies are called calves, and at birth are 15 feet (5 m) long.

Summary:

Summering each year in the north and wintering in the Gulf of California, where they give birth to their young, California gray whales spend their lives in the Pacific Ocean. From late May through October, they reside in the north, where they seem to be limited by pack ice in the Arctic Ocean. They concentrate along the coasts of Alaska and Siberia, feeding on a rich ocean harvest in shallow waters.

From the end of October through January, the gray whales move south, staying within a few miles of shore most of the time and traveling at an average rate of 115 miles (185 km) per day.

By February the gray whales have reached the warm tropical waters near the Gulf of California. Calves are born, usually in shallow lagoons. Although just 15 feet (5 m) long at birth, gray whales reach lengths of up to 42 feet (14 m) and weigh as much as 36,000 pounds (16,500 kg) as adults.

Water path:
Start: Gulf of California **End:** Off coast of Siberia or Alaska

Journey "E"

Clues:

- I am a river of water 1,000 times bigger than the Mississippi River, and I have no banks.
- England is warmer than Newfoundland because of me.
- Ships use me to increase their speed.

Summary:

The Gulf Stream originates in the Gulf of Mexico, passes through the Straits of Florida, then flows northward across the Atlantic toward Europe. Powered by ocean currents, the Gulf Stream moves as fast as 70 miles (112 km) per day and has a rate of flow 1,000 times that of the Mississippi River.

Ships ride the Gulf Stream to shorten their sailing times, and animal and plant species also hitch rides on the current. The Gulf Stream parallels the eastern coast of North America and is separated from the shore by a zone of chilly water, known to sailors as the "cold wall." By the time the Gulf Stream reaches Newfoundland, it has slowed to approximately 10 miles (16 km) per day. It continues east toward Europe, becoming the North Atlantic Current.

Much of Europe has a warmer climate than corresponding latitudes in North America. These gentler climates can be traced, at least in part, to the moderating effect of the warm Gulf Stream.

Water path:
Start: Gulf of Mexico **End:** The North Atlantic off European Coast

Journey "F"

Clues:

- I travel by water, but don't need a boat.
- I will grow into a tropical tree, associated with beaches and islands.
- My milk is used in Asian curry dishes.

Summary:

Coconuts are less dense than water, so they can float. The outer husk encloses the critical nut, which is capable of riding ocean currents for up to four months without dying. With luck, and favorable currents, the coconut will wash up on a beach, where it can sprout and send down roots.

Once established, coconut trees grow with a pronounced lean toward the sea, so that when their seeds drop, they will land in sand below the high-tide mark and be carried away on their journey.

This specific coconut voyage began on the island of Madagascar, off the east coast of Africa, and ended on a small volcanic island called Aldabra, 250 miles (400 km) away in the Indian Ocean. It rode the Equatorial Counter Current.

Water path:
Start: Madagascar **End:** Aldabra

Journey "G"

Clues:

- We are the original colonists of America's 50th state.
- Our boats were held together by coconut fiber.
- We were also the first people known to colonize New Zealand and Easter Island.

Summary:

Polynesians in the South Pacific were accomplished sailors thousands of years before Columbus was born. Because they live in a section of the world full of small islands, Polynesians have counted boats and ocean travel as a part of their culture for millennia. Evidence indicates that Polynesians purposefully explored and colonized much of the Pacific, including the Hawaiian Islands.

Polynesians traveled in double canoes capable of carrying hundreds of passengers. These boats were lashed tightly together with twine made from coconuts, and their sails were woven from other plant fibers. Their astonishing skill as navigators took them as far afield as Easter Island, New Zealand, and Hawaii. Traveling from Samoa to Hawaii required an ocean voyage of 5,000 miles (8,000 km).

Water path:
Start: Samoa **End:** Hawaii

Journey "H"

Clues:

- Sir John Franklin, along with 128 others, died trying to navigate me.
- I am icebound much of each year, and sometimes for years at a time.
- Darkness reigns over me for half of each year.

Summary:

In the late 1800s and early 1900s the quest for a Northwest Passage to the Orient fueled a feverish competition between European expeditions. Dozens of men, scores of ships, and more than a few fortunes were lost in the process. Expeditions often spent years frozen in the ice pack, suffered the effects of scurvy and other diseases, and endured the rigor of Arctic storms and six months of night, all to pioneer a route that would never result in any prize other than geographic conquest.

The islands north of the Canadian mainland bear the names of these explorers, their sponsors, and the homes they must have longed for through the long winter nights.

It was Roald Amundsen, the Norwegian who would also be the first to reach the South Pole, who finally navigated the tortuous, ice-locked Northwest Passage, during the years 1903-1906.

Water path:
Start: London, England **End:** North coast of Alaska

Journey "I"

Clues:

- I was unintentionally introduced into the United States in the late 1980s; I was carried in freshwater ballasts (loads that provide stability) of ships traveling from Europe.
- I am only about 2 inches (5 cm) long, and have a hard, striped shell; like my American cousin, I secrete tough fibers which I then use to attach myself to rocks, boats, pipes, and many other things.
- Much to the dismay of the fishing industry and water treatment plants, my population is quickly growing and expanding into each of the Great Lakes as well as to connecting rivers . . . If my population continues to grow, I may appear in a river near you!

Summary:

Zebra mussels are freshwater mollusks. It is believed they originated in the Black and Caspian Seas and were carried by ship through fresh waters in Europe. They were accidentally introduced to the United States in the mid-1980s. The mussels spread quickly down the St. Lawrence River and through the Great Lakes. They were first discovered in Lake St. Clair in 1988. They are expected to spread to a majority of United States waterways within a decade. The spread of zebra mussels throughout freshwater systems is attributed to their ability to cling like barnacles to almost any surface, some of which (boats, drifting materials, and fishing equipment) unintentionally transport the mussels to new locations. They have a high reproduction rate and lack natural predators in this new habitat.

The growing population of zebra mussels causes many problems. They colonize on pipes, clogging and contaminating water treatment systems; they remove large quantities of nutrients and outcompete native organisms; they foul beaches and jam boat engines. Communities, industries, and businesses are currently spending hundreds of thousands of dollars to eliminate zebra mussels.

Start: Black Sea **End:** Mississippi River

Global Map

Name: _____

Date: _____

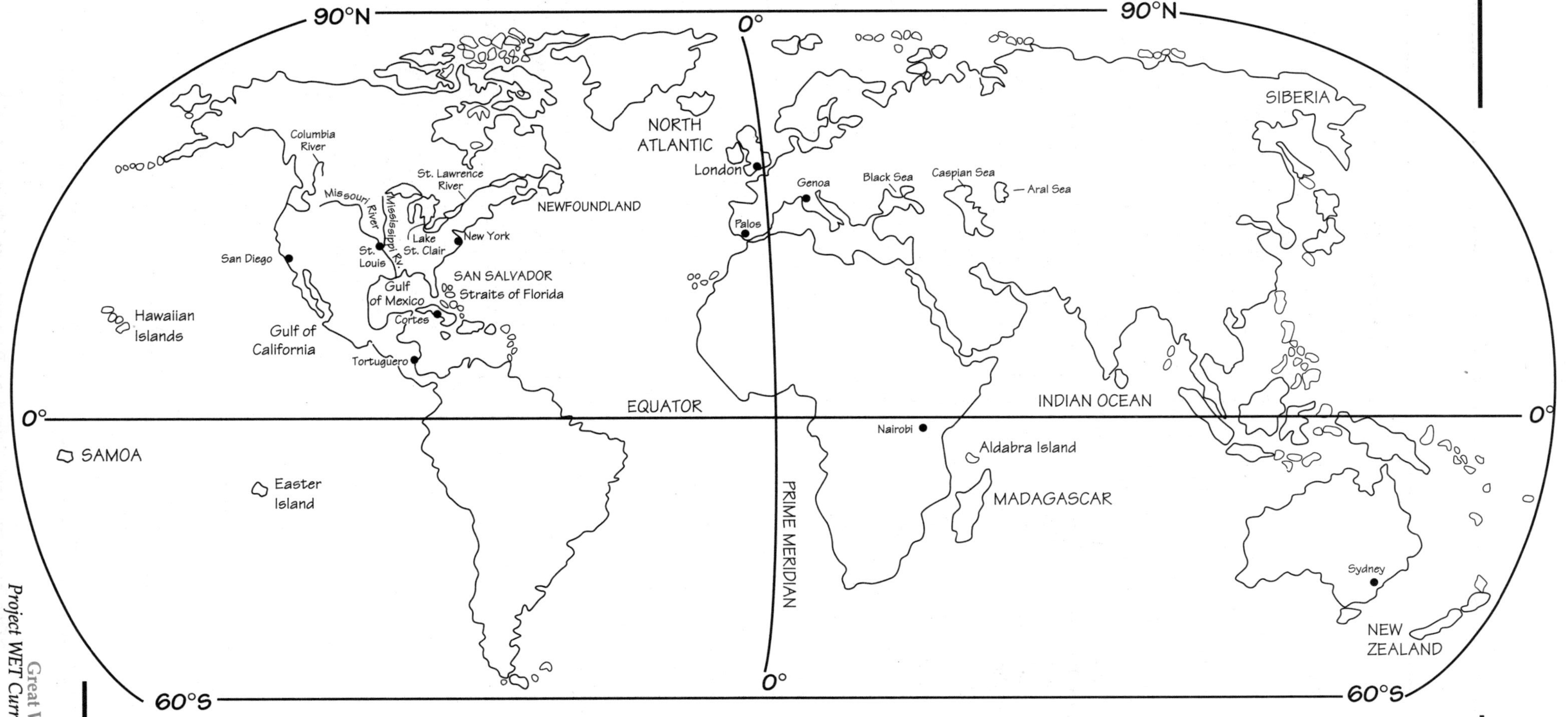

90°N

90°N

0°

0°

60°S

60°S

0°

0°

SIBERIA

Aral Sea

Caspian Sea

Black Sea

Genoa

Palos

London

NORTH
ATLANTIC

NEWFOUNDLAND

St. Lawrence
River

New York

SAN SALVADOR

Straits of Florida

Lake
St. Clair

Mississippi Rv.

St.
Louis

Gulf
of Mexico

Cortes

Missouri
River

Columbia
River

San Diego

Gulf of
California

Hawaiian
Islands

SAMOA

Easter
Island

Tortuguero

EQUATOR

PRIME MERIDIAN

INDIAN OCEAN

Nairobi

Aldabra Island

MADAGASCAR

Sydney

NEW
ZEALAND

NOTE: If possible, enlarge this map on the copier to fit a 8 ¹/₂" x 14" (legal) or 11" x 17" sheet of paper.

Irrigation Interpretation

What could cause a people to leave their homeland of a thousand years?

▼ Summary
By conducting simulations, building models, and solving a mini-mystery, students compare the economic and ecological costs of different irrigation systems.

Objectives
Students will:
- identify reasons people irrigate.
- construct a classroom irrigation system and monitor crop growth.
- describe different irrigation methods and evaluate the costs and benefits of each.
- propose explanations for an ancient culture abandoning its homeland.

Materials
- *Raincoats and shoes that can get wet*
- *Absorbent cloth or paper towels*
- *Hose attached to running water or buckets of water*
- *Used plastic trays from fast-food restaurants with small holes punched in the bottom for drainage*
- *Plastic straws, some with flexible sections*
- *Clay or wood glue*
- *Sand*
- *Potting soil*
- *Grass or bean seeds*
- *Plant food*
- *Sprinkling can*
- *Small funnels*
- *Paper cups*
- *Poster board*
- *World map*

Making Connections
The fruits and vegetables you consume likely were grown on irrigated cropland.

Without irrigated agriculture, crops such as lettuce, pineapples, oranges, soybeans, and others grown in arid parts of the world would be available in lesser quantities and at higher prices. Students may live in areas that have irrigated agriculture or may have seen it on television. Learning about different irrigation systems helps students consider the demands growing food places on water resources.

Background
People have been growing crops for a long time. In fact, some 10,000 to 12,000 years ago a cultural shift known as the agricultural revolution began in several regions of the world. This food-producing revolution involved a gradual move from a lifestyle based on nomadic hunting and gathering to one of settled agricultural communities; people learned how to domesticate wild animals and cultivate wild plants. Early growers practiced subsistence farming; that is, they grew only enough for themselves.

About 7,000 years ago the invention of the plow allowed farmers to cultivate larger areas. In some arid regions, early farmers increased crop output by diverting water from nearby streams into ditches and canals, dug by hand, to irrigate crops. This gradual shift from hunting and gathering to farming had several significant effects. Population increased as a result of greater food supplies, better living standards, and longer life spans. And people built increasingly larger irrigation systems, cleared larger fields, and organized villages.

Today, irrigated agriculture plays a critical role in providing large quantities of low-cost food for the United States and other parts of the world. Worldwide, almost 20 percent of the land farmed for crops is irrigated and produces about

■ **Grade Level:**
Upper Elementary, Middle School

■ **Subject Areas:**
Environmental Science, Anthropology, Geography

■ **Duration:**
Preparation time:
Part I: 30 minutes
Part II: 30 minutes
Part III: 10 minutes

Activity time:
Part I: 50 minutes
Part II: extended
Part III: 30 minutes

■ **Setting:**
Part I: Outdoors
Parts II and III: Indoors

■ **Skills:**
Applying (restructuring, designing); Evaluating (observing, organizing, interpreting, analyzing)

■ **Charting the Course**
Prior to this activity, students could learn how plants absorb and transport water ("Thirsty Plants" and "Let's Even Things Out"). In "Sum of the Parts," students investigate problems with runoff and nonpoint source pollution. Soil and water relations are further addressed in "Get the Ground Water Picture."

■ **Vocabulary**
irrigation, salinization

one-third of the world's food. For certain crops, the statistics for the United States' production are much higher than these.

Irrigation gives farmers and ranchers the ability to manage their lands (to add water at the appropriate time) and to increase productivity. To raise crops, people irrigate certain areas, because precipitation cannot meet plant water needs. This is especially true in the Western United States. From about the 98th meridian of longitude west to the Pacific Coast, average annual rainfall dips significantly below the 20 inches (50 cm) that normally support nonirrigated crops in the East.

Important factors when considering irrigation include:

- climate suitable for growing crop (varies from crop to crop)
- soils capable of being irrigated (irrigable soils)
- proximity to an economical source of ground or surface water (irrigation becomes less cost effective the greater the distance and height that water needs to travel to crops; governments have gone to extraordinary lengths to develop public works designed to deliver water from water-rich sources to areas of need)
- quality and quantity of water that will not adversely affect crops
- topography suitable for applying irrigated water (level, slightly sloped, or gently rolling)
- money to purchase, operate, and maintain operation systems (pipes, pumps, ditches, etc.)
- time, energy, and skills needed to set up, operate, and maintain an irrigation system
- a market for irrigated crops

"Irrigation system" is the generic term used to describe a system used to supply water to crops. A system has the following general components:

COURTESY: BUREAU OF RECLAMATION

- a source of water
- a means of retrieving water from the source (Ground water sources require a well and pump, while surface water sources need an intake pipe and pump.)
- a method of moving water from the source to the field (In some areas water is pumped directly onto the field; in other locations water is pumped long distances through pipes or canals to the site where it is applied.)
- a method of applying water onto the field such as:

  - flood irrigation (field is flooded with water)

  - ditch irrigation (pumps and pipes or siphons put water into ditches along row crops and gravity moves water throughout the field)

  - sprinkler (water is pumped into pipes that have nozzles and sprinkler heads of varying design, and water is sprinkled or sprayed on crops)

  - drip irrigation (a system of water lines is set up near the base of crops, and water is applied in exact amounts to the root systems of plants)

Irrigated land can produce crop yields two to three times those of non-irrigated land. In fact, in many dry areas if you do not irrigate, you cannot grow crops. Irrigation, however, can have its downside. Irrigation water may contain salts. In dry climates, much of the water from this saline solution evaporates, leaving behind the salts (such as sodium chloride) in the top soil. The accumulation of these salts, called salinization, stunts crop growth, lowers yields, eventually kills crop plants, and can ruin the land.

Another management problem for irrigators is waterlogging. Farmers often apply heavy amounts of irrigation water to leach salts deeper into the soil. Without adequate drainage, water accumulates underground, gradually raising the water table. Saline water eventually envelops the roots of plants and kills them.

A look at the past reveals evidence of cultures devastated by the salinization of their soil. The Hohokam people lived in the Gila and Salt River valleys (in the American Southwest) in A.D. 1300. The Salt River was named Rio Salado by the early Spanish and Jesuit explorers because of its high salt content, caused by the heavy salt formation through which the river passes about 100 miles (160 km) north of Phoenix.

The Hohokam people lived in this location for more than 1,000 years. They built complex cities and had an advanced irrigation system, consisting of ditches running from their water source, the Salt River, to their crops.

The Hohokams suddenly disappeared from the area around A.D. 1400. Some scientists think a widespread epidemic might have occurred. The people could have become frightened and fled, but no evidence supports this hypothesis. Other scientists think the area was hit by a severe drought. Perhaps the mountains received little or no rain for many years and the rivers dried up, eliminating the Hohokams' water source. Evidence exists of a drought from A.D. 1277 to 1299. Tree ring studies from both river valleys indicate little growth during these years. This may be an indication of limited rainfall. However, scientists have found that only people from the villages near the small canals moved at that time; the people living on the river, streams, and large canals remained.

Scientists believe Hohokam irrigation practices may have severely damaged the land. After years of irrigation, the soil became less absorbent and the water did not run off as quickly. The soil became

waterlogged at the surface. The high salt content of the Gila and Salt Rivers caused the roots of plants to die. Finally, the salt content was so high plants could not grow.

Irrigated lands in some areas around the world are prone to having problems with salinization today. In areas where these problems exist, landowners can reduce salinization by flushing fields or leaving fields fallow for a few years.

Procedure
▼ Warm Up
Ask students to list the essential elements that plants require for growth. One of these is water. Discuss rainfall patterns of the United States; show the map, *Average Annual Rainfall*. Have students identify the drier regions of the country. How do they think crops there get water? Have students describe agricultural lands they have seen. What irrigation methods have they seen or do they know?

▼ The Activity
Part I
1. **Take the class outside and tell students they are going to demonstrate some basic irrigation practices. Warn them that they will be getting wet.**

2. **Have students stand in rows to represent planted crops. Give each student a paper towel or an absorbent cloth. Tell them it represents soil around their roots.** They should lay the paper towel by their feet. Roots need to be surrounded by wet soil to absorb nutrients; this is represented when the cloth or towel becomes saturated.

3. **One or two students will simulate the irrigation practices. Explain that one method of irrigation is ditch irrigation, involving gravity flow systems.** Have the irrigating students allow the hose to run (or have them pour bucketfuls of water) in front of each row of students. Students representing crops

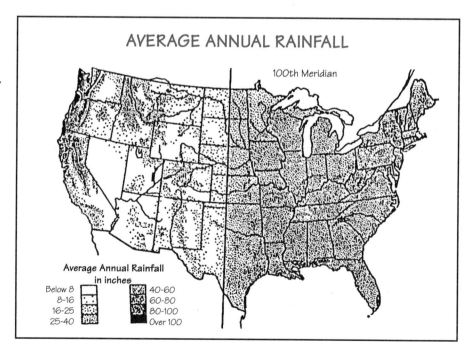

AVERAGE ANNUAL RAINFALL

100th Meridian

Average Annual Rainfall in inches

Below 8
8-16
16-25
25-40

40-60
60-80
80-100
Over 100

should find their paper towels are soon soaked.

4. **Move the crop students to a new location where the ground is dry. Have them lay a new set of cloths or towels at their feet.**

5. **The second irrigation method represents a center-pivot sprinkler system. Have the irrigating students partially block the flow of water from the hose, so that it sprays out.** They should point the hose upward so that water sprinkles over the crop students, continuing until the paper towels are saturated.

6. **Have the crop students move again to a dry location and lay down new towels.** This time the irrigating students take the hose and water each towel. They should block the flow between waterings, so that no water is lost. This represents a drip irrigation system.

Part II

1. **Students can build separate models to demonstrate each irrigation system.** For the ditch irrigation method, instruct them to plant rows of grass seed or beans in a long planter and create a furrow beside each planted row. To irrigate the plants, water is poured into the ditches (furrows) in the long planter. To simulate the center-pivot irrigation system, students should use a sprinkling water can. For the drip irrigation system, distribute plastic trays, straws, clay, sand, potting soil, plant food, a small funnel, and grass seed to small groups of students. Have the students design and build a grass farm irrigation system in a plastic dish (see *Design a Drip Irrigation System*).

2. **Discuss the three irrigation systems.** Which used the most and least water? How might evaporation affect each system? Which do

students think would be the most expensive to build and maintain? Discuss the cost of water loss compared to the cost of construction.

Part III

1. **Read or have students read the mini-mystery, *Lost Homeland*. They are allowed 20 questions to find the answer.** They may only ask questions that can be answered with a "yes," "no," or "not relevant."

2. **If students are not close to the answer after 15 questions, provide additional information about the location and the water source of these people (the Salt River).**

3. **After students have guessed or been told the solution, ask if they think modern cultures could have these problems. Discuss the benefits of and problems facing current irrigation practices.**

4. **To demonstrate how salt collects in soil, have students do the following:** Saturate some water with salt, carefully measuring the amount of salt added to the water. Poke a number of small holes in the bottom of a paper cup and fill the cup two-thirds full of soil. Pour the salt solution through the soil. Collect the water that runs through the soil; then allow it to evaporate. Compare the salt left after evaporation to the measured amount added to the water. Dry the soil and look for evidence of salt in the soil particles.

▼ Wrap Up

Discuss modern irrigation strategies with students. What types of irrigation can they identify? What technologies are used today? Have the class make a chart summarizing agricultural techniques and assessing ecological and economic benefits and costs. The chart could be posted in the hallway.

Assessment

Have students:
* demonstrate and identify irrigation systems (*Part I*, steps 3–6).
* construct classroom irrigation models, demonstrating and comparing different irrigation systems (*Part II*, steps 1 and 2).
* develop a questioning strategy to determine why a culture would abandon its homeland (*Part III*, steps 1–3).
* create a chart summarizing irrigation techniques and assessing ecological and economic benefits and costs (*Wrap Up*).

Upon completing the activity, for further assessment have students:
* research and identify on a world map locations with salinization problems.
* investigate and report what is being done to overcome salinization problems.

Extensions

Have students modify their irrigation models to demonstrate the problems of waterlogging in irrigation practices.

😊 K-2 Option

"Too Little, Too Much, Just Right"
Have students conduct an experiment using three empty milk cartons, potting soil, and three bean seeds. Fill each carton with an equal amount of soil and plant seeds according to directions on the package. (Make sure all cartons are exposed to the same amount of sunlight and temperatures.) Tell students this experiment relates to identifying the best conditions for growing crops. The first carton represents conditions with too much water. The soil in this carton should be continually saturated. The bean should not grow because of lack of air (oxygen) and because it is waterlogged. The second

Design a Drip Irrigation System

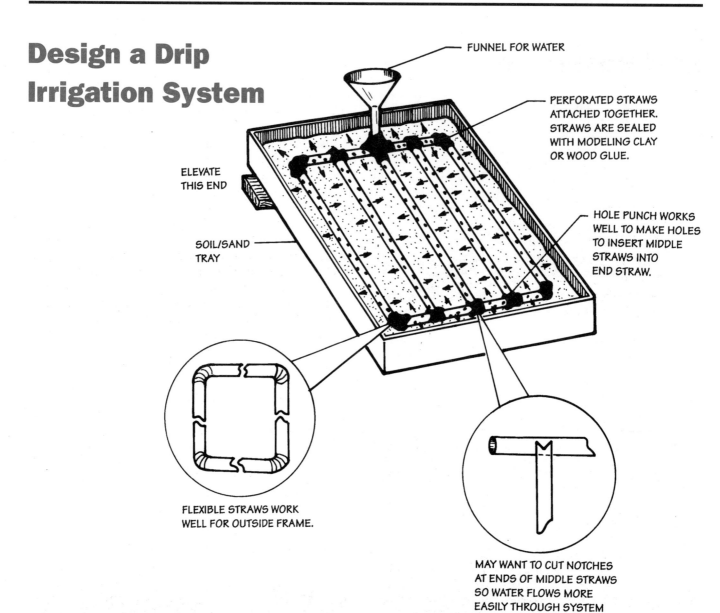

FUNNEL FOR WATER

PERFORATED STRAWS ATTACHED TOGETHER. STRAWS ARE SEALED WITH MODELING CLAY OR WOOD GLUE.

HOLE PUNCH WORKS WELL TO MAKE HOLES TO INSERT MIDDLE STRAWS INTO END STRAW.

ELEVATE THIS END

SOIL/SAND TRAY

FLEXIBLE STRAWS WORK WELL FOR OUTSIDE FRAME.

MAY WANT TO CUT NOTCHES AT ENDS OF MIDDLE STRAWS SO WATER FLOWS MORE EASILY THROUGH SYSTEM

carton demonstrates conditions with too little water. Add a few drops of water to the soil to moisten it, but no more. The plant should grow, but ultimately it will not survive. The last carton is just right. It should be watered according to seed package directions, and the plant should flourish. To demonstrate how critical good water quality is when irrigating, students may water their beans with salt water and note the results.

Resources

Dregnue, Harold E. 1985. "Aridity and Land Degradation." *Environment* 27 (8): 33-39.

Fagen, Brian M. 1990. *The Journey from Eden: The Peopling of Our World*. London, England: Thames & Hudson.

Highes, J. Donald. 1975. *The Ecology of Ancient Civilizations*. Albuquerque, N.Mex.: University of New Mexico Press.

Postel, Sandra. 1992. *Last Oasis: Facing Water Scarcity*. New York, N.Y.: W. W. Norton & Company.

Lost Homeland

Sacaton red-on-buff jar. JUDITH L. STUDEBAKER

A certain culture lived in the Southwest in A.D. 1300. The culture had been living there for more than 1,000 years.

The people had developed a huge irrigation system. They used sharp sticks to dig long, deep canals. These canals carried water across the desert. Some of the canals ran up to 12 miles (19 km) from the river; one of them was 30 feet (9 m) deep. By A.D. 1300, the canals covered approximately 150 miles (240 km).

They also built dams across the river, which were made of brush cut in the nearby mountains. These dams backed up the water and made it easier to send it into the canals. The dams also held back water to be stored for times of the year when no rain fell in the mountains.

The people grew cotton, corn, beans, squash, and pumpkins on their irrigated land. They hunted deer in the mountains. They trapped rabbits and other small game in the desert.

This was an advanced and creative culture. They made beautiful objects, like pottery. They built sturdy houses; walls and roofs were made of poles, brush, and mud plaster. At first the houses had only one story. By A.D. 1300, however, these people were building houses of several floors. They even had four-story buildings!

Sometime around A.D. 1400 these people seem to have disappeared from the area. What was the cause for their sudden departure?

Superimposed canals. HAUREY; COPIED BY ROY W. REAVES III

Casa Grande ruins, framed in dead mesquite. HANNAH

The Long Haul

■ **Grade Level:** K-12

■ **Subject Areas:**
Environmental Science, History, Mathematics

■ **Duration:**
Preparation time: 15 minutes
Activity time: 50 minutes

■ **Setting:**
Outdoor playing area with a water source

■ **Skills:**
Gathering information (calculating); Interpreting (drawing conclusions); Organizing (estimating)

■ **Charting the Course**
In "Easy Street," students compare current water use to that of a rural family in the 1890s. Students can use a "Water Meter" to monitor how they use water. "Water Concentration" and "Wish Book" compare past and modern water-use appliances and recreational equipment. Students learn about and explore water conservation strategies in "Every Drop Counts."

■ **Vocabulary**
consumptive use

You plan to go out, but first need to complete your daily tasks: wash dishes, do laundry, bathe the baby, haul 200 gallons (760 l) of water to the house. . . . Hmmm, maybe it will be a while before you can leave.

▼ Summary
Students work in teams to compete in a water-hauling game.

Objectives
Students will:
- develop an awareness of various volumes of water.
- appreciate today's readily available water supplies.
- relate how easy access to water can encourage people to use large amounts of water.

Materials
- *4 1-gallon (3.8 l) buckets*
- *2 30-gallon (114 l) garbage cans*
- *Water source or outdoor spigots*
- *Containers of different sizes*

Making Connections
Most students have seen pictures of old-fashioned wells and pumps. They may have seen movies or read books in which children's chores include drawing and hauling water. However, few children have actually experienced water hauling. Becoming involved in carrying the volume of water they use in a day promotes an appreciation of daily water consumption and modern water distribution facilities.

Background
In most modern societies, water is easily available at the turn of a tap. This was not always so. In North America less than 100 years ago, many people had to pump and haul their own water for washing, cooking, bathing, and other needs. Often the well was located several feet away from the house. Even today, in many parts of the world including places in North America, hauling water remains a common practice. Imagine how differently we would feel about water if we had to pump and carry it by hand.

The average household consumes an estimated 200 gallons (760 l) of water per day. Many people are amazed that a family of three uses this much water.

Technology has made using water extremely easy. We turn on the tap and have all the water we need. In many communities, a complex system of pipes, storage tanks and towers, treatment plants, and pumps collect, treat, and convey water. Our homes are plumbed to deliver water where it is needed. Homes with one, two, or three bathrooms are common. If three people flush four times per day, at 3 gallons (11.4 l) per flush, consuming 200 gallons (760 l) per day becomes understandable. (12 flushes x 3 gallons [11.4 l] = 36 gallons [136.8 l])

Procedure
▼ Warm Up
Discuss with the class ways they use water. Where does this water come from and how does it get to our homes? What did people have to do 100 years ago to get their water? Ask students to list chores they do after school and estimate how much time each takes. How much free time do they have after school? How much free time would they have if they had to pump their family's water and haul it home?

▼ The Activity
1. **Tell students they are going to play a water-hauling game.** Discuss what they think the purpose of the activity is.

COURTESY: PROJECT WET, MONTANA

2. **Divide the class into two teams. Each team gets two 1-gallon (3.8 l) buckets. The task is to haul water from a source (a stream or pond is ideal, but a water spigot will work fine) to a destination (garbage can) about 150 feet (45 m) away.**

3. **Organize the game as a relay race.** Team members line up at the water source. One team member fills the bucket, to represent pumping water or drawing it from a well, then carries it to the destination and pours it into the team's garbage can. He or she returns to the water source and gives the bucket to the next team member, who fills and relays it. The first team to fill its garbage can wins the race.

4. **Ask students to predict how many trips they think it will take to fill the can. How much time will it take? Record their responses for future reference. Begin the race!**

▼ *Wrap Up and Action*

Ask students how they felt about the activity. Were their predictions accurate? Based on the activity, have them determine the size, in gallons, of the garbage can. Show students a

variety of containers and have them estimate their volumes.

Discuss ways people in the past used the water hauled to their homes. (Read the story *The Bath* from the activity "Easy Street.") Compare these uses to modern practices. Do students think we use more, less, or the same amount of water? Discuss reasons we use more water now, including the ease of availability. Inform students that in the past it was often the chore of young children to haul water. How would students feel about hauling the 200 gallons (760 l) needed each day by today's average family? How would this affect how much water they used?

Involve students in designing a mural or performing a skit conveying the advantages and disadvantages of readily available water. A possible topic of the skit could be the reaction of a person from the past to the way people use water today. Students can present the skit to other classes.

Assessment

Have students:
* estimate volumes of different containers (*Wrap Up*).
* express their feelings about hauling water (*Wrap Up*).
* design a skit demonstrating the positive and negative aspects of easily available water (*Wrap Up*).

Extensions

Have someone from the municipal water service speak to the class about water delivery systems.

Technology has also dramatically enhanced the capabilities of fire departments. Fire hydrants have been added to community water systems. Alter the activity by telling students the garbage can represents a fire that needs to be extinguished. Challenge students to develop the most efficient procedure for using buckets to transport water from the source to the destination. Remember to tell students that no fire hydrants or fire trucks are available—just will power and buckets of water. Students may have seen movies set in the past, in which a bucket brigade is organized to put out a fire. Have students imagine what fire fighting would be like today without modern technology.

K-2 Option

Adjust the bucket size, the quantity of water that is hauled, and the distance between the water source and the destination.

Resources

Jones, Natalie, and Wyn Hughes. 1982. *Carrying Loads on Heads: Third World Science*. London, England: The Centre for World Development Education.

🍎 Wilder, Laura Ingalls. 1935. *Little House on the Prairie* (and other books). New York, N.Y.: Harper & Row.

Nature Rules!

■ **Grade Level:**
Middle School, High School

■ **Subject Areas:**
Language Arts, Government, Environmental Science, History

■ **Duration:**
Preparation time: 20 minutes

Activity time: three 50-minute periods

■ **Setting:**
Classroom and library

■ **Skills:**
Gathering information (researching); Applying (designing); Evaluating (critiquing); Presenting (writing)

■ **Charting the Course**
Students can do the activity "Water: Read All About It!" in conjunction with this activity. "Dust Bowls and Failed Levees" is a related activity in which students write fictional stories based on water-related disasters. Students are introduced to costs involved with natural disasters in "AfterMath."

■ **Vocabulary**
water-related disaster

Who's the boss? When nature plays rough, there's nowhere to hide.

▼ Summary
Students use visual evidence of water-related natural disasters to inspire newspaper reports.

Objectives
Students will:
- compose news stories.
- describe ways in which "Nature Rules!"
- critique newspaper reports generated by their peers.

Materials
- *Copies of* **Photo Pages**
- *Writing materials*
- *Sample newspapers*
- *Red pencils*
- *Lists of proofreader's marks* (optional)

Making Connections
Students may be able to ignore environmental conditions that surround them for weeks at a time. Living in houses, driving in cars, shopping in temperature-controlled malls, they may believe they are immune to the unpredictability of climate and weather. Students who have not experienced major environmental events may take this safety for granted and perceive that they are in control of their environment. Through historic photographs and research, students recognize the effects of extraordinary natural forces, and the potential of natural events to influence their lives.

Background
The human species is exceptional in its ability to minimize or eliminate difficult environmental conditions by employing behavioral and technological strategies. People live in every climate, from polar to tropical, and in every corner of the globe, from alpine mountains to tropical rain forests. We are ubiquitous because we can control the temperature of our buildings by burning fuels, and because we can build structures and vehicles to protect us from wind, rain, cold, and heat.

Beyond that, we have manipulated the environment to serve our needs. Dams control floods and water crops; levees protect settlements built on floodplains; irrigation systems buffer us from drought; sea walls hold back pounding ocean waves. The list goes on. This extraordinary ability to manipulate our environment can lead to a sense of complacency and confidence: attitudes that could be ruinous when "disaster" strikes.

Thinking we are safe from floods, we build cities on floodplains. Assuming that we are protected from drought, we farm in arid lands. We build homes on steep slopes with minimal vegetation and give little thought to the possibility of mudslides. Then, when exceptional floods overtop levees, when a decade of drought dries up ground water supplies, when heavy rains turn hillsides into rivers of mud, when an avalanche plows through protective barriers—we are shocked and surprised. The natural event becomes a "disaster."

These events are devastating in terms of their effects on human populations. Lives can be lost, businesses ruined, whole cities wiped out. These occurrences seem disastrous, too, because most of them are only somewhat predictable. We cannot forecast tidal waves or hurricanes with the same certainty that we can predict the seasons. These singular events strike with terrifying randomness.

But such "disasters" are, in fact, as much a part of the natural rhythm as winter and summer. They are, simply, the most dramatic and powerful expressions of our natural environment: nature's exclamation marks.

Water plays a prominent role in many of the events we call natural disasters. Hailstorms, avalanches, tidal waves (tsunamis), mudslides, river flooding—these natural events of tremendous force all require a supply of water. Even the absence of water, in the case of drought, leads to disastrous results.

These natural disasters make for riveting news. Reporters flock to scenes of disaster to relate the misfortunes and tragedies that befall people. Few stories are more sensational than disaster news.

In reporting events, journalists compete for the public's attention. They must often contend with limited time and space. Headlines have to be brief and eye-catching to pique readers' interest. A solid first line will make people want to read more, and should be followed by the essential information—who, what, when, where, and how. The body of the story can embellish the main points and discuss the larger issues at

stake (environmental impact, economic costs, human toll). The story can end with a final human note or with concluding information about the aftermath, future possibilities, etc. Ideally, the reader will be left satisfied with the facts, but not bored by detail. Finally, in a news story, a reporter must be faithful to the facts and the truth of the situation. However, this does not eliminate the need for creativity and style.

Procedure
▼ *Warm Up*
Brainstorm with students as many types of natural disasters as they can think of (mudslides, earthquakes, erupting volcanoes, major floods). Encourage specific examples. Have them recount local disasters they have experienced or have heard

about from family and friends. How many of these examples have something to do with water or the lack of water?

Have any recent water catastrophes made the news? If so, see if students can remember how these were reported on television, radio, or in the newspapers. What were the headlines? How was the essential information communicated in a limited time and space? Using events from the brainstorming session, have the class practice creating some possible news headlines.

▼ *The Activity*
1. **Tell students that they are reporters for the DRS (Disaster Reporting Service).** They travel the globe to report on the latest cata-

Aftermath of the Johnstown flood. COURTESY: LIBRARY OF CONGRESS.

strophic events. No danger is too great, no sum of money too much, no mode of travel too outrageous—nothing can thwart the public clamor for news. They have helicoptered into the craters of erupting volcanoes, sandbagged levees with floodwaters lapping over the top, and dug for avalanche victims. Danger and adventure are the daily routine for DRS reporters.

2. **For this assignment, the DRS teams are covering some great historical natural disaster scenes. Their only sources of information are single photographs with short captions. Out of this sketchy information, DRS reporters must write news stories.**

3. **Separate the class into reporting teams (three to five students).** Assign each group one of the photographs from the photo page or locate other disaster photos via a library search. Tell them that, as a group, they must fashion a headline and a one-page news story based on the picture. Refer to some of the reporting points cited in the **Background** and have several copies of newspapers available, so students can get a feel for journalistic style and headlines. Have them identify what makes an appealing headline. Suggest that their article contain possible ways the disaster might have been diverted. Had earlier decisions led to the magnitude of the catastrophe? What lessons might be learned from these events?

4. **Discuss with students how they will gather facts and information to answer these questions (interviews, history texts, periodicals, photographic archives, etc.).**

5. **After students have had an opportunity to gather this research, allot them a limited period of time to write their news stories. (This simulates the deadlines of a news room.)**

6. **Have teams of students evaluate each other's stories. Tell students to mark the stories (using proofreader's marks if desired); provide direction where possible. Tell them to use their red editor's pencils.** Remind them of the critical writing guidelines they were supposed to follow in their writing. Have the stories managed to follow the rules? Is the headline an attention-getter? Are enough facts presented? Is the reader's interest held? Stories should be interesting, but at the same time include the essential information of what, when, where, who, and how.

7. **Return the proofed articles to the original writers. Allot the teams about 50 minutes to rewrite their final copies and submit them to the Managing Editor (teacher).**

▼ Wrap Up

Have one student from each team read their story aloud to the rest of the class. Students can sketch what images they think the article conveys and compare them to the original photograph. Discuss which stories and/or headlines were most effective. What factors contributed to the best stories? Were the stories that students liked best also entirely informative news items?

Discuss the statement "Nature Rules!" In light of their articles, what do students think it means? Have students create a collage or a public display of their articles. The title of the display should read "Nature Rules!"

Assessment

Have students:
- write news stories based on historic photographs and research (step 5).
- critique and revise news stories (step 6 and *Wrap Up*).
- draw a disaster scene based on information presented in a news article (*Wrap Up*).
- interpret the statement "Nature Rules!" (*Wrap Up*).

Extensions

Organize a field trip to a newspaper office (or invite a reporter or editor as a guest speaker) to give students insight into the development of a news story.

Search local historical newspapers for water-related disasters in your region. Ask students to evaluate (edit) old news accounts for interest and content.

Study the local or regional landscape for sites that seem especially vulnerable to possible disasters. What might be done to avert disaster or to lessen the effects?

Resources

Educational materials produced by newspapers, such as "Newspaper in Education." For more information contact: Pacific Northwest Newspaper Association Foundation, P.O. Box 11128, Tacoma, WA 98411. (206) 272-3611.

The Johnstown Flood. 1989. Johnstown Flood Museum Association. Videocassette.

Lyon, George Ella. 1990. *Come a Tide.* New York, N.Y.: Orchard/ Richard Jackson.

Mayer, Larry, and D. Nash, eds. 1987. *Catastrophic Flooding.* Boston, Mass.: Allen & Unwin.

Powers of Nature. 1978. Washington, D.C.: National Geographic Society.

Project WILD. 1992. Activity "Aquatic Times." *Aquatic Project WILD.* Bethesda, Md.: Western Regional Environmental Education Council.

Simon, Seymour. 1989. *Storms.* New York, N.Y.: Morrow.

Photo Pages

Johnstown Flood. COURTESY: LIBRARY OF CONGRESS.

Dust Bowl. COURTESY: NEBRASKA HISTORICAL SOCIETY

Hurricane Andrew. COURTESY: SOUTH FLORIDA WATER MANAGEMENT DISTRICT, GENE LI

Midwest flood. FRANK OBERLE

Sum of the Parts

■ **Grade Level:**
Upper Elementary, Middle School

■ **Subject Areas:**
Environmental Science, Government

■ **Duration:**
Preparation time: 50 minutes
Activity time: 50 minutes

■ **Setting:** Classroom

■ **Skills:**
Gathering information (observing); Organizing (arranging); Analyzing (identifying components); Interpreting (identifying cause and effect); Applying (proposing solutions)

■ **Charting the Course**
Supplement this activity with activities on runoff ("Just Passing Through," "A-maze-ing Water," and "Rainy-Day Hike") and water use practices ("Common Water"). Aspects of water quality monitoring are introduced in "Macroinvertebrate Mayhem."

■ **Vocabulary**
point source pollution, nonpoint source pollution, Best Management Practices

You have just inherited valuable riverfront property with a new house and a resort on it. On the day you move in, you discover the beach polluted with oil and littered with construction materials and animal waste! Where did all this stuff come from?

▼ **Summary**
Students demonstrate how everyone contributes to the pollution of a river as it flows through a watershed and recognize that everyone's "contribution" can be reduced.

Objectives
Students will:
• distinguish between point and nonpoint source pollution.
• recognize that everyone contributes to and is responsible for a river or lake's water quality.
• identify Best Management Practices to reduce pollution.

Materials
• *Large piece of poster board or newsprint* (Using blue marker, draw and color a river on poster board, as shown below. Divide the stream in half down the middle and crosswise into sections. Each section should include a bit of river and blank space to allow room for students' drawings. The number of sections should correspond with the number of students or groups of students working together. Number the sections on one side of the river in sequential order, placing

numbers in upper left-hand corners and repeat for the other side. Cut out the sections of stream. For durability, sections can be laminated.)
• *Drawing pens and pencils*
• *Items from students' desks (e.g., pencil, paper clip, book)*

Making Connections
In math class, students add a list of figures to obtain the total or "sum" (of the parts). Most students have attended a large gathering (concert, sporting event) and have been amazed at the amount of garbage left behind. Each person in attendance probably did not leave much on the ground, but with 500, 1,000, or more people doing the same, the total amount was large. Taking a closer look at how students can positively or negatively contribute to water quality helps them appreciate their role in water quality management.

Background
The quality of water in a river (or lake) is, to a large extent, a reflection of land uses and natural factors found in its watershed. If soil near a river or lake naturally erodes, chances are the river has sediment and turbidity problems. If

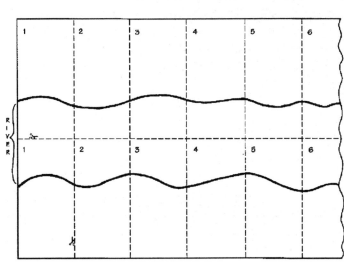

the land has stable vegetative cover, erosion is kept in check. When humans settle and develop land, water quality is affected. Breaking sod, cutting forests, building cities, mining, and other land uses make an impact upon water quality.

Everyone bears responsibility for the health of a watershed and the water systems (rivers, lakes, wetlands, etc.) within a drainage basin. Individual actions, both negative and positive, add up. Understanding a river or lake's water quality and quantity involves investigating the condition of the contributing watershed. If the watershed is polluted, the river will likely be polluted.

Watershed investigations are conducted for many reasons. Some investigations monitor changes in river and stream flows over time, to protect fisheries, to regulate floods, or to meet seasonal demands. Other studies determine the best method of protecting a river or lake from pollutants. One aim of a researcher might be to determine which areas of a watershed contribute the highest percentage of contaminants. This information is vital to policymakers and water managers when determining how best to spend money for improvements. For example, most lake improvement projects address problems in the watershed as well as those of the lake. It would prove fruitless to spend thousands (or even millions) of dollars to clean up a lake, if problems in the watershed will only pollute the lake again.

When watershed managers investigate land use practices that might affect the quality of water, they are concerned with two general sources of pollutants: point and nonpoint.

Point source pollution involves pollutants that are discharged from, and can be traced back to, an identifiable point or source, such as a

Major Sources of NPS Pollution and BMPs

Source	Best Management Practices:
Roads and Streets	• dispose of paints, solvents, and petroleum products at approved disposal sites, not in storm drains or street gutters • fix automobile oil and fuel leaks • stop oil dumping on rural roads • use nonchemical deicers (sand and ash) on roads, sidewalks, and driveways • construct a sediment catch basin to collect storm water runoff • reduce road construction runoff by building terraces and catch basins, and by planting cover crops
Agriculture	• read and follow all labels and ask for application directions before using chemicals, fertilizers, and pesticides • use conservation tillage • use contour farming • use strip cropping • leave filter strips and field borders along wetlands and streams • use a cover crop to protect exposed soil • rotate crops • plant shelter belts and windbreaks • institute pasture management • terrace areas prone to erosion • construct livestock waste collection and treatment ponds for confined livestock • use grassed waterways • seal abandoned or waste disposal wells • fence waterways to reduce riparian zone impact by livestock
Logging	• monitor water entering and leaving cut areas • prevent sediments from reaching streams and lakes by building terraces, catch basins, and natural filters • leave a vegetative buffer zone in riparian areas • maintain and restore effective watersheds • implement a plan to reduce erosion from roads
Mining	• monitor all water entering and leaving mine sites • intercept and reroute uncontaminated water away from contaminated areas (keep clean water clean!) • construct catch basins and terraces, and plant cover crops, to catch sediment and prevent erosion • catch and treat contaminated water (clean contaminated water!) • stabilize stream channels • stabilize mining waste areas to prevent release of materials to streams • maintain buffer strips along streams
Construction	• implement a sediment control plan • plant ground cover to reduce erosion • dispose of solvent, paint, and other wastes at approved disposal sites • build temporary, small dikes to slow and catch runoff • build sediment catch basins to collect construction runoff • build earth berms and filter runoff before water enters stream
Residential	• use nonchemical deicers (sand and ash) on residential driveways and sidewalks • read labels prior to using pesticides and fertilizers • consider xeriscaping • use nonchemical fertilizers (compost) on gardens • dispose of household hazardous waste at approved disposal sites • maintain septic tanks if sewers are not available

factory's discharge pipe or a sewage ditch. Nonpoint source (NPS) pollution occurs when the source of a contaminant is unidentifiable; that is, the pollutant can come from one of many places. Examples of nonpoint source pollution include runoff from agricultural fields containing fertilizers and pesticides, motor oil filtering from urban areas, and sediments from eroded stream banks.

Surface runoff and ground water can transport both point and nonpoint source pollutants. Since point source pollutants are identifiable, they are easier to monitor.

The protection of surface and ground water resources from NPS pollution presents an enormous challenge because of the widespread and diverse nature of the problem. Land and water managers rely on methods called *Best Management Practices*, or BMPs, to describe land use measures designed to reduce or eliminate NPS pollution problems. A list of nonpoint source pollution sources and suggested BMPs can be found in the side bar on the previous page.

Procedure
▼ Warm Up
Determine student knowledge about watersheds by asking them to name several major North American rivers (e.g., Mississippi, Columbia, Missouri, Hudson, and Rio Grande).

Where do these rivers originate (where are the headwaters) and end? How many states does each cross or touch?

Discuss some of the predominant types of land uses found along one river as it flows through a single state. Do students think these practices could affect the river? What do students think the attitude of downstream state residents might be about the water received from their upstream neighbors?

▼ The Activity
1. **Inform students that they have just inherited a piece of riverfront property and a million dollars. Have them list ways they could use the land and the money.**

2. **Pass out "pieces" of property and drawing pens and pencils. Explain that the blue is water and the blank space is land they own. They have one million dollars to develop their land as they wish.** They can farm or ranch; build resorts, homes, factories, or parks; plant forests, log, mine—whatever they like.

3. **When students have completed their drawings, ask them to look in the upper left-hand corner of their property for a number. Explain that each piece is actually a part of a puzzle. Starting with number one, have students assemble their pieces.**

They will construct the stream pathway and adjacent land area in proper order. (The ones should face each other, with the twos next to them, and so forth.)

4. **Have students describe how they developed their land and how they used water. They should identify any of their actions that polluted or added materials to the waterway. Have students represent each of their contributions to the river with an item from their desks (e.g., book, piece of paper, pen, pencil).**

5. **Tell students to take their item(s) and line up in the same order as their pieces of river front property. They are going to pass their pollution pieces downstream. Have them announce what kind of pollutant they are holding before they pass it on.** The ones will pass their item(s) to the twos, the twos will pass everything to the threes, and so on, until the last students are holding all the items.

▼ Wrap Up and Action
After all the items have reached the final students, discuss the activity. How did those students toward the middle or at the end of the river feel? What about their property use plans? Could a student downstream be affected by the actions of a student upstream? Could upstream users

UPSTREAM   DOWNSTREAM

Simulated point and nonpoint source pollution collected during "Sum of the Parts."

Extensions

Instead of a river, have students represent a lake system. One student represents a lake. A group of students encircle the student representing the lake; they are houses around the lake. Other students, standing in lines extending from the lake, can be streams flowing to the lake. Students pass their item(s) downstream and into the lake until all the items are held by the person in the middle who represents the lake.

Have students adapt the activity to represent a river system that includes tributaries flowing into a main channel.

Complete the main activity using real water users within the watershed where students live. Or assign roles (farmers, suburban dwellers, etc.) to students and have them develop their land accordingly. How would they manage their land to protect water resources?

Resources

Braus, Judy, ed. 1990. *NatureScope: Pollution, Problems and Solutions.* Washington, D.C.: National Wildlife Federation.

🍎 Collier, James Lincoln. 1986. *When the Stars Begin to Fall.* New York, N.Y.: Delacorte.

🍎 Gay, Kathlyn. 1990. *Water Pollution.* New York, N.Y.: Watts.

🍎 Greene, Carol. 1991. *Caring for Our Water.* Hillside, N.J.: Enslow.

Miller, G. Tyler, Jr. 1990. *Resource Conservation and Management.* Belmont, Calif: Wadsworth Publishing Company.

Myers, Carl F., and Hal Wise. 1989. "Non-Point Sources of Water Pollution: A New Law for an Old Problem." *Western Wildlands* (Winter).

alter the water quality of those downstream?

Tell students to reclaim their items. Explain that the items easily identifiable as their own simulate point source pollution. Other items (e.g., pencils, paper clips, notebook paper) may be more difficult to claim, because these kinds of pollutants originated from multiple sources. Tell students these represent nonpoint source pollution.

As a follow-up, have each student write one paragraph detailing ways to reduce the amount of pollution he or she contributed. (Share the *Major Sources of NPS Pollution and BMPs* from **Background**.) Students can research the regulations governing waterfront property in their communities. If they believe their waterways

are poorly treated, they may want to write letters to local government officials supporting environmentally sound land use legislation.

Assessment

Have students:
- express their opinions about individual contributions to total water quality (*Wrap Up*).
- write a paragraph identifying what they can do to protect water quality (*Wrap Up*).
- discriminate between point and nonpoint source pollutants (*Wrap Up*).

Upon completing the activity, for further assessment have students:
- design a community that uses Best Management Practices that allow for minimum contribution of pollutants.

Water Meter

When was the last time you thought about the amount of water you use every day?

▼ Summary
Students construct a "Water Meter" to keep track of their water use.

Objectives
Students will:
- become aware of their daily use of water.

Materials
- *5" x 7" index cards*
- *Copies of How to Make a Personal Water Meter*
- *Red ribbon*
- *White ribbon*
- *Glue or tape*
- *Scissors*
- *Ruler*

Making Connections
Students use water throughout the day. Monitoring water use helps students analyze the quantity of water they use and how they use it. Recognizing how involved they are with water on a daily basis should foster an appreciation for the resource.

Background
Water is so much a part of us and our routines that we often take it for granted. We use water every day in a variety of ways: for drinking, cooking, cleaning, bathing, watering lawns, washing cars, watering plants, rehydrating prepared foods, making ice, watering pets, filling and cleaning aquariums, and so forth. This list does not include indirect uses of water; water is vital to the manufacturing of our automobiles and the production of our CDs. In many communities water meters measure household water use. This information is used to prepare household water bills and to calculate a community's water use.

Procedure
▼ Warm Up
Have students list ways they use water. Ask them to estimate how much water they think they use each day. (Refer to *How to Make a Personal Water Meter* for water use ideas.)

▼ The Activity
1. **Have students construct a *Personal Water Meter* according to the directions on page 273. Tell them that for one week they are going to keep track of how much water they use each day.** Quantities involved in common uses of water are included with the ruler. If necessary, students may add categories for other uses and adjust the amounts to better match how much water they use. Remind students that to remain healthy, they need water and should not stint their water consumption. Their goal is to develop an awareness of their water use.

NOTE: The gallons-to-liters conversions are rounded figures. Students can more accurately convert their water use to gallons or liters by using the following conversion rates: 1 gallon = 3.785 liters, 1 liter = 0.2642 gallons.

2. **Explain that every time students use water, they should slide the ribbon to indicate the number of gallons or liters used.** The junction of the two colors of ribbon indicates the current amount. Each morning they should record yesterday's total and return the ribbon to the beginning. For water uses that involve the whole family, students can divide the amount of water by the number of family members. For example, a load of laundry uses about 40

■ **Grade Level:**
Upper Elementary, Middle School

■ **Subject Areas:**
Environmental Science, Mathematics

■ **Duration:**
Preparation time: 50 minutes
Activity time: up to one week

■ **Setting:** Classroom

■ **Skills:**
Gathering information (collecting data); Organizing (measuring, graphing)

■ **Charting the Course**
This activity serves as a good introduction to home water uses. Students should understand that water is a shared, limited resource ("A Drop in the Bucket" and "Common Water"). "Money Down the Drain" enhances this activity. Indirect uses of water ("Water Works") relate to concepts in this activity. More efficient uses of water are introduced in "Every Drop Counts," which would be an excellent follow-up to this activity.

■ **Vocabulary**
direct water use, indirect water use

gallons (152 l); if there are four family members, each member uses about 10 gallons (38 l).

3. **Students can also record their water use on a daily bar graph and supplement their measurements with journal entries.**

4. **Students may think of other water uses not listed in the data table. Encourage them to measure these amounts.** For example, many people leave water running when cooking and cleaning; have students calculate how many gallons or liters pour from their faucets each minute and multiply this amount by how long water is left running.

▼ *Wrap Up and Action*

Have students share their results. What do students think about the amount of water they use each day? In one week? Have the class combine results. Challenge students to calculate how much water they might use in a year. Students may want to compare the amount of water they use in a period of time (e.g., a week, month, year, or life-time) to known quantities. For example, an Olympic-size swimming pool contains 60,000 gallons (228,000 l) of water; 1,000 gallons of water is about 5 cubic meters; and a milk jug holds one gallon (3.8 l).

Do students believe they have accurately represented the total

amount of water used? Remind them of indirect uses, such as the water required to grow their food, make their paper, manufacture their blue jeans, produce energy for their use, and so forth. What would happen to the water meter if indirect uses of water were included?

Have students make water meters for their family and friends.

Assessment

Have students:
* monitor how much water they use each day (steps 2–4).

Upon completing the activity, for further assessment have students:

* write a newspaper article or editorial about how much water people use every day.

Extensions

Students can make a collage, with pictures cut from magazines and newspapers, identifying ways water is used.

Students may want to investigate ways they can reduce their water consumption. They can compare water use before and after imple-menting water conservation practices.

Resources

The Story of Drinking Water. Contact: American Water Works Association, 6666 W. Quincy Ave., Denver, CO 80235. (303) 794-7711.

Water Watchers: Water Conservation Curriculum for Junior High School Science and Social Studies Classes. 1989. Contact: Massachusetts Water Resources Authority, Charlestown Navy Yard, 100 First Avenue, Boston, MA 02129. (617) 242-7110.

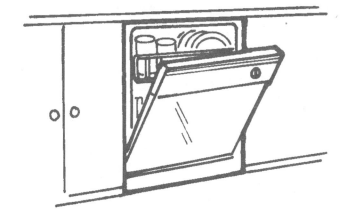

How to Make a Personal Water Meter

1. Cut out the *Personal Water Meter* ruler pattern along the heavy line and paste on an index card.

2. Cut two pieces of different-colored ribbon, each about ¹/₂ inch (2 cm) longer than the length of the ruler in the *Personal Water Meter*. Overlap ends of different ribbons and glue or tape the end of one ribbon to the end of the other.

3. Cut a slot at each end of the paper ruler. Insert the ribbon into one cut. Thread the other end of the ribbon through the other slot. Glue or tape the two ends together. The ribbon should be tight, but slide smoothly through the slots.

4. Fold the ruler along the dotted line and tape the edges together.

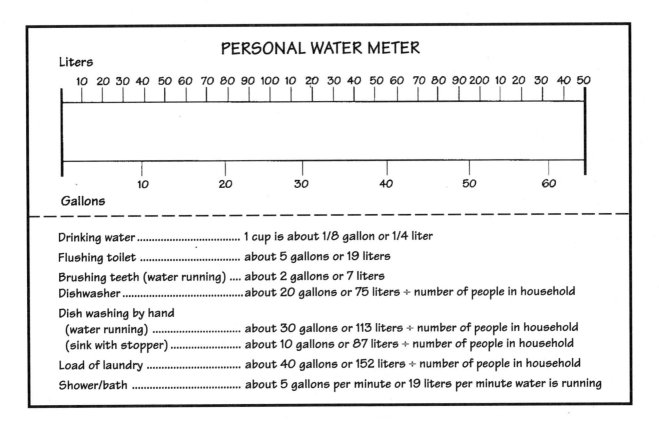

PERSONAL WATER METER

Liters
10 20 30 40 50 60 70 80 90 100 10 20 30 40 50 60 70 80 90 200 10 20 30 40 50

10   20   30   40   50   60

Gallons

Drinking water .... 1 cup is about 1/8 gallon or 1/4 liter
Flushing toilet .... about 5 gallons or 19 liters
Brushing teeth (water running) .... about 2 gallons or 7 liters
Dishwasher ....about 20 gallons or 75 liters ÷ number of people in household
Dish washing by hand
  (water running) .... about 30 gallons or 113 liters ÷ number of people in household
  (sink with stopper) .... about 10 gallons or 87 liters ÷ number of people in household
Load of laundry .... about 40 gallons or 152 liters ÷ number of people in household
Shower/bath .... about 5 gallons per minute or 19 liters per minute water is running

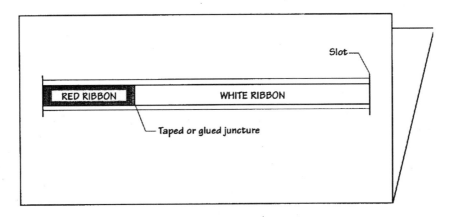

Slot

RED RIBBON   WHITE RIBBON

Taped or glued juncture

Water Works

■ Grade Level:
Upper Elementary,
Middle School

■ Subject Areas:
Government,
Environmental Science

■ Duration:
Preparation time: 30 minutes
Activity time: 50 minutes

■ Setting: Classroom

■ Skills:
Gathering information (observing); Analyzing (identifying components and relationships); Interpreting (inferring)

■ Charting the Course
Students learn that water is a common resource shared by all water users in "Common Water." "Water Meter" focuses on direct uses of water in the home. Students prioritize different community water uses in "Choices and Preferences, Water Index." In "Wet-Work Shuffle" students explore a variety of careers related to water and water resource management.

■ Vocabulary
direct water use, indirect water use

What do a loaf of bread, a sheet of paper, and an automobile have in common?

▼ Summary
Students create a "water web" to illustrate the interdependence among water users and producers.

Objectives
Students will:
- distinguish between direct and indirect uses of water.
- illustrate the interconnectedness of water users in a community.
- demonstrate the complexity of resolving water shortages among interdependent community water users.

Materials
- *Copy of **Descriptions of Water Users***
- *Index cards*
- *Marking pens*
- *Tape or string*
- *2 plastic milk jugs* (Label one jug "surface water" and the other "ground water." Tie the two handles together with string. Fill jugs with water and cap jugs.)
- *Large ball of string or yarn or index cards, cut into strips*

Making Connections
When students think of using water, they probably consider direct uses: drinking a glass of water, brushing their teeth, or taking showers. They may not realize they are using water when they eat a pear, crumple a piece of paper, or listen to the radio. The complexity of water conservation issues becomes more apparent as students experience the needs of and interconnectedness among water users.

Background
People use water for direct and indirect purposes. Direct purposes include bathing, drinking, and cooking. Indirect uses of water include the large quantities of water needed to grow grains for our bread, to process wood for making our paper, and to produce steel used in the automobiles we drive.

Agriculture, industry, and power production are society's major water users. Sometimes we are critical of the amount of water a manufacturer requires to create a product; however, we are often the major consumers of that product. To resolve this dilemma, many water users are searching for ways to maintain production but reduce water consumption.

Today, many farmers practice more efficient irrigation methods. Manufacturers use less water by incorporating recycled materials into their products or by recycling water within their factories. For example, producing a ton of recycled paper uses 60,000 gallons (230,000 l) less water than producing a ton of virgin paper. Individuals who conserve water and energy and use recycled products support the efforts of conscientious manufacturers and farmers, ensuring the availability of water for all water users.

Procedure
▼ Warm Up
Have students list the ways they use water. If students do not include indirect uses of water, ask them if they think they use water when they ride in a car or read a newspaper. Explain that producing both cars and paper requires water. Have students suggest other ways they indirectly use water.

Ask students to guess how much water is required to make each of the items listed in the box on page 275. Do not tell them if their guesses are accurate.

274

A pair of jeans made from cotton	1,800 gallons (6,840 l)
A 2-pound loaf of bread	1,000 gallons (3,800 l)
A pound of hamburger	4,000 gallons (15,200 l)
A 12-ounce can of soda	16.5 gallons (62.7 l)
The ton of finished steel used to make a car	32,000 gallons (121,600 l)
40 sheets of paper	100 gallons (380 l)

▼ *The Activity*

1.   **Instruct each student to select a water user from the** *Description of Water Users* **or from a class-generated list.** Make nametags to identify water users. (Students may research how their water user depends on this resource.)

2.   **Have each student read silently the description of his or her water user. Ask "water users" to consider how they depend on products and services supplied by other users.** For example, the steel manufacturer uses water to process steel and wash away waste materials. The production of steel requires not only water, but also energy; therefore, the car manufacturer is dependent on the power plant.

3.   **Clear an area in the room. Place two milk jugs, tied together with string at the handles, on a desk or chair in the middle of the cleared** area. **Tie the loose end of the ball of yarn to the string holding the two jugs together.** Explain that the jugs represent sources of water and the ball of yarn symbolizes the water user's need for water.

4.   **Ask students to stand in a circle around the jugs of water.**

5.   **Select a student to describe the goods or services his or her water user provides and how this product or service uses water. Run the ball of yarn to the student (who remains holding the yarn) and back to the jugs (around the string holding the two jugs together).** This indicates that this water user consumed water. This can be repeated for each student.

6.   **Choose one water user and hand him or her the ball of yarn. Ask other students to raise their hands if they use the goods or services offered by that student.**

7.   **Tell that student (Student 1) to pass the ball of yarn to one of the students (Student 2) who raised his or her hand. Ask Student 2 to describe how he or she uses the products or services of Student 1.**

8.   **Ask if other students use the products manufactured by Student 2.** Have Student 2 pass the ball to another student (Student 3). Have all students repeat the process until connections are made among all or most class members.

9.   **To emphasize the interdependencies among water users, have one student tug gently on the yarn. Ask those who felt the pull to raise their hands.** The tug symbolizes reliance on both water and that student's product.

10. **At some time during the activity, the water jugs may shift or be lifted from the chair or table.** Explain that this indicates the supply is being overextended. Ask students if they think one water user should leave the circle. What will happen if one student lets go?

NOTE: As an alternative way to make connections among water users, give each student five strips of paper. Have each student write the name of his or her water user on each of the five strips. Students may decorate the "business card" of their water user with illustrations of goods or services provided. One at a time, or in small groups, have students distribute their cards to other water users on whom they depend for goods or services. Students should end up holding strips of paper with names of other interdependent water users. Conclude by having students read aloud their cards and describe the connections they have made.

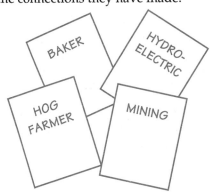

Water users demonstrate their interdependence.

▼ *Wrap Up*

Discuss the results of the activity. Have students create a diagram displaying how water users depend upon the goods and services provided by other water users.

Inform students of the quantities of water used to produce the materials listed in the *Warm Up*. Do any water users in the activity supply these materials? Do students use any of these materials? If community water supplies are overextended, how would the community decide which manufacturer should reduce water consumption? Students may find it difficult to single out one manufacturer. They may determine that causing all water users to conserve water is more fair.

Have students contact local manufacturers, asking them how they use water and what conservation measures they practice. Students can create a mural of the waterworks of their community. Include how community members use water, depend upon each other, and, if appropriate, conserve water.

Assessment

Have students:
- describe their direct and indirect uses of water (*Warm Up*).
- draw a diagram showing how water users rely on the goods and services provided by other water users (*Wrap Up*).
- create a mural illustrating the waterworks and interdependencies of their community (*Wrap Up*).

Upon completing the activity, for further assessment have students:
- conduct a town meeting where proposed solutions to a community water shortage are being discussed—highlight the difficulties of identifying one particular water user whose use should be restricted or eliminated to help solve the problem.

Extensions

Tell students a bottle of food coloring represents a source of pollution. Place a drop in the jug. Have students explain how water quality affects the quantity of water available to water users.

Have students form groups of common water users. How do groups relate to other water user groups? Although a common bond is shared in our need for water, discuss how conflicts can arise among water user groups.

Resources

🍎 Hammer, Trudy J. 1985. *Water Resources*. New York, N.Y.: Watts.

Miller, G. Tyler, Jr. 1990. *Resource Conservation and Management*. Belmont, Calif.: Wadsworth Publishing Company.

🍎 Pringle, Laurence. 1982. *Water: The Next Great Resource Battle*. New York, N.Y.: Macmillan.

276

Description of Water Users

In addition to the descriptions listed below, students may research a specific water user during the week prior to this activity.

Agriculture: Water is used to produce food and fiber for processing and consumption.

Sugar cane grower: Uses water to irrigate crops and transport chemicals (pesticides and fertilizers) to crops.

Cattle rancher: Uses water to grow food and provide drinking water for cattle, and to clean their areas for living and feeding, transporting waste to holding ponds.

Fish farmer: Uses water to raise fish to maturity in rearing ponds, and to carry waste from the ponds.

Wheat farmer: Uses water to irrigate crops.

Dairy farmer: Uses water to grow food and provide drinking water for cows, and to sanitize milking equipment and stalls.

Mining: Water is used in the extraction process of raw materials (coal, iron, gold, copper, sand, and gravel).

Miner: Uses water to carry and wash rock material during the mineral removal processes.

Sand and gravel company: Uses water to wash fine soil and rock material out of sand and gravel formations. Sand and gravel are used in cement and road construction.

Logging: Water is used to grow and harvest trees.

Forest manager: Uses water to support tree growth and control fires.

Logging company: Uses water to float rafts of logs (on rivers and lakes) to collection points.

Transporting/Shipping: Water (rivers, seas, oceans) is used to transport raw materials and finished products to points of distribution (ports).

Slurry pipeline owner: Uses water to transport pulverized coal through pipelines to distant coal-fired power plants.

Ship's crew: Uses water to haul raw materials (e.g., logs, oil, gas, wheat) and finished products (e.g., automobiles, appliances, processed food) to points of transfer.

Business/Industry: Water is used in the processing and manufacturing of goods (cars, food, medical supplies, etc.).

Steel producer: Uses large volumes of water to process iron ore into steel.

Textile manufacturer: Uses water to wash and process raw materials (e.g., wool, cotton, mohair). Dye is mixed with water to color fabric.

Soft drink company: Uses water to produce soft drinks and to sanitize equipment.

Paper mill: Uses water to transport pulp fibers for paper making and to carry away waste.

Chemical manufacturer: Uses water in the production of pesticides and fertilizers.

Wildlife: Water provides habitat for countless plant and animal species.

Mammals: Beavers, muskrats, and otters live in and near waterways.

Fish: Trout, salmon, and carp live in water and eat organisms that live in water.

Insects: Aquatic insects are a food source for many other organisms.

Vegetation: Trees and other plants use water in photosynthesis and to transport nutrients.

Recreation: People recreate in and around water for exercise and enjoyment.

Cruise ship: People travel to many parts of the world in cruise ships .

Fishing: People catch fish in rivers, lakes, and oceans.

Water theme park: Uses water to transport people on exciting and fun rides.

Scuba diver: People enjoy exploring underwater environments.

Winter sports: Snow and ice provide fun for skaters, skiers, and sledders.

Power Generation: Water is used to generate electricity.

Hydropower plant: Water flowing in rivers is stored behind dams in reservoirs. As water is released by the dam, it turns turbines that generate electricity.

Nuclear power plant: Uses water in cooling towers to maintain safe operating temperatures.

Coal-fired power plant: Burning coal produces steam heat that turns turbines, creating electricity.

Community: Water is used by community members for domestic, maintenance, and recreational purposes.

Domestic users: Water is used in a multitude of ways in and around the home.

Fire department: Uses water to extinguish fires.

Street cleaner: Uses water to wash oil, litter, and other materials from streets.

Restaurant owner: Uses water to cook meals, clean the kitchen, wash tables and floor, and water lawns.

Park: Uses water in fountains and reflecting ponds and for landscaping needs.

Where Are the Frogs?

Every spring you look forward to hearing the frogs at dusk. One year you notice the evenings are silent. What happened to the frogs?

Grade Level:
Middle School

Subject Areas:
Environmental Science

Duration:
Preparation:
Part I: no preparation
Part II: 50 minutes
Part III: 15 minutes

Activity time:
Part I: 15 minutes
Part II: up to one month (plant monitoring)
Part III: 30 minutes

Setting: Classroom

Skills:
Gathering information (measuring, collecting, observing); Organizing (matching); Analyzing (comparing and contrasting); Applying (predicting, experimenting); Presenting

Charting the Course
Students should know the components of the water molecule ("Hangin' Together"). Students can explore the implications of acid precipitation in "Whose Problem Is It?" Activities involving issue investigation include "Perspectives," "Water Court," and "Hot Water."

Vocabulary
acid precipitation, acid, base

▼ Summary

Through experimentation and a simulation, students learn how acidic water has endangered the quality of aquatic life in some parts of the country.

Objectives

Students will:
- illustrate the meaning of pH.
- analyze the effects of acidic water on plant and animal life.
- describe how acid rain can affect ecosystems.

Materials
- *Tape of frog sounds* (optional)
- *Paper to make pH labels* (see page 283)

To monitor pH and plant growth, each group will need the following:
- *3 jars with lids*
- *Lemon juice*
- *Graduated cylinder*
- *pH paper*
- *3 milk cartons* (Remove tops and punch drain holes in bottom of cartons.)
- *Potting soil*
- *1 type of seed* (e.g., marigold, tomato, bean)
- *Water*
- *Copies of pH and Plants Activity Sheet*
- *Copies of pH and Plants Observation Sheet*

Making Connections

The topic of acid rain frequently appears in the news, especially in the northeastern United States. Students may have seen pictures of statues, forests, and lakes damaged by acid precipitation. Learning about acid precipitation helps students appreciate the connections between air and water quality.

Background

Water molecules are composed of two hydrogen atoms and one oxygen atom (H_2O). Sometimes the water molecules separate or dissociate: $H_2O <\longrightarrow H^+ + OH^-$. This is called ionization. Ions have unequal numbers of protons and electrons. If an ion has more protons than electrons, it will have a positive charge; if it has more electrons, its charge will be negative. The hydrogen ion (H^+) has lost its electron to the hydroxide ion (OH^-); therefore, the hydrogen ion has a positive charge, while hydroxide has a negative charge. Very few water molecules ionize, but life processes depend on the small number that do.

When water dissociates, it produces an equal number of hydrogen ions and hydroxide ions. When another compound that ionizes is introduced, the ions of water and of the compound will react or combine with each other. Sometimes, hydrogen ions react more, other times hydroxide ions do.

If a solution (of water and another compound) has more unattached hydrogen ions than hydroxide ions, it is acidic. If more hydroxide ions remain, the solution is basic or alkaline. The level or amount of hydrogen ions in solution is measured by a pH (potency of hydrogen) scale. The scale ranges from 0 to 14. A solution with a pH of 7 is said to be neutral, because it has equal amounts of hydrogen and hydroxide ions. Bases have pH levels ranging from 8 to 14. A pH of 12 indicates a very strong base. Acids have a pH ranging from 1 to 6; a 2 is a very strong acid.

The relative levels of hydrogen and hydroxide ions are critical to organisms

Sample Range of Tolerance for pH Levels

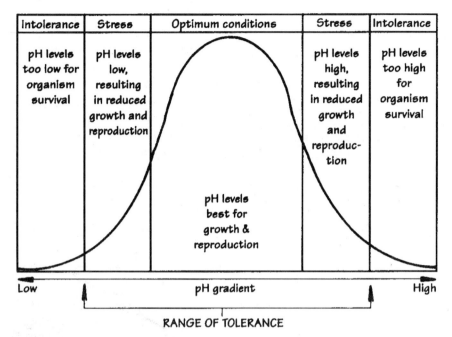

Intolerance	Stress	Optimum conditions	Stress	Intolerance
pH levels too low for organism survival	pH levels low, resulting in reduced growth and reproduction	pH levels best for growth & reproduction	pH levels high, resulting in reduced growth and reproduction	pH levels too high for organism survival

Low — pH gradient — High

RANGE OF TOLERANCE

All living organisms have a range of tolerance for varying environmental conditions—temperature, O_2 levels, salinity, pH, etc. Within the range of tolerance exist optimum conditions. Growth and reproduction are most favorable for species living under these conditions. Organisms living at either extreme of this range of tolerance can survive, but growth and reproduction may be adversely affected. Outside of this range of tolerance, species cannot survive.

Reducing the pH of lake water (increasing its acidity) harms aquatic organisms. Most fish species can tolerate a pH range of 5 to 8. A pH range of 7.1 to 7.5 represents optimum conditions for growth. Within a pH range of 5 to 6, growth and reproduction rates drop. At a pH of less than 5, fish are unable to reproduce. Most fish do not survive in water with a pH of less than 4. In addition, acidic water reacts with the substrata of the lake, either adding chemicals to or removing chemicals from the water. These chemicals further harm organisms. The organisms' ability to smell and see may be impaired, gills become clogged, and eggs do not hatch. Even when the animal is not directly harmed by acidic conditions, its life is still endangered because what it eats has been damaged or eliminated. Ironically, some beautiful lakes appear crystal clear because they are biologically dead or severely altered, their waters inhospitable to aquatic organisms. However, if conditions improve, populations can, in some cases, recover.

Some environments are more resistant to acid rain. They contain minerals such as calcium carbonates, which act as buffers and neutralize acids. Some people propose adding buffers to water sources affected by acid rain. This is called "liming"; over a long period of time, powdered

because of their effects on chemical reactions. Systems within the human body function to maintain pH balance. The pH of blood is about 7.4, gastric juices are about 2, and saliva is about 6.5.

Many parts of the world are being affected by acid precipitation. In the northeastern United States, acid rain has been cited as a probable cause for the decline of certain species of trees. Increasing levels of acidity in lakes are responsible for making these ecosystems inhospitable to many aquatic organisms. Buildings are also affected, because acid increases the rate at which minerals and metals deteriorate.

Rainwater has a pH of around 5.6; therefore, it is naturally acidic. Sometimes the pH level of rain (and other forms of precipitation, such as snow and fog) is reduced, resulting in increased acidity. This occurs when certain chemicals, mainly sulfur oxides (SO_x) and nitrogen

oxides (NO_x), mix with atmospheric water, forming sulfuric acid and nitric acid. Some Earth processes, such as volcanic eruptions, add these oxides to the air. Cars and factories introduce excess SO_x and NO_x through the combustion of fossil fuels.

The formation of acid precipitation occurs in the atmosphere's upper levels. Circulating global winds often carry clouds of acidic water droplets many miles from the source of the pollutant. As a result, the areas most affected by acid precipitation are often at great distances from large factories or urban settings.

Acid precipitation has drastically altered the quality of plant and aquatic life in some areas. Plants are damaged when acid rain falls on their leaves. Acid rain alters the chemistry of soil, making necessary minerals unavailable to plants. The trees of forests affected by acid precipitation have yellowed and damaged leaves.

limestone is added to an affected lake. However, the best solution is to correct the conditions that cause acid rain. Stricter air pollution laws (such as the Clean Air Act) and advances in technology (using scrubbers in smokestacks, prewashing coal to remove impurities, burning low sulfur coal) are beginning to reduce the amount of sulfur oxides and nitrogen oxides from industrial output and car exhaust. Because acid rain is a global issue, it requires a global response.

Procedure

▼ Warm Up

Show students a glass of water and ask them to imagine what the water molecules look like. Have them create a quick sketch. Confirm that students' molecules have two hydrogen and one oxygen atom each. Do they believe that water molecules always remain intact? What would happen if the water molecule was split?

Inform students this happens all the time. However, when the balance of the parts in the molecules becomes uneven, the quality of water changes. In some situations this imbalance is necessary for life (e.g., gastric juices for digestion). In other cases, it can produce detrimental effects, like acid rain.

Tell students that they will be acting out the splitting of a water molecule.

▼ The Activity

Part I

1. **Tell students they are going to demonstrate a special characteristic of water.**

2. **Divide the class into thirds. Indicate that students in one group are oxygen atoms, and those in the second and third groups are hydrogen**
atoms. **Have the hydrogens write the letter "e" on pieces of paper and pin them to their shirts (or place them in their pockets). The "e" represents the hydrogen's electron.**

3. **Tell students to form groups of three to represent water molecules (two hydrogens and one oxygen).** Ask the "hydrogens" to stand on either side of the "oxygen" to illustrate a water molecule. The class now represents water that has all molecules intact.

4. **Explain that water molecules do not always stay complete; sometimes molecules will break apart or dissociate. Have two or three of the groups break up into hydroxide (OH⁻) and hydrogen (H⁺) ions.** One student will be a lone hydrogen ion, and the other two students will be joined as oxygen and hydrogen in a hydroxide ion.

5. **Instruct each lone hydrogen ion to give his or her "e" to the hydroxide ion.** This represents an electron that has been lost by the hydrogen ion and gained by the hydroxide. Explain that hydrogen is a positive ion (possessing one proton and no electrons) and hydroxide is a negative ion (possessing an extra electron).

6. **Inform students that this represents a neutral water sample, because there are equal numbers of OH⁻ and H⁺. Tell students who split apart to recombine (back to water) and have another two or three groups dissociate; the solution still remains neutral.**

7. **Tell students that a compound that attracts the OH⁻ has been added to the solution. Remove three or four hydroxides from the mix. Tell students that now there are more H⁺ than OH⁻. Explain that this makes the solution acidic.** Have the hydroxides go back in solution, this time removing the hydrogen ions to make a basic solution.

8. **Describe the pH scale to students, and explain which levels are neutral, acidic, and basic. Show students pH test paper and explain how to use it.**

Part II

1. **Read students the following paragraphs:**

(If possible, have a tape of the sound of frogs ready to play in the background.)

Although Jane now lives in another part of the country, she grew up in northern New York State. She remembers enjoying beautiful fall seasons and playing in the snow. But her favorite time of the year was spring. *(Begin tape.)*

In spring, snows melted, green buds erupted from trees, and plants blossomed. With warm feelings, she remembers sitting on the screened porch at dusk with her parents, listening to the sound of frogs. *(Allow tape to play for a while, then turn the tape off.)*

Now, after many years, Jane is returning home. It is spring. Although the town has grown, the flowers and budding trees still make

Acid rain damage to trees. COURTESY: CAROLINA BIOLOGICAL SUPPLY COMPANY.

her smile. Everything smells new and fresh. In the early evening, she sits with friends on the front porch and shares memories. But as the night grows darker, Jane feels that something is not quite right, something is missing . . . then she remembers. Where are the songs of the frogs?

2. **Ask students what they think happened to the frogs.** Tell them that in some parts of the country, especially in the Northeast, populations of frogs and other aquatic species are declining. Explain that portions of northern New York State, as well as other sections of the Northeast, are affected by acid rain.

3. **Ask students to share what they know about acid precipitation. Supplement student responses with background about acid precipita-** **tion. Explain that acid rain harms trees and other sensitive organisms, such as frogs.** Students may want to collect samples of rain and snow from their area and measure the pH. Do they think their area has a problem with acid precipitation? Could their area be a source of the pollutants that cause acid precipitation?

4. **Hand out** *pH and Plants Activity Sheets* **to groups of students and have them conduct a simple experiment to investigate the effects of acidic water on the germination and growth of plants.** Have students make weekly or biweekly observations and record them on the *pH and Plants Observation Sheet.*

5. **After students have conducted the plant/pH experiment, have them discuss the following questions:**

- How did the plants react to the different types of water?
- How do the results compare with your predictions?
- How did the control plant help you determine if and how acid water affected the other plants?
- Why was it important to make sure each plant was treated the same in every way except the type of water used?
- How do your results compare to a group who used the same plant as yours? What could be reasons for any differences?
- How do your results compare to a group who used a different plant? What could be reasons for any differences? You may want to research the best growing conditions for the plants used by the class. Can some plants tolerate acidic conditions better than others?

Part III

1. To further students' understanding of the effects of acid precipitation, have them participate in the following activity.

2. Describe the following two lakes (Lake A and Lake B) to students.

Two lakes are the same size and depth. Lake A has clear water; you can see to the bottom. The water in Lake B has a greenish color, and you can't see to the bottom.

Ask students which lake they think would be best for fishing or for observing aquatic wildlife. What else would they like to know to help them make a choice? Respond to their questions with the following information. If necessary, provide clues.

Lake B has six species of fish and a variety of amphibians, including salamanders and frogs. The fish and frogs eat aquatic insects and small organisms that live in the water. An abundance of aquatic plants provides organisms with shelter and food. Lake A has none of these. The pH of Lake A is 4.2, the pH of Lake B is 6.3. Both lakes are in areas where the pH of rainfall is approximately 4. The earth around Lake B contains limestone, while Lake A is surrounded by granite.

3. Have students participate in the following demonstration to show what has happened to Lakes A and B.

4. Divide the class in half. Tell one half they represent surface water running into a lake and the other half that they are aquatic organisms. (If the number of students is uneven, the extra student should be in the water half.) Distribute pH labels for aquatic organisms to students representing aquatic organisms. (Have students hold labels in front of them.) Explain that the pH value represents ranges of pH in which the animals can live.

5. Designate a portion of the room as a lake and have the organisms "swim" or move around within the boundaries. Arrange tables or chairs in a group around the lake to symbolize soil through which water filters as it makes its way to the lake. Water students should stand on the other side of these desks.

6. Tell students Scenario 1 takes place in an area that does not receive acid rain. Distribute pH labels to students representing water (pH 6.5). Inform students that rain has recently fallen (or snow is melting).

7. The students representing water should move through the desks or chairs. When they arrive in the lake, the aquatic organisms should try to match up with water students who are within their pH range. (All aquatic organisms should find a match.)

8. Tell students to separate into two groups again. Scenario 2 takes place at Lake B; the area receives acid rain. Distribute pH values to water students (pH 4.5 should face out). What do students think will happen to aquatic organisms?

pH Labels for Aquatic Organisms

(Write these labels on notebook-sized paper or index cards; make enough copies for half of the students in the class.)

MUSSEL pH RANGE 8 TO 5.5	CLAM pH RANGE 8 TO 5.5	EEL pH RANGE 8 TO 5.5	BROOK TROUT pH RANGE 8 TO 5.5	MAYFLY pH RANGE 8 TO 5.5	SALAMANDER pH RANGE 8 TO 5.5
FROG pH RANGE 8 TO 5.5	SALMON pH RANGE 8 TO 5	BASS pH RANGE 8 TO 5	CRAYFISH pH RANGE 8 TO 5	YELLOW PERCH pH RANGE 8 TO 4.5	WATER BEETLE pH RANGE 8 TO 4.5

pH Labels for Water

(Make enough labels for each water student.)

For the first scenario, all waters should have labels reading 6.5. For the second scenario, make labels that read 4.5 on one side and 6 on the other. The pH for the third scenario is 4.5.

9. **Explain that Lake B is surrounded by thick soil that contains a rock called limestone. The rock acts like a buffer, and will reduce the acidity of solutions. Show water students how they can flip their paper to make a new pH value of 6.**

10. **Instruct the water students that their beginning pH is 4.5. They filter into the lake as before, but sometime during the process they flip their cards, so that their pH value changes to 6.** Once again, the aquatic organisms should find a match.

11. **Explain that now students are at Lake A (Scenario 3). The soil around Lake A is thin and comes from a rock called granite, which does not act like a buffer.**

12. **Distribute pH values to the water students (pH 4.5). This time, after they filter through the soil, their pH will not change.** Many of the organisms will not find matches. What do students think will happen to the aquatic organisms? Explain how acidic water affects some aquatic organisms.

▼ *Wrap Up and Action*

Have students summarize how acid rain affects living organisms and ecosystems. Have them describe what they believe a healthy lake (i.e., a lake providing optimum conditions for organisms) would look like. What would a lake with a pH of 4 look like? Describe the irony of a crystal-clear blue lake that appears "healthy," but is actually biologically dead. They should supplement their descriptions with findings from their experiment and the results of the simulation. Have students search magazines and newspapers for information about acid precipitation and create a collage that presents the impacts. They may want to contact their legislators or local industry

representatives to learn about air pollution regulations designed to limit acid precipitation. They could write a letter to these parties expressing their views about the issue of acid precipitation.

Assessment

Have students:
- demonstrate the difference between acidic and basic solutions (*Part I*, steps 4–7).
- conduct an experiment showing how plants are affected by acidic water (*Part II*, step 4).
- identify the role of a control in helping to analyze the results of an experiment (*Part II*, step 5).
- compare and contrast their predictions with the outcome of their plant/pH experiment (*Part II*, step 5).
- explain why a clear lake may not be a healthy lake (*Wrap Up*).
- create a collage that displays the effects of acid precipitation on living and nonliving things (*Wrap Up*).

Upon completing the activity, for further assessment have students:
- identify which solution has more free H^+ ions, lemon juice or ammonia.

Extensions

To study the buffering effects of various types of soil, pour water of various acidic levels through a container filled with calcium carbonate. Record the pH of the water before and after.

How do plants react to basic conditions? Have students repeat the plant experiment, using a basic solution.

Resources

Acid Rain Foundation, Inc. 1410 Varsity Dr., Raleigh, NC 27606. (919) 828-9443.

🍎 *About Acid Rain.* 1988. South Deerfield, Mass.: Channing L. Bete Co., Inc. Booklet. To order, phone (800) 628-7733 and request booklet number 45047.

🍎 Miller, Christine G., and Louise Berry. 1986. *Acid Rain: A Source Book for Young People.* New York, N.Y.: Messner (Simon & Schuster Trade).

Miller, G. Tyler, Jr. 1990. *Resource Conservation and Management.* Belmont, Calif.: Wadsworth Publishing Company.

🍎 Pringle, Laurence. 1988. *Rain of Troubles: The Science and Politics of Acid Rain.* New York, N.Y.: Macmillan.

Notes ▼

pH and Plants Activity Sheet

Name _____   Responsibilities: _____

Name _____   Responsibilities: _____

Name _____   Responsibilities: _____

Name _____   Responsibilities: _____

You will need: ☐ 3 jars with lids   ☐ Lemon juice   ☐ Graduated cylinder   ☐ pH paper   ☐ Potting soil

☐ 3 milk cartons with tops removed   ☐ 1 type of seed (for example, tomato, bean, marigold)

How do you think plants will grow when they are watered with acidic water? Select seeds of one plant type and predict how they will react to being watered with acidic water.

Plant name: _____

Prediction: _____

Prepare the testing water you will use for watering your plants.

Get three jars and fill each with 100 ml of water. Label one jar "strong acid," the second "weak acid," and the last "regular water (control)." To the first jar add 10 ml of lemon juice, and to the second add 1 ml of lemon juice. Measure the pH of each jar with pH paper. Put a lid on each of these jars and set aside.

pH of jar 1: _____

pH of jar 2: _____

pH of jar 3: _____

(If your pH paper indicates the pH level numerically, write that down. If not, describe the color of the test paper and tape it to this sheet.)

Label one milk carton "strong acid," the second "weak acid," and the third "regular water (control)." Place soil in each milk carton. Try to put the same amount of soil in each.

Moisten the soil in each carton with tap water and plant seeds according to directions on the seed package. Put the same number of seeds in each carton. If another group is testing the same plant as your group, set up your experiments identically, so you can compare results.

Put the plants in a sunny place. Check plants every day; make thorough observations every third day. When the soil is dry, use water stored in jars (water plant 1 with water from jar 1, etc.). Water all plants at the same time and with the same amount of water. If you run out of water in any of the jars, mix more using the same proportions as before.

Date watered	Amount watered

pH and Plants Observation Sheet

(Make a copy for each day you make observations.)

Name _____ Responsibilities: _____

Observations DATE:	Plant watered with strong acid	Plant watered with weak acid	Control
Height			
Number of leaves			
Color			
Other observations			
Drawing or photograph			

©The Watercourse and Council for Environmental Education (CEE).

Water resources are managed.

▼

Multiple use of water resources leads to diverse and sometimes conflicting demands, which

require water resource management practices. Management decisions

involve distribution of water resources and protection

of acceptable water quality and quantity.

AfterMath

After damage costs are calculated, what are the real losses associated with a natural disaster like a flood or hailstorm?

▼ Summary

By calculating economic loss that results from flooding in a specific area, students investigate how people are affected by floods and other weather events.

■ Grade Level:
Middle School

■ Subject Areas:
Mathematics, Environmental Science, Language Arts, Government

■ Duration:
Preparation time: 30 minutes
Activity time: 50 minutes

■ Setting: Classroom

■ Skills:
Gathering information (calculating); Organizing (mapping); Analyzing (comparing); Interpreting (discovering conclusions)

■ Charting the Course
Understanding other aspects of weather can support this activity ("Poetic Precipitation," "The Thunderstorm," and "Wet Vacation"). In "Nature Rules!" students develop news articles to report on natural disasters. Students can investigate and debate ("Hot Water") the pros and cons of living in areas prone to disasters, such as those in "AfterMath." "Back to the Future" and "Dust Bowls and Failed Levees" are also related to this activity.

■ Vocabulary
water-related disaster

Objectives

Students will:
• interpret how economic damage reports present individual and community losses from a natural disaster.
• differentiate between emotional and economic loss from a natural disaster.
• recognize why some natural events are classified as disasters.

Materials

• *Mail-order catalogues of household items*
• *Classified ads for real estate and advertisements for new and used automobiles*
• *Paper and pencils*
• *About 300 small pieces of scrap paper ($\frac{1}{2}$-inch [1cm] squares) in a bag*
• *A collection of state and national newspapers and magazines with water-related disaster stories*

Making Connections

Some students may have experienced a water-related natural event such as a flood, drought, hailstorm, hurricane, blizzard, ice storm, or maybe even a tidal wave. They may have heard or read about the economic losses of major local, national, and world water disasters. The Associated Press (AP) reports water-related natural events (floods and droughts) as top stories almost every year. Learning about the impact of these events helps students understand how it

is possible to avoid the risks associated with these disasters.

Background

When does a natural event become a disaster? While snowstorms, heavy rains, and minor flooding may be inconveniences, most people do not consider them tragedies. Weather events such as floods, hurricanes, and hailstorms are characterized as disasters when they negatively affect people through loss of life, property, or income. This perspective is human centered and based on economic principles. If a flood had occurred on the Mississippi River before human habitation, it would not have been classified as a disaster. Instead of sweeping away the accomplishments of generations, the floodwaters would have nourished the river's ancient floodplain.

The economic losses caused by water-related natural disasters can be staggering. Throughout the world, billions of dollars of damage are caused by hailstorms, floods, droughts, hurricanes, ice storms, heavy snows, and large waves in coastal areas.

After a disaster, an estimate of damages follows. ("Aftermath" literally means the result of some event—the number of houses inundated by floodwaters or the number of automobiles dented by a hailstorm.) Calculating the economic loss caused by a hailstorm, flood, or other such event is a complicated task. From a strictly analytical approach, losses can be calculated at the micro- (city block or single house) and macro- (county, state, or regional) levels. Estimates of economic losses help policymakers (city councils, county commissions, state legislative groups, and the federal government) determine those actions needed to avoid losses in the future.

These damage reports help establish the magnitude of losses that sometimes must

FRANK OBERLE

flood or hurricane is a disaster? Who makes that determination?

Ask students to think of their own bedrooms. Imagine that their rooms are on the first floor of their homes. A flood occurs in their community; the water is rising in their rooms. It is now a foot deep. Tell students that the water will not recede for two to three days. How will their personal possessions be affected? (The longer water remains in a house, the greater the likelihood of structural damage.)

Rescue workers tell students that they can take five items with them. Which personal possessions would they select? Have students discuss the "value" of these possessions. Do these items reflect an emotional or an economic worth?

be weighed against the cost of trying to stop the disaster from happening again. Floods are good examples of this rationale. Consider an area along a stream that is inundated year after year. The last flood resulted in 20 million dollars in damages to homes and businesses. The cost of a structural solution (dike, dam, or channel) or nonstructural solution (education, planning, zoning codes, and insurance) may not be practical from an economic point of view. Decision makers face difficult choices when managing populations and settled floodplains.

Insurance is available for most water-related natural events. For example, almost everyone who lives in a 100-year floodplain carries insurance because banks and mortgage companies that loan money to homebuyers require flood insurance prior to purchase. This requirement applies not only to people living along waterways but also to those in coastal areas. However, almost 99 percent of people who do not live in the floodplain and do not have this

insurance still may have to live with the aftermath of floods. Major natural disasters require huge amounts of resources to restore damaged areas, obligating funds from multiple sources.

Random weather events like hailstorms, severe rainstorms, and drought are less predictable and thus harder to manage. A farmer in a hail-prone area must weigh the cost of insurance against the economic impact of a lost crop. That is, farming in areas with documented high levels of hail damage without hail insurance is "risky business."

Procedure
▼ Warm Up
Ask students to generate a list of water-related weather events. Discuss the role of each event from an ecological perspective. What determines whether a natural event like a

▼ The Activity
1.   **Inform students that they will be part of a flood simulation and will calculate the economic losses of the aftermath. Have students arrange their chairs or desks in rows to form a grid.**

2.   **Assign each student to a square on the grid. Tell students that the square represents their home and property. Have students determine "property values" for their squares.** Distribute mail-order catalogues, magazines, and newspapers with ads for houses and automobiles. Tell each student to clip pictures of a house and two cars. Have them

select furnishings and appliances for their home. Students should record all items and associated costs and determine the value of their assets.

3. **Ask students to stand at their desks. Give a bag of paper squares to one student. Inform the student that when you say "Now," he or she should move diagonally from the upper right-hand corner of the grid to the lower left-hand corner. The student will weave among the desks and toss handfuls of paper above his or her head and from side to side. (See illustration.)** Lead students through the motions described in the activity "The Thunderstorm." When you initiate the motion "stomp your feet," say "Now" to the student holding the bag of paper.

4. **When all students are standing with open palms (last movement in "The Thunderstorm"), ask them to be seated. Have students gather as many pieces of paper (representing flood damage) as they can without leaving their seats.** Tell students that it has been an unusually wet spring. Water from melting snow and heavy spring rains has raised the level of rivers above their banks. With the last torrential rain, the river in some areas has now overflowed the levee (a barrier constructed to hold back seasonally high water). Because of land variations and differences in elevation, the amount of flooding varies.

5. **Calculate losses as follows.** Each piece of paper collected represents a $1,000 loss from floodwaters. Have students determine their individual losses. Compare their losses to the amount they calculated for their assets.

6. **Draw the grid on the board. Write the economic loss for each student in the squares on the grid. Have students connect areas of similar property loss.** These are called isolines and connect points of equal value. Have them calculate the total loss for the community. (Add the losses of all students.)

7. **Ask them how they will replace or repair their homes or cars. Some students may mention insurance.** Flood insurance is available through a government program. To cover what is considered an average home (a $100,000 house with contents worth $75,000), a homeowner would pay about $400 a year. Therefore, once the deductible is paid ($250 to $500), the insurance company would compensate the homeowner for any damages above the ground. However, the owner is responsible for damages below ground (for example, damage to a basement).

8. **Is it possible to "buy back" all items lost in a flood? What about photos, letters, family heirlooms, diaries, etc.? Have students recall the items they said they would remove from their bedrooms in a flood. Have them differentiate between economic and emotional losses.**

▼ *Wrap Up and Action*

Have students compare property losses to their locations on the grid. Discuss how people living in heavily damaged areas would feel compared to those who missed the brunt of the flood.

Have each student locate a news article describing a water-related natural disaster. Encourage students to collect both recent and historical accounts. Have them research the nature of each disaster; how much rain, snow, or hail fell; and how much damage was caused. Students should present their reports to the class.

Ask students if they think the damage estimates reported in the news articles are accurate. Discuss the difficulty of getting exact numbers and the necessity of estimating. Do these estimates include family heirlooms, old photos, or a prized flower garden that may have been washed away in a flood?

Divide students into small groups and have them develop and deliver a live-action 60-second news report on their simulated flood. They might focus on personal property and

DISTRIBUTION OF ECONOMIC LOSS

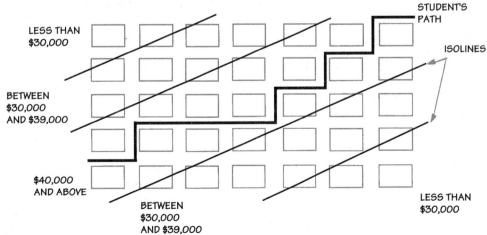

community damage. What was the total amount lost? What area got hit the worst? What area did not get hit? Videotape their presentations and have groups critique each other's newscasts.

Have students review water-related disasters that have occurred in their community over the past 25 years. Make a collection of headlines and construct community water disaster posters.

Assessment
Have students:
- explain why natural events like floods, droughts, and hailstorms are sometimes classified as disasters (*Warm Up*).
- calculate individual and community losses for a damage report (steps 5 and 6).
- assess the impact of a simulated water-related natural disaster (*Wrap Up*).
- develop and deliver a news report on a simulated flood (*Wrap Up*).
- discuss the "value" that we place on our possessions (*Warm Up* and (*Wrap Up*).

Extensions
What would your students do if you told them to expect a similar flood once every 5 years? Every 10? Every 100? Every 500 years? Which interval would cause them to take action? What action would they take?

Explain to students that many communities are not arranged in gridlike patterns. Keep the desks in order, but have students alter their positions. For example have four students per desk in one area, while another area has no students. Each student still owns the original house and two cars. Repeat the thunderstorm and the flood. The floodwaters may not crest in the area where most students (representing population) are located. How does economic loss correlate with the amount of flooding and the population density?

What other kinds of weather-related aftermaths occur? What was the aftermath of Hurricane Andrew in southern Florida in 1992? Or of Hurricane Hugo in 1991 in the U.S. Virgin Islands?

List other outcomes of water-related disasters and discuss their implications for people and the environment. Many of these are personal, such as grief, depression, disease, hunger, exposure, and death. Are there others?

Obtain newspapers from a community different from your own (i.e., if you live in a rural area, obtain papers from an urban community). Repeat the "AfterMath" activity using the new information from the newspapers. Compare this estimated damage to your own community's. Which received the most damage? Why?

Resources
Hall, A. J. 1981. *Flash Flood Forecasting*. Geneva, Switzerland: Secretariat of the World Meteorological Organization.

 Lyon, George Ella. 1990. *Come a Tide*. New York, N.Y.: Orchard/ Richard Jackson.

National Research Council (U.S.) Committee on Techniques for Estimating Probabilities of Extreme Floods. 1988. *Estimating Probabilities of Extreme Floods: Methods and Recommended Research*. Washington, D.C.: National Academy Press.

Powers of Nature. 1978. Washington, D.C.: National Geographic Society.

 Simon, Seymour. 1989. *Storms*. New York, N.Y.: Morrow.

Notes ▼

Back to the Future

How can the future be reflected in the crystal ball of the past?

■ **Grade Level:**
Middle School, High School

■ **Subject Areas:**
Earth Science, Environmental Science, Mathematics, Government

■ **Duration:**
Preparation time:
Part I: 30 minutes
Part II: 10 minutes

Activity time:
Part I: 30 minutes
Part II: 50 minutes

■ **Setting:** Classroom

■ **Skills:**
Organizing (graphing); Interpreting

■ **Charting the Course**
Students should understand the basics of watersheds ("Branching Out!"). To study how changes in a watershed affect stream discharge, have students participate in "Color Me a Watershed" and "Just Passing Through." Following this activity, students can debate the solutions to flooding and droughts in "Perspectives." "AfterMath" explores the financial consequences of living in a floodplain.

■ **Vocabulary**
discharge, cubic feet per second, floodplain, hydrograph

▼ Summary
Students analyze streamflow monitoring data to determine the safest location for a future community.

Objectives
Students will:
• analyze and interpret streamflow data.
• identify the risks and benefits of development in a floodplain.

Materials
• *News reports of floods (in the Mississippi or local river basin) or of water shortages* (optional)
• *Copies of **Streamflow Discharge Data** (**Part I** and **Part II**)*
• *A cube 12 inches on a side*
• *Graph paper*
• *Copies of **Community Planning Map***

Making Connections
Floods and droughts frequently make the news. While many disasters are unexpected, sometimes people can prepare for the future by looking into the past. Understanding and interpreting streamflow data helps students understand how people predict and prepare for times of water excess or shortage.

Background
Data collection is a critical component of most scientific investigations. Watershed managers analyze streamflow monitoring data to assess water availability, to allocate limited water supplies among different water users, and to manage flow problems (e.g., flood and drought).

Streamflow data are collected by many government agencies, including the U.S. Geological Survey and the National Weather Service. Streamflow data are a measurement of the volume of water passing a given point over a period of time. To determine streamflow, watershed managers need to know the profile of the streambed, the height or stage of the river, and the river's velocity The data are mathematically converted to cubic feet per second (cfs). This information tells watershed managers how much water is flowing in a river at a given time.

Streamflow information is collected either by electronic gauges or manually. Electronic gauges, located near bridges or dams, typically record flows around the clock, 365 days a year. Manual sites are monitored daily, weekly, as needed, or after rainfall. To take a manual reading, someone enters the stream or walks over the channel on a bridge or dock with a current meter and a gauging stick to record velocity and river depth.

Streamflow data are used to develop hydrographs, which show the amount of water flowing or discharged over time. For example, the average monthly discharge may be plotted over a one-year period (12 readings or data entries).

By monitoring a river's streamflow over many years, hydrologists learn about fluctuation patterns. For example, many rivers have low flows in the fall and winter, increased levels in the spring, and peak flows in early summer. Hydrologists use data to create models that can help predict streamflow during and after rainfall, snowmelt, and drought.

Watershed precipitation amounts or snowpack levels also help forecast possible streamflow levels. The amount of snowpack in a local mountain range directly affects the amount of water discharged in late spring or summer.

Once research hydrologists know the patterns of streamflow, they inform water resource management agencies, city planners, extension agencies, and farmers.

In addition to knowledge of slope, availability of water, soil type, and vegetation, information about flooding potential is essential for community planning. Watershed managers may recommend that people do not live in a certain location because of its frequent flooding in the past. Such an area is called a floodplain (any area that can be flooded when the water level exceeds a stream's banks). One option is to limit development in these areas or leave them in their natural state. However, such sites are often desirable for human settlement: they are fertile, level, and scenic. Dams, dikes, or levees can be built to protect an area from flooding, but these projects are costly and may still succumb to major floods.

The Midwest flood of 1993 will be remembered for many years. The flood caused the width of the Missis-sippi River to increase 10 to 20 times its normal size and covered land with 15 feet (4.5 m) of water. Fifty people were killed and over 40,000 were left homeless. Cost of damages was estimated in excess of 12 billion dollars.

What exactly does as 500-, 100-, or 10-year flood mean? Such labels are part of a classification system used to predict when a flood of a particular magnitude is *likely* to occur. Making these predictions involves studying past records of flood events and searching for a pattern. Generally, as the magnitude of a flood increases, its likelihood of occurrence decreases. This relationship exists because all the components of a large flood are unexpected, seldom occurring events (e.g., abnormally heavy rainfalls, high rates of snowmelt). Once every 100 years or so, two or more of these rare events may occur simultaneously. The result can be an abnormally large flood. However, if residents of an area experience a 100-year flood, they should not rest assured that another flood of that magnitude will not occur in their lifetimes. Hydrologists can only say that, according to past years, a flood of that magnitude occurs, on average, every 100 years. The unpredictable nature of weather patterns could result in another 100-year flood the next year, 10 years later, or 200 years later.

On the other extreme, droughts also dramatically affect our lives. Low amounts of rainfall and snowpack as well as normal fluctuations in weather patterns can result in shortages in surface and ground water supplies. Limited amounts of available water may lead watershed managers to advise against development of certain industries or types of agriculture in a particular area, unless alternate sources of water are located.

An area experiences drought conditions when it has less than an average amount of rainfall; during these times crop production is often affected, as well as availability of water supplies. For example, if one part of the country normally receives 60 inches (150 cm) of rain and another part 10 inches (25 cm), a decrease of 5 inches (12.5 cm) in the annual rainfall might result in a drought for the second region but not the first. In 1988, many parts of the United States experienced extreme drought conditions. The dry conditions resulted in failed crops, drinking-water shortages, and forest fires. Cost of damages was estimated in excess of 39 billion dollars.

Predictions of streamflow, even though they are made using scientific methods, might not be fully reliable. Significant changes in a river's watershed, like the construction of dams, levees, and water diversions, can cause flows to vary from the historical patterns. But knowing historical patterns can help people manage a river on a day-to-day basis and prepare for possible disasters.

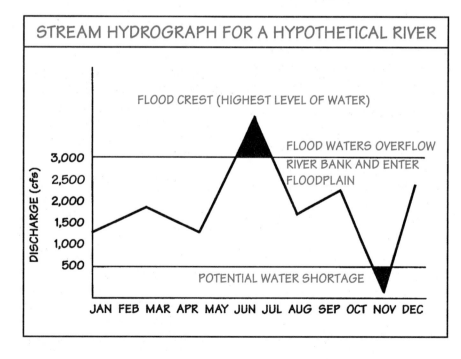

STREAM HYDROGRAPH FOR A HYPOTHETICAL RIVER

FLOOD CREST (HIGHEST LEVEL OF WATER)

FLOOD WATERS OVERFLOW RIVER BANK AND ENTER FLOODPLAIN

DISCHARGE (cfs)

3,000
2,500
2,000
1,500
1,000
500

POTENTIAL WATER SHORTAGE

JAN FEB MAR APR MAY JUN JUL AUG SEP OCT NOV DEC

294

COMMUNITY PLANNING MAP

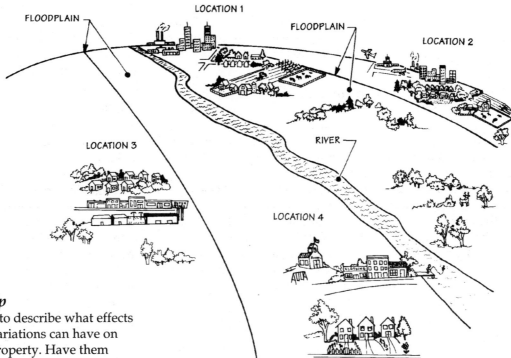

LOCATION 1

FLOODPLAIN

FLOODPLAIN

LOCATION 2

LOCATION 3

RIVER

LOCATION 4

Procedure

▼ Warm Up

Ask students to describe what effects streamflow variations can have on people and property. Have them describe events they have either heard or read about related to these variations (floods or droughts). Share news articles about these events. Have students scan the reports to discover what conditions might have led to severe flooding (for example, large amounts of rainfall in a short period of time, inadequate flood control structures) or drought (an extended period of less-than-normal rainfall).

▼ The Activity

Part I

1. **Show students the** *Streamflow Discharge Data (Part I)* **and explain that these are measurements of the quantity of water flowing past a certain point within a certain amount of time.**

2. **Explain that the measurements are in cubic feet per second (cfs). Show students a cubic foot.** If a river discharges 300 cubic feet per second, that means that 300 "boxes of water"

pass by a certain point within one second!

3. **Have students work in groups to plot the monthly averages from** *Streamflow Discharge Data (Part I)*. **There are 39 years of data. Divide the number of years by the number of groups and assign each group a set of data to graph. All data can be plotted on one graph, or, for clarity, each group can plot their data on a separate graph.** Hydrologists refer to this type of graph as a hydrograph.

4. **Discuss the following questions: During which month(s) does the greatest amount of water flow in the river? In which month(s) is the streamflow lowest?**

5. **Have students locate months when the streamflow exceeds 3,000 cfs. Tell them this is when the river is at flood stage. How many years are there between floods? Indicate instances when discharge is less**

than 600 cfs in June or July; these may be times of critical water shortage.

Part II

1. **Show groups the** *Community Planning Map.* **Normally, water stays within the river channel. When the river floods, water fills the floodplain area. Explain that a community plans to expand into a new area along this river. Four sites—Locations 1, 2, 3, and 4—have been proposed.**

2. **Provide students with the following information.** The land in the floodplain is flat and fertile, and it provides attractive views of the river. Because the area has been known to flood, land values in the floodplain are lower than land above the floodplain. The cost of transporting water from the river escalates as distance from the river increases. The volume of water normally passing

through the river makes it conducive to commercial use: certain industries want to build factories in the area so they can have access to the water for manufacturing purposes. Towns that support industry are more likely to have larger populations because factories provide opportunities for jobs. (NOTE: This information pertains to this activity's scenario and may differ in actual situations.)

3. **Have students listen to the views of four people—proponents of Locations 1, 2, 3, and 4—on where to expand the community.** Students may wish to role-play the different views. In addition to discussing where to build, consider the issue of allowing certain industries to locate their factories in the community.

4. **Ask students to list the pros and cons for building on a floodplain. Discuss the benefits and drawbacks of establishing industries in a community.** The chart *Building in the Floodplain*—presenting pros and cons—is an example of a decision-making strategy.

5. **Ask students to predict outcomes for each location (1, 2, 3, or 4). Have each group select one site for expansion and discuss the reasons for their choice.**

6. **After groups have made their selections, read the *Outcomes* in the side bar on page 297.**

7. **Provide students with the *Streamflow Discharge Data* (*Part II*). This table represents the six-year period following the community's expansion. Have students look for times when the river flooded (cfs > 3,000). Have them identify times when the community might have experienced times of water shortage (cfs for June or July < 600).** To confirm whether there is enough water for community needs, have students use the conver-

VIEWS

Location 1:
I think we should build at Location 1. The property values are low and we won't have to pay high prices to get water into our homes. The soil is great for farming and the views of the river are wonderful! I also think we should allow industries to build their factories here. There is plenty of water for their production needs, and they will provide jobs for community members. There hasn't been a flood here in over 10 years, so it's nothing to fret about.

Location 2:
Well, just because a flood hasn't happened in 10 years doesn't mean it won't. I say let's build above the floodplain. We'll have to pay more in property taxes and for water, but homes will be less expensive because we won't have to floodproof them. If we invite industries to locate here, people will have secure jobs and the city will prosper.

Location 3:
Even though we'll have to pay more, I think we should build above the floodplain. Location 3 is a good distance from the floodplain, and the land is not too steep. I don't think we should allow industry to settle here; it will use too much water and could create pollution problems. Instead, we should promote small businesses.

Location 4:
I agree that we should plan for a small community and promote small businesses instead of industry. More people will place more demands on our water supply . . . and what happens during times of drought? However, if we build in the floodplain, at Location 4, we'll have flat, fertile land, which is easier to farm and better for constructing houses. I don't think a flood will happen in our lifetime, so that shouldn't stop us from building.

Building in the Floodplain	
PRO	**CON**
low property tax	chance of flooding
flat building surface	economic and emotional impacts
scenic views	temporary or permanent:
easy access to river	- loss of home and contents
fertile soil	- business closure with loss of income
ease of transporting water	- sense of property violation
	- fear
	- injury or death

sion of 1 cubic foot per second = 0.646 million gallons per day. They can then calculate how many gallons of water the river supplies (i.e., 922 cfs x 0.646 = 595.61 million gallons per day).

8. **Students choosing Location 3 should find that they have avoided a flood and have enough water during most low discharge months.** Students may be interested in checking how other sites fared. Location 1 would have flooded and experienced water shortages. Location 2 would have experienced water shortages but would not have flooded, while Location 4 would have enough water but would have flooded.

9. **Ask students if they think their choices of locations in the activity would have been different if the interval between floods was about 50 years. What about 100 years? Or 500 years?** Provide students with information about the Midwest flood of 1993; ask students if they think homes destroyed by a flood should be rebuilt on a floodplain.

▼ Wrap Up and Action

Have students summarize how past records can help plan for the future. They may want to contact community planners and state government agencies to study their local floodplain laws.

Ask students to survey friends and family to determine if they would build their homes in a location that had reasonable property rates, attractive views, and a friendly community, even if the site was located in a 100-year floodplain. Have students tally the responses and draw conclusions from the results.

Assessment

Have students:
- graph streamflow data (*Part I*, step 3).
- interpret streamflow data to identify fluctuations in discharge (*Part I*, step 5).
- analyze the risks and benefits of living in a floodplain (*Part II*, step 4, and *Wrap Up*).

Extensions

Students may be interested in entering data into a spreadsheet software program that will plot the data for them.

Have students determine the maximum size city for which the river could constantly supply water. Assumptions: a) 75 gallons per person per day; b) no storage facilities; c) must always meet population's need—use the streamflow data to make this determination; d) 20 percent of flow must remain to meet needs of fish and wildlife.

NOTE: Calculate based on the lowest monthly average instream flow: 43 cfs.

1) convert cfs to millions of gallons per day: 43 x 0.646 = 27.7 (or 27,700,000 gallons per day)

2) 20% of flow must remain in stream (27,700,000 x .20 = 5,540,000); subtract 20% to determine how much water is available to meet population's need: 27,700,000 – 5,540,000 = 22,160,000.

3) each person requires 75 gallons per day: 22,160,000 / 75 = 295,466 (maximum population for which the river could constantly supply water)

Have an insurance representative visit the class to discuss floodplain insurance. Ask students how insurance premiums would affect the outcomes of their decisions.

Contact city planners to learn if local rivers flood or if water shortages occur. Take a walking field trip to a stream and observe the development of the surrounding area.

Resources

Leopold, Luna B. 1974. *Water: A Primer*. San Francisco, Calif.: W. H. Freeman & Co.

Patterson, Mark, and Ron Mahoney. 1993. *Environmental Education Software and Multimedia Source Book*. Moscow, Idaho: University of Idaho Agricultural Publications.

OUTCOMES

The outcome for Locations 1 and 2 is the same, except that 1 is in the floodplain and 2 is not. If you choose 1 or 2, the end result is a large community, including three factories and several farms. During the winter months, the community needs approximately 60 million gallons per day. In summer, because of agriculture and residential lawn and garden demands, water needs increase to nearly 500 million gallons per day.

The outcome for Locations 3 and 4 is the same, except that 4 is in the floodplain and 3 is not. If you choose 3 or 4, the end result is a medium-sized community, including one small factory, a number of small businesses, and several farms. During the winter months, the community needs approximately 50 million gallons per day. In summer, because of agriculture and residential lawn and garden demands, water needs increase to nearly 350 million gallons per day.

PROJECT
WET
Water Education for Teachers

Streamflow Discharge Data (Part I)

Monthly average discharge in cfs

Students should plot data until present date. After they decide on a location for the community, they should use Part II of this table to plot the rest of the data.

Year	Jan.	Feb.	Mar.	Apr.	May	June	July	Aug.	Sept.	Oct.	Nov.	Dec.
19—	147	144	150	306	802	1043	581	184	118	46	58	44
19—	43	47	61	861	1430	1158	437	159	145	207	112	85
19—	74	82	184	609	1411	937	462	150	82	113	108	75
19—	70	63	60	265	991	1648	502	168	108	144	142	157
19—	162	144	138	536	1194	863	235	54	85	86	97	81
19—	124	122	123	382	1055	1361	706	256	222	217	204	137
19—	152	172	172	910	1790	1453	820	374	203	207	169	154
19—	156	145	140	926	2708	3079	859	351	260	218	185	190
19—	199	164	200	585	755	1507	927	276	176	187	169	142
19—	149	149	157	549	1287	908	617	191	143	150	133	110
19—	108	105	99	137	694	1174	489	193	124	121	156	202
19—	178	138	180	941	2288	2132	747	291	215	227	190	163
19—	143	147	161	336	1600	1900	683	256	184	189	169	159
19—	144	146	145	386	2862	1950	692	326	240	191	183	163
19—	148	147	146	371	520	938	308	135	207	220	166	129
19—	125	115	169	545	659	751	213	101	101	107	105	92
19—	97	94	100	248	515	751	207	126	138	134	121	96
19—	99	119	117	703	952	2121	566	245	180	201	162	137
19—	120	159	146	214	1180	3608	670	257	215	206	209	158
19—	145	149	143	391	942	1437	707	259	173	169	158	197
19—	219	179	206	852	2057	2916	1759	666	438	312	247	184
19—	197	172	179	507	805	562	202	118	105	121	127	112
19—	113	113	141	269	1876	2778	1194	351	249	269	234	188
19—	172	166	216	347	516	974	355	276	229	212	185	151
19—	156	156	163	1312	2031	2010	741	314	250	243	189	168
19—	157	147	169	297	914	687	283	208	154	152	140	132
19—	146	142	154	642	1726	1662	1049	363	310	259	215	186
19—	177	170	216	568	1198	3353	449	205	152	201	194	158
19—	150	162	216	492	2393	2877	1426	500	326	304	256	220
19—	212	198	273	494	2189	2272	1550	683	426	427	430	324
19—	289	275	288	641	1755	1985	1112	469	329	283	259	224
19—	216	189	213	712	1003	749	330	219	383	265	214	196
19—	189	194	475	1178	1815	2410	694	344	290	278	226	167
19—	155	152	213	375	725	520	284	172	128	125	131	121
19—	119	119	153	343	621	715	217	133	116	120	125	115
19—	120	114	149	644	994	954	351	174	156	165	156	131
19—	126	121	157	439	464	831	359	185	152	150	146	122
19—	167	150	177	288	1107	1661	832	277	240	241	254	204
Present	212	208	334	439	1263	2550	660	315	257	266	226	161

Streamflow Discharge Data (Part II)

Monthly average discharge in cfs

For six-year period following the community's expansion

Year	Jan.	Feb.	Mar.	Apr.	May	June	July	Aug.	Sept.	Oct.	Nov.	Dec.
First	159	159	155	324	861	743	632	380	160	169	210	166
Second	181	168	279	1089	2199	3161	953	378	246	244	223	171
Third	168	158	162	209	1083	2227	1517	392	253	256	233	202
Fourth	181	181	179	492	1486	1114	615	349	312	238	183	152
Fifth	143	132	134	151	201	574	550	153	141	148	134	136
Sixth	132	131	198	623	1319	1783	955	347	346	230	196	160

The CEO

■ Grade Level:
High School

■ Subject Areas:
Government, Language Arts, Environmental Science

■ Duration:
Preparation time: 30 minutes

Activity time: three 50-minute periods

■ Setting:
Classroom, community businesses (optional)

■ Skills:
Gathering information; Analyzing; Presenting

■ Charting the Course
"Water Works" is a related activity in which students investigate the interdependence of various water users in a community. In "Perspectives," students can analyze pros and cons of suggested environmental management policies.

■ Vocabulary
Water-related issue

As the Chief Executive Officer (CEO) of a company, why should you consider how water quality relates to your liquid assets?

▼ Summary
Students assume the role of CEOs and analyze the relationship between economic profits and environmental quality.

Objectives
Students will:
• identify components of an environmental management program.
• analyze the relationship between economic benefits and environmental quality.
• apply environmental management strategies in the production of a product.

Materials
• *Paper and writing materials*
• *Newspaper or magazine articles about business and the environment*

Making Connections
Many students know that the goods they buy have been made by someone else and that the manufacturing process involves the use of water and other natural resources. They should also understand that if a company is going to stay in business, its profits must be greater than its expenses. By researching how businesses balance economic profit with environmental stability, students (tomorrow's CEOs) may better appreciate how essential the adequate supply of clean water is to the manufacturing of products they use.

Background
The relationship of the environment, the business community, and the general public is interwoven and intricate. Earth provides the resources needed to grow, process, and/or manufacture the products that people need and want: the iron to build railroads, the gas for the family car, the water used for manufacturing, even the baking soda found in some toothpastes.

People generate the demand for products. Historically, protecting the environment while providing goods and services has not been a priority of consumers or businesses. Today, a new attitude about protecting the environment has emerged among consumers. The public call is for sustainable development, "development that meets the needs of the present without compromising the ability of future generations to meet their own needs" (World Commission on Environment and Development, 1987).

Ensuring sustainable development has become a key responsibility of many companies' Chief Executive Officers. A CEO, whether of an international corporation or a family farm, must consider economical, social, political, and environmental factors. To remain in business, the costs of implementing an environmental protection program must be balanced with the margin of profit. Visionary businesses have embraced this challenge by developing corporate environmental management programs involving environmental policy, improvement, and education.

The success of a corporate environmental management program involves careful analysis of products and their life cycles. A typical product life cycle involves the following: conception and research, design and development, extraction and/or use of raw materials or resources (timber, minerals, water), a manufacturing process, product packaging, storage, distribution, marketing, use by consumers, and eventual disposal by consumers.

KEN DE YONGE

Each aspect of a product's life cycle can involve the use of water.

The environment needs the help of businesspeople and consumers alike. Becoming involved with the environment is also the smart choice from a strictly business point of view. Many consumers are trying to minimize their negative impact on the environment by using fewer resources and trying to reduce their contribution to landfills. Aware that products they use consume resources and produce wastes, many consumers are demanding that these products should be "environmentally friendly," not causing undue damage to the environment. Anticipating the public concern for natural resource conservation and implementing effective environmental management policies can significantly improve a company's goodwill and success in the marketplace.

Procedure
▼ Warm Up
Ask students to identify some of the products they use every day. Have them consider the natural resources used to manufacture these products. To what extent do students think water is required? Do the production processes impact the environment?

Do students think one person is responsible for ensuring the development, distribution, and sale of a product? Inform them that many companies have a Chief Executive Officer who does just that. Would they want to become the CEO of a company? What do students think are some of the responsibilities of a CEO? Check to see if protecting the environment and managing resources are among the list of responsibilities.

▼ The Activity
1. **Tell students they will now have the opportunity to become CEOs.** For this activity, students will focus on only one responsibility of a CEO: developing and maintaining an environmental management program.

2. **Discuss how environmental activities can affect the production of goods and services.** How will future production of goods or services be affected if the stability of the resource base is threatened? Read or review articles about business and the environment. What relationships do students recognize between economic profit and environmental quality?

3. **Before students can become CEOs of their own companies, they will need to do some research. Have students work in small groups, identifying some local businesses**

and contacting them for information. The most efficient way for them to gather information is through interviews. Discuss interviewing techniques and have the class develop a set of questions to ask community business people about creating and maintaining an environmental management program. NOTE: Protocol for conducting interviews requires sending a letter of request that states the purpose of the interview. A follow-up phone call may be necessary. Review the set of questions. Dress professionally and listen carefully. Send a thank you letter within one week of the interview. Students may be able to talk directly to the CEO or may communicate with a representative.

Students might also conduct a job-shadowing session to observe a CEO at work, or they can review company reports to gather additional information.

They should determine one or more of the following:
- purpose of the company (past, present, and future plan)
- clientele/customers
- the product's life cycle and the segments of the life cycle with which the company is directly involved (manufacturing, sales, waste management, etc.)
- how the product is manufactured (What resources are used in the production process? How is the resource obtained? Is environmental policy in place regarding resource extraction and/or use?)
- the role the environment plays in business management decisions (Are sales influenced by environmental policy? How has the company been affected by environmental regulations? Is the

company involved in environmental improvement projects?)
- environmental management record (e.g., participation in supporting sustainable development, outreach programs, partnerships with environmental groups, supporting education projects, or community service activities).

4. **Depending on time and resources, have groups do one of the following:**
- Imagine that one student in the group is the CEO of the company interviewed; the others are stockholders. Students should prepare a report about the environmental management record of the company. What are its strengths and weaknesses? What recommendations for change would they make?
- Develop and produce a simple product to sell as a fund-raiser. (Funds raised can be used for a field trip, class picnic, donation to an environmental group, support for a community service project.) Plan for each of the steps of the life cycle of the product. Develop an environmental management program to guide production processes. Describe the results of the effort in an article for the school newspaper or the business section of a local paper.

▼ *Wrap Up*
Have students summarize the responsibilities of a CEO. Is this a career path they might choose? Challenge students to explain the importance of balancing economic profit with environmental quality. Have students express their views about achieving sustainable development.

Each group could send a copy of its final report to the CEO of the real company. This would be a positive signal that young people are interested in environmental management programs and may, in some cases, lead to changes in the way the company does business.

Assessment
Have students:
- research and report on the responsibilities of a CEO regarding the management of natural resources (steps 3 and 4).
- evaluate the environmental management program of a local company (step 4).
- produce a product, utilizing environmental management strategies (step 4).
- analyze the relationship between economic profit and environmental quality (*Wrap Up*).

Extensions
If students send a copy of their report to the CEO, they could conduct a follow-up interview to ascertain the CEO's responses and recommendations.

Resources
Coddington, Walter. 1993. *Environmental Marketing: Positive Strategies for Reaching the Green Consumer*. New York, N.Y.: McGraw-Hill, Inc.

Hiam, Alexander. 1990. *The Vest-Pocket CEO*. Englewood Cliffs, N. J.: Prentice Hall.

World Commission on Environment and Development. 1987. *Our Common Future*. Oxford, England: Oxford University Press.

Dust Bowls and Failed Levees

The quivering of the solid walls was becoming a steady shaking. Water tugged at the door, slipped over the sill. The very sill was heaving. A long crack snapped across the cement floor and white water boiled through. The shaking reached to the roof. When Jimmy looked at the floor again, a whole slab of cement tilted as if a black enormous paw was working it upward.

Marjory Stoneman Douglas,
"September—Remember"

This excerpt from a short story in *Nine Florida Stories* was first published on December 7, 1935, three months after a terrible hurricane hit the Florida Keys on Labor Day.

▼ Summary

Through literature study, research, and writing, students gain a greater understanding of the effects of drought, flood, and other water-related events on people.

Grade Level:
High School

Subject Areas:
Environmental Science, Geography, History, Language Arts

Duration:
Preparation time: 30 minutes

Activity time: depends on books selected; 2 weeks to write story

Setting:
Classroom and library

Skills:
Gathering information (researching); Applying (composing); Evaluating (establishing criteria); Presenting (writing)

Charting the Course
Other activities that involve language arts skills include "Water Write" and "Nature Rules!" In "Water: Read All About It!" students create a newspaper "special edition" about water. Students study other aspects of natural disasters in "AfterMath."

Vocabulary
El Niño, levee, water-related disaster

Objectives
Students will:
- appreciate that literature reflects people's feelings about water-related events.
- illustrate the effects of drought, flood, and other water-related disasters on human lives, through creative writing.

Materials
- *Copies of **The Grapes of Wrath** (or other works of fiction involving water-related disasters)*
- *Copy of the Steinbeck entry in **Contemporary Authors: New Revision Series**, Volume 35 (optional, for teachers)*
- *Writing materials*

Making Connections
Students have all probably experienced exceptionally rainy years and dry seasons. In extreme cases, they may have had to ration water or cope with flooded basements. They know that weather patterns are inconsistent; but beyond minor inconveniences, most people have not experienced the profound life changes that can result from climatic cycles. Through a reading assignment, followed by their own research and writing, students will be aware of the tremendous impact on people of cycles of drought, flood, and other water-related events.

Background
Throughout history and around the world, human populations have both benefited from and been harmed by wet and dry climatic cycles. In northern Africa, a decade of productive, healthy years with timely rainfall and good crops can be followed by ten years of drought. Thousands of people have perished during these tragic weather episodes, and thousands more have been driven in desperation from their homelands.

In North America during the Dust Bowl era of the 1930s, drought and wind created crushing poverty and starvation, year after year, for residents of Great Plains states such as Kansas and Oklahoma. More recently, the unprecedented flooding of the Missouri and Mississippi Rivers in 1993 overwhelmed the elaborate and expensive systems of levees and dams, and produced great hardship and financial loss for residents throughout America's heartland.

These events supply sensational news and become general topics of conservation when they occur, but within a few months the media moves on to fresher news, and the images fade from our cultural memory.

Literature provides one of the few forms of documentation that lasts through the decades. Human triumph and tragedy are the stuff of great fiction, and the joy and suffering that result from wet and dry cycles of weather have furnished writers with compelling human dramas.

John Steinbeck's *The Grapes of Wrath* is far and away the best known piece of American literature from the Dust Bowl years. Steinbeck lived in California when many migrants from Dust Bowl states were arriving in search of work and the promise of a new start. The scenes of poverty and disappointment moved Steinbeck to create a work of fiction.

In 1937 Steinbeck went to Oklahoma to witness the Dust Bowl firsthand. He traveled with families on their way to California along Route 66. For two years he lived and worked with the migrant people, gathering material that would make his characters and story true to life.

Steinbeck also benefited from a relationship with Thomas Collins, who managed a model Farm Security Administration camp for migrant workers and provided Steinbeck with detailed accounts and anecdotal information essential to the authenticity of his project.

Steinbeck's powerful descriptions lend a depth and intimacy to Dust Bowl reality no news story could match. In the first pages of *The Grapes of Wrath*, Steinbeck writes:

> In the morning the dust hung like fog, and the sun was as ripe as new blood. All the day dust sifted down from the sky, and the next day it sifted down. An even blanket covered the earth. It settled on the corn, piled up on the tops of fence posts, piled

up on the wires; it settled on roofs, blanketed the weeds and trees.

The people came out of their houses and smelled the hot stinging air and covered their noses from it. And the children came out of the houses, but they did not run or shout as they would have done after a rain. Men stood by their fences and looked at the ruined corn, drying fast now, only a little green showing through the film of dust.

That *The Grapes of Wrath* has had a lasting impact on world culture is irrefutable. Nearly 15 million copies have been sold, and it has been translated into dozens of languages. Its publication was a literary event of

APPROACHING DUST STORM IN MIDDLE WEST

COURTESY: NEBRASKA STATE HISTORICAL SOCIETY

304

COURTESY: EVERGLADES NATIONAL PARK

major proportions. The book has been publicly banned and burned, debated by innumerable people, and adapted as a movie script.

Which writers will chronicle the great floods of 1993? What books will be written to ensure that the dramatic events in Illinois, Missouri, and Iowa will endure? What great weather scenes throughout history have been forgotten because no one wrote about them?

Procedure
▼ Warm Up

Ask students if they can think of climatic events that have affected human populations (El Niño, big floods, African droughts, etc.). How were people's lives changed by these weather patterns (lost homes, financial ruin, starvation, failed crops)? Discuss some of the strategies we have developed to buffer ourselves from the effects of weather (dams and levees, dryland farming techniques, irrigation systems, weatherproofed homes). Although

these measures may increase our margin of safety, extreme swings of weather can negate even the most elaborate human strategies.

▼ The Activity

1. **Discuss the role of literature in documenting cycles of flood, drought, and other water-related events, using Steinbeck's *The Grapes of Wrath* as an example.** The excerpt from *Contemporary Authors* can supplement the information provided in the **Background**. (Other biographies, autobiographies, or collections of Steinbeck's journal notes are also available.)

2. **Assign students the reading of *The Grapes of Wrath* (or another novel about a water-related event). Follow the reading with a general discussion of Steinbeck's portrayal of the human consequences of the Dust Bowl.** Did students think Steinbeck was effective? Accurate? Biased? Were they educated about the Dust Bowl and its social and economic consequences? What

makes Steinbeck's book work (compelling characters, dramatic tension, good story line, realistic dialogue, detailed descriptions)? If time is limited, an alternative is to assign excerpts from *The Grapes of Wrath*.

3. **Tell students that they will now have their chance to be Steinbecks. Discuss other climatic events that have led to human dramas. Ask students to choose one that they find fascinating to write about.** Local history might include a dramatic flood, drought, hurricane, or blizzard. Students can interview actual participants or conduct original research at local historical societies and libraries. Students who have trouble finding a topic can use the 1993 Midwest flooding. The entire class might even choose to research and write about a single event, with each student producing a unique piece of fiction. (However, this could produce a research bottleneck.)

4. **Give students time to research their topic. Encourage them to focus on their fictional-character development and the specific drama they choose to portray.** Stories could range from a family evacuating a house during a flood, to a relationship that forms between people building a sandbag retaining wall, to a defiant individual who refuses to leave his or her home, regardless of the consequences.

5. **Have students write a fictional story (at least two to five double-spaced pages), aiming to relate the human impact of cycles of drought, flood, or other water-related disasters.** Emphasize that although these events cause considerable social and economic hardship, they are nevertheless natural. People who build along rivers that regularly flood may

have good intentions; however, they will likely suffer the consequences of high water.

▼ *Wrap Up and Action*

Discuss the final stories with individuals and/or the entire class. What dramas did they find in their research? What parts of the writing were difficult? Why? How did they settle on their particular stories? How could their stories be made into books?

Collect all the stories into a "Floods, Droughts, and Other Water-Related Events Anthology" to display in the school library. A copy of the anthology could be produced for each student.

Assessment

Have students:
- appraise works of fiction to discern the effectiveness of the author's portrayal of natural disasters on human lives (step 2).
- write fictional stories based on water-related disasters. Stories can be evaluated based on:
  - accuracy (historical and scientific)
  - attention to detail (period clothing, lifestyles, architecture, transportation)
  - the range of human reactions to water-related disasters
  - sense of place
  - a consistent theme
  - realism in describing the water-related disaster (step 5).

Upon completing the activity, for further assessment have students:
- establish criteria for evaluating each other's stories.

Extensions

Have students read their stories to the class (or to a wider audience). Students can use storytelling techniques to present their work.

Encourage students to read other fiction that involves humans and climate: Rolvaag's *Giants in the Earth*, for example, or Conrad's *Typhoon*.

If students are ambitious about their stories, they can expand them or even try to create a book outline. They could also write a screenplay and produce it on videotape.

Resources

DeMott, Robert, ed. 1989. *Working Days: The Journals of The Grapes of Wrath*. New York, N.Y.: Viking Penguin Inc.

🍎 Douglas, Marjory Stoneman. 1990. *Nine Florida Stories*. Jacksonville, Fla.: University of North Florida Press.

Gillespie, John T., ed. 1990. *Best Books for Junior High Readers*. New Providence, N.J.: R. R. Bowker.

————. 1990. *Best Books for Senior High Readers*. New Providence, N.J.: R. R. Bowker.

🍎 Hemingway, Ernest. 1952. *The Old Man and the Sea*. New York, N.Y.: Scribner.

🍎 Lee, Jeanne M. 1985. *Toad is the Uncle of Heaven: A Vietnamese Folk Tale*. New York, N.Y.: Henry Holt & Co.

Lesniak, James G., ed. 1992. *Contemporary Authors: New Revision Series* (35): 452-58. Detroit, Mich.: Gale Research Inc.

Main, Edna D. 1984. "Science and Creative Writing: A Dynamic Duo." *Science and Children* 21 (4) (January): 24-26, 99-100.

🍎 Porter, Katherine Anne. 1984. *Ship of Fools*. New York, N.Y.: Little, Brown.

Powers of Nature. 1978. Washington, D.C.: National Geographic Society.

Regnier, Kathleen, Michael Gross, and Ron Zimmerman. 1992. *The Interpreter's Guidebook*. Stevens Point, Wis.: University of Wisconsin—Stevens Point Foundation Press, Inc. (See Chapter 5, "Creative Techniques, Storytelling.")

🍎 Steinbeck, John. 1939. *The Grapes of Wrath*. New York, N.Y.: Viking Penguin, Inc.

Notes ▼

Every Drop Counts

■ **Grade Level:**
Upper Elementary, Middle School

■ **Subject Areas:**
Fine Arts, Mathematics, Government, Environmental Science

■ **Duration:**
Preparation time: 50 minutes
Activity time: One week

■ **Setting:**
Classroom and home

■ **Skills:**
Gathering information (observing, collecting, measuring); Analyzing (comparing); Applying; Evaluating

■ **Charting the Course**
Prior to this activity, students can explore the amount of available fresh water ("A Drop in the Bucket") and monitor their water use ("Water Meter"). In "Easy Street" students compare the amount of water used by a family today to a family living in the 1890s. A related activity is "Irrigation Interpretation," in which students investigate irrigation practices.

■ **Vocabulary**
conservation, xeriscaping

How is conserving water like investing in the future?

▼ Summary
Students identify and implement water conservation habits to learn how this essential resource can be shared with other water users of today and tomorrow.

Objectives
Students will:
• determine how water conservation practices save water.
• identify water conservation habits they can change or adopt.
• recognize that water conservation is important.

Materials
• *Copies of* **Water Conservation Primer** (handout)
• *Copies of* **Constructing a Water Flow Cup** (student worksheet)
• *Large paper cups (about 32 oz [1 l])* (2 cups per group)
• *Heavy tape*
• *Stop watch*
• *Pin*
• *1/16-inch diameter nail*

Making Connections
The topic of resource conservation is becoming more common in schools and in other facets of our society. Television and other media often present water conservation practices. Students appreciate the need for water conservation if they or someone they know has experienced a water shortage. By participating in simple water-saving measures, students experience ways they can positively contribute to the conservation of water.

Background
Earth has a finite amount of fresh, usable water. Fortunately, water is naturally recycled (collected, cleansed, and distributed) through the hydrologic cycle. Humans have developed the technology to speed this process. However, because of diverse factors (drought, flood, population growth, contamination, etc.) water supplies may not adequately meet a community's needs. Conservation of water can ensure that supplies of fresh water will be available for everyone, today and tomorrow.

Water conservation from a practical and philosophical standpoint makes sense. The idea of using only the amount of water necessary has universal appeal. However, conserving water involves changing habits. Since many of these habits have evolved over a lifetime, they can prove difficult to alter.

People can become active in conserving water by starting simply, then gradually taking more advanced steps to reduce water consumption. The simplest habits involve turning off water whenever it is not being used. When water is needed for rinsing dishes, it can be held in a sink rather than allowing it to flow unused down the drain. An individual may simply use less water. For example, some people use a hose to "sweep" sidewalks, when a broom works well. People can shorten their shower times or reduce the amount of water they use when bathing.

Other conservation methods may initially require more effort and funds, but in the long run will save money and resources. For example, households can install low-flow showerheads with smaller holes that reduce water flow and increase pressure. A capped bottle weighted with stones takes up space in a toilet tank, reducing the amount of water available to flush.

Lawn care often requires large quantities of water. Water volume can be reduced by watering in the early morning or late evening, and by watering less often and more carefully (e.g. not watering sidewalks and streets). More advanced water conservation measures could include installing drip irrigation systems and xeriscaping: landscaping with plants that require less water.

Some regions of the United States and other parts of the world do not perceive a need to conserve because water is plentiful. However, using water efficiently has economic as well as environmental benefits. Environmentally, conserving water helps ensure that ample water will be available and reduces wastewater. Economically, water saved (or not wasted) is water that does not have to be purchased. Water conservation programs can help a municipality avoid or delay building or upgrading new drinking-water or wastewater treatment plants, potentially saving millions of dollars.

Procedure
▼ Warm Up
Have students list the ways they use water. Have students describe or draw pictures of situations in which they believe water is being wasted. Students can share their pictures and discuss ways that they would use this water more efficiently. Have them list ways water can be conserved or not wasted.

▼ The Activity
1.   Ask students to keep track of the water they use over a one-week period. They can keep journals or use "Water Meters," page 273, to monitor use. Have students design a chart to record their water use and the number of gallons or liters used. Do students think they used water wisely? Did they ever waste water?

2.   **Discuss reasons water should not be wasted.** Students could consider future water availability, sharing a limited resource, sustaining a resource, cost-effectiveness, etc.

3.   **Have students research water conservation strategies and develop a set of activities they can use to conserve water at school and home.** Their research can be supplemented with the *Water Conservation Primer* provided in this activity.

4.   **Have students identify three to five water conservation habits they can individually adopt. Ask them to write these down. For the next week, they should try to practice these habits. Instruct them to record results in their charts.** Remind students that forming new habits takes time and effort.

5.   **Students can participate in one or more of the *Conservation Capers* found in the side bar on the following page while implementing their water conservation strategies.**

▼ Wrap Up and Action
At the end of the week, ask students if their conservation practices made any difference in the amount of water used. Have students refer to their charts and compare the amounts of water used before and after conservation practices were implemented. Which practices were easy to adopt? Which were more difficult? Do they hope to adopt any other conservation habits?

Have students design posters advertising the benefits of conserving water. The posters may include a list of things people can do to save water.

Assessment
Have students:
• list and illustrate ways water can be conserved (*Warm Up* and Step 5).

• demonstrate how water-efficient products reduce the amount of water used (Step 5).
• compare amounts of water used before and after water conservation strategies are implemented (*Wrap Up*).

Upon completing the activity, for further assessment have students:
• write a paragraph or develop a TV news spot that reflects their views on the importance of water conservation.

Extensions
Students can encourage their families or the school to adopt water conservation procedures.

Visit a hardware store. Examine water conservation products. Compare the cost of the products to the amount and cost of water saved. How long would it be before the product "pays for itself"?

Contact municipalities and industries to learn how they conserve water.

Learn how government policies support water conservation practices (e.g., tax breaks). If the community lacks government support for conservation, students may want to write letters to their representatives expressing their views about conservation.

Conservation Capers

Conservation Caper One

Have students present a "Wasteful Water Charade." Refer to the list of wasteful water habits generated by the class in the *Warm Up* (e.g., leaving an unattended faucet running, flushing toilets unnecessarily, using a hose to sweep the sidewalk, allowing a faucet to leak, taking long showers). Write these on slips of paper. Divide the class into groups and give each group one of the habits. Each group should create and perform a pantomime to display the behavior written on the paper. When another group identifies the habit, this second group should create a companion pantomime to demonstrate correcting the wasteful habit.

Conservation Caper Two

Ask students if they know ways they can reduce the amount of water flowing out of their homes' faucets. Some students may be familiar with low-flow showerheads. To simulate how low-flow showerheads function, have students make water flow cups and compare the effect of flow restrictors on water quantity. (See *Constructing a Water Flow Cup*.)

Conservation Caper Three

Have students demonstrate the difference in amounts of water used by a toilet with a weighted water bottle in the tank (Toilet A) versus one with a full tank of water (Toilet B). For this activity, Toilet A uses three gallons (11.4 liters) of water per flush while, like most standard toilets, Toilet B uses approximately five gallons (19 liters).

Ask all students to stand in the back of the room to represent a common pool of water such as a city reservoir or ground water source. Each student represents one gallon (3.8 liters) of water. Two other students stand at either side of the room; acting like water meters, they will count the number of water students that pass by.

Indicate that the left half of the room represents a household with Toilet A and the right half represents one with Toilet B. The front of the room represents a wastewater treatment plant.

Tell students that both toilets have been flushed. Three students should move to the left and then to the front; while five move to the right, then to the front. Continue the process until all students have moved to the front.

Have students compare the number of gallons (liters) needed by each toilet. If a household was limited to a specified amount of water, which toilet would make that supply last longer? Which toilet would contribute to a higher water bill? Which would produce less wastewater?

Resources

🍎 Goldin, Augusta. 1983. *Water, Too Much, Too Little, Too Polluted.* San Diego, Calif.: Harcourt.

🍎 Green, Carol. 1991. *Caring for Our Water.* Hillside, N.J.: Enslow Publications, Inc.

🍎 Manner, Trudi J. 1985. *Water Resources.* New York, N.Y.: Watts.

The Montana Watercourse. 1993. *A Catalogue of Water Conservation Resources.* Bozeman, Mont: The Watercourse and National Project WET.

Water Watchers: Water Conservation Curriculum for Junior High School Science and Social Studies Classes. 1989. Contact: Massachusetts Water Resources Authority, Charlestown Navy Yard, 100 First Avenue, Boston, MA 02129. (617) 242-7110.

Water Wisdom. Contact: Massachusetts Water Resources Authority, Charlestown Navy Yard, 100 First Avenue, Boston, MA 02129. (617) 242-7110.

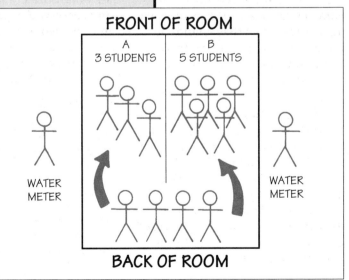

FRONT OF ROOM

A — 3 STUDENTS

B — 5 STUDENTS

WATER METER

WATER METER

BACK OF ROOM

Constructing a Water Flow Cup

- Using a nail, punch five holes into the bottom of a large paper cup. Using a pin, punch five holes in a second cup. The location of the holes should be the same for each cup. Cover the holes of each cup with a piece of sturdy tape.

- Fill the cup with the large holes with water.

- With a stopwatch handy, remove the tape and have another student time how long it takes for the water to pour out of the cup. Be careful not to squeeze the cup. Repeat the procedure two more times; make sure the water level is the same for each trial. Calculate the average time.

- Repeat the procedure for the second cup (timing the flow three times and calculating the average).

- Compare the flow rates of the two cups.

- What is the difference in the drainage times of the two?

- How do the streams of water from the cups compare?

- Would one cup make a better showerhead than the other?

- How could you use the flow restrictor data from this activity to help your family save water?

Water Conservation Primer

- Turn off the water when it is not in use. Don't leave it running when brushing teeth. Turn off the water between soaps and rinses when washing hands.

- Run the dishwasher or washing machine only with a full load.

- Keep a bottle of cold drinking water in the refrigerator instead of running water until it becomes cool.

- Limit shower time to ten minutes or less.

- Take showers instead of baths. (When taking baths, limit the amount of water used.)

- Put a capped bottle of rocks or marbles in the toilet tank to reduce water use. Do not use the toilet for a trash can.

- When washing dishes by hand, use a sink full of rinse water rather than letting the water run.

- Use a broom instead of a hose to sweep sidewalks and driveways.

- When washing the car, use a hose with an on/off nozzle or use buckets of rinse water.

- Water lawns in the mornings or evenings when water will not evaporate as quickly. Make sure the water lands on vegetation and not on streets or sidewalks. If possible, save rainwater for watering lawns.

- If you need to run water before it becomes hot, store the cool running water in a bottle for future use. Unheated water can be used for rinsing dishes, and washing vegetables and hands.

- Fix leaks!

- Install a low-flow showerhead.

A Grave Mistake

■ **Grade Level:**
Middle School, High School

■ **Subject Areas:**
Environmental Science,
History, Earth Science

■ **Duration:**
Preparation time: 30 minutes
Activity time: 50 minutes

■ **Setting:** Classroom

■ **Skills:**
Organizing (plotting); Interpreting (drawing conclusions); Analyzing

■ **Charting the Course**
In "Get the Ground Water Picture," students investigate the porosity and permeability of soil and learn about ground water systems. Students should participate in "The Pucker Effect" to understand how contaminants move underground and how testing is conducted. Students can learn how water spreads disease in "Poison Pump," "No Bellyachers," and "Super Sleuths."

■ **Vocabulary**
ground water

A few members of your community appear to have contracted a similar illness. The community is blaming a local factory for contaminating the ground water. Could the community be making a grave mistake?

▼ Summary
Students analyze data to solve a mystery and identify a potential polluter.

Objectives
Students will:
- analyze data to trace the flow of contaminants in ground water.
- conclude that past solutions, developed with the best of intentions, may create contemporary problems.

Materials
- *Glass baking dish or clear plastic lid from a salad container used by fast-food restaurants*
- *Sand*
- *Grape-flavored drink powder*
- *Spray bottle*
- *Sharp pencils*
- *Copies of the* **Community Map**

Making Connections
Too often, when trying to solve a problem quickly, people jump to the wrong conclusion. All data must be considered before making a decision about an issue. By investigating a mystery, students learn that the most obvious solution to a problem is not always the correct one.

Background
Arsenic, a naturally occurring chemical element, is currently used primarily in the production of pesticides and wood preservatives. In some areas, levels of arsenic are increasing in ground water because of seepage from hazardous waste sites. In the past, arsenic compounds were used for the treatment of certain diseases. This practice has been discontinued because of an awareness of arsenic's negative effects and because of the development of safer drugs.

Throughout the world, arsenic in ground water often comes from natural sources such as bedrock. The highest natural concentrations of arsenic in the United States are found in the Southwest, the Northwest, Alaska, and other areas near geothermal activity. Arsenical pesticide runoff also produces elevated arsenic levels in ground water.

However, another potential source of ground water contamination by arsenic is cemeteries! From 1880 to about 1910, arsenic was widely used as an embalming fluid. During the American Civil War, a physician developed an embalming fluid that preserved the bodies of thousands of dead soldiers for their long journey home; arsenic was a major ingredient. Because the only alternative was to use ice, this fluid was considered a major advancement and was soon adopted throughout the country. Of course, people in the late 1800s did not recognize the significance of concentrating large amounts of arsenic in a particular area such as a cemetery.

During this period, people were buried in wooden coffins or metal containers that degraded over time. Arsenic, a basic element, does not degrade. As water moves downward through the soils of cemeteries, it can carry arsenic through the ground water. Therefore, the potential exists for ground water contamination by arsenic in areas near cemeteries where burials were conducted from 1880 to 1910.

Arsenic poisoning may be either acute or chronic. Acute poisoning occurs when a person ingests a large quantity of arsenic at one time. This condition is characterized by vomiting and diarrhea, and may lead to shock, coma, and even death. Chronic poisoning occurs over a longer period of time. Symptoms of chronic poisoning include skin lesions that are noncancerous and tingling, and numbness of the soles and palms that develops into a painful condition called neuritis. With neuritis, reflexes in the extremities may be impaired and even lost. Upon identification and treatment of the condition, the patient generally recovers within months—although recovery is not always complete.

By sampling well water, we can assess changes in ground water quality or quantity. This is accomplished either by drilling wells specifically to secure water quality data or by sampling existing wells (e.g., city wells, individual domestic wells, irrigation wells, and stock wells). Hydrologists need ample sampling sites (wells) when investigating an area's ground water to ensure accurate results.

The exact number of wells needed to obtain reliable coverage and data is determined on a case-by-case basis. A grid pattern of wells produces excellent results. With a grid pattern, not only can cross sections be created, but also a more thorough (three-dimensional) picture of ground water systems (aquifers) can be mapped. The grid above shows

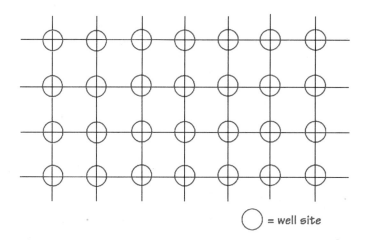

◯ = well site

the ideal situation, but, in reality, the expense of well drilling usually prohibits a perfect grid.

Monitoring a well over time allows hydrologists to observe changes in water quality and quantity. Water managers make use of the record of these changes when managing ground water systems.

Procedure
▼ Warm Up
Draw a diagram similar to the one below on the board.

Ask students: If family members living in this house find nitrates in their drinking water (which comes from a well), where should they look for the source of the contaminant? (Animal wastes are a common source of nitrates.)

To illustrate how a contaminant moves with ground water you can demonstrate a plume. (A plume is a continuous emission from a point source of contamination that has a starting point and a noticeable pathway. Contamination plumes can spread thousands of feet from a source and may persist for many years even after the contaminant is removed.)

Fill a glass baking dish with sand about 1 inch (2.5 cm) deep. Bury grape-flavored drinking powder at one end of the dish. Elevate that end of the pan 1 1/2 inches (3.75 cm). Using the spray bottle, thoroughly wet the sand. (This may require up to five minutes of misting.) Hold the container so that students can see the bottom. Ask them what conditions might have promoted this particular plume formation.

WELL

▼ The Activity

1. **Present students with the scenario in the box below:**

> You are a physician in a small community (about 1,000 residents). Yours is an old family in this area; your great-great-grandfather settled here in the 1800s and was a famous officer in the Civil War. Several members of your family are buried in the local cemetery.
>
> Over the past couple of years a few members of the community have described to you their puzzling physical symptoms. Recently, a patient presented you with similar but more serious complaints: weakness, tingling and numbness in his hands and feet, and dark warts on the palms of his hands and the soles of his feet.
>
> You listen carefully as your patient responds to questions related to his medical history. He works in the small, local factory (Private Well #6, on the *Community Map*) that produces wood preservatives. He has lived in the area for about ten years. He and his wife of ten months have a private well at their home. His wife has not exhibited similar symptoms. He quit smoking three years ago and does not drink alcoholic beverages. He takes no medications, only vitamins.
>
> You meet with members of the town council and express your suspicions—that the symptoms you have documented over the last few years are related to chronic arsenic poisoning from contaminated drinking water. You advise them that the accepted level of arsenic in drinking water is 50 parts per billion (ppb). The town council votes to budget money for ground water testing that will initially be limited to wells already in existence.

2. **Distribute copies of the *Community Map* with contamination level data (*Data Set 1*). Identify the** top right-hand corner of the map as the point of highest elevation and the low spot as the bottom left-hand corner.

3. **Have students indicate the direction ground water will move. Explain that the contamination data were collected via tests conducted at existing wells**—abandoned, private, and city wells.

4. **Instruct students to begin on the southern border of the map (the bottom) and plot contamination levels from the bottom of the map to the top. As soon as they believe they know the source of the arsenic, they should stop plotting data and alert the teacher.** (Tell students that this is a race against time; they are competing to be the first to identify the polluter.)

5. **Once consensus is reached (they will probably think Factory B is to blame), divide students into groups and ask them to discuss and write summary responses to the following questions:**
- What should your town do with this information?
- What options should the factory be given?
- This factory is a major employer of people in your community. Will this situation affect your discussions with factory owners?

6. **Have groups share their answers with the rest of the class.**

7. **Announce to the class that the factory owner was contacted by the mayor, and she has proven that her operation is not responsible for the arsenic contamination.** All arsenic coming into and leaving the factory has been accounted for.

8. **Ask students what should be done. Students may conclude that they had insufficient data. Inform students that the city has budgeted additional funds and has commissioned a water quality testing agency to locate the source.** This agency drilled test wells to confirm whether or not the factory was the source. Since the factory has accounted for all of its arsenic, other sites need to be tested.

9. **Tell students that each group represents a water quality testing agency. The goal is to see which group can locate the source of the arsenic first.**

10. **Refer students to the borders of the map, explaining how the**

Data Set 2:			
B12	= 0	B6	= 15
E12	= 0	E6	= 42
G12	= 0	G6	= 61
I12	= 0	I6	= 48
B10	= 13	B4	= 6
E10	= 20	E4	= 32
G10	= 20	G4	= 65
I10	= 18	I4	= 70
B8	= 18	B2	= 0
E8	= 38	E2	= 0
G8	= 42	G2	= 0
I8	= 33	I2	= 78

magnitudes (letters and numbers) can be used to plot coordinates on the map. Tell them that at each coordinate a test well is drilled.

11. **Tell them you will supply the data (*Data Set* 2) for each coordinate they select on the map (e.g., B10, E8, I12). They should send one representative to you with a chosen coordinate. If the coordinate is not available, have students request a different one. After the student receives the information, he or she returns to the group and helps plot the data.** After each reading, students should determine whether or not they need more data. They can request readings for more wells, but only one at a time. The groups work independently of each other, keeping their results secret until they think they have identified the source.

12. **Students will identify high arsenic concentrations north of the factory. They should find the highest levels of contamination just south of the cemetery.** Discuss other possible sources of the arsenic plume. Ask students if the cemetery could be the cause. Share with students information about embalming techniques between 1880 and 1910.

▼ *Wrap Up*

Discuss what community members should do now that the source of contamination has been identified. Have students consider special problems associated with issues surrounding cemeteries (e.g., disturbing grave sites).

Ask students how the following comment applies to this situation: "Past solutions sometimes become present problems." Can they think of any other examples?

Assessment

Have students:
- plot data to determine a source of arsenic contamination (steps 4 and 11).
- determine that insufficient data can lead to invalid conclusions (step 8).
- cite current examples that illustrate the idea: "Past solutions—present problems" (*Wrap Up*).

Extensions

Again, share the medical history of the patient with students. Have students speculate on answers to the following questions:

Why didn't the patient's wife exhibit similar symptoms? (He had been drinking the water for 10 years; she had only been consuming it for 10 months.)

The physician maintained that he had seen a few similar cases. Why wasn't arsenic poisoning immediately identified as the cause? (Many physicians would be unaware of the association of these symptoms with arsenic poisoning. Also, several people might live in the same household and be drinking the same water, but they might not all develop symptoms at the same time. People's bodies react differently to toxins, and their habits vary. Perhaps the patient drank eight glasses of water every day, while his wife usually drank milk and fruit juice.)

Students who have experience drawing isolines can use them to organize the data. How do students think these isolines would correspond with contour lines?

Have students investigate the condition of ground water in their own community. Who is responsible for testing to ensure that drinking water is safe? Do students feel that

sites or activities within their own community might be polluting ground water?

Students can visit a community cemetery and estimate the number of burials from 1880 to about 1910. Could this cemetery be a possible source of arsenic poisoning?

Resources

Ingram, Colin. 1991. *The Drinking Water Book*. Berkeley, Calif.: Ten Speed Press.

🍎 Parfit, Michael. 1993. "Troubled Waters Run Deep." *National Geographic Special Edition* (November): 78-89. Photograph of ground water test wells on pp. 80-81.

Rail, Chester D. 1989. *Groundwater Contamination*. Lancaster, Pa.: Technomic Publishing Company, Inc.

Stewart, John Cary. 1990. *Drinking Water Hazards*. Hiram, Ohio: Envirographics.

Williams, Melissa Johnson, and John L. Konefes. 1992. "Environmental Concerns of Older Burial Sites: The Use of Arsenic in Nineteenth Century Embalming Preparations." *American Cemetery* (February).

Community Map

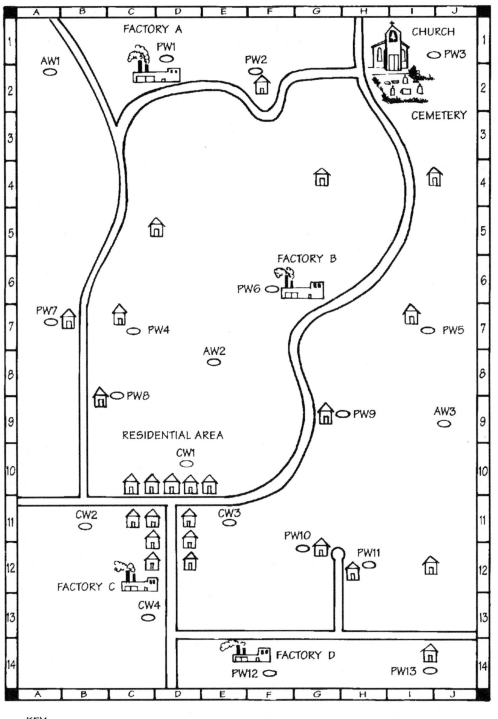

Concentration
of Contaminant
(ppb)

DATA SET I
AW1 = 0
AW2 = 39
AW3 = 9
PW1 = 0
PW2 = 0
PW3 = 0
PW4 = 24
PW5 = 35
PW6 = 54
PW7 = 12
PW8 = 21
PW9 = 30
PW10 = 12
PW11 = 3
PW12 = 0
PW13 = 0
CW1 = 22.5
CW2 = 6
CW3 = 15
CW4 = 0

DATA SET II
(provided by
teacher)

KEY:
AW# = ABANDONED WELL
PW# = PRIVATE WELL
CW# = CITY WELL

 = PRIVATE HOUSE   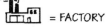 = SITE OF WELL

= FACTORY

Humpty Dumpty

What would Humpty Dumpty have looked like if they could have put him back together again?

▼ Summary
Students relate the challenges of doing environmental restoration projects to piecing together a simple puzzle.

Objectives
Students will:
- describe the challenges of restoring an altered natural environment.
- develop a restoration plan for a local site.

Materials
- *Photos of altered sites*
- *Object with multiple parts (e.g., an old clock)*

For **Option 1:**
- *Pattern for puzzle (Select a simple or more complex pattern.)*
- *Old magazines*
- *Glue*
- *Scissors*
- *Ruler*
- *Drawing materials*
- *Poster board or tagboard*

For **Option 2:**
- *Old radios, clocks, telephones, or other objects containing multiple parts*
- *Hand tools (screwdriver, wrench, hammer, pliers)*
- *Nails*

Making Connections
Some students may have tinkered with the insides of a clock or radio and learned that taking something apart is easier than putting it back together. Other students may have broken a vase or a dish. Even after it is glued back together, it is never quite the same as before. Comparing restoration projects to completing a jigsaw puzzle helps students appreciate the challenges watershed managers face as they attempt to restore altered water environments to their natural states.

Background
Many things (radios, clocks, bicycles, puzzles) can be taken apart and put back together. Other things (biological systems, watersheds) are quite difficult to restore. Superficially, each thing may look the same when put back together, but if a certain part or parts are lost, left out, or not put back in the proper relationship with the other parts, neither the timepiece—nor the ecosystem—will work effectively.

Natural systems (e.g., watersheds, ecosystems) are complex arrangements of physical factors (geology, topography, soils, climate and weather, material cycles, water, etc.) and biological components (plant and animal communities). While complexity and diversity tend to strengthen unaltered systems in nature, the more components and interrelationships those systems have, the more difficult it is to restore them if they become rearranged or damaged.

Natural systems can be altered by natural events (hurricanes, tornadoes, floods) and human activities. These activities (mining, draining and channelizing, construction, etc.) are conducted to meet the needs of growing populations. These practices often occurred before people were aware of the ecological consequences of altering ecosystems. Consequences include contamination of ground water, unabated erosion, loss of wildlife species, saltwater intrusion, and so forth.

- ■ **Grade Level:**
Upper Elementary, Middle School

- ■ **Subject Areas:**
Government, Environmental Science

- ■ **Duration:**
Preparation time:
Option 1: 15 minutes
Option 2: 30 minutes

Activity time:
Option 1: 50 minutes
Option 2: 50 minutes

- ■ **Setting:** Classroom

- ■ **Skills:**
Organizing (arranging, manipulating materials); Analyzing; Applying (planning, designing, problem solving, developing and implementing action plans)

- ■ **Charting the Course**
Students are introduced to the costs of water projects in "The Price Is Right." In "Perspectives" and "Hot Water" students present arguments supporting or opposing restoration. Long-term effects of habitat development and restoration can be explored in "Whose Problem Is It?"

- ■ **Vocabulary**
ecosystem, restoration

Ecological processes and associations, such as ecological niches, food chains, pyramids of numbers, predator-prey relationships, and various material cycles (carbon, nitrogen, sulfur, water), bind natural systems together like threads in a complex web of life. Restoration projects are undertaken in the hopes of returning ecological systems to their natural states. However, like an eggshell broken into many pieces with some crushed beyond repair, a fragmented ecosystem with permanently altered components may be difficult to "put back together again." In addition, since alterations to the system may have occurred many years ago, parts may be missing or knowledge of what the site originally looked like may be lost. Restoration is no substitute for protecting and preserving unaltered natural systems, but when systems have already been altered, the most promising solution is restoration.

Restoration of contaminated or changed water environments is a shining example of both human ingenuity and Earth's ability to heal past wounds; some land and water can be restored to near natural conditions. Laws requiring land reclamation and protection have been in existence for several decades.

Once, restoring changed land and water resources was not even given consideration. It was standard operating procedure to use the land and water, then leave it. This may seem counterproductive today; however, 100, 50, or even 30 years ago, most land and water managers were not required to restore impacted sites.

Times have changed and so have people's attitudes about restoring the environment. Many impacted areas once considered contaminated beyond recovery or permanently altered are now being reconsidered for restoration projects. New technologies, laws, shifts in societal attitudes toward the environment, and financial resources are making possible the restoration of previously forgotten or avoided sites. Government agencies, mining companies, logging firms, farmers, construction companies, developers, and other landowners are presently involved in countless restoration projects.

Restoration can be viewed as a way to reclaim the past. It offers young people hope and optimism. A single student, a family, a neighborhood, a classroom, or a school system can identify, guide, mobilize resources for, and otherwise help a restoration project. Few accomplishments would

have a more positive impact on young people than knowing that they helped restore a natural site.

Restoration is happening around the country and the world. The farmer that plugs a drain in a wetland and plants vegetation for wildlife habitat is playing a part. The industry that treats the soil and water of a polluted waste pond and turns the site into a park makes a difference. The government agency that begins the long process of restoring a hazardous waste site with plans of designating the site as a wildlife refuge makes a contribution.

One of the largest restoration projects in the world is occurring in the great Kissimmee-Okeechobee-Everglades-Florida Bay ecosystem in South Florida. Maybe if Humpty Dumpty had fallen today, he would be put back together again—not perfectly, but nevertheless, in one piece.

Procedure
▼ Warm Up
Show students pictures of altered sites. Discuss ways natural events (floods, hurricanes, tornadoes) and human activities (contaminating ground water with toxins, draining wetlands, building canals) affect natural habitats. What do students think should be done? Explain that

Kissimmee River before channelization. COURTESY: SOUTH FLORIDA WATER MANAGEMENT DISTRICT

one solution is restoration. List reasons for restoring systems (erosion control, flood control, wildlife preservation, aesthetics, preservation of water quality and quantity).

Show students an old object that contains multiple parts. Ask students to speculate how easy or difficult it might be to take it apart and put it back together again. Have them list reasons why trying to restore or replace something might be difficult.

▼ *The Activity*
Following are two options to simulate the concept of restoration.

Option 1
1. **Divide the class into small groups. Distribute to each group a copy of a puzzle pattern. (Depend-**ing on time and students' skill level, the simple or more complex pattern may be selected.) Instruct group members to glue the pattern (faceup) onto the poster board and cut around the circle. Distribute old magazines and have students locate nature scenes, preferably ones containing water. Tell them to cut out a picture and glue it to the poster board side. An alternative is for students to draw a picture of an ecosystem on the poster board.

2. **Have students carefully cut the poster board on the lines of the pattern.**

3. **Instruct students to scatter the pieces on their desk top. Explain that this represents a natural area that has been altered.**

4. **Discuss complications of putting ecosystems back together again.**

5. **Tell students to arrange their pieces so the cut-up picture is facedown. Have them switch places with another group. Without turning the pieces over, the groups should try to put the puzzles together again.**

6. **Have groups tape the puzzles together and turn the puzzles over.** Some of the pictures may be accurately reconstructed, but because of pairs of mirror images that can be interchanged (without the visual clue of a picture to guide students), some may not. This emphasizes the point that the parts of a system must fit together properly, and that incomplete knowledge of the parts

can complicate its restoration. (Even if the puzzle has been put together properly, it is still different from the original because it has been cut apart.)

Option 2

1. **Select several old, discarded items (frying pan with handle, clock, radio, toy) for students to dismantle.**

2. **Divide the class into groups equivalent to the number of objects available to dismantle.** Some objects (such as a frying pan with handle) are relatively easy to assemble once dismantled and require few resources. This is analogous to restoring a spot on the school grounds where a delivery truck has left a tire track. A few scoops of soil, a little packing, some grass seeds, and in a few weeks the spot is gone. On the other hand, some restoration projects are of monumental scope, requiring huge amounts of money, energy, and time. Use a dismantled clock to demonstrate this type of project.

3. **Direct each group to dismantle an object into its smallest pieces. The pieces should be placed in a container marked with the group's number.**

4. **Have one group attempt to reassemble another group's object. Ask them to summarize the challenges of putting the pieces together again.** Emphasize that many restoration projects are accomplished by persons other than those who dismantled or contaminated the environment.

5. **Depending on the age of the students and the difficulty of disassembly and assembly of the objects, remove several parts from each object. These removed parts represent absent plants and animals or a significant change to a site's soil, air, or water.** How would

Kissimmee River after channelization (completed 1971). COURTESY: SOUTH FLORIDA WATER MANAGEMENT DISTRICT

students propose to reassemble objects without all the parts? Could they reconstruct some of the parts?

▼ Wrap Up and Action

Discuss the relationship of the exercise to real-life restoration projects. Have students summarize why ecosystems are altered and why they are difficult to restore. Do students believe people might not alter ecosystems in the future?

Recognizing the need for humans to continue using natural resources, ask students to identify strategies for maintaining the integrity of ecosystems (inventory plant and animal species, monitor water quality, employ Best Management Practices, etc.).

Have students identify a potential water-related restoration project. Students should consider the following: establishing a restoration goal; formulating a restoration plan; predicting difficulties; analyzing costs; determining a time frame; projecting results (e.g., illustrating

Kissimmee River restoration engineering test fill, almost completed, late April 1994.
COURTESY: SOUTH FLORIDA WATER MANAGEMENT DISTRICT

the potential appearance of a restored site); maintaining restored sites. If the project proves feasible and students undertake restoration of a site, have them maintain a project diary or water log, and circulate copies to other teachers and students. Students may contact the local newspaper and ask a reporter to interview them for a feature story. Help students write a story about the project. Send the story to one or more national environmental organizations (Audubon Society, National Wildlife Federation, National Recreation and Parks Association, etc.).

Assessment

Have students:

- explain or demonstrate why some altered systems cannot be restored to their original state (**Option 1,** step 4; **Option 2,** steps 4 and 5).
- relate the challenge of assembling the pieces of an old clock (radio, puzzle, etc.) to the challenge of

real-life restoration projects (**Option 1**, step 6; **Option 2**, step 4).

- develop and participate in a restoration plan for a local site (***Wrap Up***).

Upon completing the activity, for further assessment have students:

- analyze the importance of restoration projects and the elements that contribute to success and failure.

Extensions

Have students research other water-related restoration projects that are underway locally, regionally, or nationally. Contact the Environmental Protection Agency, the U.S. Army Corps of Engineers, and the Bureau of Reclamation (Washington, D.C.) for information about environmental restoration projects. Write to Everglades National Park (P.O. Box 279, Homestead, FL 33030) and the South Florida Water Management District (P.O. Box 24680, West Palm Beach,

FL 33416-4680) requesting information about the Everglades Restoration Project.

Resources

Environmental Concern Inc., The Watercourse, and Project WET. 1995. *WOW!: The Wonders Of Wetlands.* Published through a partnership between Environmental Concern Inc., St. Michaels, Md., and The Watercourse, Bozeman, Mont.

Galatowitsch, Susan M., and Arnold van der Valk. 1994. *Restoring Prairie Wetlands: An Ecological Approach.* Ames, Iowa: Iowa State University Press.

Robinson, George B. and Sandia C. and The Watercourse staff. 1996. *Discover a Watershed: The Everglades.* Published through a partnership between The Watercourse, Bozeman, MT and The South Florida Water Management District, West Palm Beach, FL.

Puzzle Patterns

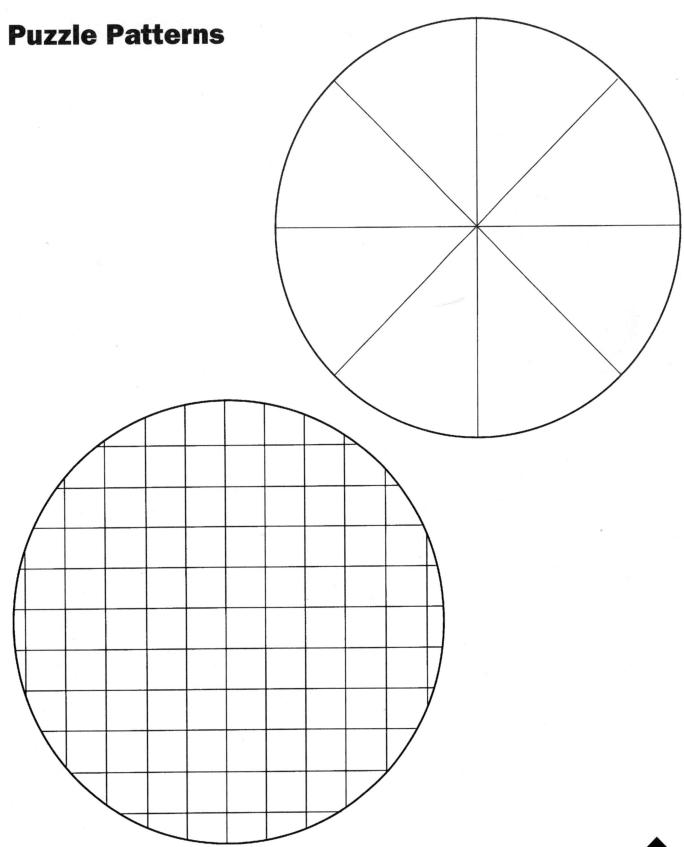

Macroinvertebrate Mayhem

How does the phrase "appearances can be deceiving" apply to the water quality of a sparkling, crystal-blue stream?

▼ Summary
Students play a game of tag to simulate the effects of environmental stressors on macroinvertebrate populations.

Objectives
Students will:
- illustrate how tolerance to water quality conditions varies among macroinvertebrate organisms.
- explain how population diversity provides insight into the health of an ecosystem.

Materials
- *Samples of macroinvertebrate organisms* (optional)
- *Resources* (texts, field guides, encyclopedia)
- ***Identification labels*** *for macroinvertebrate groups, one per student* (Divide the number of students by 7 and make that number of copies of each macroinvertebrate picture. One side of each label should have a picture of one of the seven macroinvertebrates. The other side of each label [except those for midge larvae and rat-tailed maggots] should have a picture of either the midge larva or rat-tailed maggot. For durability, the cards may be laminated. Use clothespins or paper clips to attach labels to students' clothing.)
- *Pillowcases or burlap bags*
- *Chart paper or a chalkboard*

NOTE: To adapt this activity for your area, call the state Department of Land and Natural Resources or Fish and Wildlife Service for information.

■ Grade Level:
Upper Elementary, Middle School

■ Subject Areas:
Ecology, Environmental Science, Mathematics

■ Duration:
Preparation time:
Part I: 20 minutes
Part II: 50 minutes

Activity time:
Part I: 50 minutes
Part II: 50 minutes

■ Setting:
Large playing field

■ Skills:
Gathering information (researching); Organizing (categorizing); Interpreting (relating, drawing conclusions)

■ Charting the Course
Orient students to stream ecology prior to this activity. The **Extension** of "Stream Sense" provides a variety of streamside investigations. Students can learn how nonpoint source pollutants accumulate in a stream in "Sum of the Parts." Treating polluted water is addressed in "Sparkling Water" and "Reaching Your Limits."

■ Vocabulary
macroinvertebrate, biodiversity

Making Connections
People may be able to assess the water quality of a stream by its appearance and smell. Sometimes, however, a polluted stream looks and smells clean. Students may have already learned certain ways to test water quality and may have conducted macroinvertebrate stream studies. Simulating how environmental stressors affect macroinvertebrate populations helps students relate the concept of biodiversity to the health of aquatic ecosystems.

Background
Macroinvertebrates (organisms that lack an internal skeleton and are large enough to be seen with the naked eye) are an integral part of wetland and stream ecosystems. Examples of macroinvertebrates include mayflies, stoneflies, dragonflies, rat-tailed maggots, scuds, snails, and leeches. These organisms may spend all or part of their lives in water; usually their immature phases (larvae and nymphs) are spent entirely in water. Larvae do not show wing buds and are usually very different in appearance from the adult versions of the insects. (Maggot is the term used for the larva of some flies.) Nymphs generally resemble adults, but have no developed wings and are usually smaller.

A variety of environmental stressors can impact macroinvertebrate populations. Urban and/or agricultural runoff can produce conditions that some macroinvertebrates cannot tolerate. Sewage and fertilizers added to streams induce the growth of algae and bacteria that consume oxygen and make it unavailable for macroinvertebrates. Changes in land use from natural vegetation to a construction site or to poorly protected cropland may add sediment to the water. Sedimentation destroys habitats by smothering the

322

rocky areas of the stream where macroinvertebrates live. The removal of trees along the banks of a river and alteration of stream velocity can both alter normal water temperature patterns in the stream. Some organisms depend on certain temperature patterns to regulate changes in their life cycles. Other stressors include the introduction of alien species and stream channelization.

Some macroinvertebrates, such as the mayfly and stonefly nymphs and caddisfly larvae, are sensitive (intolerant) to changes in stream conditions brought about by pollutants. Some of these organisms will leave to find more favorable habitats, but others will be killed or will be unable to reproduce. Macroinvertebrates (e.g., rat-tailed maggots and midge larvae) that may thrive in polluted conditions are called tolerant organisms. Other organisms, called facultative organisms (e.g., dragonfly and damselfly nymphs) prefer good stream quality but can survive polluted conditions.

Water quality researchers often sample macroinvertebrate populations to monitor changes in stream conditions over time and to assess the cumulative effects of environmental stressors. Environmental degradation will likely decrease the diversity of a community by eliminating intolerant organisms and increasing the number of tolerant organisms. If the environmental stress is severe enough, species of intolerant macroinvertebrates may disappear altogether. For example, if a sample of macroinvertebrates in a stream consists of rat-tailed maggots, snails, and dragonfly nymphs, the water-quality conditions of that stream are probably poor (i.e., low oxygen level, increased sediment, contaminants). If, on the other hand, the sample contains a diversity of organisms, the stream conditions are

HOWARD KARGER, N E STOCK PHOTO

likely good. However, baseline data is essential because some healthy streams may contain only a few macroinvertebrate species. A variety of food sources, adequate oxygen levels, and temperatures conducive to growth all characterize a healthy stream.

Procedure
▼ Warm Up
Review the conditions that are necessary for a healthy ecosystem. Ask students to describe what could happen to an ecosystem if these conditions were altered or eliminated. What clues would students look for to determine if an ecosystem was healthy or not?

Remind students that a stream is a type of ecosystem. Ask them how they would assess the health of a stream. Students may suggest conducting a visual survey of the surrounding area and answering the following questions: What land use practices are visible in the area? How might these practices affect the stream? Is there plant cover on the banks of the stream or are the banks eroded? What color is the water? What is living in the stream?

Identify several environmental stressors (e.g., urban and agricultural runoff, sedimentation, introduction of alien species) and discuss how they can affect the health of a stream. Review the many types of plants and animals, including insects, that live in streams. How might environmental stressors affect these organisms? Would all organisms be impacted in the same way? Why or why not?

▼ The Activity
Part I
1. **Introduce the practice of sampling macroinvertebrate populations to monitor stream quality.** Show students pictures or samples of macroinvertebrates used to monitor stream quality.

2. **Divide the class into seven groups and assign one macroinvertebrate (from *Macroinvertebrate Groups*) to each group. Have group members conduct library research to prepare a report for the class about their organism.** The report should include the conditions (e.g., clean water, abundant oxygen supplies, cool water) the organism must have to survive.

Macroinvertebrate Groups
Caddisfly larva
Mayfly nymph
Stonefly nymph
Dragonfly nymph
Damselfly nymph
Midge larva
Rat-tailed maggot

3. **Have students present their reports to the class and compare each organism's tolerance of different stream conditions.**

Part II
1. **Tell students they are going to play a game that simulates changes in a stream when an environmental stressor, such as a pollutant, is introduced. Show students the playing field and indicate the boundaries.**

2. **Have one student volunteer to be an environmental stressor (e.g., sedimentation, sewage, or fertilizer). Discuss the ways that a stream can become polluted and how this can alter stream conditions.** With a large class or playing field, more students will need to be stressors.

3. **Divide the rest of the class into seven groups to play the game. Each group represents one type of macroinvertebrate species listed in *Macroinvertebrate Groups*. Record the number of members in each group, using a table similar to *A Sample of Data From Macroinvertebrate Mayhem*.**

NOTE: Try to have at least four students in each group. For smaller classes, reduce the number of groups. For example, eliminate the

Intolerant Macroinvertebrates and Hindrances		
ORGANISM	**HINDRANCE**	**RATIONAL FOR HINDRANCE**
Caddisfly	Must place both feet in a bag* and hop across field, stopping to gasp for breath every five hops.	Caddisflies are intolerant of low oxygen levels.
Stonefly	Must do a push-up every ten steps.	When oxygen levels drop, stoneflies undulate their abdomens to increase the flow of water over their bodies.
Mayfly	Must flap arms and spin in circles when crossing field.	Mayflies often increase oxygen absorption by moving gills.

*CADDISFLY LARVAE BUILD CASES AND ATTACH THEMSELVES TO ROCKS FOR PROTECTION AND STABILIZATION.

324

A Sample of Data From Macroinvertebrate Mayhem:

ORGANISM	TOLERANCE	NUMBERS (AT START AND AFTER EACH ROUND)			
		START	ROUND ONE	ROUND TWO	ROUND THREE
Caddisfly larva	Intolerant	5	2	2	2
Mayfly nymph	Intolerant	5	4	1	0
Stonefly nymph	Intolerant	4	4	4	2
Dragonfly nymph	Facultative	5	5	4	4
Damselfly nymph	Facultative	4	4	4	3
Midge larva	Tolerant	4	6	7	9
Rat-tailed maggot	Tolerant	4	6	9	11
TOTAL		31	31	31	31

stonefly nymph and the damselfly nymph groups.

4. **Distribute appropriate identification labels to all group members.** The picture of each group's macroinvertebrate should face outward when labels are attached.

5. **Inform students that some macroinvertebrates have hindrances to crossing the field.** (See *Intolerant Macroinvertebrates and Hindrances.*) These obstacles symbolize sensitive organisms' intolerance to pollutants. Have students practice their motions.

6. **Assemble the macroinvertebrate groups at one end of the playing field and the environmental stressor(s) at midfield. When a round starts, macroinvertebrates will move toward the opposite end of the field and the stressor will try to tag them. To "survive," the macroinvertebrates must reach the opposite end of the field without being tagged by the environmental stressor.** The environmental stressor can try to tag any of the macroinvertebrates, but will find it

easier to catch those with hindered movements.

7. **Begin the first round of the game. Tagged macroinvertebrates must go to the sideline and flip their identification labels to display the more tolerant species (i.e., rat-tailed maggot or midge larva). Tagged players who are already in a tolerant species group do not flip their labels.**

8. **The round ends when all of the macroinvertebrates have either been tagged or have reached the opposite end of the playing field. Record the new number of members in each species.**

9. **Complete two more rounds, with all tagged players rejoining the macroinvertebrates who successfully survived the previous round. Record the number of members in each species of macroinvertebrates at the conclusion of each round.** Because some players will have flipped their identification labels, there will be a larger number of

tolerant species in each successive round.

▼ Wrap Up and Action
The game is completed after three rounds. Discuss the outcome with students. Emphasize the changes in the distribution of organisms among groups. Have students compare population sizes of groups at the beginning and end of the game and provide reasons for the changes. Review why some organisms are more tolerant of poor environmental conditions than others. Have students compare the stream environment at the beginning of the game to the environment at the end.

Have students investigate a nearby stream. What types of macroinvertebrates live there? How would students describe the diversity of organisms? Do students' findings provide insight into the quality of the stream? What other observations can students make to determine stream quality? They may want to report their findings to local watershed managers or water quality inspectors.

Assessment

Have students:

- analyze a stream based on a visual assessment (*Warm Up*).
- describe macroinvertebrate organisms and identify what stream conditions they need to survive (*Part I*, steps 2 and 3, and *Wrap Up*).
- explain how some organisms indicate stream quality (*Wrap Up*).
- interpret stream quality based on the diversity and types of organisms found there (*Wrap Up*).

Upon completing the activity, for further assessment have students:

- develop a matching game in which pictures of streams in varying conditions are matched with organisms that might live there.

Extensions

Supplement the students' macroinvertebrate survey of a stream with chemical tests and analyses. (See **Resources.**)

Have students design their own caddisfly case.

Have students study aspects of biodiversity by adding another round to the game. For example, add a fourth round in which all organisms are caddisflies. This round will demonstrate how a few intolerant species or a single species can be quickly eliminated.

Resources

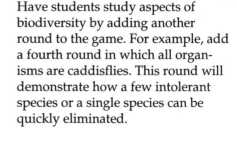 Ancona, George. 1990. *River Keeper*. New York, N.Y.: Macmillan.

Cromwell, Mare. 1992. *Investigating Streams and Rivers*. Ann Arbor, Mich.: Global Rivers Environmental Education Network (GREEN).

Delta Labs. 1987. *Adopt-A-Stream Teacher's Handbook*. Rochester, N.Y.: Delta Laboratories, Inc.

Edelstein, Karen. 1993. *Pond and Stream Safari: A Guide to the Ecology of Aquatic Invertebrates*. Ithaca, N.Y.: Cornell University.

Ellet, K. K. 1988. *An Introduction to Water Quality Monitoring Using Volunteers*. Baltimore, Md.: Citizens for the Chesapeake Bay, Inc.

Mitchell, M. K., and W.B. Stapp. 1986. *Field Manual for Water Quality Monitoring: An Environmental Education Program for Schools*. Dexter, Mich.: Thompson-Shore Printers.

Project WILD. 1992. Activity "Water Canaries." From *Aquatic Project WILD*. Bethesda, Md.: Western Regional Environmental Education Council.

Save Our Streams. Contact: Izaak Walton League of America, 1401 Wilson Blvd., Level B, Arlington, VA 22209.

The Stream Scene: Watersheds, Wildlife and People. 1990. Portland, Oreg.: Oregon Department of Fish & Wildlife.

Identification Labels

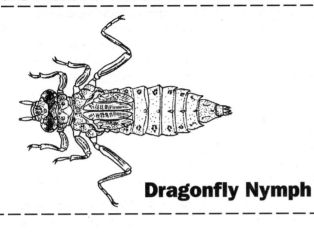

Dragonfly Nymph

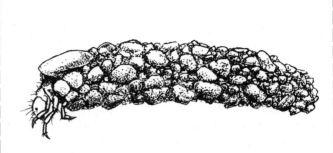

Caddisfly Larva

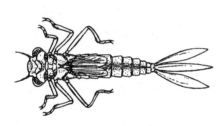

Damselfly Nymph

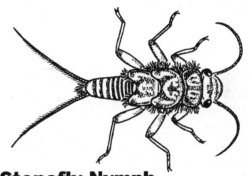

Stonefly Nymph

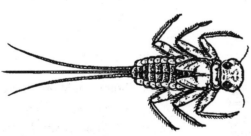

Mayfly Nymph

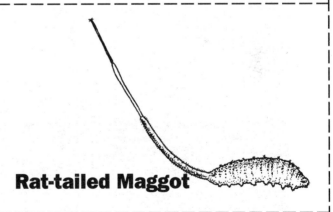

Rat-tailed Maggot

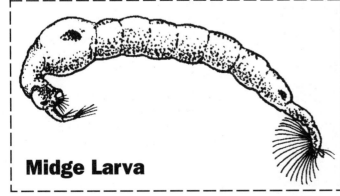

Midge Larva

Environmental Stressor

ILLUSTRATION OF MACROINVERTEBRATES USED WITH PERMISSION OF THE ARTIST, TAMARA SAYRE.

Money Down the Drain

Who would pour money down the drain?

▼ Summary
Through observation and simple calculations, students learn that a dripping faucet wastes a valuable resource.

Objectives
Students will:
- calculate the amount of water wasted by a dripping faucet.
- analyze the financial benefits of fixing leaking faucets.

Materials
- *A dripping faucet or a recording of dripping faucet* (optional)
- *3 gallon-sized milk jugs filled with 3 different colors of water.* (Put a small pin prick near the bottom of one jug, a slightly larger hole in the second, and a small nail hole in the last. Water should drip rather than stream from the holes. Cover the holes with tape until ready to begin the activity. Use more jugs for larger classes.)
- *Copies of **Money Down the Drain Worksheet** and **Answer Sheet***
- *6 Stopwatches or watches with second hands*
- *Containers to collect dripping water* (at least 1-gallon [3.8-l] capacity each)
- *A graduated cylinder*
- *Calculators* (optional)
- *A chart showing the local cost per unit of water used* (optional)

Making Connections
Unfortunately, leaking faucets are everywhere. Some students may even have one or more in their homes. Sometimes these are viewed as minor inconveniences rather than the loss of a resource. Fixing a leaking faucet is a small, inex-pensive, achievable task that can become a first step toward other water conservation measures.

Background
Plumbing systems are designed to efficiently supply water to and remove waste from homes. Pipes can develop leaks because of the age and quality of materials and construction of a plumbing system, water pressure, and/or the chemical composition of water. One of the most common causes of household leaks is the easiest to fix: replacing a worn-out washer in a faucet.

Sometimes large quantities of water can leak from a faucet or toilet over a day or week. A faucet that drips 160 drops per minute will lose over 6 gallons (22.8 l) of water per day. If a faucet leaks a small stream of water, over 25 gallons (95 l) of water per day may be lost down the drain!

Every drop of water leaking from a faucet is wasted water. To make up for this loss, municipalities are forced to treat more water to meet needs, and homeowners lose money. For example, if a faucet leaks 100 gallons (380 l) per day for 30 days, 3,000 gallons (11,400 l) will be wasted. If the water bill is $3.50 per thousand gallons (3,800 l) of water consumed, the leak will add $10.50 to the monthly bill. If the water is heated, financial losses will be even greater!

Procedure
▼ *Warm Up*
Allow a faucet to leak during a class discussion. Place a container to catch the dripping water. At the end of the discussion or when students notice the dripping faucet, show students the collected water. Ask students how many of them

---

Grade Level:
Upper Elementary, Middle School

Subject Areas:
Environmental Science, Mathematics

Duration:
Preparation time: 30 minutes
Activity time: 50 minutes

Setting: Classroom

Skills:
Gathering information (collecting data, measuring, calculating); Interpreting (inferring, drawing conclusions)

Charting the Course
This introductory activity could be done in conjunction with "Water Meter." Processes and costs involved in delivering clean water to students' homes are addressed in "Reaching Your Limits," and "The Price Is Right." Activities incorporating water conservation could follow this activity ("Easy Street" and "Every Drop Counts"). Other costs of leaks can be explored in "Whose Problem Is It?"

Vocabulary
conservation, municipal water system

---

know where they can find a leaking faucet. Have students share their views about leaking faucets. Do students notice them? Are they worth fixing? Pour collected water on plants.

NOTE: If the classroom does not have a faucet, collect an hour's worth of dripping water from any faucet. You could record the sound of a dripping faucet, and play it while you speak.

▼ *The Activity*

1. **Divide students into six groups. Assign two groups to each milk jug and instruct them to complete the *Money Down the Drain* worksheet and the answer sheet for their jug.**

2. **Arrange the three milk jugs on a table with collection buckets beneath them. Remove the tape and allow the dripping to begin.**

3. **After the worksheets are completed, have the two groups who worked on the same jug compare answers. Instruct the groups to share data and complete informa-**

tion about the other two jugs. **Compare results.**

▼ *Wrap Up and Action*

Ask students what they thought about the amount of water wasted by the drips. Do they think the amount of money lost was significant? Would they rather have used the money lost down the drain to buy something else? Ask students to list reasons why leaking faucets should be fixed.

Have students calculate how much water is lost from dripping faucets around their home or at school. Ask them to research how to fix leaking faucets or ask a plumber to demonstrate how easily a faucet can be fixed. Have them create posters presenting facts about leaking faucets. City Hall, a grocery store, or the library may post the information.

Assessment

Have students:
- calculate how much water is lost from dripping faucets (step 2).

- identify financial reasons why leaking faucets should be fixed (step 3 and *Wrap Up*).

Extensions

Many leaks occur even before water reaches the home. The water lines of many communities are over 100 years old and the materials have eroded with age. Unchecked leaks will waste water over many years and in the process cost the water user money. However, underground leaks are expensive to fix because they often require extensive excavations. When designing a water system, project planners will calculate a 10 to 20 percent water loss factor to adjust for unaccountable losses (leaks). This means that a water system must supply 10 to 20 percent more water to a community than needed, to ensure people will have enough water.

The following demonstration illustrates this. Poke holes or cut slices in a small section of a flexible water hose or surgical tubing. Bury

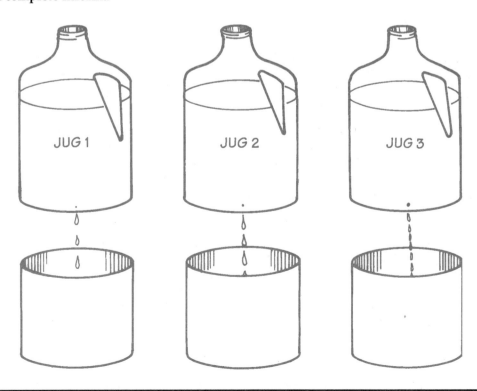

the punctured part of the tube under some sand in a shallow pan. Cut a hole in the bottom of a plastic gallon (3.8 l) jug, attach the mouth of the jug to the top portion of the tube, and seal with duct tape. Constrict the tube a few inches (cm) from where it empties into the container. This creates pressure that exists in water systems, exacerbating water loss in leaking pipes. Measure one gallon (3.8 l) of water and pour into the inverted jug. Collect the water as it comes out the other end of the tube. Do not tell students about the holes or slices in the tube. Ask students how much water they think will pour out the other end of the tube. The end result should be less than one gallon because some is lost through the leaks. Discuss how this often occurs in city water systems. Have students identify what would ensure that a gallon of water reaches the other end—pouring more water into the jug!

Take a field trip to a local water utility. Have a person at the utility talk about water treatment, its cost, and the problem of municipal water leaks. Have students compare the amount of water leaked during the activity to the amount of water stored in the municipal water tower or storage reservoir.

Resources

🍎 Pringle, Laurence. 1982. *Water: The Next Great Resource Battle.* New York, N.Y.: Macmillan.

🍎 Wald, Mike. 1993. *What You Can Do for the Environment.* New York, N.Y.: Chelsea House.

California Department of Water Resources and American Water Works Association. *Water Audit and Leak Detection Guidebook.* 1992. Guidebook may be obtained free from: State of California, Department of Water Resources, Bulletins and Reports, P.O. Box 942836, Sacramento, CA 94236-0001. (916) 653-1097.

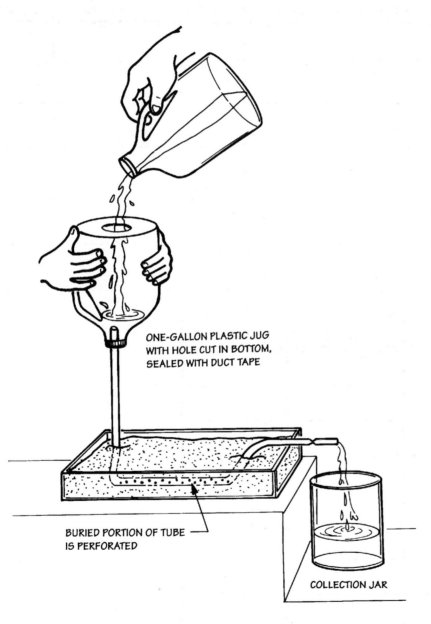

ONE-GALLON PLASTIC JUG WITH HOLE CUT IN BOTTOM, SEALED WITH DUCT TAPE

BURIED PORTION OF TUBE IS PERFORATED

COLLECTION JAR

Answer sheet for Jug # _____

Name: _____ Date: _____

Record answers to questions 1 and 2 below

	1. Drops per minute			2. Volume of water (ml) collected in 1 minute		
	JUG #1	JUG #2	JUG #3	JUG #1	JUG #2	JUG #3
Reading #1						
Reading #2						
Reading #3						
Total						
Average (Total ÷ 3)						

Record answers to questions 3, 4, 5, 7, 8, 9, 10, and 11 below. Write answer to question 6 below or on another page.

	JUG #1	JUG #2	JUG #3
3. estimate			
4. jug empty			
5. actual time			
7. ml/hour			
8. ml/day			
9. ml/week			
10. ml/month			
11. $/month			

Money Down the Drain Worksheet

Name: _____ Date: _____

INSTRUCTIONS: Complete the information for your jug, then meet with other groups to fill in the rest of the data. (**NOTE:** for simplicity, all measurements are in the metric system.)

Observe the water dripping from the jug and answer the following questions. Record your responses on the answer sheet.

1. **How many drops fall each minute?** (Take three readings and find the average. Skip this question and the next if there is a small stream instead of drips.)

   Reading **1:**_____ drops Reading **3:**_____ drops

   Reading **2:**_____ drops

   Add the above readings and divide by 3 to find the average:

   Reading **1**_____drops + Reading **2**_____drops + Reading **3**_____drops =_____

   Total drops ÷ 3 = _____average drops per minute

2. **How much water drips from the jug in a minute?** (Collect one minute's worth of water and measure the volume in a graduated cylinder. Take three readings and find the average.)

   Reading **1:**_____ ml   Reading **3:**_____ ml

   Reading **2:**_____ ml

   Add the above readings and divide by 3 to find the average:

   Reading **1**_____ ml + Reading **2**_____ml + Reading **3**_____ ml =_____

   Total ml ÷ 3 = _____ average ml per minute

3. **Estimate how much time it will take the jug to empty:**

   _____

4. **Calculate the time it will take the jug to empty.** (**NOTE:** One gallon of water equals 3,785 ml.)

   3,785 ml per gallon ÷ average amount of water collected in one minute = minutes for jug to empty:

   3,785 ml per gallon ÷ _____ ml per minute =

   _____ minutes for jug to empty

5. **Time how long it takes for the jug to actually empty** (optional) (**NOTE:** reduced pressure as water level goes down may cause some jugs not to empty completely. Do not shake or squeeze jug, stop timing after the last drop naturally falls): _____

6. **How do the answers to 3, 4, and 5 compare to each other?** Write the reasons why they are similar or different (see note in number 5 for suggestions).

7. **If this was a faucet leaking this much water, how much water would be lost in one hour?**

   Average amount of water collected in one minute x 60 minutes = ml per hour:

   ____ ml per minute x 60 minutes = ____ml per hour

8. **How much water would be lost in one day?**

   ml per hour x 24 hours = ml per day:

   _____ ml per hour X 24 hours = _____ ml per day

9. **How much water would be lost in one week?**

   ml per day x 7 days = ml per week:

   _____ ml per day x 7 days = _____ ml per week

10. **How much water would be lost in one month?** (For simplicity, assume 1 month equals exactly 4 weeks.)

    ml per week x 4 weeks = ml per month:

    _____ ml per week x 4 weeks = _____ ml per month

11. **Many people have to pay for their water. If water costs $10 for every 200 ft³* (200 ft³ equals 5,663,369 ml), and if the water dripping from the jug was a real faucet, how much would a person pay each month for this water down the drain?**

    _____ ml per month x ($10 ÷ 5,663,369 ml) =

    $_____ per month

    *Replace value with actual cost of water for your community, if known.

The Price Is Right

When you pay your water bill, what exactly are you paying for?

▼ Summary
Students learn about economics and environmental planning as they calculate the cost of building a water development project.

Objectives
Students will:
- calculate the costs involved in supplying clean water to consumers and removing wastewater.
- recognize that cost and environmental considerations influence the planning and construction of water projects.

Materials
- *Sample water bill* (optional)
- Copies of **Student Data and Instruction Sheet**
- Copies of **Water Development System Map**
- *Calculators*
- *Ruler*

Making Connections
Students who earn their own spending money likely understand the value of certain things, such as compact disks, snack foods, or gas for their cars. They have probably heard adults complain about paying bills, such as the water bill. They may wonder why we pay for water. Learning the real and sometimes hidden costs and processes involved in supplying clean water to and removing wastewater from homes helps students appreciate the value of water resources.

Background
Individuals, businesses, communities, states, and countries are all involved in water resource economics on a daily basis. The cost of water influences individual and community decisions, such as whether to take long showers, whether to purchase a new water-efficient irrigation system, and whether to upgrade a wastewater plant.

When current water supplies no longer meet the needs of a growing community or when the waste generated by this growing population becomes too much for a treatment plant to process, water management decisions must be made. Options include reducing water consumption through conservation, installing more efficient water technologies, and building new treatment facilities. People may be asked to approve an increase in taxes or an increase in water or wastewater treatment bills to cover additional costs. Whatever option is chosen, chances are public funds will be needed; therefore, citizens will have opportunities to voice their opinions and to raise concerns. Most levels of government conduct public planning forums.

There is far more to constructing a water project than meets the eye. Aside from the construction of the physical plant, surveying potential sites, engineering water lines, establishing operation systems, and maintaining production also contribute to the cost. The list in the side bar on page 335 highlights costs associated with various water projects. (Costs vary among different regions of the country.)

Procedure
▼ Warm Up
Show or describe a water bill to students. What do they think is involved in establishing the cost of water? Why does water need to be paid for? To help students appreciate the costs involved in securing water resources, have students play a price guessing game. Using the list of sample costs on page 335, ask them to guess the cost of a particular

---

▤ Grade Level:
High School

▤ Subject Areas:
Mathematics (Economics), Government, Environmental Science

▤ Duration:
Preparation time: 30 minutes
Activity time: 50 minutes

▤ Setting: Classroom

▤ Skills:
Gathering information (calculating, measuring); Analyzing (comparing and contrasting); Evaluating; Presenting

▤ Charting the Course
Students should conduct "Wet-Work Shuffle" prior to this activity to understand water treatment systems. These systems are further explored in "Reaching Your Limits" and "Sparkling Water." Other water management projects that require consideration of costs and benefits are found in "Humpty Dumpty," "Super Bowl Surge," and "Dilemma Derby."

▤ Vocabulary
easement, municipal water system, well field

Components of Municipal Water and Wastewater Treatment Systems

1. WATER SOURCE (GROUND WATER WELL FIELD)
2. UNTREATED WATER LINE
3. WATER TREATMENT PLANT
4. WATER TANK
5. WATER MAIN
6. HOUSEHOLD WATER LINE
HOMES
A. HOUSEHOLD SEWER LINE
B. COMMUNITY SEWER LINE
C. WASTEWATER TREATMENT PLANT
C1. SETTLING TANK
C2. AERATION BASIN
D. WASTEWATER TREATMENT OUTLET
SLUDGE DIGESTER

ADAPTED FROM "A WATER SYSTEM" (POSTER), BY PERMISSION. © 1988, AMERICAN WATER WORKS ASSOCIATION.

project. Instruct them to guess "higher" or "lower" until they reach the correct price.

Ask students to diagram how they think water gets from a water source to their homes, and from their homes back to the water source. Review the *Components of Municipal Water and Wastewater Treatment Systems* with students. What do students think of the costs reflected in a water bill now?

▼ The Activity
1. **Explain to students that their task is to help a community redesign their municipal water and wastewater treatment systems. A** new water treatment plant has already been built, but they need to construct water lines through which untreated water can flow from the source (a ground water well field) to the new plant. In addition, a new wastewater treatment plant must be

built and sewer lines run from the community to the plant. Both construction projects need to use Best Management Practices; "best" can be defined as the route and location that require the least costs and have fewer environmental effects. NOTE: Real-life situations would involve many other considerations for choosing the best location, including health concerns, substrate conditions, aesthetics, political matters, and so forth.

2. **Divide the class into small groups; supply each group with a copy of the *Water Development System Map* and review its contents and environmental features. Give each group a copy of the *Student Data and Instruction Sheet* and discuss.**

3. **Allow time for groups to identify what they think is the best location for each project.**

▼ Wrap Up
Have each group present its proposed plan and calculated costs for class review. Group members should summarize considerations and factors they used to help them make the decision. Encourage students to provide constructive criticism for the proposed plans. Can the class reach consensus regarding where to locate the projects?

Present students with the *Answer Key*. Do students agree with the solutions given in the key? Tell students that if this was a real-life situation, other factors and conditions would come into play, and the actual locations might be different. In other words, students may have justifiable reasons why their proposals are better.

Inform students that in some situations, citizens must pay additional taxes to fund the construction of water management projects. How do

334

Household

a. 200-foot-deep (60 m) well, $2,400
b. bathroom faucet, $65
c. dishwasher, $410
d. 16- x 32-foot (5 m x 10 m) swimming pool, $16,000
e. portable hot tub for six, $6,000
f. hot water heater, 50 gal. (190 l), gas, $350
g. septic system, $5,000

City (50,000 residents plus businesses)

a. new 6 million-gallon (22.8 million l) water storage tank or reservoir, $5 million
b. wastewater treatment plant, $45 million
c. water treatment facility (to treat drinking water), $8 million
d. water transmission mains, $370,000 (cost per mile [1.6 km])
e. full-coverage sprinkler system for 18-hole golf course, $480,000
f. sewer outfall main, $350,000 (per mile [1.6 km])
g. manhole, $2,000

County

a. 250-foot (76 m) riprap and jetty along bank of badly eroding stream, $150,000

State

a. two interstate bridges crossing river, each 300- x 75-feet (91 m x 21 m), $2.2 million

National

a. Hoover Dam Project (1935), $385 million
b. Central Valley Project (1955), $400 million
c. Panama Canal (early 1900s), $380 million
d. restoring a portion of the Kissimmee River, $400 million

Answer Key

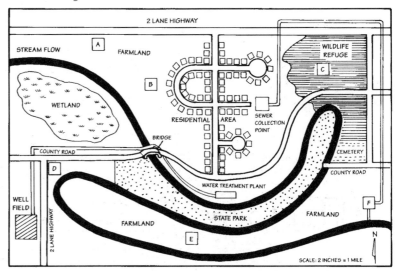

they feel about citizens incurring the cost of the project through increased taxes? Do students think they would willingly pay the price for new water supplies? Which would they rather do: change their habits and use less water, or pay more money for increased supplies? Discuss how the cost of water management projects is often a prohibiting factor to building new systems.

Have students learn about water projects in local communities. How much did they cost? Who paid for them?

Assessment

Have students:
- analyze what factors affect water use charges (*Warm Up* and *Wrap Up*).
- calculate the cost to build an untreated water line, a wastewater treatment plant, and sewer lines (step 3).
- determine the route for an untreated water line to a treatment plant, select a site for the construction of a wastewater treatment plant,

and justify their choices (step 3 and *Wrap Up*).
- evaluate other students' selected locations for water projects (*Wrap Up*).

Extension

Have students role-play bankers and project designers. The project designers request a loan for their water development system. Because the bank will only loan funds to one group of project designers, students should be well prepared to answer the banker's questions, such as "How much money do you need?" "What is your economic justification for the loan?" and "How do you intend to repay this loan?" The banker will consider the best designed project plans, proposed budget, and responses to questions when determining the loan recipient.

Resources

Barnes, D., et. al. 1981. *Water and Wastewater Engineering Systems.* London, England: Pitman Books Limited.

Cheremisinoff, Paul N. 1993. *Water Management and Supply.* Englewood Cliffs, N. J.: PTR Prentice Hall.

Student Data and Instruction Sheet

Instructions

Read the following information and refer to the map and data to find the best locations for the untreated water line and the wastewater management plant.

Untreated Water Line

- sketch possible routes for the water line

- calculate costs for each route

- assess environmental impacts of each route

- use the above information to determine the most cost-effective and environmentally sensitive route

Wastewater Treatment Plant

- consider placing the wastewater treatment plant at each of the six designated sites on the map

- assess the best location based on the following:
  - costs (of running a single major sewer line from town to the plant)
  - environmental concerns (specifically, proximity to discharge site [the river], direction of streamflow, quality of ground water being drawn into pumping wells, quality of river water that could become part of the ground water)
  - legal placement of wastewater lines (it may be unlawful to cross wetlands, public property, state parks, or wildlife refuges)
  - aesthetics and health issues (including odor, downstream flows, and landscape considerations)

- use the above information to determine the most cost-effective and environmentally sensitive location

Prepare a presentation for your classmates, including reasons why you think your routes and sites are the best.

Data

NOTE: The following are hypothetical costs; they include materials and labor. Contact local engineers, treatment plants, and construction companies to obtain costs more relevant to your community.

- untreated water line (runs from well field to plant) = $12/foot ($40/meter)

- main sewer line (runs from sewer collection point to wastewater treatment plant) = $9/foot ($30/meter)

- wastewater treatment plant = $45,000,000

- easement on farmland = $1,000 per linear mile

- construction of lines under existing two-lane highway = $100,000

- construction of line to cross river (this complicated process involves permits and completing environmental impact statements) = $500,000

- construction of line to cross existing bridge = $50,000

- construction of line to cross wetland = illegal

Water Development System Map

Name: _____   Date: _____

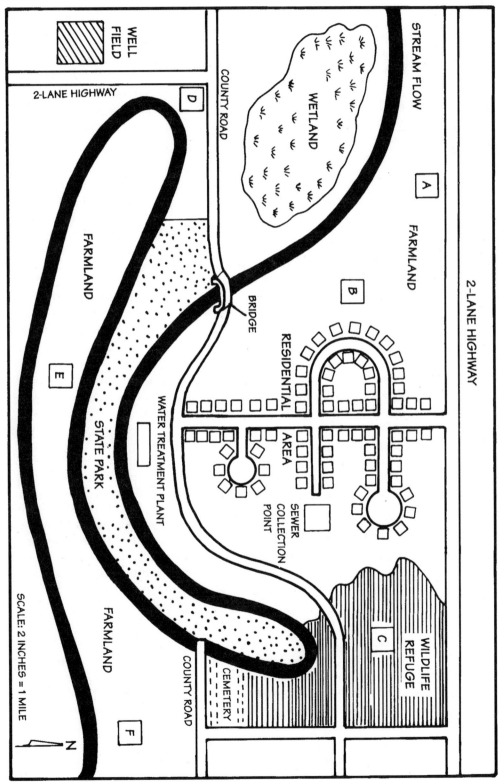

The Pucker Effect

People in your town are suffering from contaminated drinking water and are experiencing the "pucker effect"—pursed lips and sour dispositions. Your mission is to discover the source of the contamination.

▼ Summary

Students observe how ground water transports pollutants, and simulate ground water testing to discover the source of contamination.

■ **Grade Level:**
Middle School, High School

■ **Subject Areas:**
Environmental Science, Earth Science, Health, Government

■ **Duration:**
Preparation time: 90 minutes
Activity time: two 50-minute periods

■ **Setting:** Classroom

■ **Skills:**
Gathering information (observing, measuring, recording); Organizing (mapping, manipulating materials); Analyzing; Interpreting (translating)

■ **Charting the Course**
The concept of pH is discussed in the activity "Where Are the Frogs?" To gain an understanding of ground water, students should participate in "Get the Ground Water Picture." The activity "A Grave Mistake" should follow "The Pucker Effect"; it provides students the opportunity to use skills learned in this activity to solve a real problem.

■ **Vocabulary**
ground water, point source pollution, plume

Objectives

Students will:
- describe how underground point source pollutants move through ground water.
- analyze data from test wells they have "drilled" to identify point source contamination.

Materials

- *Cup of sand* (Mix grape-flavored powdered drink into the sand and poke holes in the bottom of the cup.)
- *1 clear baking pan*
- *Unsweetened grape-flavored powdered drink mix*
- *Misting bottle*
- *Water*

Each group will need the following:
- *Aluminum baking pans or fast-food salad containers*
- *Unsweetened lemonade-flavored powdered drink mix*
- *Small objects to raise end of tray one inch (2.5 cm)* (e.g., blocks of wood, books)
- *Sand* (enough to fill baking pan; an alternative is to use soil, but the results are not as dramatic)
- *Copies of* **How to Hide and Seek Your Contaminant**
- *Copies of* **Project Pucker Effect: Background, Procedures, and Data Sheet**

- *Straws*
- *13 pH papers*
- *Misting bottle*
- *Beaker of water*

Making Connections

Students may have been personally affected by contaminated drinking water or have heard of an incident within their communities. The media often report news of polluted ground water. Learning about the possible effects of point source pollution may prompt students to assume a more active role in protecting ground water in their communities.

Background

Throughout history, waste has been stored in dumps, deposited in the ocean, burned, and buried. Many years ago it became a practice to bury storage tanks underground. These tanks were used, and continue to be used, to store petroleum products (gas and oil), chemicals, and chemical waste products for manufacturers, industries, and businesses. However, many underground storage tanks have eroded, leaking their contents into ground water. When a pollutant is identified as coming from a single source, it is referred to as point source pollution.

Point source pollution of ground water can originate from a variety of situations. These include leaking pipes, faulty landfills, above-ground dumpsites, and underground storage tanks. (See *Ground Water Contamination: A True Story* sidebar on page 340.)

When contaminants dissolve in or are carried by ground water, they move in

338

the direction of ground water flow. If a well is pumping near the pathway of the flowing contaminants, the pollutants are likely to be drawn up into the well along with the water.

Contaminants seeping underground from concentrated masses are called plumes. These plumes resemble the smoke from a chimney, only underground. The concentration of the pollutant is high near the source of the contamination, and dilutes as it spreads further from its origin. The shape and size of these plumes are influenced by several variables, including the physical and chemical properties of the contaminant, the rate at which materials are added to the contaminating source, the action of wells pumping or withdrawing ground water, and the rate water moves through the substrate.

When it was discovered that pollutants from leaking underground storage tanks had been affecting ground water supplies, new legislation was established to regulate existing tanks and strengthen environmental protection criteria for new tanks. For example, the use of underground tanks requires extensive leak-monitoring equipment and less corrosive tank materials. In many instances, old tanks are removed and replaced with updated tanks (sometimes above ground), and monitoring equipment is installed along with the tank. This is done for liability purposes; it costs far less to replace tanks than to clean up after one has leaked. Millions of dollars are currently being spent to clean many sites of leaking underground tanks.

However, leaking underground storage tanks are not the only threat to ground water quality. Septic tank systems, hazardous waste sites, sanitary landfills, and wastewater disposal ponds also pose threats.

Not all contaminants have an odor. They can go undetected in a drinking water supply if it is not regularly tested. City water is frequently tested for contaminants. People who use private wells must have their water supply tested regularly.

Procedure
▼ Warm Up
Show students a cup of sand mixed with grape-flavored drink mix and ask if it appears to be clean. Pour water onto the cup and allow water to filter through; it should pick up the drink mix and turn purple. Have students ever heard of a situation where water in the ground got contaminated? How was the source of the contamination detected? Tell students that sometimes clues help to locate the origin of underground pollutants.

Fill the clear baking pan with sand to a depth of 1.2 inches (3 cm) and elevate one end of the pan 2.4 inches (6 cm). Make a small hole in the sand at the elevated end of the pan and bury a small pile of grape-flavored powder in the hole. Tell students the powder represents a substance that

has been stored underground. Ask students to predict what will happen when you spray water on the pan. List reasons for their predictions on the board.

Represent years of rainfall by gently spraying the pan with water for 5 to 10 minutes (or until the sand is saturated). Lift the pan and show the bottom. A streak of purple should originate from the source and follow the flow of water as it filters downhill. Discuss student observations. Explain that the streak of "contaminant" is called a plume. Tell students that since the source of the contamination can be identified, the pile of powder is known as point source pollution. What if a community well field or homes with private wells were pumping water from the formation through which the plume was traveling? Discuss how drinking water could be affected by the underground contaminant.

▼ The Activity
1. Ask students to form small groups. Each group is a well-drilling company (team) that tests ground water quality. Give each team an aluminum cake pan filled with 2.4 inches (6 cm) of sand. Have each group mark the outside of one end of the tray with an "X."

2. Tell students to bury a small pile of lemonade-flavored pow-

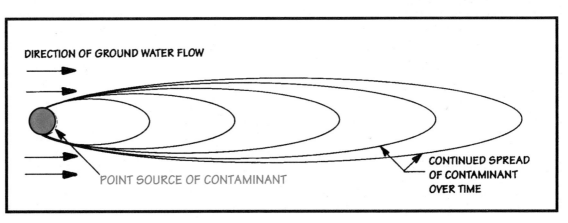

DIRECTION OF GROUND WATER FLOW

POINT SOURCE OF CONTAMINANT

CONTINUED SPREAD OF CONTAMINANT OVER TIME

dered drink mix somewhere in the sand. (See *How to Hide and Seek Your Contaminant*.) Have them sketch a map showing where they have hidden the contaminant, then switch pans with another team.

Ground Water Contamination: A True Story

People in a community noticed the smell of gas in their basements and in their well water. The fire department was notified because residents feared an explosion would occur in their homes. (A few days earlier, a manhole cover was blown off by ignited gas vapors.) Because this was an obvious public health threat, an intense effort was made to locate the source of the petroleum. Was it a leaking pipeline? Old diesel fuel tanks in the basement of a neighbor's abandoned house? The gas station at the end of the block? These were among the many possible sources of gas leaks. The health department limited the possible sources by mapping places that had identified gas odors and by determining the intensity of the fumes. They knew that as the concentration of gas smells increased, they were likely getting closer to the source. They narrowed the search further by drilling test wells to measure the gas content in ground water. After a few weeks of testing and systematic elimination of potential sources, officials located the origin: an abandoned underground gas tank. Apparently, the tank had been leaking for more than a decade before the plume reached the sewer systems and basements. The plume, flowing in the direction of ground water, was approximately one mile long, several feet wide, and several feet deep. An engineering company was contracted to clean the ground water. The process was time consuming and costly.

3. **Distribute the *Project Pucker Effect Background, Procedures, and Data Sheet*. Have students complete the investigation and record their results. Each team should compare their results to the maps made by the teams that hid the contaminant.**

▼ *Wrap Up*

Ask students to share what they observed. How did they use the results of the pH tests to locate the contaminant? Ask students if they had enough pH test papers to pinpoint the source of the contaminants. If they were given an unlimited supply, could they guarantee that the source could be accurately located? In a real situation, would testers have unlimited time and resources?

Explain that in reality underground storage tanks can contain fuel oil or radioactive materials. Discuss what problems could arise if these materials leaked into water supplies. What challenges do students think there could be to cleaning ground water?

Students may be interested in researching what steps their community is taking to avoid ground water contamination from storage tanks, septic tank systems, sanitary landfills, chemical landfills, or wastewater disposal ponds.

Assessment

Have students :
- simulate ground water testing methods (step 3).
- identify a source of contamination using simulated ground water testing methods (step 3).
- cite challenges to locating and cleaning underground contamination (*Wrap Up*).

Upon completing the activity, for further assessment have students:
- illustrate and describe the formation of an underground plume.

Extensions

Students can also compare the length and size of plume formations.

Prepare five clear baking pans as follows:
Pan #1: 1-inch (2.5 cm) depth of sand (this pan remains level)
Pan #2: 1-inch depth of sand (elevate one end about 1 inch)
Pan #3: 1-inch depth of sand (elevate one end about 2 inches [5 cm])
Pan #4: 1-inch depth of gravel (elevate one end about 1 inch)
Pan #5: 1-inch depth of a mixture of equal amounts of sand and gravel (elevate one end about 1 inch)

Make a small hole in the sand at the elevated end of each pan, and bury a small pile of grape-flavored powder in the hole. Ask students to predict what will happen when you spray water on each pan. List reasons for their predictions on the board. Spray each pan with water and discuss student observations. Ask them to summarize how the size and shape of sand particles and slope influence the shape and size of the plume.

Have students investigate the real costs of drilling test wells. Why would these costs vary among regions (depth of water table, hardness of substrate, access to site, etc.)?

Have students collect newspaper articles that convey information about ground water contamination within their own community, region, or state.

Resources

Daley, Robert B. 1986. *Earth Science, A Study of a Changing Planet*. Newton, Mass.: CEBCO.

Harte, John. 1991. *Toxics A to Z*. Berkeley, Calif.: University of California Press.

Jorgensen, Eric P. 1989. *The Poisoned Well*. Washington, D.C.: Island Press.

How to Hide and Seek Your Contaminant

HIDING THE CONTAMINANT	SEEKING THE CONTAMINANT

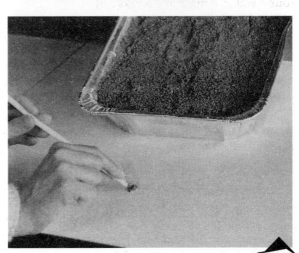

Project Pucker Effect:
Background

Your Task: Conduct water quality tests and locate the leaking underground storage tank in your community.

Background: In the fall of 1981, the ACME Lemonade Corporation closed its manufacturing facilities. This action took place amid allegations that the company had secretly been producing a highly toxic unsweetened brand of lemonade. Since the plant closed, the buildings and all above-ground evidence of the site have been removed. Recently, a few people living in the area have developed strange symptoms—puckered lips leading to sour dispositions.

The Challenge: The ACME Lemonade Corporation is suspected of abandoning a large storage tank filled with a vile, unsweetened lemonade product that has leaked into the local drinking water supply. With limited resources, you must track down and describe the extent of the spreading chemicals before the *pucker effect* strikes full force.

The Tools:
  An environmental
    TESTING DRILL RIG (a straw)

  The Hygiene-O-Matic
    SANITATION STATION (a beaker of water)

  A multi-million dollar
    TESTING LABORATORY (pH test paper)

Hints: The chemical leaked by ACME produces a telltale acidity when combined with water. Acidity can easily be measured by using a system of pH values. Ordinary tap water will leave test paper blue, while the contaminants turn it green.

WARNING: **Resources are limited.** Find the leaking underground storage tank with your allotted number of test papers or risk the pucker effect for every citizen.

Procedures

1. Write the name of your team and students' names on the data sheet.

2. Elevate the end of the pan that is marked with an "X" 1 inch (2.5 cm).

3. Sketch a picture of the pan on the data sheet, top view.

4. Fill a misting bottle with water, test the pH of the water, and record the reading on the data sheet. After the test paper has dried, affix it to the data sheet. *This is the normal color of the water without contamination.*

5. Simulate a gentle rain by misting the site with water for 5–10 minutes. MIST SLOWLY; no surface runoff should occur.

6. Fill SANITATION STATION with water. Rinse DRILL RIG with water.

7. **Begin collecting and testing as follows:**
   a. Place the DRILL RIG over the most likely location of the contaminant plume.
   b. Press the DRILL RIG down into the soil.
   c. Plug the top of the DRILL RIG with your finger. (Avoid losing any of the sample!)
   d. Lift the DRILL RIG from the soil.
   e. Place a **small** quantity of the collected sample onto the **edge** of the pH test paper (TESTING LABORATORY).
   f. Observe and record the test results.
   g. Rinse (sterilize) the DRILL RIG to eliminate contaminating the next sample.
   h. Repeat steps **a** through **g** until you have used all of your pH test papers or until you think you have found the contamination site.

8. Record the location of each test site on the data sheet by affixing the dried test paper to the location.

9. When the contamination site is found, mark the location on the data sheet with a large "X."

Project Pucker Effect:
Data Sheet

Team Name _____ Teacher: _____

Team Members _____ Date: _____

Misting Water pH Value: _____ Affix Paper Here

SITE MAP

Raised end of tray (marked "X")

Low end of tray

Reaching Your Limits

Would you like to be considered one in a million? How about one in a billion?

■ **Grade Level:**
Upper Elementary, Middle School

■ **Subject Areas:**
Environmental Science, Government, Health, Mathematics

■ **Duration:**
Preparation time: 30 minutes
Activity time: 50 minutes

■ **Setting:** Classroom

■ **Skills:**
Organizing (classifying); Analyzing (identifying relationships); Interpreting (summarizing)

■ **Charting the Course**
How pollutants enter waterways is addressed in "Sum of the Parts" and "Rainy-Day Hike." Students learn how water gets to and from their houses in "Wet-Work Shuffle." In "Sparkling Water," they explore the processes of wastewater treatment. Processes used to assess water quality are introduced in "Macroinvertebrate Mayhem." The cost involved in building treatment plants is explored in "The Price Is Right."

■ **Vocabulary**
water quality standard, parts per million, water treatment plant

▼ Summary
Through a game of "limbo," students experience the effort involved in meeting drinking-water quality standards.

Objectives
Students will:
- describe the relationship between water quality and water treatment.
- be aware of the ratio of one to a million.

Materials
- *Four 100- or 250-ml beakers*
- *Water mixed with blue food coloring*
- *Clear water*
- *10-ml graduated cylinder or pipette*
- *3" x 5" index cards*
- *Lightweight wood or metal poles, broomsticks, or metersticks*
- *Ruler*

Making Connections
Most students know that water flowing out of municipal faucets has been treated. Drinking water standards are set to ensure water is potable. Students may have experienced meeting standards, for example, when a parent has the expectation of a neat room. Students can relate to the energy involved in cleaning up a dirty room versus tidying up a neat room. Simulating how polluted water requires more energy for treatment to meet standards than cleaner water helps students appreciate the importance of keeping water supplies clean.

Background
State and federal agencies determine water quality standards. The U.S. Environmental Protection Agency (EPA) and state environmental protection or health agencies work together in monitoring the quality of surface water (streams, rivers, and lakes) and ground water sources (aquifers). These agencies and other local units of government are responsible for assessing the quality of water, setting acceptable or safe drinking-water standards, monitoring for changes, and recommending water quality improvement practices.

Water quality standards are established based on the assumption that drinking water with concentrations of organic or inorganic compounds above a designated limit could cause health problems. Scientists measure and report water contaminants in parts per million (ppm), parts per billion (ppb), and parts per trillion. Although these may seem extremely small concentrations, the toxicity of many chemicals can cause health problems above these levels. People can smell petroleum products in water at concentrations as low as 10 parts per billion.

Treating drinking water involves filtering the water, allowing sediments to settle, and adding a disinfectant (such as chlorine) to kill bacteria and other pathogens. Sources of water for treatment plants include reservoirs, rivers, ground water, etc.

Sometimes chemicals are inadvertently added to water as a result of human activities (e.g., urban and agricultural runoff, discharge from industrial plants). However, in some areas of the country, the natural or baseline water quality of a river, lake, or aquifer may have high levels of certain chemicals. For example, if the surrounding rock material contains a high concentration of a certain compound (such as arsenic), the chemical will likely be present in water.

Water quality standards have been established for hundreds of chemicals

344

(sulfate, arsenic, benzene, lead, etc.); some chemicals are not considered dangerous, while others are extremely toxic. Municipal and rural water suppliers strive to provide water to users that either meets or exceeds established drinking-water standards. If a test confirms that an established standard has been violated, a representative of the water system will be contacted and asked to take appropriate action to clean the water and meet the standard. If the water cannot be treated to meet the standard, the water provider will be asked to find a new source of water or to improve treatment capabilities. In either case, the cost is high, resulting in higher taxes or water fees.

Polluted water affects aquatic plants and animals. Unlike humans, other animals and plants do not have the option of treating the water they live in. As water quality in a river or lake degrades, plant and animal life also changes. Most fish and wildlife species have a range of tolerance within which they can survive. This could be a certain range of temperature, oxygen level, pH, or food availability. For example, if a fish is adapted to living in a cool, clear, shallow stream and feeds on insects, changes affecting these stream characteristics will affect the survival of the fish.

Water quality standards for aquatic life are established to prevent killing fish and impairing growth or reproduction. Other standards are set to prevent the accumulation of chemicals in fish flesh, which could pose a health hazard to humans who eat large quantities of contaminated fish.

Procedure
▼ Warm Up
Show students a glass of water. Ask how they know the water is safe to drink. Have students list things they

Water treatment plant. FRANK OBERLE

would like to know about the water before they drink it. Why would they drink water from a faucet, but probably not from a mountain stream?

NOTE: For simplicity, only metric measurements are used in the following demonstration.

Carefully measure out 100 ml of water mixed with blue food coloring. Tell students that this represents a pollutant. Ask them if they would like to drink it. Take 10 ml of the

pollutant and put it into 90 ml of clear water. Calculate the concentration (1 part per 10). Would they drink it? What if they were thirsty? Take 10 ml of this diluted solution and put it in 90 ml of water. What is the concentration of the pollutant? (1 part per 100). Would they drink the water now? What if they were in the desert? Dilute the pollutant one more time, 10 ml to 90 ml of clear water. What is the concentration now? (1 part per 1,000). Tell them this measurement is known as parts per thousand (ppt). Repeat three more times until you reach parts per million. Would they drink water with the pollutant now?

Remind students that although dilution is a method of reducing the concentration of a pollutant within a sample, to ensure water is safe to drink, other forms of treatment are necessary.

▼ *The Activity*

1. **Discuss reasons why water is treated. Since removing all chemicals is economically impractical, explain that the government sets standards to define how much of a pollutant is allowable in water.** Often these amounts are set at parts per million or parts per billion. For example, only five milliliters of a certain pollutant are allowed per one million milliliters of water (5 ppm). To give students a sense of this quantity remind them of the *Warm Up* demonstration and present the following example. Have them imagine a line of one million white cars. (They would stretch across the United States.) If five of these cars were blue, that would represent five cars per million, or five parts per million. Have students provide additional examples that illustrate the concept of five parts per million.

2. **Give students an example of a standard to be set for the class.** Have students count how many of them are wearing blue jeans, compared to the total number of students in class. If 6 out of 25 students are wearing blue jeans, the concentration of blue jeans would be 6 parts per 25.

How would students feel if a standard were set limiting the number of pairs of blue jeans that could be worn in class? You could set a blue jeans standard; that is, the student concentration of blue jeans on any single day could not be greater than six. To

DILUTION OF THE BLUE POLLUTANT

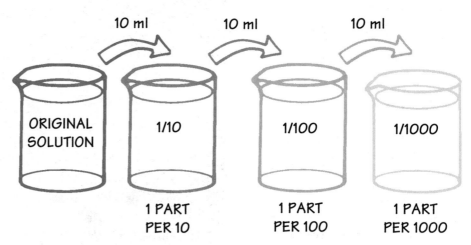

10 ml   10 ml   10 ml

ORIGINAL SOLUTION   1/10   1/100   1/1000

1 PART PER 10   1 PART PER 100   1 PART PER 1000

meet this rather silly standard, your students would have to create a system to ensure that the standard was not violated.

3. **Explain to students that this analogy relates to water quality standards.** The government sets standards for a wide range of biological and chemical parameters. A city's water department attempts to meet the standards by locating water that is as pure as possible at the source (ground water, river, or lake), and then treating it to meet or exceed the standards.

4. **Tell students the game of "limbo" will be used to demonstrate the amount of effort required to treat water to meet standards. The height of the limbo bar represents water quality. Students making it under the bar symbolize successfully treated water. As water quality declines, the bar is lowered and the effort required to meet standards increases.**

5. **Ask students to brainstorm a list of things they can do to keep water clean, and a list of things that people do that pollute water. Transfer each item from the lists to a separate index card. Mix the cards and place them face down. Put the**

cards on a table or desk near the limbo pole.

6. **Students should prepare to play the limbo game by doing some stretching exercises. Have students line up and set the bar at the median (the height at which half the students are taller and half are shorter).** Most students should be able to pass under the bar. This means little effort is needed to meet water quality standards.

7. **Before each student attempts to go under the pole, he or she should pick up a card and read it to the class. Move the bar up three inches (7.5 cm) if the card's message improves the water quality and down three inches (7.5 cm) if the message degrades the quality.** The card is reshuffled into the deck.

8. **Have each student attempt to pass under the bar, "limbo style." When students are unable to make it under the bar this means the treatment plant is taking in water that is too polluted for the plant to maintain standards for which it was designed.** Because public drinking water supplies need to ensure the water is potable, actions will be taken to meet the standards. These actions might include instituting a different

346

treatment or finding another source of water. Unfortunately, many options available to water suppliers can be expensive and time consuming, or the technology does not yet exist.

▼ Wrap Up
Discuss the results of the game. Ask students to describe feelings they experienced as the pole was lowered to levels under which they could not maneuver. What would happen if a treatment plant could not reach set standards? Discuss water contamination and waterborne diseases. Have students contact water treatment plant managers to discover what standards the water in their community must meet.

Assessment
Have students:
- write examples that illustrate the concept of one part per million (step 1).
- relate water quality to pressures on water treatment plants to meet standards (*Wrap Up*).

Upon completing the activity, for further assessment have students:
- write lyrics for an original rap or song about the importance of protecting water quality.

Extensions
To increase the challenge of the game and to better represent water treatment processes, inform students that at treatment plants, water must be monitored and treated to fall within numerous biological and chemical parameters. Demonstrate this by setting up a row of poles at the class height median. Each pole represents the presence of a different compound in water (sodium, iron, nitrate, and lead). Passing under the bar means the standard for that chemical has been met. Failure to make it under the bar means the standard has been

Limbo: How low can you go?

violated. To get the level of a compound found in water (naturally or as a result of human activities), make a set of cards labeled "same," "higher (raise bar 3 inches [7.5 cm])," "lower (lower bar 3 inches [7.5 cm])." Randomly draw a card to determine a basic level; repeat for each bar. Have students attempt to pass under the series of poles.

Several rounds can be played; each round begins with drawing cards to adjust the height of each pole. Students may want to research how these chemicals are added to water supplies.

Instead of water treatment plants, students can represent aquatic animals and plants that have certain ranges of tolerance. The limbo bar represents water quality. If students can maneuver under the bar, they can tolerate the conditions. If not, the organisms die or must relocate.

Students may obtain water test kits and analyze the quality of their school's drinking water.

Visit a water treatment plant. Have students compare the processes of

water treatment and wastewater treatment.

Resources
Cheremisinoff, Paul N. 1993. *Water Management and Supply*. Englewood Cliffs, N.J.: Prentice Hall.

🍎 Cole, Joanna. 1987. *The Magic School Bus at the Waterworks*. New York, N.Y.: Scholastic.

Ingram, Colin. 1991. *The Drinking Water Book*. Berkeley, Calif.: Ten Speed Press.

Kroehler, Carolyn. (No date). *What Do the Standards Mean: A Citizen's Guide to Drinking Water Contaminants*. Blacksburg, Va.: V.P.I. and State University.

🍎 Schwartz, David M. 1985. *How Much Is a Million?* New York, N.Y.: Lothrop, Lee & Shepard Books.

🍎 ———. 1989. *If You Made a Million*. New York, N.Y.: Lothrop, Lee & Shepard Books.

Stewart, John C. 1990. *Drinking Water Hazards*. Hiram, Ohio: Envirographics.

Sparkling Water

■ **Grade Level:**
Middle School, High School

■ **Subject Areas:**
Environmental Science, Health

■ **Duration:**
Preparation time:
Part I: 50 minutes
Part II: 10 minutes

Activity time:
Part I: two 50-minute periods
Part II: 30 minutes .

■ **Setting:** Classroom

■ **Skills:**
Organizing (charting); Applying (predicting, experimenting); Evaluating (analyzing, testing)

■ **Charting the Course**
Students can relate water treatment processes to the water cycle ("The Incredible Journey" and "Imagine!"). The basic components of a wastewater treatment system are addressed in "Wet-Work Shuffle" and "The Price Is Right." In "Super Bowl Surge" students investigate the impact of a combined sewer system overflowing during peak demand.

■ **Vocabulary**
wastewater treatment

What happens to water after it swirls down the drain?

▼ **Summary**
Students develop strategies to remove contaminants from "wastewater."

Objectives
Students will:
• describe the processes for treating wastewater.
• compare how water is cleaned in the water cycle to how it is cleaned in contemporary water treatment systems.
• list nontoxic household cleaning methods.

Materials
• *Water*
• *Safety goggles*
• *A gallon-sized (3.8 l) container*
• *Small containers, about 3-ounce capacity (100 ml)*

Wastewater materials:
• *Coffee grounds*
• *Salt*
• *Vegetable oil*
• *Soil*
• *Yeast*
• *Soap*
• *Food scraps*
• *Vinegar*

Possible water cleaning materials:
• *Screens to use as filters*
• *Coffee filters*
• *Bleach*
• *Alum* (available at grocery stores in the baking section)—see safety alert, page 352.
• *Bowls or cups*
• *Straws or pipettes*
• *Spoons*
• *Baking soda*
• *Charcoal*
• *Talc*
• *Rocks and sand*

Possible testing materials:
• *pH paper*
• *Brown paper bag*
• *Wax paper*

Making Connections
Almost every city in the United States has some kind of wastewater treatment plant—it is the law! We often take for granted those processes which ensure that water we have used is clean when released back into streams, lakes, or ground water. By attempting to clean their own sample of "wastewater," students gain an appreciation for the processes involved in keeping water sources clean.

Background
In the United States, some streams and rivers were once so polluted that one of them even burned. (So much oil and chemical waste were in the Cuyahoga River that it caught fire in 1969.) Our rivers, lakes, and even oceans were once thought to be capable of carrying off and mysteriously treating our liquid wastes. Cities pumped raw sewage from homes and businesses directly into rivers. Factories sent water that had been used in manufacturing processes, untreated, into streams, lakes, and oceans. As this practice continued and populations expanded, water supplies degraded to the point of posing serious health hazards. The country collectively and systematically tackled, initially with much controversy, this point source pollution problem.

This effort required a broad shift in attitude. Incorporating wastewater treatment into cities and businesses was costly. Citizens had to vote for higher taxes to pay for cleaner water. Factories had to raise prices to pay for new treatment equipment. (For example, the United States and Canada have spent billions of dollars in constructing water treatment plants to improve the water quality of Lake Erie.)

The process used in contemporary wastewater treatment plants is similar to the natural process by which water is cleaned while moving through the water cycle. For example, as water flows through a river into a lake, it can pick up contaminants. While in the lake, these contaminants often sink to the bottom; this process is called settling. Because soil is a natural filtering mechanism, substances can be removed from water as it moves through soil. During evaporation, water is purified when individual water molecules break away from liquid water, leaving other materials behind. This action is called distillation.

From a historical perspective, as human populations grew and areas became settled, the demand for clean water exceeded the rate at which it could be naturally purified. There-fore, wastewater treatment plants became necessary. The addition of more complicated materials to the waste stream required more elaborate treatment as well.

The simplest form of wastewater treatment (primary treatment) involves filtration and settling procedures. In addition, waste materials that float are skimmed from the top. Forty-five to 50 percent of pollutants are removed utilizing primary techniques. In addition, most developed countries have a secondary process of waste treatment. Secondary treatment, mainly a biological process, removes from 85 to 90 percent of remaining pollutants.

Wastewater treatment plant, Erie, Pennsylvania. ROBERT K. GRUBBS, N E STOCK PHOTO

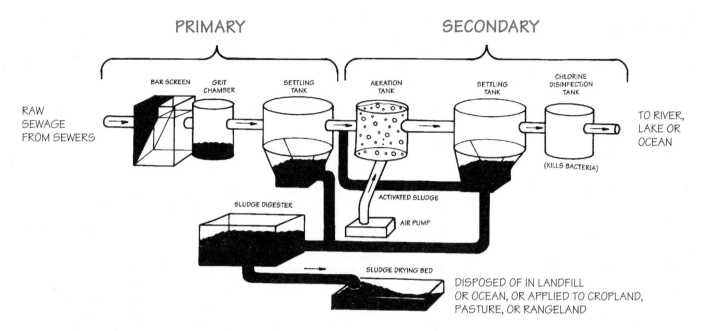

PRIMARY · SECONDARY

BAR SCREEN · GRIT CHAMBER · SETTLING TANK · AERATION TANK · SETTLING TANK · CHLORINE DISINFECTION TANK

RAW SEWAGE FROM SEWERS

TO RIVER, LAKE OR OCEAN

(KILLS BACTERIA)

SLUDGE DIGESTER

ACTIVATED SLUDGE

AIR PUMP

SLUDGE DRYING BED

DISPOSED OF IN LANDFILL OR OCEAN, OR APPLIED TO CROPLAND, PASTURE, OR RANGELAND

ADAPTED WITH PERMISSION FROM *ENVIRONMENTAL SCIENCE: SUSTAINING THE EARTH*, G. TYLER MILLER, JR. ©1991, WADSWORTH PUBLISHING COMPANY.

Helpful microorganisms consume most of the waste material in aerator tanks. Solids and microorganisms are separated from the wastewater in secondary settling tanks. Adding a disinfectant (such as chlorine) kills any remaining disease-causing organisms. The water leaves the treatment plant, to be released into nearby waterways.

Despite these processes, small amounts of undesirable materials can still remain in treated water. These include nitrates, phosphates, and heavy metals. Other chemicals, from pesticides and cleansers, may also remain in treated water. Some advanced plants have a third stage of waste treatment that helps remove most of these materials. These processes include filtration through activated carbon to remove organic materials, distillation to remove salts, and flocculation. Flocculation involves adding a coagulant or a chemical (such as alum) to water, which causes suspended particles to clump together and settle out. Unfortunately, since these advanced

treatment plants are expensive to build and operate, few communities have them. Many environmental consulting agencies are promoting the concept of engineered wetlands as a means of using natural processes to treat all wastewater.

Solid materials removed from wastewater are called sludge. In some cases sludge can be used as fertilizer for crops. At other times, it is buried or burned. If sludge is improperly treated or disposed of, it may contaminate water again.

Because some pollutants are extremely difficult to remove from wastewater, the best solution is to avoid putting them in water in the first place. Often the source of these pollutants is the kitchen, garage, or bathroom. When people pour oil, paint thinner, or pesticides down the drain, they add chemicals that may not be removed from water during treatment. Many household cleansers have caustic chemicals that lower water quality. Fortunately, alterna-

tive methods exist for keeping the house clean; many of these simply involve using baking soda and vinegar. Although such methods may require a little more work, they will not add toxic chemicals to our drinking water.

Procedure
▼ *Warm Up*
Ask students to describe the water cycle. Within the water cycle, where do students think water can be cleaned? Discuss filtering, settling, and distillation processes. Why must we treat water, instead of leaving it up to nature? Discuss human population growth and the advent of toxic chemicals. Have students ever heard of the river (the Cuyahoga) that burned in 1969? Today it is much cleaner.

Have students make a list of things that could be found in wastewater. Why are these things normally not found in lakes or streams? Ask students to write a paragraph or draw a picture describing how they think wastewater is cleaned.

▼ The Activity

Part I

1. **Involve students in making wastewater. Add soil, coffee grounds, vegetable oil, soap, salt, vinegar, yeast, and food scraps to a gallon jug of water.**

2. **Shake the jug thoroughly and distribute water in jars or beakers, one to each group of students. Each group should record its observations of the wastewater** (color, smell, pH, oil—put a drop on brown paper and see if an oil smear forms). **STUDENTS SHOULD NEVER TASTE THE WATER.**

3. **Tell students their mission is to try to clean this water. Show students the materials that can be used and instruct students on necessary safety procedures. THEY SHOULD NOT USE MORE THAN ABOUT HALF A TEASPOON (2 ML) OF THE BLEACH, ALUM, OR BAKING SODA. THEY SHOULD WEAR SAFETY GOGGLES AT ALL TIMES WHEN CONDUCTING THE TESTS AND WASH THEIR HANDS IMMEDIATELY AFTER COMING IN CONTACT WITH ANY MATERIALS.**

4. **The groups should write down the procedures they plan to use to clean the water.** Encourage them to use a series of steps, so they can evaluate each step separately. Check the proposed cleaning actions before they begin. Advise them to change their strategy if any methods appear to be dangerous.

SELECTED LIST OF NONTOXIC CLEANING SUBSTANCES	
Cleaning agent	**Alternative**
Room deodorizer	Baking soda
Drain cleaner	Boiling water, vinegar and baking soda, plunger
Window cleaner	Vinegar wiped with newspaper
Scouring powder	Baking soda and vinegar
Tarnish remover	Salt, baking soda, and a piece of aluminum foil in warm water

5. **Have students record their procedure in a table similar to the one below.**

6. **After they have attempted to clean their water, have students evaluate the results.** The groups can switch water samples to compare results. Evaluation strategies include color, smell, pH, and presence of oil. What are some contaminants they could not remove?

7. **Describe the general cleaning processes used in a treatment plant. Have students compare their procedures with what occurs in treatment plants.**

8. **Inform students of the materials that may remain even after treatment. Discuss reasons why treatment plants that can remove these contaminants are not being built.** (Reasons could include money, available resources, time, space, or practicality.)

Part II

Introduce students to a few of the alternative household cleaning materials they can use. (See table.) Encourage students to contact the department of natural resources, the health department, and environmental groups to research additional options. Have students test and use some of these methods at home and report the results to the class.

▼ Wrap Up and Action

Have students draw a diagram summarizing various ways wastewater is treated. Which of these methods are similar to natural processes in the water cycle? Compare students' diagrams to their descriptions of wastewater treatment from the *Warm Up*. Ask students to design a brochure describing alternatives to household cleaning agents. These can be distributed to friends and family.

CLEANING STRATEGY USED	DESCRIPTION OF WATER	COMMENTS ABOUT EFFECTIVENESS

Assessment

Have students:
- implement a variety of strategies to remove waste materials from water (*Part I*, steps 4-5).
- evaluate the effectiveness of their water treatment strategies (*Part I*, step 6).
- compare how water is cleaned in the water cycle to how it is cleaned in a wastewater treatment plant (*Warm Up* and *Wrap Up*).
- design a brochure highlighting alternative household cleaning agents (*Wrap Up*).

Upon completing the activity, for further assessment have students:
- discuss, "Does clear water = clean water?"

Extensions

Excess organic waste promotes the growth of microorganisms and the consumption of oxygen. To demonstrate this, mix 1/2 cup (120 ml) milk (symbolizing organic waste) in 1 cup (240 ml) of warm water. Add 10 to 12 drops of methylene blue (to indicate the presence of oxygen), and 2 tablespoons (3-5 g) of yeast (microorganisms). As the yeast consumes the milk (or organic waste), oxygen is used up. This is shown when the methylene blue color disappears. (This should occur in about 15 minutes.) Absence of oxygen affects the health of other aquatic organisms.

Visit a water treatment plant and a wastewater treatment plant or have representatives from these agencies speak to the class.

Students may be interested in testing their water for organic sediments and heavy metals. Often state departments of public health or natural resources and university laboratories can provide testing facilities. Sometimes a fee is charged. Some drugstores or school supply companies sell home water testing kits. (Lab-Aid sells a kit called "Qualitative Analysis of Water"; other examples include Nordic Ware Water Test Kit and Aqua-Pure Home Water Test Kit CW-TS; test kits can also be purchased at pet stores).

Resources

🍎 *About Wastewater Treatment.* 1988. To order, contact: Channing L. Bete Co., Inc., South Deerfield, MA 01373, or telephone (800) 628-7733, and request booklet number 45054.

🍎 Cole, Joanna. 1986. *The Magic School Bus at the Waterworks.* New York, N.Y.: Scholastic, Inc.

Household Hazardous Waste: What You Should & Shouldn't Do. 1987. Brochure. Contact: Water Environment Federation, 601 Wythe Street, Alexandria, VA 22314-1994. (703) 684-2400.

Nature's Way: How Wastewater Treatment Works for You. 1985. Brochure. Contact: Water Environment Federation, 601 Wythe Street, Alexandria, VA 22314-1994. (703) 684-2400.

Video: *The Murky Water Caper.* 1993. Distributed by: The Video Project, 5332 College Ave., Suite 1E, Oakland, CA 94618. (510) 655-9050.

Notes ▼

SAFETY ALERT

When preparing for the "Sparkling Water" activity, make certain that the alum to be used—which will be mixed with bleach—is PURE ALUM. Alum purchased at some pharmacies is ammoniated. Mixing ammonia with bleach creates a serious health hazard.

Super Bowl Surge

What do most people do during a football game's halftime?

▼ Summary

Students do in-depth research and present action plans to solve the problem of increased demands on a community's wastewater treatment plant.

Objectives

Students will:
- illustrate how demands on some treatment plants cause overflow.
- explain problems with sewage overflow.
- propose solutions to a water management problem.
- recognize how presentation strategies influence public policy.

Materials

- *Tokens or popcorn*
- *Cups*
- *A bucket or other container*
- *Copies of City of Beavertown Request for Proposals (RFP), Supplemental Form, and newspaper article, Treatment Plant Braces for "Super Sunday" Surge*
- *Chalk*

Making Connections

All over the country, millions of toilets are flushed daily. Generally the systems that collect and treat wastewater function efficiently. But when there are backups or the system becomes overextended during periods of heavy use, managers must assess the situation, make decisions, and implement them. By conducting their own investigations and making presentations, students experience the processes involved in setting management policies and practices.

Background

Most urban communities depend on wastewater treatment plants to ensure that water used by residences and businesses returns to nature clean. Engineers and city planners consider many factors when they design wastewater treatment plants. These considerations include: current and projected population growth, types of businesses, high usage periods, financial resources available to build appropriate treatment systems, and government regulations (laws and standards).

However, as populations grow (sometimes far exceeding the expectations of planners) and as the infrastructures of plants age, treatment plants may be unable to handle the increased output of residential waste. Many municipalities are familiar with surges (peaks) when a large number of people simultaneously contribute to the waste system (e.g., mornings, lunch time, and during the halftime of a Super Bowl game). In some cases, surges cause systems to overflow or back up. During times of overflow, some plants must dump excess waste directly into a body of water, such as a river or an overflow pond.

Unsightly and odorous, untreated waste leads to multiple health hazards for humans and wildlife. Sewage contains bacteria, protozoa, and viruses that normally live in the intestines of humans and other animals. Waterborne diseases such as dysentery and hepatitis are transmitted by contaminated water.

Organic waste promotes the growth of many microorganisms. When populations of bacteria and other single-celled organisms increase dramatically (bloom), they use more than their share of oxygen and nutrients. Toxins, produced by the microorganisms, and reduced oxygen levels endanger plants and animals. When sewage ends up in waterways,

- **Grade Level:**
Part I: Upper Elementary, Middle School
Part II: High School

- **Subject Areas:**
Government, Environmental Science, Health

- **Duration:**
Preparation time:
Part I: 15 minutes
Part II: 15 minutes

Activity time:
Part I: 30 minutes
Part II: up to one week

- **Setting:** Classroom

- **Skills:**
Interpreting (defining problems); Applying (problem solving; proposing solutions); Evaluating; Presenting (public speaking, persuading, reporting)

- **Charting the Course**
Prior to this activity, students should review how water is treated ("Sparkling Water") and how it gets to and leaves their homes ("Wet-Work Shuffle.") The cost involved in building new wastewater systems is addressed in "The Price Is Right." Water conservation methods are introduced in "Every Drop Counts."

- **Vocabulary**
wastewater treatment plant

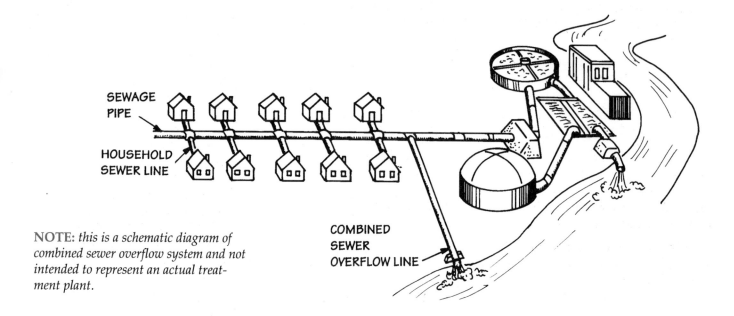

SEWAGE PIPE

HOUSEHOLD SEWER LINE

COMBINED SEWER OVERFLOW LINE

NOTE: *this is a schematic diagram of combined sewer overflow system and not intended to represent an actual treatment plant.*

humans are warned not to eat shellfish and other aquatic life because they may harbor poisons released by the microorganisms.

To treat increased amounts of waste, several alternatives are evaluated by managers. Options include building larger treatment plants or encouraging residents to reduce their water use. Residents can conserve water by limiting daily toilet flushes, placing a bottle of water in their tanks to reduce the water used per flush, and installing toilets that use very little water.

Sometimes, water management policies must change. This involves government planning boards consulting experts on methods to alleviate the problem. Boards evaluate plans based on available funds and on the needs and expectations of their communities.

Procedure
▼ Warm Up
Ask how many students watch football on Super Bowl Sunday. What do they do during halftime?

Tell students that they will participate in a simulation that demonstrates what happens to wastewater treatment systems when unusually large numbers of people simultaneously flush!

▼ The Activity

Part I

1. **Draw a chalk line down the middle of the room. Tell students this line represents a sewage pipe running underground. Near one end, draw a short line perpendicular to the first line. This represents the escape or overflow pipe that leads into a river. (A picture of a river or fish may be placed at the end of this pipe.)**

2. **Arrange chairs along each side of the line. Each chair represents a house on a street (see illustration). (The sewage pipe is buried beneath the street.) By each chair, place a cup of tokens or popcorn pieces. These tokens represent waste materials.**

3. **Place two students at one end of the line—the end closest to the**

escape pipe. They represent the treatment plant. Tell students that, in this simulation, five seconds are required for the treatment plant to clean the waste from each household. One student collects the tokens in a bucket while the other counts off five seconds.

4. **Have the remaining students stand in front of the chairs and count off by fours. Tell them that when you call "Flush!" and a number, students with that number should pick up a token, leave their homes, and walk down the pipe to the sewage plant. They should stand an arm's length from the student in front of them.**

5. **When a student reaches the sewage plant, he or she gives the token to the student representing the plant and returns home. This procedure is repeated for all students in line. If all students have their waste treated within one minute, the system has not overflowed.**

6. **Begin the activity by calling "Flush! One." Allow all number**

ones to go through the process. (This should take less than a minute.) If necessary, repeat another number.

7. **Next, call "Flush! One, Two, Three, and Four." All the students should try to move into the pipe. After about one minute, tell the class the system has backed up and students still waiting should move into the escape pipe. They drop their tokens at the end of the pipe and return to their seats. This represents untreated sewage being dumped directly into the river.**

8. **Have all students return to their seats and discuss their reactions to this simulation.** Are there times when everyone in a town may flush their toilets at once? Ask them to identify problems that arise when waste enters the river untreated.

Part II

1. **Divide the classroom into groups of four or five and provide each group with the newspaper article, Treatment Plant Braces for "Super Sunday" Surge.**

2. **Distribute the City of Beavertown Request For Proposals (RFP) form to each group. Tell students that their groups are the consulting teams. Each team will prepare a report that includes a proposed solution.** In addition to doing library research, they can contact sewage treatment plant managers and city planners to enrich their study. They may be interested in finding out if their local treatment plant has ever experienced surges during Super Bowl halftimes or other times of the day or year.

3. **Inform the teams the report must consist of the following:**
- A description of the problem and why it concerns the community (e.g., health hazards, environmental impacts).

- Individuals or groups in their community who would be affected by untreated waste overflowing into the river.

  Suggested groups:
  - Downstream communities
  - Birdwatchers
  - Friends of Beaver River
  - Beaver River Homeowners Association
  - Wildlife
  - Health department
  - Super Bowl fans
  - Livestock Association
  - Water bureau
  - U.S. Environmental Protection Agency
  - Farmers
  - Fishing enthusiasts
  - Boaters
  - Swimmers
  - Road bureau
  - Treatment plant

- Details on the effect of sewage overflow on one or more of these community groups. If possible, have each team investigate a different group. Encourage the team to conduct interviews with representatives of the groups in their own community.

- A recommended action plan for solving the potential overflow problem. The plan must address related environmental, economic, and social issues, including a report on the potential impact of sewage overflow on the community group(s) they investigated. (See *RFP* form.) Who will be affected? How will the plan ensure that community members will cooperate? What will be the cost? Who will pay? How will they pay? How much is each resident willing to pay?

4. **Each team will present their report and solution to the board. They must develop a five-minute classroom presentation illustrating their proposal. Provide each team**

Student representative from "consulting team" presents solution to the "Super Bowl Surge."

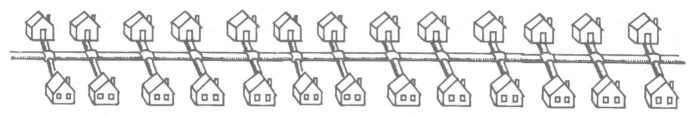

with a copy of the *Supplemental Form.* The presentation should be clear and persuasive and should involve all members of the consulting team (see *RFP* and *Supplemental Form*).

5. **Depending on the structure of the class and the desired depth of the reports, teams can be given a day or week to complete their studies and prepare reports.**

6. **Near the end of the planning process, have one member from each consulting team withdraw to form the Beaver River Water Authority Board (BRWAB).** (Each team can elect a member to leave and join the board.) The students on the BRWAB represent government officials, engineers, wastewater managers, concerned citizens, and health officials. BRWAB members will be responsible for listening to and judging each proposal. They should refer to the *Supplemental Form* for ideas by which to judge proposals. In addition, they may want to identify which concerns will particularly interest their characters. (NOTE: Consultants and potential bidders are usually not allowed to serve on boards. However, in this simulation, including students from each consulting team serves as a classroom management strategy.)

7. **Have BRWAB members design rules of conduct and establish a schedule for presentations.** They may want to provide teams with a list of judging criteria to guide the

presentations. Follow each team's presentation with a question and answer period.

8. **Conduct the mock board meeting and have teams present their reports.**

▼ *Wrap Up and Action*
Following the presentations, the BRWAB awards the "contract" to one team and explains the decision-making process used to arrive at their selection. Have the class discuss the results of the activity, commenting on how they feel about the decision-making process.

Have students contact their county or city government planning board; ask the board how and why they use consultants and which particular projects have required the use of outside experts. Also, have students share the results of their activity with their government planning board. Students may be interested in attending a public hearing on water quality issues.

Have students contact a local water quality agency for a report on the water quality of the local river. They could write letters to public officials, stating their positions on a water quality concern in the community.

Assessment
Have students:
• illustrate how a wastewater plant could overflow (*Part I*, steps 6 and 7).

• describe how overflow from a sewage plant could affect community members (*Part I*, step 8 and *Part II*, step 2).
• develop a plan of action to reduce the demands on a treatment plant (*Part II*, step 2).
• use persuasive strategies to present their proposal to a panel of judges (*Part II*, steps 3 and 7).
• evaluate proposed plans (*Wrap Up*).

Extensions
Have students request a sewage flow graph from a local wastewater treatment plant. Are there noticeable flow trends (up or down)? When do they occur?

Resources
Massachusetts Water Resources Authority. *Water Wizards.* Boston, Mass.: MWRA. (617) 242-6000.

Nature's Way: How Wastewater Treatment Works For You. 1985. Brochure. Contact: Water Environment Federation, 601 Wythe Street, Alexandria, VA 22314-1994. (703) 684-2400.

Treatment Plant Braces for "Super Sunday" Surge

Beavertown—While most of America eagerly anticipates the National Football League (NFL) Championship game, wastewater treatment plant operators at the City of Beavertown's Nutria Creek Plant dread "Super Sunday." Each year during the game, at each commercial break and at halftime, a surge of wastewater rushes into the sewer system, creating a real "super bowl" at the plant.

Nutria Creek operators jokingly refer to this phenomenon as the "rush to flush," but they quickly add that the sewer surge poses serious health, environmental, and economic problems.

"Last year we crested at 41 mgd [million gallons a day] at halftime," said plant superintendent Chuck "Red" LeSewer. "This plant was designed to handle a maximum of 40 mgd—it was a miracle we didn't have an overflow."

A raw sewage overflow into the nearby Nutria Creek and Beaver River would create a serious health, environmental, and economic disaster to the community.

The Cascadia Department of Environmental Health has required the City of Beavertown and the Beaver Creek Water Authority Board to design a solution to the potential raw-sewage overflow problem.

The city and the board have asked for consulting teams to examine the problem and propose solutions.

The Nutria Creek Plant was constructed by the city in 1977, when the sewer district's service population was 75,000. Today, more than 125,000 residents live in the district. Population growth and an aging collection system may require the city to increase capacity, at a cost of up to $40 million. The city and sanitary-sewer ratepayers hope the consulting teams will be able to propose a less costly alternative.

City of Beavertown Request for Proposals (RFP)
Potential "Super Sunday" Sanitary Sewer Surge

Background

The City of Beavertown is soliciting professional consultation to collect information and make recommendations regarding potential sewage overflow problems associated with professional football contests and other major social events.

City engineers have determined that during times of high water usage, the capacity of Beavertown's sanitary sewer system and wastewater treatment plant is nearly exceeded. This "rush to flush" phenomenon is particularly acute during halftime and at commercial breaks during the Super Bowl, as well as during Thanksgiving Day and New Year's Day televised sports events. To a lesser extent, this surge of sanitary sewage also occurs daily between the hours of six and nine in the morning.

The Cascadia State Department of Environmental Health has determined that this potential raw-sewage overflow problem poses a serious health threat, as well as a threat to the environmental and economic well-being of the Beaver Creek Basin.

The Facilities

The City of Beavertown Public Works Department provides sanitary sewer service for the urban portions of the Beaver River Basin. The city operates the Nutria Creek Wastewater Treatment Plant, which serves 50,000 homes and businesses in the basin. The Nutria Creek plant provides secondary treatment for a maximum flow of 40 million gallons per day. The effluent is discharged to the Beaver River. The Nutria Creek plant was constructed in 1977 to serve a projected population of 125,000 residents (54,000 homes and businesses).

Scope of Work

Qualified consulting teams will conduct surveys of potential affected parties, collect information on the proposed alternatives, and present recommended solutions to the Beaver River Water Authority Board of Directors (BRWAB).

Criteria

Proposed solutions to the potential overflow problem should be comprehensive and creative, and should address the concerns of all affected parties. Consulting teams should consider the environmental as well as economic costs and benefits of each proposed solution.

Consulting teams will be judged on the completeness, feasibility, creativity, and clarity of their presentations, and on the expected results of proposed solutions. Teams will also be judged on their overall presentation skills, teamwork, and study habits. Audio/visual and poster presentations are encouraged.

Time Line

Consulting team recommendations are due for presentation to the BRWAB within _____.

Supplemental Form
City of Beavertown RFP

Name of consulting team/firm: _____ Date: _____

Name of community group sponsoring the team: _____

Description of problem, including its effect on the team's sponsor (attach additional pages if necessary):

_____

_____

_____

Proposed action plan (attach additional pages if necessary):

_____

_____

_____

_____

Signatures: _____ Duties: _____

_____ _____

_____ _____

_____ _____

• •

For Board Use Only:

Criteria used to evaluate the plan: feasibility, expected results of proposed solution, clarity, effort, creativity, presentation style, etc. Assign each criterion a specified number of points, not to exceed a total of 75 points.

_____

_____

_____

For Teacher Use Only:

Study habits, cooperation, thoroughness, teamwork, etc., 25 points:

_____

_____

_____

_____

Wet-Work Shuffle

■ **Grade Level:**
Upper Elementary, Middle School, High School

■ **Subject Areas:**
Government, Environmental Science, Health

■ **Duration:**
Preparation time: 30 minutes
Activity time: 50 minutes

■ **Setting:** Classroom

■ **Skills:**
Gathering information (interviewing); Organizing (sequencing); Analyzing

■ **Charting the Course**
A variety of activities in this guide include concepts that involve careers in water resources (e.g., "Water Works," "Sparkling Water," "Humpty Dumpty," "The Pucker Effect," "Water Court" and "The CEO").

■ **Vocabulary**
water resource careers

Hydrologist, municipal planner, microbiologist: What do these titles mean to you?

▼ Summary
Students learn about different water resource occupations and place them in a sequence—from water's source, to its delivery into homes, to its return to the source.

Objectives
Students will:
- sequence water-related occupations involved in transporting water to and from the home.
- describe various water resource careers.

Materials
- *A set of **Water Career Cards** for each group of students* (Cards may be pasted to index cards for durability.)
- *Marking pens and drawing material*
- *Butcher paper*

Making Connections
Most students know that clean, safe water enters their homes with the turn of a faucet, and that a flush of the toilet expels household wastes. But they may not realize the number of people who make these services possible. Introducing students to the professions providing clean water supplies helps them appreciate their water source and makes them aware of a variety of careers related to water.

Background
Have you heard the phrase "Too many cooks spoil the broth"? This is not the case in the world of water management. By the time water has been pumped from an aquifer or diverted from a meandering river, used, and then returned to the system, it has been analyzed, gauged, protected, stored, managed, measured, and treated by a multitude of people.

First, the water supply might be predicted or measured by climatologists, hydrologists, hydrogeologists, and limnologists. When plans for its withdrawal for various uses are made, other professionals become involved: watershed planners consider regional water resource issues; engineers develop plans for the storage and transportation of water; water pollution technologists study the suitability of water for drinking; and municipal planners help determine a community's present and future needs.

At every level of government and in countless businesses, people manage water. Interest groups and those involved in the integrity of the water help ensure that fisheries and wetland habitats remain intact. Computer technicians store vital data every step of the way. Sanitarians, wastewater engineers, and wastewater treatment plant operators work to guarantee water's suitability for use and its acceptable quality when returned to the natural system.

Procedure
▼ Warm Up
Present students with the following situation. One morning they wake up, they turn on the faucet to get a drink of water, and nothing comes out. To whom would they or their parents go to find out what happened to the water supply? What if the whole community had the same problem? Ask students to list the different professions of the people involved in getting water to and from homes.

Inform them that a fictional town called "Heretothere" has identified a list of people it needs to hire to get water to and from its houses. The cards containing these job titles were arranged in correct order, but someone has dropped them! Now they need to be put back in order. Tell students their challenge will be to put the cards in proper sequence.

▼ The Activity

1. **Divide the class into small groups and give each group a set of shuffled** *Water Career Cards*. **Ask each group to arrange the cards in what they think is the best order.** Students should read the career descriptions to help them determine the correct order. If they need more help, provide them with the category headings that describe the various stages of water transport.

2. **Ask each group to explain the water career pathways and relationships they have devised. Have groups compare their arrangements, discussing whether or not the town of Heretothere will get its water.**

3. **Present students with the order given on the original** *Water Career Cards* **sheet. Ask students to evaluate their own sequencing and make adjustments.** The placement of the profession in the correct category heading is more important than the order of careers within the category. Make sure students understand that these tasks are not necessarily sequential. Activities of some workers occur simultaneously or may overlap.

4. **Remind students of the variety of careers related to water other than water supply.** These include fisheries specialist, meteorologist, marine biologist, navigator, educator, etc. Some students may be interested in adding cards to the *Water Career Cards* deck to see how all these professions are related. (For example, a water treatment plant manager needs a chemist to test water quality, or a watershed manager may confer with a wetlands specialist to help regulate surface runoff.)

▼ Wrap Up

Ask students to draw a diagram or create a wall-sized mural of water on its pathways. Include drawings of people of different professions working in appropriate settings and with appropriate equipment (i.e., a chemist located near the water treatment plant).

Instruct students to select one or more water-related careers they would like to know more about. They should contact a water professional and ask to interview him or her about a typical day at work. Some questions to ask are: 1) How did you get interested in this work? 2) What kind of education or training did you need? 3) What skills do you need? 4) What do you like the most/least about your job? 5) Is the pay scale satisfactory? and 6) Describe a typical day on the job. Based on the interview, have students pretend they are going to apply for the job and write a résumé that fits the job criteria.

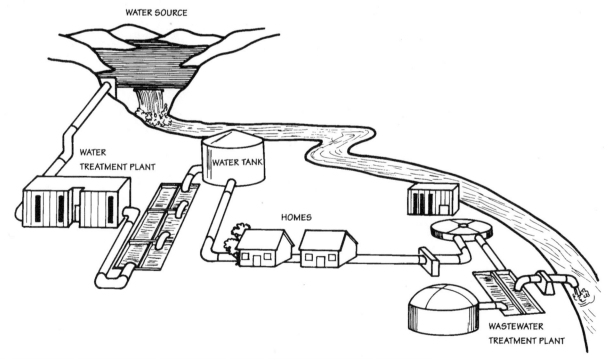

WATER SOURCE

WATER TREATMENT PLANT

WATER TANK

HOMES

WASTEWATER TREATMENT PLANT

ADAPTED FROM "A WATER SYSTEM" (POSTER), BY PERMISSION. © 1988, AMERICAN WATER WORKS ASSOCIATION.

Assessment

Have students:

• sequence the water-related professions involved in transporting water to and from the home (steps 1, 2, 3, and *Wrap Up*).

• create a résumé of a water professional (*Wrap Up*).

Extensions

Invite water-related professionals to explain their roles in water management and discuss the nature and significance of their jobs.

 **K-2 Option**

Ask students to think of a water-related career that sounds interesting to them or provide them with a list (plumber, tugboat operator, fisheries specialist, wetlands educator, etc.) from which to select their favorite. Distribute newsprint and crayons or markers to students and show them how to fold the paper into a hat.

Tell students to decorate their hats with pictures of people doing their jobs or of the environments these professionals study as part of their work. When all students have completed their hats, have them take turns role-playing in front of the class. Have them explain the pictures or materials on their hats. For example, a student whose chosen water career is a wetland research scientist may say, "I am a wetland

Water career hats.

researcher. I study the plants and animals that live in wetlands. Here is a picture of some of my wetland friends (frogs, foxes, and ducks). In this picture I am counting the number of frogs I see." After all the students have had a chance to role-play, allow them to walk around for a few minutes to look at each other's hats.

Resources

Asimov, Isaac, and Elizabeth Kaplan. 1993. *What Happens When I Flush the Toilet?* Milwaukee, Wis.: Bareth Stevens.

Bolles, Richard Nelson. 1993. *What Color Is Your Parachute?: A Practical Manual for Job-Hunters and Career Changers.* Berkeley, Calif.: Ten Speed Press.

Cole, Joanna. 1986. *The Magic School Bus at the Waterworks.* New York, N.Y.: Scholastic, Inc.

Test the Waters! Careers in Water Quality. 1991. Brochure. Contact: Water Pollution Control Federation, 601 Wythe Street, Alexandria, VA 22314. (703) 684-2400.

Video: *Careers in Water Quality.* 16 min.; 1/2" VHS. Order from: New Dimension Media, 85803 Lorane Highway, Eugene, OR 97405. (800) 288-4456. To order student and teacher guides or for more information, call: Water Pollution Control Federation, (800) 666-0206.

For further information about careers related to water supply and the education/training involved, contact: American Water Works Association, 6666 West Quincy Ave., Denver, CO 80235. (303) 347-6206.

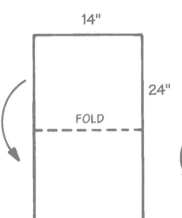

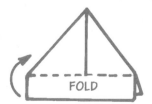

Water Career Cards

NOTE: This is a limited list of careers involved in transporting water from a source to homes and back to the source. Many more people are actually involved in this process. The arrangement of the careers is based on seven main categories. The sequence of careers within each category may vary somewhat, because the responsibilities of some careers coincide or overlap.

CATEGORY I: Careers involved in removing water from the source (river, lake, or ground water supply) and transferring it to a water treatment plant.

HYDROLOGIST
A scientist who measures the properties and movement of water, often assessing its availability.

HYDRAULIC ENGINEER
An engineer with knowledge of the mechanical properties of water who would be involved in designing or maintaining a dam or water retraction devices.

MICROBIOLOGIST
A scientist who determines the quality of the water and the health of the water source by studying microorganisms.

FISHERIES BIOLOGIST
A scientist who studies the population and behavior of fish species in relation to available habitats and quality of the water resource.

HYDROGEOLOGIST
A scientist who studies the properties and movement of ground water and aquifers.

WATER MASTER
A person who monitors withdrawal of water by water users in watersheds where supplies may be limited.

CATEGORY II: Careers involved in removing impurities from water at a water treatment plant.

CHEMIST
A scientist who tests the water to ensure its suitability for public consumption.

TREATMENT PLANT TECHNICIAN
A person who operates and maintains the water treatment plant.

CATEGORY III: Career responsible for transporting the treated water to a storage tank.

WATER WORKS ENGINEER
A person who designs systems for transport of water, often in municipal settings; can also be the person who controls the discharge of water from places of storage.

CATEGORY IV: Careers involved in planning, constructing, and maintaining distribution systems that carry water underground to homes.

WATER POLICY PLANNER
A person who studies water related problems and issues and prepares plans for consideration by agency decision makers and the public.

MUNICIPAL PLANNER
A person who works with engineers and local officials to determine the municipal needs, including the optimal water supply system for a city. This person is knowledgeable about the relevant laws.

SPECIAL INTEREST GROUPS
Groups that have special interests in the protection or use of water. They are involved as lobbyists when laws are made and have a voice at public meetings involving water.

CATEGORY V: Careers involved in monitoring quantities of water used in homes and maintaining service lines to homes.

METER READER
A person who reads the water meter at your house to determine how much water is used monthly.

PLUMBER
A person who designs a system and fits pipes for the transportation of water (both sewage and drinking) in facilities and buildings.

CATEGORY VI: Careers responsible for transporting wastewater to the wastewater treatment plant and monitoring sanitary conditions.

WATER LINE TECHNICIAN
A person who plans and installs main lines and service lines throughout the town.

SANITARIAN
A person who enforces public health, especially in relation to garbage and sewage disposal.

CATEGORY VII: Careers involved in operating wastewater treatment plants and ensuring water quality prior to its return to the source.

WASTEWATER TREATMENT PLANT OPERATOR
A person who controls and maintains equipment at a sewage treatment plant.

CHEMIST
A scientist who tests the water after it has been treated, to ensure its suitability for reintroduction into a stream.

MICROBIOLOGIST
A scientist who determines the quality of the water and the health of the water effluent or discharge by studying microorganisms.

Water resources exist within social constructs.

▼

Over time, societies develop water management systems and practices to meet the needs

of diverse water users. People's values, attitudes, and beliefs shape

political and economic systems that are dynamic.

Choices and Preferences, Water Index

Water is for all water users, isn't it?

▼ Summary

Students rank and compare different uses of water. The class develops a *water index*, an indication of the group's feelings and values about water and its uses.

- **Grade Level:**
Middle School, High School

- **Subject Areas:**
Mathematics, Environmental Science, Government

- **Duration:**
Preparation time: 30 minutes
Activity time: 50 minutes

- **Setting:** Classroom

- **Skills:**
Organizing (graphing); Analyzing (comparing and contrasting); Interpreting (drawing conclusions)

- **Charting the Course**
Basic math skills (addition and division) and an understanding of graphing will be needed to complete this activity. Students learn about the interdependence of various water users in "Water Works." The water index developed in this activity can be used to help students make decisions in several other activities ("Dilemma Derby," "Perspectives," "Water Bill of Rights"). "Hot Water," in which students conduct a debate, can follow this activity.

- **Vocabulary**
attitudes, values

Objectives
Students will:
- analyze how people perceive the value of various water uses differently.

Materials
- *Copies of **Major Water Use Chart***
- *Copies of **Student Ranking Line Graph***
- *Ruler*
- *Colored pencils* (red, blue, green)
- *Calculators* (optional)

Making Connections
People prioritize many things in their lives. Organizing a day, planning a budget, and deciding upon a career involve ranking skills. Students are often asked who their favorite musician or teacher is. In response, they may rank musicians or teachers in order of preference. Students should understand that their list of favorites may differ from another person's. Involving students in learning how their peers rank water resource uses will help them appreciate how differing opinions influence water resource management strategies.

Background
Water resources are used throughout society. Industry uses water to process materials; agriculture needs water to irrigate crops; residential areas require water for drinking, cleaning, and cooking. In many places, all water users have all the water they need. What happens when supplies are limited? Or when a particular water use decreases water quality? Is one water use the *most* important?

How people rate the importance of diverse water uses will vary based on their knowledge and experience. Often, values regarding water use are determined by geographical area, economy, community, culture, and/or family. For example, people from an agricultural region might rank water use differently than people from a region whose economy is based on recreation or industrial production. As individuals acknowledge the diversity of values and opinions surrounding water use, the need to provide water of sufficient quality and quantity to all water users becomes apparent.

An index is a reference tool used to organize concepts or topics. A water index lists water use categories arranged in order of preference or importance. This index can be used to help determine how and why a community or class values certain water uses. If indexes are produced at different times, recent indexes can be compared to earlier versions to see if preferences have changed over time.

Procedure
▼ *Warm Up*
Have the class generate a list of major water uses. Help them fit the uses into the ten categories listed in the *Major Water Use Chart*. Challenge them to relate each water category to their own lives (e.g., transportation: they use products that are shipped over water; recreation: they go sailing; industry: they play computer games).

Present the following hypothetical situation: A meeting has been called

COURTESY: NATIONAL PARK SERVICE, U.S. DEPARTMENT OF INTERIOR, RICHARD FROAR.

where representatives from agriculture, industry, recreation, energy, fish and wildlife, transportation, municipalities, and other major water use groups have assembled to ask you and your classmates one question: Which one of the water use groups is the most important and why? Your class will likely come to the conclusion that all water users are important. However, in reality, water managers and policymakers at all levels must make important decisions about allocating water.

▼ The Activity

1. **Give each student a copy of the** *Major Water Use Chart* **and have them rank the items in priority order.** "1" is the least important use, while "10" indicates top priority use.

2. **After students have completed their ranking, have them graph their scores on the** *Student Ranking Line Graph.*

3. **Have students form small groups. Ask them to average the group's rankings for each use** category. For example, if one student in a group of five students ranked energy consumption as 10, a second student gave it a 7 ranking, the third a 3, the fourth a 10, and the fifth a 5, the total of their scores would be 35. Divide 35 by the number of students in the group (5), and the result is an average of 7. Remind students to check their work.

4. **Have each student plot his or her group's averaged rankings on the graph.** How does the small-

group average compare with an individual's ranking? How do students feel if their individual top priority is ranked lower by the group?

5. **Tell students to average all the group rankings to find the class average for each category. Have students plot the class results on their graphs. Do students think the average provides an accurate representation of the choices and preferences of the class regarding water use priorities?**

6. **Have the entire class list the designated uses in the order they were rated. The highest rating first, the lowest last. This is the water index for the class.**

▼ Wrap Up and Action

Have students compare and contrast the individual, small-group, and class rankings. Why do different groups of people feel so strongly about the importance of water? Ask students what factors might cause them to rank the list in a different order. Review with students the hypothetical situation in the *Warm Up*. Will the outcome of the class ranking satisfy representatives from the other major water use groups? When decisions are made affecting large groups of people, is it possible to satisfy all individuals involved?

Have students share the class results with their families. Do all family members agree with the class, with each other, with their student family member? Students may contact a school in another geographic region, forward the activity, and exchange data. How do students account for the similarities and differences?

Assessment

Have students:
- rank major categories of water uses (step 1).

- graph scores and establish a class water index (steps 1-6).
- explain why one individual's ranking may differ from other students (step 4 and *Wrap Up*).
- interpret the graphs and water index to conclude how the class values water uses (step 6 and *Wrap Up*).

Upon completing the activity, for further assessment have students:
- suggest ways this index could be used to set water management policy within their community.

Extensions

Have students use alternate means of averaging results. They may want to find the median or mode for each ranking. The median is the middle number in a set of numbers arranged in order of magnitude. For example, if the rankings for wildlife were 3, 4, 6, 8, 8, the median is 6. In an even set of numbers the median is the average of the two middle numbers. The mode is the number that is used most frequently in the group. In the above example, the mode is 8.

Create a frequency chart by plotting the number of times each category received a ranking of 10. For example, twenty students in the class ranked energy as a 10. Three students ranked aesthetics as a 10, while six students ranked fish and wildlife 10, etc. Present the results in graph form listing the item that received the most 10s first, the category with the second most 10s next, and so forth.

K-2 Option

With fewer choices to prioritize, young children can make a water index, too. Begin the activity by orienting students to the process of how choices are made. Present students with the following scenario. Which is **most important** for an

animal, such as a pet dog or cat—water, a toy, a book, or a brush? Arranging the items in order of importance, some students may list water, brush, toy, book. Another group may select water, toy, brush, book. Discuss the reasons for their decisions.

Inform students that they can use the same criterion (degree of importance) to prioritize different uses of water. Have students list uses of water. Help them organize their suggestions into the four water use categories that are pictured (*Water Use Categories*).

Distribute copies of *Which Water Use is Most Important*. Instruct students to cut out the pictures and glue them in order of importance in the priority boxes. Discuss similarities and differences among students' arrangements and remind them that all arrangements have merit.

Resources

🍎 Hammer, Trudy J. 1985. *Water Resources*. New York, N.Y.: Watts.

Miller, G. Tyler, Jr. 1990. *Resource Conservation and Management*. Belmont, Calif.: Wadsworth Publishing Company.

Polesetsky, Matthew, ed. 1991. *Global Resources: Opposing Viewpoints*. San Diego, Calif.: Greenhaven Press, Inc.

🍎 Pringle, Laurence. 1982. *Water: The Next Great Resource Battle*. New York, N.Y.: Macmillan.

Which Water Use is Most Important?

PRIORITY BOXES

FIRST MOST IMPORTANT WATER USE   **1**
SECOND MOST IMPORTANT WATER USE   **2**
THIRD MOST IMPORTANT WATER USE   **3**
FOURTH MOST IMPORTANT WATER USE   **4**

(add more boxes if necessary)

Name: _____

Cut out the pictures and glue them in order of importance in the Priority Boxes.

WATER USE CATEGORIES

Major Water Use Chart (Alphabetical Order)

Name: _____ Date: _____

Instructions: Assign the number 10 to your highest priority and 1 to the lowest.

WATER USE	EXAMPLES	INDIVIDUAL RANKING	SMALL GROUP AVERAGE	CLASS AVERAGE
Ecological Value	Preservation, Wildlife Habitat			
Energy Development	Hydropower, Nuclear, Coal			
Fish and Wildlife	Otters, Whales, Trout, Moose, etc. . . .			
Human Consumption	Drinking Water, Washing, etc. . . .			
Irrigation	Corn, Cotton, Alfalfa, Carrots, etc. . . .			
Livestock	Cattle, Hogs, Sheep, Chickens, etc. . . .			
Manufacturing/ Industry	Automobiles, Computers, Bikes, etc. . . .			
Recreation and Aesthetics	Fishing, Camping, Floating, Boating, Sightseeing, Beauty, etc. . . .			
Transportation	Barges, Cargo Ships, etc. . . .			
Urban Development	Swimming Pools, Golf Courses, etc. . . .			

Student Ranking Line Graph

Name: _____ Date: _____

RANKING

10
9
8
7
6
5
4
3
2
1

ECOLOGICAL VALUE

ENERGY DEVELOPMENT

FISH AND WILDLIFE

HUMAN CONSUMPTION

IRRIGATION

LIVESTOCK

MANUFACTURING/INDUSTRY

RECREATION/AESTHETICS

TRANSPORTATION

URBAN DEVELOPMENT

WATER USES

Cold Cash in the Icebox

"An exterior case of antique oak, ice and provision chambers, and a drip cup based on the latest and most appropriate scientific principles: all for $22.73." Your grandparents' icebox bears little resemblance to the refrigerator in your kitchen today.

▼ Summary
Students design mini-insulators (iceboxes) in an attempt to keep ice from melting and discover the challenges of refrigeration of 100 years ago.

Objectives
Students will:
- compare the insulating properties of various materials.

Materials
- *Copies of **Stay Cool Chart***
- *Pint-size (473 ml) milk carton (1 per student, plus one extra, rinsed, with both top flaps pulled open)*
- *A variety of materials for insulating ice (straw, hay, grass, 100% cotton cloth, sawdust or crushed cedar shavings, dirt, sand, dried beans; may be provided by teachers or brought from home by students)*
- *Ice cubes*
- *Measuring spoons or graduated cylinder*

Making Connections
Almost every house has a refrigerator. Students may have parents or grandparents who once owned an icebox. By designing their own icebox, students can experience some of the challenges their ancestors faced while trying to preserve food.

Background
When temperatures reach the freezing point (32 degrees F [0°C]), water changes from a liquid to a solid state. The water in lakes and rivers freezes on the surface, while water below remains a liquid. Throughout the winter, aquatic life survives under the ice. Ice is less dense than water. Ice floats on the surface of a body of water and acts as an insulating barrier, moderating the temperature of deeper water.

To keep ice frozen, air temperature must remain at or below the freezing point. Heat energy (movement of molecules) flows from areas of warm to cold (or high energy to low). If warm air (containing faster moving molecules) comes in contact with the slower moving molecules in ice, the energy will be transferred from the air to the ice. When the water molecules in ice move faster, the ice melts. Some materials do not transfer heat energy well. (The molecules in the materials are held together strongly and are less able to move around or to transfer heat energy.) These substances are called insulators. In the case of preserving ice, insulating material such as straw is used to keep heat energy away from ice.

Before the days of electricity, ice was harvested in the winter months from frozen lakes and streams and stored in icehouses to be used for refrigeration. People cut huge blocks of ice from thick, frozen layers, using special grooving plows that had sharp blades. While humans steered the plows, horses pulled them over the ice surface again and again, until the blades had made cuts deep enough to remove the ice blocks. Later, tractors and automobiles were used in place of horses to pull the plow.

The ice was stored in well-insulated icehouses where ice blocks were packed in sawdust or straw. Ice companies sold the ice blocks to homes, to businesses such as grocery stores for their coolers,

■ **Grade Level:**
Lower Elementary, Upper Elementary

■ **Subject Areas:**
Physical Science, History, Mathematics

■ **Duration:**
Preparation time: 30 minutes
Activity time: 50 minutes

■ **Setting:** Classroom

■ **Skills:**
Applying (hypothesizing, predicting, experimenting, designing); Evaluating (analyzing, interpreting)

■ **Charting the Course**
In "Molecules in Motion" students learn how heat energy affects water molecules. In "Hangin' Together" students investigate how hydrogen bonding causes ice to be less dense than liquid water. The concept of density is explored in "Adventures in Density." A good follow-up activity is "Water Concentration."

■ **Vocabulary**
insulation, heat energy, hypothesis

and to railroads for refrigeration cars.

Ice was sold by the pound or by the block. Blocks of ice were delivered to customers in an ice wagon or truck. The driver knew when customers wanted ice because an ice card would be displayed in one of the home's windows. The customer paid for the product with cash or with ice coupons. The iceman carried blocks of ice with tongs and wore a leather apron with pockets to collect the dripping water and chips. In the homes, the blocks were stored in the icebox or ice chest, which served as a refrigerator.

Ice was placed in the ice chamber of the icebox, where air passing over the block cooled and fell directly under the provisions chambers. Warmer air rose, contacted the ice block, and fell, thus maintaining a constant flow of air. Small pieces of ice were chipped off the large block with an ice pick, to be used to cool

drinks. Ice harvesting was a lucrative business before the delivery of electricity to urban and rural homes.

In 1833, a man in New England named Frederic Tudor, owner of a successful ice harvesting business, agreed to fulfill an ice order that was to become the first international shipment of ice from the United States. His company contracted to sail 180 tons (169 tonnes) of ice to Calcutta.

Tudor prepared his vessel with a special lining of extra lumber and further insulated with straw, hay, and sawdust. Then he carefully packed the straw, hay, and sawdust between each cord of ice that was brought onto the ship. For three summer months, he sailed with the first ice cargo to ever cross the equator. When he docked in Calcutta and inspected the cargo, he found that 100 tons (91 tonnes) of ice had remained frozen during the long, hot journey.

Procedure
▼ Warm Up
Ask students if they know how people kept their food cold before electric refrigerators were available. Where did people get ice? How long do students think an ice cube can last outside a freezer?

▼ The Activity
1. **Explain to students how ice was once harvested from lakes and ponds, kept in icehouses, and used in iceboxes to keep food cold before electric refrigerators were available. Share with them the story about the first ice shipment to Calcutta.**

2. **Have students predict and record on the *Stay Cool Chart* those materials they believe would be good insulators.**

3. **Give each student or group a milk carton and an ice cube; let them choose the type of packing material they think will best preserve their ice. Students may bring materials from home or choose from items provided by the teacher.**

4. **Have them pack the ice, close and flatten the carton top, and write their name on the outside of the carton with a marking pen. On their *Stay Cool Chart*, students should draw a picture of how their ice is packed. In another milk carton, place an ice cube without packing (as a control), close the top, and write "no insulation" on the outside.**

5. **Place all iceboxes on a table, out of direct sunlight. Students check each box every two hours throughout the day, pouring out and measuring the amount of water that has collected in the box. Record measurements on the *Stay Cool Chart*.**

6. **Have them compare the preservation of ice in their icebox to the ice cube that is not insulated. An alternative to measuring is having**

Old-fashioned icebox

students draw pictures of the two cubes, to indicate their change in size over time.

▼ *Wrap Up*

How long did the uninsulated ice remain frozen? Were any of the insulated ice cubes still frozen at the end of the day? Which type of insulating material worked best? Have students draw conclusions and make recommendations on the *Stay Cool Chart*. Have students summarize the importance of ice for refrigeration before the days of electricity.

Assessment

Have students:

• predict and test the insulating abilities of different materials (steps 2, 3 and 4).

• create a mini-icebox using insulating materials designed to delay an ice cube's melting (step 4).

• evaluate designs and make recommendations for improvement (*Wrap Up*).

Upon completing the activity, for further assessment have students:

• construct a time line showing how people in the past, present, and future preserve food.

• write a catalogue description to sell an icebox in the late 1800s.

Extensions

What happens to fish and aquatic life when rivers and lakes freeze over? Water below the surface of ice is kept at a relatively constant temperature because heat energy is continually being transferred between liquid molecules and is not allowed to escape (the layer of ice traps the heat). Have students investigate how water freezes from the top down. Put some rocks in the bottom of a bowl of water and place the bowl in the freezer. After a layer of ice has

formed, poke a hole and have students look at the rocks below the ice. They should check the temperature of the water. Could a fish survive in this temperature?

Ice-Cream Making. Ice was used in many ways. It kept food cold in the icebox and it chilled drinks. In the summer, children would gather at the ice man's wagon, in the hope he would give them pieces of ice chipped from the big blocks. Ice was also used to make ice cream.

Students can make their own ice cream. Combine 1 cup (240 ml) milk, 2 tablespoons (30 ml) vanilla, 2 tablespoons (30 ml) sugar, and 2 tablespoons (30 ml) canned milk in an empty, clean 1 pound (.45 kg) coffee can. Tape the lid on the can and place in a 3 pound (1.35 kg) coffee can. Pack ice and rock salt in the space between the 1 pound (.45 kg) and 3 pound (1.35 kg) coffee can. Tape the lid on the 3 pound (1.35 kg) coffee can. Roll the coffee can back and forth for at least 15 minutes. Ice cream is ready when the liquid ingredients in the smaller can "sound" solid. Open the 1 pound (.45 kg) can and enjoy the ice cream.

What would happen if you changed some of the variables when making the ice cream? Students could test the following variations:

• Milk: amount, type (skim milk, 1% milk, 2% milk, whole milk, whipping cream, evaporated milk)

Students help an ice cube maintain its cool.

• Sugar: type, amount
• Flavorings: added before or after freezing, type, amount
• Ratio of salt to ice

Resources

Bean, Susan S. 1991. "Cold Mine." *American Heritage* (July/August).

Cuevas, Mapi M., and William G. Lamb. 1994. *Holt Physical Science.* Austin, Tex.: Holt, Rinehart & Winston, Inc.

🍎 Israel, Fred L. 1968. *1897 Sears, Roebuck Catalogue.* New York, N.Y.: Chelsea House Publishers.

Kepler, Lynne. 1992. "Make Science Matter." *Instructor* (102) 4: 74-75.

Kesselheim, Alan S., and The Watercourse and National Project WET Staff. 1993. *The Liquid Treasure Water History Trunk: Learning From the Past.* Bozeman, Mont.: The Watercourse.

Stay Cool Chart

Name: _____   Date: _____

Hypothesis	Procedure	Results		Conclusions/Recommendations
		Test	Control	
I think the following materials will insulate ice:	Draw a picture of how you packed the ice (label the materials used):	Time: Amount of water:	Time: Amount of water:	What worked? What would you do differently next time?
		Time: Amount of water:	Time: Amount of water:	
		Time: Amount of water:	Time: Amount of water:	
		Time: Amount of water:	Time: Amount of water:	
		Time: Amount of water:	Time: Amount of water:	

COPY

Dilemma Derby

It's a hot August afternoon and your city is rationing water. You're on your way to an appointment, and running late. Suddenly, you see a fire hydrant gushing water onto a street corner. Should you 1) take the time to report it and possibly miss your appointment; 2) proceed to your appointment and assume someone else will report the situation; 3) forget the appointment and play in the water? or 4) . . . ?

■ **Grade Level:**
Middle School, High School

■ **Subject Areas:**
Government, Environmental Science, Ecology

■ **Duration:**
Preparation time: 30 minutes

Activity time: 50 minutes

■ **Setting:** Classroom

■ **Skills:**
Analyzing; Interpreting (translating, relating)

■ **Charting the Course**
Students can present their feelings and values toward water in "Idea Pools" and "Choices and Preferences, Water Index." Students learn how differing viewpoints and values complicate water issue resolution in "Perspectives." In "Hot Water," students use debating strategies to present their views about an issue. Consequences of courses of action related to water management can be addressed in "Whose Problem Is It?"

■ **Vocabulary**
dilemma

▼ Summary
Students debate the pros and cons of different solutions to water management issues.

Objectives
Students will:
• outline reasons why managing water resources can create dilemmas.
• identify, analyze, and select actions related to a water resource dilemma.

Materials
• *Dilemma Cards* (These can be glued on index cards and laminated for extra durability.)

Making Connections
People confront dilemmas daily. Students may have weighed the pros and cons of completing a homework assignment versus taking the time to visit with friends. Students may also be familiar with water resource issues such as nonpoint source pollution, water shortages, and wetland restoration. As students investigate problems involving people and water, they will recognize the complexity of managing and protecting water resources.

Background
A dilemma is a problematic situation that requires a person to choose from two or more alternatives, each of which can produce desirable or undesirable effects. Managing water resources often creates dilemmas. As with most dilemmas, water resource management can involve conflicts between what one wants to do versus what one believes should be done. For example, disposing of motor oil by dumping it on the ground is easier than the environmentally sound, but more time consuming, alternative of recycling it. Taking a long, hot shower is relaxing, but a short, warm shower—though less comforting— conserves resources. Not voting on a ballot issue that would allocate tax money for water supply projects requires less effort than researching the potential impact of the projects.

People use various approaches to determine a course of action when confronted with a dilemma. These range from flipping a coin to conducting extensive research and attending high-powered meetings. However, a prudent method consists of listing the alternatives, identifying the pros and cons for each, and projecting possible outcomes. Factors to consider include cost (monetary and environmental), time, energy, persons likely affected, personal values, etc. Emotions and instincts also influence which alternative is chosen. Friends and family can help with the decision-making process as well.

Decision making and problem solving are critical thinking skills, necessary for productive and responsible citizenship. Although confronting dilemmas may not be easy, the experience (whether the outcome is positive or negative) helps people deal with similar conflicts in the future.

Procedure
▼ Warm Up
Provide students with the following scenario: Your friends have invited you to go out in their boat for an afternoon of

water-skiing, swimming, and fishing. You're really happy to be included. However, when you get to the dock and ask for your lifejacket, your friends tell you that they forgot to pack the lifejackets when they loaded the equipment early that morning. You are not a very good swimmer and you know it is illegal to go out in a boat without a lifejacket. Still, you don't want to miss out on the fun. What are you going to do?

Tell students that this is a dilemma. Ask them to list reasons why it is a dilemma. Have students describe approaches they have used to resolve similar situations. Inform them that managing water resources can also be a dilemma. What situations related to water can students recall that could be classified as dilemmas? Tell them they are going to do an exercise that introduces them to a few water-related dilemmas and tests their skills at addressing them.

▼ The Activity
Divide students into small groups and give each group one or more *Dilemma Cards*. Provide the groups with the following instructions:

- One member of the group (the reader) selects a card and reads the situation aloud. Group members identify reasons why this situation is a dilemma.
- The reader presents the list of options to the group. Group members discuss the situation and decide what to do and why. They must select one of the available options or identify an alternative course of action. One approach to making a decision is to rate each option. Rank them on a scale of 0-10, with 0 being total disagreement and 10 being total agreement. A rating of 5 indicates "no opinion" or "needs more information."

MARGO TAUSSIG PINKERTON, N E STOCK PHOTO

▼ Wrap Up
Instruct one member of each group to report their dilemma(s) to the class. He or she should identify why it is a dilemma and identify the course of action favored by the group. Students should describe the considerations involved in making their decision. Ask the class to evaluate the option that was selected, and, if applicable, provide alternatives that might be better. Do students think they will change the way they will react to real-life water dilemmas? If so, how?

Assessment
Have students:
- use a ranking system to select a course of action to solve a water-related dilemma (*The Activity*).
- decide upon a course of action to resolve a water-related dilemma and present reasons for their choice (*Wrap Up*).
- explain why the management of water resources can create dilemmas (*Wrap Up*).

Upon completing the activity, for further assessment have students:
- identify water-related dilemmas in their community and present alternative courses of action, citing pros and cons of each.

Extensions
Have students research the dilemmas presented in the activity and determine if this additional information causes them to change their course of action.

Invite a community planner or water resource manager to speak to the class about a local water-related dilemma and to discuss the processes involved in addressing the dilemma.

Resources
Miller, G. Tyler, Jr. 1991. *Environmental Science: Sustaining the Earth*, 3rd ed. Belmont, Calif.: Wadsworth Publishing Company.

Polesetsky, Matthew, ed. 1991. *Global Resources: Opposing Viewpoints*. San Diego, Calif.: Greenhaven Press, Inc.

DILEMMA CARDS

DILEMMA 1: You've changed the oil in your car. You know the hazards of oil seeping into ground water, yet you are in a hurry to attend a meeting. How will you discard the used oil?

1. Put it in the back of the garage.
2. Place it in a garbage can for disposal in the city/county landfill.
3. Pour it on the ground somewhere out of sight while no one is looking.
4. Burn it.
5. Take it to an approved oil-disposal facility in your area.
6. Other?

DILEMMA 2: You are the mayor of a city which has an area known to flood. A developer wants to build houses on the floodplain. These houses will have a great view of the river, will be conveniently located near the business district, and will entice prosperous people to move to your struggling community. You must make the final decision on the developer's request. Which option will you choose?

1. Inform the developer no building will be allowed.
2. Let the developer build in the flood area.
3. Insist the developer elevate the houses on piles of gravel in hopes of avoiding flood damage.
4. Instruct the developer to find an alternative building location out of the floodplain.
5. Other?

DILEMMA 3: You own a cabin on a lakeshore and there are 400 other cabins facing the lake. Several residents around the lake have been complaining because they think the lake's water quality is poor. (There has been an increase in algae growth and unpleasant odors.) A public service announcement informed the community that these problems likely are caused by septic tanks leaking sewage into the ground water that feeds into the lake. The announcement advised that septic systems should be checked every three years. It has been almost ten years since yours has been checked, and you know other cabin owners have not checked theirs recently either. Checking your septic tank and fixing the problem could be costly. A fine could be imposed if your septic tank is found to be defective, although it is not likely the tank will be checked. What are you going to do?

1. Sell the cabin.
2. Do nothing; your tank probably isn't leaking—and if it is, the fine can't be that bad, and you can appeal it.
3. Have your septic tank checked; and if it's leaking, pay to have the sewage pumped and hauled to a safe place.
4. Have your septic tank checked, and if it's leaking, sell the cabin.
5. Have your septic tank checked; fix it if it's leaking, and form a homeowner's association to encourage everyone else to check their tanks, too.
6. Rally the public works system to develop a community water and sewage system and pay to have your cabin hooked up.
7. Other?

DILEMMA 4: You and a friend are hiking, and you see someone dumping a 55-gallon (209-l) drum of a dark liquid into a shallow stream. What should you do?

1. Go over and ask what is going on.
2. Run home and call the police.
3. Wait until the person leaves, then investigate by smelling and feeling the liquid.
4. Take down the license plate number of the nearby truck and report the situation to the fire department.
5. Other?

DILEMMA 5: You are the governor of your state. Many streams are drying up because water is being diverted for municipal, industrial, and irrigation uses. This has resulted in fish kills. Furthermore, people who like to canoe, raft, and kayak have sent letters of complaint. Industry and agriculture are major sources of income in your state, but you also like its reputation of being a "quiet place" where people can explore scenic rivers. What action will you take?

1. Ask water users to stop using water.
2. Locate and publicize other rivers around the state where people can fish and canoe.
3. Establish a committee to study the problem.
4. Propose constructing a dam and reservoir to store water for release when needed.
5. Buy out the water users so they will have to move to new locations.
6. Establish a water conservation program with incentives.
7. Other?

DILEMMA 6: Your friends have spread a plastic tarp on a hill and are spraying it with a hose. This creates a great water slide. However, sliding repeatedly kills the vegetation on the hillside, and large amounts of water are consumed during the game. Your community has experienced water shortages, but there have been no notices about conserving water for almost a year. You have been invited to take a dive down the hill. What should you do?

1. Report the game to the local authorities and have them cut off the water supply.
2. Change into your bathing suit and join the fun.
3. Try to encourage your friends to do something else, like play basketball or go skateboarding.
4. Join the activity, but only for a short while, encouraging your friends to stop with you.
5. Refuse to join in, and go home to watch television.
6. Lecture your friends on the reasons not to waste water.
7. Other?

DILEMMA 7: You are the head of a household. You are trying to save money; because your water bills have been large, you have decided to practice water conservation methods to reduce water consumption by family members. Although you have installed low-flow faucets on your showerheads and sinks, your family still insists on taking long, hot showers (sometimes over 20 minutes). What are you going to do?

1. Hold a family meeting to discuss why conservation is important, and ask that shower times be reduced.
2. Order family members to cut down their shower times to five minutes, or else you will turn the hot water heater down or off.
3. Figure the cost of water per gallon and how many gallons flow out of the showerhead each minute. Tell the family you will time their showers, and they will be charged (or their allowances reduced) for each minute over five minutes they shower.
4. Tell family members that you will compare monthly water bills, and if a bill is lower than the previous one, the money saved will go toward a family trip or entertainment event.
5. Nothing. Your family has a right to bathe for as long as they want.
6. Other?

 COPY

DILEMMA 8: You are a city council member for a community located adjacent to a large, privately owned wetland. The wetland is home to rare wildlife and migratory birds; some wetland managers indicate that the wetland helps control surface runoff. The owner has decided to sell her land and move to a new location. The land is in an area surrounded by lucrative businesses, where land prices are high and parking is an issue. What should you encourage the council to do?

1. Provide tax incentives to a local development consortium, to help them purchase the land around the wetland and seek permits to develop it for business.
2. Launch an initiative to have the city purchase the land. This will require new taxes and protect the wetland forever.
3. Apply for a permit to fill the wetland with soil from a local hill, developing the wetland into a parking garage and community park.
4. Leave the fate of the wetland to the desires of the community's special interest groups.
5. Wait and see who buys the wetland, and then decide what to do.
6. Other?

DILEMMA 9: You have moved across country. You love to fish, and you are known for your skill at catching a particular species. This species is not found in the lakes and streams around your new home. A friend from your old neighborhood has offered to bring a tank of these fish to introduce into one of your local streams. You have heard that introduced organisms (such as starlings, zebra mussels, and purple loosestrife) are competing with native species for resources. However, you have not found the local fishing practices appealing. How should you respond to your friend's offer?

1. Tell your friend to bring the fish; you can't wait to get a population growing.
2. Tell your friend you are already learning how to catch a new species of fish, so not to bother.
3. Check with a local fish and wildlife agent to learn if the introduced fish will compete with native fish.
4. Tell your friend to bring the fish; fry up a few and release the rest—they'll probably die anyway.
5. Other?

DILEMMA 10: You are a taxpayer in a coastal state that owns large tracts of land which historically were wetlands. Through complex engineering, the land has been drained to provide flood protection and to open the area for development and agriculture. These accomplishments have saved lives and improved the standard of living for many residents, while increasing revenues from crop exports. However, populations of some organisms living in the wetlands (such as scarlet ibis, wood storks, and panthers) and along coastal areas (such as coral reefs, lobsters, and shrimp) have been greatly reduced. Shrimpers and other fishing industries have suffered from low harvests, and the number of tourists has declined. There is a proposal to restore the historic water flow pattern in some of these areas. This action will increase your taxes. What should you do?

1. Vote down the tax; you pay enough in taxes already.
2. Vote for the tax; a restored, healthy ecosystem is good for everyone.
3. Vote down the tax because communities will be flooded.
4. Vote for the tax because your best friend says you should.
5. Other?

Easy Street

Grade Level:
Middle School

Subject Areas:
Mathematics, Language Arts, History, Environmental Science

Duration:
Preparation time:
Part I: 15 minutes
Part II: 15 minutes

Activity time:
Part I: 50 minutes
Part II: 30 minutes

Setting: Classroom

Skills:
Gathering information (reading, calculating); Analyzing (comparing and contrasting); Interpreting (identifying cause and effect)

Charting the Course
Students can learn more about historic water use in "Water Crossings" and "The Long Haul." Changes in water use habits are explored in "Wish Book" and "Water Concentration." "Water Meter" takes a closer look at current water use practices. "Every Drop Counts" introduces students to water conservation strategies.

Vocabulary
conservation

You use about 50 to 100 gallons (190 to 280 liters) of water a day . . . how much did your great-great-grandparents use?

▼ Summary
Students compare the quantities of water used by a contemporary family to one in the late 1800s, and investigate changes in water use habits.

Objectives
Students will:
* compare and contrast contemporary and historical water uses.
* identify water conservation strategies.

Materials
* *Copies of Drought Days Simulation*
* *Copies of Water Use Calculations Worksheet*
* *Calculators*
* *Copies of Cool Clear Water and The Bath*

Making Connections
People often use water without thinking about the implications. Comparing present access to water to that of the late 1800s, helps students appreciate how convenience can lead to increased use of a resource.

Background
Too often, we take water for granted. It easily flows from taps, spurts from the ends of garden hoses, flushes down toilets. Because water is convenient, it is also easy to think of water as plentiful, almost limitless.

This was not always so. In North America less than 100 years ago, many people had to pump and haul their own water for washing, cooking, bathing, and other needs. A dependable well or spring was a critical factor in choosing a homesite, and an inadequate supply of water caused daily hardship. In many parts of the world, including some regions of North America, hauling water remains a common practice.

Imagine how differently we would feel about water if we had to pump and carry it by hand. Imagine, also, the effects of drought or pollution on the life-giving supply we too-easily think of as infinite.

Procedure
▼ Warm Up
Ask students to guess how much water their families use every day. Have them gather and compare estimates from individual family members. If necessary, review math skills needed to complete the *Water Use Calculations Worksheet*.

▼ The Activity
Part I
1. **Ask students to work through the *Drought Days Simulations*, starting with the present day, then moving to the 1890 family, and record their computations on the *Water Use Calculations Worksheet*.**

2. **Discuss results. Do students think the average household in 1890 would consume 200 gallons (760 liters) of water per day (not including water for livestock), as many households do today? Ask students to list several reasons why they would or would not.**

Part II
1. **Give the class time to read the short selections, *Cool Clear Water* and *The Bath*.**

2. **Discuss the following questions:**
* Why do students think homesteaders recycled so much of their water?
* How would students feel if they had to haul water to their house every day

instead of simply turning on a tap?

- Do students know that in some places in the world people still have to carry water to their homes?
- What lifestyle impact do students think hauling water has on people who live in less-developed parts of the world?
- Do students think they would alter the amount of water they use every day if they had to haul it themselves?

▼ Wrap Up and Action

Ask students to estimate again how much water their families use per day and compare with their original guesses. Have the class brainstorm conservation ideas. Encourage students to discuss water conservation at home. Have them talk with grandparents or other older relatives about times when they had to haul water or do without indoor plumbing.

Assessment

Have students:
- compare and contrast water use habits from the 1890s and the present (*Part I*, steps 1 and 2).
- provide reasons why a modern family might use more water than one in the 1890s (*Part I*, step 2).
- analyze a story about water use in the past to evaluate their own use of water (*Part II*, step 2).
- develop strategies for water conservation (*Wrap Up*).

Extensions

Calculate what students' monthly water bills would be without any conservation measures, then figure the savings after changes are instituted (using their figures from the calculation worksheet).

Ask students to get a copy of their families' last water bill, then institute several water conservation measures

with the help of their parents. See if these changes are reflected in the next bill.

Have students research their family histories to determine when their ancestors stopped hauling water and installed indoor running water.

Visit a local retirement home to interview residents about their water use experiences before modern plumbing. Students can tape their interviews.

Bring in a local expert from the water commission or city water board to discuss local and regional water use problems.

Resources

🍎 Cramer, Marian. 1984. *Lantern Glow*. Contact: Marian Cramer, RR 1, Box 147, Bryant, SD 57221.

Kesselheim, Alan S., and The Watercourse and National Project WET Staff. 1993. *The Liquid Treasure Water History Trunk: Learning From the Past*. Bozeman, Mont.: The Watercourse.

🍎 Wilder, Laura Ingalls. 1935. *Little House on the Prairie* (and other books). New York, N.Y.: Harper & Row.

**Notes ▼**

Drought Days Simulation

Name: _____ Date: _____

1890 Family

This scenario is based on a homesteading household in the American West. You are a family of eight persons: two adults and six children (a 9-month-old boy, a 3-year-old girl, a 6-year-old boy, an 8-year-old boy, a 10-year-old girl, and a 15-year-old girl). You live in a wooden house with three rooms.

You get your water from a well located near the barn, 150 feet (45 m) from your house. Your dad recently dug a pit for an outhouse. Your family has five horses (consuming 12 gallons [45.6 l] of water per horse per day), two hogs (3 gallons [11.4 l] per hog per day), and four cows (12 gallons [45.6 l] per cow per day). Also, you rely on a garden for most of your family's vegetables.

Problem 1: You have noticed that the well is unable to meet your family's water needs during prolonged periods of hot and dry weather. If dry weather conditions persist, you will have to decrease your water consumption or take some other action.

On the *Water Use Calculations Worksheet*, list the ways your family uses water. Remember, there was no running water or electricity in 1890. In addition, water was often recycled for several purposes. For example,

bath and dish tub rinse water were used to water the garden.

Problem 2: How much water do you think your family of eight would consume in one day?

How much of this total would be consumed by livestock?

Why do you think the well was dug closer to the barn than to the house?

If the family had to decrease water consumption, how would they do it? List your ideas on the worksheet.

GALLONS OF WATER CONSUMED BY COMMON USES
Before Running Water

Water Use	Gallons	Liters
Toilet (outhouse)	0	0
Wash basin	1	3.8
Washing dishes by hand	2	7.6
Drinking water (see present-day common uses)		
Washing clothes by hand	5	19
Watering the garden	10-20	38-76
Bathtub	30	114

WATER USE CALCULATIONS WORKSHEET — Past

Water Use	Gals.	1st Change	Saved
TOTAL USE			

Drought Days Simulation

Name: _____ Date: _____

The Present

Think of your family and its water use. Typically, a person uses about 50 to 100 gallons (190 to 280 liters) of water every day. Using that figure as a guide and referring to the chart, *Gallons of Water Consumed by Common Uses,* calculate how much water your household requires daily.

Consider the following two problems and perform calculations:

Problem 1: The area in which you live is beginning to experience a water shortage because of persistent hot, dry weather. Your water department has requested that each household voluntarily reduce water consumption by 20 percent. Decide how you will deal with the request. List the ways your family commonly uses water and determine quantities. Identify five changes you can make in your water use habits. Record your computations on the *Water Use Calculations Worksheet.*

Problem 2: Two weeks have passed. Hot and dry conditions continue to plague your area. The water department has asked each household to decrease water consumption another 20 percent. On the *Water Use Calculations Worksheet,* list an additional five changes you can make and figure the result.

GALLONS OF WATER CONSUMED BY COMMON USES Present-Day		
Water Use	**Gallons**	**Liters**
Brushing teeth (water running)	2	7.6
Drinking water (1 quart/ 50 lbs. [1 l/22.5 k] body weight/day)	_____	_____
Flushing toilet	5-7	19-26.6
Dishwasher	10	38
Shaving (water running)	20	76
Leaky faucet (per day)	25-30	95-114
Washing dishes by hand (water running)	30	114
Bath	35	133
Ten-minute shower (without water-saving head)	25-50	95-190
Washing machine (large load)	60	228
Watering lawn (10 minutes)	75	285
Washing car (hose running)	180	684

WATER USE CALCULATIONS WORKSHEET — Present

Water Use	Gals.	1st Change	Saved	2nd Change	Saved
TOTAL USE					

Cool Clear Water

Kerwhump-squeak, kerwhump-squeak. The cold water gushed from the pump. Was any drink ever as sweet as that you caught in an improvised hand-cup dipper and sucked up noisily?

Towering above the well was the windmill, sentinel of the prairie. Kicked into gear she whipped her AEROMOTOR or DEMPSTER tail away from the wind and pushed her wheel to catch the breeze. With a clank of gears the pump-stick began its up and down rhythm lifting cool water from the depths of earth, sending it splashing into the wooden stock-tank or waiting buckets.

It took very little wind to operate the mill. Ten to fifteen miles an hour would keep things going nicely.

The well was the hub of the farm. If possible the barn was located nearby. This was best for labor if not hygienic reasons. All livestock had a mighty thirst.

Children of the bygone era were, as now, loved for themselves but they filled a real need in the family unit. A child was measured, not only on the kitchen door where heights were carefully charted, but in the chores they were able to accomplish. A child could take pride in and know he was really growing up and amounting to something when he could help with the watering.

It began with a small bucket dipped full from the tank and lugged drippingly beside Dad who swung along with two five-gallon pails hanging light as feathers from his powerful fingers. Gradually you progressed to a twelve-quart galvanized pail that only had to be set down a couple of times as you watered the chickens.

That nice pail-full of water offered many youngsters their first practical lesson in physics. How fast must you windmill your arm, swinging the pail in a complete circle to prevent any water from spilling? No one mentioned centrifugal force; it was called "Spin the Pail."

You knew you had arrived the day Dad said, "Use the five-gallon pail beside the barn and water the pigs, I'll feed the calves."

It was a feeling of sheer power to stand by the fence, alone, pouring water into the hog trough as the squealing porkers fought noisily for a drink. The livestock, your family needed you!

The importance wore a bit thin as you made possibly ten trips. It was an incentive to keep trying to haul two pails at one time and cut the trips to five.

If the well and water tank were in the best possible position it might be possible to arrange fences so that at least two yards had access to it.

The water tank, because of its importance and danger, had an unofficial set of rules for children. For toddlers ... "Stay away from the tank. You may fall in and drown."

For middle sized children . . . "Yes, you may sail stick boats on it but take them out when you are done and DON'T stir up the water. The horses will be in from the field at noon and need a good, fresh drink."

If by chance a few days of calm descended on the farm the hand pump would be pressed into service. Farm boys with an inclination for arithmetic could tell how many strokes it took to fill the tank.

Farm children were and are notorious dreamers of big dreams. Pumping water was a chore that required almost no concentration and visions of wonder flashed through active minds as they pumped away. Not one of the most accomplished, wildest dreamers envisioned a farm where water fountains supplied every pen and barn with an automatic supply of water, warmed and kept from freezing in cold weather; center-pivot irrigation units watering a quarter-section of land; or rural water systems with mains crossing the countryside bringing water to every farm.

If such notions had been proposed to a B.E. (Before Electricity) farm kid he would surely have laughed and answered . . . "Ya, come with me; I'll race you to the foot of the rainbow."

—Marian Cramer, *Lantern Glow*

The Bath

Ma took down the wash-boiler from the back-porch wall about three o'clock on Saturday afternoon and summoned her chief water-hauler, a boy about ten years old. He must fetch four pails of water for the boiler.

Though washday was past or coming whichever way you looked at it, this was Saturday—the night of the bath.

Ma and the girls would start things off with a head-wash every second week. Since their hair was long it was nice to do that in the afternoon as it would be completely dry by bedtime.

After supper the boiler steamed away on the stove. In winter the steam that collected on the windowpane quickly froze to thick, white frost but near the stove it was cozy.

Some families had tin bath tubs you could soak in. Some used the round rinse-tub from washday in which you stood and scrubbed; some used a wash basin. It was sort of a matter of tradition and using what you had.

The kitchen was hot with the stove really fired up. Ma brought out a big hooked rug and put it right in front of the open oven door. The turns usually went from the youngest to the oldest ending with Pa. Sometimes a boy or girl of courting age might have Saturday night plans and they could be worked in the early part of the schedule. During summer when the whole family went to town on Saturday night the bath hour was moved up so the baths came before town.

In winter Ma laid out neat piles of clean underwear and night clothes for each member of the family. With a pail of cold water at hand to blend with the hot water it was bath time.

Ma presided over scrubbing the small children until they were considered old enough to manage themselves and then they could bathe alone and be checked afterwards.

Privacy was honored. No one interfered as one by one the family members took their turn enjoying the nice hot water. It usually wasn't emptied between bathers, but more water could be added to keep it nice and warm. Homemade soap was used for scrubbing, but sometimes there was a bar of town-soap with its good smell.

There would be at least three bath towels for family use. These would be nice, soft, terry cloth, not the hard huck toweling used for everyday. As one towel got wet it could be draped over the oven door to dry and later used again. Ma had likely cut and hemmed the wash rag from a bath towel gone thin in the middle.

There might be a bottle of lotion set on the table to smooth on elbows and rough heels.

Pa, the last one in the bath, took care of emptying the water into slop pails. He would wipe out the tub and hang it on the back-porch wall by the boiler.

Ma would come in quietly wearing her night clothes with her hair braided into one big braid down her back. She picked up the piles of discarded clothes for her washbox and tidied up the kitchen for tomorrow was Sunday.

Sunday could come. Her family was all clean for another week.

—Marian Cramer, *Lantern Glow*

COURTESY: NEBRASKA STATE HISTORICAL SOCIETY

Hot Water

■ **Grade Level:**
High School

■ **Subject Areas:**
Environmental Science, Government, Language Arts

■ **Duration:**
Preparation time: 30 minutes

Activity time: two 50-minute periods

■ **Setting:** Classroom and library

■ **Skills:**
Gathering information (researching); Organizing; Analyzing; Interpreting; Applying (designing, composing); Evaluating; Presenting (debating)

■ **Charting the Course**
Students can investigate the scope and duration of water-related issues in "Whose Problem Is It?" Exploring water values and dilemmas helps students understand issues involving water ("Choices and Preferences, Water Index," "Dilemma Derby," and "Perspectives"). In conjunction with this activity, students can participate in "Idea Pools." Other forms of conflict resolution are presented in "Water Court."

■ **Vocabulary**
debate

Have you ever had to talk your way out of hot water?

▼ Summary
Using debate strategies, students learn how to present a valid argument regarding a water-related issue.

Objectives
Students will:
- apply basic principles and strategies in debating water resource issues.
- recognize the effectiveness of reason-based versus emotion-based presentations.

Materials
- *4 x 6 inch (10 x 15 cm) note cards*
- *Copies of **Debate Ballots***
- *Video of actual debate (optional)*

Making Connections
Students will be able to recall at least one time when they had a disagreement with a friend, parent, or teacher. They may have been in conflict over a minor incident, yet found themselves determined to win the argument. Participating in a formal debate helps students practice skills— such as impromptu speaking, effective listening, critical thinking, and sound reasoning—that help them to express their point of view and support their side of an argument.

Background
Every day, thousands of debates occur on water issues around the world— debates on topics that range from personal concerns to major issues, such as the loss of wetlands. For every water resource issue, a variety of individual views exist regarding how to resolve a problem. Interested parties, such as resource managers, community mem-

bers, and business, or agricultural representatives, desire to have their solution enacted. However, if they cannot communicate their positions effectively, their views will not be well received and may not be taken seriously. Never in the history of resource management has communication been more important than it is today.

Debate provides an opportunity for individuals to present their respective views regarding an issue. Debate involves two kinds of speeches: constructive and rebuttal.

Constructive speeches support and defend a viewpoint, while rebuttal speeches refute an opposing one. In other words, during the constructive speeches, each debater presents arguments supported by evidence (acquired through research and written on note cards) in favor of his or her viewpoint; and during the rebuttal speeches, each presents arguments, supported by evidence, to disprove or discredit the opposing viewpoint.

Procedure
▼ *Warm Up*
Present and review with students a well-known issue, such as capital punishment or the reintroduction of wolves. Discuss different viewpoints people may have regarding these issues.

Have students brainstorm a list of controversial water topics that are characterized by two opposing viewpoints. Write the ideas on the board, presenting each issue in the form of a proposition. (For example, "There should be no further large-scale hydro-electric development in the United States.") Other examples of topics include: pros and cons of water storage, use of pesticides and herbicides, drought management, and water rights.

▼ *The Activity*

1. **Inform students that they are going to conduct a debate about an issue. Review debating procedures and related terminology.** (Refer to **Background** and the following steps.)

2. **Explain that the purpose of a debate is to provide an opportunity for two opposing sides to defend or argue a given proposition (viewpoint).** One side will present positive support, and the other will argue against the proposition. Whichever side presents the strongest evidence will influence the action taken regarding this particular proposal.

3. **Have students pair up. Assign each pair of students the responsibility of representing a particular viewpoint (pro or con) of a specific issue.** For example, you may assign two students to argue for hydroelectric development and two to argue against; two for recreational uses of streams and two against (perhaps favoring irrigation uses, etc.). An alternative is to organize students into groups and assign two groups to opposite sides of the same issue. Group members work together to research and prepare their position on the issue. One member of each group is appointed spokesperson. Be sure each issue has both affirmative and negative representation.

4. **Have students research their assigned water issue and record pertinent information on note cards.** The evidence they collect must either support the particular viewpoint they are representing or refute opposing arguments.

5. **Two pairs of students assigned to opposite sides of an issue will sit at the front of the classroom; students should stand when speaking. The remaining students will act as judges, keeping score and deciding who wins. The debaters will**
present their arguments in accordance with the following form (based on the *Oregon Style of Debate*):

SIMPLIFIED DEBATE SCHEDULE FOR 2 SPEAKERS (based on the Oregon Style of Debate)	MINUTES (MIDDLE SCHOOL)	MINUTES (HIGH SCHOOL)
Affirmative Constructive Speech	4*	8*
Cross-examined by the Negative	2	3
Negative Constructive Speech	4	8
Cross-examined by the Affirmative	2	3
Negative, Rebuttal	2	3
Affirmative, Rebuttal	2	3

* maximum time allowed in minutes

6. **Toss a coin to determine who (affirmative or negative) gives their constructive speech first. Either speaker may give the first rebuttal. Preparation time for rebuttal may be allowed, but such time shall not exceed three minutes.**

7. **The judging will be done by assigning values from 1 to 4 (with 1 being the most convincing argument and 4 being the least convincing) for both the constructive and rebuttal sections.** During the debate the judges will take notes on the arguments. At the end of the debate the results are tabulated, and the team with the lowest cumulative number of points wins.

In scoring, consider the following:

ANALYSIS:	getting to the heart of the question
PROOF:	supporting contentions with sufficient and convincing evidence
ARGUMENT:	sound reasoning; logical conclusions
ADAPTATION:	clashing with or responding to the opposition
REFUTATION:	destroying opponents contentions; reinforcing your own
ORGANIZATION:	clear, logical presentation of material
SPEAKING:	effective delivery; favorable impact on audience

NOTE: Remember that although one team has been determined the "winner," both teams have contributed to a deeper understanding and appreciation of water issues and the controversies involved.

▼ *Wrap Up*

Ask students how they felt about the outcome of each debate. Have them summarize which approach worked (and which did not work) in the debate. Discuss how strategies and skills acquired during the debate can be applied to other areas of students' lives.

Assessment

Have students:

- design an affirmative or negative constructive argument using well-reasoned evidence (step 4).
- present an affirmative or negative constructive argument and participate in cross-examination and rebuttal on a water-related issue (step 5).
- evaluate the proceedings of a debate (step 7 and **Wrap Up**).

Extensions

Have students apply their skills to write a constructive letter to the editor of a newspaper, expressing their views about a water issue. (Remind students that they will be submitting their work to the editor as individuals; they should not imply that their school supports their opinions, unless they receive permission to do so.)

Resources

Basic Debate: For the Novice Debater. Contact: National Textbook Company, 4255 W. Touhy Avenue, Lincolnwood, IL 60464-1975.

Debate video. 1986. Contact: Dale Publishing Company, P. O. Box 151, Grandview, MO, 64030. Topic: 1986; Resolved, that the federal government should establish a comprehensive national policy to protect the quality of water in the United States.

An Introduction to Debate. Contact: National Federation of State High School Associations, 11724 Plaza Circle, P.O. Box 20626, Kansas City, MO 64195

Miller, G. Tyler, Jr. 1990. *Resource Conservation and Management.* Belmont, Calif.: Wadsworth Publishing Company.

Project WILD. 1992. Activities "To Dam or Not to Dam" and "Facts and Falsehoods." *Aquatic Project WILD.* Bethesda, Md.: Western Regional Environmental Education Council.

Graves, William, ed. 1993. "Water: The Power, Promise, and Turmoil of North America's Fresh Water." *National Geographic Special Edition* (November).

Debate Ballot

Team's Name:_____   Judge's Name: _____

Affirmative Number_____   Negative Number_____   Round_____

DIRECTIONS: Circle the number that best describes the debater(s) you judged, and record your comments below. Remember, a score of 1 = the most convincing argument, and a score of 4 = the least convincing argument.

Overall Affirmative:	1	2	3	4	**Overall Negative:**	1	2	3	4
Constructive Speech:	1	2	3	4	**Constructive Speech:**	1	2	3	4
Cross Examination of Negative:	1	2	3	4	**Cross Examination of Affirmative:**	1	2	3	4
Rebuttal:	1	2	3	4	**Rebuttal:**	1	2	3	4
Comments:					**Comments:**				

I determine the debate to have been won by _____. Reasons for my decision are:

_____
Judge's Signature

Pass the Jug

■ **Grade Level:**
Middle School

■ **Subject Areas:**
Social Studies, Environmental Science, History, Government

■ **Duration:**
Preparation time:
Part I: 15 minutes
Part II: 15 minutes

Activity time:
Part I: 30 minutes
Part II: 30 minutes

■ **Setting:** Classroom

■ **Skills:**
Organizing (formulating questions); Analyzing; Applying (problem solving)

■ **Charting the Course**
"A Drop in the Bucket" helps students appreciate that water is a limited resource. In "Wet Vacation" students compare amounts of precipitation in different parts of the country. Debates and conflicts regarding water rights could follow (e.g., "Hot Water," "Perspectives," and "Water Court").

■ **Vocabulary**
riparian areas, water rights, water allocation, consumptive use, nonconsumptive use

Imagine you have just bought a bag of candy and have six friends who want some. How are you going to divide it up? Do you give everyone an equal amount, do you give some to the first person who asks, or do you give your best friend more?

▼ Summary
Students simulate and analyze different water rights policies to learn how water availability and people's proximity to the resource influence how water is allocated.

Objectives
Students will:
- describe historical and current aspects of water rights.
- illustrate how water rights are used to allocate water.
- evaluate water rights allocation systems.

Materials
- *Paper cups or glasses* (1 per student plus extras)
- *Water jug* (e.g., apple cider or gallon milk container)
- *Water Users (Descriptions)* (cut into strips)
- *Funnel*

Making Connections
Water is a resource needed by everyone, and people have invested considerable time, energy, and money to ensure that they have ample supplies of water. However, sometimes demands on the resource require that water be allocated. Some students have experienced water shortages in their lives and are familiar with rationing. Simulating how water resources are allocated helps students appreciate the value of this shared, limited resource.

Background
Water rights provide an organized and systematic manner for allocating water. A water right allows a person, business, community, or other group to use a specified amount of water. People receive only the right to use the water; they do not own the water.

The history of water rights is related closely to settlement and land ownership. Settlers in the East adapted a water rights policy similar to what the populace used in England. The Riparian Rights or Common-Law Doctrine gives people who own land bordering a water source the right to use that water however they choose. A more recent version of the doctrine requires people to justify their uses as reasonable. They must also ensure that landowners downstream have their fair share of water.

East of the Mississippi, average annual rainfall is more plentiful than in the West. This is apparent from a geographical view. From about the 98th meridian of longitude west to the Pacific coast, average annual rainfall dips significantly below the 20 inches that normally sustain nonirrigated crops in the East.

Scarcity generates westerners' preoccupation with water and water rights. Western water rights were developed for the needs of 19th century settlers. They evolved from the customs and practices of miners from about 1848, who developed systems for protecting their claims to land and minerals. More than one hundred years later, after investing billions of dollars to build water diversion and storage projects such as ditches, dams, and reservoirs, westerners remain strongly committed to ensuring a continued supply of water for their irrigation and mining needs.

In many parts of the West, the Prior Appropriation Doctrine regulates water rights. This doctrine maintains "first come, first served," or "first in time is first in right." In other words, whoever uses the water first has the "prior" or first right to the supply of available water. If all the water in a stream is allocated, no new users are allowed.

Exceptions to the state-based Prior Appropriation Doctrine are federal and tribal reserved water rights. Reserved water rights were created to provide adequate water for lands owned by the federal government and Native American nations. Unlike state rights allocated under the Prior Appropriation Doctrine, reserved rights on federal and tribal lands do not have to be used to be valid.

In the last 20 years, many changes have added new dimensions to water rights and water allocation programs. Irrigated agriculture is a large consumer of water. Individuals and corporations invest millions of dollars in irrigation systems to grow crops for people and for livestock. Cities also need water to meet the needs of residents, businesses, and industries. Water for recreation and for fish and wildlife is receiving growing attention. Many communities depend on water resources for

HOWARD KARGER, N E STOCK PHOTO

energy production methods such as hydroelectric and thermoelectric generation plants. The challenge of meeting today's growing demand for water will involve nontraditional allocation strategies. Several methods, such as water rights transfers, water rights changes, water marketing, and water leasing, have evolved as considerations to satisfy 20th century needs.

Average Annual Rainfall in inches

Below 8
8-16
16-25
25-40
40-60
60-80
80-100
Over 100

100th Meridian

Procedure
▼ Warm Up
Present students with the scenario described in the **Teaser**. Ask them how they would divide the candy.

▼ *The Activity*

Part I

1.   **Arrange students' seats in a row or around a table and give each student a cup. Starting at one end, have the first student pour out as much water as he or she needs and pass the jug to the next student in line.** Because of the limited amount of water in the jug, there might not be enough to go around.

2.   **Ask students (those who received water and those who did not) to express how they feel. Tell them that sometimes there is not enough water available to meet everyone's needs.**

3.   **Ask students what they could do to make sure they all get water. Have them repeat the activity and put their plan into action.**

4.   **Provide students with a brief description of riparian rights. Ask them to explain how passing the jug relates to riparian rights.**

Part II

1.   **After students have emptied their cups, inform them they will now simulate the allocation of water rights in many places in the West. Explain how the Prior Appropriation Doctrine gives people who originally moved into an area and started using water the right to use water first, whether or not their land borders the water source.**

2.   **Have each student write down his or her birth month and day on a piece of paper and display it so everyone can see. Then distribute** *Water Users (Descriptions)* **by handing the strips out in the order of students' birthdays (from January 1 to December 31). This represents the concept of first in time, first in right.**

3.   **Explain that the descriptions are numbered. The student with description number one is the first person who moved into the area**

("first in time"). **Along with the right to use the water, each description also states how the water is used and how much is needed.** NOTE: An alternative is for students to make up their own water use and quantities needed.

4.   **Pass around the jug of water in the order of the numbered cards. Have students read aloud how they use water. Each student must take the amount of water indicated on his or her card.** Some water users, such as fisheries and hydroelectric power plants, utilize water without reducing water quantity; water managers call these users nonconsumptive. (However, reservoirs associated with hydroelectric power plants do lose some water to evaporation.) Students who represent these water users should pour water into their cups and then funnel it back into the jug.

5.   **When water runs out, have students express their opinions about this system.** What are the benefits of this system? (It protects the investments [money, time, and energy] and the rights of first water

users.) What are some shortcomings? (It restricts new or different water users' access to water.) How or why would students change the system?

▼ Wrap Up and Action

Have students summarize the two general approaches to allocating water rights and how each evolved. Encourage students to investigate options for individuals or groups of people who do not have enough water. For example, they could promote conservation, invest in engineering projects that collect or divert water supplies, etc.

Have students research water allocation in their community. (They should contact a city or state water works manager or the public health department.) Suggest that they create a display for the school outlining their community's and/or state's water rights system (e.g., "Our Water Rights Made Simple").

Assessment

Have students:
• develop a strategy to distribute a limited resource (e.g., a bag of

candy, an hour of television time, a five dollar bill) among students in the class (*Warm Up* and *Part I*, step 3).

- compare and evaluate different approaches to allocating water rights (*Part II*, step 5 and *Wrap Up*).
- summarize how water rights practices evolved (*Wrap Up*)

Extensions

To simulate annual fluctuations in streamflow, change the amount of water in the jug. Some years have heavy streamflow; in other years the river runs dry.

To demonstrate how pollution affects water users, have students add a drop of food coloring or dunk a tea bag in their cups—simulating their "use" of the water. Students will return some of this used water to the jug (demonstrating runoff and discharge). Add a sugar lump to symbolize invisible chemicals that are carried in water. Have students list how water quality can affect water quantity.

To simulate snowpack, freeze colored water in layers in a plastic liter bottle. The layers represent the amount of water that is frozen or "held" in snowpack over the winter. The first layer, colored green, represents November, the second, colored red, symbolizes December, and so on through to the top clear layer, March. (The colored layers will remain distinct as long as each freezes solid before the next layer is added. The four colors in a box of food coloring plus one clear layer will make up the five layers [or months] necessary.)

Arrange students in a circle and distribute cups and tell them that you will "pass the jug" once again. Hand the first student the frozen bottle of water and suggest that he or she pour into the cup whatever is needed. When students express

confusion, ask them what must happen before they can share this water. Inform them that in some parts of the country snow accumulates in the mountains through the winter months (November through March) and results in "snowpack." In spring, warmer temperatures melt this snow and the water is released. Streams are often swollen (sometimes overflowing their banks) during the spring thaw. This water is critical for irrigating crops, for providing lush vegetation for grazing wildlife and livestock, and for filling reservoirs that may have been drawn down over the winter months.

Remind students that snowpack is often referred to as a "water bank." That is, water is "saved" until the rise in temperature (above 32 degrees F [0°C]) "opens the bank." Ask students to speculate on what conditions might exist in the spring if there was very little precipitation during the winter and a reduced snowpack.

Simulate a drought by asking students not to drink water one hour prior to the activity. You might even take a short hike to generate thirst.

Have students adapt "Pass the Jug" to demonstrate how federal reserved water rights could affect water allocation. These rights are designed to ensure that public lands (e.g., parks) and Native Americans receive the water they need. Their demands can sometimes supersede other water rights systems (e.g., riparian, prior appropriation).

Demonstrate needs of in-stream flows for fish and wildlife by placing a fish bowl at the end of the line of students. Explain that at least one cup of water must be poured into the fish bowl to meet this requirement. How do your students adjust to meet this new need?

K-2 Option

A simplified version of this activity emphasizes the value of sharing water. During snack time, provide the class with a jug of flavored water. Begin filling students' cups or hand the jug to students and have them fill their own cups. Tell them not to drink until each student has water in his or her cup. When you run out of water, assess the reactions of students who did and did not receive something to drink. Tell them this is all the available water. Ask for suggestions to make sure that everyone gets water. Help them to consider the idea of evenly distributing the water among the students. Have students summarize the importance of sharing water and other resources.

Resources

Getches, David. 1990. *Water Rights in a Nutshell*. St. Paul, Minn.: West Publishing Co.

Marstib, Betsy. 1987. *Western Water Made Simple*. Washington, D.C.: Island Press.

Wolfe, Mary Ellen. 1994. *A Landowner's Guide to Western Water Rights*. Bozeman, Mont.: The Watercourse.

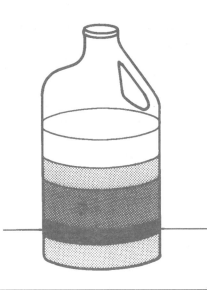

Water Users (Descriptions)

Number 1	You are a descendant of the first homesteader that moved into the area. You own a goat dairy farm and grow alfalfa and corn.	use 2 cups
Number 2	Your ancestor was heading toward California during the great gold rush, but got distracted by the flowers. While picking daisies, he found a huge deposit of copper and started a copper mining company. Your family runs this small, but lucrative, operation.	use 2 cups
Number 3	Your great-great-grandmother came out to teach the children of the copper miners. You still live on the property she bought and need water for personal use and crop irrigation.	use 1 cup
Number 4	You represent a small community of families who work in the mine. You use water for daily domestic and irrigation purposes. Your water needs may increase as the town grows.	use 2 cups
Number 5	Your grandparents left their farm in Iowa to start a farm here. You help meet the needs of the growing community. Your grandfather is still alive and resists using modern farming practices.	use 5 cups
Number 6	To avoid the competition in the big city, your father moved his coat hanger factory to this growing community. The industry provides a means of income for community members.	use 2 cups
Number 7	You represent a hydroelectric company with a dam upstream of the town. The water you use passes through the dam to generate electricity. Show this by pouring three cups of water back into the jug.	use 4 cups
Number 8	You represent a town that grew as more people escaping the city moved to the countryside. Consequently, your town has become a city. You use water for domestic and irrigation purposes.	use 3 cups
Number 9	You are a high-tech farmer that has moved here to supply food to the growing communities.	use 2 cups
Number 10	You have decided to start an industry that you think meets a growing need: shoulder pad storage racks.	use 1 cup

The rest of the user cards can be copied and numbered in any order. If the community is allocated only one jug of water, there will probably be no water left by this time.

	Small farmer	1 cup
	Industry	1 cup
	Small town	1 cup
	Rancher	1 cup

©The Watercourse and Council for Environmental Education (CEE).

Perspectives

Think of an argument you had with your best friend. Did your friend understand your point of view? Did you understand your friend's? Disputes often involve people's differing values.

■ **Grade Level:**
Middle School, High School

■ **Subject Areas:**
Government, Environmental Science

■ **Duration:**
Preparation time:
Part I: 20 minutes
Part II: 10 minutes

Activity time:
Part I: 50 minutes
Part II: two 50-minute periods

■ **Setting:** Classroom

■ **Skills:**
Gathering information (researching, listening); Organizing information (categorizing); Applying (decision making)

■ **Charting the Course**
Prior to this activity, students could create a class water index ("Choices and Preferences, Water Index"). The activity "Whose Problem Is It?" can help students investigate the scope and duration of the issue. "Perspectives" relates to a variety of activities in this guide (e.g., "A Grave Mistake," "Where Are the Frogs?" and "Humpty Dumpty").

■ **Vocabulary**
values, water-related issue

▼ **Summary**
Students analyze public values toward water issues to help them evaluate approaches to managing water resources.

Objectives

Students will:

• recognize that people have differing values regarding water resource management issues.

• evaluate strengths and weaknesses of proposed solutions to water resource management issues.

• describe purposes of diverse advocacy groups and summarize their similarities and differences.

Materials

• *Reference material relating to one or more water issues* (newspapers, magazines, encyclopedias, video recordings of news events)

• *Blackboard and chalk or butcher paper and markers*

Making Connections

Problem-solving and decision-making skills are integral abilities of responsible citizens. Because water plays a central role in human lives, water issues provide an excellent source of activities designed to develop those skills.

Background

Fundamental to problem-solving and decision-making skills is the ability to analyze an issue. Environmental issues arise when differing values converge regarding resource management strategies. Because of the differing viewpoints of the people involved, most issues do not have simple solutions.

Finding, proposing, and implementing solutions to environmental issues often requires an understanding of values. When this understanding is lacking, attempts to resolve the issues often meet with resistance.

Values are expressed through feelings and sometimes lead to actions. Often taking years to develop, values are influenced by culture, family, and the social and physical environment. Values are usually well established and form an integral part of an individual's pattern of living. When water resource issues involve conflicting values, solutions are usually difficult to formulate and implement. Resolution often requires that those involved participate in a group decision-making process. This decision-making process should include an understanding of ecological and economic factors that relate to the issue. In addition, the views and opinions of the people affected by the issue should be considered.

The variety of views regarding the resolution of water-related issues often prompt people who support a particular path of action to group together. Sometimes these groups share a similar career or live in the same part of a town. Because these groups support a certain cause or policy, they are referred to as advocacy groups. Advocacy groups may range from grass roots to national organizations. Local groups may form to promote the cleaning of a hazardous waste site or to protect water designated for irrigation. People who share a career, watershed managers for example, may join together to support statewide water conservation practices, or a national environmental group may lobby Congress to enforce a water quality protection bill.

PERSPECTIVES
The pros and cons of various solutions to community flooding.

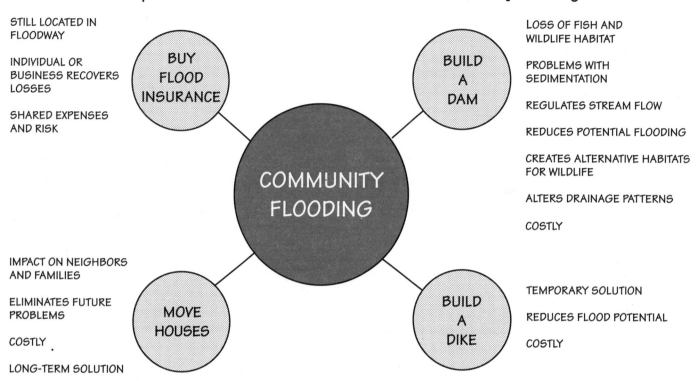

STILL LOCATED IN
FLOODWAY

INDIVIDUAL OR
BUSINESS RECOVERS
LOSSES

SHARED EXPENSES
AND RISK

BUY FLOOD INSURANCE

BUILD A DAM

LOSS OF FISH AND
WILDLIFE HABITAT

PROBLEMS WITH
SEDIMENTATION

REGULATES STREAM FLOW

REDUCES POTENTIAL FLOODING

CREATES ALTERNATIVE HABITATS
FOR WILDLIFE

ALTERS DRAINAGE PATTERNS

COSTLY

COMMUNITY FLOODING

IMPACT ON NEIGHBORS
AND FAMILIES

ELIMINATES FUTURE
PROBLEMS

COSTLY

LONG-TERM SOLUTION

MOVE HOUSES

BUILD A DIKE

TEMPORARY SOLUTION

REDUCES FLOOD POTENTIAL

COSTLY

Procedure
▼ Warm Up
Ask students to define a public issue. Discuss issues common to students' lives or present a scenario that demonstrates the complexities of an issue. For example, students can role-play an adult trying to get another family member to take shorter showers. Students should appreciate that issues arise because people have differing views about a situation.

▼ The Activity
Part I
1.   **Discuss several problems concerning water quality and/or quantity. Assign or have students select a local water resource issue.** News articles about issues can be made available for reference.

2.   **Have students describe the cause of the issue, determining if it was a natural or human-made occurrence. Or it could be a combination of the two.** For example, ocean currents carry dumped waste materials thousands of miles up and down coastlines. If necessary, time can be allotted for students to research the issue.

3.   **Determine whom this issue affects. Discuss the values of each of the people or groups involved.**

4.   **In the center of the board, write the water resource issue and circle it.**

5.   **Brainstorm or discuss potential solutions to the issue. Write solutions on the board around the circle enclosing the issue statement. Circle each solution; these**

are the "perspectives."

6.   **Have students evaluate each solution, listing pros and cons under each.** Students can consider values, cost, time, resources, ecological balance, jobs, wildlife habitat, wilderness, historic perspectives, etc., when evaluating the solutions. Might a proposed solution benefit some people, while making the situation worse for others? Might a proposed solution actually create more problems in the long run? (If your students developed a class water index in "Choices and Preferences, Water Index," they can use priorities to help evaluate solutions.)

7.   **Have students rank the solutions. Taking into consideration their own values, students should explain the reasoning behind their rankings.**

Part II

1. **After students have created a "Perspectives" diagram for a water-related issue, discuss the different viewpoints. Ask them if they think certain groups would support one solution over another.** Explain that when a water-related issue arises, people who support a certain viewpoint often come from a particular group or will form a new one if none exists.

2. **See if students can assign a local, state, and/or national advocacy group to each viewpoint.**

3. **Assign groups of students to research certain advocacy groups.** They should look into the group's mission, the demographics of the membership (for example, size and local, state, national, and/or international involvement), and its primary methods of issue resolution. In addition, students can report on the history of the group. (Has the size, philosophy, or course of action changed over the years, or has it maintained consistency?)

4. **Each student group should prepare a class presentation about its researched advocacy group. Included in the report should be an evaluation of the advocacy group's success.** What are the group's accomplishments? What are its weaknesses? Do students think the group has effectively contributed to water resource management decision-making processes?

▼ Wrap Up

Discuss how managing water resource issues often involves the interactions of advocacy groups. Have students summarize why people might form groups to support a certain viewpoint. What do they consider potential benefits and dangers of aligning with a certain advocacy group? (Benefits could consist of strength in numbers, increased awareness, and networking. Problems could include conflicts of interest, financial needs, and increased responsibilities.)

Assessment

Have students:

*   identify the values of people affected by water resource issues (*Part I*, step 3).
*   evaluate the strengths and weaknesses of proposed solutions to an issue (*Part I*, step 6).
*   rank suggested solutions to a water resource issue based on their evaluations (*Part I*, step 7).
*   present a report on the background and accomplishments of advocacy groups regarding the management of a water-related issue (*Part II*, step 4).
*   identify pros and cons of working with an advocacy group (*Wrap Up*).

Upon completing the activity, for further assessment have students:
*   apply the "Perspectives" format to identify and evaluate solutions to a different water resource issue.

Extensions

This activity can be completed as a role-playing activity as well, in which students role-play people with different perspectives involved in a water resource issue. Students can choose whom they want to represent, or they can be assigned to play the role of a person whose views are counter to their own. At the end of the activity, students can describe what it was like to play that character.

Discuss the difference between structural solutions (dikes, dams, levees, and water systems) and nonstructural solutions (education, planning, water conservation, relocating people, purchasing land, and so forth) in resolving community water issues. Have students analyze the drawbacks and merits of each approach.

Resources

Caduto, M. 1985. *A Guide on Environmental Values Education.* UNESCO-UNEP International Environmental Education Program, Environmental Education Series, no. 13. Paris, France: UNESCO.

Coughlan, B., and C. Amor. 1990. *Group Decision-Making Techniques for Natural Resource Management Applications.* Resource publication 185. Washington, D.C.: U.S. Department of the Interior, Fish & Wildlife Service.

Decision Making: The Chesapeake Bay. 1985. An Interdisciplinary Environmental Education Curriculum Unit, 2nd ed. College Park, Md.: Maryland University, Sea Grant Program.

Hungerford, Harold, et al. 1992. *Investigating and Evaluating Environmental Issues and Action Skill Development Modules.* Champaign, Ill.: Stipes Publishing Company.

Polesetsky, Matthew, ed. 1991. *Global Resources: Opposing Viewpoints.* San Diego, Calif.: Greenhaven Press, Inc.

Water: Read All About It!

*"Local Students Clean Up Beach." "Town Worries Ground Water Supplies May Be Running Out." "Children Plan a Water Festival." Create headlines for your own **Water Special Edition**.*

▼ Summary
Students assume the roles of various people on a newspaper's staff and develop their own special edition on water.

Objectives
Students will:
- recognize that water is a frequent subject in the news.
- demonstrate skills needed to publish a newspaper special edition on water.
- critique their *Water Special Edition.*

Materials
- *A variety of local, state, or national newspapers*
- *Tabloid-sized paper* (Rolls of newsprint are sometimes available from local newspapers.)
- *Pens, pencils, marking pens*
- *Tape, rubber or glue stick*
- *Scissors*
- *Computers and word-processing programs* (optional)
- *Computer graphics program or a hand waxer and grid paper* (optional)

Making Connections
Students may turn to newspapers to find sports scores, movie and television schedules, and the "funnies." But, newspapers are also a main source of information about local and world events. By creating a newspaper about water, students learn how they can inform themselves and others about important water issues.

Background
The bad news and the good news about water—its ebb and flow, availability, quantity and quality—are often topics in newspapers. Newspapers allow people everywhere to stand on the common ground of shared knowledge of current events. In recent years newspapers have chronicled heavy rainfall and mudslides in Southern California, record snowfall and ice storms in the Northeast, the 1993 Midwest floods (Missouri and Mississippi Rivers), the Exxon *Valdez* oil spill, Hurricane Andrew, and other stories related to water.

Newspapers juxtapose fact with opinion and interpret reality through the use of words and images. They focus on current events, yet they have connections with the past. Newspapers are journals that record much of our history. Through editorials and letters to the editor, newspapers provide forums for the exchange of disparate human ideas and opinions. Through newspapers people can exercise their constitutional rights to free expression.

Newspapers are a collective effort on the part of many people, each with special skills and designated tasks. Newspapers serve as ideal vehicles for interdisciplinary explorations. They combine a diverse range of skills including writing, photography, word processing, graphics, organization, and editing. Gathering the news is just the beginning of a complex process, regulated by deadlines (the times that all parts of the process must be completed in order to get papers printed and delivered on time each day).

The publisher is the person (or persons) who owns the paper and pays for it to be produced. Most newspapers divide the labor among many people: editors, reporters, photographers, artists, cartoonists, proofreaders, composers, typographers, etc.

■ **Grade Level:**
Middle School, High School

■ **Subject Areas:**
Language Arts, Environmental Science, Government, History

■ **Duration:**
Preparation time: 30 minutes
Activity time: 1 week

■ **Setting:** Classroom

■ **Skills:**
Gathering information (researching); Applying (designing, composing, restructuring); Evaluating; Presenting (writing)

■ **Charting the Course**
Prior to this lesson students could investigate their own values toward water (e.g., "Idea Pools," "Choices and Preferences, Water Index"). Through this activity students can investigate water-related concepts and issues presented in this guide (e.g., "Where Are the Frogs," "Humpty Dumpty," "Sum of the Parts," and "The Pucker Effect").

■ **Vocabulary**
Water-related issue

Reporters work on the front line. They seek and gather information about the events they are assigned to "cover"—their "beat," as it is called. Reporters write (and rewrite if necessary) the "copy" (article, story, or column). Often, reporters are accompanied by photographers who capture images to illustrate the stories.

Writing for newspapers differs from other forms of journalism. There is usually little time (short deadlines) and the traditional journalistic questions—who, what, when, where, why, and how—must be answered in an intriguing and concise style. Considering the restraints of time and space, reporters must be disciplined writers.

Editors determine which breaking stories (events currently unfolding) or newsworthy items (things that can be expected to interest readers) are most important and assign reporters to them. They also review rough drafts of stories and comment on additions or corrections that should be made. Advertisements are an important part of any newspaper because they generate funds that keep the presses rolling. The ad manager works with the managing editor to determine where stories will be placed in relation to the ads. The managing editor or page editor lays out and arranges the stories in logical order.

Newspapers are usually divided into sections, and any section could contain news related to water. The *news/features* section of the paper includes most of the major breaking stories (e.g., "City Water Supply Contaminated") and usually has an index indicating the page location of other stories. The *weather* section reports current and projected weather conditions (e.g., "Major Snow Storm Expected to Hit Area"). Exchanges of opinion and stands

taken by the newspaper on important issues are found in the *editorials* section (e.g., "Chronicle Supports New Water Policy"). Movie and television schedules and comic strips are placed in the *entertainment* and *recreation* sections (e.g., "The Ice Pirates, matinee, 1:30" or "Tips on Fly Fishing"). In the *sports* section rain delays of ball games are reported. In the *ads* you might find a plumber, pool services, or irrigation systems.

Procedure
▼ *Warm Up*
Ask students why people read newspapers. Which section do they or their parents read first? How are newspapers important to our society? Discuss why water is a "newsworthy" subject. Ask if they can recall water-related issues that have been in the news. Students can clip articles related to water from different newspapers for one week.

▼ *The Activity*
1.   **Provide students with a variety of local, state, or national newspapers. Ask them to list the different sections of the newspapers. Discuss the parts of a newspaper and what information each contains.**

2.   **Tell students they are going to develop a newspaper focusing on the theme of water. The primary emphasis will be on local and regional water-related topics and issues.** These could include water rights issues, recreation, pollution, water uses, conservation, and so forth.

3.   **Discuss the different jobs involved in newspaper development.** Students may want to call the local newspaper office to get detailed descriptions of these positions.

4.   **Divide the class into groups and have each group choose a section of the newspaper.** These sections could include: 1) news/features, 2) weather, 3) editorial, 4) entertainment, 5) sports, 6) advertising. More than one group should choose the news/features section.

5.   **Each group should have an editor and reporters. Other personnel include photographers, word processors, and researchers.**

6.   **The groups should brainstorm topics that are of interest to them and that relate to their section. The editors from each group should then meet to decide which subjects should be pursued.**

7.   **Discuss with students how reporting differs from other types of writing.** They will be under pressure to produce researched and well-written articles within a short time period. Ideally, all writing should be completed and saved on computer disks.

8.   **Review interview techniques with students.** Make sure they write or call in advance to schedule interviews. Help them design a set of questions concerning the topic. Students can practice their questions with each other. They should take careful notes during the interview. If a tape recorder is used, have them

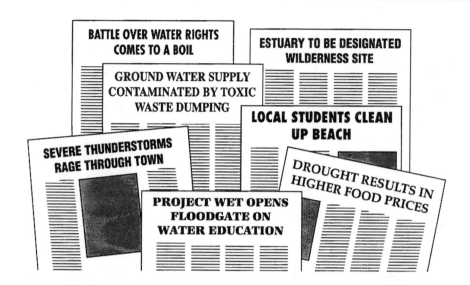

secure permission *before* turning it on. Permission must also be obtained for any quotations used in the newspaper. A thank-you letter should follow the interview.

9. **Tell students they have a deadline of five days to complete the newspaper.** (This can be adjusted for simpler or more extensive projects.) They have three days to research a topic (including interviews and references) and write drafts of the articles. The last two days are needed for the editors to proofread the articles and prepare the newspaper layout. NOTE: Graphic layout can be done by a few students using a computer or they can manually lay out the articles on a display board. A hand waxer can be used to wax the backs of special paper which can be placed on a page and moved to different locations.

▼ *Wrap Up and Action*

When students have completed the newspaper, have them evaluate their work and express how they felt about creating a *Water Special Edition*. What were the rewards and frustrations of publishing a newspaper under a deadline? Depending on the desired quantity, papers can be reproduced in-house on a photocopier or taken to a printer. Post the

newspaper in the classroom. Students may want to distribute newspapers to other classrooms or around the community. Encourage students to read the newspaper at home and discuss issues about water and the environment with their parents.

Assessment

Have students:
- explain why water is a subject of interest in the news (*Warm Up*).
- work cooperatively to develop a section of a newspaper (steps 4-9).
- assume a specific task related to newspaper development (steps 5-9).
- evaluate the quality of the newspaper (*Wrap Up*).
- recount the rewards and frustrations of producing a newspaper (*Wrap Up*).

Extensions

Have students send the *Water Special Edition* to community, county, state, or national leaders. These people may respond with their thoughts on this class project.

Invite the publisher or editor of the local or county newspaper to speak to students. The editor should discuss the role of the newspaper in relaying information to the public.

Arrange for a field trip to a local newspaper or call for free classroom materials (curriculum modules on specific subjects, videotapes, etc.).

Have students collect photographs, articles, cartoons, editorials, and advertisements about water from local, regional, and national newspapers and place them in a "Water in the News" scrapbook.

Explain to students that water is often a subject of other forms of writing, such as music, poetry, fiction, nonfiction, and television and motion picture screenplays. Ask students to think of some examples (e.g., "The Rime of the Ancient Mariner" [poem], *A River Runs Through It* [book and film], "River of Dreams" [song]).

Resources

Educational materials produced by newspapers, such as "Newspaper in Education." For more information, contact: Pacific Northwest Newspaper Association Foundation, P.O. Box 11128, Tacoma, WA 98411. (206) 272-3611.

Project WILD. 1992. Activity "Aquatic Times." From *Aquatic Project WILD*. Bethesda, Md.: Western Regional Environmental Education Council.

There are several computer programs (grades 6-12, **ClarisWorks**; grades K-8, **KidPix** and **KidPix Companion**; grades 8-12, **Pagemaker**) for layout or graphics.

NOTE: Several of the ideas for this activity were provided by Butch Beedle of J. C. McKenna Middle School in Evansville, Wis. Students at J. C. McKenna produce the *Tropical Tribune*, which provides extensive news and features about rain forests. These newspapers have been distributed throughout the United States and around the world.

402

Water Bill of Rights

■ **Grade Level:**
Middle School, High School

■ **Subject Areas:**
History, Government, Environmental Science

■ **Duration:**
Preparation time: 10 minutes

Activity time: two 50-minute periods

■ **Setting:** Classroom

■ **Skills:**
Gathering information (listening); Applying (proposing solutions, designing); Presenting (writing, persuading, debating)

■ **Charting the Course**
Prior to this activity, students should explore all the different ways they need and use water ("Easy Street"), including indirect uses of water ("Water Works"). Students should understand that water is a finite and shared resource ("A Drop in the Bucket" and "Common Water"). In "Choices and Preferences, Water Index" students debate and prioritize the different uses of water; this could precede or complement the development of a water bill of rights.

■ **Vocabulary**
Bill of Rights

Is the freedom to have clean, ample water an "inalienable right?"

▼ Summary
Students speculate on their rights to sustainable water resources.

Objectives
Students will:
- appreciate the value of the United States Bill of Rights in their lives.
- structure a Water Bill of Rights that ensures water of quality and quantity for all people.

Materials
- *Copies of the **United States Bill of Rights***

Making Connections
Students may have heard the terms *right to free speech* and *right to public trial*. The right to use natural resources is often taken for granted. Because water is a resource in high demand, sometimes limitations are imposed through water rationing and water right policies. Developing a Water Bill of Rights helps students consider and debate what they perceive as their fundamental rights to availability and use of this resource.

Background
The American Bill of Rights was written out of concern for the individual, to ensure that in the quest for a government-controlled democracy, certain inalienable, or absolute, rights and freedoms would not be wrested from that individual.

In 1787, the American Constitution was awaiting ratification by at least nine of the 13 colonies. A number of states balked at ratification because the Constitution lacked a bill of rights to protect citizens against federal tyranny and to

guarantee civil liberties. When John Hancock agreed to endorse ratification in Massachusetts, he proposed that nine amendments be added to protect citizens against such federal tyranny.

In an impassioned speech to the Virginia State Convention, Patrick Henry portrayed the new Constitution as dangerous to liberty. Under it, he claimed, the citizen would be abused, insulted, and tyrannized. "The Constitution reflects in the most degrading and mortifying manner on the virtue, integrity and wisdom of the state legislatures," he declared. "It assumed that the chosen few who go to Congress will have more upright hearts, and more enlightened minds, than those who are members of individual legislatures."

However, the Federalists, a political party that supported a strong federal government, resisted the addition of the Bill of Rights. They argued that most states already had their own bill of rights, and the Constitution prevented the government from interfering with states' rights. Others argued that since the Constitution made the federal government superior to state rule, a Bill of Rights, protecting individual freedoms, was a crucial addition.

Thus, although the Constitution was ratified without amendments recognizing individual rights, such amendments were soon added. An understanding was reached that if the states would approve the Constitution, the First Congress would submit a series of amendments adding a bill of rights. Congress promptly proposed 12 amendments in 1789. Ten of these were ratified by the states and became part of the Constitution in 1791.

The First Amendment establishes the basic freedoms of religion, speech, press, assembly, and petition. The Second and

Third Amendments are concerned with the right to bear arms and the quartering of soldiers. Amendments Four through Eight prescribe just procedures in the treatment of persons accused of crimes. The Ninth and Tenth Amendments reaffirm the principle that the federal government possesses limited powers.

Other amendments have been added since the Bill of Rights was written. These amendments have helped the government solve special problems that have arisen as the nation has grown.

Around the world, people are beginning to recognize their right to a clean environment and to adequate resources (e.g., clean water). International meetings, such as the 1992 United Nations Conference on Environment and Development (UNCED), focus on national and individual rights related to a sustainable future and develop action plans to address these rights. Perhaps in the future, national and international bills of rights related to natural resources, including water, will become common.

Procedure
▼ Warm Up

Briefly review the United States Bill of Rights. Have students discuss or write a brief paper about what they think their lives might be like without these rights. Students can include an overview of all the rights or chose one or two to consider. Some students may have read George Orwell's *1984* . Others may be familiar with *Lord of the Flies* (Golding), *Fahrenheit 451* (Bradbury), *Brave New World* (Huxley), or *Invisible Man* (Ellison). Passages from each of these books could be related to the discussion.

Ask students if they have ever considered their right to use water. Do students believe that a bill of rights related to water or other natural resources is necessary? What would life be like if their rights to use water were restricted? Students might be familiar with water rights doctrines and water rationing policies that do regulate water use. Encourage students to express their personal expectations for water rights and privileges, both for themselves and for those in other parts of the country or world. List

these suggestions on the blackboard or butcher paper.

▼ The Activity

1.   **Inform students that they are going to draft their own Water Bill of Rights based on their personal expectations regarding access to and use of water.**

2.   **Have students refer to the list generated in the *Warm Up*. Students can work in small groups or as a class to identify the most important suggestions, consolidate the list, and delete rhetorical or unnecessary items.** Multiple viewpoints may result in heated discussions and debates. For example, is the proposed right practical? What if two rights contradict or challenge each other?

3.   **Encourage students to finalize ten rights for their bill. Students can use persuasive arguments and presentations to convince other students to support certain rights.** Remind students that like the original Bill of Rights, the Water Bill of Rights *must* be acceptable to the majority of people. If necessary, take a class vote and select the ten most popular items.

A student generated Water Bill of Rights might include:
*   The right to drink and use water without concern for health hazards.
*   The right to live in a region or community that has citizen guidelines for water use and conservation and that enforces water laws and regulations.
*   The right to learn about and practice one's cultural heritage relating to water.
*   The right to an education that includes water awareness and citizen responsibilities.
*   The right to compensation for damages to or destruction of water resources.

404

- The right to public forums in which citizens may express concerns about water resources.
- The right to a sense of personal power to address and correct water problems.

▼ *Wrap Up and Action*

Discuss the process and outcome of the development of the rights. How do students feel about the need for a bill of rights related to water? What if some of the rights listed were taken away? Have students develop an action plan to ensure these rights are maintained.

Distribute the Water Bill of Rights to other classes, post it on bulletin boards, and contact local newspapers about printing it. Present the Water Bill of Rights to local, regional, national, or international conservation organizations (the Sierra Club, the National Association of Conservation Districts, the Wilderness Society, the National Farmers Union, the National Audubon Society, the Cousteau Society, etc.). Many of these organizations have programs and publications for young people.

Present the Water Bill of Rights to local water management authorities. This will provide water managers with an understanding of young people's expectations for water resources in the future. This will also give managers an opportunity to

Notes ▼

explain current water management practices within a historical context.

Students may want to send the Water Bill of Rights to congressional representatives (and the president), so that government leaders may understand the concerns of young people.

Assessment

Have students:
- describe what life would be like if a United States Bill of Rights did not exist (*Warm Up*).
- develop a Water Bill of Rights that addresses their expectations regarding the right to clean water supplies (step 3).
- write a brief essay describing what should be done to secure individual rights related to water (*Wrap Up*).

Extensions

To focus the attention of other students and teachers on the issue, collect headlines, articles, cartoons, and photographs (from newspapers and magazines) that deal with water quality problems. Create a hallway display by pasting these items on a long piece of brown wrapping paper or newsprint.

Research water laws that attempt to address the national need for clean, ample water.

Attend a public meeting where formalized parliamentary procedures are practiced, to learn how people debate, vote or come to consensus on, and decide issues.

Resources

American Journey: The Quest for Liberty Since 1865. 1992. Englewood Cliffs, N.J.: Prentice Hall.

🍎 Bradbury, Ray. 1993. *Fahrenheit 451.* New York, N.Y.: Simon & Schuster.

🍎 Ellison, Ralph. 1993. *Invisible Man.* New York, N.Y.: Random House, Inc.

🍎 Golding, William. 1992. *Lord of the Flies.* Cutchogue, N.Y.: Buccaneer Books, Inc.

🍎 Huxley, Aldous. 1991. *Brave New World.* San Bernardino, Calif.: Vorgo Press.

Keating, Michael. 1990. *The Earth Summit's Agenda for Change: A Plain Language Version of Agenda 21 and Other Rio Agreements.* Ottawa, Ontario: Canadian Youth Foundation.

🍎 Orwell, George. 1949. *1984.* New York, N.Y.: New American Library.

World Commission on Environment and Development. 1991. *Our Common Future.* Oxford, England: Oxford University Press.

United States Bill of Rights

Amendment 1

Congress shall make no law respecting an establishment of religion, or prohibiting the free
exercise thereof; or abridging the freedom of
speech, or of the press, or the right of the people
peaceably to assemble, and to petition the Government for a redress of grievances.

Amendment 2

A well-regulated militia being necessary to the
security of a free State, the right of the people to
keep and bear arms, shall not be infringed.

Amendment 3

No soldier shall, in time of peace, be quartered in
any house without the consent of the owner; nor
in time of war, but in a manner to be prescribed
by law.

Amendment 4

The right of the people to be secure in their
persons, houses, papers, and effects, against
unreasonable searches and seizures, shall not be
violated, and no warrants shall issue, but upon
probable cause, supported by oath or affirma-
tion, and particularly describing the place to be
searched, and the persons or things to be seized.

Amendment 5

No person shall be held to answer for a capital or
otherwise infamous crime, unless on a present-
ment or indictment of a grand jury, except in
cases arising in the land or naval forces, or in the
militia, when in actual service in time of war or
public danger; nor shall any person be subject for
the same offense to be twice put in jeopardy of
life or limb; nor shall be compelled in any
criminal case to be a witness against himself, nor
be deprived of life, liberty, or property, without
due process of law; nor shall private property be
taken for public use without just compensation.

Amendment 6

In all criminal prosecutions, the accused shall
enjoy the right to a speedy and public trial, by an
impartial jury of the State and district wherein
the crime shall have been committed; which
district shall have been previously ascertained by
law, and to be informed of the nature and cause
of the accusation; to be confronted with the
witnesses against him; to have compulsory
process for obtaining witnesses in his favor, and
to have the assistance of counsel for his defense.

Amendment 7

In suits at common law, where the value in
controversy shall exceed twenty dollars, the right
of trial by jury shall be preserved, and no fact
tried by a jury shall be otherwise re-examined in
any court of the United States, than according to
the rules of the common law.

Amendment 8

Excessive bail shall not be required, nor excessive
fines imposed, nor cruel and unusual punish-
ments inflicted.

Amendment 9

The enumeration in the Constitution of certain
rights shall not be construed to deny or dispar-
age others retained by the people.

Amendment 10

The powers not delegated to the United States by
the Constitution, nor prohibited by it to the
States, are reserved to the States respectively, or
to the people.

Water Concentration

Sometimes living in the past seems romantic ... but would you exchange your daily hot shower for a dip in an icy stream?

▼ Summary

Through the familiar game of Concentration, students make connections between modern and past water use practices and discuss how attitudes toward water changed as water use practices evolved.

Objective

Students will:
- analyze why water use practices have evolved over time.
- compare efficiency of past and present water use practices.

Materials

- *Copies or overhead of* **Water Comes Home**
- **Water Use Cards** (Cut cards into squares; cards may be glued on cardboard and laminated for durability.)
- *Some of the items displayed on the cards* (e.g., a chamber pot, washboard, bucket, etc.) (optional)

Making Connections

With modern appliances, dishes and clothes are washed with an ease that was unimagined 100 years ago. Students may have become familiar with simpler water use practices through trips to museums or from watching movies about the past. Learning the history of modern appliances may encourage students to appreciate clean, ample water supplies.

Background

It has often been said, "Necessity is the mother of invention." Human needs and wants related to water have promoted advanced technology to ensure clean, plentiful water supplies.

For instance, when people settled at greater distances from water supplies (rivers, streams, lakes, or areas where ground water was plentiful), the means to collect, store, and transport water were needed. Reservoirs, storage tanks, aqueducts, and pumps were invented. In the past, sparsely populated communities could dump their sewage into the river with limited ill effects. When crowded cities followed those same practices, diseases such as cholera and typhoid developed. Consequently, laws were enacted requiring that sewer systems and wastewater treatment plants be constructed. For many cultures in the past, the river was the center of activity where families met, bathed, washed dishes, and did laundry. (Even today rivers are focal points for some cultures.)

As lifestyles changed, people demanded more convenient and efficient methods to complete their tasks. Therefore, inventors and early engineers devised easier methods of collection, cleaning and distribution of water, both in the community and in households. A long list of conveniences including indoor plumbing, washing machines, and dishwashers were invented.

These technological advances have made life healthier and easier. However, in some cases, these conveniences have also created complex problems. For example, simpler water use practices depended on human energy; modern appliances usually require electrical power, which creates greater demands on our natural resources.

Water quality and quantity issues have caused people to become more aware of their water use practices. While it is unrealistic for modern societies to do

■ **Grade Level:**
Upper Elementary

■ **Subject Areas:**
History, Language Arts, Environmental Science

■ **Duration:**
Preparation time:
Part I: 30 minutes
Part II: none needed

Activity time:
Part I: 50 minutes
Part II: 30 minutes

■ **Setting:** Classroom

■ **Skills:**
Organizing (sequencing); Analyzing (identifying components and relationships); Presenting (writing)

■ **Charting the Course**
Prior to this activity, have students analyze how they use water ("Water Meter"). How people used water in the past is addressed in "Easy Street," "The Long Haul," "Water Crossings," and "Wish Book." Following this activity, students could investigate more efficient uses of water in the home ("Every Drop Counts").

■ **Vocabulary**
conservation, water use practices

laundry by hand and take sponge baths, the need to use this shared resource more thoughtfully is a reality. Consequently, water conservation measures are being exercised in many homes and communities.

Procedure
▼ Warm Up
Have students read the story *Water Comes Home*, about a family's first encounter with indoor plumbing. Ask students to summarize how the characters in the story felt.

- Why was the grandfather's reaction different from that of the young boys?
- Would students like to live in places without indoor plumbing?
- Can students list places in the world where community members still carry their water from a common well or stream?
- What other water use practices have evolved over time and may have had similar introductions into homes?

▼ The Activity
Part I
1. **After shuffling the *Water Concentration Playing Cards*, lay them face down in rows, four cards in each. Review the game of Concentration with students.** A player turns over two cards and, if they are related, keeps them.

2. **To determine if the cards are related, students need to explain how both cards display pictures of similar water use practices.** One of the two cards should depict a more modern method of using water (for example, a person bathing in a water hole and a shower). Students can also match icons.

3. **If the cards do not match, they are turned facedown. This process is continued until all cards are matched.** Memory and observation skills will be needed to recall where the cards are placed.

4. **After all the cards have been matched, challenge students to relate two pairs of cards to each other to make a set of four. Instruct students to arrange the four cards from earliest to most recent inventions.** Each series of four cards has the same icon. NOTE: For older students the icon may be removed to make the activity more challenging.

Part II
1. **Ask students to form groups and assign a set of four cards to each. Ask them to discuss the following questions:**
- What water use practice is represented?
- Which method involved the most time?
- What supplied the energy for each method?
- What spurred the need or desire for new technologies to be developed?
- What resources were used to construct tools or appliances?
- What waste materials were generated by each method?

2. **From their set of four cards, have students write a short story or draw a picture depicting each method, highlighting the time and energy involved and possible problems or shortcomings. Have them identify which method they prefer and why.**

▼ Wrap Up and Action
Have students review current water use practices in their homes and community and relate them to past practices. Instruct them to research ways appliances should be used to promote energy efficiency and conservation of water and other resources. (Suggest running the dishwasher only when it is full, not leaving the refrigerator door open, installing low-flow showerheads, etc.)

408

Have students create a display comparing past and present water use practices. Critiques of current water use habits and suggestions for using water more wisely should be included.

Assessment

Have students:

• arrange water use practice cards from older to more modern (*Part I*, steps 1-4).

• write a story concerning the efficiency of current and past water use practices and methods (*Part II*, step 2).

• identify reasons why water use practices have evolved (*Part II*, steps 1 and 2, and *Wrap Up*).

• critique current water use practices in the areas of resource use and waste production (*Part II*, step 1 and *Wrap Up*).

Extensions

Have students write stories of what their lives would be like if they used simpler appliances and practices.

Students can do a community survey to determine if their community has remnants of past water systems (e.g., canal, old well field, icehouse or ice company, or pumping house).

Have students research what life was like in a different time period regarding water use practices. For example, in the Middle Ages perfume was invented because people rarely bathed and large hats were worn to prevent sewage from landing on their clothes when it was thrown from windows.

Have students search periodicals for pictures of current water use practices of cultures around the world. They may collect these pictures in their portfolios and plan a special "water and cultures" display for a social studies unit or school-wide International Day. As part of their display they may mold water pots or other water-carrying vessels.

Have students design cards for other water use practices. Ideas are listed in the chart below.

Have students project what water use practices will be like in the future. Students can develop a fifth card for each series of cards.

Resources

Fenner, Carol. 1991. *Randal's Wall.* New York, N.Y.: Margaret K. McElderry Books, Macmillan.

Kesselheim, Alan S., and The Watercourse and National Project WET Staff. 1993. *The Liquid Treasure Water History Trunk: Learning From the Past.* Bozeman, Mont.: The Watercourse.

Kittredge, William, and Annick Smith, eds. 1988. *The Last Best Place: A Montana Anthology.* Helena, Mont.: Montana Historical Society Press.

Wilder, Laura Ingalls. 1935. *The Little House on the Prairie Books.* 9 volumes. New York, N.Y.: Harper Collins Children's Books.

OTHER WATER USE PRACTICES

Water Use	Methods			
Purifying water	clean water from source	boil water	treatment plant	home water purifier
Waste disposal	dump site or streets	cesspool or ditch	septic tank	treatment plant
Fire fighting (protecting personal property)	let it burn	bucket brigade	fire truck with water tank	fire hydrants throughout city
Water transport	raft	paddle-powered	wind-powered	gas-powered
Bridging water	log	raft and pulley	simple bridge	suspension bridge

Water Comes Home

An entire family of eight is squeezed tightly into the small, newly constructed bathroom. No one is about to miss this first demonstration. The youngest two boys complain loudly that they can't see, until they shove their way up to the front and latch their hands eagerly on the rim of the gleaming sink.

The honor of performing this first test has been awarded to grandfather. His gnarled, arthritic hand is already closed around the spigot marked COLD. He looks over the fidgeting ranks of his family, drawing out the anticipation until the little boys are jumping up and down with the tension. He quiets them with a stern look, then turns the handle sharply.

For a moment nothing happens. There is a faint sound of rushing air and eight people hold their breath. Then a torrent of water gushes out of the faucet. It sputters and spurts, runs rusty with sediment, then settles into a clear, strong flow. Water whirls quickly down the drain, magically disappearing into pipes. It is bedlam for a moment, with the tap rushing full blast and everyone shouting and trying to touch the miraculous stream.

Everybody gets a turn. The hot water is tested, every faucet tried out, the new toilet flushed. Grandfather escapes from the confusion and retreats to the front parlor, where he stands at the window facing the street.

The celebration recedes as his thoughts drift back. No more trips to the backyard privy, he muses. No more worry about fumes and contamination or outbreaks of waterborne disease. No more chamber pots, water buckets, bickering over whose turn it is . . . .

The scope of the project still astonishes him: pipes laid all over the city, running into each home, supplying fresh water at a turn of the wrist, carrying away waste. He wonders absently how many gallons of water he has toted in his long life, but when he starts to calculate in his mind, the number grows so quickly that he gives up.

He can feel the exact weight of the bucket pulling on his arm, the way the water dipper rests across the palm of his hand. And he wonders how long it will be before those indelible memories start to fade.

Water Use Cards

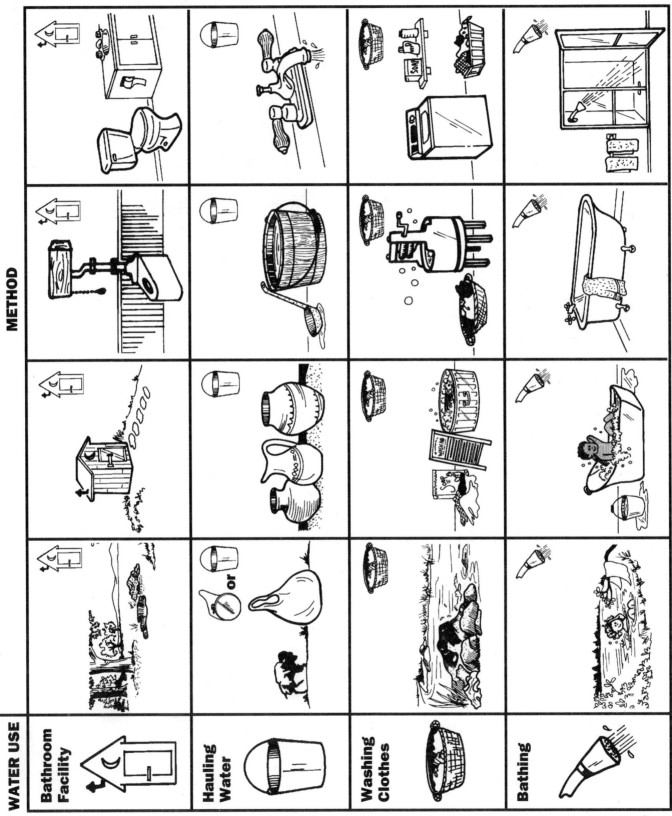

Water Use Cards

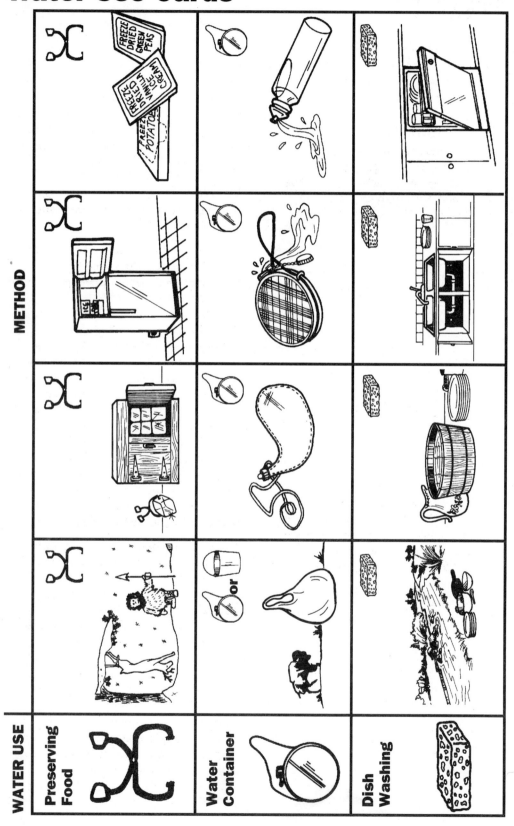

Water Court

The Brown family accuses the Dinn family of using more than its fair share of water; the Dinns disagree. Where can these two families go to settle their differences?

▼ Summary
Students learn how conflicts involving water quality and quantity (and other issues) can be resolved through mediation and litigation.

Objectives
Students will:
- demonstrate how disputes regarding water quality and quantity can be settled through mediation or litigation.
- develop and present an argument supporting their view relevant to a water-related issue.
- evaluate arguments presented by people on opposing sides of an issue.

Materials
- *Resources and materials regarding court cases involving water* (Check the *Environmental Law Journal* and *U. S. Water News* for water-related court cases. Ask government representatives for summaries of relevant state and federal laws) (optional)
- Copies of **Student Mediation Worksheet**

Making Connections
From *Perry Mason* to *L.A. Law*, the public has been fascinated with the United States trial system. By participating in mediation and a mock courtroom trial, students learn the roles of participants and the procedures in resolving conflicts (water-related or otherwise).

Background
Our country is governed by laws that prescribe what is and is not allowed in our society. Water pollution and allocation laws have been developed to protect water quality and quantity. Sometimes people perceive these laws as unconstitutional or feel that their rights are being compromised. When this occurs, a lawsuit (alleging abridgment of constitutional rights regarding a water issue) is possible.

Resource managers increasingly attempt to settle disputes through conflict resolution methods such as mediation prior to entering a court of law. The idea behind conflict resolution is to open new lines of communication. A mediator (neutral or non-biased third party) is consulted to help the disputants resolve their argument. The mediator's ultimate goal is to end mediation with both parties believing that they have won or settled the dispute fairly. Mediation can save disputants time and money, and can eliminate the perception of winner and loser, which usually results from a trial. If an argument cannot be successfully resolved through mediation, the parties may choose to settle in court.

Trials occur when people feel they have been wrongly accused or when two parties cannot settle a dispute through compromise or mediation. Using the judicial system to settle a dispute usually requires that each side hire an attorney. The client pays the attorney to research the background of the case thoroughly and to present the client's view effectively in a court of law. A background search involves finding similar cases that relate to the current situation and locating witnesses who can support the client's position. The outcome of a water-related trial can reshape laws and policies governing how water and other natural resources are used and protected.

■ **Grade Level:**
High School

■ **Subject Areas:**
Environmental Science, Government

■ **Duration:**
Preparation time:
Part I: 20 minutes
Part II: 20 minutes

Activity time:
Part I: 50 minutes
Part II: two 50-minute periods

■ **Setting:** Classroom

■ **Skills:**
Applying; Evaluating; Presenting (debating, persuading, public speaking)

■ **Charting the Course**
Students should understand that people have differing views and values related to water ("Pass the Jug," "Sum of the Parts," "Choices and Preferences, Water Index," "Dilemma Derby," etc.). Alternate forms of resolving water-related issues and conflicts are explored in "Perspectives" and "Hot Water."

■ **Vocabulary**
water allocation, mediation, litigation, conflict resolution

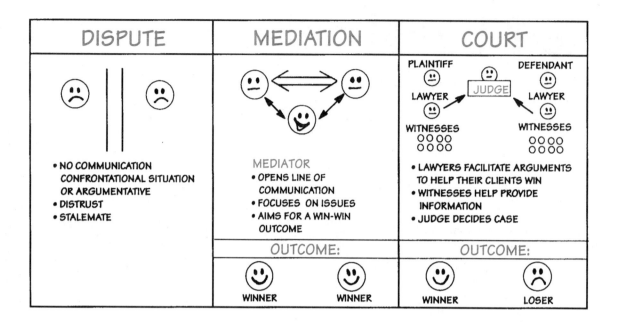

DISPUTE	MEDIATION	COURT
• NO COMMUNICATION CONFRONTATIONAL SITUATION OR ARGUMENTATIVE • DISTRUST • STALEMATE	MEDIATOR • OPENS LINE OF COMMUNICATION • FOCUSES ON ISSUES • AIMS FOR A WIN-WIN OUTCOME	• LAWYERS FACILITATE ARGUMENTS TO HELP THEIR CLIENTS WIN • WITNESSES HELP PROVIDE INFORMATION • JUDGE DECIDES CASE
	OUTCOME: WINNER WINNER	OUTCOME: WINNER LOSER

NOTE: Very few water-related cases are presented to a jury. Most water-related cases involve the disputants presenting their claim to a judge who makes the decision. However, to involve all students in a class, a more extensive courtroom procedure is described in this activity.

Participants in a trial include a judge, a petitioner or plaintiff (the party bringing forth the lawsuit), the respondent or defendant (the party arguing against the suit or claim), attorneys for the plaintiff and the defendant, witnesses, and a jury.

The judge's primary job is to determine which laws pertain to the case. He or she gives written and oral instructions to the jury to use the law in reaching their decision. The role of the attorney for the petitioner is to prove that a legitimate claim has been filed and that action must be taken. Both attorneys will call on witnesses to provide testimonies that present their views about the issue. Witnesses can be experts in certain fields (e.g., water chemists, watershed managers, medical professionals) who provide relevant information, or they can be people who can

provide factual information about what they have seen or heard firsthand regarding the case.

The procedures for a court case include the following. The judge and the topic of the trial are introduced to the courtroom. The attorney for the petitioner presents an opening statement, and is followed by the respondent's lawyer who provides their view. The petitioner's attorney calls witnesses to the stand who support the position of the petitioner. The respondent's attorney is provided the opportunity to cross examine each witness. The defendant's attorney tries to find weaknesses in the witness's information. Witnesses for the defendant follow, once the plaintiff has called all witnesses, and the prosecutor may cross examine these.

When one attorney is questioning a witness, the other attorney listens carefully. If a question is irrelevant or leads the witness to answer a certain way, an attorney can call an objection. An objection can also be called if it seems the witness is being harassed or is not qualified to answer a certain question. The judge listens

to the objection and decides if it should be supported (sustained) or rejected (overruled).

The judge must also monitor the behavior and cooperation of the courtroom members. If a party or witness acts in an unruly manner or refuses to answer a question, the judge can hold the person in contempt of the court. This usually involves a fine and sometimes a short sentence. Judges can also reprimand lawyers and jury members if they do not comply with rules of conduct.

After witness testimonies, the attorneys provide closing statements. The intention is to summarize the proceedings and the perspectives of their client and to persuade the jury to accept their client's view. The jury receives further instructions on the law from the judge, if necessary, and then deliberates or leaves the courtroom to make a decision. The decision is based on the law as presented by the judge, the presentation skills of the attorneys, and the credibility of the evidence provided by the witnesses. The jury evaluates the testimonies and evidence, considering logic, contradictions, coherence, and sincerity. After determining the facts, jurors apply the legal instructions to the facts to reach a decision. They present the judge with the outcome or verdict.

Procedure
▼ Warm Up
Ask students to share what they know about the judicial system. Have students ever heard of cases concerning water being debated in court? Inform them that the majority of such cases are settled through mediation (a process occurring outside the courtroom). Tell students they are going to participate in a form of conflict resolution commonly practiced with water issues.

▼ The Activity
Part I
1. **Have students brainstorm 10 to 15 issues that could arise between two parties.** If possible, these should relate to water, such as a dispute over water rights, an argument between neighbors about lawn watering, or a disagreement between the city council and water users concerning a perceived exorbitant water rate increase.

2. **Divide the class into groups of three. Have each group select an issue and decide who will be the mediator and the two disputants.**

3. **Distribute and discuss the** *Student Mediation Worksheet.* **Explain that they are to conduct a mock mediation following the steps provided on the worksheet; they should record their statements.** Encourage students to be creative and open minded.

4. **Allow groups up to 20 minutes to complete their mediation session.**

5. **Have groups summarize to the**

Venango County Courthouse, Northwest Pennsylvania. JIM SCHWABEL, N E STOCK PHOTO

class how successful they believe their mediation was. What could be the advantages of resolving a conflict through mediation rather than going through a court case? (You would be saving time and money.) Tell them that although few water-related cases are presented to a jury, students will now conduct a mock trial to investigate this alternate method of resolving issues.

Part II

1. **Provide students with background about a water-related lawsuit (*Generic Water Cases*), or have them create their own lawsuit.**

2. **Have students brainstorm background information they would need for this case.** The class can research actual laws and statutes relevant to the case (e.g., state and federal water allocation laws, Safe Drinking Water Acts, Clean Water Acts, national effluent standards, water treatment processes), or they can generalize the background based on common knowledge.

3. **Ask the class to choose two students to act as witnesses for each viewpoint.** The attorneys and clients can research their roles to determine their specific parts in the trial, or they can generalize these roles.

4. **Review courtroom procedures with the class.** If possible, invite a lawyer or judge to speak to the students.

5. **Assign or have students choose different roles to play.** The judge should be someone who is unbiased and mature, and can manage people and outbursts. Work with the judge to develop a set of rules for courtroom behavior and policies. (The attorneys for each side usually propose instructions on the application of the law to the judge. The judge then decides which instructions should be given to the jury.)

Students who do not play major roles (judge, plaintiff, defendant, attorneys) can be jury members, witnesses, court reporter, bailiff, etc. Most juries are comprised of twelve members, but because of average class size, the jury for this mock trial may include more than the usual twelve.

6. **Allow both sides time to build their cases.** Suggest that attorneys interview witnesses and research the background for the case. Witnesses can research their roles and locate information. Jury members should refrain from discussing the case among themselves and with other students. Instead, jury members and other court members can establish what criteria should be used to evaluate the court proceedings of the mock trial.

7. **For the day of the mock trial, encourage students to dress and behave as they would in an actual courtroom. Following normal trial procedures, students should present the mock trial.** Jury members can be given deliberation time to make a decision or can be requested to take a vote immediately following the closing statements. Jury members should write their opinions (valid/not valid; or liable/not liable) on pieces of paper; one member or the judge can tally the vote.

▼ *Wrap Up*

Discuss the outcome with the class. What could be the real-life implications of the ruling? What fines might be involved? How would the ruling be enforced? Would there likely be an appeal?

Review and evaluate courtroom procedures. What have students learned about water rights and/or water quality laws? What additional information would have helped with the case? What influenced the

outcome of the trial? What were the strengths and weaknesses of the evidence and witnesses, and of the attorney's presentations?

Assessment
Have students:
- mediate a water-related issue (*Part I*, step 4).
- evaluate the mediation process (*Part I*, step 5).
- choose a character in a trial scene, then research and present that character in a mock trial (*Part II*, step 5-7).
- resolve an issue based on court proceedings (*Part II*, step 7).
- evaluate the performances and proceedings of a mock trial (*Wrap Up*).

Extensions
Students may be interested in attending an actual mediation or court case. They can discuss the components and evaluate the process and outcomes. How does the real situation compare to their classroom simulation?

Resources
Getches, David H. 1990. *Water Law In a Nutshell*, 2nd ed. St. Paul, Minn.: West Publishing Company.

🍎 Goldfarb, Theodore, D. 1993. *Taking Sides: Clashing Views on Controversial Environmental Issues*, 4th ed. Guilford, Conn.: Dushkin Publishers.

Popp, T. E. 1991. "A Mock Trial Program for the Junior High School Classroom." *The Clearing House* (64) 3: 179-84.

Student Mediation Worksheet

1. **Initial Contact**—a phone contact initiated by the mediator to gain information and to make plans with both parties. (This means the parties desire to resolve the issue and enter mediation in a spirit of cooperation.) (Assume this has already taken place.)

2. **Arranging for Mediation**—mediator contacts parties to confirm meeting time and place, and to review the mediation process with them. (Assume this has already taken place.)

3. **Opening Statement by Mediator**—to describe role of the mediator and the mediation process (speaking order, opening statements, issues and needs, etc.). (The mediator explains his or her role in the mediation process; that is, the mediator has no authority to impose a settlement and only assists the parties in settling their differences.)

4. **Opening Statement by Both Parties**—to further clarify points of concern from each party. (Each party records statements; and includes the events that resulted in this issue.)

5. **Establishing an Agenda**—to clarify the issues (not positions) and to summarize areas of agreement. (The mediator separates the real issue from personal positions. He or she also identifies areas of common interest and agreement. Disputants may comment if a point is missed.)

6. **Collaborative Problem Solving**—for each issue, a review of areas of agreement or options for agreement. Parties work to identify common ground and solutions based on number 5. The mediator summarizes information, listing points of resolution and helping parties review cost and benefits [pros and cons] of each option. Discussion is encouraged between the disputants, but the mediator must always remain impartial.

7. **Agreement**—after reviewing a potential agreement for each issue, have a discussion of the feasibility of carrying it out, followed by a final agreement (or, if no agreement, moving on to the next issue). Parties analyze and evaluate each option and choose the solution that is satisfactory to both parties. The mediator reads the agreement aloud and includes methods for enforcing or monitoring the agreement.

8. **Debriefing and Follow-up**—review what was decided/learned; determine if additional sessions are needed. (Summarize the process. Was resolution accomplished?)

DISPUTE	MEDIATION	COURT
		PLAINTIFF DEFENDANT
		LAWYER JUDGE LAWYER
		WITNESSES WITNESSES
• NO COMMUNICATION CONFRONTATIONAL SITUATION OR ARGUMENTATIVE • DISTRUST • STALEMATE	MODERATOR— • OPENS LINE OF COMMUNICATION • FOCUSES ON ISSUES • AIMS FOR A WIN-WIN OUTCOME	• LAWYERS FACILITATE ARGUMENTS TO HELP THEIR CLIENTS WIN • WITNESSES HELP PROVIDE INFORMATION • JUDGE DECIDES CASE
	OUTCOME:	OUTCOME:
	WINNER WINNER	WINNER LOSER

Generic Water Cases

RASPBERRY RIVER (UPSTREAM)

CASSET FAMILY

DINN FAMILY

NEW LAND

BROWN FAMILY

RASPBERRY RIVER (DOWNSTREAM)

PENN FAMILY

Generic Case 1: Water Rights

The water in Raspberry River has been adjudicated (partitioned out) among various water users. The adjudication process was based on the parameters (pleas) presented by the water users 30 years ago. All pleas involved irrigation practices. Raspberry River has an average flow of 25 cfs, and there are four main water users. The Dinns were the first to move into the area. The Dinns were decreed (allotted) 7.5 cfs of water and the Casset family 5 cfs. The Browns were decreed 7.5 cfs, while the Penns were allotted 5 cfs. Since then, the Dinn family has purchased new land from a neighbor that has the most recent decree to use 5 cfs.

After unsuccessful mediation attempts, the Casset, Brown, and Penn families have brought suit against the Dinn family. The petitioners (Cassets, Browns, and Penns) claim that the Dinns are using more water than was originally allotted to them (7.5 cfs), based on the "first in time is first in right" water rights doctrine. They maintain that the Dinns should be allowed to withdraw the originally agreed upon 7.5 cfs, but should only be able to remove the additional 5 cfs **after** the Cassets, Browns, and Penns have taken their allotments. The Dinns claim that the new water right (5 cfs) has become part of the old water right (7.5 cfs).

Both parties believe they have a case. However, the users still want to use more water than is available in the river. A possible solution is to divert water from another drainage basin, but then environmental impact statements and cost issues have to be considered.

A suggestion for this case is to have students assume the roles of the petitioners and the respondents. Several students can draft a version of the law and detail the process of allocating water rights to the people on the Raspberry River. They should describe how the parties use the water allotted to them and why they do or do not need more water. The jury will need to decide if the claims of the parties are valid.

Generic Case 2: Riparian Land Ownership

When territory X gained statehood in the late 1800s, federal law claimed that the river bed of any unnavigable waters would become the property of the United States Government. Consequently, a certain portion of the Mountain Do River runs through federally owned property. Over the years, the State has been trying to claim ownership of the land but to no avail. Now the federal government plans to lease the land to certain companies for gas and oil development.

An environmental impact statement found that no species living in the area would be endangered by the development. Therefore, the government has proceeded with the leasing process.

The current strategy of the State is to prove that the waters were actually navigable at the time of statehood. It is presenting its case to a federal district court.

Have certain students represent the State and others present the views of the United States Government. They should consider how a waterway would be determined navigable in the late 1800s (journals, letters, newspaper articles recording log floats, canoeing expeditions, etc.). Any evidence the petitioners present must be shared with the respondents (the United States Government) for their examination. Students representing the United States Government should provide reasons why gas and oil development is necessary. The judge needs to decide if the arguments presented by the petitioners are valid or not.

Generic Case 3: Water Quality Issues

The village of Odiferous is suing the Paxty Pencil Sharpener Production Plant. The plant has been accused of violating its permit by failing to decrease the amount of waste effluent it annually deposits into the local river. According to the permit, issued 15 years ago, Paxty was to have developed a new technology or production means by the beginning of this past year, which would reduce the amount of waste discharged into the river by 80 percent. Water tests have shown that the quantity of wastes produced have only been reduced approximately 50 percent. In addition, new pollutants are being added, ones not addressed in the original permit.

The Paxty Plant claims that the conditions prescribed in the permit are not realistic. The company has implemented all the latest technologies (within its financial means) as they have been developed, but it has been unable to reduce waste quantities within the prescribed time limit. Paxty pencil sharpeners now use a new material that is cheaper to produce and more durable. While different waste materials are produced, environmental studies have shown that fish and other aquatic life are not adversely affected by these substances. Paxty is requesting an extension on its permit and increased government funding to purchase more advanced pollution control devices.

Generic Case 4: Nonpoint Source Pollution Controls

The agricultural district of Cowmoo County is bringing suit against new state laws, claiming they are unconstitutional. The new laws require a landowner whose agricultural operation has the potential to contribute waste runoff to the drainage basin to develop and implement a pollution control plan within a five-year period. Landowners are willing to promote farming practices that will reduce waste; however, they contend that the law does not provide sufficient funding or incentive for them to enact these practices. Enforcement of these new laws will require research, new technology, and may involve a reduction or change in fertilizer and pesticide quantities presently being used. The landowners want the State to institute a cost-sharing program, whereby the State covers 75 percent of the cost needed to develop, test, and implement the new strategies.

Students can represent the agricultural district and the State. The State believes there are low-cost runoff control measures that farmers can implement. The farms are already subsidized for erosion control measures, and the State argues that runoff control measures fall under this funding.

Management practices for runoff control include soil testing, no-till cropping, and the construction of manure storage tanks. Buffer strips must be planted along the banks of rivers to capture runoff. The State argues that these practices will actually save farmers money.

Important Water Resource Legislation: A Short List

Rivers and Harbor Act (1826) - Gives authority to the U.S. Army Corps of Engineers

Swamp Act (1850) - Encourages draining of wetlands for development

Homestead Act (1862) - Opens the West to settlement and water development

Desert Lands Act (1877) - Promotes sale of 640-acre tracts to those who promise to speculate land in the West

Quarantine Act (1893) - Prevents the interstate spread of contagious disease

Carey Irrigation Act (1894) - Grants public lands to states for irrigation

Rivers and Harbors Act (1899) - Prohibits discharge of solids into navigable rivers

Reclamation Act (1902) - Establishes the Reclamation Service, which later becomes the Bureau of Reclamation

Reclamation Act (1906) - Authorizes sale of surplus power from reclamation projects

General Dam Act (1906) - Regulates private dam construction on navigable streams

Public Health Service Act (1912) - Authorizes the study of river contamination and sets up the Public Health Service

Raker Act (1913) - Authorizes the construction of Hetch Hetchy Dam in Yosemite National Park

Federal Water Power Act (1920) - Empowers the Federal Power Commission to regulate private power and regulate power from federal projects

Oil Pollution Act (1924) - Prohibits the discharge of oil into marine waters

Rivers and Harbors Act (1925) - Authorizes the U.S. Army Corps of Engineers to survey all navigable waters and formulate general water use plans

Tennessee Valley Authority Act (1933) - Establishes the Authority

Fish and Wildlife Coordination Act (1934) - Considers wildlife protection provisions in federal projects

Flood Control Act (1936) - The first nationwide flood control act; introduces cost-benefit analysis

Reclamation Project Act (1939) - Authorizes the planning of multipurpose projects

Flood Control Act (1944) - Recognizes the priority of flood control over irrigation, recreation, and power production

Water Pollution Control Act (1948) - Provides technical assistance to municipalities for wastewater treatment

Small Watershed Act (1954) - Sets up a small watershed program under the Soil Conservation Service

Federal Water Pollution Control Act (1956) - Increases federal assistance for wastewater treatment

Fish and Wildlife Act (1956) - Sets up the Fish and Wildlife Service

Fish and Wildlife Coordination Act (1958) - Requires equal consideration of wildlife protection at federal water projects

Water Supply Act (1958) - Deems future municipal supply an equal purpose in the planning of multi-purpose projects

Water Resource Research Act (1962) - Establishes water resource research institutes in each state and territory with a $100,000 grant for each

Wilderness Act (1964) - Preserves regions of federal lands from development

Water Resources Planning Act (1965) - Establishes the Water Resources Council and river basin commissions

Water Quality Act (1965) - Establishes the Federal Water Pollution Control Commission

Endangered Species Act (1966) - Protects endangered species

National Environmental Policy Act (1970) - Sets up Council on Environmental Policy; requires Environmental Impact Statements

Clean Water Act (1972) - Authorizes substantive grants to urban municipal sewage treatment; sets up National Pollutant Elimination Discharge System; regulates dredge and fill

Coastal Zone Management Act (1972) - Provides federal funds for setting up state coastal zone management programs

Federal Water Pollution Control Act amendments (1972) - Institutes a national permit system for point-source discharges; puts U.S. Army Corps of Engineers in charge of regulating discharge of dredge and fill material

Safe Drinking Water Act (1974); amendments (1986) - Coordinates monitoring and training for safe drinking water; sets up drinking-water standards

Clean Water Act amendments (1977, 1981, 1987) - Authorizes more grant money for states

Food Security Act (1985) - Establishes erosion control programs for agricultural lands; denies federal farm benefits to farmers harvesting from converted wetlands

Water Resources Development Act (1986, 1988, 1990, 1992) - Authorizes new construction projects, with cost-sharing

Wild and Scenic Rivers Act (1987) - Protects instream flows for rivers designated wild and scenic

Water Quality Act (1987) - Requires EPA to regulate storm water runoff and states to prepare nonpoint source management programs

Water Crossings

Grade Level:
Upper Elementary, Middle School, High School

Subject Areas:
Geography, History, Language Arts

Duration:
Preparation time:
Part I: 15 minutes
Part II: 50 minutes

Activity time:
Part I: 50 minutes
Part II: two 50-minute periods

Setting: Classroom

Skills:
Analyzing (identifying patterns); Applying (designing, building); Evaluating (testing)

Charting the Course
Other activities related to water resources in the past and comparisons to current water uses are found in "Easy Street," "Water Concentration," and "Wish Book." Students investigate water travels around the world in "Great Water Journeys."

Vocabulary
water crossing

It is the late 1800s, your wagon is packed, and you are traveling west. You arrive at a raging river, 1 mile (1.6 km) wide. Now what?

▼ Summary

Students participate in a water-crossing contest in which they must move their possessions (a hard-boiled egg) across a span of water (a cake pan).

Objectives
Students will:
- analyze the influence of river crossings on settlement patterns.
- describe the water-related transportation problems that faced early explorers and settlers.
- design and build water-crossing conveyances.

Materials
- *Copies or overhead of excerpt from* **The River of the West**
- *Map of the United States or local map*
- *State road maps*
- *Hard-boiled eggs, rocks, or tennis balls*
- *Student collected natural materials (e.g., twigs, dried grass, reeds, bark, cork)*
- *String or twine*
- *Waterproof glue*
- *Cake pan, bucket, or dish pan*

Making Connections
Water crossings and the technology involved in bridging rivers have had a major impact on exploration and settlement patterns throughout history. Student understanding of the challenges posed by water crossings, and of the various historic methods used to overcome these obstacles, leads to a greater appreciation of the efforts of early explorers and pioneers.

Background
Pioneers crossing North America faced many challenges. While today there are interstates and highways, back then the land was untamed and relatively unchanged by people's influence. The cross-country trip would have taken many months on roads that often were no better than trails. People traveled by steamboat and railroad, on horseback, in wagons pulled by horses or oxen, and on foot.

River crossings were common challenges. Consider crossing the Mississippi or Ohio Rivers today at a spot where no bridge exists. Consider, too, the dilemma facing a family encumbered by a wagon filled with all of their possessions, as they overlooked the Colorado River in 1890.

Rivers without crossings have a natural damming effect on travelers. A safe and efficient crossing acts like a funnel, drawing people from far and wide. Towns and cities all across the nation were established at river crossings. Riverboats and ferries added prosperity to local economies.

Successfully crossing waterways demanded innovation, hard work, group coordination, and luck. Sometimes a section of river could be found that was shallow enough to allow a ford. In other cases, ferries or cable and pulley systems were rigged to transport people and material. During winter, people could cross on the ice, once it had reached sufficient thickness. If a river's course ran in generally the same direction as a party's travel route, boats or rafts could be made and the river used as a roadway. Once a sufficient level of population and resources had been amassed at a crossing site, a bridge could be built to span the water. Even after a bridge was

*Arrived at the Yellowstone with his company, Smith found it necessary, on account of the high water, to construct Bull-boats for the crossing. These are made by stitching together buffalo hides, stretching them over light frames, and **paying** the seams with elk tallow and ashes. In these light **wherries** the goods and people were ferried over, while the horses and mules were crossed by swimming.*

*The mode usually adopted in crossing large rivers was to spread the **lodges** on the ground, throwing on them the light articles, saddles, etc. A rope was then run through the **pin-holes** around the edge of each, when it could be drawn up like a **reticule**. It was then filled with the heavier camp goods, and being tightly drawn up, formed a perfect ball. A rope being tied to it, it was launched on the water, the children of the camp on top, and the women swimming after and clinging to it, while a man, who had the rope in his hand, swam ahead holding on to his horse's mane. In this way, dancing like a cork on the waves, the lodge was piloted across; and passengers as well as freight **consigned**, undamaged, to the opposite shore. A large camp of three hundred men, and one hundred women and children were frequently thus crossed in one hour's time.*

Excerpt from Frances Fuller Victor's book, *The River of the West*

built, its life expectancy was jeopardized by spring floods and floating ice.

Procedure
▼ Warm Up

Ask the students if any of them have taken lengthy trips across the country. Compare their experiences to travel during the pioneer days. Have them identify the hazards pioneers faced during their journeys. If students have been exposed to early American history, review Native Americans' need to cross rivers, early European explorations, and historical transportation routes.

Have students read the excerpt from Frances Fuller Victor's book, *The*

River of the West. The author describes a crossing of the Yellowstone River by a group of trappers and traders led by Jedediah Smith in 1829.

Some of the words in the excerpt may be unfamiliar to students. (See bold type.) Have students guess the meaning from the context of the sentence and story. Compare students' and author's meanings.

Ask if any students have had to cross bodies of water where no bridges existed. What were their feelings? How did they solve the problem? What factors had to be taken into account (safety, time of year, building materials, alternative routes, etc.)?

▼ The Activity

Part I
1. **Have students study a map of the United States or their local region and identify several major cities located at river crossings. Why are river crossings often associated with towns? List the positive and negative impacts of a crossing site on the development of a region.**

2. **Using a road atlas, have students select a river or stream in their state and count the number of bridges/crossings.** What factors are likely to influence their number and location?

3. **Have students write a short fictional story about approaching a**

422

river and needing to get to the other side. Encourage them to use their imaginations when describing the river. They should explain the characters' feelings and indicate how they would cross the river.

Part II

1.   Tell students they are about to gain insight into some of the challenges pioneers faced when they arrived at a river; they are going to participate in a water-crossing contest! The goal of the contest is for small groups of students to plan, design, and construct a means of carrying a load across a body of water. The competition should encourage a variety of interesting approaches.

2.   Divide the class into small groups. Each team will build a water-crossing conveyance from natural materials collected from front yards, city parks, and school

grounds. Since each team gets only one chance to succeed, encourage groups to discuss their options (e.g., a ferry, raft, wherry [a light, swift boat built for one person], etc.) before beginning construction.

3.   Inform students that the load to be transported is a hard-boiled egg (or rock or tennis ball). Once each team has built its conveyance, an egg is placed on the center and the whole floated in a bucket or dish pan. The conveyance must support

the load for two minutes, while not touching the sides or the bottom of the bucket. If the structure does not crack, capsize, or fall apart within two minutes, the team has succeeded in crossing the barrier. To increase the challenge and simulate treacherous crossing conditions, rock the pan, sprinkle water, or create wind with a fan.

4.   Have students vote on the most successful strategy and brainstorm improvements in raft designs for

A stagecoach fords the Lamar River in Yellowstone National Park at the turn of the century. COURTESY: U.S. DEPARTMENT OF THE INTERIOR

another contest. Students can also vote on the most aesthetic, innovative, or unique design. Try to make every team a winner.

▼ Wrap Up

Discuss with students the impact of water crossings during the travels of early explorers and pioneers. With the benefit of what they now know, how would students have chosen to cross the country in the past? Have students interview family members about their experiences with water obstacles.

Assessment

Have students:

- relate settlement patterns to river crossings (*Part I*, step 1).
- write a story illustrating problems explorers and early settlers faced in water-related transport (*Part I*, step 3).
- design, build, and test water-crossing conveyances (*Part II*, steps 2-3).
- judge the effectiveness of peers' water-crossing conveyances (*Part II*, step 4).

Extensions

Look at the routes of historical trails and recognize the effects of water obstacles on their course. Have students map a *pioneer trail* across America, minimizing water obstacles. Compare historical trails to the modern highway system and discuss the differences and similarities regarding rivers and lakes. Are modern bridges located at some of the same places as the historical crossings?

Conduct a bridge-building contest. Divide the class into small groups and provide each with the same set of materials (e.g., four 6-inch [15-cm] sticks of balsa wood, 20 popsicle sticks, waterproof glue, box of toothpicks, 20-inch [50-cm] length of string or twine). The bridge must span 10 inches (25 cm) and be at least 2 inches (5 cm) wide. There is no height limitation. Allow students a set amount of time to construct their bridge. The roadbed of the bridge must have an opening for the test load. The test load will be applied to the center of the bridge and consists of a block of wood (2 1/2″ x 2 1/2″ x 1″ [6.25 cm x 6.25 cm x 2.5 cm]) through which a 6-inch (15 cm) eyebolt has been screwed. A bucket is hooked onto the eyebolt. The load is applied by a student adding cups of sand to the bucket until a failure occurs. The weight of the bucket and the results are recorded.

The contest has two categories for winning bridges: strongest (supporting the most weight) and most aesthetically pleasing.

Resources

🍎 Collins, James I. 1989. *Exploring the American West*. New York, N.Y.: Watts.

Victor, Frances Fuller. 1983. *The River of The West*. Missoula, Mont.: Mountain Press.

🍎 Gorsline, Marie, and Douglas Gorsline. 1982. *The Pioneers*. New York, N.Y.: Random LB.

🍎 Harvey, Brett. 1988. *Cassie's Journey: Going West in the 1860's*. New York, N.Y.: Holiday.

🍎 Hilton, Suzanne. 1980. *Getting There: Frontier Travel Without Power*. New Orleans, La.: Westminster.

A bamboo bridge crosses a gorge in Nepal. JENNIE LANE

What's Happening?

Perhaps someone has said to you, "Everyone knows that!" But how do you know when that statement is really true?

▼ Summary

Students conduct a survey to determine what the community thinks and feels about an important water resource issue.

Objectives

Students will:

- develop and conduct a survey.
- recognize that surveys can reveal current public understanding, knowledge, feelings, or involvement related to a water resource topic or issue.
- interpret results of a survey to provide information about a water-related topic or issue.

Materials

- *Newspaper and magazine articles about water-related issues*
- *Sample opinion polls* (optional)
- *Telephone book* (optional)
- *Random numbers table* (optional)
- *Paper* (enough to make copies of surveys for sample population)
- *Computer with word-processing program* (optional)
- *Photocopier*
- *Calculator*
- *Stamps and envelopes* (if surveys are mailed)
- *Clipboards* (if students are polling people)

Making Connections

Students often encounter water-related interests and issues in their community (e.g., water sports, winter sports, water shortages, wetlands, ground water contamination). Community planners frequently use information about public opinion and actions regarding these issues; sometimes this information is collected through surveys. Conducting a survey helps students discover what is happening in their community, how people think and feel about what's happening, and how survey results can be used to help make decisions.

Background

Sometimes when an issue arises in a community, people want to know what others think or are doing about it. One way to obtain information about people's thoughts and actions regarding an issue is through a survey.

Surveys can be used to solicit facts from people and to determine people's opinions about a topic. Opinions include personal beliefs, attitudes, and values. For example, people can indicate whether or not they like something, if they think something is important, or if they agree or disagree with another opinion or statement. Facts include background information such as age, education, experience, and place of employment. Facts can also include a report of activities, such as if people do a certain thing and how often, if they have visited a place, if they purchased something in the past, etc. Facts can also be obtained by surveying objects or locations. This type of survey is more like an inventory. For example, students can survey the number of leaking faucets in the school. How many households in a 10-block area have sprinklers operating on a hot sunny afternoon? How many lawns in the community use xeriscaping?

Surveys often provide information helpful to solving a problem or answering a question. The purpose of the survey is often expressed as a research question. Research questions should be clearly written, should be reasonable in scope, and should provide insight into

■ **Grade Level:**
Upper Elementary, Middle School, High School

■ **Subject Areas:**
Depends upon activity

■ **Duration:**
Preparation time: 50 minutes
Activity time:
Depends upon activity

■ **Setting:**
Classroom, school, and community

■ **Skills:**
Gathering information (interviewing); Organizing (calculating, graphing, categorizing); Interpreting; Applying (designing, implementing); Evaluating; Presenting (writing, reporting)

■ **Charting the Course**
Students can use surveys to investigate how people think and feel about water-related concepts and issues they study in other Project WET activities. Involving students in community education and action can follow ("Water Actions").

■ **Vocabulary**
attitudes, water-related issue

the purpose of the survey. Examples of research questions include: "How many students recycle their car oil?" "How concerned are students about acid rain (or other forms of pollution)?" "Do male students or female students report that they take longer showers?" "How many people visit the local waterfall (or another scenic site) in the summer?"

After the research questions are developed, the best methods for answering them must be determined. This involves deciding who will be surveyed and structuring the survey to include items that address the research question.

Although people who conduct surveys will have certain expectations, these must not bias their study. For this reason, survey questions are carefully designed and evaluated to ensure that they are stated clearly and do not lead the respondent to answer one way or another. Even though a survey is usually limited to a geographic area, randomly selecting survey participants helps to provide a clearer view of what a sample population thinks and feels.

After surveys have been administered and returned, the collected data (responses to the survey questions) need to be interpreted. One of the simplest procedures is to tally responses and find frequencies. For example, if 20 people were asked if they turn the water off when they brush their teeth, 12 people might respond yes; six indicate that they do not; and two say they are not sure. Sometimes a survey report will describe what proportion of a population responded a certain way to the questions. In the above example, the results would be reported as: 60 percent (12 people divided by 20—the number of people who answered the question) of the respondents turn off the water, 30 percent do not, and 10 percent are not sure. (The sum of the proportions should equal 100.) Without more advanced statistical analysis, it is best not to make claims such as "the majority says," or "an insignificant number of people feel" because this could lead to false assumptions or bias the results.

Surveys only query a portion of the population at a specific time. The results of a survey might vary if other people were approached, if the questions were asked differently, or if the survey was conducted at another time. If the results of a survey indicate that people think or feel a certain way, this information can be used to support or oppose a plan of action. For example, if an organization is trying to promote water conservation and a survey finds that people in the community do not think water conservation is important, the organization might conclude that a conservation education program is needed. However, surveys are only one of many tools people can use to make decisions. Other factors, such as financial costs, time, and available resources, should also be considered.

Procedure
▼ Warm Up
Have students brainstorm a list of water issues or topics they feel are important to them and their community. Interests or issues might include community involvement in water sports, leaking faucets in the school, funding for a town fountain, water quality of a local stream, etc.

Ask students to collect newspaper and magazine articles that pertain to these interests or concerns. Do students think the messages contained in these articles are accurate? Have students discuss what they could do to learn how their school or community feels about these water issues. Guide the discussion to the use of surveys for collecting information about the community and people's thoughts, feelings, and actions related to a water topic or issue.

▼ The Activity
1. **Have students describe surveys or polls that they are familiar with (e.g., Nielsen TV ratings and polls in popular magazines).** Hand out sample opinion polls if available. Discuss what the results of the survey mean to students. How does the information make them feel? How could it be used?

2. **Have students divide into groups and each group select one water-related issue or topic. Tell them they are going to survey their class (school or community) to determine people's thoughts about the issue.**

3. **Help each group develop a simple research question regarding their issue. (What exactly do they want to find out?) Check the questions for clarity, precision, logic, and relevance to the purpose of the study.**

4. **Discuss the information presented in *Survey Development* (opposite page) to determine how groups will answer the research question.**

5. **Have groups administer the survey. Make sure they keep good records of the responses.** The amount of time allotted for the survey depends on the size of the sample population and the length of the survey. Surveying can continue until a desired number of people are polled or until a certain time limit has been reached.

6. **After the survey is conducted, students tabulate and analyze the**

SURVEY DEVELOPMENT

With which people do you intend to talk?

As a safety precaution, students may consider polling only people they know. Most students will sample people in their neighborhood. If other students are being surveyed, this can be done before and after school. These are both samples of convenience. For a more sophisticated study, students may consider collecting a random sample. Students could use a phone book to choose names randomly (picking the 17th name on every 6th page), or a random numbers table found in statistics books. Students can also stand in a public place and talk to every fifth person who walks past.

How will you conduct the survey?

Mailed surveys, face-to-face interviews, and phone calls are a few of the options a student might use to collect information. Discuss the pros and cons of each. Cost is one consideration; encouraging participation is another. Although with face-to-face interviews and phone calls responses are immediate, students may encounter people who refuse to take part in the survey. Students should practice skills necessary to approaching potential respondents successfully. Mailing surveys eliminates face-to-face confrontations, but some people may not bother to return the survey. To encourage a high response rate, students could compose a creative cover letter requesting participation. Mailing costs also discourage use of mailed surveys. Some schools hold fund-raisers, such as a bake sale, to buy stamps.

What questions will you ask?

Each group should generate a list of questions—or items—that could be used in the survey. (Make sure the responses to the items will help answer the research questions for the study.) For simplicity's sake, students should limit the survey to 10 questions.

Involve groups in designing their survey. If copies of other surveys are available, use these for reference. Have students consider whether they will be collecting facts, opinions, or both. Write several examples of each on the board and discuss the difference between facts and opinions (see examples below).

Facts

- How many minutes long is your average shower?
- Did you visit the waterfall this summer?
- Do you change your own car oil? If yes, what do you do with the old oil?

Opinions

- It is important to conserve water.
  Agree   Neutral   Disagree
- The community should preserve wetlands.
  Agree   Neutral   Disagree
- Why do you like to visit the waterfall?

Encourage groups to test the questions for clarity and to make sure they are not biased. The survey can be tested by asking a friend to listen to the questions. Does the item provide information that helps answer the research question? Does the question make sense? Did the question make the person feel he or she should answer a certain way (in other words, was the tone of the question threatening, condescending, or leading?)

How will the results of the survey be analyzed?

Close-form items (e.g., agree/disagree, multiple choice) are easier to analyze than open-form items. (Open-form items are those to which the participant responds in his or her own words. Examples include the following: How do you feel about water pollution? Why is water conservation important?).

For close-formed questions, students can report the frequency of responses by tallying the number of people who responded to each question. Students can also calculate the group average or what percent of the sample answered a certain way (by dividing the number of people who responded a certain way by the total number of respondents). Analyzing open-ended responses involves carefully studying (listening to, reading, reviewing) all responses and looking for common messages that can be used to summarize the statements.

results. The class might want to work as a whole and combine results, or different groups can conduct separate surveys and compare results. Depending on the extent of the survey, data can be recorded and tabulated on a computer statistics program; pencils and calculators work fine for small-scale surveys.

7. **Have the groups prepare a report of their results.** Advise them to find a snappy title that incorporates or relates to the research question, and to include any background information explaining the issue, a description of how the survey was conducted, results (tables, charts, and graphs make results more visually appealing), and conclusions. They can also express what they did and did not like about the survey process and what recommendations they would have for someone conducting a survey in the future.

▼ *Wrap Up and Action*

Have the groups present and discuss the survey and its results. Were the results what they expected? What do they know now that they did not know before? If opinions about an issue were collected, was there a variety of different opinions or did people think and feel in a similar manner?

Now that students have completed the survey, what will they do with the information? They may want to write a letter summarizing the results and send it to the local newspaper or to their state legislators.

Assessment

Have students:
- design a survey to learn how a population thinks and/or feels about a water-related issue or topic (steps 3 and 4).
- administer the survey (step 5).

- analyze results of the survey (step 6).
- prepare an accurate and concise research report on the study (step 7).

Extensions

Another way water managers secure input from citizens is through public meetings. The public meeting is advertised. A brief overview of the issue or topic is presented. Citizen comments are recorded. This is not a public debate. Have students select an issue and conduct a class public meeting.

Once students have analyzed the opinions and facts regarding an issue, they can begin to form a plan of action to correct a community water resource problem.

K-2 Option

Young children can conduct surveys, too. They could ask friends and neighbors simple questions, such as: Do you like snow? What is your favorite season? Safety concerns demand that children only poll other students, teachers, or people that they know.

Resources

Alreck, P., and R. Settle. 1985. *The Survey Research Handbook.* Homewood, Ill.: Richard C. Irwin, Inc.

Dilman D. 1978. *Mail and Telephone Surveys: The Total Design Method.* New York, N.Y.: John Wiley & Sons.

Hungerford, H. R. et al. 1992. *Investigating and Evaluating Environmental Issues and Actions Skill Development Modules.* Champaign, Ill.: Stipes Publishing Co.

Lewis, Barbara. 1991. *The Kids Guide to Social Action.* Minneapolis, Minn.: Free Spirit Press.

Student conducts a survey to find out what's happening.

Whose Problem Is It?

■ **Grade Level:**
Middle School, High School

■ **Subject Areas:**
Government, Environmental Science

■ **Duration:**
Preparation time: 20 minutes
Activity time: 50 minutes

■ **Setting:** Classroom

■ **Skills:**
Gathering information (listening and collecting); Organizing (classifying); Analyzing (comparing, discussing, and contrasting); Interpreting (defining problems, generalizing, drawing conclusions)

■ **Charting the Course**
This activity could be conducted at the beginning of a unit to assess concerns or at the end of a unit to evaluate changes in student perceptions of water-related issues. The activity "Perspectives" complements this activity. Conduct "Idea Pools" prior to this activity to access students perceptions of water-related problems and "What's Happening" and "Water Actions" can follow if students want to further investigate or analyze an issue.

■ **Vocabulary**
water-related issue

Why should the world care about a leaky faucet in your home? Why should you care about a drought in central Africa?

▼ Summary
Students analyze the scope and duration of a variety of water-related issues to understand the relationship between local and global issues.

Objectives
Students will:
- analyze how water issues affect individuals as well as world populations, and how these issues can have short- and/or long-term implications.
- illustrate the scope and duration of water-related issues.

Materials
- *News reports on water-related issues* (can be collected by students)
- *Copies of Water Issue Analysis Chart*
- *Chalkboard and chalk, or butcher paper and markers, or overhead transparency and markers*

Making Connections
Too often people become so involved in everyday problems that they forget to pay attention to issues that are of a statewide, national, or international scope. While it is important for young people to focus inward and learn about themselves, they should also be aware of the community and world around them. Analyzing water issues of concern to students helps them understand that local issues have global implications and global issues affect individuals.

Background
Ensuring that human activities sustain, rather than damage, water resources involves ecological and consequential thinking. That is, we need to understand the processes by which balanced ecosystems are maintained and to develop long-term thinking and our planning skills. Employing these understandings and skills enables us to predict how actions might affect water resources in the future. Students may develop these qualities by considering how the scope and duration of water-related problems can simultaneously affect the individual, the community, and the world.

The scope of water-related problems ranges from local to global. Local problems usually involve a small number of people and take place in a limited area. However, if left unchecked, local issues may affect other communities. For example, if individuals in one town carry a waterborne disease, the bacteria could multiply and spread to other towns. A drought in one part of the world may raise prices of certain foods at your grocery store.

Global problems affect the lives of individuals. For example, many scientists predict that if changes in global climate increase world temperatures, sea levels will rise. This would bring a global problem to the direct attention of individuals living in coastal areas.

The duration of water-related concerns may be short-term (e.g., within a week's time), long-term (e.g., over 500 years from now) or both. A leaky roof creates a short-term problem if fixed within a reasonable amount of time. Toxic wastes dumped into oceans will remain an issue for humans many years into the future. A hurricane may pass through a town in a few hours, but it may take several years for people to recover from the damage to property and a lifetime to mourn the loss of life.

People are more likely to act on issues that affect them directly. The challenge

for educators is to help people appreciate how they can be personally affected by global problems and how individual actions can help solve not only local, short-term problems but also broad-scale concerns.

Individuals resolving local problems (cleaning trash out of a river, landscaping a hillside to prevent erosion, etc.) contribute to the well-being of the planet. Individuals can also act directly on global issues (educating others about environmentally responsible behavior, lobbying a government official about the nation's water quality laws, etc.). Local actions may produce immediate results, but an individual working to resolve global issues may not see the result of his or her efforts for many years, if at all.

Procedure
▼ Warm Up
Ask students to think of a problem they face. When posing the following questions, have students raise their hands to indicate a positive response: Does the problem affect their lives directly? Will it concern them during the upcoming week? Does the problem concern their family? Will it be an issue a year from now? Does it concern the community? The nation? The world? Will it still be on their minds in five years? Most students will raise their hands for the first questions, fewer for the last.

▼ The Activity
1. **Have the class brainstorm a list of current issues related to water.** (This can be supplemented by news articles collected by students.) A current-events bulletin board or wall could be designed in the room.

2. **Have students, working in groups, choose a water-related issue. Ask them to discuss the following questions:**
    - What caused the problem?
    - Who is affected by the problem (a few individuals, an entire town, the population of a country, etc.)?
    - How long has the problem persisted?
    - Can the problem be resolved in the near future or will it take a long time for a solution to be found?
    - Will the solution be costly?
    - How realistic is the solution? (For example: "Air pollution could be reduced if everyone stopped driving cars." Is this practical?)

3. **Provide each group with the *Water Issue Analysis Chart*, or have them draw the chart on butcher paper or an overhead transparency.**

4. **Ask students to decide in which box of the chart the issue belongs.** Decisions will be based upon the issue's scope (who is affected: individual, community, state, etc.) and duration (how long the problem will affect those involved: weeks, months, years, etc.). For example, students may conclude that a leaky faucet in a house will affect the *individual/family* in the next *week*—until the faucet is fixed. The issue of acid rain affects several countries and may take many years to correct; therefore, students may place it at the intersection of *international* and *over 100 years*.

5. **Discuss why students categorized issues as they did.** Was there any debate among the students about the scope and duration? Did students find the task easy or difficult? Challenge students to see that a single issue may vary in scope and duration. (For example, what if the leaky faucet is not fixed? What about the individual property owner whose trees are affected by acid rain?)

▼ Wrap Up

Have the groups share results with other groups and transfer their conclusions to a master copy of the chart posted on the board, wall, or overhead. Ask the groups to discuss similarities and differences among findings. Is there a correlation between who is affected and which issues get the most attention in the media? Do global or local issues get mentioned more frequently in the media?

Ask students to rank 10 of the water-related concerns from most to least important. What criteria did they use? Did they consider scope and duration? Which of the issues do students think affect them the most? Why? Students can review periodicals and news reports to learn how the media address these issues.

Have students draw pictures or cut photographs and articles from newspapers to create a collage for each of the issues. The collage should reflect who is affected by the issue (scope). A time line can be incorporated into the collage, showing when the problem originated and how long it likely will persist. Student work can be posted in the school hallway or sent to local or national government officials.

Assessment

Have students:
- analyze the scope and duration of water-related issues by using the *Water Issue Analysis Chart* (step 4).
- create a collage and coordinate it with a time line to show how water-related local issues can have global implications and how world-wide issues can affect the individual (*Wrap Up*).

Extensions

Divide students into groups and have students pretend to be members of a think tank or conservation group focusing on particular issues. Groups can study issues that affect different levels of society. What are possible solutions? How would students persuade people to participate in resolving these problems? Will local, state, and global issues require different approaches?

Ask students to imagine they work for an advertising agency developing a campaign to motivate people to become involved in local or global water issues. Different groups can be assigned different types of issues. For example, one issue could involve a toxic waste site near a stream within an inner city; another could focus on water sanitation in a developing country, and a third on preserving wetlands. Groups can compare strategies they used to involve individuals for each type of issue. Have students use the results of the advertising campaign activity to publish a brochure for the school or community.

Considering geographic and cultural differences, students may investigate the unique perspectives and approaches of other countries in avoiding and solving water issues. If students have a sister school in another country, they may contact the school to learn how water resources are managed and protected.

Resources

Hungerford, Harold R., et al. 1992. *Investigating and Evaluating Environmental Issues and Actions Skill Development Modules.* Champaign, Ill.: Stipes Publishing Co.

Notes ▼

Water Issue Analysis Chart

Name: _____ Date: _____

Issue: _____

DURATION

SCOPE	1 WEEK	SEVERAL MONTHS	1 YEAR	OVER 5 YEARS	OVER 10 YEARS	OVER 50 YEARS	OVER 100 YEARS	OVER 500 YEARS
Individual/family								
Community								
Statewide								
National								
International								
Global								

Explanation:

_____

_____

_____

_____

_____

_____

_____

_____

Water resources exist within cultural constructs.

▼

Cultures express connections to their unique water environments through art,

music, language, and customs. Cultures around the world hold

similar and contrasting views toward water.

Raining Cats and Dogs

If someone told you that it was "raining cats and dogs," would you call the Humane Society or don a raincoat?

▼ Summary

Students analyze and interpret water sayings—through a card game, skits, pantomime, and creative writing—to compare figures of speech across cultures and climate zones.

Objectives

Students will:
- distinguish between figurative and literal translations of various water sayings.
- analyze water-related sayings of diverse cultures.

Materials

- Copies of **Water Sayings, Water Illustrations,** and **Water Scenarios** (Cut cards into squares. Cards may be glued onto cardboard and laminated for durability.)
- Copies of **Water Sayings From Around the World**
- **Bartlett's Familiar Quotations** (optional)

Making Connections

Through conversation and literature, students encounter sayings related to water. Although the origins of the sayings may not be known, students may have a regional or cultural understanding of their meanings. Students may broaden their understanding of regional and cultural perspectives and practices related to water by studying water-related proverbs.

Background

Sayings, proverbs, or adages exist in all cultures. They express the beliefs, values, and lifestyles of the people. Although proverbs are common to all cultures, their expression and interpretation are unique. Proverbs are rich in tradition; they are generally passed from generation to generation and often represent the collective wisdom of a culture.

In Africa, proverbs are used for debate, storytelling, and daily conversation. In fact, in Africa it is said that talking without using proverbs is *"like going on a journey without rice in your bag."*

Because we are all dependent on water, proverbs related to observations about water pervade all cultures. The interpretation of a proverb often reflects ideas about how a person should live within that culture.

In some African cultures, for example, these water proverbs apply to knowing one's place:

"Even if you sit on the bottom of the sea, you cannot be a fish."

"If a crocodile deserts the water, he will find himself on a spear."

In speaking about endurance, one might say:

"If there is a continual going to the well, one day there will be a smashing of the pitcher."

Sometimes the sayings or proverbs from two different countries may have a similar meaning, but different modes of expression. For example, some Japanese water sayings have an English equivalent. In Japan one might say, *"Fukusui bon ni kaerazu,"* or *"Spilt water never returns to the tray."* In English one would comment, *"It's no use crying over spilled milk."* A possible interpretation for both of these sayings is that one should not have regrets over what has already occurred. In Japan if someone were advising you to be prepared for an event, he or she might add, *"Have an umbrella ready before you get wet."*

■ **Grade Level:**
Upper Elementary, Middle School

■ **Subject Areas:**
Language Arts, Culture, Ecology

■ **Duration:**
Preparation time:
Part I: 15 minutes
Part II: 15 minutes

Activity time:
Part I: 50 minutes
Part II: 30 minutes

■ **Setting:** Classroom

■ **Skills:**
Gathering information (listening); Organizing (matching); Analyzing (identifying); Relationships and components (discussing)

■ **Charting the Course**
This is an excellent introduction to any activity exploring various cultures and their relationships with water. "The Rainstick" could follow this activity, and "Piece It Together" would complement it with emphasis on the three climate zones and desert ecosystems.

■ **Vocabulary**
proverbs

Several English adages are associated with observations about rain, snow, dew, etc. For example, "Save it for a rainy day" refers to thriftiness, and "You're skating on thin ice" warns of trouble. In the 1700s, Ben Franklin wrote, "You won't miss the water till the well runs dry." This simple and direct saying could be interpreted to apply to conservation of resources.

Proverbs or sayings provide insight into a culture and indicate a people's awareness of and relationship with water. A German philosopher of the 1700s wrote: "Proverbs mirror the thinking of a nation."

Procedure
▼ Warm Up
Open the discussion of proverbs or sayings by writing a few examples on the board. Ask students to share any proverbs that they have heard within their own families. Have them be more specific by citing any sayings that are related to water. (See *Water Proverbs/Sayings*.)

Have students discuss the characteristics of proverbs. Relate how proverbs pass from generation to generation, occur in most cultures, and reflect the values and beliefs of the people. Explain how proverbs have been used to teach a lesson or moral or to indicate how individuals should conduct themselves within a culture.

Ensure that students understand the difference between literal and figurative meanings. For example, the literal translation of "raining cats and dogs" entails household pets falling from the sky. Figuratively, the saying implies a heavy rainfall. Have them identify the literal and figurative meanings of some of the proverbs listed on the board.

▼ The Activity
Part I
1. **Show students the list of** *Water Proverbs/Sayings* **provided in this activity. Ask students to review the water sayings from different countries. Do they understand what they mean? Have students discuss why so many sayings relate to water.**

2. **Divide the class into groups of four. Distribute to each group one set of** *Water Sayings* **and one set of** *Water Illustrations* **cards. Each set has twelve cards. Six of the cards illustrate literal interpretations of the sayings written on the six remaining cards.**

3. **Have the group sit in a circle and determine who will be the "reader." The reader holds the six** *Water Sayings* **cards and places the six** *Water Illustrations* **cards faceup (pictures showing) in the center of the circle.**

4. **The reader will select a card and read aloud the saying that is written on it. Players must touch the picture card that they believe shows the literal translation of the saying. If a player touches the correct card, he or she keeps the saying and the picture card. (The reader consults the** *Answer Key* **to be sure the players are correct in their selec-**

tions.) If a match is incorrect, the reader will inform the player immediately, and that player must return the cards and may not guess again until a new saying is introduced.

5. The game is played until all sayings and pictures have been matched. The player holding the greatest number of cards wins!

6. Students will play the game again, but this time will determine the figurative interpretation. Have students select a new reader. Give the reader the six *Water Scenario* cards. Place the six *Water Sayings* cards faceup in the center of the four students.

7. Have the reader state the scenario aloud. The other three students will touch the saying that they believe completes the scenario. Once again, if the choice is correct, the player collects both cards. The player holding the most cards at the end of the game wins!

8. Have students design a skit demonstrating the literal and/or figurative interpretation of a proverb selected by their group. After students perform, classmates should guess the proverb being illustrated.

Part II
1. **Have students remain in their groups. Give each group a copy of** *Water Sayings From Around the World*.

2. **Tell students their task is to match each group of sayings to the region where they originated (polar, tropical, desert, temperate). Have students respond to the following questions within their own group to help them match the sayings with the region. Do the sayings:**
- provide any clues to temperature?
- indicate seasons?
- reference locations of water?

- reflect scarcity or abundance of water?
- reference land forms?
- identify forms of water?

3. **Discuss the matches students have determined and their reasons for them. Share the answers with students (Region A = polar, Region B = temperate, Region C = tropical, Region D = desert).**

▼ Wrap Up and Action

Have the class discuss several of the proverbs or sayings and speculate how they evolved in view of the culture's relationship with water.

Have students collect proverbs and sayings related to water with their family and friends. If possible, have them contact schools or communities from other regions or cultures to find out if they have different water-related proverbs. They may want to compile sayings in a booklet, "Water Sayings of Our Community" (county, state, or region).

Assessment

Have students:
- distinguish between the literal and figurative meanings of various water sayings (*Part I*, steps 3-8).
- analyze water sayings to explore how language expresses a culture's relationship with water (*Part II*, steps 1-3 and *Wrap Up*).

Extensions

Riddles are another form of expression that reveals insight into various cultures and their relationships with water. Riddles are very popular in African cultures. Share the following examples with your students.

NOTE: African riddles are not in the form of questions, but are declarative. "A slender staff touches earth and sky at the same time." Answer: Rainfall.
"They tell him to bathe and he

bathes; they tell him to stop and he weeps." Answer: Sponge.

Have students create their own water-related riddles and attempt to stump their classmates. This would make an excellent family project.

Resources

Corwin, Charles, ed. 1980. *A Dictionary of Japanese and English Idiomatic Equivalents.* Tokyo, Japan: Kodansha International, Ltd.

Jablow, Alta, and Paul Goodman. 1961. *Yes and No, The Intimate Folklore of Africa.* New York, N.Y.: Horizon Press.

Williams, Terry Tempest, and Ted Major. 1984. *The Secret Language of Snow.* New York, N.Y.: Pantheon Books.

Water Proverbs/Sayings

- A drop in the bucket
- A flood of . . . (tears, mail)
- A stepping stone to . . .
- Blood is thicker than water
- Bogged down
- Break the ice
- Crying buckets
- Don't change horses in mid-stream
- Down the drain
- Even if you sit at the bottom of the sea, you cannot be a fish (Africa)
- Feeling swamped
- Finding your sea legs
- Get your feet wet
- Get your ducks in a row
- Have an umbrella ready before you get wet (Japan)
- Having a ripple effect
- Icy stare
- If a crocodile deserts the water, he will find himself on a spear (Africa)
- If there is a continual going to the well, one day there will be a smashing of the pitcher (Africa)
- In hot water
- It's all water under the bridge
- Jump in with both feet
- Like water off a duck's back
- Little by little the cup is filled (Spain)
- Make a big splash
- Mind in a fog
- On cloud nine

- One hand washes the other
- Pull the child out of the water before you punish it (Africa)
- Raining cats and dogs
- Sink or swim
- Somebody is all wet
- Something smells fishy
- Something snowballs
- Steamed up
- Still waters run deep
- The stone in the water knows nothing of the hill which lies parched in the sun (Africa)
- The well's run dry
- Today is the elder brother of tomorrow, and a heavy dew is the elder brother of rain (Africa)
- Took hook, line, and sinker
- Treading water
- Troubled waters
- Wash my hands of the whole matter
- Watered down
- Wet behind the ears
- Wet your whistle
- When it rains it pours
- When our ship comes in
- With too many rowers the ship will crash into the mountain (Japan)
- You are not the alligator's brother, though you swim well by his side (Africa)
- You won't miss the water till the well runs dry

Water Sayings

Skating on thin ice	Tip of the iceberg
We'll cross that bridge when we get there.	Like a duck to water
Madder than a wet hen	You can lead a horse to water, but you can't make it drink.

Water Illustrations (Literal Interpretations)

Water Scenarios (Figurative Interpretations)

"Mom, I played well this week, but what about the game next week? What if I miss a fly ball? What if I strike out? What if a grounder gets past me?"

"Juan, don't worry, . . ."

Answer: We'll cross that bridge when we get there.

"I can't believe Phyllis has broken up with Mark. She was crazy about him. It must be because he embarrassed her in the cafeteria yesterday."

"No, Phyllis has been telling me about their problems for a long time. The blow-up in the cafeteria was just the . . ."

Answer: Tip of the iceberg.

"So, what happened when your mom got home and saw the mess we made at your house? I bet she wasn't too happy about the cherry soda we sprayed on the curtains, or the chocolate sauce we smeared on the white carpet, or the rec room that we filled with the garden hose—I was sure we could make an indoor swimming pool."

"She was . . . She said I was grounded until I was a grandfather—that's about another 60 years!"

Answer: Madder than a wet hen.

"Did you go to Nyasha's piano recital last night?"

"Yes, it was wonderful. Did you know she has only been taking lessons for one year?"

"Wow! she has taken to the piano . . ."

Answer: Like a duck to water.

"I can't believe Yasu. The music was awesome at the dance; the girl he wanted to ask was there; and he stood by the refreshment table all night. He didn't even ask one person to dance."

"Well, you know what they say. . . . ."

Answer: You can lead a horse to water, but you can't make it drink.

"Mom, can I have four quarters for a video game?"

"No, son, we don't have time."

"Please, Mom, I'll hurry; I only need four quarters.

"No, we're already late for dinner."

"Come on, Mom, you always say that. Please, just four quarters."

"That's enough, Garrett, you're . . ."

Answer: Skating on thin ice.

Water Sayings From Around the World

Region A

1. Ice three feet thick is not frozen in a day.

2. What lay hidden under the snow comes to light at last.

3. Much February snow, a fine summer doth show.

4. No one thinks of the snow that fell last year.

Region B

1. Up a creek without a paddle.

2. After a storm comes a calm.

3. The sea refuses no river.

4. Little drops of water make the mighty ocean.

Region C

1. Till you are across the river, beware how you insult mother alligator.

2. Store up the water while it rains.

3. Don't empty your water jar until the rain falls.

4. What is written on sand is washed out by the tide.

Region D

1. A trickle of water is better than no water.

2. Putting the water back in the well is not waste.

3. If you go first you will not drink muddy water.

4. Gently flowing water will hollow even a rock.

Answer Key (For *Part I*, step 4)

Water Sayings	Water Illustrations Drawing of:
Skating on thin ice	Boy on skates
Tip of the iceberg	Iceberg
We'll cross that bridge when we get there	Boy and girl and bridge
Like a duck to water	Duck with towel
Madder than a wet hen	Chicken
You can lead a horse to water, but you can't make it drink	Horse and girl and tub of water

The Rainstick

Can you use the materials around you to create the sound of rain?

▼ Summary
Students build a rainstick out of materials in their own environment and, like people of ancient cultures, imitate the sound of rain.

Objectives
Students will:
- relate the sound produced by an instrument to the type and quantity of materials used in its construction.
- recognize how other cultures create rainsticks from materials found within their own environments.
- imitate the sound of rain with various materials.

Materials
- *Tape recordings of nature sounds, including rainfall*
- *Simple instruments* (e.g., rattles and bells)
- *An actual rainstick* (optional)
- *A premade rainstick with removable ends*
- *Copies of* **Build Your Own Rainstick**
- *Goggles*

Materials for making rainsticks:
- *Cardboard tubes of a variety of widths and lengths—from toilet paper, paper towels, giftwrapping, or mailing tubes. If these tubes have caps on the ends, save them to seal the tube. Otherwise, use masking tape.* (One-inch [2.5 cm] diameter tubes are sturdy and do not require a large quantity of fill. Paper and mailing supply companies carry tubes.)
- *A tool to make holes in the tube* (If using a drill, select a bit that creates a hole into which a toothpick fits snugly. An awl may also be used to punch holes in the tube.)
- *Toothpicks or other similar thin pieces of material* (Flat-head nails may also be used. With a 1-inch diameter tube, use a 7/8-inch [2.2 cm] nail.)
- *Wood glue*
- *Scissors or wire cutters*
- *Masking Tape*
- *A large quantity* (at least a cup [240 ml] per student) *of dry seeds, beans, pebbles, rice, macaroni, beads, etc.*
- *Funnels* (optional)
- *A variety of materials for decorating the tubes: sand, leaves, twine, yarn, shells, dried herbs, etc.*
- *Watercolor paints and brushes*
- *Pictures of rain forest and/or desert communities*

Making Connections
Students may be aware of rhythm- or sound-producing instruments, such as drums, wooden flutes, or rattles, that imitate natural sounds. Through *National Geographic* magazine, *Discover* programs, and

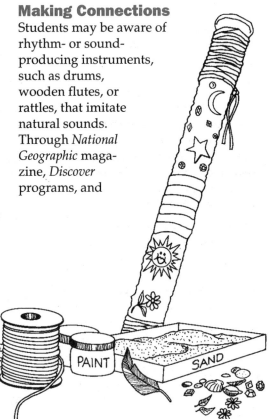

Sidebar

■ **Grade Level:**
Upper Elementary, Middle School, High School

■ **Subject Areas:**
Fine Arts, Geography, History, Anthropology

■ **Duration:**
Preparation time: 50 minutes

Activity time: up to one week

■ **Setting:**
Classroom or outdoors (This is a messy activity.)

■ **Skills:**
Gathering information (listening); Organizing (manipulating materials); Analyzing (comparing and contrasting); Applying (building); Presenting

■ **Charting the Course**
Other aspects of precipitation are explored in "Poetic Precipitation" and "The Thunderstorm." The effect of climate on cultures is discussed in "Piece It Together." The activity "Water Celebration" also explores cultural influences of water. "Raining Cats and Dogs" demonstrates how cultures express relationships with water through language.

■ **Vocabulary**
rainstick, culture

442

other media, students may already have made the connection that diverse cultures produce these instruments from elements available within their own environments. Experiencing how ancient cultures developed instruments to imitate the sound of rain encourages students to explore their own perception of water more closely.

Background

The rainstick is a type of tubular rattle, a sound-producing instrument that belonged to the earliest cultures. Throughout time, the rainstick has been used by diverse cultures in various ways. It has served ceremonial purposes and has been made and played by children. People continue to use the rainstick today. In some parts of the world it has cultural meaning as a traditional instrument associated with the onset of rain, and in other places it is simply played as a percussion instrument.

The rainstick is a hollow tube with an unusual internal structure. An interior matrix formed of cactus spines, wooden pegs, bamboo, or palm slivers distinguishes the rainstick from other tube rattles. The cylinder is filled with pebbles, hard seeds, beans, sand, rice, or tiny shells. The ends of the tube are sealed. The rattle may be decorated with paint and feathers or sheathed with a woven cover.

The rainstick is a product of the environment in which it is found. Rain forest people create rainsticks from bamboo or the midrib of a raphia palm frond. A section of the center stem is cut from the palm frond, split lengthwise, and hollowed out. Material is left at each end of the tube so that the ends are closed. The tube is filled with rice and fastened together with palm slivers.

The palm rainstick imitates the timbre of rain in the forest. Grains of rice tapping against each other, the slivers, and the sides of the tube create the muted sounds of raindrops on ferns, leaves, and the damp forest floor. In desert communities rainsticks have been constructed from various species of cactus.

The sound produced by a rainstick is determined by the material from which the tube is constructed, its length and circumference, the tiny objects enclosed, and the position of the internal needles. The needles or pegs may bisect the tube or only extend halfway through, like the spokes in a wheel.

The way in which the rainstick is "played" affects its sound. Sometimes the tube is shaken like a rhythm instrument. The angle at which the stick is held determines not only the quality but also the duration of the sound.

Some musicologists believe that the rainstick evolved in different parts of the world at the same time. A tubular rattle with pegs has been found in Northern China. However, other investigators maintain that the rainstick was developed in West Africa and introduced to other areas, such as South America, where it is also found today.

Procedure
▼ Warm Up

Ask students to list sounds from the natural environment. Have them listen to music that incorporates these sounds. Guide students to understand that many musical instruments were designed to imitate natural sounds. Have simple instruments on display (e.g., gourd, baby rattle, bell, mouth harp, drum, wooden whistle or flute). Discuss how these are made and the sounds that they produce.

▼ The Activity

1. **Play the rainstick. Ask students what sounds in nature they think the instrument imitates and compare it to recordings of rain.** Another approach is to tell a story about rain or read *The Rainstick, A Fable* and demonstrate the rainstick.

2. **Discuss the use of the rainstick.** Ask students how ancient cultures might have used the rainstick (for ceremonial reasons to celebrate the rain, for musical accompaniment, for children's toys).

3. **Ask students to hypothesize how the rainstick is constructed and what materials were used to make it.** How would using different fill materials affect the sound? Using a premade rainstick with ends that open, ask students to predict the sound before you add new material. Test their predictions. Have students suggest other materials from their environment that could be used to make rainsticks. Have them speculate what materials ancient people in rain forest or desert communities might have used. (Show pictures of these communities for clues.)

4. **Explain and demonstrate how to design a rainstick. Have students build their own rainsticks.** (See *Build Your Own Rainstick.*)

NOTE: Depending on time and students' skill levels, drilling can be done in advance or as part of the activity. If done during class time, adults or responsible students can supervise the drilling at specified work stations. Students can plan how to decorate their rainsticks or write stories or poems about rain while waiting for their sticks to be drilled.

Students with drilled sticks can begin the next step. If they use nails, drilling holes is not necessary.

For hearing-impaired students, larger fill material may be used so that the vibrations can be felt. You may obtain clear PVC pipe from a hardware store and get the school shop to drill holes.

▼ Wrap Up

Have students compare the sounds produced by their rainsticks. Challenge students to arrange their rainsticks in order from a *light* to a *heavy* rain. Have them perform a rainstick medley. Discuss how the sound of rain affects people differently. A gentle rain might create a sense of comfort and well-being, whereas a violent storm can evoke fear and anxiety.

Assessment

Have students:
- predict the sound a rainstick will produce based on its construction and fill materials (step 3).
- speculate about the materials that cultures of diverse environments might have used to create rainsticks (step 3).
- build a rainstick (step 4).
- arrange rainsticks on a sound scale (*Wrap Up*).

Upon completing the activity, for further assessment have students:
- express the personal significance or special meaning of their rainsticks.

Extensions

A rainstick can be a type of journal. Students may decorate rainsticks with items that have personal significance. On a field trip students may create a "natural journal" by collecting material and decorating their rainsticks. They may also design rainsticks that reflect particular environments (e.g., an ocean

rainstick or a forest rainstick). Caution students to collect materials only where such activity is allowed. Also, feathers should not be collected because of legal restrictions involving most bird species.

This instrument may be used to study sound. Students can investigate how the rainstick's sound varies by changing: the diameter of the tube; the length of the tube; the spacing of the internal pegs; the number of internal pegs; the weight of fill material (a heavy substance like corn compared to a lighter material like rice); or the outer coating of the tube.

Resources

Fraginals, Manuel Moreno, ed. 1984. *Africa in Latin America.* New York, N.Y.: Holmes & Meier Publishers, Inc.

Izikowitz, Karl Gustav. 1934. *Musical and Other Sound Instruments of the South American Indians, A Comparative Ethnographical Study.* Göteborg, Sweden: Elanders Boktryckeri Aktiebolag.

Martin, Claude. 1991. *The Rainforests of West Africa: Ecology/Threats/Conservation.* Basel, Switzerland: Birkhäuser Verlag.

Nketia, J. H. Kwabena. 1974. *The Music of Africa.* New York, N.Y.: W. W. Norton & Company.

🍎 Robinson, Sandra C. 1994. *The Rainstick, A Fable.* Published through a partnership between Falcon Press Publishing Co., Inc., Helena, Mont. and The Watercourse, Bozeman, Mont.

Von Hornbostel, E. M. 1933. "The Ethnology of African Sound Instruments." *Journal of the International Institute of African Languages and Cultures* 6 (2).

Build Your Own Rainstick

As people build rainsticks from materials found in the environments in which they live, you too can create your own rainstick with things available within your home.

What you'll need
- *Cardboard tubes from paper towels, gift wrapping or mailing tubes*
- *A tool to punch holes in the tube, such as a drill or awl*
- *Small hammer*
- *Toothpicks or flat-head nails (1-inch diameter tube, $^7/_8$ inch nail)*
- *Glue*
- *Masking tape*
- *Wire cutters or sturdy scissors*
- *"Fill" seeds, pebbles, rice, dried beans, shells, beads and so forth.*
- *Materials to decorate the outside of the tube: paint, crayons, sparkles, sand, etc.*

The Steps

1. Drill or poke holes in the cardboard tube. Be careful not to collapse the tube by pressing too hard. Drill the holes through one side only or all the way through both sides of the tube. If you are using nails, it is not necessary to drill holes.

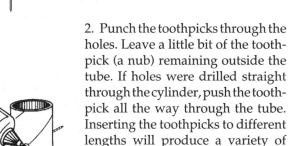

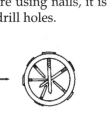

4. Seal one end of the tube with masking tape. Pour in the fill. Cover the open end of the tube with your hand and invert it. Close your eyes and listen. Add more fill or take some away to create a sound that is pleasing to you. Cover the other end of the tube with masking tape.

2. Punch the toothpicks through the holes. Leave a little bit of the toothpick (a nub) remaining outside the tube. If holes were drilled straight through the cylinder, push the toothpick all the way through the tube. Inserting the toothpicks to different lengths will produce a variety of sounds.

If you are using nails, insert nails that are slightly shorter than the diameter of the tube in a spiral pattern. A small hammer may be useful.

3. Apply glue to the nubs and allow to dry. Cut off the nubs if they stick out more than $^1/_4$ inch from the tube. Or, seal the nail heads with glue or wrap the entire tube with masking tape.

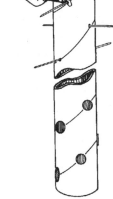

5. You may wish to decorate your rainstick by coating it with glue and rolling it in sand. (Messy, but it provides a wonderful texture for the surface of your instrument.) After it dries, you may paint and decorate it with natural objects from your own part of the world. Be creative!

When you slowly turn your rainstick end to end, listen for the sound of the rain.

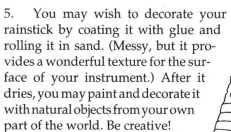

Water Celebration

■ Grade Level:
Upper Elementary, Middle School

■ Subject Areas:
History, Anthropology, Fine Arts, Language Arts, Geography

■ Duration:
Preparation time:
Part I: 10 minutes
Parts II: Depends on extent of fair or celebration

Activity time:
Part I: 50 minutes
Parts II: Depends on extent of fair or celebration

■ Setting:
Indoors, outdoors, classroom

■ Skills:
Gathering information; Analyzing (comparing, identifying patterns); Applying (planning, designing); Presenting

■ Charting the Course
Students can focus on a specific cultural expression of rain in "The Rainstick" and "Water Messages in Stone." "Piece It Together" is a related activity that introduces how different cultures adjust to water availability.

■ Vocabulary
rainstick

What do contemporary students have in common with ancient Pueblo people of the American Southwest?

▼ Summary
Students plan a water celebration.

Objectives
Students will:
- communicate their knowledge of water through a water celebration.
- appreciate how some cultures celebrate water.
- plan and implement a school, community, or state water celebration.

Materials
- *Reference material*
- *Colored pencils, crayons, paint, and paper*
- *Materials depend on the activity selected for the water celebration*
- ***Water Celebration! A Handbook*** (optional—available from the Project WET office)

Making Connections
Students may be familiar with rain dances or other cultural events and expressions associated with water. They may have attended a community Water Celebration. Comparing and contrasting their culture's water symbols with those of other cultures will provide a greater awareness of people's historical and present dependence on water.

Background
Literature provides many examples of water ceremonies and celebrations among diverse cultures. People through the ages—particularly those in areas receiving unpredictable amounts of rain and experiencing floods or droughts—have recognized their dependence on water. They knew from stories of their ancestors, if not from their own experiences, that unwatered crops shriveled and died, and that the people suffered. Rain was a mysterious and special phenomenon, because it connected the earth with the sky. An African riddle states: "A slender staff touches earth and sky at the same time." The answer is rain.

Within a culture, special people and objects were associated with rain. Many parts of Africa had rainmakers; sometimes these were village chiefs. They were responsible for bringing the rain or, in some areas (such as wet coastlines), stopping it. When things were going well (that is, sufficient rainfall and bountiful harvests), the rainmaker enjoyed respect and wealth. However, in times of drought, an unsuccessful rainmaker was cast out and in some cases killed.

Many cultures adopted objects or instruments related to their need for rain. Sometimes these objects reflected the belief that if the people (or the rainmaker) imitated rain, then it would surely come. Water was sprinkled over special stones that were thrown into the air; the stones then fell to the ground, like rain. Selected branches were dipped into water and the drops scattered. The rainstick, a tubular rattle which when inverted produces the sound of rainfall, was used by cultures in South America to call for rain.

Rain dances have long been performed by many Native American groups. Members of a sacred buffalo society among the Omaha filled containers with water and then danced. The Shawnee plunged a buffalo tail in water and shook it, attempting to solicit rain. The Kachina dances of the Hopi in the American Southwest often involve rain. Rain symbols are painted on the hands of dancers, who also wear rain sashes. Shells are worn that imitate the beat of raindrops as the dancer moves. The Hopi also perform the Snake Dance (which is not a Kachina ritual); this prayer for rain involves live, and sometimes venomous, snakes.

People of Thailand celebrate their new year, and the end of the dry season, with a Water Festival that begins April 15 and lasts three days. During these days, people use buckets or bowls to scoop up water and then toss it on each other. Children, believing that acts of kindness carry great merit, carry fish in their bowls to the river and release them during this holiday. Peru's water-throwing carnival involves water and flour being tossed from balconies onto unsuspecting people passing below.

Students, teachers, parents, and community members can conduct their own Water Celebration. A Water Celebration is a free, one- to three-day event to entertain and educate a community about the importance of water. Many celebrations have been organized as one-day events for 4th through 6th grade students and their teachers; however, a Water Celebration can be tailored to meet the needs of any audience or age group.

A celebration can range from a special one-hour class in school, to a half-day event in a park, to a week-end-long water fair at a convention center. It can target school children, a special interest group, or an entire community.

Themes for a Water Celebration might include: wetlands, watersheds, the water cycle, water conservation, ground water, environmental water history, water and culture, etc. Organizers may wish to select a title that reflects their theme, such as: Conservation Sensation, Ground Water Celebration, Water Fun Day, Xeriscaping Demonstration Days,

Water Rights/Your Rights, Water Invention Convention, Liquid Treasure—Learning From the Past, An International Celebration of Water.

A Water Celebration, a high-profile educational activity, increases a community's awareness and appreciation of water resources and issues. Celebrations for school children can include classroom activities, exhibit areas, contests, games, and teacher networking opportunities. A Water Celebration for adults can range from water conservation conventions, to forums on wise water use, to

public debates on water rights.

So, what is a Water Celebration? It's education. It's networking. It's fun!

Procedure
▼ *Warm Up*
Have students list reasons why water is important. How can they tell that cultures value water? Students may consider news media, songs, art-work, dances, and celebrations. Ask them if their culture observes holi-days that celebrate water. If students know how cultures celebrate water, have them describe events to the class.

Tukwinong (Cumulus Cloud Kachina) is a messenger to summer thunderheads, bringing water to the dry fields of the Hopi. ILLUSTRATED BY PETER GROSSHAUSER

▼ The Activity

Part I

1. From the **Background**, share with students cultural information about water. Have students conduct research to learn how different cultures, past and present, celebrate water and the rain symbols associated with these celebrations. Family members may be interviewed.

2. Students may write a paragraph, draw a picture, or create a song, poem, or legend to illustrate the relationship of a culture and water.

3. Have each student create a cultural symbol that expresses his or her connection with water.

4. Students may show and interpret their symbols to the class. Are there similarities among students' symbols?

5. Have students share their research about ancient rain symbols. Have them compare and contrast their modern designs with those of other cultures.

6. Students may select one logo (or symbol) and create class T-shirts, hats, or buttons.

Part II

Following are two approaches for conducting a Water Celebration.

Option I

Students may be interested in creating and conducting their own Water Celebration. Discuss ways water is used in their community and how they could organize a festival around these uses. Ideas include water conservation, water careers, water fun, etc. A Water Celebration can be simple or complex, depending upon the resources, time, and interest of the class. The celebration may occupy an hour or a half-day, or full day and involve one class or several schools. Students may be divided into small groups, to plan a Water Celebration or Fair. After the class has determined the scope of their celebration, have them consider the following:
- appropriate date (Earth Day or the birthday of a famous conservationist)
- theme
- logo
- activities

Details on planning, organizing, and conducting a water celebration are thoroughly discussed in *Water Celebration! A Handbook* (see **Resources**).

Option II

Students may wish to plan and produce a Project WET Water Celebration. Have students select their favorite Project WET activities and plan an afternoon or a day when they conduct them for other classes in their school. Students should select activities based upon the location of their celebration (indoors or outdoors), availability of materials for large numbers of participants, activity time, etc. Students should enlist the help of parents in planning and implementing their Project WET Water Celebration. See *Possible Floor Plan for a Project WET Celebration.*

▼ Wrap Up and Action

Have students discuss how the water needs of ancient people and other cultures are similar to their own. Ask them to compare to what degree our culture controls its environment compared to our ancestors. Could early people predict when it would rain; can we?

If students decide to put on a Water Fair—even an hour in duration—have them share it with other classes or the community. As they study other cultures in social studies units or celebrate other countries for International Day, have them incorporate water-related material.

Assessment

Have students:
- write a paragraph, song, or legend describing how early cultures celebrated water (*Part I*, step 1).
- identify the water symbols of early cultures (*Part I*, steps 1 and 5).
- design a symbol representative of their dependence on water (*Part I*, step 3).
- organize and conduct a Water Celebration (*Part II*, Option I).
- teach others about water through a Project WET Water Celebration (*Part II*, Option II).

Extensions

Students may choreograph their own dance to celebrate rain, or they may construct instruments from materials in their environment to imitate the sound of rain, a river, or a waterfall. Students could research and construct ancient and modern instruments that imitate natural sounds (rainstick, bullroarer, etc.) and create a Water Symphony.

Resources

Baylor, Byrd. 1986. *I'm in Charge of Celebrations.* New York, N.Y.: Charles Scribner's Sons.

Chapelle, Delores L., and Janet Bourque. 1973. *Earth Festivals.* Silverton, Colo.: Finn Hill Arts.

Robinson, Sandra C. and The Watercourse Staff. 1994. *The Rainstick, A Fable.* Helena, Mont.: Falcon Press Publishing Co., Inc.

The Watercourse and Project WET Staff. 1993. *Water Celebration! A Handbook.* Bozeman, Mont.: The Watercourse and Project WET.

Possible Floor Plan for a Project WET Celebration

*Indicates Project WET Activity

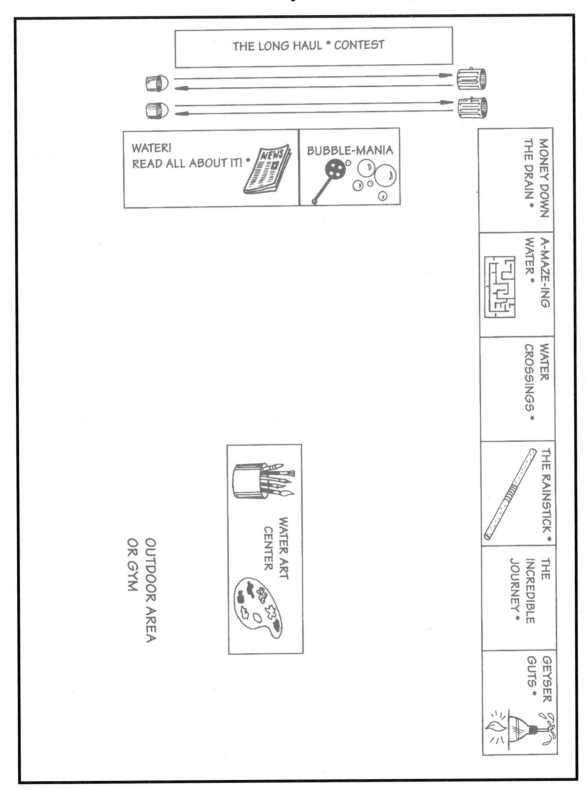

W∆te℞ in Mo⊤ion

Why do people pull off the highway to watch a cascading waterfall, or pause along a trail to listen to a stream?

▼ Summary
Students create artwork to help them appreciate the movement and sound of water in their environment.

Objectives
Students will:
- recognize reasons why people find the sound and movement of water pleasing.
- demonstrate how wind, pressure, and gravity move water.
- design artwork that incorporates the movement and sounds of water.

Materials
- *Rectangular clear baking pan*
- *Blue-colored water*
- *Battery-operated or electric fan*
- *Aluminum pie plate with holes pierced through bottom*
- *Cardboard*
- *Aluminum foil*
- *Tape*
- *Photograph of fountain (provided)*
- *Sand*
- *Plastic jar*
- *Flexible tubing (about 3 yards [1 m] long)*
- *Wood glue or duct tape*
- *Student-supplied building materials such as scraps of wood, aluminum foil, clay, tubing, jars with lids, rocks, hammer, nails, waterproof glue, etc.*

Making Connections
Water's movement in natural settings—crashing waves, cascading waterfalls, and rolling rivers—influences many forms of artistic expression found in cities. Fountains and water sculptures imitate the aesthetic characteristics of water in nature. By recognizing this relationship, students identify not only their physiological but also their emotional need for the soothing effects of water's movement and sound.

Background
All around the world, water is in motion. Gravity, the sun's energy, and Earth's rotation cause rivers to rush downstream or plunge over ledges to create spectacular waterfalls; they induce lakes and ponds to swirl below their surfaces, and draw the ocean waves to shore. People travel to Niagara Falls, Old Faithful Geyser, or Maui to enjoy the beauty and power of water in motion.

Gravity causes all free-running water to flow downhill. Falling rain is also influenced by this force. Raindrops fall from clouds when water vapor cools and condenses into droplets that are too heavy to be suspended by air molecules.

Wind also contributes to the movement of water. Because Earth's surface is made up of a variety of materials, it heats unevenly. The heat from the surface warms the air above it. Warmer air rises and is replaced by denser, colder air, creating wind. When wind blows over water, it produces waves.

Sounds are generated by the motion of water; these sounds can either alarm us (waves crashing or thundering) or soothe and comfort us (brooks babbling, rainfall softly pattering).

In the natural world, water not only sustains plants and animals, but also entertains and inspires people. Many architects and landscape designers have recognized the pleasing qualities of water in nature and have re-created

Grade Level:
Upper Elementary

Subject Areas:
Fine Arts, Physical Science, History

Duration:
Preparation time:
Part I: 30 minutes
Part II: 30 minutes
Part III: 10 minutes

Activity time:
Part I: 30 minutes
Part II: 30 minutes
Part III: two 50-minute periods

Setting:
Classroom or outdoors (activity can be messy)

Skills:
Gathering information (observing); Applying (designing); Presenting

Charting the Course
The sounds of water in art are also incorporated into the activity "The Rainstick." The use of flowing water to produce energy is presented in "Energetic Water," which is a related activity.

Vocabulary
gravity, water pressure

them in steel and stone in cities. Fountains and water sculptures mimic the sights and sounds of waterfalls and bubbling creeks.

Fountains have been built for thousands of years. While many modern fountains are activated by pumps, earlier designs utilized water pressure. The source of the water was elevated above the level of the fountain, and gravity and the weight of water upon itself created the pressure. Traditionally, artists used naturally flowing water for their fountains. Today, many fountains, such as those designed for libraries, malls, and hotels, use water that is recycled by generators.

Procedure
▼ Warm Up
Ask students why people like to visit waterfalls, rivers, and beaches. Have students list the sounds these water bodies produce. Do they find these sounds pleasing or not? Ask students to describe what causes water to move and the sounds that are created.

▼ The Activity
Part I
1. **Fill a baking pan one-third full of blue-colored water and proceed with the following activities.**

- Place a battery-operated fan in front of the pan. (If using an electric fan, caution students about the hazard of water and electricity.) Ask students to predict what will happen to the water when you turn on the fan. Start the fan and have the students record their observations. Ask them to identify the energy source used to create these waves. (The first response is wind power; ultimately, however, the energy comes from the sun.)
- Hold the aluminum pie plate with

holes punched in the bottom over the pan of water and pour a small amount of water into the pie plate. Ask students what this demonstration simulates. Have them identify the force of nature that pulls atmospheric water down to Earth.

- Fold a piece of cardboard lengthwise. Wrinkle a sheet of aluminum foil and tape it to the cardboard. Hold the board almost vertically over the pan and slowly pour water over the surface of the aluminum foil. Ask students to describe the sounds when the water flows over the aluminum foil and falls into the pan of water.

2. **Ask students where they might find the sounds created by moving water in a city building or a park. Show students pictures of fountains and discuss why people are attracted to fountains and why fountains are built in many public places.**

Part II
1. **Demonstrate how to mimic a fountain.** Fill a pan with sand. Cut a hole in the lid of a plastic jar and thread one end of a flexible tube through the hole. Seal the spaces around the tube with wood glue or duct tape. Put the lid on the jar. Bury the other end of the tube under the sand leaving the end pointing upward above the surface. (See diagram.) Lift the jar above the level of the pan and pour water into the hole in the base of the jar.

2. **Have students observe water flowing upward and explain that this is the basic structure used by artists to create fountains. Have them identify what causes the water to flow upward, against the pull of gravity.**

Part III
1. **Divide the students into groups and tell them they are architects or landscape designers. Challenge them to locate various building**

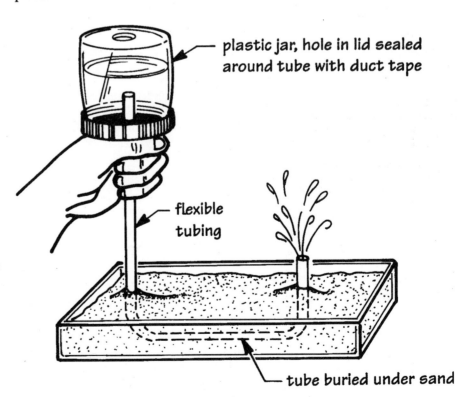

plastic jar, hole in lid sealed around tube with duct tape

flexible tubing

tube buried under sand

Fountain at Missouri Botanical Garden, St. Louis, MO.
FRANK OBERLE

guides, providing viewers with information and background about the designs.

Assessment
Have students:

- describe how water moves in nature (*Part I*, step 1).
- design art forms that incorporate moving water (*Part III*, step 1).
- list reasons why people find the sound of moving water in natural and human-made settings appealing (*Part I*, step 2 and *Wrap Up*).
- critique water designs (*Part III*, step 2 and *Wrap Up*).

reading and studying. Conversely, fountains in Las Vegas create excitement, and in attracting people may contribute to the economy of the city.

K-2 Option
CREATE A WATER TABLE! Set up a "water table" or center in the room so students can create a variety of water movement structures and learn math (e.g., volume) and physical science (e.g., density) concepts as well. Include the following items at the water table: large basins, measuring cups and spoons, squeeze bottles, bowls, straws, funnels, sieves, sprinkling cans, sponges, blocks of wood, plastic and metal, tubes, etc. Focus students' attention by giving them task cards. (See *Water Task Cards.*) When placing the water table, consider students' safety, freedom of movement, accessibility to running water, and ease of clean up. Encourage students to wear raincoats or plastic aprons when working at the table. Have students record their observations and conclusions by writing or drawing in a "Water Log" or journal and presenting their work to the class.

materials to create their own functional design that incorporates flowing water. Student designs could include water sounds, sights, and motions.

2. **Have each group test and demonstrate their creation by pouring water through, on, or over it.**

▼ Wrap Up and Action
Have students review and interpret the artwork created by other groups. How did the artists create water movement? Do they think the artists were trying to elicit a feeling or thought with their designs? Do the structures have symbolic meaning?

Have students organize an art show to exhibit their work. This display should include information about the artists and reviews or interpretations of their designs. Students can act as

Extensions
Water has been an integral part of architecture since the time of ancient Greece. Have students examine art and architecture books to find examples of fountains and other designs that incorporate water (e.g., water clocks, water drums). Students may research and model a particular design.

If a kiln is available, students may want to create a clay sculpture that incorporates rainfall. This functional design could be placed in the school yard or nature center.

Have students discuss how fountains may be designed to create a particular atmosphere to influence people's behavior. For example, fountains have been constructed in libraries where the sound of flowing water is conducive to quiet activities—

Resources
Campbell, C. S. 1978. *Water in Landscape Architecture.* New York, N.Y.: Van Nostrand Reinhold.

Martin, Bill, Jr., and John Archambault. 1988. *Listen to the Rain.* New York, N.Y.: Harry Holt & Company.

Praegor, Frederick A. 1958. *The Praegor Picture Encyclopedia of Art.* New York, N.Y.: Praeger Publishers.

Robb, David M., and June J. Garrison. 1963. *Art in the Western World.* 4th ed. New York, N.Y.: Harper & Row.

K-2 Option

Water Task Cards

Can you make water squirt upward?

How many spoons of water fill a cup?

Can you make a waterfall?

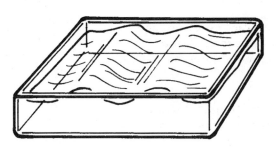

Can you create big and small waves?

 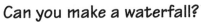

wAteR in moTion
Project WET Curriculum and Activity Guide

Water Messages in Stone

Could you interpret this message if it were left for you?

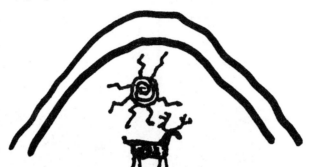

▼ Summary

Students replicate rock paintings and carvings to learn about ancient cultures' relation to water and to create their own water-related expressions.

Objectives

Students will:
- demonstrate how ancient cultures drew messages to express their relation to water
- discern characteristics of pictographs and petroglyphs

Materials

- *Photographs of petroglyphs* (optional)
- *Drawing paper and pencils*
- *Chalk and chalkboard*

Materials needed to create painted pictograph:
- *Flat surface such as plastic, rock, or paper*
- *Watercolors or other painting media*
- *Paint brushes*

Materials needed to create petroglyph:
- *Flat surface such as soap, plastic, a soft rock, plaster of Paris*
- *Nails*
- *Protective gloves*
- *Goggles*

Making Connections

People leave messages to each other on notes and answering machines. Often messages relay information of value to the sender and receiver (e.g., appointments, requests). Learning about and interpreting prehistoric messages left in stone helps students understand the value ancient cultures placed on water and other natural resources.

Background

Throughout the world evidence exists of early peoples' attempts to communicate their ideas or to record their histories through pictures. Among the most ancient and enduring of these messages are pictures painted and carved on rocks. Many archaeological and historic sites throughout North America contain ancient and historic rock paintings and carvings.

Each painted image or incised symbol can be viewed as a work of art and a sensitive reflection of the culture that produced it. Some European and African works were crafted thousands of years ago. These creations provide insight into ancient lifestyles and ideas.

A pictograph communicates through pictures on stone that are chipped, carved, or painted. The earliest form of pictograph is the petroglyph, in which images are pecked or chiseled into rock surfaces with hard stone and bone tools. To create such an image, the carver wields a heavy stone to hammer a sharp rock into a stone surface. This was an exacting process, requiring up to 100 tiny chips of rock to create just one square inch of an image. Prehistoric people later learned to create paints by grinding minerals (e.g., red from iron, white from gypsum, and black from charcoal) and plant material (e.g., red-to-yellow colors from ochre). Sometimes chipping and painting were combined.

Archaeologists are scientists who investigate past cultures, locating and analyzing materials such as pictographs to help understand history. Archaeologists are able to learn how pictographs were made, but are rarely able to determine why they were made. This is because the people who created such images lived long ago, and their lives and perspectives differed greatly from ours. Nonetheless, through complex processes similar to detective work, archaeologists look for themes and try to decipher these messages. However, if three different scientists study the same pictograph, they likely will have three different interpretations.

In general, archaeologists believe that images created by early peoples represent information about harvests, location of herds of animals, social hierarchies, etc. Archaeologists have concluded that several pictograph images represent water. This finding suggests that early people valued water. The reproductions of pictographs on the previous page might relate to water.

PROJECT WET

Procedure
▼ *Warm Up*
Have students list ways they leave messages for other people. Why do people leave messages? Have students describe how messages have been conveyed through time (e.g., telegrams, smoke signals, stone tablets). Display pictures in the classroom of ancient pictographs or petroglyphs or use representations provided on this page and on the previous two pages. Ask students to write what they think the original creator of the image intended. Discuss the meaning with the class.

▼ *The Activity*
1. **Discuss the characteristics of a pictograph, and clarify that a petroglyph is a type of pictograph.**

2. **On drawing paper, have students design symbols that they think represent water.** Encourage them to consider clouds, steam, water drops, rain, snow, thunderstorms, oceans, etc. Some of these symbols may be concrete, such as a water drop or a wave crashing on the beach. Others may be more abstract, such as wavy lines suggesting the surface of a lake.

3. **Have each student come to the front of the room and draw one of** his or her symbols on the board. See if the class can guess its meaning.

4. **Instruct students to choose one or more symbols and create their own pictographs. They can make a painted pictograph or a petroglyph. Following are instructions for each:**

   • Painted pictograph: Students can use paints to transfer their sketched image to a flat surface. Students might want to experiment making their own paints out of plant materials and minerals.

   • Petroglyph: Symbols can be carved or chipped into soap, plaster of Paris, or some other flat surface using a nail. If a hard material is used, students should wear goggles and heavy, protective gloves.

▼ *Wrap Up*
Ask students to identify the characteristics of pictographs. What messages about water are people recording today that could be found in the future? What messages are we leaving for people in the future about our attitudes toward water? Examples might include fountains, dams, water slides, interpretive signs located near water-related nature scenes, hot tubs, billboards containing water scenes, etc.

Have students create a display for their pictographs. Students can interpret each other's messages and write small descriptions for each display. How are the interpretations alike? How are they different? Students can discuss reasons for the variations.

Assessment
Have students:
• design water symbols and simulate pictographs and petroglyphs (steps 2-4).
• describe how pictographs are used by cultures (*Wrap Up*).
• interpret possible messages presented in other students' pictographs (*Wrap Up*).

Upon completing the activity, for further assessment have students:
• sequence several pictographs in order to communicate a message.

Extensions
Encourage students to investigate other materials archaeologists use to decipher the past (e.g., tools, stored seeds, pottery). How many of these relate to water?

Another technique to create a pictograph or other artifact involves using modeling dough. (See the activity "A-maze-ing Water" for recipe.) Roll out dough until it is about 1 inch (2.5 cm) thick and 6 inches (15 cm) in diameter. Students can press figures into the dough or shape the dough to create three-dimensional images. Allow to dry, and paint if desired. These also make wonderful gifts.

Resources
Barnes, F. A. 1992. *Prehistoric Rock Art*. Salt Lake City, Utah: Wasatch Publishers.

Schaafsma, Polly. 1990. *Indian Rock Art of the Southwest*. Santa Fe, N. Mex.: School of American Research Press.

Smith, Shelley J., et al. 1993. *Intrigue of the Past: A Teacher's Activity Guide for Fourth through Seventh Grades*. Washington, D.C.: United States Department of Interior, Bureau of Land Management.

🍎 Stokes, William M. 1980. *Messages on Stone*. Salt Lake City, Utah: Starstone Publishing Co.

Water Write

■ **Grade Level:** K-12

■ **Subject Areas:**
Language Arts, Science, Fine Arts

■ **Duration:**
Preparation time:
Part I: 30 minutes
Part II: 15 minutes

Activity time:
Part I: depends upon exercise selected
Part II: depends on book selected

■ **Setting:** Classroom

■ **Skills:**
Analyzing; Applying (problem solving); Presenting (writing)

■ **Charting the Course**
In the analysis of literature, students may want to consider the activities, "Adventures in Density" and "Dust Bowls and Failed Levees." Writing skills also are utilized in "Water: Read All About It," "Nature Rules," and "Water Log."

■ **Vocabulary**
critical analysis

Toning and shaping exercises are not just for the body—they're also for the brain!

▼ Summary
Through a variety of writing and reading activities, students explore their feelings for and understanding of water-related topics.

Objectives
Students will:
- express, through writing, their knowledge of, feelings about, and values related to water.
- evaluate literature based on the presentation of water-related concepts.

Materials
(depend upon exercise selected)

- *Paper*
- *Pencil*
- *Yarn*
- *Tape*
- *Tape recorder*
- *Jigsaw puzzle* (about 20 pieces with a water theme)

Making Connections
Older students may have read the works of novelists, poets, or journalists who have written eloquently about water and its characteristics. Younger students may have been exposed to stories with a water message. Students of all ages may benefit from exercises that stimulate them to think and write about water by looking at the resource in a different way.

Background
The famous naturalist Loren Eiseley wrote, "If there is magic on this planet, it is contained in water. . . . Its substance reaches everywhere; it touches the past and prepares the future; it moves under the poles and wanders thinly in the heights of air. It can assume forms of exquisite perfection in a snowflake, or strip the living to a single shining bone cast up by the sea."

Children's authors Bill Martin, Jr., and John Archambault wrote in *Listen to the Rain*, "Listen to the rain, the singing of the rain, the tiptoe pitter-patter, the splish and splash and splatter, the steady sound, the singing of the rain."

Students may wonder where writers get their ideas. Some authors maintain that their ideas come from stories in newspapers, from conversations with friends or strangers, and from dreams and their own imaginations. Friends and relatives of writers often find bits and pieces of their own personalities adapted to a character in the writer's book. Writers have often admitted to eavesdropping. Some writers keep notebooks with snatches of dialogue (particularly for accents or dialects) or lists of names. Many authors maintain journals of ideas for future books.

Sometimes writers may suffer from "writer's block." This "affliction" causes them to stare blankly at a computer screen or to chew the ends off pencils while they contemplate a blank piece of paper for days. Writers sometimes find themselves unable to express their ideas on paper. One cure for this condition is mentally "stepping back" and looking at the subject in a different way. Whether students are suffering from writer's block or simply would like to look at a subject from a fresh perspective, writing exercises can be helpful and fun. The exercises that follow focus on water, but they can be adapted to any number of subjects.

The Rainbow Goblins · 20,000 Leagues Under the Sea · DUNE · Listen to the Rain · Paddle to the Sea · e for Environment

Procedure

▼ Warm Up

Ask students to think of books, movies, cartoons, or comics that they particularly enjoy. Can they recall any references to water in these resources? As water is pervasive in our lives, it often serves as a back-drop for stories and sometimes provides the motivation for characters. In *The Milagro Beanfield War*, the story pivots on one man's struggle to water his field although he doesn't own the water right. The science fiction classic, *Dune*, is based on water scarcity. In *A River Runs Through It*, the river and the art of fly-fishing are metaphors for a man's examination of the relationships of his youth. *The Rainbow Goblins* is a fable about how rainbows were formed. *e for Environment* contains excellent children's literature related to the environment (including water). Your librarian may have additional suggestions. Tell students that they will participate in writing games or exercises that will stretch their thinking and writing about water.

▼ The Activity

Part I

From the following list, select exercises that are appropriate to the grade level, curriculum, needs, and interests of your students.

Water Message:
A daily message about water can be written on the board to be used as a reading and writing activity. Inform students that their task is to determine if the message is true or false or to locate any spelling, grammar, or punctuation errors. Examples include:
- *Water can be found in four forms (or states).*
- *Plants use their leaves to absorb water.*
- *It is important for me to drinks water everyday.*
- *Yesterday, it rains very hard.*

Water Yarn:
Every foot-and-a-half on a long strand of yarn, attach a tag with a water word or phrase written on it (e.g., blizzard, snow skier, avalanche, snowcapped mountain). Coil the yarn in the bottom of a box. Have students sit in a circle; hand the box to the first student. Tell the student to pull the yarn out of the box until the first tag appears. Have the student read the word, then create a sentence using it. Pass the box to the next student and repeat the process. Tape record the sentences. Write the sentences on paper; make copies and distribute them to students. Working in pairs, students should try to arrange the sentences into a logical story or paragraph. They may throw out one sentence and write one of their own. Record students as they read their stories aloud. Award prizes for the best Water Yarns. Younger students may read the word and think of rhyming words.

Water Puzzle:
Either create or use a commercial jigsaw puzzle with a water theme (preferably a child's version that has about 20 pieces). Do not show the class the complete puzzle. Separate the pieces and give one to each student (or pair of students). Have students write descriptions of their puzzle pieces and take turns reading them aloud. Can the class guess the design of the complete puzzle?

Water Super Hero:
Discuss with students super heroes that they see in cartoons or read about in comic books. Have students describe: their appearance (Do they wear a costume?), their abilities (Do they possess "super powers"?), their background (How did they become super heroes?), and their character (Are they motivated to do good or evil?). Discuss briefly with students the qualities of water (it can change form; it can erode mountains and rearrange shorelines; it is necessary for all living creatures). Have students create a Water Super Hero. Have them write a one-page profile (physical description, special powers, history, and character) and illustrate their "Evapo-Man" or "Transpire-Woman."

Water Trekkies:
Tell students that they live in the year 2020, the era of the "water card." Individuals must have water cards, that allow them to use only a certain amount of water every day. When people have consumed their allotment, alarms go off and the water card no longer activates

faucets, toilets, water fountains, washing machines, etc. Ask students to describe their lives in the year 2020, using their knowledge of water concepts to write this science fiction thriller.

Water Invention Convention:
Have students design appliances for the future that conserve water. Have them draw plans and write instructions for assembling their inventions.

Starters:
Allow students to select from the following "starters" or create their own. Have them write a paragraph, a page, or a book—whatever it takes to tell the story. However, some people can actually tell a story better than they can write it. Some authors tape record their stories, play them back, and write them down. Some students may want to try this.

It had been raining all day and I was tired of being cooped up in the house. I threw on my raincoat and left through the back door. As I walked along the street, I came to a large puddle. Out of habit I checked it out. I sharply sucked in my breath and did a double take. I looked at my reflection in the puddle, but it was not I who looked back. It was . . .

We had just finished playing our soccer game; I was pretty happy because our team had won. I shivered slightly as I walked home; it had rained lightly on and off throughout the game. I looked up at the sky as the sun broke through the clouds, and there was the most beautiful rainbow I had ever seen. But my admiration turned to amazement as I watched the colors of the rainbow change to black and white . . .

Part II

Have students present a critical analysis of a book based on their knowledge of water-related concepts. Give students the following questions and have them record answers as they read popular selections. Have them present an oral report to the class.

- How is the topic of water incorporated into the book?
- Is water just part of the scenery or is it integral to the plot?
- Does water have a symbolic meaning?
- What concepts related to water are introduced (e.g., density, reflection, latent heat)?
- Has the author accurately presented the concepts?
- Is the author using water or water-related concepts to convey his or her message?
- How did your knowledge of water enhance your understanding of the reading?

▼ Wrap Up and Action

Have students share stories, analyses, and illustrations with the class. Students may wish to create bulletin boards or combine stories into collections that can be placed in the school library, and checked out by other students. Stories may be submitted for possible publication to school or local newspapers, newsletters, or magazines.

Assessment
Have students:
- express their thoughts and feelings about water resources through writing exercises (**Part I**).
- analyze popular literature to evaluate their knowledge of water-related concepts (**Part II**).

Extensions
Have students generate additional water writing exercises. Older students can write reviews of popular fiction based on their analysis of the accuracy with which water concepts are presented.

Resources
🍎 Dunn, Sara, and Alan Schofield, eds. 1991. *Poetry for the Earth*. New York, N.Y.: Fawcett Columbine.

Gillespie, John T. 1990. *Best Books for Junior High Readers*. New Providence, N.J.: R. R. Bowker.

—. 1990. *Best Books for Senior High Readers*. New Providence, N.J.: R. R. Bowker.

🍎 Herbert, Frank. 1965. *Dune*. Philadelphia, Pa.: Chilton Books.

🍎 Koch, Kenneth, and Kate Farrell, (comps.). 1985. *Talking to the Sun: An Illustrated Anthology of Poems for Young People*. New York, N.Y.: The Metropolitan Museum of Art/Henry Holt Co.

Maguire, Jack. 1985. *Creative Storytelling: Choosing, Inventing and Sharing Tales for Children*. New York, N.Y.: McGraw-Hill Book Co.

🍎 Nichols, John Treadwell. 1974. *The Milagro Beanfield War*. New York, N.Y.: Ballentine Books.

Sinclair, Patti K. 1992. *e for Environment*. New Providence, N.J.: R. R. Bowker.

Ziegler, Alan. 1984. *The Writing Workshop*. Vol. 2. New York, N.Y.: Teachers & Writers Collaborative.

Wish Book

■ **Grade Level:**
Upper Elementary, Middle School, High School

■ **Subject Areas:**
History, Environmental Science

■ **Duration:**
Preparation time: 30 minutes

Activity time: 50 minutes

■ **Setting:** Classroom

■ **Skills:**
Gathering information (reading, researching); Organizing (categorizing); Analyzing (contrasting); Interpreting

■ **Charting the Course**
To understand how water uses have evolved, students may want to play "Water Concentration." "Easy Street" compares the quantities of water used 100 years ago to today.

■ **Vocabulary**
water-related recreation

"Wool soap" . . . "Nerve and brain pills" . . . "Ventriloquism Self-Taught" . . . "Ice shredder"? You can find these among the 5,996 items in the Wish Book of 1897.

▼ Summary
Using catalogue selections from the late 1800s and the present, students compare and contrast the role of water in the leisure time of people, past and present.

Objectives
Students will:
* compare and contrast the water-related sports and other recreational activities of the past and present.
* become aware of sources of information for learning about the past.

Materials
* *Photos of water-related recreation in the past* (optional)
* *Historical newspapers* (optional)
* *Copies of page from* **1897 Sears, Roebuck Catalogue**
* *Current catalogues that include recreation and sports paraphernalia*
* *1897 Sears, Roebuck Catalogue (see* **Resources**) (optional)
* *Colored pencils*
* *Paper*

Making Connections
Most students have perused modern catalogues for clothing, stereos, and sports and camping equipment. Just as these catalogues reflect the present culture, catalogues of the past provide insight into the lifestyles and habits of our ancestors. Students may have been exposed to old photographs or artwork that also illustrate early people and their recreational connection to water. Learning about connections among past and

present uses of water for recreation helps students appreciate the evolution of water resource use over time.

Background
Water is a major ingredient in many of today's diverse forms of outdoor recreation. Swimming, canoeing and kayaking, scuba diving, fishing, sailing, windsurfing, ice-skating, sledding, skiing, and snowboarding are all popular water sports. However, water recreation does not always involve getting into water or onto ski slopes. Bird watchers with binoculars scan the grassy waters of wetlands, sunbathers flock to beaches, and picnickers and dreamers spread their blankets on the shores of lakes.

Surprisingly, many of the water activities that we enjoy today have evolved over hundreds of years. How did our ancestors take advantage of water resources during their leisure time?

Although they likely served a utilitarian as well as a recreational purpose, the first skis were made of bone and were strapped to the skier's boots with strips of leather. Early skiing was cross-country because the loose leather bindings would not hold the ski to the boot on downhill runs. The practice of skiing began thousands of years ago in northern Europe and Asia. Modern downhill skiing began in the mid-1800s with the development of the first stiff bindings. With the invention of ski lifts, more people took up skiing in the 1930s. The increasing popularity of downhill skiing today—sometimes resulting in crowded slopes and long waits at lifts—has prompted many people to return to the oldest form of skiing, cross-country.

Snowshoeing was popular many years ago, not only for recreation but also for transportation. Snowshoes are usually at least 3 feet (91 cm) long and from 1 to

1¹/₂ feet (30 to 46 cm) wide. A person wearing snowshoes can travel across deep snow because the snowshoes distribute the wearer's weight over a large area. In the 1800s, adults and children alike would strap on their snowshoes after dinner and enjoy a walk in the moonlight with friends.

In rural and urban areas, ice-skating has long been popular. In cities, ponds became ice rinks and attracted crowds on pleasant days. In fact, in the mid-1800s, ice-skating was one of the few outdoor sports in which both men and women could participate. In rural locations, an ice rink might be constructed at the schoolyard. After the ground was frozen, snow would be scraped to the side, forming a border around the rink. Hauling pail after pail of water from the pump, students would flood the rink. The area would be flooded weekly to keep the surface of the ice smooth. Students fashioned their own sticks from carefully selected branches and played ice hockey during recess.

Whether at a fancy seaside resort or the local pond, swimming has always been a favored water pastime. In the 1800s, swimming in mixed company was considered "daring." Some beaches strictly segregated men and women. Wherever they swam, women wore "swimming costumes" that covered them from neck to ankle.

Fishing has always been a popular outdoor water sport. Fly-fishing, a type of fishing that involves the creation of artificial lures that imitate a living creature, was widespread in the 1800s. In fact, fly-fishing is reported to have been practiced by the early Romans. Fly-fishing anglers create artificial lures to attract fish that feeds on insects, minnows, or crustaceans. Diverse species of fish are sought by people who fly-fish: sunfish, bass, trout, bluefish, shark,

Will students find what they are looking for in a Wish Book from 1897?

sailfish, salmon, catfish, etc. However, fly-fishing is usually associated with trout and salmon in streams. In fact, most Atlantic salmon rivers of North America require the use of fly-fishing gear exclusively. This sport is enjoyed all across the United States.

Certain technological improvements have expanded the scope of some types of water recreation. As outboard motors became more powerful, interest in boating increased and water-skiing became possible. As snorkeling and scuba diving equipment became safer and less cumbersome, more people visited underwater areas.

In the late 1880s, the 1890s, and the early 1900s most people worked at their jobs about ten hours a day, six days a week, usually 51 weeks a year. However, their lives were not without recreation. They enjoyed holidays and sports, but because travel was limited, most of their celebrations occurred locally. People of financial means took summer

holidays at beach resorts or spas, where visitors "took the waters" (that is, bathed in or drank mineral waters). At Niagara Falls, tourists donned rubber coats and hats and took the famous boat trip below the falls.

Since World War II, recreation has become an important element in people's lives. Better incomes, paid vacations, and improved working conditions and transportation have provided greater numbers of people with increased opportunities (i.e., money, time, and mobility) for recreation.

Today, recreation is a multi-billion-dollar industry. Besides its contribution to the economy, recreation is important for the mental and physical health of individuals. Because of water's significance to recreation, our continued enjoyment of fishing, swimming, skiing, and other outdoor sports depends on maintaining the quality and quantity of water resources.

Procedure

▼ Warm Up

Ask students to name recreational activities. Which activities do they personally enjoy? Which of these involve water? Have students recall parents' or grandparents' stories about recreational activities they participated in as children. Show students photographs of recreation from the past (see *Water Recreation in the Past*). Can they imagine their grandparents doing these things?

Discuss with students the resources that can be used to learn about the habits and lifestyles of people of 100 years ago. Books are an important resource. Publishers generally print books that they believe are interesting to the public, so they often reflect those subjects particularly appealing to people of a certain era. Catalogues, sometimes called consumer guides or *Wish Books*, are also indicators of people's interests. Old photographs, magazines, and newspapers illustrate the activities of our ancestors. Local museums and libraries have materials about the past, and antique stores display artifacts. Parents, grandparents, and others can provide information via interviews.

▼ The Activity

1. **Distribute the page of selected items from the *1897 Sears, Roebuck Catalogue* to pairs of students. Tell students these were items related to water recreation found in the 1897 edition of the catalogue, which is over 700 pages long.** If a copy of the catalogue is available, have students look through the book themselves. Students may also research old newspapers, magazines, and photographs.

2. **Have students read the captions for each item, then place the items in categories such as swimming, fishing, boating, ice-skating.**

3. **Distribute current catalogues. Have students identify items that are related to water recreation and place them in categories.**

4. **Have students compare the categories of past and present water-related activities and answer the following questions:**
- Which categories are common to both past and present?
- Which categories belong to the past but not the present?
- Which categories belong to the present but not the past?
- Which single items are part of the past but not the present?
- Which items appear in the current catalogue but not in the 1897 edition?
- How has technology changed our water-related activities from the past to the present?

▼ Wrap Up and Action

Have students discuss the water needs of present-day recreational users. What are students' opinions of current recreational practices? Discuss reasons why water-related activities and sports have evolved as they have.

Invite individuals who participate in water-related recreational activities to the classroom to discuss their sports with students. Perhaps someone could instruct students in fly tying or demonstrate fly-fishing; scuba shop owners may be willing to discuss scuba diving and certification requirements; contact canoeists to demonstrate their skills. Students can select a particular water-related activity, research it, and demonstrate learned skills to classmates, family, or community members.

Assessment

Have students:
- categorize recreational water uses from the past and present (step 3).
- compare and contrast past and current recreational uses of water (step 4).
- provide reasons for changes in water recreation practices (*Wrap Up*).
- research a water-related sport or activity and report to the class (*Wrap Up*).
- demonstrate the skills of a water-related sport or activity to class, family, or community members (*Wrap Up*).

Upon completing the activity, for further assessment have students:
- survey their school or community to discover popular water-related sports or activities of their area.

Extensions

Have students predict the recreational water uses of people 100 years into the future. They may want to produce a *Wish Book* with illustrations and captions for the year 2090 or beyond. Have them discuss how water users of the future will share the resource and maintain its quality.

Resources

Dodds, John W. 1965. *Everyday Life in Twentieth Century America*. New York, N.Y.: G. P. Putnam's Sons.

🍎 Israel, Fred L. 1993. *1897 Sears, Roebuck Catalogue*. New York, N.Y.: Chelsea House Publishers. (This reproduction of the Sears, Roebuck and Co. Consumers Guide is available from the Museum of the Rockies, Montana State University, Bozeman, MT 59717.)

Jakle, John A. 1985. *The Tourist*. Lincoln, Nebr.: University of Nebraska Press.

Wright, Louis B., and Elaine W. Fowler. 1972. *Everyday Life in the New Nation*. New York, N.Y.: G. P. Putnam's Sons.

1897 Sears, Roebuck Catalogue

McIntosh Wading Pants.

No. 31448. McIntosh Wading Pants, dead grass color, with stocking feet, net lined. Sizes, 5 to 11; weight, 70 oz.
Per pair................**$9.00**
No. 31449. Dull Finish Rubber Wading Pants, on drill, with stocking feet, best quality. Sizes. 5 to 11; weight, 72 oz.
Per pair................ **$5.00**
No. 31450. McIntosh Wading Pants, dead grass color, net lined, with boots, extension edge. Sizes, 5 to 11; weight, 101 oz.
Per pair................**$10.00**

No. 81136. Bathing trunks, fancy colored cotton in stripes, assorted sizes. Per pair................$0.20
No. 81137. Bathing trunks, heavy, fancy colored cotton in stripes, assorted sizes. Each........$0.30

Special Bargains in Bob Sleds.

Our Bob Sleds are made and shipped from Abingdon, Ill., by a concern who have a reputation in this line second to none. The manufacturers of these goods are recognized by all dealers as the makers of the best bobs in the country, and only the best are good enough for us to offer to our trade. We contracted for this line of goods, for the reason that we learned by investigation that nothing but the best of material entered into the construction of this work, that this line of bobs was the best on the market regardless of price.

These Sleighs are all covered by the most binding two years' guarantee, during which time, if any piece or part gives out by reason of defect in material or workmanship, we will replace it free of charge. With care they will last a natural lifetime.

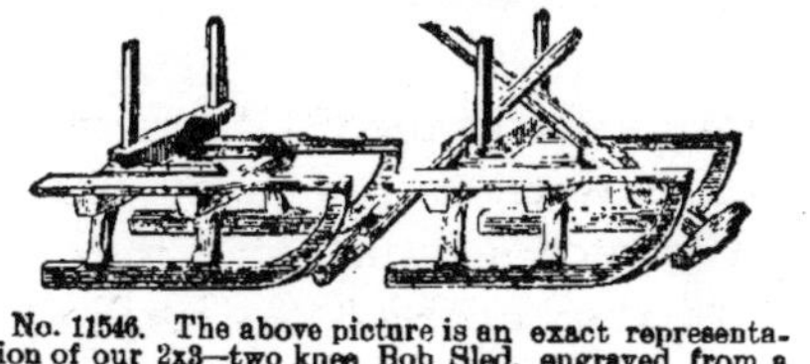

No. 11546. The above picture is an exact representation of our 2x3—two knee Bob Sled, engraved from a photograph.
Our Bobs are made of the very best selected material throughout; best workmanship, painted in four coats vermilion paint, striped, ornamented and varnished.
Our special offer price on the above Bob Sled complete is **$11.90**. Well ironed throughout; complete in every respect.

Ice Skates.

All of our skates are carefully mated, inspected and packed. The material which we use is of the highest grade which can be obtained. Our aim is to retain the reputation of selling superior goods.

We guarantee all our skates to be equal to the very best goods made, and any not proving to be, may be returned to us.

When ordering skates, the best and surest way to obtain the right size skate is to always send us the length of boot or shoe in inches. Below we give the size of skates compared with the sizes of shoes by numbers:
Skates, inches, 7 7½ 8 8½ 9 9½ 10 10½ 11 11½
Number of shoe, 9½ 11 12½ 1 2 4 5½ 7½ 9 10½

No. 14682. This skate runner is made from the best rolled cast steel; plates, clamps, etc., of cold rolled steel, bright finish. The runners are highly polished. The easy work and sure-grip lock-lever will fit large or small boot heels. Always give size of skate wanted in inches when ordering. Sizes 8 to 12 inches. Price, per pair....**25c**

Ladies' Skates.

No. 14648. Ladies' Club Skate, with rolled cast steel polished runners, bright steel toe and heel plates, russet leather straps. Size, from 7 to 10 inches. Always give sizes in inches when ordering. Price per pair......**62c**

THE KOSHKONONG HUNTING SKIFF.

"Sets on the water like a duck."

No. 62288. The celebrated Koshkonong Hunting Boat is without doubt the best in the world, all things considered. Fifteen feet long, three feet beam, cockpit five feet long, two feet wide, pointed at both ends, deck boarded and canvas covered—can walk all over deck. Folding canvas wing around cockpit. Overlocks not fitted, can put on any kind of locks desired. Water and air tight chamber in each end, good in open rough, as well as shallow water. Can not be tipped over, easy rowing, foot rack in bottom, made especially for running easily over grass and weeds, sets low on the water. Capacity, 1,200 to 1,500 pounds. Just what every hunter and fisherman has been looking for; "easy as a rocking chair." Weight about 90 pounds. Boat only................**$22.00**

LIFE PRESERVERS.

No. 81902. "Never Sink," cork jackets, adopted as standard and the government inspector's stamp on each one, and easily put on, durable and has great buoyancy. Weight, 9 pounds;
each..............$ 1.25
Per dozen 13.50
No. 81903. Life belts, in squares, similar to the "Never Sink" and buckles on the same way. One of the best in the market; safe and durable. Weight, 9 pounds; each...........$ 1.10
Per dozen 10.20

Ice Shredder.

The operation of our shredder requires no explanation, being simply to draw the blade upon a piece of ice—the pressure applied producing fine or coarse pieces, as desired. To remove the finely cut ice from the cup, grasp the shredder firmly in the right hand and strike it, inverted, upon the left, at the same time being careful to keep the lid closed. Then scrape the ice into some convenient receptacle. It is not necessary to take the ice out of the refrigerator, as you may reach in and fill the cup from the side, end or top of a cake of ice without disturbing anything or wetting your hands. Its use will be appreciated for fruits, drinks, oysters and clams on the half shell, olives, celery, radishes, iced tea, sliced tomatoes, etc., and for many purposes in the sick room. It is also adapted for use in making "snow balls," which are variously flavored and sold to children on the streets and at their schools, also to the general public at fairs. Men engaged in making "snow balls" are making from $5 to $9 per day.
No. 15475. Price, each, tinned..................**50c**

SPLIT BAMBOO RODS.

Our rods may vary in length from 6 in. to 1 ft. We endeavor to fill orders as ordered.

Our split bamboo rods we wish particularly to call attention to, as they have been selected from the very best we have been able to secure all over the country. Do not judge the quality of the rods by the exceedingly low prices we have them catalogued at, as we are able to obtain these prices by the large quantities we buy and know that all the rods we send out in this line will be a lasting advertisement for us. Our "Split Bamboo" prices are 50 to 100 per cent. lower than the regular retail prices, and any rods not found just as represented can be returned at our expense, provided you do so immediately.

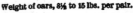

No. 81290. Split and glued bamboo fly rod. Silk-wound rings, with alternate silk wrappings of red and green silk. This rod is one of the best rods we know of in the country for the money. Price, each... ....**$1.05**

WHITE ASH OARS.

Weight of oars, 8½ to 15 lbs. per pair.

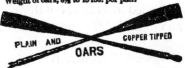

PLAIN AND OARS COPPER TIPPED

COPPER TIPPED ASH OARS.

No. 81878. Length...	6 ft.	6½ ft.	7 ft.	7½ ft.	8 ft.
Per pair	$0.88	$0.94	$1.00	$1.12	$1.20
Length...	8½ ft.	9 ft.	9½ ft.	10 ft.	
Per pair...	$1.25	$1.32	$1.39	$1.46	

PLAIN ASH OARS.

No. 81880. Length...6 ft.	6½ ft.	7 ft.	7½ ft.	8 ft.
Per pair...$0.78	$0.82	$0.88	$0.95	$1.04
Length...8½ ft.	9 ft.	9½ ft.	10 ft.	
Per pair...$1.10	$1.16	$1.19	$1.25	

LANDING NETS.

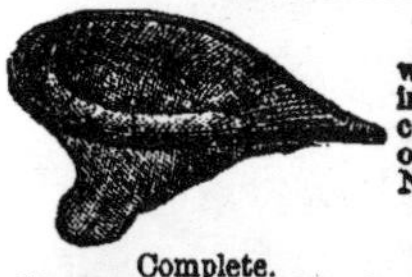

This is a fac-simile of our wooden frame landing net, 12 inch screw-off handle; a very complete and necessary part of a fishing outfit.
No. 81886. Wooden frame landing net with 12 inch handle. Weight, about 3 lbs. Each................85c
Complete.
No. 81838. Wood frame landing net, with 3 foot screw-off handle, complete with net. Weight, about ¾ lb. Each................46c
No. 81840. Landing net, cane bow, wound handle, 6 inch handle, bow 9 inch diameter, complete with net. Each................55c

TROUT BASKETS.

Weight, 1 to 1¾ lbs.

No. 81818. 7½x10¾ inches on back, 70c; capacity 6 lbs.
No. 81820. 7½x12 inches on back, 80c; capacity 9 lbs.
No. 81822. 9x13 inches on back, 96c; capacity 12 lbs.
No. 81824. 9¼x14½ inches on back $1.25; capacity 20 lbs.
No. 81826. 16x16 inches on back, $1.45; capacity 25 lbs.

ARTIFICIAL BAITS.

No. 81728. Bumble bee, cockchafer, beetle, caterpillar, fly-minnow, wasps, blue bottle, lady bird, spider, cricket and house fly; assorted colors. Each......15c.
Grasshopper, small, each................15c.
Grasshopper, large, each................25c.
No. 81730. Frogs, small; soft rubber. Each........20c.
No. 81732. Frogs, large; soft rubber. Each........25c.

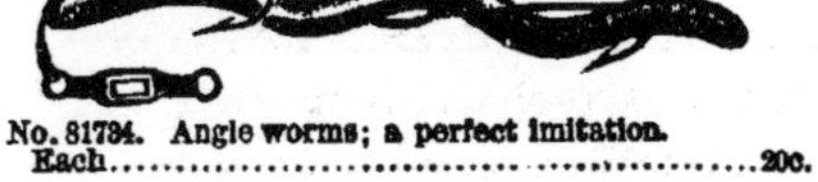

No. 81734. Angle worms; a perfect imitation. Each................ ....20c.

Water Recreation in the Past

Spelunking in an ice cave. COURTESY: LIBRARY OF CONGRESS

Guide and climbers hike to the summit of Mt. Rainier, Washington. COURTESY: LIBRARY OF CONGRESS

Bathers at the beach. COURTESY: COLLECTION OF THE NEW-YORK HISTORICAL SOCIETY

A successful catch! COURTESY: U.S. DEPARTMENT OF INTERIOR

464

Acknowledgments

On behalf of The Watercourse, the Western Regional Environmental Education Council, the Project WET Advisory Council members and staff of Project WET, I would like to thank everyone who contributed to the development and publication of the Project WET Curriculum and Activity Guide.

The following is a list of people and organizations acknowledged for their contributions to Project WET since its inception in 1984.

Dennis Nelson,
Director of Project WET

State of North Dakota

The North Dakota State Water Commission under the leadership of Vern Fahy, Former State Engineer; David Sprynczynatyk, State Engineer, and Gene Krenz, Director of Planning and Education Division, provided the administrative support and funding to develop the original Project WET program. Special thanks are extended to these State Water Commission staff: Bill Sharff (current coordinator of Project WET North Dakota), Lee Klapprodt, Linda Weispfenning, Larry Knudtson, Melissa Miller (former), Brenda Bosworth, Frank Johnson, Milton Lindvig, Steve Pusc, Dave Ripley, Matt Emerson (former), Roy Putz (former), Randy Binegar (former), Tim Fay, Bill Hanson (former), and Jeff Klein. The following people and organizations provided assistance and guidance to Project WET North Dakota during the program's formative years: Robert Heintz, (Former Extension Forester), North Dakota State University; Stanley Griffin, Teacher and Project WET Facilitator; David Jensen, Project WILD Coordinator, North Dakota Game and Fish Department; Ted Upgren, Chief of Interpretation and Education, North Dakota Game and Fish Department; and Mike Dwyer, Executive Director, North Dakota Water Users Association. Special thanks to the Project WET and Project WILD facilitators who conducted hundreds of water education events for thousands of teachers across the state.

The Watercourse (formerly the Western Watercourse)

Special thanks to Susan Higgins, former Associate Director of The Watercourse, for co-leading the development and implementation of Project WET during the program's pilot phase—Susan's steadfast support and enthusiasm for water resources education has been an inspiration; Mary Ellen Wolfe, Coordinator of the Montana Watercourse led Project WET Montana through the program's development years; members of the original Western Watercourse advisory council; Dr. John Amend, Montana State University; Bob Briggs, formerly of the Montana Office of Public Instruction; Gary Fritz, Montana Department of Natural Resources and Conservation; Richard Opper, Missouri Basin States Association; and Dr. Howard Peavey, formerly of Montana State University for their guidance and encouragement to expand Project WET beyond the pilot states.

Montana State University

Montana State University houses and provides administrative support for the national headquarters of Project WET. This support has been critical to the program's development. Specific thanks to Dr. Robert Swenson, Vice President for Research; Gordon Stroh, Director, Grants and Contracts. Dr. Howard Peavy, Former Director of the Montana University System Water Resources Research Center and currently Professor of Civil Engineering at the University of Idaho, and Dr. John Amend, Professor of Chemistry, are acknowledged for their vision in seeing Project WET's potential and for guiding the program's development during its pilot phase (1989-1991). Dr. Peavy and Dr. Amend raised the funds and provided the guidance and support necessary to expand and test the Project WET concept in the three pilot state programs.

Project WET Pilot States

The following people and organizations worked with Project WET to establish the three state pilot programs (1991-1992): Dr. Hanna Cortner, Director, and Larry Sullivan, Associate Director, of the Arizona Water Resources Center; Dr. Howard Peavy; and Dr. Roy Mink, Director of the Idaho Water Resources Research Institute. Pilot state Project WET program coordinators are, in Montana: Greg Smith (former) and Gina Morrison (current); in Idaho: Karla Falter (former) and Dottie Kunz Shuman (current); and in Arizona: Larry Sullivan and Lin Stevens-Moore.

Western Regional Environmental Education Council

Special thanks to Josetta Hawthorne, Executive Director of WREEC for her friendship, guidance, and tireless work on behalf of Project WET; to Rudy Schafer, founder of WREEC, for his vision, leadership, and enduring faith in educators worldwide who deliver Project Learning Tree, Project WILD, and now Project WET, to young people; and to WREEC members Bob Briggs and John Gahl for introducing Project WET to WREEC members in 1991. The following presidents of WREEC provided vision and leadership in helping Project WET during the developmental years: Daphne Sewing (1991), Bob Briggs (1992), John Gahl (1993), Dave Sanger (1994), and Mark Hilliard (1995). Special thanks to the WREEC members who voted to form a partnership with The Watercourse to develop Project WET at their 1991 annual meeting.

Project WET Staff

In 1992 Project WET assembled a team of people to lead the development of the program. The Project WET staff has gone above and beyond the call of duty throughout the development of this program. Special thanks to Sandra Robinson, Jennie Lane, Nancy Carrasco, and Linda Hveem for their limitless energy, professionalism, and enthusiasm.

Project Learning Tree and Project WILD

The outstanding accomplishments of Project Learning Tree and Project WILD programs have been invaluable to the development of Project WET. Special thanks to Kathy McGlauflin, Director of Project Learning Tree, and Betty Olivolo, Director of Project WILD, for their friendship and support, and for their leadership in environmental education.

Regional Writing Workshop Participants (Project WET Crew Members)

Bolded names indicate workshop hosts

MID-ATLANTIC REGION, Smith Lake, Virginia. William Hall, Lewes, DE; Penny Hall, Georgetown, DE; Janet Parsons, Bethany Beach, DE; John Reiher, Wilmington, DE; Venita Bright, Frankfort, KY; Lucian Doyle, Fairdale, KY; Tricia Kerr, Frankfort, KY; Julie Ritchie, Cynthiana, KY; James Roessler, Parksville, KY; Karen Aspinwall, Havre de Grace, MD; Kimberly McPhillips, Baltimore, MD; Joanne Roberts, Owings, MD; Jennifer Smith, Annapolis, MD; Margene Versace, Fallston, MD; Joyce Bland, Beaufort, NC; Nancy Evans, Greenville, NC; Tonya Hancock, Raleigh, NC; Terry Cook, Dyersburg, TN; Mike Edmonds, Gray, TN; Devonda Eiklor, Gray, TN; Patricia Borkey, Mechanicsville, VA; Barry Fox, Petersburg, VA; **Kathy Sevebeck,** Blacksburg, VA; Ann Skalski, Richmond, VA; Karen Snavely, Hartwood, VA; Almetta Hall, Washington DC; Romanita Harrod, Upper Marlboro, MD; Genevieve Bardwell, Mt. Morris, WV; Emily

Graphton, Morgantown, WV; Lesley Klishis, Morgantown, WV; Judy Werner, Morgantown, WV

NORTHCENTRAL REGION, Custer State Park, South Dakota. Ginny Elliott, Tama, IA; Beverly Ellis, Urbandale, IA; Esther Korporal, Osceola, IA; Randi Montag Peterson, Cedar Falls, IA; Letitia Laske, Brainerd, MN; Shannon Arens, Princeton, MN; Karen Vogt, Staples, MN; Jim Olsen, Wayzata, MN; Susan Morse, Havre, MT; Gina Morrison, Bozeman, MT; John Scheuering, Miles City, MT; Laurie Hamilton, Great Falls, MT; Susan Clendenin, Billings, MT; Kristen Gottschalk, Wahoo, NE; Marlene Rasmussen, Litchfield, NE; Shirley Trout, Waverly, NE; Diane Rivers, Omaha, NE; Arlene Hanna, Lincoln, NE; Doris Hartsoch, Minot, ND; Beverly Sandness, Bismarck, ND; Bill Sharff, Bismarck, ND; Ann Hauer, Bismarck, ND; Harriet Howe, Hettinger, ND; Michelle Keller, Bisbee, ND; Stanley Griffin, Oberon, ND; Max Laird, Thompson, ND; Tracy Norman, Aberdeen, SD; Roy Richardson, Pierre, SD; Jerry Siegel, Brookings, SD; Phillip Heubner, Rapid City, SD; Joe Vogler, Cheyenne, WY; Tom Farrell, Cheyenne, WY; Tom Cech, Greeley, CO; Denese Wierzbicki, Billette, WY; Patty Stevens, Cheyenne, WY.

NORTHEAST REGION, Woods Hole, Maine. Sandra Brown, Glastonbury, CT; James Lucey, Easton, CT; Carol Matuszewski, Southbury, CT; Robert Sepanik, Clinton, CT; Don Cass, Bar Harbor, ME; James Chandler, South Paris, ME; Jon Kerr, Islesboro, ME; Judy Markowsky, Orono, ME; Mary Ann McGarry, Machias, ME; Bob Barlow, Yarmouth Port, MA; Leslie Ellis Beaulieu, Beverly, MA; Neil Clark, Boston, MA; Barbara Offenhartz, Acton, MA; Chuck Roth, Newton, MA; Barbara Waters, Barnstable, MA; Karolina Bodner, Barrington, NH; Barbara Fife, Lincoln, NH; Jim McMahon, East Kingston, NH; Carol Plummer, Wolfboro, NH; Warren Tomkiewicz, Plymouth, NH; Karen Bage, Stone Harbor, NJ; Kate Daniels, Cranford, NJ; Paul Daniels, Cranford, NJ; Rachael Salas Didier, Fort Hancock, NJ; Jerry Schierloh, Branchville, NJ; Mary Anderson, Thiells, NY; Karen Edelstein, Ithaca, NY; Laurence Rand, Ellenville, NY; Laura Van Vleet, Ithaca, NY; Jean Devlin, Harrisburg, PA; Rance Harmon, Dingmans Ferry, PA; Sue Taylor, Duncansville, PA; Christine Dudley, West Kingston, RI; Gloria Heltshe, Wakefield, RI; Nancy LaPosta-Frazier, Narragansett, RI; Judith Allard, Burlington, VT; Donald Jarrett, St. Albans, VT

SOUTHWEST REGION, Las Vegas, Nevada. Kristina Allen, Phoenix, AZ; Randy Magie, Chandler, AZ; Dan Smith, Flagstaff, AZ; Linda Stevens-Moore, Phoenix, AZ; Larry Sullivan, Tucson, AZ; Ann Testa, Mesa, AZ; Cindy Cowen, South Lake Tahoe, CA; Christina Gonzales, San Bernardino, CA; Patricia Rutowski, Monterey, CA; Judy Wheatley, Sacramento, CA; Chris Bridges, Denver, CO; John Kaliszewski, Denver, CO; Kimberley Knox, Denver, CO; Donald Maxwell, Colorado Springs, CO; Thomas Chun, Honolulu, HI; Barbara Klemm, Honolulu, HI; Deborah Ward, Hilo, HI; Ann Weaver, Honolulu, HI; Rod Ottenbreit, Billings, MT; Tom Cates, Reno, NV; Cojean Herrin, Reno, NV; Everett Jesse, Carson City, NV; Bob Lawson, Reno, NV; Gini Mitchell, Las Vegas, NV; Janet Parigini, Sparks, NV; Bob Walsh, Boulder City, NV; Arlene Bobelu, Zuni, NM; Jennifer

Huntsberger, Anthony, NM; Kristy Krahl, Santa Fe, NM; Dolores Maez, Cuba, NM; Patty Roberts, Los Alamos, NM; Bonnie Trujillo, Las Vegas, NM; Lynette Ferrell, Syracuse, UT; Jack Greene, Smithfield, UT; Ron Hellstern, Logan, UT; Virginia Jensen, Salt Lake City, UT; Nola Ostraff, Alpine, UT; Rosalee Riddle, Richfield, UT; Barry Wirth, Salt Lake City, UT.

SOUTHEAST REGION, Blackwater, Florida. Jerry deBin, Montgomery, AL; A. Ross Hobbs, Selma, AL; Patti Hurley, Montgomery, AL; Lloyd Scott, Mobile, AL; Terri Todhunter, Maylene, AL; Hazel Wilson, Dauphin Island, AL; Cynthia Clark, Tallahassee, FL; Mary Ann Davis, Tampa, FL; Nancy T. Davis, Panama City, FL; Bob Frease, Melbourne, FL; Julianne Gerlach, Miami, FL; Laura Jodice, Lake City, FL; Roy King, West Palm Beach, FL; David LaHart, Tallahassee, FL; Valerie LaHart, Woodville, FL; David Makepeace, Islamorada, FL; Karen Yanchunis, Dade City, FL; Nancy Cox Beck, Dunwoody, GA; Susan Gannaway, Dahlonega, GA; Elizabeth Lackey, Monticello, GA; Gail Marshall, Lithia Springs, GA; Eleanor Abrams, Baton Rouge, LA; John Trowbridge, Baton Rouge, LA; Laura Beiser, Jackson, MS; Debra Brown, Gulfport, MS; Martha Cooper, Jackson, MS; June Hollis, Brandon, MS; Jeannine May, Pearl, MS; Lynn Slade, Pass Christian, MS; Sharon H. Walker, Ocean Springs, MS; Moises Camacho, Aguadilla, PR; Mildred Joan Guerrero-Griffin, Ponce, PR; Laura Blind, Loris, SC; Julie Cliff, Mt. Pleasant, SC; Garrison Hall, Taylors, SC; Linda McBride, Columbia, SC; Denise Parsick, Beaufort, SC; Margaret Walden, Columbia, SC; Bonnie Stapp, St. Thomas, VI; Gloria Ayot, St. Croix, VI.

SOUTHCENTRAL REGION, Red Rock, Oklahoma. Jeanette Campbell, Billings, MT; Jamye Barnes, Prescott, AR; Beth Carnes, Rogers, AR; Lynne Hehr, Fayetteville, AR; Pat Knighten, Little Rock, AR; Ellen Neaville, Rogers, AR; Gregg Patterson, Little Rock, AR; Lynn Almer, Denver, CO; Don Hollums, Denver, CO; JoNell How, Indian Hills, CO; Jean Palmer-Moloney, Frisco, CO; Sandra Stokley, Denver, CO; Lisa Bietau, Manhattan, KS; Donna Erpelding, Manhattan, KS; Captola Taylor Harris, Kansas City, KS ; Fran Irelan, Manhattan, KS; Susan Krotzinger, Independence, KS; Gail Shroyer, Manhattan, KS; Sue Ellen Lyons, New Orleans, LA; Pam Sanders, Lafayette, LA; Roxson Welch, Baker, LA; Joe Pitts, Jefferson City, MO; Herbert Turner, Waynesville, MO; Rhonda Brooks, Albuquerque, NM; Alice Darilek, Santa Fe, NM; Beth Dillingham, Albuquerque, NM; Gabrielle Reil, Albuquerque, NM; Mary Stuever, Placitas, NM; Todd Carter, Forgan, OK; Carol Erwin, Coweta, OK; Robert Gibbs, Moore, OK; Ted Mills, Stillwater, OK; Lori Painter, Enid, OK; Dan Sebert, Oklahoma City, OK; Pamela Smith-Umsted, Madill, OK; Deidra Wakeley, Tulsa, OK; Brenda Weiser, League City, Texas; Gayla Wright, Moore, OK; Andrea Cantu, Port Aransas, TX; Marilyn Cook, Port Aransas, TX; Bobbye Estes, Austin, TX; Jennifer Houghton, Austin, TX; Robert Jones, Houston, TX; Ann Miller, Austin, TX; Isobel Stevenson, Austin, TX; Pam Stryker, Austin, TX.

GREAT LAKES REGION, Hillsdale, Michigan. Larry Anglada, Zion, IL; Judy Duzan, Hindsboro, IL; Nancy Eskew, Ashmore, IL; Marilyn Lisowski, Charleston, IL; Marty Alenduff, Indianapolis, IN; Jon

Bennett, Bluffton, IN; James Hoffman, Indianapolis, IN; Elvia Solis, Indianapolis, IN; Cynthia Addison, Kalamazoo, MI; Marjane Baker, Livonia, MI; Dave Chapman, Okemos, MI; Steven Fryling, Vicksburg, MI; Diane Cantrell, Columbus, OH; Rosanne Fortner, Columbus, OH; Charlotte Greenfelder, Massillon, OH; Paula Hanely, Cincinnati, OH; Pam Lamkin, Cincinnati, OH; Karen Landis, Columbus, OH; James Morris, Columbus, OH; Jean Morris, Columbus, OH; David Klindienst, State College, PA; Tod McPherson, State College, PA; LeAnn Chase, Port Edwards, WI; Sara Hilgers, Stevens Point, WI; Cindy Halter, Onalaska, WI; Benjamin Senson, Madison, WI; Al Stenstrup, Madison, WI; Suzanne Wade, Madison, WI.

NORTHWEST REGION, Corbett, Oregon. Barbara Braley, Fairbanks, AK; Dale Lackner, Northway, AK; Sassa Peterson, Dillingham, AK; Cynthia Brown, Barrigada, Guam; Mark Hilliard, Boise, ID; Dorothea Kunz Shuman, Moscow, ID; Lori McCollim, Bozeman, MT; Mary Ellen Wolfe, Bozeman, MT; Steve Andrews, Beaverton, OR; Rand Fisher, Portland, OR; Ronald Gaither, Monument, OR; Lin Howell, Beaverton, OR; Mark Jockers, Hillsboro, OR; Marion Rice, Portland, OR; Dan Tilson, Roseburg, OR; Vivienne Torgeson, Salem, OR; Forrest Warren, La Grande, OR; Shann Weston, Portland, OR; Patrick Willis, Hillsboro, OR; Don Wolf, Corvallis, OR; Julie Bradley, Selah, WA; Tom DeVries, Vashon, WA; Rhonda Hunter, Olympia, WA; Kathy Sider, Seattle, WA; Laurie Usher, Bainbridge Island, WA; Robert Halliday, Regina, SA; Dave Jensen, Bismarck, ND.

National Field Test and Review

Special thanks to field test coordinators, educators, and reviewers whose efforts and expertise helped ensure the accuracy and effectiveness of Project WET activities.

Field Test Evaluation Coordinators. Center for Science Education, Western Michigan University: Cynthia Halderson, Research Assistant; Kathleen Kutter, Project Assistant; Dr. Robert Poel, Professor and Director; Kay Shearer, Administrative Assistant. Science and Mathematics Program Improvement (SAMPI), Western Michigan University: Dr. Zoe Barley, Assistant Professor and Co-Director; Dr. Mark Jenness, Senior Research Associate and Co-Director.

Regional Field Test Workshop Coordinators. Mid-Atlantic: Kathy Sevebeck, Virginia Polytechnic Institute and State University; North Central: Gina Morrison, Project WET Montana; Bill Sharff, Project WET North Dakota; Dottie Kunz Shuman, Project WET Idaho; Michael Brody (former), Project WET; Northeast: Warren Tomkiewicz, Plymouth State College; Southwest: Virginia Jensen, Utah Department of Natural Resources; Southeast: Mary Ann Davis, University of South Florida; Southcentral: Gail Shroyer, Kansas State University; Great Lakes: Diane Cantrell, Ohio Department of Natural Resources; and Northwest: Lin Howell, Saturday Academy (Oregon).

Field Test Coordination Team. Zoe Barley, Michael Brody, Diane Cantrell, Mary Ann Davis, Cynthia Halderson, Lin Howell, Mark Jenness, Virginia Jensen, Jennie Lane, Dennis Nelson, Bob Poel, Sandra

Robinson, Kathy Sevebeck, Gail Shroyer, and Warren Tomkiewicz.

Project WET's Expedition Field Scouts (Field Test Educators). John Adamontis, Rosemore Junior High School, Whitehall, OH; Janis A. Adams, Sheridan Elementary, Junction City, KS; Suzy Adams, Prescott Schools, Prescott, WA; Joanne Alex, Stillwater Montessori School, Old Town, ME; Arlene J. Andersen, Pahvant Elementary, Richfield, UT; Cindy Anderson, Amanda Arnold Elementary School, Manhattan, KS; Debbie Anderson, Portland, OR; Randy Andreasen, North Sevier High School, Salina, UT; Rebecca Arenson, Hancock Field Station/OMSI, Fossil, OR; Carolyn Asar, Pieces of Nature, Reynoldsburg, OH; Cynthia Atkinson, 4-H Camp Ohio, St. Louisville, OH; Jennifer Austin, Oxford University School, Oxford, MS; Karen Jane Bailey, Hawthorne, Bozeman, MT; Linda Bair, Lewiston Elementary, Lewiston, UT; Kathy Balan, Mineral City Elementary, Mineral City, OH; Andrea K Balas, Pieces of Nature, Reynoldsburg, OH; Donna Ball, Clear Creek Middle School, Gresham, OR; Betsy Bangley, Wood County Park District, Bowling Green, OH; Deb Barnes, Fort Riley Middle School, Fort Riley, KS; Linda Bass, Avalon Elementary, Columbus, OH; Neil Bauer, Blue Mountain Junior High School, John Day , OR; Penny Baz, Crest Line Elementary, Vancouver, WA; Vern Beeson, Banks High School, Banks, OR; Earl Behrens, Fargo, ND; Jerry Belcher, St. Helens High School, St. Helens, OR; Mindy Bell, Logan High School, Logan, UT; Barb Bennett, Jefferson Elementary, Fort Riley, KS; Kit Bennett, Almo Elementary, Almo, ID; Anne Jex, Benson, Edgemont Elementary, Sandy, UT; Marilyn Bernstein, Ottawa River School, Toledo, OH; Andrea Berrigan, Spotswood Elementary, Harrisonburg, VA; Marilyn Berry, Ware Elementary, Fort Riley, KS; Sheila Berry, Boswell Elementary, Auburndale, FL; William Besaw, Westbrook Middle School, Westbrook, CT; Teresa Bettac, Willis Intermediate School, Delaware, OH; Penny Bettas, Jefferson Elementary School, Pullman, WA; Virginia Bidwell, Christa McAuliffe Elementary School, Woodbridge, VA; Lisa Bietau, Amanda Arnold Elementary School, Manhattan, KS; Deb Bigelow, Knox SWCD, Mt. Vernon, OH; Muffie Bilyeu, Whittier Elementary, Bozeman, MT; Cheryl Birkhimer, Kent State Salem Campus, Salem, OH; Jo Birley, Sifton Elementary School, Vancouver, WA; Carole Bjornson, Griggs County Central, Cooperstown, ND; John Boehm, Centerburg Elementary, Centerburg, OH; Ann L., Bogar, W. Springfield High School , Springfield, VA; Jeanine Boldt, Welches School, Welches, OR; Bob Bordelon, Brooks Elementary School, Brooks, OR; Susan Bosco, Woodrow Wilson Elementary, Manhattan , KS; Lucy G. Bourgeois, Washington Annex, Junction City, KS; Ron Bowerman, Donnell Middle School, Findlay, OH; Phyllis J. Brewer, Smith Elementary, Delaware, OH; Nancy Bridges, Amanda Arnold Elementary, Manhattan, KS; Betsey Brighton, Hardin Middle School, Hardin, MT; Sandee Brown, Hebron Elementary School, Hebron, CT; Suzanne Brown, Loudoun Soil & Water Conservation Dist., Leesburg, VA; Lisa Bruns, La Center Intermediate School, La Center, WA; Cheryl Bryner, Holt Elementary, Clearfield, UT; Warren H. Bucknell, Kennett High School, Conway, NH; Nancy Burritt, Willson, Bozeman, MT; Marlo Byberg, New Rockford Central, New Rockford, ND; Tammy Calhoun, Lake Ridge Middle School, Woodbridge, VA; Kelly Cameron, Columbia River High School, Vancouver, WA; Steve Camp, North Sevier High School, Salina, UT; Ann Cannata, Chief Joseph Middle School, Bozeman, MT; Stephanie Cannon, Woodmoor Elementary, Bothell, WA; Gail Cape, Cheldelin Middle School, Corvallis, OR; Sarah E. Carpenter, OSU Extension Service, Bucyrus, OH; Lisa Carter, Belgrade Intermediate, Belgrade, MT; Ann B. Cayce, Sikes Elementary, Lakeland, FL; Dale Champion, Oakland High School, Oakland, OR; Pam Champion, Scott Lake Elementary, Lakeland, FL; Bernadette Chapman, Murphy Elementary, Haslett, MI; Melissa Charlton, Lacey Spring, VA; Janet Charnley, The Evergreen School, Seattle, WA; Candice Chatfield, Waverly East Intermediate School, Lansing, MI; Emily Chidester, ECO Discovery, Maumee, OH; Joyce Chiotti, Kennedy School, Butte, MT; Randy Christensen, Spring Creek Middle School, Providence, UT; Gail Christianson, Rita Murphy School, Bismarck, ND; Mary K. Clanahan, Pleasant Valley Elementary School, Harrisonburg,VA; Fred Clark, Phoenix High School, Phoenix, OR; Rod Clark, Merrimack High School, Merrimack, NH; Susan Clendenin, Meadowlark, Billings, MT; Mickie Cline, Pickerington Elementary, Pickerington, OH; James Colbert, Winona Junior High, Winona, MS; Barbara Coleman, Fairfield Elementary School, Maumee, OH; Susanne Conijn, Samantha Smith Elementary, Redmond, WA; Mike Cook, Mill City Middle School, Mill City, OR; Robert E. Cooley, Joel P. Jensen, West Jordan, UT; Carol Coombs, Monroe Elementary, Monroe, UT; Faye C. Cooper, The Wildlife Center of Virginia, Weyors Cave, VA; Marilyn Cottle, Harding Gibbs Middle School, Firth, ID; Richard Cox, William Knight Elementary School, Canby, OR; Pat Crandall, Eliot Middle School, Clinton, CT; Linda Crane, Willson, Bozeman, MT; Barbie Crone, Ridgecrest Elementary School, Largo, FL; Roxa Crowe, Irving Elementary, Bozeman, MT; David Dahlberg, Valley View Middle School, Snohomish, WA; Walter Darr, Williston Junior High School, Williston, ND; Franklin Daugherty, Maumee Valley Country Day School, Toledo, OH; Chris Davidson, Fairfield Elementary School, Maumee, OH; MarJean Davis, Loa Elementary, Loa, UT; Randall Davis, Selah Middle School, Selah, WA; W. Kim Davis, West Valley School Dist. #1, Kalispell, MT; Nancy DeBruin, Highland, Sylvania, OH; Kim DeLong, Girl Scouts, Kincheloe, MI; Mary DeLong, Highland View Middle School, Corvallis, OR; Susan DeRuwe, Prescott Schools, Prescott, WA; Diane DeYonker, Agriculture Education Center, Toledo, OH; William J. Dean, Emmett High School, Emmett, ID; Susan Debauche-Markle, OLPH, Toledo, OH; Angelika Decker, Lee Elementary School, Manhattan, KS; Kristin Dickerson, Wilson Elementary, Logan, UT; Christa Dillabaugh, Bexley Middle School, Bexley, OH; Debbie Dixon, Chester, VA; Stella Doak, Fairfield Elementary, Maumee, OH; Barbara Doenecke, Sacajawea Elementary School, Vancouver, WA; Annette Doktor, Marsteller Middle School, Manassas, VA; Margie Donnelly, P. K. Yonge Developmental Research Sch., Gainesville, FL; Franka Drake, St. Patrick's Catholic School, Spokane, WA; Joyce Dresbach, Walnut Elementary, Ashville, OH; Lori Drummond, East Lake High School, Tarpon Springs, FL; Agnes Drzal, Kinawa Middle School, Okemos, MI; Jan Durbin, St. Francis Education Center, Sylvania, OH; Peter Durbin, Blissfield High School, Blissfield, MI; Anne Dutton, Butte View Elementary, Emmett, ID; Diane Ellison, Stewart Elementary, Centerville, UT; Sue Emerine, Wayne Trail Elementary, Maumee, OH; Roland Erikson, Prescott High School, Prescott, WA; Amy M. Evans, Fulks Run Elementary School, Fulks Run, VA; Mary Evans, John R. Graham School, Veazie, ME; Beth Evener, Etna Road Elementary School, Whitehall, OH; Bruce Evener, Robinwood, Whitehall, OH; Lynnette Ferrell, Holt Elementary, Clearfield, UT; Barbara S. Fife, Lin-Wood Public School, Lincoln, NH; Marilyn Fisher, Jackson Elementary, Circleville, OH; Kerry Fitzharris, Northside Elementary, Sandpoint, ID; Amy Lynn Flygare, Chief Joseph Middle School, Bozeman, MT; Beth Foisy, Red Hills Middle School, Richfield, UT; Rick Foster, Azalea Middle School, Brookings, OR; Barry W. Fox, Virginia State University, Coop. Ext., Petersburg, VA; Sharon Freeman, Kalama Elementary School, Kalama, WA; Bev Froemming, Wasco County Union High School, Maupin, OR; Ken Fuller, Estacada High School, Estacada, OR; Kathy Funk-Mills, Columbia River High School, Vancouver, WA; Camille Gambles, Upland Terrace Elementary, Salt Lake City, UT; Holly Gardner, West Linn High School, West Linn, OR; Anne Gariano, John Pattie Elementary, Dumfries, VA; Sandy Garst, Patrick Henry High School, Roanoke, VA; Dennis Garvin, City of Toledo, Div. of Parks & Forestry, Toledo, OH; Sandy Geer, Dorothy Fox Elementary School, Camas, WA; Nancy Geesey, Emily Dickinson Elementary, Bozeman, MT; Virginia George, Bismarck High School, Bismarck, ND; Andrew Gilford, Hancock Field Station, Fossil, OR; Gary Gillespie, Waverly East Intermediate School, Lansing, MI; Kate Gillow-Wiles, Oaklea Middle School, Junction City, OR; Dan Goehring, Meadowdale Middle School, Lynnwood, WA; Jack Greene, Logan High School, Logan, UT; Charlotte Greenfelder, Pfeiffer Middle School, Massilon, OH; Barbara Gries, St. Joseph, Sylvania, OH; Stephanie Griffin, Amanda Arnold Elementary, Manhattan, KS; Jaci Guilford, Cynthia Mann Elementary, Boise, ID; Jodi L. Gwin, Cherry Valley Elementary, Newark, OH; Margaret Hackler, Virginia Cooperative Extension, Palmyra, VA; Mildred Hackler, Jefferson Elementary, Fort Riley, KS; Joan Hackworth, River Grove Elementary School, Lake Oswego, OR; Anna Haffner, Morris Hill Elementary, Fort Riley, KS; Karen Hailey, Fred Lynn Middle School, Woodbridge, VA; Mary Halda, Eisenhower Elementary School, Manhattan, KS; Robbye Hamburgh, Morning Star School, Bozeman, MT; James E. Hamilton, East Derry Memorial, Derry, NH; Barbara C. Hamlin, Milo Elementary School, Milo, ME; Tani Hamm, Kalama Elementary School, Kalama, WA; Doris Hampton, Grandview Elementary, Junction City, KS; Cynthia Hancock, Skyline Soil & Water Conservation Dist., Christiansburg, VA; Melisa Hancock, Woodrow Wilson Elementary, Manhattan, KS; Curt Hanks, Spring Creek Middle School, Providence, UT; Manisha S. Hariani, Roanoke Valley Governor's School, Roanoke, VA; Romanita Harrod, Paul Jr. High School, Washington, DC; Frank Hatcher, Wickliffe Elementary, UpperArlington, OH; Andrea Hayes, Jefferson Elementary, Fort Riley, KS; Stephen Heath, Ashland Middle School, Ashland, NH; Mikell

Hedley, Central Catholic High School, Toledo, OH; Daune Heft, River Oaks Elementary, Woodbridge, VA; Carol A. Heiser, Virginia Dept.of Game & Inland Fisheries, Richmond, VA; Ron Hellstern, North Cache Jr. High, Richmond, UT; Wendy Hellstern, North Park Elementary, Logan, UT; Susan Henry, CC Wells Elementary School, Chester, VA; Ed Henthorn, Parkside Middle School, Manassas, VA; John E. Hermsmeier, Tandem School, Charlottesville, VA; Judy Herr, Whiteford Elementary, Toledo, OH; Macio H. Hill, Jr., Virginia Cooperative Extension, Charlottesville, VA; Eric Hoeppner, Maitland Middle School, Maitland, FL; Suzanne Holland, Hidden Oaks Nature Center, Annandale, VA; Timera Holly, Centerburg Elementary School, Centerburg, OH; Mary Hopkins, Pickerington Elementary, Pickerington, OH; Kim Hosen, Nature's WonderWorld, Woodbridge, VA; Harriet Howe, Hettinger Public School, Hettinger, ND; Sue Hu, Kenmore Middle School, Arlington, VA; Rebecca Huffman, Mt. Clinton Elementary School, Harrisonburg, VA; LaVar Hult, North Park Elementary, Logan, UT; Tim Huntley, Crook County High School, Prineville, OR; Anna Lou Hutchings, Loa Elementary, Loa, UT; Jaclyn Hutchings, Jones Middle School, Upper Arlington, OH; Vera Hylsky, Longfellow Elementary, Idaho Falls, ID; Jann Hypes, Osbourn High School, Manassas, VA; Frances Irelan, Lee Elementary School, Manhattan, KS; Don Iverson, Orting Middle School, Orting, WA; Billie Jagers, Garrettsville, OH; Julie James, Sylvania Northview, Sylvania, OH; Steve James, Mohican School In the Out of Doors, Danville, OH; Scott Jamieson, Lakeside Middle School, Seattle, WA; Sally Jean Jensen, Holderness Central School, Plymouth, NH; Nell Jeschkowski, Selah Middle School, Selah, WA; Laura Jodice, Corvallis, OR; Brad Johnson, Richfield, UT; Barbara Johnson, Elkton Elementary School, Elkton,VA; Candy Johnson, Washington Elementary, Junction City, KS; Marla Jones, Merrimack High, Merrimack, NH; Suzanne Jones, Schoolfield Elementary School, Danville, VA; Laura Kasley, John Marshall Soil & Water Conservation, Warrenton, VA; Janet Kearsley, Island County Education, Coupeville, WA; Susan Keenan-Farrelly, Rundlett Junior High School, Concord, NH; Michelle Keller, Bisbee-Egeland High School, Bisbee, ND; Janet Kellog, Amanda Arnold Elementary School, Manhattan, KS; Emily Kelly, Holderness Central School, Plymouth, NH; Thomas Kemp, Anthony Wayne High School, Whitehouse, OH; Jon Kerr, Isleboro Central School, Islesboro, ME; Paul Kiely, New Durham Elementary, New Durham, NH; Becki Kilkenny, Cornelius Elementary School, Cornelius, OR; Sue Kircher, Osbourn Park High, Manassas, VA; William H. Knee, Londonderry High School, Londonderry, NH; Lorrie Knies, Wintergreen Resort - Outdoor Center, Wintergreen, VA; Joyce Knowles, Longfellow Elementary, Idaho Falls, ID; Marti Kolb, City of Newark, Newark, OH; Craig Kramer, Bexley High School, Bexley, OH; Suzanne Krause, Burnt Bridge Creek Elementary, Vancouver, WA; Mike Krebill, Whitmore Lake Middle School, Whitmore Lake, MI; Marcia Kreinbrink, Whitehouse, OH; Michael E. Kremer, Blake Junior High School, Tampa, FL; Thomas Kwiatkowski, DeVeaux Jr. High School, Toledo, OH; Sallie LaCava, Christa McAuliffe Elementary School, Woodbridge, VA; Nancy Lam, Port Republic Elementary, Port Republic, VA; Linda

Lamkin, Prillaman Spencer-Penn Elementary, Spencer, VA; Phill Lanasa, USDA Forest Service, Harrisonburg, VA; Gerry Landon, Williams Soil & Water Conservation Dist., Bryan, OH; Diana Lanfare, Stranahan Elementary, Toledo, OH; Susan Last, Stewart Elementary, Centerville, UT; Lisa Lawton, Whittier Elementary, Bozeman, MT; Jean Legge, Litchville-Marion High School, Marion, ND; Kert Lenseigne, Canyon Park Junior High School, Bothell, WA; Dawn Lewis, Garfield High School, Woodbridge, VA; Vivian Linden, Chief Joseph Middle School, Bozeman, MT.; Linda Litzkow, P. K. Yonge Developmental Research Sch., Gainesville, FL; Bonnie Lock, La Center Intermediate School, La Center, WA; Tracie Lockhart, Hillcrest Elementary, Logan, UT; Anagene Loebick, Highland East Elementary, Sparta, OH; Ilone D. Long, Edith Bowen Laboratory School, Logan, UT; Dianna Lony, Bennett Woods, Okemos, MI; Jack Lowers, Scio High School, Scio, OR; Joann Lucan, Hardin Intermediate/Hardin Primary, Hardin, MT; David J. Lymanstall, Westside Montessori Center, Toledo, OH; Jane Malatak, King Elementary, Woodbridge, VA; Kristi Manian, Amanda Arnold Elementary, Manhattan, KS; Bonnie Mann, Fairview Magnet School, Roanoke, VA; Carol Matuszewski, Chalk Hill Middle School, Monroe, CT; Susan Maughan, Longfellow Elementary, Idaho Falls, ID; Sherline Maxfield, Monte Vista School, Farmington, UT; Danna May, Oxford University School, Oxford, MS; Julie McBride, Bickleton Elementary School, Bickleton, WA; Lynn McCluskey, Ware Elementary, Fort Riley, KS; Art McEldowney, The High Desert Museum, Bend, OR; Shannon McGinnis, Nocatee Elementary School, Nocatee, FL; Stacy McGarity, Lee Elementary School, Manhattan, KS; Patricia McIlvain, Loudoun Soil & Water Conservation Dist., Leesburg, VA; Emmi McLarty, Sacajawea Elementary School, Vancouver, WA; Earlene F. McLaurin, John Philip Sousa Middle School, Washington, DC; Roz McLean, Outdoor Lab/ Arlington Schools, Arlington, VA; Jim McMahon, East Kingston Elementary, East Kingston, NH; Jim McNulty, Brooksville, FL; Marty McTigue, Worthington Schools Outdoor Educ. Dept., Worthington, OH; Mike Melin, Tahoma High School, Kent, WA; Kathleen Mello, Seminole Middle School, North Seminole, FL; Linda S. Melton, Garfield High School, Woodbridge, VA; Marlex Memmel, Hazelwood Elementary School, Lynnwood, WA; Cathy Mielke, Burr Road Middle School, Wauseon, OH; Eric Mihata, William Knight Elementary School, Canby, OR; Roger Mikota, Burnt Bridge Creek Elementary, Vancouver, WA; Denielle Miller, Morning Star Elementary, Bozeman, MT; Jim Miller, Madison Plans Middle School, London, OH; Rena Mincks, Jefferson Elementary School, Pullman, WA; Diane Mirosh, Selah Middle School, Selah, WA; Frank Mitchell, University of New Hampshire, Durham, NH; Sandy Mitchell, Schoolfield Elementary School, Danville, VA; Jon Miya, Kaysville Junior High, Kaysville, UT; Sharon Miya, Davis High School, Kaysville, UT; Phylis Moore, Amanda Arnold Elementary, Manhattan, KS; JoAnn Morris, Homedale Elementary, Homedale, ID; Pam Morrison, Groveport Madison High School, Groveport, OH; Mary Elizabeth Mund, Lake Pend Oreille High School, Sandpoint, ID; Marcia Nagy, Chase Elementary, Toledo, OH; Robert Neal, Reedsport High School, Reedsport, OR; Pat Nebeker,

Midvalley Elementary, Midvale, UT; Joan Neff, Stone Spring Elementary, Harrisonburg, VA; Debra Nelson, Bottineau High School, Bottineau, ND; Tamara Holmlund Nelson, Snohomish High School, Snohomish, WA; Linda Neth, Groveport Elementary, Groveport, OH; John W. Neth, III, Groveport Madison High School, Groveport, OH; Terridee Newman, La Center Intermediate School, La Center, WA; Ellen Newton, Taylorsville Elementary, Salt Lake City, UT; Jon Noyes, Corvallis, OR; Jim O'Connell, Inza R. Wood Middle School, Wilsonville, OR; Jennifer O'Ryan, Valley View Middle School, Snohomish, WA; Vicki Olsen, Wilson Elementary, Logan, UT; Colleen Osborne, Kennedy Elementary, Butte, MT; Beth F. Osgood, Carpenter School, Wolfeboro, NH; Marcia Ostendorff, Stonewall High School, Manassas, VA; Nola Ostraff, Loranger High School, West Valley City, UT; Carolyn Otto, Lee School, Manhattan, KS; Sue Packer, Wilson Elementary, Logan, UT; Maria Passante, Jared Eliot Middle School, Clinton, CT; Bruce Patterson, Harrison Community Schools, Harrison, MI; Thomas K. Payne, North Sevier Middle School, Salina, UT; Martha J. Peck, Gahanna Middle School, West Gahanna, OH; Teri Peery, Lincoln Elementary, Hyrum, UT; Douglas Pennington, Port Hope High School, Port Hope, MI; Barbara Pepper, Environmental Center, Birmingham, MI; Scott Perkes, North Park Elementary, Logan, UT; Janet Petersen, Lewiston Elementary, Lewiston, UT; Traciann Petite, Custer Hill Elementary, Fort Riley, KS; Linda Pettit, Franklin Soil and Water Conservation, Columbus, OH; Wendy Pierce, Chief Joseph Middle School, Bozeman, MT; Ronald Pilatowski, Thomas Worthington High School, Worthington, OH; Jane Poole, Mill Pond Intermediate School, Yelm, WA; Elizabeth M. Postlewaite, Sedomocha Middle School, Dover-Foxcroft, ME; Nancy Pottroff, Woodrow Wilson Elementary, Manhattan, KS; Douglas L. Poulson, Bingham Middle, Bingham, UT; Kimberly A. Preske, Reston Association, Reston, VA; Katherine T. Ptak, Christ the King Parochial School, Tampa, FL; Vicki Radcliff, New Concord, OH; Ruth Rahla, McKinley School, Toledo, OH; Jeanne Raines, John Wayland Elementary, Bridgewater, VA; Judy Rank, St. Adalbert School, Toledo, OH; Shauna Rasmussen, Red Hills Middle School, Richfield, UT; Ann Regn, Dept. of Environmental Quality, Richmond, VA; David Reichle, Jackson Middle School, Portland, OR; Robyn Reidhead, OMSI, Cascade Science School, Bend, OR; Todd Reighley, Roanoke City Parks and Recreation, Roanoke, VA; Deb Reinke, Richmond, VA; Theresa Reis, Gorrell Elementary, Massillon, OH; Vincent Reis, Greentown Elementary, North Canton, OH; Gladys Remnant, Port Republic Elementary, Port Republic, VA; Kathy Rice, Bend High School, Bend, OR; Rosalie Riddle, Red Hills Middle School, Richfield, UT; Lorraine Ritchie, Anderson Island School, Steilacoom, WA; Claudia Robertson, Woodrow Wilson Elementary School, Manhattan, KS; Jean Robinson, Irving Junior High School, Pocatello, ID; Sharon A. Robinson, Lake Ridge Middle School, Woodbridge, VA; DaNece Robson, Hillcrest Elementary, Logan, UT; Collin Rose, South Sevier High School, Monroe, UT; Stan Rosenblatt, Bolivar, OH; Rita Ross, Amanda Arnold Elementary School, Manhattan, KS; Bruce Rothweiler, Jefferson Elementary School, Port Angeles, WA; Angela Roufs, Corvallis, OR; Pam

Royer, Myrtle Crest Elementary School, Myrtle Point, OR; Carol Runyon, Emily Dickinson Elementary School, Bozeman, MT; Tonya Russell, Southwest Elementary, Lakeland, FL; Kara Sample, Cherry Annex, Toledo, OH; Kathleen Sand, Lopez Elementary School, Lopez Island, WA; Juanita Sattler, Fallen Timbers Middle School, Whitehouse, OH; Deborah P. Scales, Drewry Mason Middle School, Ridgeway, VA; Susan Schenk, Jefferson High School, Portland, OR; Glen Schmidt, Phoenix High School, Phoenix, OR; LeRoy Schultz, Minter Bridge Elementary School, Hillsboro, OR; Yvonne Schultz, USFWS, Mason Neck National Wildlife Ref., Woodbridge, VA; Cindy Seely, City Middle School, Junction City, KS; Beth Seiber, Allen SWCD, Lima, OH; Terry Selby, Philomath High School, Philomath, OR; Patricia Sepanik, Daisy Ingraham School, Westbrook, CT; Stephen F. Seymour, Gackle-Streeter High School, Gackle, ND; Dawn C. Shank, Dept. Of Conservation and Recreation, Richmond, Va; Ann W. Shelton, Schoolfield Elementary School, Danville, VA; Paul Sherman, West Linn High School, West Linn, OR; Krista Shifflett, Lacey Spring, VA; Paige Shiller, Northern VA Soil & Water Conservation, Fairfax, VA; Rachel Simpson, Toledo High School, Toledo, WA; Dennis Slotnick, Clay High School, Oregon, OH; Martha Slover, Garfield Senior High School, Woodbridge, VA; Cindy Smith, Prince William Soil & Water Conservation, Manassas, VA; Hans Smith, Crater High School, Central Point, OR; Pat Smith, Vae View, Layton, UT; Patricia Smith, Sifton Elementary, Vancouver, WA; Sarah Smith, Dale City Elementary, Woodbridge, VA; L. Frank Smith, Jr., Edgemont Elementary, Sandy, UT; Karen Snavely, Gayle Middle School, Falmouth, VA; Jill Snyder, Chiloquin Elementary School, Chiloquin, OR; Rod Snyder, Prairie View, Conrad, MT; Penny Sorrell, Perry Soil and Water Conservation Dist., Somerset, OH; Sue Southwick, Ashman Elementary, Richfield, UT; Jill Spackman, Cedar Ridge Middle School, Hyde Park, UT; Joyce Sparks, Ottawa River Elementary, Toledo, OH; Darrell Spendlove, Lewiston Elementary, Lewiston, UT; Doug Springer, Napavine High School, Napavine, WA; Elizabeth Stagner, Orting School District, Buckley, WA; Pam Stalker, Oscoda Middle School, Oscoda, MI; Allen Stastny, Valley High School, Hazelton, ID; Tina Stephens, Stony Point Elementary, Keswick, VA; Linda D. Stover, Roanoke Valley Governor's School, Roanoke, VA; Janet Struble, Regina Coeli, Toledo, OH; Don Sudweeks, Ashman Elementary, Richfield, UT; Betsy Sullivan, Pearl Junior High, Pearl, MS; Kathleen Sullivan, Spotswood Elementary School, Harrisonburg, VA; Timothy J. Sullivan, Kimball Elementary School, Concord, NH; Timothy Taglauer, Shenandoah National Park, Luray, VA; Jackie Taylor, Holt Elementary, Clearfield, UT; Lisa Terrall, Welches School, Welches, OR; Diane Thompson, Sylvan Elementary, Sylvania, OH; Larry Tibbs, Klamath County 4H Program, Klamath Falls, OR; Scott Torgeson, Clear Lake Elementary School, Keizer, OR; Andrea Trank, University Montessori, Charlottesville, VA; Carol Trimble, Wyandot Run Elementary, Delaware, OH; Bernard G. Tschiderer, Oak Grove Middle School, Clearwater, FL; Kathi Tullis-Grant, Irving School, Bozeman, MT; Debby Turner, Homedale Elementary, Homedale, ID; Debora Tuzzolino, East Detroit High School, Eastpointe, MI; Duane Uusitalo, Meadowdale Middle School, Lynnwood, WA; Kathleen VanSlyke, Lincoln Elementary, Hyrum, UT; Rita M. Vasquez, Baypoint Middle School, St. Petersburg, FL; Sherri T. Vaughn, Willis Elementary, Willis, VA; Lucy Vernile, DeVeaux Jr. High School, Toledo, OH; Elly Veyera, Wy'East Junior High School, Vancouver, WA; Christy Vines, Virginia Cooperative Extension, Charlottesville, VA; Judi Virost, Fairfield Elementary, Maumee, OH; Norm Wachlin, Clear Creek Middle School, Gresham, OR; Connie Walker, Amanda Arnold Elementary, Manhattan, KS; Sandy Wallentine, North Park Elementary, Logan, UT; Margaret Walker, Lee Elementary School, Manhattan, KS; Mary Ann Walsh-Studer, Homeschool, Grand Rapids, OH; Karen Ward, 4-H/Melville School, Springdale, MT; Meg Ward, Sheridan Elementary, Junction City, KS; Jane Watanabe, Bonneville Junior High, Salt Lake City, UT; Kathleen Watts, Capital High School, Olympia, WA; Susan Wayment, Cedar Ridge Middle School, Hyde Park, UT; Mike Weatherby, Kilo Junior High School, Auburn, WA; Denise Wecker-Seipke, The Greening of Detroit, Detroit, MI; Lita Weingart, Lakewood High School, St. Petersburg, FL; Eileen Weinstein, McKinley, Toledo, OH; Myrna Weis, Washington Annex, Junction City, KS; Michele Wendel, Rundlett Junior High School, Concord, NH; Vivian Werner, Jefferson Elementary, Pullman, WA; Barbara Whitaker, Hillcrest Elementary, Logan, UT; Howard Whitten, Nokomis Regional High School, Newport, ME; Tess Wieland, Elmwood School, Lansing, MI; Sandy Wilcox, Byrd Elementary School, Goochland, VA; Kenneth Wild, Cascade Elementary School, Marysville, WA; Nancy Wilkes, Keezletown Elementary, Keezletown, VA; Cindy J. Wilkins, Hanksville Elementary, Hanksville, UT; Kent Wilkinson, West Valley Junior High School, Yakima, WA; Julie Williams, Hillcrest Elementary, Logan, UT; Pat Williams, Boswell Elementary, Polk City, FL; Mary Wills, Lake Ridge Elementary, Woodbridge, VA; Bonnie S. Wilson, Virginia Museum of Natural History, Martinsville, VA; Elizabeth Wilson, St. Patrick's Catholic School, Spokane, WA; Mary Wilson, Chamberlain High School, Tampa, FL; Rebecca Wilson, Avalon Elementary, Columbus, OH; Tara Wilson, Grandview Elementary, Junction City, KS; Terri Wiseman, Parkside Middle School, Manassas, VA; Regina Wohlke, Joel School, Clinton, CT; Linda Wolf, Glencoe High School, Hillsboro, OR; Lorrie Wolverton, Alkali Creek School, Billings, MT; Gretchen Woodhull, Hawthorne, Bozeman, MT; Fred Woods, Scio Middle School, Scio, OR; Dianne Woodward, John Wayland Elementary, Bridgewater, VA; Paula Worley, Jefferson Elementary, Fort Riley, KS; Bill Wysham, Madras High School, Madras, OR; Georgia Yamaki, Chesapeake Bay Foundation, Richmond,VA; Julie Yothers, Hardin SWCD, Kenton, OH; Kathi Jo Young, Eisenhower Elementary School, Junction City, KS; Carol Zimmer, Chief Joseph Middle School, Bozeman, MT; Pat Zwiebel, Flint Northwestern High School, Flint, MI.

Expert Reviewers.

Project WET Crew Members. Eleanor Abrams, Louisiana Sea Grant College Program, Baton Rouge, LA; Cynthia Y. Addison, Kalamazoo Area Math & Science Center, Kalamazoo, MI; Marty Alenduff, Indiana Department of Education, Indianapolis, IN; Judith L. Allard, Burlington High School Science Dept., Burlington, VT; Lynn Almer, Bureau of Reclamation, Denver Office, Denver, CO; Steve Andrews, Beaverton School District, Beaverton, OR; Larry Anglada, Zion Benton Township High School, Zion, IL; Shannon Arens, Princeton Middle School, Princeton, MN; Gloria Ayot, Charles H. Emanual School, St. Croix, VI; Robert J.G. Barlow, Yarmouthport, MA; Jamye S. Barnes, Prescott Middle School, Prescott, AR; Nancy Cox Beck, Chattahoochee River National Recreation Area, Dunwoody, GA; Laura Cook Beiser, MS. Dept. of Environmental Quality, Jackson, MS; Chris Bridges, Water Conservation Board, Denver, CO; Venita Bright, Western Hills High School, Frankfort, KY; Rhonda Brooks, Albuquerque Academy, Albuquerque, NM; Moises Camacho, I.A.U. of Puerto Rico, Aguadilla, PR; Todd Carter, Seward County Community College, Liberal, KS; Tom Cech, Central Colorado Water Conservancy District, Greeley, CO; LeAnn M.L. Chase, Port Edwards Public Schools, Port Edwards, WI; Marilyn Cook, Port Aransas I.S.D., Port Aransas, TX; Terry Cook, Dyersberg Primary School, Dyersburg, TN; Mary Ann Davis, Chamberlain High School, Tampa, FL; Tom DeVries, Vashon Island High School, Vashon, WA; Judy Duzan, Lake Crest Grade School, Hindsboro, IL; Karen Edelstein, Cornell Cooperative Extension, Ithaca, NY; Donna Erpelding, Marlatt Elementary, Manhattan, KS; Carol L. Erwin, West Middle School, Muskogee, OK; Nancy Eskew, Lake Crest Elementary School, Ashmore, IL; Nancy F. Evans, D.H. Conley High School, Greenville, NC; Barbara S. Fife, Linwood Public School, Lincoln, NH; Rosanne Fortner, Ohio State University, Columbus, OH; Barry W. Fox, Virginia Cooperative Extension Service, Petersburg, VA; Steven Fryling, Vicksburg Community Schools, Vicksburg, MI; Susan P. Gannaway, North Georgia College, Dahlonega, GA; Christina Gonzales, North Verdemont Elementary School, San Bernardino, CA; Charlotte Greenfelder, Pfeiffer Middle School, Massillon, OH; Paula Hanley, Career in Teaching Program, Cincinnati, OH; Arlene L. Hanna, University of Nebraska, Lincoln, NE; Rance Harmon, Pocono Environmental Education Center, Dingmans Ferry, PA; Romanita Harrod, Paul Junior High School, Washington, DC; Ann Hauer, Roosevelt School, Bismarck, ND; Ross Hobbs, Byrd Elementary School, Selma, AL; James Hoffman, Indianapolis, IN; Don Hollums, Colorado Department of Education, Denver, CO; JoNell How, Parmalee Elementary, Indian Hills, CO; Harriet T. Howe, Hettinger High School, Hettinger, ND; Tom Hruby, Washington Department of Ecology, Olympia, WA; Jennifer Huntsberger, Gadsden High School, Anthony, NM; Patti Hurley, Alabama Dept. of Environmental Management, Montgomery, AL; Fran Irelan, Lee Elementary School, Manhattan, KS; Virginia Jensen, Utah Division of Water Resources, Salt Lake City, UT; Laurie Jodice, Head Start, Corvallis, OR; John R. Kaliszewski, Colorado Water Conservation Board, Denver, CO; Michelle Keller, Bisbee-Egeland High School, Bisbee, ND; Lisa Knauf, Oklahoma Conservation Commission, Oklahoma City, OK; Esther Korporal, Clarke Community School, Osceola, IA; Lucretia Krantz, Wildfowl Trust of North America, Grasonville, MD; Dorothea Kunz Shuman, Idaho Water Resources Research Institute, Moscow, ID; Nancy LaPosta-Frazier, Wickford

Middle School, North Kingstown, RI; Max Laird, Community High School, Grand Forks, ND; Karen Landis, Hamilton Alternative Elementary School, Columbus, OH; Marylin Lisowski, Eastern Illinois University, Charleston, IL; Sue Ellen Lyons, Holy Cross High School, New Orleans, LA; Randy Magie, Sirrine Elementary, Chandler, AZ; Judy Markowsky, Parks, Rec. & Tourism Prgm., So. Annex B, Orono, ME; Carol Matuszewski, Chalk Hill Middle School, Monroe, CT; Donald E. Maxwell, Biological Sciences Curriculum Study, Colorado Springs, CO; Jeannine May, USDA Soil Conservation Service, Pearl, MS; Lori McCollim, Bozeman School District #7, Bozeman, MT; Terry Messmer, Department of Fisheries & Wildlife, Logan, UT; Ann Miller, Lake Travis Middle School, Austin, TX; Gini Mitchell, ST&P Building, Suite 207, Las Vegas, NV; Randi Montag Peterson, University of Northern Iowa, Cedar Falls, IA; Jean B. Morris, Columbus, OH; Gina Morrison, Project WET Montana, Bozeman, MT; Lori Painter, Monroe Elementary School, Enid, OK; Jean Palmer-Moloney, Summit High School, Frisco, CO; Janet M. Parsons, Indian River School District, Bethany Beach, DE; Joe Pitts, Missouri Department of Natural Resources, Jefferson City, MO; Marlene Rasmussen, Litchfield Public Schools, Litchfield, NE; Gabriele Reil, Moriarty High School, Moriarty, NM; Julie M. Ritchie, Harrison County High School, Cynthiana, KY; Patty Roberts, Los Alamos National Laboratory, Los Alamos, NM; John Scheuering, Garfield Elementary School, Miles City, MT; Jerry T. Schierloh, Montclair State College, Branchville, NJ; Lloyd Scott, Mobile County Public School System, Mobile, AL; Dan Sebert, Oklahoma Conservation Commission, Oklahoma City, OK; Benjamin J Senson, James Madison Memorial High School, Madison, WI; Kathy Sevebeck, VA Water Resources Research Center, Blacksburg, VA; Anne Skalski, VA Dept. of Game & Inland Fisheries, Richmond, VA; Dan Smith, J.Q. Thomas Elementary School, Flagstaff, AZ; Pamela Smith-Umsted, Milburn Elementary, Coleman, OK; Karen Snavely, T. Benton Gayle Middle School, Falmouth, VA; Patty Stevens, Laramie County School District #1, Cheyenne, WY; Lin Stevens-Moore, Water Resources Research Center, Tucson, AZ; Sandy Stokely, Ellis Elementary, Denver, CO; Sue Taylor, Hollidaysburg Area Senior High, Hollidaysburg, PA; Captola Taylor, Harris Central Middle School, Kansas City, KS; Ann Testa, City of Mesa, Water Conservation Office, Mesa, AZ; Vivienne Torgeson, Governor's Watershed Enhancement Board, Salem, OR; Shirley Trout, Trout Communications, Waverly, NE; John Trowbridge, Louisiana State University, Baton Rouge, LA; Margene Versace, Deerfield Elementary School, Edgewood, MD; Joe Vogler, Wyoming Game & Fish Department, Cheyenne, WY; Deidra Wakeley, Edison Middle School, Tulsa, OK; Deborah J. Ward, Univ. of Hawaii, Cooperative Extension Service, Hilo, HI; Barbara S. Waters, Cape Cod Cooperative Extension, Barnstable, MA; Ann B. Weaver, University of Hawaii,, College of Education, Honolulu, HI; Judy Wheatley, Water Education Foundation, Sacramento, CA; Denese Wierzbicki, Alternative Transitional Center, Gillette, WY; Don Wolf, Lawrence, KS.

WREEC Members. Steve Andrews, C. E. Mason School, Beaverton, OR; Bob Ellis, Utah Division of Wildlife Resource, Salt Lake City, UT; CeCe Forget,

U.S. Environmental Protection Agency Region VIII, Denver, CO; John Gahl, Idaho Fish and Game Department, Boise, ID: Mark Hilliard, Bureau of Land Management, Boise, ID; Don Hollums, Colorado Department of Education, Denver, CO; June McSwain, Associate WREEC member, Arlington, VA; Gini Mitchell, Nevada Cooperative Extension, Las Vegas, NV; Dave Sanger, Nevada Department of Wildlife, Reno, NV; Rudy Schafer, founder of WREEC, Sacramento, CA; Vivienne Torgeson, Oregon Water Resource Department, Salem, OR; Bob Warren, School of Education, Liberal Arts and Science, University of Alaska, S.E., Juneau,AL.

Project WET State Coordinators. Chris Bridges, Colorado Water Conservation Board, Denver, CO; Virginia Jensen, Department of Natural Resources, Salt Lake City, UT; Rosanna Long, Department of Environmental Protection, Charleston, WV; Philip Osborne, Schools Coordinator, Little Rock, AR; Peder Otterson, Department of Natural Resources, Division of Water, St. Paul, MN; Dottie Kunz Shuman, University of Idaho, Moscow, ID; Judy Wheatley, Water Education Foundation, Sacramento, CA.

Other Education Specialists. Ralph Baldwin, Romig Junior High School, Anchorage, AK; Ray DePriest, Colony Middle School, Palmer, AK; Trisha Herminghaus, O'Malley Elementary School, Anchorage, AK; John Koutsky, Houston Junior/ Senior High School, Big Lake, AK; Lori Koutsky, Iditarod Elementary School, Wasilla, AK; Kellie Marie Litzen, Alaska Department of Natural Resources, Division of Water, Anchorage, AK; Sue Perin, Project WET Idaho Workshop Coordinator, Moscow, ID; Collin Smith, Scenic Park, Anchorage, AK; Heidi Solper, Project WILD state coordinator, AZ; Peg Stout, Baxter Elementary School, Anchorage, AK; Jim Sumner, Indian, AK.

Expert Content Reviewers. Paul Azevedo, Project Manager, The Montana Watercourse, Bozeman, MT (Geology); Amy Bender, Science Consultant, Berrien County Intermediate School District, Berrien Springs, MI, (Chemistry); Steve Brewer, Doctoral Student; Science Studies, Western Michigan University, Kalamazoo, MI, (Biology/Ecology); Jo Brunner, Montana State Water Chairperson, Power, MT, (Watershed Management/Hydrology); Katherine Caputo, Key Largo School, Key Largo, FL (Primary Education); Chris Cauble, Falcon Press, Helena, MT, (Journalism/Writing); Dr. Dean Cooke, Department of Chemistry, Western Michigan University, Kalamazoo, MI, (Chemistry); Dr. Stan Derby, Department of Physics, Western Michigan University, Kalamazoo, MI, (Physics); Dr. Joseph Engemann, Biological Sciences Department, Western Michigan University, Kalamazoo, MI, (Biology/Ecology); Deby Everton, Ventura, CA (Primary Education); Barbara Glillespie-Washington, Wiley School, Urbana, IL (Primary Education); Dr. Joe Heimlich, University Extension; Ohio State University, Columbus, OH, (Resource Management/Community Planning); Barbara Hudson, Department of Microbiology, Montana State University, Bozeman, MT, (Pathology/Epidemiology); Rick Hutchinson, Yellowstone National Park, Old Faithful, WY, (Earth Science); Dr. Alan Kehew, Department of Geology, Western Michigan

University, Kalamazoo, MI (Water Quality); David J. Kinsey, Policy Analyst, Air Division, Department of Environmental Quality, Richmond, VA (Meteorology/Climatology); Dr. Martha Kronholm, Elementary Teacher, Wisconsin Rapids, WI (Assessment); Tina Laidlaw, Winchester, VA, (Water Quality); Joe Moreland, District Chief; U. S. Geological Survey, Helena, MT (Earth Science); Doug Plasencia, Flood Plain Planning, Department of Conservation and Recreation, Richmond, VA (Disaster/Risk Assessment); Dr. Don Powers, Elementary Education, Western Illinois University, Macomb, IL, (Physical Science); Sandra Reiger, Monroe Elementary School, Enid, Oklahoma (Primary education) Bonnie Sachatello-Sawy, Museum of the Rockies, Bozeman, MT (Culture/Anthropology); Lynn Scalia, Willson Science and Technical School, Bozeman, MT (Primary Education Consultant); Paul Schullery, Yellowstone National Park, Yellowstone National Park, WY (Social Science/History); Dan Sivek, Wisconsin Center for Environmental Education; University of Wisconsin—Stevens Point, Stevens Point, WI (Environmental Action); Dr. Marian Smith, Department of Geology, Western Michigan University, Kalamazoo, MI (Earth Science); Anne Sullivan, Bozeman High School, Bozeman, MT (Debate); Andrea Swanson, Plover Creek Center, Northfield, MN (Primary education); Dr. Robert A. Thomas, Vice President for Environmental Policy, Audubon Institute in New Orleans, New Orleans, LA (Wetlands); John Thorson, Arizona Stream Adjudication, Phoenix, AZ (Law/Politics); Mary Ellen Wolfe, The Montana Watercourse, Montana State University, Bozeman, MT (Social Science/History); Douglas Wood, Trails, Nitro, WV (Resource Management/Community Planning).

Reviewers of the Guide's Front and Back Materials. Dr. Diane Cantrell, Office of Public Information and Education, Ohio Department of Natural Resources, Columbus, OH; Cynthia Halderson, Center for Science Education, Western Michigan University, Kalamazoo, MI; Josetta Hawthorne, Western Regional Environmental Education Council, Houston, TX; Dr. Mark Jenness, Center for Science Education, Western Michigan University, Kalamazoo, MI; Virginia Jensen, Department of Natural Resources, Division of Water Resources, Salt Lake City, UT; Kathryn Sevebeck, College of Forestry and Wildlife Resources, Virginia Polytechnic Institute and State University, Blacksburg, VA.

Final Reviewers. Judy Braus, Director of Environmental Education, World Wildlife Fund; Josetta Hawthorne, Executive Director, Western Regional Environmental Education Council; Debra Nickerson, Educator, Tumwater, Washington; Dr. John Paulk, Executive Director, Global Network for Environmental Education Centers and Former Manager, International Programs Network, Tennessee Valley Authority; Dr. Robert Raze, Office of Environmental Education, Florida Department of Education; Dr. Rick Wilke, Associate Dean of the College of Natural Resources and Director of the National Environmental Education Advocacy Project, University of Wisconsin-Stevens Point; and Debra Wood, Educator, Yelm, Washington.

Project WET Curriculum Framework

The Project WET Curriculum Framework consists of three major areas: conceptual, affective, and skills. The framework is based on current educational research, water-related curricula, and national education reform efforts. It incorporates key concepts related to learning about water and water resources.

Conceptual Framework

Water has unique physical and chemical characteristics.

• The water molecule has a specific structure.

• The structure of the water molecule gives water characteristic properties.

• The properties of water lead to unique chemical and physical behaviors.

Water is essential for all life to exist.

• Chemical processes of life occur in a water solution.

• Life processes are based on water quality.

• Life processes are based on water quantity.

• Water is a limiting factor of life.

Water connects all Earth systems.

• Water is an integral part of Earth's structure.

• Water plays a unique role in Earth processes.

• The water cycle is central to all Earth systems.

Water is a natural resource.

• Water resources are based on supply.

• Water resources are used by all living things.

• Multiple uses of water can lead to water resource issues.

Water resources are managed.

• Water resources are managed by individuals and communities of people.

• Water resource management sets objectives based on needs and issues.

• Water resource management develops strategies to resolve issues.

• Water management effectiveness is determined by assessing progress toward expected outcomes.

Water resources exist within social constructs.

• Water resource use has changed over time.

• Water resources have value based on economic systems.

• Water resources are governed through political systems.

Water resources exist within cultural contexts.

• Different cultures often express different beliefs about water.

• Cultural beliefs about water resources change over time.

• Cultural beliefs about water vary within a society.

• Cultures express their connections to water through art, music, language, and customs.

• Various cultures influence our understanding of water resources.

Affective Framework

NOTE: The following affective components of water education are interrelated; they are not necessarily listed in sequential order. People's attitudes and values are constantly evolving; classifying them and placing them in discrete categories can be difficult. The categories listed below are based on arrangements presented by various professional environmental educators (Caduto 1985; Engleson 1994; Marcinkowski 1993).

• People's awareness of and sensitivity toward water and water-related concepts and issues.

• People's attitudes (opinions, likes, dislikes) toward water and water-related concepts and issues.

• People's values (consideration of worth, need to cherish, importance) toward water and water-related concepts and issues.

• People's behavior toward and expression of water and water-related concepts and issues, influenced by awareness and sensitivity, attitudes, and values.

References

Caduto, M. 1985. *A Guide on Environmental Values Education*. UNESCO-UNEP International Environmental Education Program, Environmental Education Series, no. 13. Paris, France: UNESCO.

Engleson, D. 1994. *A Guide to Curriculum Planning in Environmental Education*. Madison, Wis.: Wisconsin Department of Public Instruction.

Marcinkowski, T. 1993. "Assessment in Environmental Education." In *Environmental Education: Teacher Resource Handbook*. R. Wilke, ed. Millwood, N.Y.: Kraus International Publications.

Skills Framework

Following is a list of thinking and process skills utilized when learning about water and water-related concepts and issues. The skills listed are based on those advocated by the Association for Supervision and Curriculum Development and the American Association for the Advancement of Science.

The organization of skills is based on the scientific method of investigation and Bloom's Taxonomy of cognitive thinking skills. The structure is logical and efficient for identifying skills within the Project WET activities. The first four skill areas involve learning, assimilating, and processing information. The last three pertain to applying information, evaluating, and presenting results. While learning often progresses in the order in which the levels are presented, this sequence will vary in certain situations.

• *Gathering information* includes: reading, observing, listening, collecting, researching, interviewing, measuring, computing, calculating, recording.

• *Organizing information* includes: matching, plotting data, graphing, sorting, arranging, sequencing, listing, classifying, categorizing, estimating, mapping, drawing, charting, manipulating materials.

• *Analyzing information* includes: identifying components and relation-

ships among components, identifying patterns, comparing, formulating questions, contrasting, discussing.

• *Interpreting information* includes: generalizing, summarizing, translating, relating, inferring, making models, drawing conclusions, defining problems, identifying cause and effect, confirming.

• *Applying learned information* includes: planning, designing, building, constructing, composing, experimenting, restructuring, inventing; predicting, hypothesizing, proposing solutions; problem solving, decision making, developing and implementing investigations and action plans.

• *Evaluating application of learned information* includes: establishing criteria, verifying, testing, assessing, and critiquing results.

• *Presenting evidence of learning from application and evaluation processes* includes: demonstrating, writing, drawing, describing, public speaking, reporting, persuading, debating.

COURTESY: EVERGLADES NATIONAL PARK

Development of Project WET Activities

Regional Writing Workshops

The Project WET staff conducted writing workshops from September 1992 through April 1993. Over 300 educators, resource managers, and specialists from all fifty states, the District of Columbia, the U.S. territories, and Canada were selected by their peers to participate in one of eight regional workshops. Participants, called *Crew Members*, gathered at sites in the following states: Virginia, South Dakota, Massachusetts, Nevada, Florida, Oklahoma, Michigan, and Oregon. Mindful of their states' curriculum guidelines and local water issues, educators generated interdisciplinary activities based on concepts they considered critical for inclusion in a water education curriculum. Guided by the Project WET activity format, participants produced more than 500 activities.

Activity Writing and Development Process

Ideas and activities created by the writing workshop participants were consolidated and organized according to the curriculum framework, and refined by Project WET staff. Researchers gathered resources and contacted consultants in water resource management, natural and physical sciences, and other content areas to supplement background information. During activity development, procedures were tested and the activities were analyzed for content. After preliminary drafts were edited and proofread, the activities were field-tested.

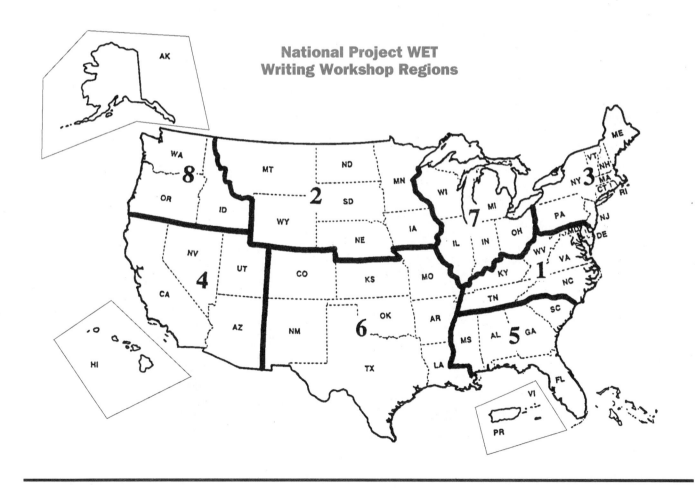

National Project WET Writing Workshop Regions

National Fieldtest and Review

Fieldtest and Review Team Western Michigan University and Project WET

Activities in this guide were "tested" in a variety of classrooms and other educational settings, and they were reviewed by recognized content experts and practitioners from many fields. Results were analyzed and the activities were revised.

The national fieldtest and expert review were conducted by science educators and program evaluators from the Western Michigan University Center for Science Education and Science and Mathematics Program Improvement (Kalamazoo, Michigan). The evaluation consisted of a two-step process: 1) gathering information from classroom teachers, nonformal educators, and recognized experts and practitioners regarding the appropriateness, "teachability," and accuracy of the fieldtest versions of the activities and 2) compiling and analyzing data. The Project WET staff applied the information to revise and strengthen the activities.

Participants in the fieldtest and expert review included:

- 399 classroom teachers

- 63 nonformal educators

- 140 environmental educators (Crew Members, WREEC members, State Project WET coordinators, and eight Alaska educators)

- 32 content expert reviewers

- 7 final reviewers

These reviewers came from 45 states, the District of Columbia, Puerto Rico, and the Virgin Islands.

Fieldtest and Review Process

Educators from across the country conducted fieldtests of 104 activities and provided feedback. Each fieldtester, called an *Expedition Field Scout*, participated in one of eight regional fieldtest workshops and received five lessons, appropriate to grade level, to conduct and evaluate. Using a 20-item evaluation form, they responded to activity use, format and content, and effectiveness. A sample of teachers was also asked to have their students complete an evaluation of selected activities. Regional *Fieldtest Coordinators* organized the workshops and the distribution and retrieval of "tested" activities.

Classroom Teachers Fieldtest

In all, 399 teachers fieldtested the Project WET activities. Who were these teachers and their students?

- They came from 15 states and the District of Columbia.

- They were evenly divided among rural, suburban, and urban districts.

- They represented grades pre-kindergarten through twelve.

- The teachers' classroom experience ranged from 1 to 45 years: 1-5 years (86); 6-15 years (157); 16-25 years (127); more than 25 years (27); No response (2).

- The teachers rated their own knowledge about water and water-related topics as a 4.0 on a 5-point scale; they rated their familiarity with water education programs as 3.7.

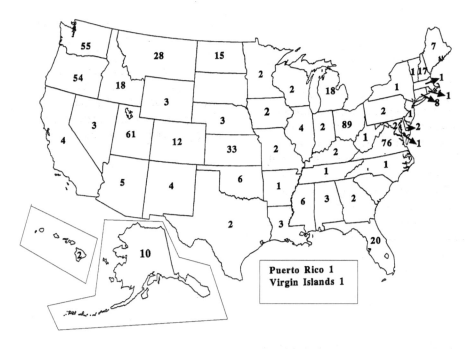

Fieldtesters and Reviewers

- Approximately 34,000 students from 2,051 classes participated in the fieldtest. The group was about equally divided between females and males.

- About 180 teachers indicated their classes were made up of more than 25 percent nonwhite students; 74 of the classes were made up of more than 50 percent nonwhite students.

Nonformal Educators Fieldtest

Sixty-three nonformal educators also taught and reviewed Project WET activities. Twenty-one were from nature, outdoor, or environmental education centers; 13 from soil and water conservation districts; 8 from universities or cooperative extension services; and 6 from 4-H clubs. In addition, three home-school educators fieldtested activities. The remaining nonformal educators represented a variety of city, state, and national organizations. Many taught the activities in school classrooms, but several taught in less formal settings.

Environmental Educator Review

Project WET Crew Members (from the original writing teams), WREEC members, state Project WET coordinators, and other environmental educators from across the United States also had an opportunity to review and provide feedback on the activities. One hundred forty reviewers each completed between one and five activity feedback forms.

Content Review

Content reviewers from universities, museums, government agencies, and schools were asked to examine the content of the activities for accuracy and thoroughness, and to evaluate lesson procedures, graphics, and resources. Twenty-six experts received activities pertinent to their fields of study: chemistry, physics, life science, pathology, wetlands, earth science, meteorology, hydrology, natural resource management, social studies, anthropology, law and politics, assessment, environmental action, and writing. For several activities, **K–2 Options** were written and reviewed. The **K–2 Options** present alternate, more concrete approaches to concepts for kindergarten through second-grade students. Highly recommended K–2 teachers were selected to review these options.

Final Review

A final review was conducted by respected environmental and science educators from around the country, to evaluate the cohesiveness and efficacy of the entire guide. Reviewers based their assessments on the needs of educators in specified categories, including formal education, nonformal education, preservice education, in-service education, and water resource management.

Compilation and Data Analysis

Quantitative and qualitative data from 2,759 activity evaluation forms were compiled and analyzed. From this information, 312 separate reports—three for each activity reviewed—were prepared, representing feedback from classroom teachers and nonformal educators, Crew Members, and environmental education specialists. Additionally, 100 reports were prepared, based on student feedback. Survey responses from the content and final reviewers were analyzed individually to evaluate and revise the activities to which they applied.

Use of Fieldtest Results and Review to Revise Activities

Results of the fieldtest were used to confirm or to correct designated grade levels, subject areas, and durations for the activities. In addition, teachers' responses and suggestions were used to rewrite activities. Special attention was given to any concerns about safety, cultural bias, excessive time requirements, or difficulty obtaining materials. Content reviews were used to fortify the accuracy of the background and conceptual information of the activities. Following the revisions of the activities, objectives were checked to ensure that each was addressed within the activity. Assessment strategies were amended to reflect any revised objectives.

Continuing Evaluation of Activities' Effectiveness

A full report of the fieldtest and review has been prepared and is available from the Project WET office upon request. The Project WET staff will continue to review and revise activities as it receives feedback from educators, students, and others concerning the "usability" of the activities.

The developers of this guide appreciate the efforts of the more than one thousand formal and nonformal educators and resource managers from around the country and U.S. territories who helped ensure the accuracy, effectiveness, usefulness, and appeal of these activities.

Meeting Standards

As societies are further influenced by technological, social, political, and economic changes, the need grows for responsible and effective science and environmental education programs. Goals 2000, a national strategy to "build a nation of learners," defines the challenges and calls on everyone to work toward providing sound education for all children. In response to this call, local, state, and national efforts are underway to develop standards, guidelines, and frameworks for realizing important educational goals. These standards set levels of conceptual understanding and skill attainment that all students are expected to meet.

At the national level, standards for specific content areas have been developed or are being developed, such as *Benchmarks for Science Literacy* from the American Association for the Advancement of Science, Project 2061, and *Standards for School Mathematics* from the National Council of Teachers of Mathematics.

In most states, curriculum frameworks exist or are being designed to incorporate national standards. These frameworks set goals and describe learning expectations, thereby helping local districts develop high-quality curricula that meet the needs of their students. Educators are encouraged to select and use teaching materials that will help students meet these goals.

Project WET used appropriate standards, such as the *Benchmarks for Science Literacy*, in developing activities. For example, the activity "Molecules in Motion" specifically addresses physical science benchmarks related to the structure of matter. "Irrigation Interpretation" addresses the benchmarks for the technological system of agriculture, specifically the relationship between irrigation and crop production. (See *Using Project WET Activities to Meet Standards*, below.)

Subsequently, as teachers develop and/or implement curricula designed for their classrooms, schools, and districts, they will find Project WET activities appropriate and effective in helping to meet goals and objectives. (See *Using Project WET Activities to Supplement an Existing Curriculum* on page 477.) Project WET encourages educators to select activities from the *Project WET Curriculum and Activity Guide* to meet national educational standards and local curricula expectations, in order to "build a nation of learners."

Using Project WET Activities to Meet Standards

Project WET activities can be used or adapted to address the objectives or standards within the scope and sequence of existing education programs. Following is an example showing selected objectives for Science Literacy* and the Project WET activities that address them.

K-2

Observing things can help you learn about your environment ("Stream Sense")

Living things need water, food, air and light ("The Life Box")

3-5

Heating and cooling causes changes in the properties of materials ("Molecules in Motion")

Gravity pulls objects, including water, towards Earth's center ("wAteR in moTion")

6-8

Many substances dissolve in water ("What's the Solution")

Animals and plants have diverse physical appearances and behaviors that help them retain and/or live in water ("Water Address")

9-12

The chemical composition of the water molecule determines its

JENNIE LANE

properties ("Hangin' Together")

How data is presented often influences how it is interpreted and accepted ("Super Bowl Surge")

adapted from the Benchmarks for Science Literacy

Using Project WET Activities to Supplement an Existing Curriculum

Following are examples of how Project WET activities can be used to help meet the objectives of a social studies or health curriculum.

Selected objectives for Social Studies and Project WET activities that address them.

K-2

The geographic characteristics of a land area form connections between home, school, and community ("Rainy-Day Hike")

People have similarities and differences of opinion regarding water resources, and people can learn from each other in many ways ("Idea Pools")

3-5

Past events influence contemporary communities, and information about communities can be obtained from many sources ("Water Crossings")

Community members are dependent upon each other for many goods and services ("Water Works")

6-8

Location and availability of resources influence how people manage these resources ("Pass the Jug")

Aspects of culture are influenced by geographical features, including climate ("The Rainstick")

9-12

Managing water resource issues involves critically analyzing information to consider all sides of the issue ("Perspectives")

The rights and responsibilities of citizens should be carefully considered and presented in a logical manner ("Water Bill of Rights")

Selected objectives for Health and Project WET activities that address them.

K-2

Water is an important nutrient for our bodies ("Aqua Bodies")

We have five senses that help us observe our environment ("Stream Sense")

3-5

Healthy habits help prevent the spread of disease ("No Bellyachers")

Individuals and communities can contribute to or prevent water pollution ("A-maze-ing Water")

6-8

The diffusion of water through our cells helps transport nutrients ("Let's Even Things Out")

Water quality is related to health through drinking water ("The Pucker Effect")

9-12

Waterborne diseases are caused by a variety of microorganisms and exhibit a variety of symptoms ("Super Sleuths")

Water-related issues can affect individuals and global communities within both the short-term and long-term time frames ("Whose Problem Is It?")

Cross Reference and Planning Charts

Following is a series of charts containing further information about activities, to assist with activity selection and unit planning.

Topics

Subject Areas

Time Required

Grade Levels

Setting

Teaching Methods

Topics

Activity	Physical Properties	Water Cycle	Ground Water	Surface Water — General	Surface Water — Watershed	Surface Water — Wetlands	Atmospheric — Weather	Atmospheric — Climate	Health
Adventures in Density (25)	▼								
AfterMath (289)				▼					
A-maze-ing Water (219)				▼					▼
Aqua Bodies (63)									▼
Aqua Notes (66)									▼
Back to the Future (293)				▼					
Branching Out! (129)					▼				
Capture, Store, & Release (133)					▼	▼			
The CEO (300)									
Check It Out! (3)				Depends on activity					
Choices & Preferences . . . (367)									
Cold Cash in the Icebox (373)	▼								
Color Me a Watershed (223)					▼				
Common Water (232)									
Dilemma Derby (377)									
A Drop in the Bucket (238)			▼	▼					
Dust Bowls . . . (303)				▼			▼		
Easy Street (382)									
Energetic Water (242)	▼								
Every Drop Counts (307)									
Get the Ground Water . . . (136)			▼						
Geyser Guts (144)			▼						
A Grave Mistake (311)			▼						
The Great Stony Book (150)				▼					
Great Water Journeys (246)				▼					
H₂Olympics (30)	▼								
Hangin' Together (35)	▼								
Hot Water (388)									
A House of Seasons (155)							▼	▼	
Humpty Dumpty (316)						▼			
Idea Pools (7)				Depends on activity					
Imagine! (157)		▼							
The Incredible Journey (161)		▼							
Irrigation Interpretation (254)				▼					
Is There Water on Zork? (43)	▼								
Just Passing Through (166)				▼					
Let's Even Things Out (72)	▼								▼
Let's Work Together (9)				Depends on activity					
The Life Box (76)									▼
Life in the Fast Lane (79)						▼			
The Long Haul (260)									
Macroinvertebrate . . . (322)									
Molecules in Motion (47)	▼								
Money Down the Drain (328)									
Nature Rules! (262)							▼		
No Bellyachers (85)									▼

Topics (cont.)

Natural Resource					Water History	Management				Activity
Uses Historic	Current	Misc.	Issues Point	Non-Point		General	Quality	Conservation	Career	
										Adventures in Density
		▼				▼				AfterMath
			▼	▼			▼			A-maze-ing Water
										Aqua Bodies
										Aqua Notes
		▼				▼			▼	Back to the Future
										Branching Out!
										Capture, Store, & Release
		▼				▼			▼	The CEO
		Depends on activity								Check It Out!
	▼									Choices & Preferences . . .
▼										Cold Cash in the Icebox
		▼				▼			▼	Color Me a Watershed
▼	▼	▼						▼		Common Water
	▼	▼				▼				Dilemma Derby
										A Drop in the Bucket
▼		▼				▼				Dust Bowls & Failed Levees
▼								▼		Easy Street
	▼					▼				Energetic Water
								▼		Every Drop Counts
		▼					▼		▼	Get the Ground Water . . .
										Geyser Guts
			▼		▼		▼		▼	A Grave Mistake
										The Great Stony Book
		▼			▼					Great Water Journeys
										H$_2$Olympics
										Hangin' Together
		▼				▼				Hot Water
										A House of Seasons
		▼				▼			▼	Humpty Dumpty
		Depends on activity								Idea Pools
										Imagine!
										The Incredible Journey
▼		▼				▼		▼		Irrigation Interpretation
										Is There Water on Zork?
						▼				Just Passing Through
										Let's Even Things Out
		Depends on activity								Let's Work Together
										The Life Box
										Life in the Fast Lane
▼	▼							▼		The Long Haul
				▼			▼		▼	Macroinvertebrate Mayhem
										Molecules in Motion
		▼						▼		Money Down the Drain
		▼			▼					Nature Rules!
										No Bellyachers

Activity	Physical Properties	Water Cycle	Ground Water	Surface Water General	Surface Water Watershed	Surface Water Wetlands	Atmospheric Weather	Atmospheric Climate	Health
Old Water (171)				▼					
Pass the Jug (392)									
People of the Bog (89)						▼			
Perspectives (397)									
Piece It Together (174)								▼	
Poetic Precipitation (182)	▼						▼		
Poison Pump (93)									▼
The Price Is Right (333)									
The Pucker Effect (338)			▼						
Raining Cats and Dogs (435)									
The Rainstick (442)							▼		
Rainy-Day Hike (186)					▼				
Reaching Your Limits (344)									
Salt Marsh Players (99)						▼			
Sparkling Water (348)									
Stream Sense (191)				▼					
Sum of the Parts (267)				▼					
Super Bowl Surge (353)									
Super Sleuths (107)									▼
Thirsty Plants (116)	▼	▼							
The Thunderstorm (196)							▼		
Water: Read All . . . (400)									
Water Actions (12)									
Water Address (122)				▼					
Water Bill of Rights (403)									▼
Water Celebration (446)									
Water Concentration (407)									
Water Court (413)									
Water Crossings (421)				▼					
wAteR in moTion (450)	▼								
Water Log (19)				Depends on activity chosen					
Water Match (50)	▼								
Water Messages . . . (454)									
Water Meter (271)									
Water Models (201)	▼	▼						▼	
Water Works (274)									
Water Write (457)									
Wet Vacation (206)							▼	▼	
Wet-Work Shuffle (360)									
Wetland Soils . . . (212)						▼			
What's Happening? (425)									
What's the Solution? (54)	▼								
Where Are the Frogs? (279)	▼								
Whose Problem Is It? (429)									
Wish Book (460)									

| Natural Resource | | | | | Water History | Management | | | | Activity |
| Uses | | Misc. | Issues | | | General | Quality | Conser-vation | Career | |
Historic	Current		Point	Non-Point						
					▼					Old Water
▼		▼				▼				Pass the Jug
										People of the Bog
		▼				▼				Perspectives
										Piece It Together
										Poetic Precipitation
					▼					Poison Pump
						▼			▼	The Price Is Right
							▼		▼	The Pucker Effect
	▼									Raining Cats and Dogs
					▼					The Rainstick
			▼	▼			▼			Rainy-Day Hike
							▼		▼	Reaching Your Limits
										Salt Marsh Players
						▼	▼		▼	Sparkling Water
										Stream Sense
				▼			▼			Sum of the Parts
		▼					▼		▼	Super Bowl Surge
										Super Sleuths
										Thirsty Plants
						▼				The Thunderstorm
	▼	▼								Water: Read All About It!
	▼	▼				▼			▼	Water Actions
										Water Address
	▼					▼				Water Bill of Rights
					▼					Water Celebration
▼	▼	▼				▼				Water Concentration
						▼				Water Court
					▼					Water Crossings
										wAteR in moTion
				Depends on activity						Water Log
										Water Match
					▼					Water Messages in Stone
	▼							▼		Water Meter
										Water Models
	▼				▼				▼	Water Works
	▼									Water Write
									▼	Wet Vacation
						▼			▼	Wet-Work Shuffle
										Wetland Soils . . .
	▼	▼								What's Happening
										What's the Solution?
				▼						Where Are the Frogs?
		▼				▼				Whose Problem Is It?
▼	▼									Wish Book

Subject Areas

Activity	Fine Arts	Language Arts	History/Anthropology	Geography	Government	Math	Earth	Physical	Life	Environmental	Ecology	Health
			Social Studies				Science					
Adventures in Density (25)		▼						▼				
AfterMath (289)		▼			▼	▼				▼		
A-maze-ing Water (219)										▼		▼
Aqua Bodies (63)						▼			▼			▼
Aqua Notes (66)	▼								▼			▼
Back to the Future (293)					▼	▼	▼			▼		
Branching Out! (129)				▼			▼					
Capture, Store, & Release (133)				▼			▼				▼	
The CEO (300)		▼								▼		
Check It Out! (3)					Depends on activity							
Choices & Preferences . . . (367)					▼	▼				▼		
Cold Cash in the Icebox (373)			▼			▼		▼				
Color Me a Watershed (223)			▼			▼				▼	▼	
Common Water (232)			▼							▼		
Dilemma Derby (377)					▼					▼		
A Drop in the Bucket (238)				▼		▼	▼					
Dust Bowls . . . (303)		▼	▼	▼						▼		
Easy Street (382)		▼	▼			▼				▼		
Energetic Water (242)			▼					▼		▼		
Every Drop Counts (307)		▼			▼	▼				▼		
Get the Ground . . . (136)					▼	▼	▼			▼	▼	
Geyser Guts (144)				▼			▼					
A Grave Mistake (311)			▼	▼			▼			▼		
The Great Stony Book (150)							▼					
Great Water Journeys (246)			▼	▼			▼					
H₂Olympics (30)						▼		▼				
Hangin' Together (35)								▼				
Hot Water (388)		▼			▼					▼		
A House of Seasons (155)	▼						▼					
Humpty Dumpty (316)					▼					▼	▼	
Idea Pools (7)					Depends on activity							
Imagine! (157)	▼	▼					▼		▼		▼	
The Incredible Journey (161)							▼				▼	
Irrigation Interpretation (254)			▼	▼						▼		
Is There Water on Zork? (43)								▼				
Just Passing Through (166)							▼			▼	▼	
Let's Even Things Out (72)								▼	▼			
Let's Work Together (9)					Depends on activity							
The Life Box (76)									▼			
Life in the Fast Lane (79)							▼		▼		▼	
The Long Haul (260)			▼			▼				▼		
Macroinvertebrate . . . (322)							▼			▼	▼	
Molecules in Motion (47)								▼				
Money Down the Drain (328)						▼				▼		
Nature Rules! (262)		▼	▼		▼					▼		
No Bellyachers (85)									▼			▼

484

Activity	Fine Arts	Language Arts	History/ Anthropology	Geography	Government	Math	Earth	Physical	Life	Environmental	Ecology	Health
			Social Studies				Science					
Old Water (171)	▼		▼			▼	▼					
Pass the Jug (392)			▼		▼					▼		
People of the Bog (89)			▼						▼		▼	
Perspectives (397)					▼					▼		
Piece It Together (174)		▼	▼	▼			▼				▼	
Poetic Precipitation (182)		▼					▼					
Poison Pump (93)			▼						▼			▼
The Price Is Right (333)					▼	▼				▼		
The Pucker Effect (338)				▼			▼			▼		▼
Raining Cats and Dogs (435)	▼	▼	▼	▼								
The Rainstick (442)	▼		▼	▼								
Rainy-Day Hike (186)				▼			▼			▼		
Reaching Your Limits (344)					▼	▼				▼		▼
Salt Marsh Players (99)	▼	▼									▼	
Sparkling Water (348)										▼		▼
Stream Sense (191)	▼	▼					▼					
Sum of the Parts (267)		▼			▼					▼		
Super Bowl Surge (353)					▼					▼		▼
Super Sleuths (107)				▼					▼			▼
Thirsty Plants (116)						▼			▼			
The Thunderstorm (196)		▼					▼					
Water: Read All About It! (400)		▼								▼		
Water Actions (12)	Depends on activity											
Water Address (122)		▼		▼					▼		▼	
Water Bill of Rights (403)			▼		▼							
Water Celebration (446)	Depends on activity											
Water Concentration (407)	▼	▼	▼							▼		▼
Water Court (413)					▼					▼		
Water Crossings (421)		▼	▼	▼								
wAteR in moTion (450)	▼		▼						▼			
Water Log (19)	Depends on activity											
Water Match (50)									▼			
Water Messages . . . (454)	▼		▼									
Water Meter (271)						▼				▼		▼
Water Models (201)				▼			▼	▼			▼	
Water Works (274)					▼					▼		
Water Write (457)	▼	▼										
Wet Vacation (206)	▼	▼		▼			▼					
Wet-Work Shuffle (360)					▼					▼		▼
Wetland Soils . . . (212)							▼				▼	
What's Happening? (425)		▼			▼					▼		
What's the Solution? (54)								▼				
Where Are the Frogs? (279)									▼	▼	▼	▼
Whose Problem Is It? (429)					▼					▼		
Wish Book (460)		▼	▼									

KEY:
I = Time to conduct Part I of activity
 (if there is no II listed, then the activity only has one part)
II = Time to conduct Part II of activity
 (if there is no III listed, then the activity only has two parts)
III = Time to conduct Part III of activity
OI = Time to conduct Option I of activity
OII = Time to conduct Option II of activity

Activity	30 minutes or less	50 minutes or less	100 minutes or less	Three hours or less	Several days	Up to one week	Extended time period
Adventures in Density (25)		I, II					
AfterMath (289)		I					
A-maze-ing Water (219)	OI				OII		
Aqua Bodies (63)	I, II, III						
Aqua Notes (66)	I						
Back to the Future (293)	I	II					
Branching Out! (129)			I				
Capture, Store, & Release (133)		I, II					
The CEO (300)					I		
Check It Out! (3)	Depends on activity						
Choices & Preferences (367)		I					
Cold Cash in the Icebox (373)		I					
Color Me a Watershed (223)	OI	OII, OIII					
Common Water (232)		I					
Dilemma Derby (377)		I					
A Drop in the Bucket (238)	I						
Dust Bowls . . . (303)	Depends on activity						
Easy Street (382)	II	I					
Energetic Water (242)	Depends on activity						
Every Drop Counts (307)						I	
Get the Ground Water . . . (136)	I, II	III					
Geyser Guts (144)	I, II						
A Grave Mistake (311)		I					
The Great Stony Book (150)							I
Great Water Journeys (246)		I					
H₂Olympics (30)			I				
Hangin' Together (35)	I, III	II					
Hot Water (388)			I				
A House of Seasons (155)		I					
Humpty Dumpty (316)		OI, OII					
Idea Pools (7)	I						
Imagine! (157)	I						
The Incredible Journey (161)			I				
Irrigation Interpretation (254)	III	I					II
Is There Water on Zork? (43)		I, II					
Just Passing Through (166)	I, II, III						
Let's Even Things Out (72)		I					
Let's Work Together (9)	Depends on activity						
The Life Box (76)		I					
Life in the Fast Lane (79)		II				I	
The Long Haul (260)		I					
Macroinvertebrate . . . (322)		I, II					
Molecules in Motion (47)		I					
Money Down the Drain (328)		I					
Nature Rules! (262)				I			

Activity	30 minutes or less	50 minutes or less	100 minutes or less	Three hours or less	Several days	Up to one week	Extended time period
No Bellyachers (85)	I, II						
Old Water (171)			I				
Pass the Jug (392)	I, II						
People of the Bog (89)							I
Perspectives (397)		I	II				
Piece It Together (174)	I, II, III						
Poetic Precipitation (182)	I	II					
Poison Pump (93)		I					
The Price Is Right (333)		I					
The Pucker Effect (338)			I				
Raining Cats and Dogs (435)		I					
The Rainstick (442)						I	
Rainy-Day Hike (186)		I, II					
Reaching Your Limits (344)		I					
Salt Marsh Players (99)		I					
Sparkling Water (348)	II		I				
Stream Sense (191)			I				
Sum of the Parts (267)		I					
Super Bowl Surge (353)	I						
Super Sleuths (107)		I				II	
Thirsty Plants (116)	I	II					
The Thunderstorm (196)	I	II					
Water: Read All About It! (400)						I	
Water Actions (12)			Depends on activity				
Water Address (122)		I					
Water Bill of Rights (403)			I				
Water Celebration (446)			Part I: 50 minutes; Part II: Depends on activity				
Water Concentration (407)	II	I					
Water Court (413)		I	II				
Water Crossings (421)		I	II				
wAteR in moTion (450)	I, II		III				
Water Log (19)							I
Water Match (50)	II	I					
Water Messages . . . (454)		I					
Water Meter (271)						I	
Water Models (201)			I				
Water Works (274)		I					
Water Write (457)			Depends on activity				
Wet Vacation (206)		I				II	
Wet-Work Shuffle (360)		I					
Wetland Soils . . . (212)		I	II				
What's Happening? (425)			Depends on activity				
What's the Solution? (54)		I					
Where Are the Frogs? (279)	I, III						II
Whose Problem Is It? (429)		I					
Wish Book (460)		I					

KEY:
LE=Lower Elementary (K-2)
UE=Upper Elementary (3-5)
MS=Middle School (6-8)
HS=High School (9-12)
(KO)=K-2 Option provided (K-2 Options provide alternate, more concrete approaches to illustrate concepts for kindergarten through second-grade levels.)

*Grade levels indicated in the activity were determined by the results of the national fieldtest. Based upon the individual educator's assessment of students' understanding, activities may be adapted for the span of grade levels referenced in this chart.

Activity	K-2 LE	3-5 UE	6-8 MS	9-12 HS
Adventures in Density (25)		▼	▼	▼
AfterMath (289)		▼	▼	
A-maze-ing Water (219)	▼	▼	▼	
Aqua Bodies (63)	▼	▼		
Aqua Notes (66)	▼	▼		
Back to the Future (293)		▼	▼	▼
Branching Out! (129)	KO		▼	
Capture, Store, & Release (133)		▼		
The CEO (300)				▼
Check It Out! (3)	▼	▼		
Choices & Preferences (367)	KO		▼	▼
Cold Cash in the Icebox (373)	▼	▼		
Color Me a Watershed (223)				▼
Common Water (232)	KO	▼	▼	
Dilemma Derby (377)			▼	▼
A Drop in the Bucket (238)	KO	▼	▼	▼
Dust Bowls . . . (303)				▼
Easy Street (382)		▼	▼	▼
Energetic Water (242)	▼	▼	▼	
Every Drop Counts (307)			▼	
Get the Ground Water . . . (136)			▼	▼
Geyser Guts (144)		▼	▼	
A Grave Mistake (311)			▼	▼
The Great Stony Book (150)			▼	
Great Water Journeys (246)			▼	▼
H₂Olympics (30)		▼	▼	
Hangin' Together (35)		▼	▼	▼
Hot Water (388)				▼
A House of Seasons (155)	▼			
Humpty Dumpty (316)		▼	▼	
Idea Pools (7)	▼	▼	▼	▼
Imagine! (157)		▼	▼	
The Incredible Journey (161)		▼	▼	
Irrigation Interpretation (254)	KO	▼	▼	
Is there Water on Zork? (43)		▼	▼	▼
Just Passing Through (166)		▼	▼	
Let's Even Things Out (72)		▼	▼	▼
Let's Work Together (9)	▼	▼	▼	▼
The Life Box (76)	▼	▼		
Life in the Fast Lane (79)		▼	▼	▼
The Long Haul (260)	KO	▼	▼	▼
Macroinvertebrate . . . (322)		▼	▼	
Molecules in Motion (47)	▼	▼	▼	
Money Down the Drain (328)		▼	▼	
Nature Rules! (262)			▼	▼

Activity	LE	UE	MS	HS
No Bellyachers (85)		▼	▼	
Old Water (171)		▼	▼	
Pass the Jug (392)	KO	▼	▼	▼
People of the Bog (89)			▼	▼
Perspectives (397)			▼	▼
Piece It Together (174)		▼	▼	
Poetic Precipitation (182)	KO	▼	▼	
Poison Pump (93)		▼	▼	
The Price Is Right (333)				▼
The Pucker Effect (338)			▼	▼
Raining Cats and Dogs (435)		▼	▼	▼
The Rainstick (442)		▼	▼	▼
Rainy-Day Hike (186)	KO	▼	▼	
Reaching Your Limits (344)		▼	▼	
Salt Marsh Players (99)		▼		
Sparkling Water (348)		▼	▼	▼
Stream Sense (191)	▼	▼	▼	
Sum of the Parts (267)		▼	▼	
Super Bowl Surge (353)			▼	▼
Super Sleuths (107)			▼	▼
Thirsty Plants (116)			▼	
The Thunderstorm (196)	▼	▼	▼	▼
Water: Read All About It! (400)			▼	▼
Water Actions (12)			▼	▼
Water Address (122)	KO	▼	▼	▼
Water Bill of Rights (403)		▼	▼	
Water Celebration (446)		▼	▼	
Water Concentration (407)		▼	▼	
Water Court (413)				▼
Water Crossings (421)		▼	▼	▼
wAteR in moTion (450)	KO	▼	▼	
Water Log (19)	▼	▼	▼	▼
Water Match (50)	▼	▼		
Water Messages . . . (454)		▼	▼	
Water Meter (271)		▼	▼	
Water Models (201)		▼	▼	
Water Works (274)		▼	▼	
Water Write (457)	▼	▼		▼
Wet Vacation (206)			▼	▼
Wet-Work Shuffle (360)	KO	▼	▼	▼
Wetland Soils . . . (212)		▼	▼	▼
What's Happening? (425)	KO	▼	▼	▼
What's the Solution? (54)		▼	▼	
Where Are the Frogs? (279)			▼	
Whose Problem Is It? (429)			▼	▼
Wish Book (460)			▼	▼

488

Setting

The following lists identify activities that require special settings. Activities not listed can be adapted for a variety of settings (indoor or outdoor).

Activities that involve use of lab equipment

Adventures in Density, A Drop in the Bucket, Energetic Water, The Great Stony Book, Hangin' Together, Is There Water on Zork?, People of the Bog, Sparkling Water, The Pucker Effect, H₂Olympics, What's the Solution?, Where Are the Frogs?

Activities that use cards or pieces of paper that might blow away outdoors

A House of Seasons, Poison Pump, Raining Cats and Dogs, Super Sleuths, Water Address, Water Concentration, Water Match, Wet-Work Shuffle

Activities that require a large playing space

A-maze-ing Water, Just Passing Through, Incredible Journey, Life in the Fast Lane, The Long Haul, Molecules in Motion, No Bellyachers, Poetic Precipitation, Reaching Your Limits, Salt Marsh Players, The Thunderstorm, Water Celebration, Water Works

Activities that must be conducted outdoors

Common Water, Irrigation Interpretation, Life in the Fast Lane, The Long Haul, Rainy-Day Hike, Stream Sense, Thirsty Plants, Wetland Soils in Living Color

Activities that involve students going out into the community

Perspectives, Water: Read All About It!, Water Actions, Water Celebration, Water Meter, What's Happening?, The CEO

Teaching Methods

Activity	Whole-body	Hands-on	Art form	Inquiry	Reading	Writing	Calcu-lations	Record data	Graph/map
Adventures in Density (25)		▼			▼			▼	
AfterMath (289)	▼						▼	▼	▼
A-maze-ing Water (219)	▼	▼							
Aqua Bodies (63)			▼				▼		
Aqua Notes (66)	▼		▼			▼			
Back to the Future (293)							▼		▼
Branching Out! (129)		▼		▼		▼		▼	
Capture, Store, & Release (133)		▼							
The CEO (300)							▼	▼	
Check It Out! (3)				Depends on activity					
Choices & Preferences . . . (367)				▼			▼	▼	▼
Cold Cash in the Icebox (373)		▼		▼				▼	
Color Me a Watershed (223)							▼		
Common Water (232)		▼							
Dilemma Derby (377)				▼					
A Drop in the Bucket (238)							▼		▼
Dust Bowls . . . (303)					▼	▼			
Easy Street (382)				▼	▼		▼	▼	
Energetic Water (242)		▼		▼					
Every Drop Counts (307)	▼	▼	▼				▼	▼	▼
Get the Ground Water . . . (136)	▼			▼			▼		▼
Geyser Guts (144)									
A Grave Mistake (311)								▼	
The Great Stony Book (150)		▼						▼	
Great Water Journeys (246)					▼	▼			▼
H₂Olympics (30)		▼		▼				▼	
Hangin' Together (35)		▼	▼						
Hot Water (388)				▼	▼				
A House of Seasons (155)		▼	▼						
Humpty Dumpty (316)		▼		▼					
Idea Pools (7)				▼		▼			
Imagine! (157)			▼			▼			
The Incredible Journey (161)	▼			▼		▼		▼	▼
Irrigation Interpretation (254)	▼	▼						▼	▼
Is There Water on Zork? (43)		▼		▼				▼	
Just Passing Through (166)	▼								
Let's Even Things Out (72)	▼			▼					
Let's Work Together (9)				Depends on activity					
The Life Box (76)				▼					
Life in the Fast Lane (79)	▼	▼		▼		▼		▼	
The Long Haul (260)	▼				▼	▼	▼		
Macroinvertebrate . . . (322)	▼						▼	▼	
Molecules in Motion (47)	▼								
Money Down the Drain (328)							▼	▼	
Nature Rules! (262)						▼			
No Bellyachers (85)	▼						▼	▼	

Debate	Role-play	Simula-tion	Model	Game	Experi-ment	Research	Demon-stration	Large group	Small group	Activity
					▼				▼	Adventures in Density
	▼							▼		AfterMath
		▼		▼		▼		▼	▼	A-maze-ing Water
						▼			▼	Aqua Bodies
								▼		Aqua Notes
▼									▼	Back to the Future
			▼					▼	▼	Branching Out!
			▼						▼	Capture, Store, & Release
		▼				▼			▼	The CEO
				Depends on activity						Check It Out!
▼								▼	▼	Choices & Preferences, Water Index
		▼			▼				▼	Cold Cash in the Icebox
		▼						▼	▼	Color Me a Watershed
		▼						▼		Common Water
▼								▼	▼	Dilemma Derby
							▼	▼	▼	A Drop in the Bucket
						▼		▼	▼	Dust Bowls & Failed Levees
								▼	▼	Easy Street
			▼				▼	▼	▼	Energetic Water
		▼						▼	▼	Every Drop Counts
			▼					▼	▼	Get the Ground Water Picture
		▼	▼				▼	▼		Geyser Guts
		▼						▼	▼	A Grave Mistake
		▼	▼					▼	▼	The Great Stony Book
				▼		▼		▼	▼	Great Water Journeys
					▼				▼	H$_2$Olympics
	▼	▼							▼	Hangin' Together
▼						▼		▼	▼	Hot Water
									▼	A House of Seasons
		▼				▼			▼	Humpty Dumpty
▼						▼		▼	▼	Idea Pools
			▼					▼		Imagine!
		▼		▼				▼		The Incredible Journey
		▼			▼	▼		▼	▼	Irrigation Interpretation
					▼			▼		Is There Water on Zork?
		▼						▼		Just Passing Through
		▼						▼		Let's Even Things Out
				Depends on activity						Let's Work Together
								▼		The Life Box
		▼		▼		▼		▼	▼	Life in the Fast Lane
		▼				▼		▼		The Long Haul
		▼				▼		▼		Macroinvertebrate Mayhem
		▼						▼		Molecules in Motion
		▼				▼		▼	▼	Money Down the Drain
						▼			▼	Nature Rules!
		▼		▼				▼		No Bellyachers

Teaching Methods (cont.)

Activity	Whole-body	Hands-on	Art form	Inquiry	Reading	Writing	Calcu-lations	Record data	Graph/map
Old Water (171)			▼				▼		
Pass the Jug (392)									
People of the Bog (89)		▼		▼				▼	
Perspectives (397)				▼					
Piece It Together (174)					▼				▼
Poetic Precipitation (182)	▼				▼	▼			
Poison Pump (93)					▼				▼
The Price Is Right (333)							▼		▼
The Pucker Effect (338)		▼		▼				▼	▼
Raining Cats and Dogs (435)					▼	▼			
The Rainstick (442)		▼	▼						
Rainy-Day Hike (186)				▼				▼	▼
Reaching Your Limits (344)	▼								
Salt Marsh Players (99)	▼		▼			▼			
Sparkling Water (348)		▼		▼				▼	
Stream Sense (191)		▼	▼	▼		▼		▼	
Sum of the Parts (267)		▼	▼	▼		▼			
Super Bowl Surge (353)	▼				▼	▼			
Super Sleuths (107)								▼	
Thirsty Plants (116)		▼					▼	▼	
The Thunderstorm (196)	▼	▼			▼		▼	▼	
Water: Read All About It! (400)		▼		▼	▼				
Water Actions (12)	Depends on activity								
Water Address (122)				▼	▼	▼			
Water Bill of Rights (403)						▼			
Water Celebration (446)	▼	▼	▼			▼			
Water Concentration (407)				▼	▼	▼			
Water Court (413)				▼	▼	▼			
Water Crossings (421)		▼		▼	▼	▼			
wAteR in moTion (450)		▼	▼						
Water Log (19)		▼		▼	▼	▼	▼	▼	
Water Match (50)									
Water Messages in Stone (454)		▼	▼						
Water Meter (271)							▼	▼	▼
Water Models (201)		▼	▼			▼			▼
Water Works (274)		▼			▼	▼			
Water Write (457)					▼	▼			
Wet Vacation (206)			▼					▼	
Wet-Work Shuffle (360)					▼				
Wetland Soils . . . (212)		▼						▼	
What's Happening? (425)				▼	▼	▼	▼	▼	▼
What's the Solution? (54)		▼		▼					
Where Are the Frogs? (279)	▼	▼		▼			▼	▼	
Whose Problem Is It? (429)				▼	▼			▼	
Wish Book (460)						▼			

492

Teaching Methods (cont.)

Debate	Role-play	Simulation	Model	Game	Experiment	Research	Demonstration	Large group	Small group	Activity
						▼		▼		Old Water
	▼	▼						▼		Pass the Jug
			▼		▼	▼		▼		People of the Bog
▼	▼					▼		▼		Perspectives
						▼		▼	▼	Piece It Together
		▼						▼	▼	Poetic Precipitation
				▼				▼		Poison Pump
▼		▼						▼	▼	The Price Is Right
		▼							▼	The Pucker Effect
				▼				▼		Raining Cats and Dogs
					▼			▼	▼	The Rainstick
									▼	Rainy-Day Hike
		▼		▼				▼		Reaching Your Limits
	▼	▼				▼		▼		Salt Marsh Players
		▼			▼			▼	▼	Sparkling Water
									▼	Stream Sense
	▼	▼						▼		Sum of the Parts
▼	▼	▼				▼		▼	▼	Super Bowl Surge
				▼		▼		▼		Super Sleuths
						▼	▼	▼	▼	Thirsty Plants
		▼						▼		The Thunderstorm
▼						▼		▼	▼	Water: Read All About It!
				Depends on activity						Water Actions
				▼		▼			▼	Water Address
						▼		▼	▼	Water Bill of Rights
		▼	▼	▼		▼		▼	▼	Water Celebration
				▼					▼	Water Concentration
▼	▼	▼				▼		▼	▼	Water Court
		▼	▼	▼	▼			▼	▼	Water Crossings
			▼		▼				▼	wAteR in moTion
						▼		▼		Water Log
				▼					▼	Water Match
									▼	Water Messages in Stone
								▼		Water Meter
			▼			▼		▼	▼	Water Models
						▼		▼		Water Works
						▼			▼	Water Write
						▼		▼	▼	Wet Vacation
				▼		▼		▼		Wet-Work Shuffle
								▼		Wetland Soils in Living Color
						▼			▼	What's Happening?
					▼				▼	What's the Solution?
		▼		▼	▼			▼		Where Are the Frogs?
▼						▼		▼	▼	Whose Problem Is It?
						▼		▼	▼	Wish Book

Assessing Student Learning

Assessing student learning is a vital component of education. Assessments for Project WET activities were carefully developed to provide strategies for measuring student accomplishment of learning objectives. These types of assessments are summative: they help the educator determine what students know, can do, or believe after completing an activity. Opportunities for monitoring student learning are incorporated into Project WET activities. These creative and practical evaluation strategies are summarized in the **Assessment** section of each activity; the particular location within the activity during which each assessment can occur is noted in parentheses. Occasionally, suggestions for post-activity assessments are provided.

Assessment of student learning from a Project WET activity can proceed in the following manner. During the *Warm Up*, assessment begins when teachers identify what students currently know or do not know about the topic. (For further information about preassessment strategies, see the activity "Idea Pools.") Assessment continues as students participate in the activity itself (e.g., through teacher observation, discussion, and examination of student work). In addition to bringing closure to the lesson, the *Wrap Up* suggests several ways to discover what students have learned from the activity. Students' responses in the *Warm Up* and *Wrap Up* can be compared to determine what progress has been made.

The diverse assessment strategies used in Project WET activities are categorized into five areas and presented in the **Assessment Chart** which follows. The five areas are:

- Observation (noting how students perform during the activity, whether they follow directions, how they cooperate with other students, etc.);

- Product (evaluating a tangible object, such as an art project or poem, or observing a student's performance during a play);

- Communication (appraising students' expressions of what they know through speaking, writing, or drawing);

- Demonstration of Skill (observing students demonstrate a particular skill while performing an activity);

- Self and/or Peer Evaluation (complementing teacher assessment with students' judgments or assessments of their own or each other's work).

As a vital component of Project WET activities, students use thinking and process skills to obtain and express knowledge about water; this can provide a means to assess student learning. The Project WET curriculum framework includes a **Skills Framework**. A **Skills Chart** identifies activities that address specific skills within the framework.

When several Project WET activities are organized into a unit, teachers may employ a comprehensive assessment strategy to determine students' overall learning experiences. Comprehensive strategies are described in several activities, such as "Idea Pools," "Water Log," and "Check It Out!" These activities are identified by the Teaching Strategy icon.

In addition to the assessment strategies described within each Project WET activity, the following list includes more suggestions to help evaluate student learning:

Have students:
- build a three-dimensional model of what they have learned.

- create a photographic essay about what they have seen.

- invent a board game using new concepts.

- develop a picture book to express their thoughts and feelings.

- write a letter to their friends describing their experiences.

- conduct interviews to discover what other people think about similar experiences.

- produce a scene from a movie or play which dramatizes a water topic.

- design a mobile displaying objects they have created.

- draw a comic strip which presents concepts to a friend.

494

Assessment Strategies

Activity	Obser-vation	Product	Communication			Skills*	Self/Peer Evaluation
			verbal	written	drawn		
Adventures in Density (25)	▼		▼	▼		▼	
AfterMath (289)			▼	▼		▼	
A-maze-ing Water (219)			▼				
Aqua Bodies (63)		▼	▼			▼	
Aqua Notes (66)		▼	▼			▼	
Back to the Future (293)			▼		▼	▼	
Branching Out! (129)				▼	▼	▼	▼
Capture, Store, & Release (133)			▼	▼			
The CEO (300)		▼				▼	
Check It Out! (3)			Depends on activity				
Choices & Preferences . . . (367)			▼			▼	▼
Cold Cash in the Icebox (373)		▼		▼		▼	▼
Color Me a Watershed (223)		▼	▼			▼	
Common Water (232)	▼	▼	▼	▼	▼		
Dilemma Derby (377)			▼			▼	
A Drop in the Bucket (238)			▼			▼	
Dust Bowls . . . (303)		▼		▼		▼	▼
Easy Street (382)			▼	▼		▼	
Energetic Water (242)		▼	▼			▼	
Every Drop Counts (307)	▼			▼		▼	
Get the Ground Water . . . (136)			▼			▼	
Geyser Guts (144)		▼			▼	▼	
A Grave Mistake (311)			▼			▼	
The Great Stony Book (150)	▼		▼		▼	▼	
Great Water Journeys (246)	▼		▼			▼	
H₂Olympics (30)	▼		▼		▼	▼	
Hangin' Together (35)	▼	▼	▼	▼		▼	
Hot Water (388)	▼		▼			▼	▼
A House of Seasons (155)		▼			▼	▼	▼
Humpty Dumpty (316)	▼		▼			▼	
Idea Pools (7)	▼				▼		
Imagine! (157)	▼			▼	▼		
The Incredible Journey (161)	▼		▼	▼	▼		
Irrigation Interpretation (254)		▼	▼			▼	
Is There Water on Zork? (43)			▼			▼	▼
Just Passing Through (166)	▼		▼	▼		▼	
Let's Even Things Out (72)	▼		▼			▼	
Let's Work Together (9)			Depends on activity				
The Life Box (76)			▼				
Life in the Fast Lane (79)	▼		▼	▼		▼	
The Long Haul (260)		▼	▼			▼	
Macroinvertebrate . . . (322)		▼	▼			▼	
Molecules in Motion (47)	▼		▼	▼		▼	
Money Down the Drain (328)			▼			▼	
Nature Rules! (262)		▼		▼	▼	▼	▼
No Bellyachers (85)	▼		▼				

Assessment Strategies (cont.)

Activity	Obser-vation	Product	Communication			Skills*	Self/Peer Evaluation
			verbal	written	drawn		
Old Water (171)		▼			▼	▼	
Pass the Jug (392)	▼		▼			▼	
People of the Bog (89)			▼			▼	
Perspectives (397)	▼		▼			▼	
Piece It Together (174)			▼	▼		▼	
Poetic Precipitation (182)	▼	▼		▼	▼		▼
Poison Pump (93)						▼	
The Price Is Right (333)			▼		▼	▼	▼
The Pucker Effect (338)			▼			▼	
Raining Cats and Dogs (435)			▼			▼	
The Rainstick (442)		▼					
Rainy-Day Hike (186)	▼		▼		▼	▼	
Reaching Your Limits (344)		▼	▼	▼		▼	
Salt Marsh Players (99)	▼	▼	▼	▼		▼	
Sparkling Water (348)		▼	▼			▼	
Stream Sense (191)	▼	▼		▼	▼	▼	
Sum of the Parts (267)			▼	▼		▼	
Super Bowl Surge (353)		▼		▼		▼	▼
Super Sleuths (107)	▼		▼			▼	
Thirsty Plants (116)			▼	▼	▼	▼	
The Thunderstorm (196)	▼		▼	▼	▼		
Water: Read All About It! (400)		▼	▼	▼		▼	▼
Water Actions (12)	▼	▼	▼	▼	▼	▼	▼
Water Address (122)		▼	▼			▼	
Water Bill of Rights (403)		▼	▼	▼			▼
Water Celebration (446)		▼				▼	
Water Concentration (407)	▼	▼	▼	▼		▼	
Water Court (413)	▼		▼			▼	▼
Water Crossings (421)		▼		▼		▼	▼
wAteR in moTion (450)		▼	▼	▼			▼
Water Log (19)			Depends on activity				
Water Match (50)	▼		▼			▼	
Water Messages in Stone (454)		▼	▼			▼	
Water Meter (271)				▼		▼	
Water Models (201)		▼	▼		▼	▼	▼
Water Works (274)	▼		▼		▼		
Water Write (457)		▼		▼	▼	▼	
Wet Vacation (206)		▼				▼	▼
Wet-Work Shuffle (360)				▼		▼	
Wetland Soils . . . (212)				▼		▼	
What's Happening? (425)	▼	▼		▼		▼	
What's the Solution? (54)	▼		▼			▼	
Where Are the Frogs? (279)		▼	▼			▼	
Whose Problem Is It? (429)		▼				▼	▼
Wish Book (460)			▼	▼		▼	

*Skills are categorized further in the Skills Chart on page 497

496

Skills

Activity	Gather	Organize	Analyze	Interpret	Apply	Evaluate	Present
Adventures in Density (25)	▼	▼	▼	▼	▼		
AfterMath (289)	▼	▼	▼	▼	▼		
A-maze-ing Water (219)		▼					
Aqua Bodies (63)	▼	▼	▼				
Aqua Notes (66)	▼			▼	▼		
Back to the Future (293)		▼	▼	▼	▼	▼	
Branching Out! (129)		▼	▼		▼	▼	
Capture, Store, & Release (133)	▼				▼		
The CEO (300)	▼		▼				▼
Check It Out! (3)			Depends on activity				
Choices & Preferences . . . (367)	▼	▼	▼	▼			
Cold Cash in the Icebox (373)					▼	▼	
Color Me a Watershed (223)	▼		▼	▼			
Common Water (232)	▼	▼	▼	▼	▼		
Dilemma Derby (377)			▼	▼			
A Drop in the Bucket (238)	▼	▼	▼				
Dust Bowls & Failed Levees (303)	▼				▼	▼	
Easy Street (382)	▼			▼	▼	▼	
Energetic Water (242)		▼	▼	▼	▼	▼	▼
Every Drop Counts (307)	▼			▼	▼	▼	
Get the Ground Water Picture (136)		▼	▼	▼	▼		
Geyser Guts (144)	▼	▼		▼	▼		
A Grave Mistake (311)		▼		▼	▼		
The Great Stony Book (150)	▼	▼		▼			
Great Water Journeys (246)	▼	▼	▼	▼	▼		▼
H₂Olympics (30)	▼	▼	▼	▼			
Hangin' Together (35)	▼			▼			▼
Hot Water (388)	▼	▼	▼	▼	▼	▼	▼
A House of Seasons (155)	▼	▼	▼				▼
Humpty Dumpty (316)		▼	▼		▼		
Idea Pools (7)	▼	▼	▼	▼			
Imagine! (157)	▼	▼		▼	▼		
The Incredible Journey (161)	▼	▼	▼	▼			
Irrigation Interpretation (254)				▼	▼		
Is there Water on Zork? (43)	▼	▼	▼	▼	▼	▼	
Just Passing Through (166)	▼		▼	▼			
Let's Even Things Out (72)	▼			▼			
Let's Work Together (9)			Depends on activity				
The Life Box (76)			▼				
Life in the Fast Lane (79)	▼	▼	▼	▼			
The Long Haul (260)			▼	▼	▼		
Macroinvertebrate Mayhem (322)	▼	▼	▼	▼	▼		
Molecules in Motion (47)	▼			▼			
Money Down the Drain (328)	▼	▼	▼		▼		
Nature Rules! (262)	▼					▼	▼
No Bellyachers (85)	▼		▼		▼	▼	

Activity	Gather	Organize	Analyze	Interpret	Apply	Evaluate	Present
Old Water (171)		▼	▼	▼	▼		▼
Pass the Jug (392)	▼	▼	▼		▼	▼	
People of the Bog (89)	▼		▼	▼			
Perspectives (397)	▼	▼	▼				
Piece It Together (174)	▼	▼	▼	▼	▼		
Poetic Precipitation (182)	▼	▼	▼	▼			
Poison Pump (93)		▼	▼	▼	▼		
The Price Is Right (333)	▼		▼	▼		▼	▼
The Pucker Effect (338)	▼	▼	▼	▼			
Raining Cats and Dogs (435)	▼	▼	▼				
The Rainstick (442)	▼		▼		▼		▼
Rainy-Day Hike (186)	▼	▼	▼	▼	▼		
Reaching Your Limits (344)		▼	▼	▼			
Salt Marsh Players (99)	▼	▼	▼	▼	▼		
Sparkling Water (348)		▼			▼	▼	
Stream Sense (191)	▼	▼					
Sum of the Parts (267)	▼		▼		▼		
Super Bowl Surge (353)	▼	▼	▼	▼	▼	▼	▼
Super Sleuths (107)			▼	▼			
Thirsty Plants (116)	▼	▼	▼	▼	▼		
The Thunderstorm (196)	▼			▼	▼		
Water: Read All About It! (400)	▼	▼	▼	▼	▼	▼	▼
Water Actions (12)				▼	▼		▼
Water Address (122)	▼			▼	▼		▼
Water Bill of Rights (403)	▼	▼	▼		▼		▼
Water Celebration (446)	▼	▼	▼	▼	▼	▼	▼
Water Concentration (407)		▼	▼	▼	▼	▼	
Water Court (413)					▼	▼	▼
Water Crossings (421)			▼		▼	▼	
wAteR in moTion (450)	▼			▼	▼	▼	▼
Water Log (19)	Depends on activity						
Water Match (50)	▼	▼		▼			
Water Messages in Stone (454)				▼	▼		▼
Water Meter (271)	▼	▼					
Water Models (201)	▼		▼	▼			▼
Water Works (274)		▼	▼				
Water Write (457)		▼	▼		▼		
Wet Vacation (206)	▼	▼	▼	▼	▼	▼	▼
Wet-Work Shuffle (360)	▼	▼	▼				
Wetland Soils in Living Color (212)	▼	▼	▼	▼			
What's Happening? (425)	▼	▼		▼	▼	▼	▼
What's the Solution? (54)			▼	▼	▼		
Where Are the Frogs? (279)	▼	▼	▼	▼	▼		▼
Whose Problem Is It? (429)	▼	▼	▼	▼			
Wish Book (460)	▼		▼	▼	▼	▼	

Environmental Education and Project WET

The need to educate young people about the environment continues to gain national attention. Currently, the North American Association for Environmental Education (NAAEE) is establishing national standards for environmental education. Project WET has used the framework presented in a draft NAAEE document to create a reference chart demonstrating how Project WET activities can address environmental education standards.

The components of the NAAEE framework are as follows:

Affect: environmental sensitivity, attitudes toward environmental issues, motivation to participate in environmental improvement and protection, moral reasoning, and values clarification

Ecological Knowledge: understanding of major ecological concepts (e.g., ecosystems, biogeochemical cycles, energy transfer), knowledge of natural systems, appreciation of limitations

Sociopolitical Knowledge: awareness of economic, social, political, and ecological interdependence; appreciation of cultural influences on the environment; understanding of relationships among beliefs, political structures, and environmental values of various cultures; geographic knowledge

Knowledge of Environmental Issues: understanding of various environmentally related problems and issues, including water quality and quantity (water pollution; resource use and management)

Skills: ability to define problems; to analyze, synthesize, and evaluate information; and to plan, implement, and evaluate action

Determinants of Environmentally Responsible Behavior: locus of control (similar to empowerment— assuming that one's action will have an effect, rather than thinking that results occur by chance), assumption of personal responsibility

Environmentally Responsible Behaviors: active participation aimed at solving problems and resolving issues

Reference

Simmons, Deborah. 1994. *The NAAEE Standards Project: Working Papers on the Development of Environmental Education Standards.* Troy, Ohio: NAAEE.

NOTE: This is a condensed version of the framework (from pages 48-51 of the *NAAEE Standards Project*). For a more complete description of the environmental education framework proposed by NAAEE, contact NAAEE, P.O. Box 400, Troy, OH 45373. Phone and fax: (513) 676-2514.

Environmental Education Framework

Activity	Affect	Ecological Knowledge	Socio-Political Knowledge	Knowledge of Env. Issues	Skills	Determinants of Env. Responsible Behavior	Environmentally Responsible Behavior
Adventures in Density (25)					▼		
AfterMath (289)	▼		▼	▼	▼		
A-maze-ing Water (219)	▼	▼	▼	▼		▼	▼
Aqua Bodies (63)	▼	▼					
Aqua Notes (66)	▼	▼					
Back to the Future (293)		▼		▼	▼	▼	
Branching Out! (129)		▼					
Capture, Store, & Release (133)		▼		▼			
The CEO (300)			▼	▼		▼	
Check It Out! (3)			Depends on activity				
Choices & Preferences . . . (367)	▼		▼		▼		
Cold Cash in the Icebox (373)		▼	▼		▼		
Color Me a Watershed (223)		▼	▼	▼	▼		
Common Water (232)	▼	▼	▼	▼		▼	▼
Dilemma Derby (377)	▼			▼	▼	▼	
A Drop in the Bucket (238)		▼		▼			
Dust Bowls & Failed Levees (303)	▼	▼		▼	▼	▼	▼
Easy Street (382)			▼	▼	▼		
Energetic Water (242)			▼				
Every Drop Counts (307)			▼	▼	▼	▼	▼
Get the Ground Water Picture (136)	▼	▼		▼			
Geyser Guts (144)	▼	▼	▼				
A Grave Mistake (311)				▼	▼		
The Great Stony Book (150)		▼	▼				
Great Water Journeys (246)			▼	▼			
H₂Olympics (30)					▼		
Hangin' Together (35)					▼		
Hot Water (388)	▼		▼	▼	▼	▼	
A House of Seasons (155)	▼	▼					
Humpty Dumpty (316)		▼	▼	▼	▼	▼	▼
Idea Pools (7)	▼	▼					
Imagine! (157)		▼					
The Incredible Journey (161)		▼					
Irrigation Interpretation (254)		▼	▼	▼	▼		
Is There Water on Zork? (43)					▼		
Just Passing Through (166)		▼		▼			▼
Let's Even Things Out (72)		▼					
Let's Work Together (9)			Depends on activity				
The Life Box (76)	▼	▼					
Life in the Fast Lane (79)		▼			▼		
The Long Haul (260)	▼		▼	▼			
Macroinvertebrate Mayhem (322)		▼		▼	▼	▼	
Molecules in Motion (47)		▼					▼
Money Down the Drain (328)	▼			▼			
Nature Rules! (262)	▼		▼	▼	▼		
No Bellyachers (85)		▼					

Activity	Affect	Ecological Knowledge	Socio-Political Knowledge	Knowledge of Env. Issues	Skills	Determinants of Env. Responsible Behavior	Environmentally Responsible Behavior
Old Water (171)	▼	▼					
Pass the Jug (392)			▼	▼			
People of the Bog (89)	▼	▼		▼			
Perspectives (397)	▼				▼	▼	
Piece It Together (174)		▼	▼				
Poetic Precipitation (182)	▼	▼					
Poison Pump (93)			▼	▼			
The Price Is Right (333)			▼	▼	▼		
The Pucker Effect (338)			▼	▼	▼		
Raining Cats and Dogs (435)	▼		▼				
The Rainstick (442)	▼		▼				
Rainy-Day Hike (186)		▼		▼			▼
Reaching Your Limits (344)			▼	▼			
Salt Marsh Players (99)	▼	▼					
Sparkling Water (348)				▼	▼	▼	▼
Stream Sense (191)	▼	▼					
Sum of the Parts (267)	▼		▼	▼		▼	▼
Super Bowl Surge (353)				▼	▼	▼	
Super Sleuths (107)		▼					
Thirsty Plants (116)		▼			▼		▼
The Thunderstorm (196)					▼		
Water: Read All About It! (400)	▼		▼		▼		▼
Water Actions (12)					▼	▼	▼
Water Address (122)		▼					
Water Bill of Rights (403)	▼		▼		▼	▼	
Water Celebration (446)	▼				▼	▼	▼
Water Concentration (407)			▼	▼			
Water Court (413)			▼	▼	▼	▼	
Water Crossings (421)			▼				
wAteR in moTion (450)	▼						
Water Log (19)	▼				▼	▼	
Water Match (50)		▼					
Water Messages in Stone (454)			▼				
Water Meter (271)	▼	▼				▼	
Water Models (201)		▼	▼				
Water Works (274)			▼	▼			
Water Write (457)	▼						
Wet Vacation (206)		▼	▼				
Wet-Work Shuffle (360)			▼			▼	
Wetland Soils in Living Color (212)		▼			▼		▼
What's Happening? (425)	▼		▼		▼	▼	
What's the Solution? (54)					▼		
Where Are the Frogs? (279)		▼	▼	▼	▼		▼
Whose Problem Is It? (429)	▼		▼	▼		▼	
Wish Book (460)			▼				

Metric and Standard Measurements

Metric Conversions

When You Know	Multiply By	To Find
Length		
inches (in.)	2.5	centimeters (cm)
feet (ft.)	30.0	centimeters (cm)
yards (yd.)	0.9	meters (m)
miles (mi.)	1.6	kilometers (km)
centimeters (cm)	0.4	inches (in.)
meters (m)	3.3	feet(ft.)
meters (m)	1.09	yard (yd.)
kilometers (km)	0.6	mile (mi.)
Area		
square inches (in.²)	6.5	square centimeters (cm²)
square feet (ft.²)	0.09	square meters (m²)
square yards (yd.²)	0.84	square meters (m²)
square miles (mi.²)	2.6	square kilometers (km²)
acre (a.)	0.4	hectares (ha)
square centimeter (cm²)	0.16	square inches (in.²)
square meter (m²)	10.8	square feet (ft.²)
square meter (m²)	1.2	square yards (yd.²)
square kilometer (km²)	0.4	square miles (mi.²)
hectare (ha)	2.5	acres (a.)
Mass		
ounces (oz.)	28.35	grams (g)
pound (lb.)	0.45	kilograms (kg)
short ton (2,000 lbs.)	0.9	tonnes—metric ton (t.)
grams (g)	0.035	ounces (oz.)
kilograms (kg)	2.2	pounds (lbs.)
tonnes (t.)	1.1	short tons (2,000 lbs.)

When You Know	Multiply By	To Find
Volume		
teaspoons (tsp.)	5.0	milliliters (ml)
tablespoons (tbs.)	15.0	milliliters (ml)
fluid ounces (fl. oz.)	30.0	milliliters (ml)
cups (c)	0.24	liters (l)
pints (pt.)	0.47	liters (l)
quarts (qts.)	0.95	liters (l)
gallons (gal.)	3.8	liters (l)
cubic feet (ft.³)	0.03	cubic meters (m³)
cubic yards (yd.³)	0.76	cubic meters (m³)
milliliters (ml)	0.2	teaspoons (tsp.)
milliliters (ml)	0.7	tablespoons (tbs.)
milliliters (ml)	0.3	fluid ounces (fl. oz.)
liters (l)	4.2	cups (c)
liters (l)	2.1	pints (pt.)
liters (l)	1.06	quarts (qts.)
liters (l)	0.26	gallons (gal.)
cubic meters (m³)	35.0	cubic feet (ft.³)
cubic meters (m³)	1.3	cubic yards (yd.³)

Temperature

When You Know	Multiply By	To Find
degrees Celsius (°C)	$(9/5 \times °C) + 32$	degrees Fahrenheit (°F)
degrees Fahrenheit (°F)	$5/9 \times (°F-32)$	degrees Celsius (°C)

Flow Rate

1 gallon per minute	$= 2.23 \times 10^{-3}$ cubic feet/sec. (cfs)
	$= 4.42 \times 10^{-3}$ acre feet/day
	$= 6.31 \times 10^{-5}$ m³/sec.
	$= 5.42$ m³/day

1 cubic foot per second	$= 449$ gallon/min. (gpm)
	$= 0.0283$ m³/sec.
	$= 2450$ m³/day

1 cubic meter per second	$= 1.58 \times 10^{4}$ gpm
	$= 35.3$ cfs
	$= 8.64 \times 10^{4}$ m³/day

1 cubic meter per day	$= 0.183$ gpm
	$= 4.09 \times 10^{-4}$ cfs
	$= 1.16 \times 10^{-5}$ m³/sec.

Velocity

1 foot/second	$= 0.682$ miles/hour
	$= 0.3048$ meters/second
1 mile/hour	$= 1.467$ feet/second
	$= 1.609$ kilometers/hour
1 meter/second	$= 3.6$ kilometers/hour
	$= 3.28$ feet/second
	$= 2.237$ miles/hour
1 kilometer/hour	$= 0.621$ miles/hour

Length

Unit	Number of Meters
kilometer	1,000
hectometer	100
decameter	10
meter	1
decimeter	0.1
centimeter	0.01
millimeter	0.001

Area

Unit	Number of Square Meters
sq. kilometer	1,000,000
hectare	10,000
are	100
centare	1
sq. centimeter	0.0001

Volume

Unit	Number of Liters
kiloliters	1,000
hectoliter	100
decaliter	10
liter	1
deciliter	0.1
centiliter	0.01
milliliter	0.001

Mass

Unit	Number of Grams
metric ton or tonne	1,000,000
kilogram	1,000
hectogram	100
decagram	10
gram	1
decigram	0.1
centigram	0.01
milligram	0.001

U.S. Customary System of Measurement (Conversions)

Linear

12 inches	=	1 foot
3 feet	=	1 yard (yd.)
1,760 yds.	=	1 mile

Area

144 square inches	=	1 square foot
9 square feet	=	1 square yard (sq. yd.)
4,840 sq. yds.	=	1 acre
640 acre	=	1 square mile

Weight

1 ounce	=	1/16 pound (lb.)
2,000 lb.	=	1 ton

Liquid

60 drops	=	1 teaspoon (tsp.)
3 tsp.	=	1 Tablespoon (tbs.)
8 ounces (oz.)	=	1 cup
16 oz	=	1 pint
2 pints	=	1 quart
4 quarts	=	1 gallon

Dry

2 pints	=	1 quart
8 quarts	=	1 peck
4 pecks	=	1 bushel

International Metric System (Conversions)

Linear

10 millimeter (mm)	=	1 centimeter (cm)
10 cm	=	1 decimeter (dm)
10 dm	=	1 meter (m)
1,000 m	=	1 kilometer

Area

10,000 square meters	=	1 hectare
100 hectares	=	1 square kilometer

Weight

10 decigrams	=	1 gram
1,000 grams	=	1 kilogram (kg)
1,000 (kg)	=	1 metric ton

Liquid

1,000 milliliters (ml)	=	1 liter

Supplementary Resources

Resources available from The Watercourse and Project WET complement and enrich many of the activities in the Project WET Curriculum and Activity Guide. *These resources include several publications (guides, booklets, modules) and a ground water flow model.*

Publications

Newsletter, Guides, and Books

Celebrate Wetlands!

Published in cooperation with Wild Outdoor World (W.O.W.), this 16-page full-color booklet is for upper elementary and middle school aged students. Through hands-on investigations, games, intriguing articles, a poster, and other activities, readers learn about the types and functions of wetlands; the plants, animals, soil, and water found in wetlands; and the relationship of people and these special places through language and culture.

Exploring the Waters of Our National Parks: Everglades, an Educator's Guide

Developed by The Watercourse with The National Park Foundation and the Interpretive Staff of Everglades National Park, the fun and informative activities in this resource offer ways for educators and 4th through 6th grade students to learn more about the role of water in one of the largest wetland ecosystems in the world. Participants may journey through the hydrologic cycle, create an alligator hole in their classroom, or design a newly authorized Wetlands National Park and explore the concept of the "national park idea." This supplement reinforces the activities, "The Incredible Journey," "The Life Box," "Water Address," and "Humpty Dumpty."

The Liquid Treasure Water History Trunk: Learning From The Past

This 64-page booklet contains stories, activities, and information for procuring artifacts needed to assemble a water history trunk. Other less expensive and time-consuming options are suggested for developing a water environmental history program, such as creating a water history scrapbook or building a water history home. This resource may be used with the following activities: "Old Water," "Water Messages in Stone," "Water Crossings," "The Long Haul," "Easy Street," "Water Concentration," "Wish Book," and "Cold Cash in the Icebox."

Water Celebration! A Handbook

A water celebration is a one- to three-day event to entertain and educate a community, a school, or a single class about the importance of water. This 32-page booklet provides schedules, funding suggestions, sample letters, flyers, press releases, and ideas for games, exhibits, and presentations; it supplements the activity, "Water Celebration."

Getting to Know the Waters of Yellowstone, an Educator's Guide

Produced by The Watercourse in cooperation with the National Park Service, *The Waters of Yellowstone* is a supplement containing activities and reference material for Expedition Yellowstone, an environmental education curriculum of Yellowstone National Park. This work celebrates the park's water resources, its geothermal features, rivers, and waterfalls, and relates how plants and animals adapt to Yellowstone's unique water environments. This supplement reinforces the activities "Geyser Guts," "The Great Stony Book," and "Water Address."

Water, A Gift of Nature

See the many faces of water: clouds, rain, hail, snow, icebergs, geysers, rainbows, and waterfalls. Meet the animals and plants that depend on water: from wetland beavers to the

desert chuckwalla, from a coral reef to a saguaro cactus. Co-published with K. C. Publications, Inc., *Water, A Gift of Nature* is grounded in the social and natural sciences. It provides interpretive text and full-color photographs that illustrate subjects found in the *Project WET Curriculum and Activity Guide.*

A Landowner's Guide to Western Water Rights

Produced with Roberts Rinehart, Publishers, this guide provides the layperson with a user-friendly introduction to western water rights systems. It includes a reference section on western water rights, commonly asked questions (and answers) about water rights with cautions for prospective landowners, information on federal and tribal reserved water rights, and profiles of western states' water rights systems. This booklet will afford the secondary-through-adult educator additional background information for the activities "A Drop in the Bucket," "Wet Vacation," and "Pass the Jug."

The Rainstick, A Fable

Produced with Falcon Press Publishing Co., Inc., *The Rainstick, A Fable* is drawn from the riddles, myths, and traditions of West African people as well as from descriptions of tropical rain forests by early adventurers and present-day scientists. The book contains a fable about a young boy's journey from the savanna to the rain forest to solve the riddle, "A slender staff touches earth and sky at the same time." Factual information about this early sound instrument and easy-to-follow directions to build a rainstick are included. With its full-color illustrations of West Africa, this book will enrich the activity, "The Rainstick."

The Water Story

This 16-page full-color supplement, published in cooperation with *Wild Outdoor World (W.O.W.)* is for upper elementary and middle school aged students. In telling the story of water, this publication provides young readers with a variety of creative, hands-on activities, projects, games, a poster, and valuable information about water. Distinguished Achievement in Educational Publishing, EdPress Award Winner.

Conserve Water

This colorful 16-page booklet designed for upper elementary and middle school aged students was published in cooperation with the Wild Outdoor World (W.O.W.) magazine of the Rocky Mountain Elk Foundation. Through engaging graphics and text, students are challenged to participate in investigations such as assembling a sun-powered still or experimenting with catchment. Activities challenge students to "soak up" intriguing water facts; play a board game to learn how water moves through their homes and how they can conserve it; conduct a simple home water audit; and discover how a person's latitude can affect their attitude about water conservation.

Modules—resources containing a reference section and 15 to 50 activities focused on a single topic.

WOW!: The Wonders Of Wetlands

This module, co-developed by The Watercourse and Environmental Concern Inc., is based on the highly successful *WOW!: The Wonders Of Wetlands* activity guide for K–12 educators originally created by EC. The new *WOW!* guide includes a reference section, new activities (in addition to the originals), and a new format. This resource complements the activities "Capture, Store, and Release," "Wetland Soils in Living Color," "Salt Marsh Players," and "Life in the Fast Lane," and provides the educator with material to create wetlands units.

Discover a Watershed: The Everglades

Developed for formal and nonformal educators of middle and high school students (and beyond!), this comprehensive guide is divided into three parts: a reference section that includes the natural and human history of the watershed; contemporary issues and potential solutions; and learning activities. Build a model of the Kissimmee-Okeechobee-Everglades watershed or plot a hurricane and predict if it will make landfall. Explore a unique and endangered watershed where unprecedented solutions are being tested to "find the balance." Produced through a partnership with the South Florida Water Management District, this resource provides examples of restoration concepts introduced in the activity "Humpty Dumpty."

Water Conservation Module for Educators

Developed for middle and high school educators, The *Water Conservation Module* provides background material, case studies, and activities on the topic of water conservation. Case studies are based on water conservation scenarios ranging from a rancher in west Texas to an ice cream factory in Massachusetts, and from water's role on the space shuttle to the survival of a sailor adrift in the Atlantic. These real-life examples encourage students to use decision-making skills to work through issues related to water use and conservation. Sidebar material, illustrations, charts, and a selection of activities complement the background chapters and case studies. This resource supplements the following activities: "A Drop in the Bucket," "Water Meter," "Easy Street," "Piece It

Together," "Water Concentration," and "Common Water."

Ground Water Flow Model Package

The Ground Water Flow Model is a popular and easy to use teaching tool for both youth and adult educators. The model is constructed with a clear Plexiglas front, which allows observers to watch water and contaminants introduced into the system move through underground rock formations. The model can also be adapted to demonstrate how surface sources like rivers or wetlands can be connected to ground water. The model enables students to learn about porosity, permeability, water tables, confined aquifers, contamination, and other important ground water concepts. This package includes a model, users guide and video, and everything needed to conduct a ground water education class or

workshop. The activities "Get the Ground Water Picture," "The Pucker Effect," and "A Grave Mistake" help learners gain a greater understanding of ground water concepts.

Other Suggested Resources

Taking Action! An Educator's Guide to Involving Students in Environmental Action Projects

This guide, intended for educators of grades 5-12, will enable teachers to help students translate their interest in wildlife and environmental concerns into environmental action projects. It includes steps for facilitating student efforts, ways to connect action projects to the curriculum, suggestions for assessment, and a description of diverse action projects undertaken by students and teachers across the U.S. Available from Project WILD.

Exploring School Nature Areas Video

The *Exploring School Nature Areas* video was produced in cooperation with St. Olaf College's School Nature Area Project and KTCA-TV of St. Paul, producers of "Newton's Apple," a science education program. The video, targeted for teachers and administrators, will demonstrate the value of "school sites" or "school nature areas" and will show students in action at these school sites. The purpose of the 12-minute video is to motivate educators and students to initiate environmental action projects that will improve habitats for wildlife and people. Available from Project WILD.

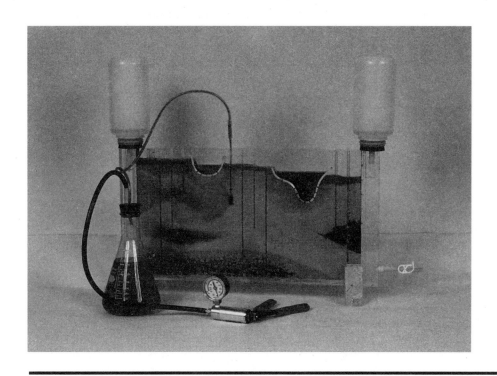

Glossary

A number in **bold** indicates the page on which a word is defined in the text.

Acid. Any substance that has a pH level below 7, or that has more free hydrogen ions (H^+) than hydroxide ions (OH^-). 90, 146, **279**, 279-286, 340-343

Acid precipitation (acid rain). Precipitation (e.g., rain, snow) that has a lower pH level than normal. Acidic precipitation is created when atmospheric water combines with sulfur dioxide and nitrous oxide emissions. These emissions are by-products of the combustion of fossil fuels. Acid precipitation can harm plant and animal life and alter soil conditions. **280**, 279-286

Action. Applying awareness, knowledge, attitudes, values, and skills toward preventing and resolving water-related issues at all levels (home, community, state, country, etc.) xii, 12-18, 377-381

Adaptation. The modification, over time, of the structure, function, or behavior of an organism, which enables it to be better suited to its environment. 90-91, 99-106, **122**, 122-126, 174-181

Adhesion. The attraction of water molecules to other materials as a result of hydrogen bonding. **30**, 30-34, 36, 116-120

Aerobic. Able to live only in the presence of air or free oxygen; conditions that exist only in the presence of air or free oxygen. 89-92, 212-214

Anaerobic. Able to live and grow only where there is no air or free oxygen; conditions that exist only in the absence of air and free oxygen. **89**, 89-92, 212-214

Aquifer. An underground bed of saturated soil or rock that yields significant quantities of water. **136**, 136-143, 312, 344

Archeology. The discovery, recovery, and study of material evidence or artifacts (i.e., structures, tools, clothing, implements, and burial sites in various states of preservation) of past human life and culture. 90-92, 455-456

Assessment. A teaching strategy used to determine students' understanding of, or competencies related to, a certain concept. x, xii, **3**, 3-6, 7-8, 11, 19-22

Atmosphere. The layer of gases surrounding Earth; composed mainly of nitrogen and oxygen. 76, 146, 157-160, 161-165, 171-172, 182-185, 201-202, 280

Attitudes. The opinions, feelings, or beliefs that people have about something. 3-6, 19-22, 155, 182-185, 221, 349, 367-372, 425-428, 456

Bacteria. Single-celled microorganisms that are either free-living or grow on and derive nourishment from dead or decaying organic matter. Some bacteria cause disease in plants and animals. 85-88, 90, 93-98, 107-115, 141, 344, 353

Base. Any substance that has a pH level above 7, or that has more free hydroxide ions (OH^-) than hydrogen ions (H^+). **279**, 279-286

Best Management Practices. Methods adopted by resource users designed to mitigate harm to the environment that might result from their activities. 166-169, **269**, 267-270, 319, 334

Bill of Rights. A document listing the fundamental rights of a group of people; such a document is attached to the U. S. Constitution. **403**, **406**, 403-406

Biodiversity. A measure of the distinct characteristics, qualities, or elements of plant and animal life in a defined area; a measure of biological differences. 322-327

Body water content. That portion of the body composed of water; expressed as a percentage of total body volume. 63-65, 69

Bog. An area of soft, water-saturated ground with a spongy, acidic substrate composed mostly of sphagnum moss and peat, and in which water-tolerant shrubs, herbs, and trees usually grow. **89**, 89-92

Boiling point. The temperature at which a liquid boils. For water, it is 212 degrees Fahrenheit (100° Celsius) at sea level. 50, 144

Capillary action. The means by which water is drawn through tiny spaces in a material, such as soil, through the processes of adhesion and cohesion. **31**, 31-34, 36, 116-120

Climate. The meteorological elements, including temperature, precipitation, and wind, that characterize the general conditions of the atmosphere over a period of time at any one place or region of Earth's surface. Earth has three climate zones: Polar, Temperate, and Tropical. Climate zones are further classified into ecosystems and biomes. 174-181, 201-203, 206-212, 238-240, 246, 255-256, 262-266, 303-306

Cohesion. The attraction of water molecules to each other as a result of hydrogen bonding. **30**, 30-34, 36, 116-120

Collection site. A stream, lake, reservoir, or other body of water fed by water drained from a watershed. 186, 223

Concentration. The amount of a specific substance dissolved in a given amount (volume) of another substance. **72**, 72-75, 339, 344-346

Condensation. The process by which a vapor becomes a liquid; the opposite of evaporation. 35, 43-46, 117-120, 157, 161-165, 172, 182-185, 201-205

Confined aquifer. A water-saturated layer of soil or rock that is bounded above and below by impermeable layers. **140**, 137-143

Conflict resolution. The act of arbitrating differences of belief or opinion about a given set of conditions or circumstances. 413-420

Conservation. The use of water-saving methods to reduce the amount of water needed for homes, lawns, farming, and industry, and thus increasing water supplies for optimum long-term economic and social benefits. 117-120, 198, 224, 226, 232-237, 274-278, 307-310, 328-332, 333-335, 380, 382-387, 399, 408-412, 436

Consumptive use. The use of a resource that reduces the supply (e.g., removing water from a source such as a river or lake without returning an equal amount). Examples are the intake of water by plants, humans, and other animals and the incorporation of water into the products of industrial or food processing. 232-237, 238-241, 260-261, 271-273, 274-278, 382-387

Contaminant. Any substance that when added to water (or another substance) makes it impure and unfit for consumption or use. 50, 93-98, 107-115, 136-141, 163, 186-190, 219-222, 240, 268-270, 311-315, 338-343, 344-347, 348-352, 353

Control. A standard for comparing, checking, or verifying the results of an experiment or activity. 109, 114-115, 282-286, 374

Cooperative learning. A teaching strategy designed to promote productive and mutual learning among a group of students. **9**, 9-11

Critical analysis. Careful, exact evaluation and judgment. 93-98, 388-392, 397, 459

Cubic feet per second (cfs)/cubic meters per second (cms). Units typically used in measuring streamflow that express rate of discharge. The measurement is equal to the discharge in a stream cross section one foot wide and one foot deep (or one meter wide and one meter deep), flowing with an average velocity of one foot (or meter) per second; 1 cfs = 44.8 gallons per minute (gpm); 1 cms = 1,000 liters per second. **224**, 224-228, 293-299

Culture. The collective body of understanding, belief, and behavior among a given group of

people; depends on the human capacity for learning and transmitting knowledge from one generation to another. 174-181, 182, 248, 431, 435-441, 442-445, 446-449, 454-457

Debate. To engage in argument through the expression of opposing points of view. 388-392, 435

Decomposition. The breakdown or decay of organic matter through the digestive processes of microorganisms, macroinvertebrates, and scavengers. 89-92, 99, 213

Density. The compactness or crowdedness of matter (e.g., water molecules) in a given area. **25**, 25-29, 35-42, 43-46

Depletion. The loss of water from surface water reservoirs or ground water aquifers at a rate greater than that of recharge. 198, 232-238

Deposition. The process of laying down sediment or accumulating layers of material carried in suspension. 150-154, 166-169

Diffusion. The movement of a substance from an area of high concentration to an area of low concentration. **72**, 72-75

Dilemma. A situation in which a choice must be made from among different alternatives; a difficult or complex set of circumstances. **377**, 377-381

Direct water uses. Uses of water that are apparent (e.g., washing, bathing, cooking). 271-273, **274**, 274-278

Discharge. An outflow of water from a stream, pipe, ground water system, or watershed. 134, 137, 224, 293-299, 395

Divide. See ridge lines. **129**, 129-131, 186

Downstream. In the direction of a stream's current; in relation to water rights, refers to water uses or locations that are affected by upstream uses or locations. 108, 269-270, 336

Drainage basin. See watershed.

Drought. An extended period with little or no precipitation; often affects crop production and availability of water supplies. 240, 262, 289, 294, 303-306, 382, 384-385, 395, 446

Easement. A legal document that makes it possible to give, sell, or take certain land and/or water rights without transfer of title (e.g., the passage of utility lines). 336

Ecology. The study of the relationships of living things to one another and to the environment. 79-80, 254, 290, 316-321

Ecosystem. A community of living organisms and their interrelated physical and chemical environment; also, a land area within a climate. 79-80, 91, 123, 174-181, 201-203, 232-237, 279-286, 316-321, 322-327, 429

Electromagnetic forces. The fields created by positive and negative charges of atoms, which influence the formation of molecules and the attraction or repulsion (push and pull) of molecules to and from each other. 35-42, 161-165, 196, 201, 279

El Niño. A periodic warming of the ocean surface off the western coast of South America caused by the absence of the normal upwelling of cold, nutrient-rich water. El Niño occurs every 4 to 12 years, causing plankton and fish to die and affecting weather. 305

Energy. The capacity to perform work, or the potential for power and activity. 72-75, 76-77, 137, 182-184, 242-245, 373

Environment. All of the external factors, conditions, and influences that affect an organism or a biological community. 74, 80, 102, 122-126, 150-152, 201, 246, 262-263, 300-302, 316-321, 322-326, 442-445, 458

Epidemic. An outbreak of a contagious disease that spreads rapidly and widely. 93-98, 107-115

Epidemiology. The study of the incidence, transmission, distribution, and control of infectious disease (including waterborne disease) in large populations. 93-98, 107-115

Erosion. The wearing down or washing away of the soil and land surface by the action of water, wind, or ice. 77, 131, 150-154, **166**, 188, 200, 224, 267

Evaporation. The conversion of a liquid (e.g., water) into a vapor (a gaseous state) usually through the application of heat energy; the opposite of condensation. 35-42, 43-46, 66, 116-121, 130-131, 134, 157-160, 161-165, 201-205

Evapotranspiration. The loss of water from the soil through both evaporation and transpiration from plants. **117**, 117-121

Excretion. The act or process of removing waste material from living organisms. 66-71, 162-165

Flood. Any relatively high streamflow overtopping the natural or artificial banks of a stream. 99-106, 131, 150, 196-200, 213, 223-226, 240, 262-266, 289-292, 303-306, 379, 398, 446

Floodplain. Any normally dry land area that is susceptible to being inundated by water from any natural source; usually lowland adjacent to a stream or lake. 166, 223, 262, 289-290, 293-297, 379

Freezing point. The temperature at which a liquid freezes; for water, this occurs at 32 degrees Fahrenheit (0° Celsius). 50, 373

Fresh water. Water with less than 0.5 parts per thousand dissolved salts. 25-29, 238-241

Gas (gaseous). The state of water in which individual molecules are highly energized and move about freely; also known as vapor. 25-29, 37-42, 47-49, 50-53, 54-60, 66, 76-77, 117-121, 144-149, 157-160, 161-165, 171-172, 174-176, 201-205

Geyser. A geothermal feature characterized by periodic eruptions of superheated water and steam. 144-149

Gradient. A measure of a degree of incline; the steepness of a slope. 137, 188-189

Gravity. The natural force of attraction exerted by Earth on objects or materials on its surface that tends to draw them down toward its center. 31-34, 137, 157-160, 161-165, 201, 243-244, 255, 450-453

Ground water. Water found in spaces between soil particles underground (located in the zone of saturation). iii, 89, 133-135, **136**, 136-143, 161-165, 223, 233, 255, 311-315, 338-343, 344

Ground water system. All the components of subsurface materials that relate to water, including aquifers (confined and unconfined), zones of saturation, and water tables. 134, 136-143, 222

Habitat. The environment where a plant or animal grows or lives. 26, 99-106, 123, 246, 323

Headwaters. The source of a stream. **131**

Heat energy. Energy that pertains to the movement of molecules within a material or object. As heat is added to a material, the movement of molecules within the material increases. 25-29, 37-42, 47-49, 66, 117-121, 157-160, 161-165, 182-183, 196, 201, 206, 373, 450-451

Heat sink. A substance to which heat energy is transferred. A heat sink has a lower level of heat energy (slower moving molecules) than the surrounding material; heat energy travels from an area of high concentration to that of a lower concentration. **42**

Humidity. The degree of moisture in the air. 117, 155, 158, 175-181

Hydroelectricity. Electric energy produced by water-powered turbine generators. 146, 242-245, 278

Hydrogen bond. A type of chemical bond caused by electromagnetic forces, occurring when the positive pole of one molecule (e.g., water) is attracted to and forms a bond with the negative pole of another molecule (e.g., another water molecule). 31, **35**, 35-42, 117

Hydrograph. A representation of water discharge over time. **293**, 293-299

Hydrologic cycle. See water cycle. 307

Hydrology. The study of Earth's waters, including water's properties, circulation, principles, and distribution. 200, 293-297, 312, 360, 363

Hypothesis. A potential explanation for a condition or set of facts that can be tested through further investigation. 44, 376, 444

Impermeable layer. A layer of material (e.g., clay) in an aquifer through which water does not pass. **140**, 137-143

Indirect water uses. Uses of water that are not immediately apparent to the consumer. For example, a person indirectly uses water when driving a car because water was used in the production process of steel and other parts of the vehicle. 271-273, 300

Instream flow. The minimum amount of water required in a stream to maintain the existing aquatic resources and associated wildlife and riparian habitat. 297, 395

Instream use. Uses of water within a stream's channel (e.g., by fish and other aquatic life, or for recreation, navigation, and hydroelectric power production). 246-254, 277-278, 367-372, 394

Insulation. Anything that prevents the passage of heat (or light, electricity, or sound) from one medium to another. 27, 123, 175, 373-376

Investigation. The process of using inquiry and examination to gather facts and information in order to solve a problem or resolve an issue. xii, 43-46, 54-60, 93-98

Irrigation. The controlled application of water to cropland, hay fields, and/or pasture to supplement that supplied by nature. 200, 232, 254-259, 262, 308, 393

Isohyetal line. A line drawn on a map or chart connecting points that receive equal amounts of precipitation. **200**

Journal. A personal record of experiences, observations, thoughts, and ideas, usually kept in a diary or other written form. 3, 19-22, 163, 192, 308, 400, 444, 457

Kinetic energy. The energy of motion, determined by an object's mass and speed. **47**, 47-48, 183-184, 242-244

Levee. An embankment or raised area that prevents water from moving from one place to another. 262, 294, 303, 399

Liquid. The state of water in which molecules move freely among themselves but do not separate like those in a gaseous state. 25-29, 35-42, 47-49, 50-53, 54-60, 66, 157-160, 161-165, 373

Litigation. The act of carrying on a legal contest through a judicial process. 413-420

Macroinvertebrates. Invertebrate animals (animals without backbones) large enough to be observed without the aid of a microscope or other magnification. **322**, 322-327

Mediation. The process of intervening between two or more parties in conflict to promote reconciliation, settlement, or compromise. 413-420

Metabolism. The physical and chemical processes in an organism that produce energy and that result in the production, maintenance, or destruction of materials in the body. Many metabolic processes involve water. 37, 66-71, 77, 116-120, 122

Meteorology. The study of the atmosphere, including weather and climate. 184

Migration. The periodic movement of animate things from one area to another, often in response to seasonal change. 80, 100, 123, 200, 246-253

Municipal water system. A network of pipes, pumps, and storage and treatment facilities designed to deliver potable water to homes, schools, businesses, and other users in a city or town and to remove and treat waste materials. 108, 158, 219-222, 260-261, 308, 328-332, 333-337, 344-347

Nonconsumptive use. Instream use of water that does not reduce the supply; or, removing water and returning it to the source without reducing the supply (e.g., navigation and fisheries). 394

Nonpoint source pollution. Widespread overland runoff containing pollutants; the contamination does not originate from one specific location, and pollution discharges over a wide land area. 166, **186**, 186-190, 219-222, 267-270, 419

Observation. The act of watching something attentively; a record or notation of the act. 3-6, 19-21, 155, 191-195

Organic. Of, related to, or derived from living organisms. Organic substances contain carbon. 76, 89-90, 151, 166, 212-214, 344, 352, 353

Osmosis. The diffusion of water through a membrane. 66-71, **72**, 72-75, 116-120

Parts per million (ppm)/parts per billion (ppb). Units typically used in measuring the number of "parts" by weight of a substance in water; commonly used in representing pollutant concentrations. 344-347

Pathogen. A disease-producing agent, especially a microorganism. **85**, 85-88, 94, 107-115, 344

Permeable. Capable of transmitting water (e.g., porous rock, sediment, or soil). 92, 201, 227

Permeable layer. A layer of porous material (rock, soil, unconsolidated sediment); in an aquifer, the layer through which water freely passes as it moves through the ground. 92, **140**, 136-143

Petroglyph. An image pecked or chiseled into a rock surface with a hard stone and bone tools; the earliest form of pictograph. **455**, 454-457

pH. A classification of acid or base materials on a scale of 0 to 14, with 7 representing neutrality; numbers less than 7 indicate increasing acidity, and numbers greater than 7 indicate increasing alkalinity (basic conditions). 43-46, **279**, 279-286, 340-343, 351

Photosynthesis. The process through which green plants (and certain other organisms) produce simple sugars by combining carbon dioxide and water using light (sunlight) as an energy source and producing oxygen as a by-product. (Some forms of photosynthesis do not release oxygen.) **76**, 76-78, 92, 116

Pictograph. A picture that was chipped, carved, or painted on stone by prehistoric peoples to represent a word or idea. **454**, 454-457

Plume. A continuous emission from a point source of contamination that has a starting point and a noticeable pathway. **312**, 312-314, 339-343

Point source pollution. Pollutants discharged from any identifiable point, including pipes, ditches, channels, sewers, tunnels, and containers of various types. **186**, 186-190, 267-270, 338-343, 348-352

Polar. Having to do with, or characterized by possessing, oppositely charged electric poles. **35**, 35-42, 54-55

Pollution. An alteration in the character or quality of the environment, or any of its components, that renders it less suited for certain uses. The alteration of the physical, chemical, or biological properties of water by the introduction of any substance that renders the water harmful to use. 17, 50-53, 77, 137-143, 163, 166, 186-190, 194, 219-222, 240, 267-270, 279-286, 311-315, 322-326, 338-343, 344-347, 348-352, 379, 382, 395

Portfolio. A teaching strategy that involves students (and/or teachers) maintaining a record or collection of student work. **19**, 19-22

Potential energy. Stored energy such as that found in water that is retained in a reservoir or kept from flowing downhill. When released (allowed to move), potential energy changes to kinetic energy. **243**, 243-244

Pre-assessment. A teaching strategy that is used to determine students' level of understanding or competencies related to a concept prior to instruction. Pre-assessments are often compared to assessments performed after instruction to determine if progress has been made. xii, **7**, 7-8

Precipitation. Water falling, in a liquid or solid state, from the atmosphere to Earth (e.g., rain, snow). 117-121, 133-135, 140, 144, 155, 157-159, 171-172, 174-181, 182-185, 196-200, 201, 206-212, 219, 240, 255-256, 279-286, 442-445, 446-449

Proverb. A short saying or statement in frequent and widespread use that expresses a basic truth or practical precept. **435**, 435-441

Rainstick. A common term for a type of tubular rattle that mimics the sound of rainfall; a primitive musical instrument in which sound is produced by the movement of particles (sand, stones, etc.) through a hollow tube with an internal matrix that is closed on each end. **443**, 442-445, 446-449

Respiration. The act or process by which an organism exchanges gases with its environment; in animals with lungs, the process of inhaling and exhaling, or breathing. Cellular respiration involves the release of energy from food through chemical reactions. 66-71, 77, 162-165

Restoration. The act or process of bringing something back to a previous condition or position. 316-322

Ridge lines. Points of higher ground that separate two adjacent streams or watersheds; also known as divides. **129**, 129-131, 186

Riparian areas. Land areas directly influenced by a body of water; usually have visible vegetation or other physical characteristics showing this water influence. Stream banks, lake borders, and marshes are typical riparian areas. 131, 166

Runoff. Precipitation that flows overland to surface streams, rivers, and lakes. 17, 119, **129**, 129-131, 137-143, 169, 186-189, 200, 202, 219-222, 223-231, 232-235, 311, 324, 395

Salinization. The condition in which the salt content of soil accumulates over time to above the normal level; occurs in some parts of the world where water containing high salt concentration evaporates from fields irrigated with standing water. **255**, 254-259

Salt marsh. A low coastal grassland frequently inundated by the tide. **99**, 99-106

Salt water. Water that contains a relatively high percentage (over 0.5 parts per thousand) of salt minerals. 25-29, 239-241

Season. A period of time during the year classified by length of day and weather conditions. 102, 155-156, 163, 185, 206-212

Sediment. Fragmented organic or inorganic material derived from the weathering of soil, alluvial, and rock materials; removed by erosion and transported by water, wind, ice, and gravity. 141, 150-154, 224, 267, 324, 344

Soil. The top layer of Earth's surface, containing unconsolidated rock and mineral particles mixed with organic material. **76**, 76-78, 133-135, 157-160, 161-165, 166-169, 201, 212-216, 224, 255-259, 280

Solid. The state of water in which molecules have limited movement. 25-29, 35-42, 47-49, 50-53, 54-59, 66, 157-160, 161-165, 373

Solute. A substance dissolved in another substance (the solvent) to create a solution. 55, 72-75

Solution. The mixture of a solute (a solid, liquid, or gas e.g., sugar, alcohol, or carbon dioxide) with a solvent (e.g., water). The solute mixes thoroughly with the solvent and appears to become a part of the solvent. 35-41, **54**, 54-60, 72-75

Solvent. A material such as water that dissolves another substance (the solute) to form a solution. **55**

Stomata. Tiny pores in the epidermis or surface of plant leaves or stems through which gases and water vapor are exchanged with the environment. **116**, 116-120

Storm drain. Constructed opening in a road system through which runoff from the road surface flows into an underground sewer system. 17, 219-222

Stream. Any body of running water moving under gravity's influence through clearly defined natural channels to progressively lower levels. 17, **129**, 129-132, 157, 161, 167-169, 191-195, 219-222, 223-228, 322-327

Streamflow. The discharge of water from a river. 224, 268, 293-299

Sublimation. The transition of a substance from the solid phase directly to the vapor phase, or vice versa, without passing through an intermediate liquid phase. 51, **201**

Substrate. A layer of material beneath the surface soil. 136-143, 280, 334

Surface tension. The attraction among water molecules at the surface of a liquid; creates a skinlike barrier between air and underlying water molecules. **31**, 30-34, 36, 43-46

Surface water. Water above the surface of the land, including lakes, rivers, streams, ponds, floodwater, and runoff. 111, 133-135, 186-189, 255, 344

Temperature. The measurement of the average kinetic energy of moving molecules within a substance. 26, 43-46, 47-48, 55-60, 99-100, 174-181, 182-185, 201-205, 206-212, 373

Temperature regulation. The processes through which an organism's temperature is adjusted to certain metabolic requirements or conditions in its environment. 66-71, 206-212, 262, 373-376

Temporary wetland. A type of wetland in which water is present for only part of the year, usually during the wet or rainy seasons (e.g., spring); also called vernal pools. **79**, 79-86

Transpiration. The process by which water absorbed by plants (usually through the roots) is evaporated into the atmosphere from the plant surface (principally from the leaves). **116**, 116-120, 157, 162, 202

Tributary. A stream that contributes its water to another stream or body of water. **130**, 130-132, 223

Unconfined aquifer. An aquifer in which the upper boundary is the water table. **140**, 136-143

Upstream. Toward the source or upper part of a stream; against the current. In relation to water rights, refers to water uses or locations that affect water quality or quantity of downstream water uses or locations. 269-270

Values. Principles, standards, or qualities considered worthwhile or desirable by the person who holds them. 3-6, 7-8, 12-15, 182-185, 367-372, 397-399, 425-428, 435-441, 444, 445, 457

Vapor. See gas.

Virus. Any of various infectious agents that are so small they can only be seen with an electron microscope. Viruses are unable to reproduce without a host cell and are not considered living organisms. 85-88, 107-115, 353

Wastewater. Water that contains unwanted materials from homes, businesses, and industries; a mixture of water and dissolved or suspended substances. 108, 219-222, 308, 333, 347, 348-352, 353-359

Wastewater treatment. Any of the mechanical or chemical processes used to modify the quality of wastewater in order to make it more compatible or acceptable to humans and the environment. 50-52, 219-222, 232, 308, 333-337, 348-352, 353-359, 407

Water (H_2O). An odorless, tasteless, colorless liquid made up of a combination of hydrogen and oxygen. Water forms streams, lakes, and seas, and is a major constituent of all living matter. The word **water** and important concepts related to water appear on almost every page of this text. i, 47

Water allocation. In a hydrologic system in which there are multiple uses or demands for water, the process of measuring a specific amount of water devoted to a given purpose. 232-238, 293-299, 367-372, 392-396, 413-420

Waterborne disease. Any illness transmitted through ingestion of or contact with water contaminated by disease-causing organisms (e.g., bacteria, viruses, or protozoa) or chemicals. 85-88, 93-98, **107**, 107-115, 347, 353

Water crossing. A commonly used route for crossing a river or stream. 246-253, 421-424

Water cycle. The paths water takes through its various states—vapor, liquid, and solid—as it moves throughout Earth's systems (oceans, atmosphere, ground water, streams, etc.). Also known as the hydrologic cycle. 50, 116-121, 157-160, 161-165, 201-205, 307, 348-352

Water molecule. The smallest unit of water; consists of two hydrogen atoms and an oxygen atom. 25-28, 30-34, **35**, 35-42, 47-49, 54-60, 72-75, 117-120, 138-141, 157-160, 161-165, 182-184, 247, 279-281

Water pressure. The downward force of water upon itself and other materials; caused by the pull of gravity. 26, 450-453

Water quality. The chemical, physical, and biological characteristics of water with respect to its suitability for a particular use. 16, 17, 93-98, 107-115, 137-143, 166-169, 194, 232-235, 267-270, 300-302, 311-315, 319, 322-326, 338-343, 344-347, 356, 379, 396, 404-405, 419

Water quality standard. Recommended or enforceable maximum contaminant levels of chemicals or materials (e.g., chlorobenzene, nitrate, iron, arsenic) in water. These levels are established for water used by municipalities, industries, agriculture, and recreationists. 344-347

Water-related disaster. A cyclic event involving water during which there is threat to or loss of human life or property (e.g., flood, hurricane, tsunami). 211, 262-266, 289-292, 303-306

Water-related issue. An environmental problem involving water that is complicated by the disagreement of two or more parties over the cause, effect, and/or resolution of the problem. i, 12-18, 293-297, 300-302, 377-381, 388-392, 397-399, 400-402, 413-420, 425-428, 429-432

Water-related recreation. Leisure and sports activities that occur in, on, or around water or snow. 188, 211, 278, 380-381, 460-464

Water resource careers. Professions or vocations involved in the protection, allocation, development, or management of water. 17, 293-299, 360-364

Water resource management. The decision-making, manipulative, and nonmanipulative processes by which water is protected, allocated, or developed. 133, 166, 293-299, 312, 316, 367-372, 377-381, 397-399, 413-420

Water right. A legal right to use a specified amount of water for beneficial purposes. 234, 388, **392**, 392-396, 404, 415, 418, 458

Watershed. The land area from which surface runoff drains into a stream channel, lake, reservoir, or other body of water; also called a drainage basin. **129**, 129-132, 133-

135, 161, 166, 186-189, 198, 219, 223-231, 248, 267-270, 316

Water table. The top of an unconfined aquifer; indicates the level below which soil and rock are saturated with water. **140**, 137-143, 198, 255

Water treatment plants. Facilities that treat water to remove contaminants so that it can be safely used. 95, 108-109, 344-347

Water use practices. Direct, indirect, consumptive, and nonconsumptive uses of water. These include domestic practices (e.g., washing, cooking, drinking), navigation, wildlife habitat management, irrigation practices, recreation activities, industrial uses, and hydroelectric power generation. 232-237, 254-259, 260-261, 271-274, 274-278, 307-310, 382-387, 407-412, 460-464

Weather. The composite condition of the near-Earth atmosphere, including temperature, barometric pressure, wind, humidity, clouds, and precipitation. Weather variations in a given area over a long period of time create climate. 155-156, 174-181, 182-185, 187, 196-200, 202, 206-212, 238, 262-266, 289-292, 293-297, 303-306

Well field. An area in which productive wells are drilled (similar to an oil field). **334**, 334-337, 409

Well log. A record of the depth and type of rock material in a well. **137**, 137-143

Wetlands. Lands where water saturation is the dominant factor determining the nature of soil development and the types of plant and animal communities. Other common names for wet-

lands are sloughs, ponds, and marshes. 79-84, 89-92, 99-106, 133-135, 140, 166, 212-216, 322, 381

Work. The application of force (a push or a pull) to an object to create movement; the result of such a force. **243**, 243-244

Xeriscaping. A form of landscaping that utilizes a variety of indigenous and drought-tolerant plants, shrubs, and ground cover. **117**, 116-120, 308

Xylem. The supporting layer of tissue in vascular plants that conducts water and nutrients from the roots to other parts of a plant. **116**, 116-120

Zone of aeration. The unsaturated surface layer of the ground in which some of the spaces between soil particles are filled with water and others are filled with air. Some of the water in the zone of aeration is lost to the atmosphere through evaporation. **140**, 140-143

Zone of saturation. The part of a ground water system in which all of the spaces between soil and rock material are filled with water. Water found within the zone of saturation is called ground water. The water table is the top of the zone of saturation. **140**, 140-143

ORDER FORM
(PRICES SUBJECT TO CHANGE)

Send to: (please print)

Name_____

Street Address_____

City_____State_____Zip_____

Telephone Number_____

Quantity	Item and Unit Cost	Total
	The Liquid Treasure Water History Trunk: Learning From the Past ($7.50)	
	Water Celebration! A Handbook ($3.50)	
	Getting to Know the Waters of Yellowstone: An Educator's Guide ISBN 1-888631-01-5 ($9.95)	
	Water, A Gift of Nature ($7.95)	
	A Landowner's Guide to Western Water Rights ISBN 1-57098-093-4 ($16.95)	
	The Rainstick, A Fable ISBN 1-56044-284-0 ($9.95)	
	The Rainstick, A Fable T-shirt ($12.00) Natural color only ☐ L ☐ XL ☐ XXL	
	The Water Story (30 copies for $13.50)	
	Celebrate Wetlands (30 copies for $13.50)	
	Conserve Water (30 copies for $13.50)	
	WOW!: The Wonders Of Wetlands ISBN 1-888631-02-3 ($15.95)	
	Discover a Watershed: The Everglades ISBN 1-888631-00-7 ($15.95)	
	Exploring the Waters of Our National Parks: The Everglades ISBN 1-888631-03-1 ($9.95)	
	Ground Water Flow Model Package (Call for options and prices)	
	Water Conservation Module for Educators (Available Summer 1999)	
	Project WET T-shirt ($12.00) White Only ☐ L ☐ XL ☐ XXL	
	Project WET cap ($12.00) Khaki Only—One Size Fits All	
TOTAL COST:		

Shipping Costs (see box below)...+$_____

TOTAL..$_____

Method of Payment: ☐ Check ☐ VISA ☐ MasterCard ☐ Purchase Order
Please make checks payable to: **The Watercourse**

P.O. Number: _____

Card Number: _____ Exp. Date: _____

Card Holder's Signature: _____

Return to: The Watercourse
PO Box 170575
Montana State University
Bozeman, MT 59717-0575
406-994-5392 Fax 406-994-1919

SHIPPING	
Merchandise	*Shipping Charges*
Total to $20.00	$4.50
$20.01 - $40.00	$6.50
$40.01 - $60.00	$8.50
$60.01 - $80.00	$10.50

More Than $80.00 or if sent UPS, actual charges will be billed. For shipping on international orders please contact The Watercourse.